Critique & Praxis

Critique & Praxis

A Critical Philosophy of Illusions, Values, and Action

Bernard E. Harcourt

Columbia University Press
New York

Columbia University Press
Publishers Since 1893
New York   Chichester, West Sussex
cup.columbia.edu

Library of Congress Cataloging-in-Publication Data

Names: Harcourt, Bernard E., 1963- author.
Title: Critique and praxis / Bernard E. Harcourt.
Description: New York : Columbia University Press, [2020] |
Includes bibliographical references and index.
Identifiers: LCCN 2019049171 (print) | ISBN 9780231195720 (hbk) |
ISBN 9780231551458 (ebk)
Subjects: LCSH: Critical theory. | Political science—Philosophy. |
Political participation. | Social action.
Classification: LCC HM480 .H37 2020 (print) | LCC HM480 (ebook) |
DDC 142—dc23
LC record available at https://lccn.loc.gov/2019049171
LC ebook record available at https://lccn.loc.gov/2019049172

Columbia University Press books are printed on permanent
and durable acid-free paper.

Printed in the United States of America

Cover design: Lisa Hamm

Contents

Critique & Praxis

Critique & Praxis

The Primacy of Critique and Praxis

To change the world: The ambition of critical philosophy since its inception in the nineteenth century has always been to transform human existence.[1] Not just to make the world more safe and secure for private possessions or for the free pursuit of self-interest, as Thomas Hobbes, John Locke, or Adam Smith aspired to earlier. Not just to make it more rational, self-conscious, or orderly, with Immanuel Kant, G. W. F. Hegel, or Max Weber. Nor simply to make men more virtuous or life more pleasurable, as Aristotle, Epicurus, Seneca, and the ancients envisaged millennia before. But rather, to create a more just and equal society, with less domination and social differential, and to materialize the opportunity for each and every one of us to flourish and achieve our greatest potential. To realize a world of equal citizens, in which all human beings can fulfill their talents and aspirations, in which all are nurtured, educated, and cared for generously and respectfully by each other, tending not only to their dreams and ambitions, but also humbly to everyone else's.

"The philosophers have only *interpreted* the world, in various ways," Karl Marx wrote in his notebooks in 1845, "the point, however, is to *change* it."[2] These now-famous words sealed the birth certificate of critical philosophy, although many had foreshadowed it earlier, including Jean-Jacques Rousseau, the Levellers, Saint Francis, or even, on some readings, the prophetic traditions long before. What they all shared—and would share with later critical theorists such as Max Horkheimer, Michel Foucault, Angela Davis, Judith Butler, and Gayatri Chakravorty Spivak—was the ambition to infuse the world with the values of compassion, equality, solidarity, autonomy, and social justice. To turn the contemplative philosophical tradition into a practice of emancipation. To push thought in the direction of action and toward human liberation. To convert theory into practice.

From antiquity, philosophers had conceived of the two—theory and practice—as two fundamentally different ways of living, different ways of being human. The ancient Greeks referred to them as *theoria*, meaning contemplation, and *praxis*, the ethical and political form of being. The former, *theoria*, predominantly involved understanding and comprehension—in essence, knowing. It was oriented toward wisdom. The latter, *praxis*, revolved around activity, action, performance—in essence, doing. It was geared toward proper behavior in ethical and political life. For the ancients, these represented two different modes of engaging the world—two among others, *poiesis*, or artistic creation, being another.

These categories helped shape human experience ever since. They entered our common lexicon and structured our way of being.[3] Over the centuries, philosophers continued to interrogate and explore the nexus of theory and praxis. Early theologians drew on these categories in their struggle to square contemplative faith with works of charity. Medieval scholars explored the possibility of practical applications of theoretical knowledge. Enlightenment philosophers—from Descartes through the German idealists—tilted the field toward reason and rationality, toward theory and away from practice, generating new debates over the relation between mind and body, between private reason and public action, and over the self-actualization of the human spirit.[4]

Philosophers, almost by definition—by the very etymology of their creed as "lovers of wisdom"—naturally tended to favor theory, contemplation, and inquiry over action. This orientation traced far back in history. In the *First Alcibiades* and Plato's *Statesman*, Socrates reenacted the age-old preference for knowledge over practice. Confronting young men who wanted to live the life of praxis rather than contemplation, Socrates quickly made them realize that they did not actually know that much about doing justice or governing others, and that they first needed to gain knowledge. Socrates convinced them to know themselves first, giving philosophical expression to the ancient Delphic maxim *gnōthi seauton*, "know thyself." Politics in practice, it turns out, is a skill that requires a *technē*, a technique, a craftsmanship—a set of knowledges. Like the captain of a ship or the shepherd of a flock, the political practitioner must first acquire knowledge. There are skills to be learned and knowledge to be had. There must be wisdom first—which, naturally, pushed the inquiry back to the realm of contemplation. It returned the young men of praxis to Socrates' discussion of justice from the *Republic*. Praxis, it turns out, must defer to true wisdom.

It was against this tendency, continually replicated throughout the ages and especially stark in the modern rationalist tradition from Descartes to Kant to Hegel, that critical philosophers in the nineteenth century struggled to invert the relationship and correct the imbalance—the Left Hegelians first among them, as so strikingly encapsulated in Marx's *Theses on Feuerbach*.[5] The second thesis: "The question whether objective truth can be attributed to human thinking is not a question of theory but is a *practical* question." The eighth: "Social life is essentially *practical*." And, then, of course, the eleventh.

With his bold language and clear vision, Marx epitomized the critical turn in philosophy. It was at the heart of his philosophical and personal quest for human emancipation, above and beyond simply ensuring civil and political rights. It was the basis, first, of Marx turning idealism into materialism so that the motor of history would no longer be the evolution of reason or the rationalization of society, but rather the material contradictions in capitalism that would ultimately lead to the emancipation of all women and men; and second, of his turning classical political economy into an analysis of the crises of capital accumulation. In both periods, the young and the mature Marx inaugurated a critical turn in philosophy by attempting to convert the *contemplative* tradition into a *practice* of emancipation.

Yet Marx was by no means alone in his ambition to convert philosophy into praxis. Waves of critical theorists took on the mantle enthusiastically. Rosa Luxemburg propelled the analysis of capital accumulation further, toward a theory of radical democracy, and in the process enacted her own philosophical commitments into revolutionary praxis. Max Horkheimer demonstrated how critical theorists, themselves the product of their own historical conditions, seek to transform their society: Critical theory "never aims simply at an increase of knowledge as such," Horkheimer declared; "its goal is man's emancipation from slavery."[6] Hannah Arendt privileged the *vita activa* in her study *The Human Condition* before turning, only in later years, to the contemplative realm in *The Life of the Mind*. Frantz Fanon transformed his philosophical ambitions into a revolutionary practice and advocated for an anticolonial war of liberation. Jean-Paul Sartre privileged praxis as well, serving as prosecutor and judge at popular tribunals while searching for a method for praxis in his writings; in the colonial context, Sartre also embraced revolution.[7] Foucault wrote *Discipline and Punish* "for users, not readers," as he famously said—for educators, wardens, magistrates, and conscientious objectors.[8] Davis reoriented her philosophical commitments toward an abolitionist practice.[9]

Butler developed a theory of gender performativity with the normative aim and political goal, in her own words, to "let the lives of gender and sexual minorities become more possible and more livable."[10] Chantal Mouffe confronted "the sterile academic debate" to advocate for a praxis of left populism.[11] Sara Ahmed issued a killjoy manifesto and survival kit to offer practical tools to live a feminist life.[12]

The object of critical philosophy "is not simply the theory of emancipation," Horkheimer emphasized in 1937; "it is the practice of it as well."[13] This ambition unfolded in a variety of ways and under myriad rubrics, from debates over "dirty hands" in the postwar years, to privileging distribution over recognition (or vice versa), to calls for the "unity" of theory and praxis.[14]

Yet a series of historical setbacks, failures, and catastrophes during the twentieth century led critical philosophy to beat retreat from its practical ambitions. These seismic shifts in history—the rise of fascism and the Holocaust, the gulag archipelago and collapse of Soviet communism, the eclipse of the student and worker revolts of May 1968, the hegemonic emergence of global neoliberalism—all chastened the critical impulse and pushed critical theory into a safer, epistemological direction. Safer, at least, for philosophers and critical thinkers. Critical theory took an epistemological detour and moved away from praxis.

Max Horkheimer's own trajectory is undoubtedly illustrative. Before the war, and even at first in exile at Columbia University in New York City, Horkheimer vigorously embraced, in his own words, "the unity of theory and practice." Writing from his institute in exile in 1937, Horkheimer extolled "the idea of a theory which becomes a genuine force, consisting in the self-awareness of the subjects of a great historical revolution." This, he maintained, was something that traditional philosophers simply could not grasp because of their adherence to "the Cartesian dualism of thought and being." The mind-body dichotomy prevented traditional philosophers from comprehending the unity of theory and practice: "Reflecting on themselves men see themselves only as on-lookers, passive participants in a mighty process which may be foreseen but not modified." The resulting passivity thwarted traditional intellectuals from thinking of themselves as agents of change. By contrast, Horkheimer portrayed the critical theorist as one who enlightened and guided the masses—who engaged in praxis. Critical intellectuals thus played a pivotal role in helping the masses recognize and activate their interests. They were the ones who could pierce the veil of false consciousness. They had a "real function," Horkheimer wrote: to facilitate "the historical process of proletarian emancipation."[15]

By the end of the war and faced with the horror of the Holocaust, however, Horkheimer retreated from praxis. He prefaced his book *Eclipse of Reason*—a set of lectures he delivered at Columbia in the spring of 1944—by emphasizing that he "is not trying to suggest anything like a program of action."[16] Horkheimer emphasized (writing as he did in the third person), "On the contrary, he believes that the modern propensity to translate every idea into action, or into active abstinence from action, is one of the symptoms of the present cultural crisis: action for action's sake is in no way superior to thought for thought's sake, *and is perhaps even inferior to it*."[17] The experience of the war utterly fractured the potential unity of theory and praxis. The "core of dialectical theory," Horkheimer would now declare, is "the basic difference between the ideal and the real, between theory and practice."[18] Horkheimer concluded *Eclipse of Reason* on the following note: "This age needs no added stimulus to action. Philosophy must not be turned into propaganda, even for the best possible purpose. . . . The concentrated energies necessary for reflection must not be prematurely drained into the channels of activistic or nonactivistic programs."[19]

Horkheimer was, at this point, at the zenith of the dialectic of enlightenment and eclipse of reason—distrustful, to the maximum degree, of man's claims to progress. The position he took, in consequence, was decidedly *anti*-praxis: "Today even outstanding scholars confuse thinking with planning," he emphasized. "Shocked by social injustice and by hypocrisy in its traditional religious garb, they propose to wed ideology to reality, or, as they prefer to say, to bring reality closer to our heart's desire." That effort, however, was doomed to failure, Horkheimer maintained: "Philosophical theory itself cannot bring it about that either the barbarizing tendency or the humanistic outlook should prevail in the future." No, do not count on critical philosophy to guide praxis; it should chasten, rather than encourage, action and planning.[20]

The action imperative repelled Theodor Adorno as well, perhaps with even greater intensity. In the aftermath of the student revolts of 1968, Adorno stressed the utter contradiction of theory and practice. The tradition of critical philosophy, Adorno maintained in his "Marginalia on Theory and Praxis," was not one of unity, but of dialectical contradiction between theory and practice. Marx himself had offered "no program for action" in *Capital* and "by no means surrendered himself to praxis," Adorno remonstrated.[21] In his own works, Adorno professed—in

Dialectic of Enlightenment and *The Authoritarian Personality*—there was no praxis intended: those books "were written without practical intentions," he declared. Adorno attacked the "error of the primacy of praxis." He further decried "the question 'what is to be done?'" as an "automatic reflex to every critical thought before it is fully expressed, let alone comprehended." "It recalls the gesture of someone demanding your papers," Adorno wrote, scathingly.[22]

In this, Foucault too ultimately agreed—one of the few instances of substantial overlap with Horkheimer and Adorno. In the late 1970s, after a period of engaged militancy and confronted with the perceived failure, or at least fatigue, of post-1968 protest movements, Foucault distanced himself from the praxis imperative—at least in contrast to his earlier involvement in the prison abolitionist movement, the *Groupe d'information sur les prisons* (GIP), in 1970–1971; to his more marxisant period in 1972–1973;[23] or, for that matter, to his engagement with the French Communist Party in 1950–1952.[24] In an interview with the psychiatrist David Cooper and others published in 1977, when asked whether, after criticism, there could be "a stage at which we might propose something?" Foucault carefully demurred:

> My position is that it is not up to us to propose. As soon as one "proposes"—one proposes a vocabulary, an ideology, which can only have effects of domination. What we have to present are instruments and tools that people might find useful. By forming groups specifically to make these analyses, to wage these struggles, by using these instruments or others: this is how, in the end, possibilities open up.
>
> But if the intellectual starts playing once again the role that he has played for a hundred and fifty years—that of prophet, in relation to what "must be," to what "must take place"—these effects of domination will return and we shall have other ideologies, functioning in the same way.[25]

For Foucault, the action imperative had become not only a critical contradiction, but a dangerous proposition—one that reproduces ideology and domination. To have to answer the question "What is to be done?" was disciplinary, not emancipatory. The role of the critical philosopher was instead to craft ideas for others to deploy, as instruments or tools, if they deemed them useful. By the late 1970s, praxis was reserved for political actors, not philosophers—this was further reinforced, for Foucault, by the political backlash he received to his writings on the Iranian Revolution in 1978–1979. As Foucault noted at the end of his interview with Cooper, "It is simply in the struggle itself and through it that positive conditions emerge."[26] It is the praxis of militants, as opposed to that of critical philosophers, that opens possibilities.

And in later years, paradoxically, the closer Foucault got to forms of practice—to the practices of the self—the more contemplative his philosophy appeared.[27] In *The Hermeneutics of the Subject* and the final volumes of *The History of Sexuality*, Foucault increasingly turned critique toward techniques of the self, or what he called "care of self;" but the political implications gradually became less evident. Foucault reinterpreted the *First Alcibiades* as a dialogue less focused on knowledge of the self and more on care of the self. From there, he pivoted our attention to the permanent practices of the self in the Stoics and Epicureans. And from then on, his analysis was trained on dimensions of subjectivity that enriched, but at the same time concealed his earlier analyses of power. Foucault's ambition was to augment his theory of knowledge-power through an exploration of the subjective dimension of self-formation, or what he called "the history of desiring man." His goal was to "investigate how individuals were led to practice, on themselves and on others, a hermeneutics of desire."[28] His aim was, ultimately, to produce a critical philosophy along three axes: knowledge, power, and subjectivity. And it is indeed possible that the integrative work would come next, but it was cut short by his untimely death in 1984. As a result, Foucault's later work on subjectivity, although focused on practices of the self, stands for many readers at somewhat of a distance from their political engagements.[29]

The historical setbacks effectively pushed critical philosophy down an epistemological path. With Antonio Gramsci's idea of cultural hegemony, the Frankfurt School's critique of ideology, Louis Althusser's notes on ideological state apparatuses, Foucault's theories of knowledge-power and, later, regimes of truth, and Derrida's deconstructive practices, critical philosophy took a sharply epistemological turn.

Here too, the long-term ambition may have been to transform human existence, not merely to interpret it; but critical philosophers needed first to understand—to contemplate—how human beings come to believe what they believe, how their desires are shaped, how their subjectivity is formed.[30] The agents of revolution may be in the best position to feel their exploitation, given their placement in the hierarchy of modern capitalist society; but that does not ensure that they can properly understand it. "Even the situation of the proletariat is, in this society, no guarantee of correct knowledge," Horkheimer proclaimed. "Even to the proletariat the world superficially seems quite different than it *really* is."[31]

So it fell to the critical philosophers to clear the epistemological ground, to unveil the ideological interferences, and to let others see properly. This would give birth to decades of philosophical discourse on ideology critique, *epistemes*, knowledge-power, and *différance*—all of which put primacy back on *theoria* rather than praxis, and on the contemplative intellectual rather than the critical practitioner.[32]

The epistemological work was certainly productive. New ways of thinking about truth and ideology emerged, liberated from the deceptive charms of analytic philosophy. In the ensuing epistemological investigations, relations of power took on an increasingly important role, especially as the triad that Foucault elaborated in his quest to analyze truth—knowledge/power/subjectivity—took hold of the critical imagination. The problems of false consciousness and genuine interests generated productive challenges to liberal theory. The concept of epistemes and the paradigm of an archaeology of knowledge opened new vistas, as did the genealogical method. The turn to subjectivity and the history of desire proved fertile ground to denaturalize phenomena ranging from sexuality to political assembly.

But the epistemological questions took precedence over praxis, and critical theory descended into petty internecine epistemological battles and struggles of influence over the correct epistemological sensibility to guide critique—with Marxian and Althusserian conceptions of science and history opposing postcolonial, subaltern, critical race, feminist, or queer theories on the constructed nature of society, all of which contested Deleuzian, Lacanian, Foucaultian, or Derridean approaches to social reality. Cliquish epistemological politics replaced healthy debate over praxis, as the main question no longer was "What is to be done?" but rather how to interpret the social landscape in light of the deep conflict between the various approaches of ideology critique, epistemes, deconstruction, postcolonialism, and other critical theories. The criticality of critical philosophy itself—focused on the unintended consequences of well-intentioned programs—also made many critical philosophers hesitate to engage praxis, especially as egalitarian experiments continued to miscarry around the globe, from Mao's Cultural Revolution to the Cambodian killing fields. These historical catastrophes chastened critical philosophers even more, pushing them further away from praxis and into the safer terrain of epistemology.

Instead of debating praxis, the more pressing—and anodyne—question became how people came to believe what they believe and desire what they desire, including fascism or totalitarianism, whether Nazi- or Soviet-style. Critical philosophers sought refuge in epistemology, almost as if to protect themselves and keep their hands clean. And part of the resistance to praxis was surely a necessary corrective to the know-it-all intellectual telling everyone what they should do. The figure of the universal intellectual, implicating himself in every controversy, bullhorn at his mouth blaring Marxist or Maoist dogma, was broadly and rightly attacked. The apparent asymmetries of clairvoyance between the public intellectual and the masses became somewhat problematic, resulting in introspective critiques of critical theory by thinkers such as Jacques Rancière, Luc Boltanski, Sharon Marcus, Bruno Latour, and others.[33]

These critiques of critical theory could have generated productive debate over praxis, as they had done earlier. But instead, they led to a further withdrawal of critical philosophy into the academy and a form of entrenchment. As Didier Fassin shows, critical theory withdrew to a handful of academic departments in higher education.[34] The space of critique, previously more public, narrowed to the critical professoriate at effete universities and colleges, and even there to the margins of power in rhetoric and English departments, or at the fringes of professional schools.

The epistemological battles subtly diverted critical philosophy from its true ambition—to change the world. The task, once again, was to know it. To analyze it on proper epistemological foundations. To offer new understandings of how desire or power shapes knowledge and makes people want things that hurt them. To make sense of how the new spirit of capitalism might coopt cultural and artistic revolutionary impulses. To identify, analyze, and diagnose our contemporary crises. This was so much the case, in fact, that the words *crisis* and *critique*—*Krise und Kritik*—became homologues. From Walter Benjamin and Bertolt Brecht's proposal for a new journal titled *Krise und Kritik* in 1930, to Reinhart Koselleck's 1959 book *Kritik und Krise*, to the current redeployment of those conjoined terms, the analysis of crises soon became the primary focus of critical philosophy.[35] Critical philosophy folded back into epistemology and crisis identification. Critical contemplation *alone* became praxis.

Many critical philosophers today—even some of the leading critical theorists of our time—now openly resist the call to praxis. Axel Honneth's book *The Idea of Socialism*, published in 2017, is a good illustration. An intervention seeking to rehabilitate the idea of socialism and to breathe new life back into the concept, *The Idea of Socialism* is a deeply committed engagement and presents itself as a veritable *crie de cœur*. Yet right up front, on the fifth page, Honneth warns:

> I make no attempt to draw connections to current political constellations and possibilities for action. I will not be dealing with the strategic question of how socialism could influence current political events, but solely how the original intention of socialism could be reformulated so as to make it once again a source of political-ethical orientations.[36]

"No attempt" to discuss "possibilities for action": the question of praxis has fallen by the wayside. Changing the world is no longer the task of the critical philosopher—now it falls to the political actor and strategist. The critical theorist proposes ideas and diagnoses crises, but others may have to find some use for all this. The task of critical philosophy has come full circle once more: not to change the world, but to critically understand it.

Today, for the most part, praxis has taken a back seat to theory. Practice, practical knowledge, and clinical activity have become the handmaids of theoretical knowledge—not only in the traditional disciplines and sciences, like law, engineering, or physics, but now, paradoxically, in the one domain that sought to overturn the relationship: critical philosophy. This is so much the case that, today, in the one realm that was designed to transform the world, we laud critical theories but are incapable of properly identifying critical praxis.

The collapse of critical philosophy and of its ambition to change the world, not just interpret it, could not have come at a worse time. It coincides with the most pressing crises that humans have ever faced: the looming cataclysm of global climate change, the hegemonic rise of neoliberalism and growing inequalities within nations, the surge of a fascist New Right at the international dimension, the emerging threat of pandemics, nuclear proliferation and conflict between rogue nations. We are living through one of the most critical periods, if not *the* most critical, in human history—with critical taken in its most formative etymological sense. Our politics, our world, our very Earth are in critical condition and are situated at turning points from which we may never recover.

After more than four decades of global neoliberal governance and a generalized grab for the commons—including Earth and her resources—we face perils unparalleled in time and along multiple dimensions. Growing domestic inequality has fueled extreme-right populist movements around the globe, as exemplified by the growing popularity of right-wing populist leaders in the United States, Brazil, Turkey, India, and across Europe. Xenophobic sentiment is mounting in quarters around the world, and strongmen political leaders are gaining power on the back of a global "war on terror." Meanwhile, global climate change threatens the planet, and world leaders such as U.S. president Donald Trump deny the science. It is fair to say, with Bruno Latour, that "it is as though a significant segment of the ruling classes (known today rather too loosely as 'the elites') had concluded that the earth no longer had room enough for them and for everyone else."[37] As I write, the fragile democratic process and inclusive politics of the United States—as faulty as they are—teeter on the verge of collapse, and it is no longer unimaginable that the country may be headed toward authoritarianism.

The global crises could not be greater, and yet critical theory is missing in action. Having disdained the question "What is to be done?" critical theory has little to offer by way of critical praxis. Critique is failing at the time it is needed most—producing a real crisis in critical theory itself. This has given rise to an unexpected quiescence, even a low-grade paralysis, among critical thinkers, at least in contrast to the more vocal resistance of liberal critics and organizations such as the American Civil Liberties Union (ACLU), Human Rights Watch, or the Center for Constitutional Rights in the United States. The critical response, by contrast, sounds muffled. The critical Left, as opposed to the liberal Left, appears disarmed.

When it has mobilized, the critical Left has tended to use predominantly liberal measures and has folded back on liberal institutions. In the United States at least, the principal forms of critical resistance to the Trump administration involved, first, civil rights litigation in federal courts aimed at blocking executive orders on everything from immigration to sexual orientation in the military, to the citizenship question on the census; second, protest marches, from the Women's March held the very day after Trump's inauguration to even a March for Science; and third, online petitions, letters, editorials, and statements of protest by individuals and their institutions. The principal resistance to Donald Trump reposed in a special counsel investigation by Robert Mueller, a former director of the Federal Bureau of Investigation (FBI), and House impeachment proceedings. Paradoxically, the FBI, the Central Intelligence Agency (CIA), career diplomats, and other intelligence agencies became the critical Left's strongest allies.

For the most part, critical resistance took the path of liberal democratic forms of resistance, even among the most critically oriented. The resistance to the administration's immigration ban—a Muslim ban despite the administration's reluctance to call it that—followed precisely a liberal civil and political rights model: civil rights lawyers, and even state attorneys general, went to court and sued President Trump, while critical theorists volunteered their expertise as area experts or translators for asylum hearings and public challenges. The same is true for the critical fight on global climate change. In effect, critical resistance predominantly used the courts and liberal institutions as an attempted bulwark against these unprecedented assaults.

I am not pointing fingers. I say this fully conscious that my own critical praxis in these times of crisis has deployed predominantly liberal-legal weapons—litigation, protest marches, petitions, editorials, and electoral politics. Days after he signed the Muslim ban, Tom Durkin and I sued Trump on behalf of a young Syrian doctor denied entry into the country, challenging his executive order on the grounds of the establishment of religion. A few months later, I took the case of a dual national, a Libyan-British young man, whose visa was being denied, and pursued administrative appeals and applied political pressure. I marched down New York's streets in the Women's March and other protests. I rallied law professors to oppose the confirmation of an unfit Supreme Court nomination. I doubled down representing inmates who were on death row or condemned to life imprisonment without parole in Alabama. Noah Smith-Drelich and I sued North Dakota law enforcement for their unconstitutional repression of protest and assembly at the Standing Rock reservation. I advised a Democratic presidential candidate as well as I could. I employed every weapon at my disposal to resist the tide of xenophobia and neo-fascism, and many of these indeed were liberal-legal methods.

And to be sure, the liberal toolkit has had positive effects in critical times like these. It is surely more desirable than raw authoritarianism and serves as a necessary corrective in these times of crisis. It has even had some success—for instance, blocking or stalling some of the worst executive orders and regressive political actions. But it is not necessarily critical praxis and does not necessarily offer a critical solution. In all likelihood, it merely postpones reckoning with the crises, especially if the right-wing populist wave eventually engulfs Congress and packs the judiciary as well.

These liberal remedies are not bulwarks against encroaching right-wing populism. They are temporary measures and are easily appropriated by the New Right. They are no more than stopgap measures in an ongoing political struggle. They stand on fragile footing. They rest, for the most part, on illusions that may well have contributed to the crises in which we find ourselves today. The rule of law, for instance, is far more malleable than its proponents imagine and can easily be distorted in the hands of autocratic leaders, as happened under the Third Reich or in post-9/11 America. (Recall the infamous torture memos produced by the Justice Department during the George W. Bush administration that immunized unconscionable practices like waterboarding, stress positions, and inhumane deprivations.) Facts—particularly social facts—also are far more malleable than we would like to admit. Many legal facts, for instance, depend on contested notions of materiality, proximity, or intent that are more influenced by relations of power than by objective measurement. Truth, it turns out, is not immune to politics; there is no wall, but instead a tight relationship between truth, knowledge, and power—hopefully, the epistemic detour has taught us that much.

We face unprecedented critical times at a very moment of critical failure. Now, it is time to return to the task of critical philosophy: not to merely interpret the world, but to change it—to develop critical praxis appropriate to these critical times.

Critical theory is up to the task. In fact, it is precisely in crisis moments that critical theory grew the most and has been the most productive. During the 1920s and 1930s, the United States, France, and Germany especially, confronted economic turmoil amid the rise of fascism. The Cold War, colonialism, and the nuclear arms race rippled across the continents in the 1960s, causing wars, civil conflicts, and student and worker revolutions in May 1968 and thereafter. In both of these periods, the critical times renewed critical theory and gave birth to new forms of critical praxis. The 1920s, especially during the fall of the Weimar Republic, gave rise to the Frankfurt School and a whole generation of innovative critical theorists—many of whom would emigrate in exile around the world and spawn a critical diaspora.[38] The 1960s, with its global student uprisings and government repression, stimulated another wave of critical theory and praxis, giving way to a formidable decade of critical thought. The 1970s was particularly fertile for critical theory and praxis, with critics such as Althusser, Arendt, Deleuze and Félix Guattari, Cornelius

Castoriadis, Foucault, and others upending formerly established ways of thinking. The critical debates over praxis in the 1970s were truly remarkable—stimulated by a series of global political upheavals.

It is now time to steer critical philosophy back on track so that we can attend to the most pressing matter: to change this world in these times of utter crisis. These times could not be more pressing. They demand a renewed critical philosophy—one that draws on the epistemological detour to reconstruct itself into a critical praxis. It is time to chart new directions for critical praxis.

In times past, critical theory would have had a ready-made answer. For much of its history, Marxist thinkers dominated the critical Left. Critical theory was tethered to class struggle and historical materialism. Critical practice—what became known as *praxis*, in fact—was oriented toward proletarian revolution. There were, of course, heated debates over tactics. There were severe disagreements over revolution versus parliamentary reform, famously between Rosa Luxemburg and Eduard Bernstein, or over vanguardism versus democratic forms, famously between Lenin and Luxemburg.[39] Yet the broad outline of the path forward was well defined: class struggle, international solidarity, and radical social transformation.

This vision of praxis shaped the first generation of the Frankfurt School and represented a common horizon for the critical Left in the early to mid-twentieth century. But with peasant and anticolonial insurrections in the East and Global South at midcentury, and in the wake of the repression following May 1968, many critical voices began to fracture any such consensus. The decline of syndicalism and of more radical factions of the international labor movement gradually transformed and pacified labor movements during the second half of the twentieth century. The events in the 1950s and 1960s, especially in Hungary and the Eastern bloc, unveiled some of the illusions of critical theory itself, as did the experience of May 1968, where the vitality of the student and worker movements slammed against the rigidity of Leftist parties, especially the Western communist parties still beholden to the Soviet Union. At that point, the grip of Marx's philosophy of history began to loosen. And once that hold dissolved, the critical prescriptions got muddied. Since that time, critical praxis has lacked its earlier coherence—leaving many critical thinkers today somewhat disarmed in the face of renewed right-wing populism.

There is today no longer an intelligible or coherent critical response to the question "What is to be done?" In fact, the question itself has become repugnant to many critical theorists. Apart from a dwindling core, few critical theorists pose the question this way, and even fewer would explicitly advocate the answers that most on the critical Left would have imagined in the early or mid-twentieth century. Today, right-wing populist movements have cannibalized segments of the proletarian base of the former Left, turning old-style class warfare into anti-immigrant, xenophobic, and ethnoracist conflict. The cleavage is no longer between the workers and the bourgeoisie, but rather between a populist white class and minorities and immigrants (or children of immigrants), predominantly persons of color. In the United States, it is between impoverished whites and destitute blacks and Latinos. The problems that this raises today are acute.

This book offers a way forward. It is time—I argue, past time—to imagine a new critical praxis theory for the twenty-first century. There is today an urgent need to rethink critical praxis and reframe the very questions that it poses. This is the task that I have set for myself in these pages: to counter decades of contemplative complacency and to return critical praxis to its central place in critical philosophy. In doing so, this project will strive to reformulate, for a more self-reflective critical age, the action imperative "What is to be done?"

In approaching the praxis imperative in this way, I do not intend by any means to return to Lenin, nor to side with Lenin in his debate with Luxemburg. My intention, on the contrary, is to displace the question; however, in originally approaching the praxis question from this tradition, I mean to resist as strongly as possible the seduction and temptation of contemplation in critical theory. To resist as much as possible the safety of retreating to questions of knowledge and epistemology, or crises diagnoses, rather than confronting as directly as possible the action imperative—with all its difficulties. I intend to resist the move that allows critical philosophy to consider itself simply a form of praxis. To resist the temptation to gradually return the discussion to epistemology or contemplative philosophy, rather than critical praxis. To resist the gradation that ultimately disparages and disdains the practical dimensions, the programs of action, the possibilities for action. Far too many critical thinkers today protect themselves, refuse to take the risk of praxis, and fail to put their ideas (and reputations) honestly at stake. Far too often, we do so by resisting the praxis question. We propose instead to identify the crisis and offer sophisticated critical analysis, but refuse to go any further and engage the question of critical praxis. We claim to be engaged in praxis but refuse to articulate a practice or program. And inevitably, contemplation takes the place of critical theory and praxis.

No more. The problem needs to be addressed at its heart. Today, the praxis imperative must be reformulated. The question "What is to be done?" cannot be asked as a way to check anyone's identification papers. Neither is it a way to distribute reward or locate blame, nor as a way to silence others or crowd anyone out. The question must be rethought and reformulated and nevertheless pursued because, in the end, the aim of critical philosophy is to change the world—not just to change ourselves, although that may be a prerequisite, but to remake our society along lines of compassion, equality, solidarity, and social justice.

Twentieth-century critical theory, especially discourse analysis, demonstrated that even within our own intellectual communities, certain people are heard and others not. It revealed that our own critical practices often serve to reinforce invidious social order and hierarchies. It is precisely for this reason that Foucault's early praxis attempted to resist these tendencies and make space for marginalized voices to be heard. The idea was to enable silenced discourse to become audible. Especially with Foucault's prison abolition efforts with the GIP in the early 1970s, the strategy revolved around creating a space for others to be heard—the prisoners themselves—rather than telling them what to do or what to believe. One can hear this throughout the tracts of the GIP, like this one, from March 15, 1971:

> It is about letting speak those who have an experience of prison. It is not that they need help in "becoming conscious": the consciousness of the oppression is absolutely clear, and they are well aware of who the enemy is. But the current system denies them the means of formulating things, of organizing themselves.[40]

Discourse analysis made us acutely aware of the privilege of certain speakers. The postcolonial critique alerted us to the privilege even of radical critical theorists; and Gayatri Chakravorty Spivak's further critique in "Can the Subaltern Speak?" challenged even the ability of subaltern scholars to hear the voice of the subaltern, underscoring the need for even more vigilance and attention.[41] These are necessary correctives. As we learned, as Foucault did not tire of reminding us, and as Spivak highlights in her own critique of Foucault, the most affected among us do not need a public intellectual to tell them what they want: "the masses no longer need him to gain knowledge: they *know* perfectly well, without illusion; they know far better than he and they are certainly capable of expressing themselves."[42]

Spivak may well be right in her searing critique of this sentence: "The ventriloquism of the speaking subaltern is the left intellectual's stock-in-trade."[43] But even if so, that does not diminish the concern that we, critical theorists, should no longer be speaking for others.

In this sense, the question "What is to be done?" must be reformulated today. Critical theory cannot speak for others. It must instead foster a space for everyone who shares the critical ambition to speak and be heard. The solution to the problem of speaking for others is not to silence anyone, but the opposite: to collaborate and cultivate spaces where all can be heard, especially those who are most affected by our crises today. This reflects as well a new writing style and grammar today. We no longer write in the third person, as Horkheimer did at midcentury. We do not write in universal form either, as Marx or Hegel did before that. Neither do we hide behind the passive tense. No, today, each and every one of us must write in the first person. And that means that we can no longer ask, passively, "What is to be done?" but must actively reformulate the very question of critical praxis for ourselves. For me, it becomes: "What more shall I do, and what work is my praxis doing?"

To change the world through critical praxis: this book calls for a profusion of critical debate over our own critical practices. In the process, it seeks to valorize the work of those critical voices who have stayed true to the ambition of critical praxis. This includes critical philosophers like Angela Davis, who engages in critical praxis through organizations like Critical Resistance and her writings *Are Prisons Obsolete?* and *Freedom Is A Constant Struggle*; Michael Hardt and Antonio Negri, who tell us how to organize, how to assemble, how to revolt, how to seize power, and how to transform society in their book *Assembly*. "Smash the state," they write. "Blow the dam!" "Take power."[44] It includes Chantal Mouffe, who advocates for left populism. "To stop the rise of right-wing populist parties," she proclaims in *For a Left Populism*, "it is necessary to design a properly political answer through a left populist movement that will federate all the democratic struggles against postdemocracy."[45] It includes Stefano Harney and Fred Moten, who tell us, in *The Undercommons: Fugitive Planning & Black Study*, to burn it all down and start over; and Jack Halberstam, who exclaims: "We refuse to ask for recognition and instead we want to take apart, dismantle, tear down the structure that, right now, limits our ability to find each other, to see beyond it and to access the places that we know lie outside its walls. We cannot say what new structures will replace the ones we live with yet, because once we have torn shit down, we will inevitably see more and see differently and feel a new sense of wanting and being and becoming."[46] And Sara Ahmed, who offers a militant, engaged, constant, and unbending vision to create a new world for women and persons of color to inhabit, to live, to find themselves.[47] And Ruth Wilson Gilmore, who not only brilliantly diagnoses the crisis of racialized mass incarceration but weds that diagnosis to her militancy for abolition and racial justice.[48]

These are the critical works that this project seeks to valorize—not to agree with in every respect, but to highlight and engage. They are, however, outliers in critical theory—and most often, they are excoriated for being too praxis oriented, for risking to change the world, for putting themselves out there and addressing praxis head on. By contrast, for the most part, critical philosophers influenced today by the leading strands of critical thought shy away from praxis. They seek shelter in *theoria*. But that is no longer tenable. And so, it is to these others—these courageous others—that we must turn. The ambition of this book is to help create a space where every critical thinker can propose how to rethink critical theory and share how they are doing critical praxis, with the ultimate aim of changing the world.

I will not stop there, though. I will not simply call for a new critical praxis without placing myself at risk. In what follows—and first in summary fashion in the following chapter—I will set forth my own position for a renewed critical praxis theory, in order to fulfill my own challenge and put myself on the line. I do not intend to abuse the author's prerogative, but I will not shirk my responsibility either. I will set out my views as schematically as possible in the next chapter, in order to respond honestly to my own call, before articulating a thorough reconstruction of critical theory and praxis in three parts, which will elaborate a reconstructed critical theory (part I), a reimagined emancipatory horizon (part II), and a renewed critical praxis (part III).[49] I will then return to my own critique and praxis in chapter 18 and elaborate them throughout part IV. And I hope and pray, in an agnostic way, that you will join and lead in cutting a new path for critical theory and praxis in the twenty-first century.

Toward a Critical Praxis Theory

This work, *Critique & Praxis*, is not named after Marx, or for Marx—although both terms, and especially *praxis*, are so closely associated with him. With Marx, that is, and with other critical thinkers who used Marx, such as the early Frankfurt School, Jean-Paul Sartre, the members of the Praxis School, or the contributors to the *Praxis* journal and, later, *Praxis International*. No, this is not a Marxist project, nor a project about Marxism. Marx's philosophy of history no longer holds today, and his analysis of political economy is dated. In many ways, the reconstructed critical praxis theory proposed here, with its emphasis on illusions and values, may be closer to Nietzsche than to Marx, even though just as much of Nietzsche's philosophy also must be set aside, ruthlessly—especially its misogyny and aristocracy. In any event, this is by no means a Marxist manifesto.

But Sartre, Marx, and those other praxis thinkers—whatever their faults—manifested in their intellectual engagements, in their lives, in their very being, a distinct attitude or way of doing critical philosophy that I aspire to. A way of doing critique oriented toward both intellectual emancipation *and* social change. It is *that* way of thinking, of being, of living, of doing that I would like to recover. It is a way of being that draws on other valuable modes of engaging the world—the more contemplative mode of philosophy, the creative mode of *poiesis*—but that revolves more centrally around political activity, in essence, around political doing. As both Nicholas Lobkowicz and Richard Bernstein underscore, this political way of life, as far back as Aristotle, captured the performative dimension of action in the political sphere—performative in the sense that *poiesis* involved making something, whereas *praxis* entailed doing something.[1] It involved a political and ethical form of being.

All three ways of being were intended to be active forms of living, as Lobkowicz and Bernstein emphasize. In other words, the contrast was not intended to be between active and inactive ways of living, but between different active ways of living. *Theoria* was not intended to be merely passive reflection, as opposed to the active doing of praxis. For the ancients, they were instead, as Bernstein suggests, "two dimensions of the truly human and free life."[2] In fact, on Bernstein's reading of the ancients, especially Aristotle, the two ways of living were intended to be joined.[3] The good life was one where there is a harmony. That is quite an ideal—and perhaps I share it. But even a harmony requires rebalancing at times. The ambition of critical philosophy, at least since the nineteenth century, has been to rebalance that harmony and invigorate the praxis imperative. Critical philosophy was born of a desire to push theoretical inquiry in the direction of practice as a more robust mode of being.

You will recall that Foucault, reading Kant's essay "An Answer to the Question: 'What Is Enlightenment?'" identified what he called an "attitude of modernity." Foucault identified in Kant the beginning of a new way to think critically in relation to the present.[4] It consisted of a new philosophical attitude that is oriented, genuinely, to the contemporary moment. "By 'attitude,'" Foucault explained, "I mean a mode of relating to contemporary reality; a voluntary choice made by certain people; in the end, a way of thinking and feeling; a way, too, of acting and behaving that at one and the same time marks a relation of belonging and presents itself as a task."[5] According to Foucault, this attitude of modernity would bring together philosophical inquiry and critical thought focused on contemporary historical actuality. The contemporary moment—most notably, the French Revolution, for Kant—became the object of critical thought. Foucault placed Marx in the wake of this new attitude of modernity.

In a similar way, I suggest, Marx inaugurated a "*practical* attitude of modernity," pivoting the attitude of modernity not just onto the contemporary moment, but from theoretical to practical engagements—from *theoria* to praxis. Richard Bernstein traces this to the writings of the young Marx, where he documents three stages of the turn to praxis. The first, Marx's early call in 1843 for a new attitude and role for the intellectual to awaken self-consciousness about the need for revolutionary change through the "*relentless criticism of all existing conditions*, relentless in the sense that the criticism is not afraid of its findings and just as little afraid of the conflict with the powers that be." The idea was that critique must serve as the way to awaken a new sense of human dignity and bring about social change.

The second, when Marx materializes this relentless criticism and actualizes it by tapping into our deepest passions—when he explicitly argues, "Material force must be overthrown by material force. But theory also becomes a material force once it has gripped the masses"; or, more directly, when he writes: "Theory is actualized in a people only insofar as it actualizes their needs." The final, third moment, when Marx pens the eleventh thesis. As Bernstein writes, "The critique of philosophy had dialectically led Marx to the conclusion that only a correct, detailed understanding of existing social reality could effect such a revolution." At that point, Marx goes beyond philosophy to the critique of political economy, and—no mere coincidence—the term *praxis* almost disappears from Marx's vocabulary.[6]

My fear is that today, that practical attitude of modernity, inflected in praxis as a mode of being, has dissipated such that critical philosophy now has become too contemplative. One might think of the history of critical philosophy as being punctuated by praxis moments—first by the Left Hegelians's call for philosophy to become a practical activity that would directly influence social life; then by Rosa Luxemburg; later by Frantz Fanon and Sartre's *Critique of Dialectical Reason*; later by Foucault and the young maoists.[7] Faced with these critical times today, I would argue, we desperately need a renewed praxis moment—a corrective. That is the ambition of this intervention. But it entails rethinking critical theory, its horizon, and its relation to praxis.

My ambition here is not to inspire critical theorists to become activists. It is not to make theorists drop their pens and turn to direct action. I am fond of Daniel Defert's story of how, during May 1968, he threw his doctoral thesis to the pavement—"*jeté aux pavés*," as he said—and turned to Maoism. But that is certainly not my intention here, particularly because, in the end, I do not believe in influencing others. I do not even believe in the idea of "influence." Critical thinkers, as I will show, are not "influenced" by others. They use and deploy their own interpretations of others' writings and practices to pursue their own political interventions. But also, and more important, because critical philosophy is not about telling others what to do, or even trying to signal that or subliminally hint at that. Critical philosophy, in the end, is a personal praxis. My ambition, then, is to instantiate a personal corrective moment—to push myself back toward praxis and to confront my praxis with critical theory.

In the same way in which Marx's encounter with Hegel's philosophy, when he was a young student at the University of Berlin, was a traumatic experience that produced a type of conversion or life change to praxis,[8] I would like the current moment of political crisis to serve as an alarm bell. We face today an unprecedented set of crises: the global climate crisis, the rise of extreme-right populist movements, the international impact of neoliberal policies, the threat of pandemics, increased xenophobic expressions and attacks on minorities, and the fallout of a global war on terror. We are in the midst of a rare historical epoch of worldwide political turbulence. In these times, now more than ever, I feel compelled not only to diagnose these crises, but to answer the most pressing question: What am *I* to do, what more shall *I* do, and how will it work?

I fear that even my own diagnosis of crises is no longer sufficient. I must supplement it with a more engaged confrontation of my own critical practices. Even if, as Aristotle believed and Bernstein underscores, *theoria* is active, it alone is not active *enough* for me. I need to engage in *critique and praxis*—not just to answer the question "What should be done?" but to confront my ongoing practice with theory and vice versa, and in the process to enrich both my praxis and my critical theory.

The fact is, the concept of praxis in Marx's early thought had a much thicker and richer nature than just theorizing the question "What is to be done?" in the face of our diagnosed crises today. Human practice and real existence, for Marx, were sources of knowledge. Through human interactions—the same set of human clashes and struggles that Hegel anthropomorphized as spirit (*Geist*)—we can learn things about our present. For the young Marx, practice taught him about the feelings of alienation from being separated from the product of one's labor, about feelings of recognition, and so on. As Bernstein demonstrates in his chapter on Marx in *Praxis and Action*, Marx operated a transformation of Hegelian thought that inverted the relationship between the consciousness of a world spirit or rationality and the actions of human beings. Rather than spirit and its peripeteia being the motor of history and human progress, it is human action and interaction, as praxis, that constitute our political condition and our history.[9]

What this suggests is that the relationship between theory and practice cannot just be the thin *application* of critical theory to actual circumstances—thin in the way in which we tend to say that our political actions have to be "guided" by political principles or theories or reason, or that we "apply" theory to practice. The simple direction of movement from one pole of the spectrum to the other—from theory or from practice—has a significant effect on where we end up: if we start from contemplation, it becomes too easy to propose that we merely apply our theories, or simply theorize what is to be done. If we start from the other direction, from praxis, it becomes too easy to suggest that our political practices could enlighten the crises that surround us.

This entails the need to develop a space of critical theory that does not merely theorize practice, nor that simply starts from praxis, but that is genuinely and simultaneously a space of *critique and praxis*: genuinely a space where practice and critical thought confront each other constantly, so that we do away with notions like applying theory, or drawing implications, or theorizing practice. In fact, the notions of a separation or of a dichotomy of theory and practice are not productive ways to proceed. Instead, it must be a constant confrontation that ends up creating, in effect, a unified space. It is the unity in constant confrontation that pushes both our critical practices and our critical theory. It is this space that I call *critique and praxis.*

In this book, I chart a path forward to the space of critique and praxis. It requires, I argue, a reconstruction of critical theory, as well as a reimagination of the critical horizon and a reconceptualization of critical praxis. I offer those in parts I, II, and III. But I refuse to shirk my own call to praxis. I refuse to refrain from putting myself at risk. So, in effect, I will start at the end, as promised. I will start by revealing my hand. In this chapter, I will set out, first, my position on critical praxis; second, my view of the proper relationship between theory and praxis; and third, my outline for a reconstructed critical philosophy for the twenty-first century—what I call a *critical praxis theory.*

Reformulating the Praxis Imperative

It feels odd starting at the end, but to do otherwise would undermine the ultimate point—namely, first, that the question "What is to be done?" may well capture the action imperative at the heart of critical philosophy, but in these times of heightened reflexivity, it needs to be updated and reformulated. Second, that the reconstruction of critical philosophy cannot serve as a universal or as a model for others, but only as a subjective enterprise and intervention. The work of reconstruction has to be done by each critical thinker for herself or himself. The value of reconstruction is in the work of reconstruction itself. In other political traditions, political movements can and often do thrive on leadership, emulation, and influence. Some political traditions in fact depend on charismatic leadership and authority. But the critical approach typically does not, and a critical political movement typically cannot. It has, at its root, an inextricable element of reflexivity that does not make "following" easy. There are, naturally, exceptions, such as recent calls for a left populism that are not allergic to charismatic leadership.[10] But this is precisely what riles so many critical theorists. It is, at least, what I object to.

So the question, for me, cannot be "What is to be done?" in the sense of telling others what to do, how to organize, whom to follow, when to submit, or how to revolt. It always has to be a question that one poses to *oneself*—or rather, that *I* pose to *myself.* This is, I would argue, both a liability and the strength of critical philosophy. Because of its reflexivity, critical theory does not lend itself well to organization or militarization. When there is unity, it is fractious. It is contested. It is constantly challenged by another layer of critical thought. In my view, however, critical philosophy has no choice but to make a virtue out of this necessity—and to turn the question onto oneself.

I would reformulate the question "What is to be done?", a question usually addressed to others, as a question addressed only to myself: "What more am I to do, and how does what I am doing work?" That is the reflexive question and posture that I will take. What is *my* critical praxis, and what work is it doing? Does it work, and if so, how? How does it pursue the critical ambition to change the world? How does it survive and confront critique? How does it affect the world? The question "What more am I to do?" places the emphasis and the onus on my own praxis. It places the focus on *my* actions. And it carries a number of connotations. By asking myself how my *own* praxis works, or what work my praxis is doing, I want to challenge myself to critically understand what in fact I am trying to accomplish with my actions. I also want to focus, equally, on the *what* in the question: to focus on the object that is, precisely, *what* I am doing and *how* it works.

In the end, the unity of theory and praxis does not mean that theory can dictate praxis, as if it were simply applied thought. Neither does it imply that I abandon theory and just start from praxis. It means that I must constantly confront the two and leave neither unscathed, for I cannot theorize when I am not engaged, and I cannot act without critical reflection. I must constantly engage and reengage in praxis *and* critical theory, and *confront the two.* If I, as a critical thinker, am not actively engaged in political contestation, I am not being honest either to myself or to critical philosophy. Critical theorizing alone, for me, is not a praxis. Writing critical theory, even writing critical interventions and teaching critical theory alone, for me, are not praxis. My critical theory has to confront, nourish, and be challenged by my own critical praxis. I need to be struggling, writing, litigating, marching, organizing, fighting—and if I am not doing that, I am no longer, in my eyes, a critical theorist. I've become a contemplative philosopher. I surely cannot tell anyone else how to act, nor do I espouse action for action's sake. I am simply saying that I have to engage in praxis and confront theory and praxis. Critical theory is not just about diagnosing crises. It is not just about *Krise und Kritik.* It is about *critique and praxis.* Especially in these times of acute crises, I must engage in critical praxis and confront my praxis with critical theory.

My answer, then, to the question "What more am I to do?" is this: I litigate, I militate, I organize, I write, I advocate, I organize, I teach, I convene—and throughout, at all times, I brutally confront my own praxis with critical theory, and vice versa. As I discuss in chapter 18—a more personal account of my struggles since, there, I will directly respond to my own reformulation of the action imperative—my critical praxis has evolved in confrontation with critical theory to the point where, today, it embraces an abolitionist ambition aimed not only at ending the death penalty in the United States, where I started my litigation praxis, but at the broader goal of abolishing our punitive paradigm of governing in this country—of abolishing our punitive society.

Through conflict and friction, and the constant back-and-forth between praxis and theory, I have gradually enlarged my field of action to address evolving and growing crises, and now constantly challenge my own engagements—whether they are litigating on behalf of the condemned, suing President Donald Trump to enjoin the Muslim ban, organizing opposition to a judicial nomination, challenging repressive police practices, or advocating against racial profiling and biased algorithms. Having spent more than three decades as a public-interest litigator and organizer, and as a critical theorist and writer, having dedicated years to building critical conversations and collectives, I have learned to confront my praxis with theory and my theory with praxis, and to push both to their maximum. I deploy that conflict toward social justice and the emancipatory ideals at the heart of critical philosophy—not always with success, but always with passion. In all this, I aspire to create a space to live the way of the critical theoretic practitioner and critical praxis theorist.

As such, I aspire to an ideal that differs from the model of the universal, specific, or even singular intellectual. I aspire to a way of being, as a critical praxis theorist, that has not yet been entirely conceived—at least not with the exact same sensibility that I envisage. It differs from the other models that have been articulated, especially in relation to Foucault.

In an essay on forms of truth-telling titled "*Dire, contredire*" (Speak, contradict), Étienne Balibar explores the relationship, in Foucault's late lectures, between Foucault's study of forms of truth-telling (or what Foucault referred to, using the ancient Greek term, as *parrhesia*), the evolution in Foucault's understanding of critique, and Foucault's unique position or self-understanding as an intellectual.[11] By connecting these three dimensions, Balibar proposes that the practice of speaking truth—especially the formula of speaking truth to power, of frank speech, or even of fearless speech, and of the courage of truth, to which Foucault often returned—was central to his distinctive way of defining critique as the act of resistance to being governed in a particular way. Speaking out, breaking silence, and frank speech become, in Foucault's late lectures, forms of praxis or ways of being that appear valuable to political existence.

Balibar locates in this way of being a distinct and peculiar element: a form of resistance or contrarianism associated with the notion of contradiction, of counterconduct, of opposition to ordinary discursive practices. It is an agonistic form of truth-telling—a contrarian one. Balibar emphasizes the element of counterspeech, underlining the hidden syntax of contradiction as "*contra-diction*," with diction, naturally, indexing speech.[12] Balibar marshals the multiple expressions, throughout Foucault's writings, of this counterconduct in speech and of the use of the term *counter*. Balibar associates this counterpositionality with a certain agonistic relationship or resistance to ordinary democratic processes. He associates it with the figure of Diogenes, the cynic, one of the truth-tellers whom Foucault studied (with some admiration).

Balibar suggests, between the lines, that this form of *contra-diction* may be essential to democracy as a vital counterweight—and that Foucault valued it as a form of counterconduct. Balibar refers to the "necessity of a disruptive intervention to restore democracy."[13] He imagines it as a ballast to Habermasian discourse ethics. Along these lines, Balibar proposes that Foucault may have understood these forms of counterspeech and contradiction as a method of critique and, even more, that Foucault understood himself, as an intellectual, in this counterpositionality. (This notion of "counter," which recurs throughout Balibar's essay and writings, as well as those of Foucault, is extremely productive, and I will come back to it in chapter 6 of part I.)

In discussing "*contra-diction*" as a form of praxis and critique, Balibar offers an alternative way to conceive of Foucault's role as intellectual—an alternative, that is, to the usual distinction between what is called the "universal" and the "specific" intellectual. Regarding the latter, Foucault himself had outlined the model of the specific intellectual, as opposed to the universal intellectual—a somewhat derogatory term, aimed mostly at Sartre and intended to capture the intellectual actor who always has a position (and typically the same position) on all political issues. The specific intellectual, by contrast, weighs in more selectively and develops unique positions deeply immersed in the specific context of any particular political conflict. Foucault at times identified as a specific intellectual.

In light of the idea of "*contra-diction*" as critique, Balibar proposes a third model of the intellectual, an alternative model, which he calls the "singular intellectual." The singular intellectual makes countermoves in order to preserve political life. This is the truth-teller who negotiates the space of politics and philosophy, of both governing others and oneself, and who, Balibar writes, "engages historical *singularities*, in other words moments of actuality: an intellectual who is neither 'universal,' nor 'specific,' but situates himself *beyond* that metaphysical distinction in his way of living and of discourse. An intellectual who tries to say things about the present, about his rights and obligations, about the intolerable, and about the possibilities that may emerge."[14]

Balibar cautions that this model risks veering toward what he calls the "counter-expert" or the "counselor to social movements" (analogous to the counselor to the prince). It is a risky position, he warns. The danger is becoming a backseat driver to political movements—an armchair advisor to resistance. When it works, it can change everything; at other times, it is useless and derisory.[15] What it promises, though, is a corrective to the democratic form, an agonistic counterpoint to too-facile agreement—assuming, Balibar notes ominously, that the political conditions still allow for the singular intellectual.

Balibar contrasts this model with the Habermasian ideal of communicative action: there is, with the singular intellectual, no attempt to universalize any principles, but rather to challenge and give voice to contradiction. It is, in this sense, the very counterpoint of a Habermasian discourse ethic. It does not seek rational agreement or eventual convergence on norms. It serves instead to contradict and contest—but in that contradiction, it keeps the political space alive. It has conflict, not consensus, as its guiding star. The idea is that contradiction is essential to maintaining political life.

The model of the singular intellectual that Balibar proposes intrigues me. It has something that is attractive, but also worrisome. From a first impression, it feels too self-absorbed, and I find the model of the truth-teller a bit too self-righteous. What I am telling is not the truth, but an interpretation, as I will show—one that is tied to my political project. To be sure, the universal intellectual has little appeal to me because of the problems of universalization—I will get to those. But in addition, both the specific and the singular intellectual have problems. They are too likely to veer into the role of "counselor in uprisings." It is that model I want to resist. I cannot counsel uprisings. I cannot tell others what to do. I cannot advise militants. I can only confront my own praxis.

So instead, I propose the model of the critical praxis theorist or critical theoretic practitioner: a reflexive way of being that *turns the analysis entirely on my own practices and confronts only my praxis and my critical theory.* To theoretically confront my actions and practically confront my theorizing—that is the way of being to which I aspire. And it carries with it an obligation, for me, to engage in critical praxis, not just critical theory.

So, for instance, in the face of the Yellow Vest movement in France in 2018–2019, many critical thinkers had a lot to say about the movement itself and what it should do. The fact is, many of the protesters expressed a desire for greater equality and fair treatment, especially for the disadvantaged in society and the precarious, as well as anger at the country's neoliberal policies and a desire for plebian institutions, such as a citizen-initiated referendum process. As a result, many critical thinkers on the Left supported the movement. Étienne Balibar and Antonio Negri aptly described it as a "*contre-pouvoir*" (counterpower), perhaps one of the only counterpowers in French politics at the time.[16] In an early essay published on December 13, 2018, Balibar presented a diagnosis of the movement, locating it within the present crisis of neoliberalism and drawing its Gramscian element as a potential "reversal of hegemony." He ended that piece by offering guidance as to how the movement could gain momentum, suggesting that mayors and municipalities should "open their doors to the local organization of the movement, and declare[] themselves ready to pass on its demands or proposals to the government."[17]

I would take a different angle. I have no standing, nor any interest in assuming the position of the counselor to uprisings—whether as a general, specific, or singular intellectual.[18] I do not consider myself—nor would I want to present myself—as a public intellectual advisor; instead, I am simply someone who acts, who implicates himself, who rises up at times, breaks silence at others, and litigates most often. I cannot counsel or critique other people's struggles. I can only critique my own political engagements. I cannot do critical philosophical work on other people's political engagements, only on my own. This imposes on me, I believe, a duty to act—to engage politically, to perform praxis, as the very precondition to critique, but critique and praxis *of my own actions.*

So the questions that I would raise are different, but pointed, and pointed at myself: When I was at the Étoile in Paris myself during one of the *Actes* of the Yellow Vest movement, why did I not sport a yellow vest? Why did I not consider myself part of the movement? Why did I decide to be an observer, or at most an ally, and not a protester? Those are the questions, or the form of engagement, that I demand of myself. It is not to advise or give counsel, not merely to diagnose, and not to theorize their praxes, but to confront my own actions with critical theory; and not to presume that where I come out will be useful to others. I feel that I must do this for my own praxis and theory—for a critical praxis theory.

After all, the Yellow Vest movement at the time challenged many of the contemporary political formations that I target in my own political interventions and writings. It aimed at the ills of neoliberalism and the start-up, Uberized culture that does not provide for the welfare of ordinary people. It targeted police excess and the police state. I've been challenging that in the United States for decades. If you listen closely, for a moment, to some of the grievances of the Yellow Vests, you clearly hear those of the Occupy Wall Street movement. So the question that I want to pose to myself is not "What should they do?" but rather, "Why am I not donning a yellow vest?"

This reflexivity, I would argue, is the point of departure for critical theory. It lay at the origin of Max Horkheimer's intervention: to understand how the critical theorist, located in and shaped by history, can transform history through theory and practice. It is central to Foucault's genealogical method and to the new wave of critical theory in the 1960s.[19] It is, as I will show in chapter 5, at the core of the interventions of later critical theorists, such as Edward Said, Gayatri Chakravorty Spivak, Seyla Benhabib, Amy Allen, and Rahel Jaeggi. It is at the heart of critical philosophy and transcends all of the later internecine epistemological battles between the Frankfurt School, poststructuralists, postcolonial and queer theorists. And in terms of its implications for the role of the intellectual, it motivates an alternative even to Balibar's singular intellectual.

Foucault, as you recall, was not in favor of proposing. As he explained in an interview with Christian Panier and Pierre Watté in Louvain, on May 14, 1981, he did not believe in telling others what to do, or even signaling by his own commitments what others should do: "I confess that I do not subscribe to the idea of the intellectual intervening or assuming the role of someone who gives lessons or advice regarding matters of political choice—it doesn't sit well with me. I think people are grown-up enough to choose for themselves who they vote for. To say: 'I am an intellectual and I vote for Mr. So-and-so, and therefore you should vote for Mr. So-and-so,' strikes me as a rather astonishing attitude, a kind of arrogance of the intellectual."[20] On the other hand, as you will recall, Foucault was comfortable with his books serving others if they found something of interest in them. As he said at times, he wrote for users, not readers. He hoped, perhaps aspired, that his books could be useful to others, that his ideas would have resonance. So he told Panier and Watté: "On the other hand, if for any number of reasons an intellectual thinks that his work, his analysis, his reflections, his way of acting or thinking about things can shed light on a particular situation, social domain, or conjunction of circumstances, and that he can bring to bear his theoretical and practical contributions on them, then in that case one can draw political consequences. . . . I think that if he wants to, the intellectual can contribute important elements to the perception and critique of things, from which certain political choices would then naturally follow, if people are so inclined."[21]

To me, even this is too arrogant. It still views critical work as giving lessons or advice, but for others to discover. It still anticipates that the critical theoretic work will be useful to *others*. It merely displaces the didactic element onto the reader.

I would like to carve out a different space: my theoretical work is intended to push me and my praxis. I do not believe or presume that any readers will think that it sheds light on theirs. Then why publish, you may ask? Why discuss this critical praxis theory in public? The answer is: to stake out a personal space opposed to all those who think they can tell me what is to be done, without giving up on the ambition to critical praxis. It is not to serve as an illustration, an exemplar, or a loadstar; not to shed light for others; nor to serve as a Diogenes. The purpose, it turns out, is to create a space for me to proceed differently and to create space to hear others.

In his discussion with Panier and Watté at Louvain in 1981, Foucault put the theory-praxis question in terms that are pretty close to the space that I am trying to carve out for myself. I will cite the full passage, as it is important, before drawing the distinctions:

> When I was a student, I was struck by the fact that during that period we were in a profoundly Marxist atmosphere where the problem of the link between theory and practice was absolutely at the center of all theoretical discussions.
>
> It seems to me that there was perhaps an easier way, or I would say a more immediately practical way, of posing the question of the relationship between theory and practice correctly, and that was to carry it out directly in one's own practice. In this sense, I could say that I have always insisted that my books be, in one sense, fragments of an autobiography. My books have always been my personal problems with madness, the prison, and sexuality.
>
> Second, I have always insisted that there take place within me and for me a kind of back and forth, an interference, an interconnection between practices and the theoretical or historical work I was doing. It seemed to me that I was all the more free to reach deeper and farther into history because I also tied the questions I was asking to practice, in an immediate and contemporary way. It was because I spent a certain time in psychiatric hospitals that I wrote *The Birth of the Clinic.* With regard to prisons, I began to do a certain number of things, and then I wrote *Discipline and Punish.*
>
> I also took a third precaution: during the period when I pursued these theoretical and historical analyses exclusively in relation to the questions that I had specifically asked myself, I always insisted that this theoretical work not dictate rules with regard to contemporary practice, and that it pose questions. Take the book on madness, for example: its description and analysis end in the years 1814 to 1815. Thus, the book did not appear to be a critique of contemporary psychiatric institutions, but I knew their functioning well enough that I could question their history. It seems to me that the history I wrote was sufficiently detailed for it to pose questions for those who currently live in the institution.[22]

There is much that I admire in this formulation, but I would not embrace it as is. I definitely agree with the overarching ambition to live the relationship between theory and praxis in one's own practice. I also agree that theory should not dictate rules to praxis or vice versa. But I am not satisfied with turning first and foremost to my books as illustrations of practice, nor merely to lived experience.[23] I am also concerned about the notion of autobiography *tout court.* Overall, I worry that

Foucault's formulation does not push enough toward critical practice. The balance seems off, in my view, or at least for myself. I am not suggesting what anyone else should do, but for myself, the resulting balance does not feel as if it is sufficiently engaged in political action.

I must continue to litigate, to advocate, to militate—in addition to researching and writing books that engage practices and institutions and to teaching and creating critical space. By *litigate*, I do not simply mean filing lawsuits and representing clients. That is too often merely defensive or reactive, and not sufficiently proactive. Plus, if the courts are stacked and impenetrable, these actions may be pointless. I use this term to refer to using the law proactively, in a country where the rule of law is the compass—even if that principle is only an illusion. By *advocate*, by *militate*, I set no limits. By *writing*, I intend to confront my praxis with critical theory and also to imagine ways forward. By *teaching*, I express the hope that I can support and encourage students to become social justice warriors as much as possible. By *creating a critical space*, I mean to animate a space of critical praxis theory that allows others to speak equally and be heard.

Contrary to the Enlightenment, to liberal tenets, or even to Habermasian communicative theory, there are no rational principles, no universal charters of civil and political rights, and no universalizable maxims that will protect us from a downward spiral into authoritarianism. There is no institutional fix, no discursive principle, no permanent or lasting legal protection against tyranny. Reason has been eclipsed far too often. Ideal theory is just that—ideal. And the rule of law will not save us; it is plied instead by brilliant lawyers who bend it to the will of their handlers, as we witnessed so starkly during the presidency of George W. Bush.

Our political condition does not achieve the kind of equilibrium characterized by liberal political theory. Instead, it is a constant, never-ending struggle to shape distributions of resources. It is an unending political competition, one that never reaches a stable equilibrium, but rather churns endlessly, dramatically, and often violently, redistributing wealth, security, influence, liberty, well-being—and, yes, life itself. This is a central insight of a critical praxis theory, and it remains as sound today as it was 100 years ago: our political condition is a constant battle to realize contested visions and ambitions for life and social existence. We are steeped in these ongoing political struggles. We are shaped by them. We are implicated in them. We transform them.

These struggles are most often fought, and won, on the basis of illusions: by getting people to believe so deeply in the truth of social facts that they are then willing to sacrifice their lives for their beliefs. In recent decades, with the collapse of communism and the rise of neoliberalism, the illusion of free markets has done most of the work. But today, the specter of immigrant invasion, of loss of white identity, and of the Islamification of the West is increasingly driving many more people to join extreme-right populist movements. We know this. Critical theory has labored over these epistemological matters for decades. We no longer need to fight among ourselves over these basics. We no longer need to replow these epistemological points.

Instead, we need now to turn to the most difficult task at hand—the ambition of critical theory: to reframe and articulate a new critical praxis theory. I offer in part IV an idiosyncratic and individual proposal for critical praxis. And, somewhat like Bruno Latour, I too will end my urgent call for critical theory and praxis in these urgent times with an invitation:

> There, I've finished. Now, if you wish, it's your turn to present yourself, tell us a little about where you would like to land and with whom you agree to share a dwelling place.[24]

I might not say it in exactly the same way as Latour. Perhaps I might emphasize not just with whom, but how you might agree to share your existence. But the invitation remains open.

I have many firm convictions that will come out in the course of this book. For instance, I don't believe in a Marxian philosophy of history, nor in the idea of human progress. In fact, I think that, with the global climate crisis and the threat of pandemics, we are in a worse position than ever before. I don't believe that a revolution would succeed now in the United States, but I do believe that we face a Counterrevolution. I don't believe in physical violence, although I know all politics are inevitably violent. But these specific positions are all secondary to the larger ambition of this work: I believe that I must act and engage in praxis. I believe that I cannot do critical theory unless I am engaged in critical practice. I believe I must confront my critical praxis with critical theory, and my critical theory with critical praxis.

Rethinking the Relation Between Theory and Praxis

In reformulating the question "What is to be done?" as "What more am I to do?" I propose a specific relationship between theory and praxis: a constant confrontation between my critical practices and critical theory. Paradoxically, the vision I propose overlaps theoretically with the relationship that Adorno espoused in 1968–1969: a continuous and unresolved dialectical contradiction between theory and praxis. But I embrace it with an entirely different sensibility to action than Adorno had, and I intend to push it in an entirely different direction: I propose to constantly collide and clash my praxis and theory on the model of the Large Hadron Collider at CERN. My goal, in effect, is to collide theory and praxis as if in the Large Hadron Collider.

Some critics might respond that it would be better to do away with the dichotomy altogether, that the theory/praxis divide merely replicates the Cartesian body/mind problem. Jack Halberstam, for instance, directly contests the theory-praxis divide. He challenges the privileged position from which any critical theorists could declare what is to be done or how to change the world. Presuming or accepting the theory-praxis opposition has negative effects, Halberstam argues. When we start from that dichotomy, Halberstam writes, "we cement the opposition between theory and practice and make it seem as if this bounded zone were real, as if people were just waiting to hear from on high about the proper interpretation of Marx's 'Theses on Feuerbach,' as if the correct definition of the general strike would resolve the question of how to change things." Halberstam emphasizes that the distinction creates unnecessary hierarchies and counterproductive expectations. He underscores that "getting it right is not a prelude to change; the general strike is ongoing and everywhere, it is spontaneous (contra Luxemburg) and lasting in its form and impact. Furthermore, critique is not the road to enlightenment; enlightenment is not the goal; and the undercommons is not a route to a new politics but the end of politics as such." In a direct rebuke, Halberstam declares: "Denizens of the undercommons do not recognize the distinction between theory and practice that . . . preoccupies our most canonical political thinkers such as Marx, Lenin, Foucault, and Arendt."[25]

This represents, to my mind, the most direct challenge to this project of a critical praxis theory—or at least the most important challenge that I am drawn to. I am less concerned about the liberal or conservative critique, as both are reactionary.

But I am mobilized by the undercommons critique because, at times, I espouse it.[26] I agree that knowledge is the product of the hierarchies we inhabit. I agree that meritocracy is an illusion and a product of regimes of truth. I reject the ranking, the hierarchy, and the exploitation of our universities. So the underlying critical theory seems right to me. Yet I would like to imagine that the model of the Large Hadron Collider does not reify the dichotomy but rather blasts it apart. It creates a unified field of critical praxis theory that deconstructs the divide. In this way, the constant contradiction and confrontation produce a fused space of critical praxis, something like a unity of theory and practice—perhaps that unity of theory and practice that Horkheimer aspired to before moving away from it after World War II, or that Marcuse spoke of. It may be possible to avoid the pitfalls that Jack Halberstam identifies if we speak, in this Marcusian way, of a unified field of theory and praxis.

I too would like to imagine that praxis does not wait for theory. I would like to believe that I can and must act first, and that there is no legitimacy to theorizing about praxis, to critical theory itself, absent a militant engagement. I can and should theorize only about *my* actions. I also want to imagine that we can instantiate now something beyond politics—an end of politics. That was, in part, what I believed that the Occupy movement was doing so brilliantly. So I say: Accentuate the tension and contradiction because they are so productive. They reveal so much about what we are doing and thinking. They do so much. Rather than dissolve, I say accentuate and put them into a virtual Large Hadron Collider. Smash them to pieces. I believe that this idea of a "unified field" is possible and can be distinguished from the other four ways of relating theory and praxis. As I will demonstrate, those other four models are more grounded on the dichotomy.

Critical Theory as Praxis

The first model views critical theoretic work itself—for instance, the diagnosis of crises moments, the exercise of exposing illusions, the work of ideology critique—as a form of critical praxis in its own right. This is different than pure contemplation or traditional philosophy. It is more than pure philosophical practice that does not even engage the real world or the present times, more than abstract theory or philosophy for its own sake—a form of philosophy that antedates the "attitude of modernity," does not concern itself with the present, and does not seek to address social problems. Critical theory as a form of praxis, by contrast, considers that the critical work itself affects or transforms reality. The reflective nature of critical theory means that the theorist is necessarily situated within a historical transformation that he or she forms part of and fuels. So critical thinking itself is an active task. Other practitioners, afterward and elsewhere, may find something to use—but that is not part of the critical theoretic work. Theorists need look no further than their own conceptual work to see practice in action. There is, in this sense, an autonomy to critical theory.

This resonates with the earlier statement of Foucault: he is providing ideas and tools, and it is up to others to find something of value in them (if they do). I think you also hear this in Horkheimer and Adorno and their resistance to action. It is also reflected in the passage, given earlier, from Honneth. When he writes in *The Idea of Socialism*, "I make no attempt to draw connections to current political constellations and possibilities for action. I will not be dealing with the strategic question of how socialism could influence current political events," he is essentially drawing a line between the critical intellectual work and implementation or praxis: it will be up to others to figure out how these ideas might be put into action.[27]

As I will make clear in this work, I reject this first model as too contemplative. Critical theorizing alone is not, in my opinion, sufficiently active and alone does not amount to critical praxis.

Critical Theoretic Implications for Praxis

Alternatively, one could view the task of critical theory as guiding and informing practice. On this view, praxis should be understood as applied theory: the theoretical work comes first, and it has implications for what we should do. This model recalls the Enlightenment view: reason effectively guides our action. Paradoxically, there is a sense in which Horkheimer, in his article "Traditional and Critical Theory," is doing just that—paradoxically because later, in 1944, he would come down so hard on instrumental reason (the core of his and Adorno's critique in the *Dialectic of Enlightenment*). But in 1937, when Horkheimer writes that the proletariat is suffering from illusions and that the task for the theorist is to help the proletariat see straight and bring about social transformation, this can be described fairly as an applied theoretical approach.

Here, critical theory focuses not merely on diagnosing present crises or reformulating critical ideas, but also on proposing avenues and actions to address the crises and bring about social change. This might be something of an equilibrium point on the theoretical side between *theoria* and praxis, where we theorize practice and formulate strategies to address current crises.

The work of Michael Hardt and Antonio Negri well illustrates this second approach. Their book *Assembly* (2017) functions as a manual for assemblies intended not just to analyze or theorize, but to counsel, advise, and encourage assembly-style social movements. It is a how-to guide, with concrete instructions on how to seize power, organize leadership, and restructure subjectivity and economic production. Hardt and Negri draw on the practices of existing social movements, but not so much to learn from them as to give them direction and correction based on their theoretical work. In other words, their theory is driving their praxis recommendations, rather than the praxes of others driving their theory.

They locate the productivity of "assembly" as a new mode of politics within the power of the "multitude"—the notion that grounded a previous book of theirs—in effect suggesting that contemporary social movements are verifying or actualizing their conception of the multitude. In the process, they hope to stimulate and guide these insurrectional social movements. Their work is, in the words of Joshua Smeltzer, "a blueprint for empowering the multitude as the means of establishing a more just society."[28] Their strategies, such as inverted leadership and claimed entrepreneurship, are individually to be viewed "as a simple operator of assembly within a multitude that is self-organized and cooperates in freedom and equality to produce wealth."[29] Hardt and Negri propose a list of concrete organizational advice (almost commands) for Leftist revolt, derived primarily from their theoretical work, as well as from Negri's Marxist militant background.

Confronted with leaderless social movements like Occupy Wall Street or the Arab Spring, Hardt and Negri advise against giving up on leadership. Rather than going leaderless, they argue that one should "transform the role of leadership by inverting strategy and tactics": let the multitude decide on strategy, but the leaders decide on tactics. Do not give up on institutions and organizations, they declare; instead, build new institutions—specifically nonsovereign ones. They continue, "Smashing the state means . . . creating political and administrative institutions that immanently organize the collective, democratic decision-making of the entire population."[30]

Most important, Hardt and Negri argue that social movements today need to seize power. They write that many of the current social movements focus all their attention on the movement itself, its general assemblies, and the insulated world of the resistance movement rather than on taking power from the state. Many groups create a hermetically sealed space of protest and militancy—*en vase clos*—separate and independent from ordinary politics and political power. With Occupy, for instance, there was a palpable and deliberate resistance to power, legislative politics, or party politics—to any engagement with conventional political representation and practices. Hardt and Negri push in a very different direction: Leftist movements must take power. They must seize the conventional instruments, institutions, and pathways of politics. "We have little sympathy with those who want to maintain their purity and keep their hands clean by refusing power," they proclaim. "In order to change the world we need to take power."[31]

In other words, Hardt and Negri do not merely theorize what is going on. They draw on their critical theory to counsel, advise, and revise the strategies of these movements. It is in this sense that we could say that they are *applying* critical theory to praxis. There is, however, a vanguard intellectualism here that seems out of date and somewhat unconvincing. Hardt and Negri are, without doubt, brilliant theorists, but there is no reason to believe that they are good strategists or authoritative practitioners, or that the implications of their brilliant theorizing are right. There is no reason to follow them into battle. And that's the problem, often, with applied theory: a lack of credibility. Slavoj Žižek falls victim to this as well. He advocates for a direct relationship from theory to praxis; his is the model of critical theory telling us what to do. In his essay in *The Idea of Communism*, volume 3, Žižek writes, "There are numerous cases in which representing (speaking for) others is a necessity."[32] Žižek does not abide by the "step back" idea. Instead, he embraces a form of Leninism that dictates practice. The problem, again, is that there is no basis to trust his strategic judgment, no reason to defer to his application of critical theory.

Theorizing Praxis

Toward the other end of the spectrum, some critical theorists theorize praxis: practice is something that we interpret, essentially after the fact. Theory comes in afterward to help us understand practices, make sense of them. In this view, it is not that theory can guide practice, but rather that practice has a certain kind of autonomy and independence, which allow it to be interpreted and theorized. We can learn things from praxis. There is often, in this approach, a thoughtful valorization of the practices in a manner that showcases them as a possible way of moving forward. The practices that are studied serve as exemplars. Without advocating for them explicitly, theorizing them serves to showcase them. The exercise, in this sense, is not purely theoretical. It has a veiled action orientation.

Banu Bargu's theorizing of death fasts and forms of self-immolation, and Massimiliano Tomba's writings on insurgent universalities and his ongoing project on struggles over water rights in South America, are undoubtedly illustrative of this approach.[33] Bargu's book, *Starve and Immolate: The Politics of Human Weapons*, published in 2014, serves as a powerful illustration of this relationship. She analyzes forms of resistance that she categorizes under the rubric of the "weaponization of life": the hunger strike or death fast, self-mutilation and self-immolation, and other forms of human sacrifice. Bargu calls these "necroresistance" and analyzes them in relation to the structures of power within which they emerge, which she calls "the biopoliticization of sovereignty."

Bargu performs, in essence, a kind of autopsy of a philosophical nature of the actions that produce death in order to make sense of them and our present political condition. From the perspective of the relation of theory and praxis, she theorizes praxis to understand it. The directionality of her project is *from* praxis *to* theory in order for theory to enlighten praxis. This is evident throughout her methodological discussion. Bargu writes, for instance, "This book therefore explores the death fast struggle by placing self-destructive techniques of political action at the center of its inquiry *in order to theorize this highly particular form of struggle in which life is forged into a weapon.*" "In order to theorize": the objective is to understand by means of critical theory. The set of questions that guides Bargu's inquiry is equally revealing: "What are the reasons for choosing such tactics? What are the justifications provided for this choice? What are their ethical and political implications?"[34]

Bargu engages in categorization, distinguishing defensive from offensive uses of human weapons. She engages in interpretation, suggesting that these forms of death fasts are *not* nonviolent. She is concerned "with understanding their relation to the conditions out of which they emerge." She is engaged in an interpretive task—not to judge but to understand. Specifically, the task is to understand "in order to deploy [these] findings toward the theorization of this emergent repertoire of action that increasingly stamps the radical struggles of our present." We are firmly in the space of the theorization of praxis: "I theorize the self-destructive practices that forge life into a weapon as a specific modality of resistance." Listen to the ultimate payoff: "Through this inquiry, the book attempts to interpret the growing centrality of a novel set of practices of resistance that have entered the political scene in Turkey and to scrutinize their meaning, function, and effects, without whose analysis both the opposition of political prisoners and the reaction of the Turkish state are bound to remain opaque."[35]

Bargu's theoretical work enriches our understanding not only of how power circulates in society today, but also of how resistance circulates, so we see the resistance as not simply trying to "make life better" in opposition to biosovereignty and the regulation of life, but to implicate and draw out the centrality of death as well. But what it does, principally, is theorize praxis. Perhaps this is essential in a charged context like this—one situated between, on the one hand, the total domination of life in solitary confinement in supermax prisons, and on the other hand, the only remaining weapon to resist the domination, life itself. In any event, though, this work represents the *theorization* of practice.

Similarly, Tomba's book *Insurgent Universality: An Alternative Legacy of Modernity* seeks to unearth alternative forms of praxis and theorize them in order to showcase them—from the Paris Communards' use of medieval types of self-government, to the peasant communities and workers' councils in 1918 Russia, to the Zapatistas' experiments in self-government in Mexico.[36] Moreover, Tomba and Bargu's larger ongoing project at the University of California, Santa Cruz, has the ambition of discussing actually-existing critical practices that arise globally in both the South and the North from activist interventions, and to analyze them as a way to highlight them—in other words, to theorize new forms of praxis and offer them as exemplars.

The Autonomy of Praxis

Furthest along the spectrum, some critical theorists believe that praxis is essentially autonomous of critical theory and our theoretical inquiries will have (and can have) no effect on praxis. The idea is not to theorize forms of praxis as a way to potentially guide our actions, but simply a way to demonstrate the autonomy of action.

Joshua Clover is a good illustration. His work documents where praxis is headed. It has a predictive element because he is able to show the independent factors—the forces that drive praxis. But his analysis does not and will not have a feedback effect on our actions: the praxis that he identifies will happen, regardless of whether we theorize it, regardless of whether we even see it. In this sense, from this perspective, practice itself may be considered autonomous, and theory superfluous. Theory is derivative of practice. Practice happens regardless of whether we theorize.

That autonomy is central to Clover's intervention in *Riot. Strike. Riot.* In conversation with Clover, I proposed to him that his book could be interpreted as advocating the autonomy of praxis—to which he responded that on the contrary, it more likely represented the autonomy of theory. Praxis goes on, regardless of our theorizing. It is the theorizing that is autonomous—and in that sense, perhaps, irrelevant to the ongoing praxis. Critical theory is so immanent, it is almost outside the space of praxis. As Clover writes in his introduction: "Theory is immanent in struggle; often enough it must hurry to catch up to a reality that lurches ahead."[37]

In his work, Clover traces the increasing practice of riots and looting as forms of uprising tied to our current political-economic condition of neoliberal consumption capitalism. According to Clover, this represents a parallel history of praxis and political economy—a history in which modalities of uprising are shaped by economic conditions and evolve as a result of the necessary evolution of economic history.

Clover offers a three-part story: During the medieval and early modern periods, marked by an economy of circulation of goods, forms of uprising were dominated by the mob riot, the type of violent event described and theorized through the lens of moral economy by the English historian E. P. Thompson. Early capitalism and the Industrial Revolution brought about an economy of production accompanied by labor movements, syndicalism, and the modality of the strike as the dominant form of struggle against capitalism. With the neoliberal turn in the 1970s and the transformation of the advanced capitalist economy into a service economy dominated once again by the circulation of goods, revolt turned to a new form of riot, what Clover calls "riot prime," that involved urban youth attacking the commercial symbols of consumption. These included the London riots of 2011, the *émeutes* of the French *banlieues* in 2005 and 2009, and the rioting in Ferguson, Missouri, in Baltimore, and elsewhere in the United States. These are the direct product of the crises of capitalism at the turn of this century: "*crisis signals a shift of capital's center of gravity into circulation, both theoretically and practically, and riot is in the last instance to be understood as a circulation struggle, of which the price-setting struggle and the surplus rebellion are distinct, if related, forms*," Clover emphasizes.[38]

The historical trajectory that Clover describes, then, is directly reflected in the title of his book, *Riot. Strike. Riot*: "riots" during the medieval and early modern period of a circulatory economy, "strikes" throughout capitalism, and now the "riot prime" in our age of postindustrial neoliberal capitalism. What is important in his thesis is that the economic dimension drives the praxis: forms of uprising are determined by economic conditions and evolve regardless of human intervention—or critical theory. We face a distinct future of praxis, regardless of theory. "The riot, the blockade, the barricade, the occupation. The commune. These are what we will see in the next five, fifteen, forty years. The list is not new."[39] The space of praxis is, in this sense, autonomous. History has its direction. We theorists are just observers who will not affect or change the direction of history. Praxis will happen, whether we theorize or not.

Confrontation and the Unified Field

Somewhere, distinct from these four approaches, lies a fifth path, where theory and praxis can be interpreted as being so much in confrontation that they form a unified field: the two form an irreconcilable tension, a constant contradiction that nourishes both but does not entail any directionality from one to the other. This could be described as a dialectical opposition, or even a confrontation imagined through the lens of pure negativity, as in Adorno's negative dialectics.[40] But it need not carry such a theoretical burden, nor such negativity, as I will argue in chapter 5. The relation is more immediate, constant, and productive, a pure collision that can produce a unified field. Critical theory does not guide practice or enlighten us about practice. It challenges praxis by trying to layer categories and concepts on it, but in the resistance to those efforts, theory grows and changes shape. On the other hand, praxis also confronts critical theory, and in that encounter, it too changes and grows. This may be close to the idea of a contradiction and confrontation that Adorno had in mind in his "Marginalia on Theory and Praxis" and that Horkheimer expressed in *Eclipse of Reason*. But I push it in a fundamentally different direction, with a sharply different sensibility to action.

Collision, contradiction, and confrontation: this is where I would situate myself. As I detail in chapter 18, it is in the conflict between my praxis and critical theory that I develop and push both. By participating in the Occupy movement and speaking at the open university at the foot of the Chicago Board of Trade, by supporting protesters and counseling those arrested at Grant Park, I confronted notions of civil disobedience and ungovernability and developed a critical theory of political disobedience to understand the new grammar of occupation and leaderlessness. By struggling alongside the Yellow Vest movement, I confronted and resuscitated the practice of the fellow traveler. By working with Noah Smith-Drelich on our §1983 civil rights lawsuit against North Dakota law enforcement for violating the assembly and protest rights at the Standing Rock reservation, we confronted critical theory with legal practice, deploying the new language of water protectors rather than protesters. In my decades of representing the condemned in Alabama, I tackled the contradictions within legal-liberalism and ultimately expanded my target to the punitive society writ large. The process of theorization challenges and pushes my own praxis and vice versa: trying to imagine political disobedience, comparing Occupy Wall Street to Gandhi, King, or Thoreau, ends up highlighting and problematizing features of my own praxis. But the praxis also confronts my critical theories and challenges them. It is a constant struggle back and forth.

Ultimately, there is only one viable space for me: the confrontation, the clash. As a critic, I must engage, I must practice, and I must critique and reflect. I agonize over this relation between theory and praxis. That is critical theory to me. When I am not doing that, I am not a critical theorist—I am merely an academic. In the end, the first model of contemplation as praxis is too docile, too chastened, too unengaged. The fourth model is a phantasm: the idea that history marches on its own and that praxis will just evolve in coordination with history is an illusion. And the second model, the idea that theory could guide praxis, is pure hubris. It privileges intellectuals over militants and practitioners. I need to act, to litigate, to militate in order to change the world. I need to theorize. I need to place the two in conflict—without telling others what to do. I need to theorize and contest my own actions. In the end, I cannot tell other people what to do. I have to reformulate the very question: no longer "What is to be done?" but rather "What more shall I do? What work am I doing? How is what I am doing working—or not?"

Constructing a New Critical Praxis Theory

While the aim of this work is to push critical theory back toward praxis, the starting point must be to propose a resolution of the internecine battles and struggles for influence that currently plague critical philosophy. As I mentioned earlier, critical theorists have been bogged down for decades in an epistemological detour that now has given rise to clannish politics between its various branches—Frankfurt School, Foucaultian, deconstructive, Lacanian, feminist, postcolonial, queer—or worse, has descended to mere gossip about its illuminati. Critical theory today is itself in crisis—and that has to be resolved first.

I am by no means the only one to diagnose this malaise. Amy Allen also has taken it as her point of departure in *The End of Progress: Decolonizing the Normative Foundations of Critical Theory*, published in 2016. Allen maintains that the inheritors of the Frankfurt School are wedded to a foundationalist belief in progress that is at odds with other critical theories and has prevented them from engaging in dialogue with those other branches. Their belief in progress, Allen argues, has resulted in "the failure of Frankfurt School critical theory to engage substantively with one of the most influential branches of critical theory," namely postcolonial and decolonial theory, critical race theory, and queer theory.[41] Allen decries the "long-running feud" and denounces "the ongoing family quarrel between Frankfurt School critical theory and French critical theory."[42] Seyla Benhabib also recognizes the factious nature of the critical theory field today. She too refers to "the contentious plurality of approaches caught between the critical theory of the Frankfurt School proper, on the one hand, and Foucaultian genealogy and Derridean deconstruction, on the other." These are precisely the factions vying for influence today—in Benhabib's words, a "contentious and rivalrous plurality."[43] I would argue that they are more than mere rivalries today. The contentions have become roadblocks.

How, then, can we get past these long-running feuds? That is one of the most important challenges today for critical philosophy. One approach would be to allow every faction to bloom. At times, Benhabib seems to embrace that route, writing that "we have to accept the *legitimate pluralization of critical theory approaches* today."[44] But I believe that it would be better to resolve the epistemological disagreement and get back to the task at hand: trying to change the world. Accordingly, in this work, I will first elaborate a reconstruction of critical theory and its reorientation toward praxis. I will propose that we understand critical theory, at its core, as an exercise in stripping illusions that lays bare and calls for an assessment of values, as well as an analysis of strategies and tactics, to achieve an egalitarian form of human emancipation. In this final section, I will prefigure the reconstructive argument as succinctly as possible.

Critical theory has been wracked, at least since the early twentieth century, by a deep tension between two originary tendencies: the first toward a reflexivity and historical constructivism, and the second toward emancipatory horizons, such as Marxism, that bore an element of scientism. It is that very tension that pushed first-generation critical theorists like Horkheimer into an epistemological direction in order to reconcile how the subjective self-understanding of workers obstructed the Marxian march of history. This led Horkheimer and the early Frankfurt School toward a critique of ideology and, later, toward discourse ethics, both of which served to normatively ground the enterprise; but it also brought wave after wave of antifoundational challenges, counterpositivist reactions, and critical efforts aimed at the elements of scientism and Marxism originally inserted in critical theory. These latter challenges sought to loosen the hold of Marxian epistemology, producing theories of knowledge-power, of *epistemes*, of desire, of deconstruction, of regimes of truth, and embroiling critical theorists in infinite epistemological debate and controversy.

The various epistemological approaches, however, all belabored a similar set of points that could be stripped of their Hegelian clothing and of their normative foundationalism: first, people's beliefs about their conditions—about their social, political, and economic conditions—have effects of reality and shape their behavior. People are even willing to sacrifice their lives for what they believe in, politically or ethically. Second, people's beliefs are shaped by historical conditions. People are shaped by the political, economic, and social conditions that they themselves interpret and study. The reflexivity thereby precludes any universal truths in these domains; it only allows for historically situated contexts. However, third, there is no necessary direction of change, nor any universal metric or criterion to judge the truth-value of these beliefs. There is no teleology to history: we are not necessarily headed toward the collapse of capitalism or neoliberalism, nor are we necessarily headed toward autocratic or fascistic regimes. Here too, humans can shape their political reality. We are not necessarily headed to climatic apocalypse either. Humans can intervene and change the course of history.

What people believe and consider true, then, shapes and is shaped by their social, economic, and political conditions—and it changes. These conditions are powerful in that they shape people's behavior; but as they evolve and change—as people evolve and change—people's beliefs get denaturalized and show themselves to have been illusions: illusory beliefs that prevent people from realizing change or reshaping history and their world. What people consider true today, politically or socially, may be shown to be an illusion. In fact, it most likely will be shown to be an illusion at some future point in history.

At the heart of critical theory, then, is this reflexivity, originally introduced into critical theory, which calls for a radical theory of illusions. Whether we ultimately call this a theory of ideology or of regimes of truth matters little—so long as we do not reinfuse that concept with necessity (i.e., with the idea that there is a necessary contradiction inherent to the object of critique that necessarily will push history in any particular direction).[45] The label is not important. What matters is that we do not reify what is unveiled or stop being reflexive. What matters is that we not turn critical theory into a touchstone.

Precisely because of its reflexivity, historicity, and constructivism, critical theory is not a *basanos* that creates and tests truth, but a constant critique that unveils recurring illusions. *Basanos* refers originally to the touchstone that was used in ancient practice to test the purity of gold. This was the practice of the moneychangers—and there is undoubtedly a link between these practices and money itself as a measure of truth.[46] But we must ensure that critical theory does not become a method for truth. We need to get beyond the idea that critical theory, as the unmasking of illusions, unveils the truth. Rather, it unveils a situation that itself eventually needs to be reexamined. Rather than get stuck in internecine battles over epistemology and truth, we need to get beyond them—and back to the main ambition: to change the world.

First, then, a reconstructed critical theory precisely represents an endless unveiling of illusions to demonstrate how our beliefs distribute resources and material conditions. It traces the effects of reality of our beliefs and material practices, recognizing that, as it unveils illusions, it creates new ones that will need to be unpacked later. It is relentless in this way. It engages in a form of recursive unmasking—an infinite regress—that endlessly exposes the distributional effects of belief systems and material conditions. It entails, in this sense, *a radical critical philosophy of illusions.*

It may feel at times, especially today in these times of utter crisis, that we could dispense with critical theory and the unveiling of illusions. The rise of such explicit hatred and prejudice as we have seen with the New Right, some suggest, no longer calls for subtle critical analysis. As Stephen Best and Sharon Marcus observed in 2009, "Eight years of the Bush regime may have hammered home the point that not all situations require the subtle ingenuity associated with symptomatic reading."[47] The tools of critique, to many, have begun to appear unnecessary in the pitch of battle. "The assumption that domination can only do its work when veiled, which may once have sounded almost paranoid, now has a nostalgic, even utopian ring to it," Best and Marcus note.[48] But this, I will argue, is precisely the wrong approach. Rather than abandon, it is time to rejuvenate and reformulate critical theory, because, as I will show, it is the only theoretical tradition that pursues equality, social justice, and autonomy. It is always at the darkest moment that critical theory rises from the ashes. It is that time again.

Second, in the same way that reconstructed critical theory, understood as a radical theory of illusions, liberates us from unfounded scientistic foundations and tendencies, it also frees us from the foundational constraints of the old utopias of critical philosophy. The proposed resolution of the epistemological controversies can serve as a model and can motivate and guide the normative analysis. When we unmask and unveil, we are in fact proposing. Exposing an illusion is itself a proposition. It involves an affirmative choice: what to unveil and how? That moment of critique itself represents a choice that will undoubtedly, eventually, recirculate power and impose a new form of domination. It must, of course, inevitably. When we unmask, indeed, we propose a vocabulary, a grammar, new ideas and ideologies that will eventually have effects of domination. Yes, in this, Foucault was surely right. When we propose, we inevitably impose. But when we critique, we also propose and impose. So we cannot stop there. We must evaluate and assess what we are doing, and also act, constantly reevaluating and critiquing how our actions reshape relations of power and the critical vision for the future. To believe that we could avoid these effects of domination is to ignore the reality of critique. So we cannot stop there. We need to constantly address and reexamine the critical horizon—or what historically had been called utopia.

It turns out that there is no unique form of political economy that satisfies the ambition of critical theory. There is no one type of economic arrangement that fulfills the utopian vision—not socialism, Keynesianism, post-Keynesian economics, or even (at least so I would argue) the idea of communism. All actually existing economies are regulated, each in their unique way, and they each produce material distributions that are the direct result of the particular microrules and regulations of that particular economic arrangement, and not of the abstract regime type. A state-controlled economy can distribute to its *apparatschik*, just as a privately owned corporation can distribute to its workers: it is not the abstract regime type, but the detailed mechanisms and regulations of the specific regime, that shape the social order. All that we can judge, as critical theorists, is how close an actually existing economic arrangement approximates the values and ideals of critical philosophy. In this sense, critical theory calls for judgment about the values that a political economic arrangement instantiates through its material outcomes and distributions, not for a particular type of political economy.

Hand-in-hand with a radical theory of illusions, then, reconstructed critical theory must be agnostic about the abstract type of political economic regime, but adamant about the values it produces. It entails, in this sense, *an unswerving evaluation and assessment of values.* It addresses, head on, Nietzsche's question of the value of values and responds: the value of these critical values is the creation of a more just and equal society, marked by less domination, oppression, and social differential, and by the opportunity for each and every person to flourish and achieve her or his greatest potential. The value of critical values is achieving this more just and equal society. It calls, in this sense, for *a radical critical philosophy of values.*

Third, in terms of critical praxis, a reconstructed critical theory also distances itself from the anointed practices from the past—vanguard parties and proletariat revolution. It calls instead for entirely situated and contextualized analyses of how to push specific, really existing political economic arrangements—whether they can be labeled capitalist, post-Keynesian, socialist, or communist—in the direction of our critical values. Each historical, geographical, and political situation is different, calling for different strategies and tactics—with nothing off the table. Politics is a constant battle over values, and we are all inevitably in a state of competition to realize our ideals. In such a contested space, it is possible to develop tactics only in a situated and contextualized way. Because there is no war to be won, but rather an endless series of struggles, critical theory must focus on strategies and tactics. These are not portable or generalizable. What might have been appropriate in 1930s Germany was completely different from what worked in 1940s India. In the latter context, nonviolent resistance may have been appropriate; in the former, it would have been madness. The methods of struggle cannot be universalized. The answer is not a vanguard party, a leaderless movement, nonviolent resistance, or any general mode of uprising, in the abstract. There is no one right way to proceed in general terms. We immediately go off track when we seek one generalizable or universal answer to the question. Instead, the question must be answered differently for each situation, specified and contextualized in space and time. There must be a GPS-, a time-, and a date-stamp for every answer.

The upshot is that there is no single, abstract, or universal—or universalizable—answer to the praxis question. In the same way in which reconstructed critical theory overcomes unfounded scientistic foundations, the classic question "What is to be done?" must be deanchored and reformulated—and reformulated by each and every one of us in our different time and space. In this sense, reconstructed critical praxis calls for *a radical critical philosophy of strategies and tactics.*

In this book, I propose one such time-, place-, and date-stamped reformulation. In part IV, I reformulate this question by turning it on myself and asking myself what I am doing—in other words, by confronting my own praxis. My answer has to come from my own confrontation of theory and praxis. I hope that others will reformulate and answer the question with their own time-, place-, and date-stamps wherever they are now—and I aspire to support a forum for those reformulations and answers. Critical theory cannot simply understand our crises and unveil our illusions. It cannot content itself with reflection or contemplation as a form of practice. It must articulate tactics and praxis. Critical times call for radical revaluation. That is what I propose here: a new vision of critical praxis theory for the twenty-first century.

PART I

Reconstructing Critical Theory

To return critical philosophy to its main task and true ambition—to change the world, not just to interpret it—requires first resolving the epistemological controversies that still plague the critical enterprise today, in order second to reconstruct a critical praxis theory.

Critical theory originally wove together different elements in terms of its method and conception—and, most often, it still does today. Most critical theories were grounded on a reflexive understanding of the critical theorist as an actor situated in history with the capability to affect the course of history through critical praxis. Most of them deployed immanent critique and defetishizing or unmasking critique to try to achieve the goal of human emancipation, recognizing the significant role of beliefs and ideas in the production of oppression and inequality.

From its inception, however, there was a deep tension within critical theory between, on the one hand, aspects of immanent critique and a philosophy of history that pushed in the direction of scientism, and, on the other hand, aspects of defetishizing critique and reflexivity that pushed in the opposite direction of ethics. The first aspects were far more foundational, in an epistemological and normative sense, insofar as they grounded the correctness of the critical theory or the truth of the outcome of the critical analysis on the certainty of a historical trajectory and on quasi-scientific notions of the overcoming of necessary internal contradictions. On the basis of the unfolding of history and a correct social theory, the critical theorist could know for certain the accuracy of the analysis and prescription. By contrast, the second aspects were far less foundational—even antifoundational at times. The unmasking in defetishizing critique did not necessarily reveal truth, but simply unmasked illusions; and reflexivity, in combination with a more fluid conception of history, allowed some contingency both in the facticity of present circumstances and in the way in which critical theorists could transform history.

This deep tension was present in the earliest expressions of critical philosophy—already in Marx's analysis of commodity fetishism, but more importantly in Horkheimer's original vision for critical theory in 1937. There, one can already find the elements of reflexivity and historical constructivism that were potentially at odds with the scientism of the Marxian analysis, which also was present in Horkheimer's early writings. That paradoxical combination of reflexivity, historical constructivism, and scientism ultimately pushed critical theory into its epistemological impasse. The *aporia* traverses the long history of critical philosophy, the generational shifts of the Frankfurt School, and the clash with poststructuralist, postcolonial, queer, critical race, and other contemporary critical theories.

In her book *The End of Progress*, Amy Allen traces this tension and the resulting conflict between later generations of the Frankfurt School and thinkers such as Gilles Deleuze, Michel Foucault, and postcolonial, queer, and decolonial theorists to the former's abiding faith in the concept of progress. The notion of moral and political progress as a fact and imperative, Allen argues, prevented critical philosophers such as Jürgen Habermas, Axel Honneth, and Rainer Forst from properly engaging the other strands of postcolonial and queer critical theories. Allen's thesis is compelling, but, if anything, should be broadened from the specific matter of the concept of progress to the larger question of epistemological foundations. Adorno did not hold a notion of progress (which Allen recognizes—Adorno's quip that "progress occurs where it ends" is the source of Allen's book title and epigraph[1]) and Horkheimer essentially gave up on progress after the war, both of which suggest that the crux of the problem is broader than the controversy over the idea of progress. Instead, it goes to the overarching problem of a recurring foundationalism in later iterations of Frankfurt School critical theory that expressed itself in both the historiography and normativity of the writings. The real source of the tension—and what pushed critical theory into its epistemological detour—is the recurring struggle over the problem of foundations.

Part I of this work offers a way to reconstruct critical theory as a critical method that indexes the original reflexivity, historicity, and counterpositivism of critical theory, but also liberates it from its tendency to revert to scientism and foundationalism, in an effort to get us beyond the epistemological detour and make possible a more contextual, nimble, and powerful critical approach oriented toward praxis. A reconstructed critical theory embraces the challenge that was at the root of critical philosophy: the idea of a "ruthless" unveiling of illusions.[2] That impulse toward an unending, pitiless critique existed since the young writings of Marx, but it went underground at times and must now be rejuvenated. It should remain, today, at the core of critical theory.

This part calls for the constant, ruthless, and unending unveiling of illusions to expose how belief systems and material conditions redistribute resources in society, attuned to the fact that that very unveiling will produce new illusions that themselves need to be unmasked and exposed. It proposes an unapologetic theory of illusions and calls for an ongoing and unrelenting theoretical stance of resignification, reinterpretation, and reevaluation as a way to then push the critical discussion to its main objectives: pursuing its critical horizon and determining practically how to get there. It offers a resolution of the epistemological quagmire, allows us to get beyond it, and lets us return to praxis.

It also will retrace the history of the tension that has wracked critical theory since its inception, in order to demonstrate a way forward through a reconstructed critical praxis theory. Chapters 1–4 approach the problem first from a historical perspective. They trace the conflict back to the origin of critical theory in 1937 to demonstrate the source of the problem, and then forward to its actual manifestation today. The following three chapters (chapters 5–7) will then articulate the conceptual and theoretical conflict between the various methods of critique and propose a reconstructed critical theory that goes beyond the problem.

In beginning with the historical context, the point of the analysis is not to demonstrate historical progression or a learning process in critical thought. Neither is it to suggest that there has been intellectual growth or a process of self-realization along the lines of Hegel's *Phenomenology of Spirit.* It by no means rehearses the Hegelian method of a learning process, like the one that Honneth deployed in his historical narration of the evolution of critical theory in *The Critique of Power*, or that Rahel Jaeggi returns to in her *Critique of Forms of Life.*[3] No, critical theory has not learned or grown in the process. It has stumbled. But it is vitally important to locate where it went wrong, where it faltered, in order to push it forward and past those fault lines and avoid those pitfalls.

This is not a story of progress, a Hegelian history of philosophy, or a learning process. It is a cartography of shoals and rocky coasts to avoid. It is an effort to move past prior failures to get back to praxis—knowing full well that the process will surely produce regressions and require rethinking in the future. This is a reconstructed critical theory for these times and for our historical context: a reconstructed critical praxis theory for the twenty-first century.

CHAPTER 1

The Original Foundations

When Max Horkheimer articulated his vision for a new program of critical research in 1937 while the Frankfurt School was in exile at Columbia University, he put in motion a tension between two sensibilities that has plagued critical theory ever since: on the one hand, a commitment to reflexivity and a type of historical constructivism that was potentially postfoundational, and on the other hand, an allegiance to scientific knowledge that was deeply Marxian and bore a clear scientistic tendency. The tension, inscribed in Horkheimer's formative article "Traditional and Critical Theory," led to an instability that would tilt critical theory one way or the other over the rest of the twentieth century. Frankfurt School critical theory could have gone in either direction, and had it gone in the first, it would have been far closer to poststructuralism, postcolonialism, and critical race, queer, and other late-twentieth-century theories. But in the 1930s, the members of the Frankfurt School were predominantly Marxian, and this pushed the original generation instead in a more scientistic direction. Later generations would move away from Marxism, but nevertheless they replaced those epistemological and normative foundations with others—some more Kantian, others more Hegelian. If anything, the chasm between later generations of the Frankfurt School and poststructuralism, postcolonialism, and queer and other critical projects deepened as time went by and as the various critical theories confronted one another more brutally—despite the fact that most critical thinkers moved further and further away from Marx.

Horkheimer's classical articulation of critical theory in 1937 contains the seeds of today's predicament. Paradoxically, his article contains an internal contradiction: two intellectual instincts at odds with each other, two instincts melded together that, separately, would have pushed critical theory in very different directions.

I say "paradoxically" because the idea that contradiction is a driving force of history was an integral part of the Marxian method and central to the form of immanent critique that the Frankfurt School drew from Hegel to deploy for its own use. It would be tempting to call this original tension in Horkheimer an inherent contradiction within critical theory that now calls for overcoming and sublation, but frankly, that would be presumptuous hubris—and undermine the very point of this intervention. The tension was not in fact inherent or necessary. The contradiction was not inextricably linked to critical theory. It was, instead, a historical artifact of Horkheimer's situation in 1937, the historical position of Marxism at the time, and the geopolitics before, during, and following World War II. It was, in the end, a deep and historically situated tension unique to the mid-twentieth century—and one from which we need to extricate ourselves today. Let me explain.

Marxian Normative Foundations :: Max Horkheimer

The tension at the heart of Horkheimer's project for critical theory stemmed from the conflict between two intellectual tendencies laid on top of a specific normative ambition—namely, human emancipation. The first tendency was a certain type of reflexive and historical constructivism; the second, a deep commitment to Marx and an aspiration to scientific Marxism. The confrontation between the two pushed early critical theory toward a scientism that was entirely at odds with its own constructivism and antipositivism.

The backdrop, most importantly, was the normative ambition. By contrast to traditional scientists, Horkheimer explained, critical theorists do not aim simply to describe the world accurately or objectively, infer universal laws and rules that determine reality, or predict external outcomes or behavior with precision. The goal is not simply to make correct prognostications based on scientific discovery of external objective phenomena. The ambition, instead, is to emancipate humans from their self-incurred slavery—from the forms of domination inherent in early-twentieth-century capitalism. The goal, in other words, is to change the world that critical theorists study.

For Horkheimer, the world as presently ordered, "the world of capital," is marked by oppression, war, and barbarity. It is a world without reason and is inhuman, characterized by "a new barbarism." In the face of this reality, critical theorists pursue the goal, no different than that of human activity more generally, of achieving "a reasonable organization of society that will meet the needs of the whole community." Or, as Horkheimer states elsewhere in the article (he repeatedly and clearly articulates the ambition of critical theory throughout), the goal is to achieve "the rational state of society"; "a future society as a community of free men"; "the right kind of society"; "an association of free men in which each has the same possibility of self-development"; "a society without injustice"; "a rationally organized future society"; "a state of affairs in which there will be no exploitation or oppression"; and "a world which satisfies the needs and powers of men." Critical theory has "the happiness of all individuals as its goal." The "real function" of critical theorists is precisely to be a force within their concrete historical situation "to stimulate change."[1]

With these objectives in mind, critical theory took on two very different guises. On the one hand, Horkheimer infused critical theory with a deep reflexive and constructivist tendency: the core difference that distinguishes critical from traditional theory is that critical theorists understand themselves to be the product of the historical conditions and modes of production. They understand that they and their scientific knowledge are the products of, in Horkheimer's words, "the mode of production practiced in particular forms of society."[2] In other words, both the objects that critical theorists perceive and the very "perceiving organ" of the critical theorist are shaped by historical circumstances.[3] As a result, there is no universality to the phenomena that they study. Their understanding of the world and their theories are historically situated. These will vary depending on the historical and economic context and especially depending on the modes of production in society. Reality is different in a feudal versus an industrial context. Critical theorists see differently at any historical moment and see different objects. Moreover, because of the normative ambition, critical theorists try to shape their historically situated reality in specific ways. They are not only historically situated but also, at the very same time, transforming history and themselves. The idea is not simply to interpret reality accurately but to transform it in specific ways that are inflected by the normative ambition of critical theory. Insofar as reality is entirely situated and must be understood in such a way as to push it in a particular normative direction, there is not only no universality but also no objectivity to the analysis: it is impossible to maintain a fact-value distinction. Interpretation serves the ambition of social transformation.

This forms one main distinction between critical and traditional theory. The latter is founded, by contrast, on the notion of objectivity, insofar as the objects of study are all taken to be "external to the theoretical thinking"—that is, not historically shaped by humanity, not "the product of human work." "This alienation," Horkheimer writes, "finds expression in philosophical terminology as the separation of value and research, knowledge and action, and other polarities."[4]

The reflexivity of critical theory means that critical theorists must constantly measure their reality simultaneously on the basis of their own self-transformations, the changes in historical and economic conditions, and the surrounding social reforms and transformations. There is a fluidity and constant motion to critical theory. It is never static; it never remains the same. It is constantly evolving as both its objects and its horizon change. And that change is human-made: the critical attitude understands that, in contrast to biological or physical laws, any notion of necessity in critical theory is affected by human conduct. The theorist is part of the transformation and must participate in bringing about that change. They have agency: as Horkheimer writes, this is "the idea of a state of affairs in which man's actions no longer flow from a mechanism but from his own decision." If there is change, it is the product of critical theorizing. This is the idea of critical theory being "a genuine force, consisting in the self-awareness of the subjects of a great historical revolution."[5] In this sense, critical theory does not rest on solid foundations other than its normative ambition of emancipation. The normativity is its only foundation. This is why, in part, Amy Allen charges the Frankfurt School with an unfounded faith in progress: progress, Allen argues, is its normative foundation. Insofar as Horkheimer is (in 1937 at least) still Marxist, Allen's charge is compelling, at least with regard to the 1937 article; but after the war, Horkheimer's relation to progress changed.

On the other hand, Horkheimer's vision for critical theory aspired to a scientific paradigm modeled on the natural sciences. It was also Marxian. It is actually the combination of these two elements that creates the greatest tension, given that the article in fact embraces a scientific Marxism rather than the earlier, more philosophical Marx or what is often referred to as the Young Marx. The article venerates the model of the hard sciences and places critical theory in the scientific tradition. That, in itself, is remarkable and has significant effects on the texture of critical theory that Horkheimer articulates. It means that critical theory is about hypothesis testing and the formulation of scientific theories. From this perspective, it has a relation to facts and truth that is inherently foundational: critical theories can be tested to check their validity and truth value.

Horkheimer frames his article in terms of scientific theory. He begins by defining theory in the most scientific way, drawing on mathematics and physics. For Horkheimer, theory is the derivation of propositions from primary principles, in a Cartesian sense. Its validity (or rather its "real validity," in Horkheimer's words) "depends on the derived propositions being consonant with the actual facts."[6] Now, to be sure, critical theory differs from traditional theory, in Horkheimer's view, precisely because of its contextualism and the self-reflectivity of the critical theorist. But—and this is the important point—critical theory aspires to the same scientificity as all other theory. Horkheimer emphasizes this—and it is, in fact, the reason that he frames the entire article on the paradigm of scientific theory. "The individual steps within [critical] theory are," Horkheimer stresses, "at least in intention, as rigorous as the deductions in a specialized scientific theory."[7] In large part, Horkheimer does so to shield critical theory from the usual charge that, insofar as it is not objective in the usual sense of science, it is nothing more than "an aimless intellectual game, half conceptual poetry, half impotent expression of states of mind" or that it appears "to be subjective and speculative, one-sided and useless," as well as "biased and unjust."[8]

"As rigorous as the deductions in a specialized scientific theory": that is a remarkable statement and ambition for critical theory that would orient the early Frankfurt School toward a particular type of scientism (specifically, toward Marx). Marxian analysis would provide the rigor and scientific backbone to Horkheimer's article. The article is grounded on the reality of class struggle and on the necessity of proletarian revolution. It embraces a Marxian theory of history based on dialectical materialism and the driving force of internal contradictions. Horkheimer could not be clearer about this—as evidenced, for instance, in the following passage:

> To put it in broad terms, the [critical theory of society] says that the basic form of the historically given commodity economy on which modern history rests contains in itself the internal and external tensions of the modern era; it generates these tensions over and over again in an increasingly heightened form; and after a period of progress, development of human powers, and emancipation for the individual, after an enormous extension of human control over nature, it finally hinders further development and drives humanity into a new barbarism.[9]

Horkheimer explicitly follows Marx and Engels on a number of points. First, he expressly adopts their thesis that the proletariat is best situated to perceive the contradiction between capitalist modes of production and a just society. Second, he specifically embraces the "Marxist categories of class, exploitation, surplus value, profit, pauperization, and breakdown," as well as "commodity, value, and money." Horkheimer implicitly follows Marx and Engels with regard to social classes, modes of production, and their philosophy of history and in believing that the objective of critical theorists forms "a dynamic unity with the oppressed class." Or, even further, that the thinking of critical theorists must "serve" the oppressed class. And that a capitalist economy of commodity exchange "must necessarily lead to a heightening of those social tensions which in the present historical era lead in turn to wars and revolutions."[10]

Horkheimer adopts all three key building blocks of Marxian thought. First, undergirding the entire project is a belief in the importance of the Marxian category of "class conflict." Horkheimer argues that, by contrast, the natural sciences are "not directly connected with class conflicts," which has a direct implication on their construction of facts.[11] Second, Horkheimer also accepts and assumes Marx's theory of alienation. In a bourgeois society, he writes, people's "work and its results are alienated from them." Third, Horkheimer embraces Marx and Engels's thesis that the proletariat are best situated to do the immanent work, from their working experiences, to achieve social transformation. In sum, critical theory, as a way of knowing, is based "on Marx's critique of political economy," Horkheimer declares in the "Postscript" to his article, also in 1937. This gives Horkheimer's thesis a real sense of historical determinism. His critical theory of society is correct, he maintains, and necessary: "the most advanced form of thought at present is the critical theory of society and every consistent intellectual movement that cares about man converges upon it by its own inner logic," Horkheimer contends.[12]

These two tendencies in Horkheimer's vision for critical theory clashed. The first was profoundly constructivist; the second, deeply scientistic. And given the importance of the second, which infuses and realizes his normative ambition, Horkheimer's article ends up sounding proto-positivist and, thus, foundationalist.

To reconcile this conflict, Horkheimer oriented critique in an epistemological direction, toward the critique of ideology.[13] In the article, he argued that the proletariat, although in the best position to understand the contradictions of capitalism, could not see its own interests properly or envision the future and, thus, the critical intellectuals needed to show the proletariat the proper way.

The proletariat, Horkheimer wrote, is prevented from seeing because of ideological interference: "this awareness is prevented from becoming a social force by the differentiation of social structure which is still imposed on the proletariat from above and by the opposition between personal class interests which is transcended only at very special moments." The result is that the proletariat does not achieve "correct knowledge": "Even to the proletariat the world superficially seems quite different than it really is." This then imposes an obligation on the critical theorist to become "a critical, promotive factor in the development of the masses."[14]

The critical theorist, in Horkheimer's view, plays a vanguard role and "can find himself in opposition to views prevailing even among the proletariat." Horkheimer embraces an almost Leninist ideal: "The theoretician whose business it is to hasten developments which will lead to a society without injustice can find himself in opposition to views prevailing even among the proletariat."[15] He resolves that tension by taking an epistemological route.

The result is that critical theory became twined with ideology critique. As Raymond Geuss explained in 1981 in his analysis of critical theory, "The very heart of the critical theory of society is its criticism of ideology. Their ideology is what prevents the agents in the society from correctly perceiving their true situation and real interests; if they are to free themselves from social repression, the agents must rid themselves of ideological illusion."[16] This is what allows Horkheimer to talk about individuals in capitalist regimes following their "untrue interests" and acting "as mere functions of the economic machine"; of the proletariat having its "own true interests"; or of the world as "it really is."[17] It is what allows Horkheimer to characterize fidelity and solidarity as being "elements of the right theory and practice"; to speak of critical theory as "true theory"; or, even more, to claim that "the future of humanity depends on the existence today of the critical attitude."[18] These are proto-positivist statements, made possible by a belief in the necessity of Marxian theory but fundamentally at odds with the constructivist strand of his critical theory.

In sum, Horkheimer articulates in 1937 a critical theory that is reflexive (in the sense that critical theorists view themselves as historically situated and changing the course of history) and historically constructivist (in the sense that people are the product of their times and reality is historically constructed), but then he inflects it with a Marxian philosophy of history that makes critical theory scientistic. The normativity in the theory is Marxian. Horkheimer embraced a highly scientific conception of knowledge influenced by Marx—one in which all scientific theories, traditional and critical, are the product of the social conditions and modes of production attendant to determinate historical circumstances. Thus, knowledge can be situated only within the context of what he calls "real social processes."[19]

Theorists who are not critical do not understand or recognize this, Horkheimer argues. Instead, they universalize and render permanent their theories—which then become reified and a form of ideology. These traditional scientists believe that they are acting freely, when in fact they are shaped by social mechanisms.[20] In this sense, they are subject to "false consciousness," in Horkheimer's words. "The false consciousness of the bourgeois savant in the liberal era" is precisely to believe that they are free and discovering scientific truths, when in fact everything is determined by social conditions and modes of production.[21] By contrast, critical theorists both understand that they and their object of study, society, are shaped by historical conditions, and correctly view themselves as agents of revolutionary change. This creates a tension that pushes Horkheimer toward ideology critique as a way to address and resolve the lack of a proletarian revolution. The critical task became to overcome the false consciousness of the proletariat to ensure that history progresses along the lines outlined by Marx and Engels.

It is important to realize how central Marx was to the first generation of the Frankfurt School because that is what inflected the original critical theory and created the lasting tension within critical theory. This was true even for the most interpretive critical theorists—even for someone like Walter Benjamin.

The Reach of Dialectical Materialism ⁘ Walter Benjamin

Walter Benjamin's "Theses on the Philosophy of History"—his final essay, written in 1940 shortly before he took his life—is situated at a great distance from Marx's philosophy of history, as are many of his other writings.[22] The essay is messianic, perhaps; esoteric, certainly. Benjamin writes that there is no telos in history. He distances himself from Marx's view and makes plain that he does not believe in the inevitability of a revolution giving rise to communism. There and elsewhere, Benjamin resisted dialectical materialism, worried that it would lead to a form of quietism.

But if one looks more closely at Benjamin's political-intellectual engagements, he, like Horkheimer, was caught in the mesh of dialectical materialism. This is illustrated well by Benjamin's project, with Bertolt Brecht and others, to launch a new journal, *Krise und Kritik*, in 1930: the critical scaffolding was firmly embedded in a Marxian register.[23] "The journal is political," the memoranda of intent declared. "By that is meant that its critical activity is consciously anchored in the critical situation of present society—that of class struggle."[24]

In January 1930, Benjamin and Brecht planned the launch of *Krise und Kritik*, along with the writer Bernard von Brentano and the drama critic Herbert Ihering. The critical framework was firmly Marxian. They all agreed on what was needed: scientific expertise by critical intellectuals to demonstrate the validity of the dialectical materialist method, the foundational role of class struggle, and their implications for understanding the crisis—and even perhaps contributing to it. They understood (at least Benjamin clearly did) that the economic and political crises had begun to produce or, in Benjamin's own words, "*must* produce manifestations of crisis in the superstructure."[25]

Benjamin's plans for *Krise und Kritik* were starkly positivist, even foundationalist. The role of the critical intellectual, Benjamin declared in conversation with Brecht, was not to lead the proletariat but rather to fulfill "a subordinate function" of proving the validity of the dialectical materialist method—essentially, of providing scientific research to solidly establish the proper and necessary sociological positions.[26] The journal was intended, Benjamin maintained, to publish the scientific expertise of scholars and to engage not in journalism but in academic research and demonstration. The program that Benjamin and Brecht set was clear: "The journal's field of activity is the present *crisis* in all areas of ideology, and it is the task of the journal to register this crisis *or bring it about, and this by means of criticism*."[27]

"Interventionist thinking" was the order of the day. "Inconsequential thought" was to be avoided. *Krise und Kritik*—which also for a short time was called *Kritische Blätter* (literally "Critical Pages" but more metaphorically "Critical Notebooks" or "Critical Papers")—was to be a journal that would permit "an active, interventionist role, with tangible consequences, as opposed to [the] usual ineffectual arbitrariness."[28] Benjamin clearly expressed what he had in mind for *Krise und Kritik* as follows:

> The journal was planned as an organ in which experts from the bourgeois camp were to undertake to depict the crisis in science and art. This was meant to demonstrate to the bourgeois intelligentsia that the methods of dialectical

> materialism are dictated to it by its own most necessary characteristics—necessities of intellectual production, research, and existence. The journal was meant to contribute to the propaganda of dialectical materialism *by applying it to questions that the bourgeois intelligentsia is forced to acknowledge as those most particularly characteristic of itself.*[29]

The project was thus deeply positivistic in a scientific, Marxian sense. Critique would lay the foundation for revolutionary political change. As Brecht wrote in the context of that projected journal, the concept of *Kritik* was "to be understood in the sense that politics is its continuation by other means." It should not come as a surprise that Erdmut Wizisla, who published the extensive materials recording the planned publication of *Krise and Kritik*, compared, as "near equivalents," the intended method of Benjamin and Brecht with the logical positivism of the Vienna School.[30]

Benjamin was really taken by the project. "A new journal is at issue, and indeed the only one to have overcome my firmly rooted conviction that I could never again get involved in anything like it . . . and it will be called *Krise und Kritik*," he wrote in a letter to Gershom Scholem in October 1930.[31] It created friction with the larger orbit of the Frankfurt School. Brecht was perhaps too crude or vulgar theoretically for Theodor Adorno, Max Horkheimer, or Friedrich Pollock and troublingly supportive of Stalin; the Institute members were perhaps too bourgeois still for Brecht; and Benjamin was a source of concern for all as he navigated between them.[32] But everyone was working in the same register of class struggle, dialectical materialism, and a certain kind of scientism.

Ultimately, this positivist ambition foiled the project. Benjamin felt that the first three articles to be published were not in fact expert science. They had not lived up to the ambition of the journal and could not "claim to have been written by an expert authority." For instance, the German translation of an article by Georgi Valentinovich Plekhanov, a Russian Marxist who died in 1918, titled "Idealist and Materialist World Views," was decades old and outdated. If it could have claimed expert authority, Benjamin wrote, that would have been twenty-five years earlier. Benjamin withdrew from the project at the end of February 1931, followed by Ihering and then by the financial collapse of the publishing house Rowohlt and the emergency press restrictions of July 1931, which finally ended the project.[33]

The terms *Krise* and *Kritik* would be taken up again and again and eventually became twined—ultimately displacing the term *praxis*. For most of the following decades, they retained a Marxian connotation. Reinhart Koselleck's book *Kritik und Krise*, published in 1959 and written explicitly for a postwar "state of permanent crisis," had already begun to distance itself from Marx.[34] Koselleck focused there instead on the way in which the Kantian conception of critique had so influenced the utopianism that would, apparently and recurrently, at least according to Koselleck, lead to terror. But throughout the 1930s and 1940s still, critical theory and the primacy of crisis and critique remained tied to dialectical materialism for the most part.

Consolidating the Foundations :: Theodor W. Adorno

Theodor Adorno's intellectual sensibilities regarding scientific knowledge, social science, and philosophy differed sharply from Horkheimer's. Adorno came to critical theory from a more interpretive philosophical background, steeped in Husserl, Freud, and Kierkegaard and influenced by musical composition, art, and musicology. From the outset, from his inaugural lecture delivered to the philosophy faculty at the University of Frankfurt in May 1931, titled "The Actuality of Philosophy," Adorno questioned the very premise that human inquiry could comprehend reality. Adorno took as his point of departure a radical break in philosophy: contemporary philosophy, he argued, could no longer aspire to understand the world in its totality. The actual could not be rendered rational. The systematic and total theories of earlier German philosophy were things of the past. "Philosophy," Adorno said, "must learn to renounce the question of totality." The philosophical enterprise itself was an interpretive exercise, by contrast to science. Adorno could not have been clearer. "Plainly put: the idea of science (*Wissenschaft*) is research; that of philosophy is interpretation." Accordingly, Adorno cut critical philosophy down to size: rather than aim to render society rational, he proposed searching for middle-level concepts and interpretations that could solve punctual problems—conceptual tools that lay somewhere between the minute analyses of the Vienna Circle and of positivism and the comprehensive, totalizing analyses of German idealism. These concepts, he argued, could serve as interpretive keys to resolve social problems and thereby trigger the demand for change. The task of critical philosophy, Adorno proposed, was to discover and construct those interpretive keys.[35]

Despite the different sensibilities, Adorno shared with Horkheimer an attachment to Marxian theory. The only two examples of promising concepts that Adorno offered were the Marxian categories of commodity structure and class analysis. These interpretive keys, in his view, led directly to praxis—in an unmediated way. Referring specifically to the praxis imperative in Marx, Adorno explained:

> When Marx reproached the philosophers, saying that they had only variously interpreted the world, and contraposed to them that the point was to change it, then the sentence receives its legitimacy not only out of political praxis, but also out of philosophic theory. Only in the annihilation of the question is the authenticity of philosophic interpretation first successfully proven, and mere thought by itself cannot accomplish this [authenticity]: therefore the annihilation of the question compels praxis.[36]

The tension between interpretive philosophy and Marxian theory would push Adorno to focus his theoretical research on the negative moment of the Hegelian dialectic, leading to the publication in 1966 of *Negative Dialectics*. Before that, however, in conversation with and under the influence of his intellectual collaborations with Horkheimer, Adorno found himself pulled even deeper into the same tension reflected in Horkheimer's writings—one that was accentuated by the historical circumstances of the war.

On the one hand, the reality of fascism and the Holocaust pushed Adorno to an even more negative position about the potential of critical philosophy. The historical circumstances had a marked effect on Horkheimer as well, who became far less sanguine about the prospect of a proletarian revolution. Indeed, Horkheimer became less confident about the prospect or even the very possibility of progress.

In their notes appended to the *Dialectic of Enlightenment* completed during the war in May 1944, Horkheimer and Adorno took a dark view of history, at odds with the prospect of a communist horizon. Even as they foresaw the demise of fascism, they did not predict a progressive future but rather more of the same, if not worse. When fascism is over, they wrote, "there is nothing to prove that a spirit of freedom will spread across Europe; its nations may become just as xenophobic, pseudocollectivistic, and hostile to culture as Fascism once was when they had to fight against it. The downfall of Fascism will not necessarily lead to a movement of the avalanche."

As if that were not sober enough, Horkheimer and Adorno added: "The principle of liberal philosophy was that of 'both/and.' Today the principle of 'either/or' seems to apply, but as though a decision had already been taken for the worse."[37]

In these dark passages, *Dialectic of Enlightenment* reinforces the earlier aspect of historical constructivism with an even larger dose of contingency. Marx's determinist philosophy of history is absent. The prospects are bleak. Critical theory, Horkheimer and Adorno would later emphasize in their new preface in April 1969, "holds that the core of truth is historical, rather than an unchanging constant to be set against the movement of history." There are no universals, but now there are no teleologies either. In fact, two decades after they wrote the book, they already had different views of the correct interpretation of their historical circumstances. "In not a few places," they write in 1969, "the reality of our times is formulated in a way no longer appropriate to contemporary experience."[38] Critical analysis, in this sense, has to be punctual and historical and can be valid only in its immediate, concrete historical context.

"There is nothing to prove that a spirit of freedom will spread across Europe": One might have thought that this revisionism would have broken the grip of the Marxian conception of history and liberated those elements of constructivism embedded in Horkheimer's earlier vision for critical theory. But surprisingly not: even Horkheimer and Adorno's writings during World War II retained elements of scientific Marxism. On the other hand, then, and somewhat surprisingly, *Dialectic of Enlightenment* also continued in the furrow of Marxian categories and logics. The discussion of Odysseus and his confrontation with the Sirens, from book 12 of the *Odyssey*, is telling. In their essay on Odysseus and the Sirens, Horkheimer and Adorno lay on top of the relationship between Odysseus and his oarsmen a dialectic modeled on the Marxian relationship between the capitalist managers and factory workers. As you recall, Odysseus' encounter with the Sirens is a test by means of which Odysseus conquers nature and his own nature. He does so by dominating his men—through the complete dominion over his oarsmen who, with wax in their ears and strict orders to continue rowing no matter what, cannot hear him beseech them to release him from the chains that tied him to the mast. It is only through the thoroughgoing oppression of his men that Odysseus' plan succeeds and he can overcome nature.

Horkheimer and Adorno impose a Marxian interpretation on the myth of the Sirens by equating Odysseus to a capitalist head of industry and the oarsmen to workers. They achieve this in gradual steps that retrace Marx's philosophy of class conflict. First, they make an allusion to feudalism. Odysseus is first compared to "the seigneur who allows the others to labor for themselves." Right after that, they introduce the next historical period and the arrival of the early bourgeoisie. Odysseus is compared to "the burghers," who, like him, "would deny themselves happiness all the more doggedly as it drew closer to them with the growth of their own power." Then the capitalist proprietor enters the stage. They describe Odysseus "as [the] proprietor, [who] finally renounces even participation in labor." Finally, the stage is set for the last phase of capitalism, characterized by capitalist managers and directors of industry. They compare Odysseus to the captains of industry. They write about "rulers from the cunning Odysseus to the naïve managing directors of today."[39] The historical trajectory is Marxian: from the feudal seigneur, to the burgher, to the proprietor, to the manager, to the captain of industry.

In fact, the last two stages reflect precisely the historical analysis that Horkheimer laid out in "Traditional and Critical Theory." In that article in 1937, he had specifically elaborated on Marxian history to develop a new, final stage in which the proprietors of capital were displaced by managers and directors. As he explained there, capitalism had evolved since the nineteenth century and since Marx's analysis, to the point where, as a result of the concentration of capital, the legal owners of capital had begun to take a back seat to the managers and directors of corporations, in fact to the point where (in 1937 at least) directors who did not even own part of the business were more powerful than the capitalists: "Owners become increasingly powerless before the directors and their staffs." This was accompanied by a rise of ideologies grounded on notions of great personalities and management skills. "The end result of the process," Horkheimer wrote in 1937, "is a society dominated no longer by independent owners but by cliques of industrial and political leaders."[40] This same progression, from proprietor to director, is reflected in their elaboration of Odysseus and the myth of the Sirens.

Horkheimer and Adorno elaborate a similar historical progression for the oarsmen. At first, they are described as mere "laborers" toiling for their seigneur. But soon, "the world of prehistory is left behind," and all of a sudden, the oarsmen are compared to the proletariat. Horkheimer and Adorno refer to their "manual labor," and then they write, in very Marxian terms: "The stopped ears which the pliable proletarians have retained ever since the time of myth have no advantage over the immobility of the master." Following that, we witness the same progression from the mid-nineteenth century to the present. The oarsmen are compared to factory workers today: "The oarsmen, who cannot speak to one another, are each of them yoked in the same rhythm as the modern worker in the factory," Horkheimer and Adorno write.[41]

Like the recurring master-slave dialectic, Horkheimer and Adorno actualize the domination of Odysseus over his men by mapping it onto a Marxian history of the present. The myth ultimately reflects the relation between the "managing directors of today" and "the modern worker in the factory." The mode of production is coerced and alienated labor: the workers are deafened and turned into human machines that cannot even see themselves in their work. Horkheimer and Adorno write that these "men—despite their closeness to things—cannot enjoy their labor because it is performed under pressure, in desperation, with senses stopped by force. The servant remains enslaved in body and soul; the master regresses."[42] This is, of course—and the authors draw explicitly on it—Hegel's *The Phenomenology of Spirit* and its famous dialectic of the lord and bondsman. And along those lines, "the master," Odysseus, maintains his superiority and position of domination but regresses as a moral agent.

The Hegelian master-slave dialectic—perhaps the most privileged trope of Marxist critical thinkers in the 1950s and 1960s—is the heart and soul of this dialectic of enlightenment. Horkheimer and Adorno are explicit about this: "Measures such as those taken on Odysseus' ship in regard to the Sirens form presentient allegory of the dialectic of enlightenment." Enlightenment, as mastery over our natures and emancipation from our self-incurred immaturity, entails forms of domination that are inescapable and destructive and inevitably lead to regression. In Horkheimer and Adorno's words, this reflects "the inescapable compulsion to social domination of nature."[43]

Horkheimer and Adorno, then, continued to meld together radically different epistemological sensibilities. They retained a Marxian conception of class struggle and the idea of internal contradictions to capitalism that enacted a Left Hegelian dialectic, but at other times, they gave up entirely on the progress narrative in Marx. There emerged during and shortly after the war a Left Hegelian logic stripped of its optimism and sublation. "Adaptation to the power of progress involves the progress of power, and each time anew brings about those degenerations which show not unsuccessful but successful progress to be its contrary," they wrote. "The curse of irresistible progress is irresistible regression."[44] As the tragic historical circumstances took their toll on Horkheimer, as well as Adorno, they both sank into a dark dialectic. Humanity, they believed, "is sinking into a new kind of barbarism," from which it seemed it would not recover.[45] Even the defeat of fascism would not lighten the forecast, as we saw earlier. The dialectic of enlightenment was ruthless. They faced, in their words, "the indefatigable self-destructiveness of enlightenment," to the point where, they wrote, "enlightenment becomes wholesale deception of the masses."[46] Horkheimer's lectures at Columbia University from the spring of 1944, published in 1946 under the title *The Eclipse of Reason*, retained the same mixture of Marxism without a notion of progress. They too were dark, leading him to practically give up on the ambition of critical praxis.

Two Versions of the Frankfurt School

The deep tension within the first generation of the Frankfurt School—between, on the one hand, the reflexivity, constructivism, and historicism marked by negation and contingency and, on the other hand, the type of scientism typically associated with Marxism, especially scientific Marxism—produced two versions of early Frankfurt School critical theory.

The first variation is critical theory as *critique of Marxism*. Drawing on the elements of reflexivity and constructivism and highlighting Adorno's writings in particular, this version unwinds dialectical materialism, liberates itself from the historical determinism of political economy, and weakens the necessity and inherence of internal contradictions and the formality of the Hegelian dialectic. This first version tries *to salvage critical theory from Marxism*. It highlights the younger Marx—the Marx that Paul Ricœur, Geuss, and others grouped together with Nietzsche and Freud under the umbrella of the "hermeneutics of suspicion." It highlights the moment of unveiling and unmasking. The effort here is to put epistemology in service of critical theory. And it allows later Frankfurt School scholars to portray the Frankfurt School and the whole tradition of critical theory as being opposed to rigid Marxism and instead as being much closer to poststructuralism, postcolonialism, and queer and critical race theories. It is what allows a philosopher such as Martin Saar to rearticulate critical theory as a "critique of power" under the rubric of "social philosophy" and argue that there is no fundamental tension with Foucault's work; that the Frankfurt School was always sufficiently copious, flexible, and open to absorb its antifoundational critics.[47]

The second version is critical theory as *corrective to Marxism.* Drawing on the more scientistic elements of the first generation, this version recuperates dialectical logics to rehabilitate Marx, or at least rejuvenate a more foundational leftism—one that is true and normatively correct. The ambition here is to preserve the normative correctness of the Hegelian dialectic by means of concepts such as rationality, acceptability, and learning processes. This version tries *to salvage Marxism (or a proto-positivist leftist politics) from critical theory.* It returns to the Hegelian dialectic. It highlights and rehabilitates immanent critique. It revives the critique of ideology and the idea of false consciousness—in the belief that, if we get past ideological veils and can see our real interests, we can resuscitate Marxism or a real Left politics. The effort here is to put epistemology in service of a Marxian or new leftist orientation. It is what allows a philosopher such as Rahel Jaeggi or a critical thinker such as Steven Lukes to revive notions of ideology or false consciousness in the service of correct forms of life or true politics.[48]

It is this controversial and divisive space—the epistemological refuge that critical theory sought—that would explode in the 1960s. It would push critical philosophy into its prolonged epistemological detour.

CHAPTER 2

Challenging the Frankfurt Foundations

In his 1962 monograph, *Nietzsche and Philosophy*, the French philosopher Gilles Deleuze proposed a radically different version and genealogy of critical philosophy. Deleuze turned elsewhere: not to Marx, nor back to Hegel or Kant, but instead to Nietzsche. In Deleuze's hands, Nietzsche becomes *the* critical philosopher—the founder, the inventor of, in Deleuze's words, "*la philosophie critique*."[1] Nietzsche is the one who pointed the way to the truly critical question about the value of truth—to interrogate what value truth serves in politics and philosophy, and what value values have.

"The search for new means of philosophical expression was inaugurated by Nietzsche."[2] Thus opens Deleuze's most demanding of philosophical texts, *Difference and Repetition*, published shortly before May 1968. If his book with Félix Guattari four years later would be called *The Anti-Oedipus*, then his towering work from 1968 could have been called *The Anti-Dialectic*. And Nietzsche, in his capacity as antidialectician, would serve as Deleuze's loadstar. In the new age of philosophy, Deleuze writes, "difference and repetition have come to supplant identity and negation, identity and contradiction."[3] Critical philosophy, for Deleuze, is unique and uncompromising, totally at odds with Kant, but also with Hegel. "There is no possible compromise between Hegel and Nietzsche," Deleuze writes. "The philosophy of Nietzsche forms an absolute anti-dialectic, and sets out to denounce all the mystifications that find refuge in the dialectic."[4] Naturally, Deleuze was aiming directly at Marx as well.

Deleuze turns to Nietzsche as an antidote to Hegel, to the Hegelian dialectic, to the concepts of necessity and overcoming, and to the notion of truth underlying the dialectic. He deploys Nietzsche to question the motivation for truth: to interrogate the will to truth and ask what animates the claim to truth in the dialectical method, in the notion of internal versus external values, in the idea of necessary contradictions and transformations of values. Deleuze displaces Kant as the source of critique, but he retains and relocates that critical impulse to expose the work that truth and illusions do. He draws on Nietzsche to propose what he calls real critique: not just to identify the criteria to distinguish truth from falsity, but to document the work that the concept of truth does.

In the period 1967–1973, Michel Foucault also drew on and confronted Nietzsche's writings to develop a genealogical method for his critical philosophy and a theory of knowledge-power. As Daniel Defert recounts, Foucault turned to Nietzsche in 1967 to distance himself from Marx, as he had done in the early 1950s to free himself from Marxism and the French Communist Party.[5] In the process, Foucault developed a theory of knowledge that directly confronts Marxian notions of ideology and the early writings of the Frankfurt School. He proposed a radical critique of knowledge that aimed to unmask the idea that it was ever possible to sever knowledge from relations of power and, accordingly, to reach a solid normative foundation, even through ideology critique.

Foucault's theory of knowledge-power presents the most direct challenge to the epistemological and normative foundations of a Marxian philosophy of history or of Horkheimer's critique of ideology. Knowledge and normativity can never be severed from relations of power in Foucault's view and, therefore, there is no escape from reflexivity and historical constructivism by way of Marx. As if he were writing directly against Horkheimer, Foucault declares in his 1973 Rio lectures on "Truth and Juridical Form":

> This great myth needs to be dispelled. It is this myth which Nietzsche began to demolish by showing that, behind all knowledge, behind all attainment of knowledge, what is involved is a struggle for power. Political power is not absent from knowledge, it is woven together with it.[6]

That great Western myth, Foucault declares, had to be, in his words, "*liquidé*"—liquidated, a far more forceful expression than *dispelled*, as in the official English translation. Foucault's intervention is a searing critique of the possibility of achieving the kind of powerless knowledge that would be necessary in order to know what the workers' "own true interests" are, or what political reality looks like as "it really is."[7] Foucault explicitly contests the Frankfurt School's concept of ideology.[8] Foucault's critical philosophy directly challenges the idea of an epistemological foundation, calling instead for a constant reexamination of how power circulates through society, always questioning the categories through which critics can even analyze relations of power, and always reexamining the ways in which power and subjectivity are transformed.

Foucault, Deleuze, and others in the 1960s confronted the epistemological and normative foundations of early critical theory—it would be important to add Pierre Klossowski, Jacques Derrida, Sarah Kofman, and other critical philosophers as well.[9] These confrontations challenged critical theory on the terrain of epistemology and pushed critical philosophy down an epistemological path—a path that Nietzsche had forged with his own radical interventions on the value of truth. "What, then, is truth?" you will recall Nietzsche asking, and answering: "a sum of human relations that have been poetically and rhetorically intensified, translated, and embellished, and that after long use strike a people as fixed, canonical, and binding: truths are illusions of which one has forgotten that they are illusions."[10] Other brilliant critical theorists, such as Edward Said, Gayatri Chakravorty Spivak, Judith Butler, and others, would up the ante in the following decades with more pointed postcolonial and queer challenges to the universalism, Eurocentrism, and protoscientism not only of traditional and critical philosophy, but of those very challenges to early critical theory as well.

In subsequent work, beginning at the turn of the 1980s, Foucault would open another front against epistemological foundationalism. Having freed himself at that point of Marx and debates over Marxism, and having in the process left Nietzsche behind as well, Foucault traced the origins of critical philosophy further back: first, to the fifteenth and sixteenth centuries and the pastoral arts of governing—and conversely, the critical attitude of not being governed in those ways—and then, much earlier, to the fifth century BCE and the birth of the philosophical puzzles of truth-telling and *parrhesia*. Those origins would lead Foucault to write a history of truth-making and also push his final version of critical philosophy further down an epistemological path—focused not on the criteria of truth, but instead on the orthogonal question of the production and power of truth: on how truth is manufactured and what authority and weight truth-telling has in politics and society.[11]

There is a telling passage from one of Foucault's intellectual mentors, Georges Dumézil, to which Foucault returned at formative moments of his intellectual life. It is a passage from the 1943 volume of Dumézil's series on *Roman Myths*, titled *Servius and Fortuna: An Essay on the Social Function of Praise and Blame and on the Indo-European Elements of the Roman Census*.[12] Foucault invokes it on at least two pivotal occasions: first, in the February 3, 1971, session of his first lecture series at the Collège de France, his *Lectures on the Will to Know*;[13] and again nearly ten years later, as the epigraph to his 1981 lecture series at the Catholic University of Louvain, *Wrong-Doing, Truth-Telling: The Function of Avowal in Justice*—two formative bookends, almost, to his history of truth and truth-telling. The passage reads:

> Looking back into the deepest reaches of our species' behavior, "truthful speech" [*la parole vraie*] has been a force few could resist. From the earliest moments, truth was one of man's most formidable verbal weapons, most prolific sources of power, and most solid institutional foundations.[14]

The power of truth: Foucault had promised a book with that title in an enigmatic footnote in 1976 and did not deliver specifically on that promise, but he did dedicate most of the years between 1971 and 1984 to precisely that: a historical analysis of truth-making, of truth-telling, and of how truth functions, what it achieves.[15] This would represent a deeply antifoundational challenge to earlier forms of critical philosophy, which pushed against the question of truth versus falsity, in order to interrogate instead the operation itself of dividing truth from falsity—the function of the critical judgment that divides truth from falsity and becomes a basis for governing others. This alternative genealogy of critical philosophy, once again, pushed squarely into the terrain of epistemology.[16]

In the sections that follow, I will trace these various challenges to the Frankfurt School foundations, beginning in this chapter with Deleuze and Foucault, followed by Said, Spivak, and Butler, before turning, in the next chapter, to Foucault's alternative genealogy of critical philosophy from his lectures at the Collège de France (1970–1984). But before I do so, let me present, in as sharp a contrast possible, the confrontation represented by Foucault's challenge to earlier critical theory.

The Confrontation with Marx

The confrontation comes alive in Foucault's critique of Marx at the conclusion of his 1973 Rio lectures, "Truth and Juridical Forms." There, Foucault discusses the theory of alienated labor—the claim, which he attributes to Marx, that workers feel alienated in the capitalist mode of production given that "man's concrete essence is labor."[17] Foucault does not provide a pin cite, but we could point to the *Economic and Philosophical Manuscripts of 1844*, where Marx defines what is quintessentially human (as opposed to animal) as precisely laboring freely and productively—a thesis that was itself the product of a denaturalizing move.[18]

Foucault critiques Marx's thesis—specifically the claim that man's essence is labor—arguing first that this is by no means true. "Labor is absolutely not man's concrete essence." Second, he proposes that people come to believe in its truth only by means of certain practices that are intimately connected to capitalist relations of production themselves. These are the practices, Foucault argues, that shape the body and render bodies docile. He refers to them in his Rio lectures as "infrapower": "a set of political techniques, techniques of power . . . by which people's bodies and their time would become labor power and labor time so as to be effectively used and thereby transformed into [surplus value]"; a "web of microscopic, capillary political power . . . at the level of man's very existence . . ."; "the whole set of little powers, of little institutions situated at the lowest level," in contrast to the state, or even to a notion of class.[19] Marx's theory of capital accumulation, on Foucault's reading, depends on these disciplinary techniques (which are themselves intimately connected with capitalist production) to shape bodies and render workers docile.

Foucault develops this insight two years later in *Discipline and Punish*, where, specifically citing Marx's *Capital* (vol. I, chap. XIII), he argues that the economic revolutions that made possible the accumulation of capital during the nineteenth century cannot be separated from the production of these docile bodies—or what he refers to as "the methods for administering the *accumulation of men*." These methods are the disciplinary techniques at the heart of *Discipline and Punish*; the forms of discipline that displaced sovereignty—in Foucault's words, those "traditional, ritual, costly, violent forms of power, which soon fell into disuse and were superseded by a subtle, calculated technology of subjection." In Foucault's view, these disciplinary methods were as important to capitalist production and the exploitation of surplus value as the modes of production.[20]

Drawing on Georg Rusche and Otto Kirchheimer's *Punishment and Social Structure*—published in 1939 under the auspices of the Frankfurt School in exile at Columbia University—Foucault transforms traditional Marxian political economy into a "'political economy' of the body," effectively into "a history of bodies" that focuses on the "political investment of the body" and the "political technology of the body."[21] These disciplinary forms—themselves embedded equally in relations of production—rendered docile the modern body, simultaneously making possible factory workers *and* the idea that free labor is man's essence. As Foucault would say in *Psychiatric Power*, "disciplinary power, and this is no doubt its fundamental property, fabricates subjected bodies; it pins the subject-function exactly to the body. It fabricates and distributes subjected bodies; it is individualizing [only in that] the individual is nothing other than the subjected body."[22] These disciplinary techniques "bring[] about the maximum possible use of individuals. They make all of them usable"; they "make possible the accumulation not only of these forces, but equally of time"; and "this triple aspect of the techniques of the accumulation of men and of the forces of work, is, I think, the reason why the different disciplinary apparatuses were deployed, tried out, developed, and refined. The extension, movement, and migration of the disciplines from their lateral function to the central and general function they exercise from the eighteenth century are linked to this accumulation of men and to the role of the accumulation of men in capitalist society."[23]

Foucault could not have been clearer—or more challenging to Marx: the idea that "man's concrete essence is labor" is *itself* fabricated, alongside these docile bodies, by disciplinary techniques that are embedded in relations of production and that themselves make those relations of production possible. Those disciplinary techniques also produce feelings of alienation because they deprive workers of the rich, substantive meaning that their lives could have. Those disciplinary techniques give rise to knowledges—such as the idea that labor is "the essence of man," but more broadly, the idea of man as an object of science. In his Rio lectures, Foucault specifically proposes that this infrapower "gave rise to a series of knowledges—a knowledge of the individual, of normalization, a corrective knowledge—that proliferated in these institutions of infrapower, causing the so-called human sciences, and man as an object of science, to appear."[24] This rehearses the argument at the end of *The Order of Things* from 1966—the image of man written in sand, disappearing under the waves—or even earlier, the final paragraph of Foucault's introduction, in 1960, to Kant's *Anthropology*.

As Foucault explains in Rio: "If what I have said is true, it cannot be said that these forms of knowledge [*savoirs*] and these forms of power, operating over and above productive relations, merely express those relations or enable them to be reproduced." The reason is that these ideologies themselves are made possible both by the disciplinary techniques and by relations of production, which are themselves made possible by knowledge-power. There is no priority of relations of production that would privilege or place first production or capital as the driving force of history. Ideas and beliefs embedded in these disciplinary techniques are necessary to enable political economy. The relations of production are themselves shaped by conceptions of the self that enable the docile bodies that work the factories. Modes of production, knowledge, and relations of power are interlocking. Foucault writes: "In order for the relations of production that characterize capitalist societies to exist, there must be, in addition to a certain number of economic determinations, those power relations and forms of operation of knowledge. Power and knowledge are thus deeply rooted—they are not just superimposed on the relations of production but, rather, are very deeply rooted in what constitutes them."[25]

In Foucault's view, then, it is not possible to speak of humanity's essence that would be, in some sense, foundational, or to speak of any genuine or true interests. Instead, conceptions of self are shaped by relations of power and are historically situated at all times. They make possible the modes of economic production within which they find themselves interwoven. They are not exterior to relations of production in any way. It is possible to show how they are born and maintained and evolve, and to what effect. Despite all that, for Foucault, they have real force and staying power. They cannot easily be lifted like a veil. They have real effects—*des effets de vérité*. They cannot easily be proven wrong. They are not susceptible to demonstrations of falsity. And it may take a whole series of complex techniques of knowledge and relations of power, deeply embedded in relations of production, for other beliefs to form.

On both approaches, to be sure, there is a form of enlightenment and emancipation—but by different means. For the first, access to truth, to facts—and thereby emancipation from illusions—is achieved by acquiring the right social theory. In Horkheimer's words, "one must possess the key to the historical situation, the right social theory."[26] This allows a foundation to make claims to truth and correctness about ways of being, or real interests of people, or forms of life.[27] In Foucault's view, on the other hand, there is no access to powerless knowledge or right social theories. There can be at best an unveiling of current forms of oppression or relations of power, achieved through the denaturalization of dominant ideas. In this second view, we do not achieve a resolution or progress, but rather reach another place from which we will again need to emancipate ourselves. We do not escape relations of power; we never do. We are always embedded in them. In unveiling illusions, we simply bring about a new condition that will itself need to be reassessed and reexamined so that we can understand how power recirculates anew. When we shed illusions, when regimes of truth shift, we are merely at another place where power relations are thickly at play, may be problematic, and may become entrenched—and where we will need to revalue how we are governing and being governed.[28]

This represents a philosophical tug of war between, on the one hand, a normatively correct solution to a social problem that reflects an overcoming, an improvement, a rational or better solution to a social situation, and, on the other hand, an unveiling that does not generate a normative solution or grounding. The difference, at its core, is that the first approach—which, as I will show in chapter 5, maps onto immanent critique—maintains that there are internal values that are necessarily transformed and remain internal to the practices and constellations that are the object of critique. In other words, the normativity is internal and comes from within the original complex, whereas with Foucault, any normativity would have to come from outside, and therefore the criticism would remain external and calls for relentless critique. But before turning to this conceptual analysis of the problem (in chapter 5) and how to resolve it (in chapters 6 and 7), let me return first to the historical account and trace the challenges to early Frankfurt School foundations, beginning with Gilles Deleuze in the 1960s.

Challenging the Value of Truth :: Gilles Deleuze

Deleuze locates in Nietzsche's writings a pure form of critique, the very essence of critical philosophy, its core: namely, questioning the value of truth. Nietzsche alone raised the question of the value of values and of morality. The *critical* element, Deleuze writes—italicizing the word "*critique*" in "l'élément *critique*"—is precisely "the creative element of meaning and of values." And so Deleuze defines the problem of critique specifically as the value of values, their evaluation, and the problem of their creation. In the process, Deleuze displaces even Kant—who is conventionally considered the source of critique—because, as Deleuze tells us, Kant missed his target and did not do "real critique." In Deleuze's reading, Nietzsche's overarching project was "to introduce the notions of meaning and value into philosophy." In this sense, Nietzsche shaped critical philosophy. He reoriented modern philosophy away from the straightforward question of truth and falsity and toward the categories beyond good and evil: "The categories of thought are no longer truth and falsity, but *the noble and the vile, the high and the low*, in the nature of the forces that seize thought itself."[29]

By posing the question in terms of values rather than truth versus falsity or the limits of reason, Nietzsche founded a genuine critical philosophy: one that questions the value of values, that raises the question about the creation of values and of the meaning of evaluation, thus performing the reversal that *is* critique. In Deleuze's reading, Kant never got close to doing this, and as a result never fully grasped the idea of critique. Kant never engaged in true critique, Deleuze argues, because Kant "did not know how to pose the problem of critique in terms of values."[30]

Deleuze places his critical approach under the sign of "genealogy," and for him, the critical philosopher himself becomes a genealogist.[31] Genealogy captures the critical element, insofar as it challenges the value of values by seeking the origin of values. In this, it comprises a double movement: the origin of the values and the value of the origins. It should come as little surprise that Deleuze's *Nietzsche et la philosophie* begins with the header "*le concept de généalogie*" on the very first page.

At its most radical, then, critique challenges the value of truth. Deleuze returns to Nietzsche's later work, from 1887, *On the Genealogy of Morals*, and specifically the passage in the third essay, §24: "Let us thus define our task—we must attempt once and for all to put in question the value of truth." Deleuze systematizes Nietzsche as a thinker, presenting his main ideas in a rigorous, interconnected, and coherent manner. Deleuze tries to fix the terminology, to anchor the metaphors, and to refine the logic and argument. It was necessary, he maintains, because "all the rigor of this philosophy, of which we often suspect, to our detriment, the systematic precision," depended on this type of analytic work.[32] Deleuze pays special attention to the *Genealogy of Morals*—more so than many before him, such as Georges Bataille or Maurice Blanchot—in large part because, for Deleuze, the *Genealogy* represents the most systematic of Nietzsche's books, and it grounds his critical philosophy.

At the heart of Deleuze's genealogy, there is a certain distantiation, or distance, or difference. This notion of difference reflects the genealogical distance from the origin: the search for both origins and the distance from origins. These would be core terms that Deleuze would continue to explore and develop—and also appropriate in his work a few years later, in 1968, in *Difference and Repetition.* Deleuze returned to Nietzsche throughout his philosophical writings, first with a conference at Royaumont in 1964, which he would preside over and offer the concluding remarks; and then in his shorter monograph, titled *Nietzsche*, in 1965; then in 1967, in his presentation of Léopold von Sacher-Masoch's *The Venus in Furs*—a presentation that rivals the breadth and length of Sacher-Masoch's own book; and then again in 1986, in his *Foucault.* In effect, he did so throughout his life and career, through at least 1993 in *Critique et Clinique*.[33] In practically every work, Nietzsche reappears as a central interlocutor, offering a pathway to critical philosophy.

Deleuze uncovered in Nietzsche a way to emancipation. Bataille had recuperated Nietzsche from the fascists decades earlier, in 1937. At the very same moment that Martin Heidegger began lecturing on Nietzsche at the University of Freiberg, in the winter of 1936–1937, Bataille and a handful of his closest intellectual collaborators—the artist André Masson and the philosophers Jean Wahl and Pierre Klossowski, among others—published the second volume of their new review, *Acéphale: Religion, sociologie, philosophie*.[34] The date of publication: January 1937, the same year as Horkheimer's article. The title: "*Nietzsche et les Fascistes: Une Réparation*"—a reparation, a repair. Illustrated by Masson's drawings of these headless and groinless figures of Man—or rather, not groinless, but rather castrated and sculled figures.[35] The 1937 volume was dedicated to recuperating Nietzsche from the fascists. The lead article—"*Nietzsche et les Fascistes*"—was a violent diatribe against Elisabeth Föerster-Nietzsche (somewhat curiously renamed "Elisabeth Judas-Föerster"), as well as thinkers who, according to Bataille, had distorted and abused Nietzsche's words, including Georg Lukacs on the left, but mostly Alfred Rosenberg, Alfred Baeumler, and other contemporary fascist thinkers who had misappropriated Nietzsche's work, pilfered quotations out of context, and betrayed his ideas. The volume could be retitled, in light of an earlier untimely meditation, "The Uses and Abuses of Nietzsche for Death." Through this *Acéphale* journal and other collective projects, such as the Collège de Sociologie (1937–1939), and later the review *Critique*, Bataille and his collective built a bulwark to maintain and entrench their critical reading of Nietzsche.

If Bataille recuperated Nietzsche from the fascists and made war reparations to him, and if Maurice Blanchot would later return to Nietzsche the revolutionary potential of the act of writing, then Deleuze, we could say, turned Nietzsche into *the critical philosopher*, the one who most directly challenged claims of truth and the will to truth, and in so doing, offered a path to human emancipation. This was an entirely different basis for critical theory than the one that the Frankfurt School had developed, and it pushed hardest against the protoscientism of the Marxian elements of the first generation. The confrontation was primarily along epistemological lines, which would push the controversy onto the question of normative foundations.

Instead of grounding critical theory, Deleuze pushed it in an ethical direction—the opposite of validity and truth. In this regard, he turned to Nietzsche's concept of eternal return.[36] Deleuze first elaborated the notion of eternal return in his 1962 monograph *Nietzsche et la philosophie*, then developed it at Royaumont in 1964, and returned to it again and again after then.[37] Deleuze understood Nietzsche's idea of eternal return through the notion of "becoming" and the priority of becoming over being. He rejected, in most strenuous terms, the idea that the eternal return represented "an old idea, borrowed from the Greeks, the Hindus, the Babylonians," or that it is "a cycle, or a return of the same, a return to the same."[38] Instead, he understood it as an ethical concept: the eternal return is the equivalent of a Kantian maxim to help guide our actions. Rather than the categorical imperative, it is the threat of recurrence: act so that you would be willing to always have your actions recur. Deleuze, in fact, states that "the eternal return dictates to the will a rule as rigorous as the Kantian rule."[39] Or, as he proposes, "in terms of ethics, the eternal return is the new formulation of a practical synthesis: *Whatever you will, make sure to will it in such a manner that you will its eternal return.*"[40] Deleuze finds and rehearses the specific passage from *The Will to Power* (IV, §242), where Nietzsche sets this out: "If, in all that you will you begin by asking yourself: is it certain that I will to do it an infinite number of times? This should be your most solid center of gravity."[41] Deleuze adds later, to confirm and emphasize, "*L'éternel retour est l'être du devenir.*"[42]

For Deleuze, the eternal return is an ordeal, a test—"*une épreuve*," he says.[43] It forces us to face our weaknesses, our laziness. It confronts us with their potential repetition. And for this reason, the eternal return lifts us to greater heights. It makes us better. It improves us. It is, in this sense, an ethical ordeal.[44] It does not lead in the direction of normative validity or justifiability, but rather of ethical choice. It also reveals something central about the will to power: specifically, that it is not a desire for domination but the power of the will. Deleuze had developed this idea in his monograph in 1962. He returns to it in *Difference and Repetition*, where he emphasizes that, for Nietzsche, the eternal return, like the *Übermensch*, is an ambition, an aspiration, a drive toward virtuous excellence.[45]

The power of the will, and specifically the power of the will to truth: That is what makes Nietzsche such a threat and such a contrast to the early Frankfurt School. One cannot sever normative order from the power of the will to truth. One cannot sever it from will or from desire. Ultimately, Deleuze would violently upend theories of ideology and history, Marxist and even post-Marxist ones. One can hear it clearly in his conversation with Foucault, published in 1972, in which he dismisses class interests and discusses instead the role of desire and of libidinal investments. The concepts of will and desire replace ideology and class struggle as the foci of analysis. Deleuze is particularly brilliant in that exchange, challenging the Marxist privileging of class struggle and showing instead the libidinal investments that are in play:

> Perhaps, this is because in terms of *investments*, whether economic or unconscious, interest is not the final answer; there are investments of desire that function in a more profound and diffuse manner than our interests dictate. But of course, we never desire against our interests, because interest always follows and finds itself where desire has placed it. We cannot shut out the scream of Reich: the masses were not deceived; at a particular time, they actually wanted a fascist regime! There are investments of desire that mold and distribute power, that make it the property of the policeman as much as of the prime minister; in this context, there is no qualitative difference between the power wielded by the policeman and the prime minister. The nature of these investments of desire in a social group explains why political parties or unions, which might have or should have revolutionary investments in the name of class interests, are so often reform oriented or absolutely reactionary on the level of desire.[46]

It was at around this time, pushing even further on the Reichian theme, that Deleuze and his coauthor, Félix Guattari, penned their famous (or infamous) attack on the concept of ideology.[47] In this debate and at that time, Nietzsche served for Deleuze as the emancipatory path from Marxism and an alternative source for critical philosophy.

Infinite Interpretation :: Michel Foucault

Foucault turned to Nietzsche's writings as a way to open new possibilities and push his own critical projects in new directions. At important junctures, he drew on Nietzsche to distance himself from Marx. As noted earlier in this chapter, the first period was in 1952–1953, at the time that he was leaving the French Communist Party. Those first encounters with Nietzsche—mostly through Heidegger, Bataille, and Blanchot—inspired Foucault to deliver lessons on Nietzsche at the École normale supérieure in 1953-1954 and to write a series of experimental essays and drafts on Nietzsche's work.[48] Those manuscripts reveal that Foucault was experimenting, probing the words, expressions, and turns of phrase of Nietzsche's writings in an effort to think through questions of dialectic, of repetition, of knowledge, of becoming, of reason and madness, of will, of the dangers of knowledge. Knowledge already lay at the heart of these epistemological investigations, as Foucault began working and reworking—as he would throughout his intellectual life—that enigmatic passage in Nietzsche: "To perish from absolute knowledge could well form part of the basis of being."[49]

Foucault returns to Nietzsche six years later as a way to loosen the hold of phenomenology, and especially existential phenomenology—the dominant mode of philosophical discourse on the Continent at the time, notably represented by Jean-Paul Sartre's unique blend of Marxism, phenomenology, and existentialism. In a ten-part introduction to his translation of Kant's *Anthropology*—written in 1959–1960 and accepted as his secondary doctoral thesis, but not published until long after his death in 2008[50]—Foucault explores the relationship between Kant's lectures on anthropology and the notion of critique. He argues that the transcendental illusion that Kant tried to resolve by means of his critique of pure reason was itself replicated by the anthropological illusion in Kant's work and, more generally, in post-Kantian phenomenological thought. Phenomenology and existential phenomenology (Husserl, Sartre, Heidegger, Merleau-Ponty, and others) simply replicated that illusion, Foucault argues. Phenomenologists claimed to analyze subjects who construct themselves and their environment, but they fall back into the trap of naturalizing the subject. It is not that they believed in human nature—they certainly did not—but that they placed the human subject once again at the very heart of their analyses.

Late in the argument, Foucault turns to Nietzsche (first ironically, but then experimentally) as a way to pry open existential phenomenology. Foucault's text is testing, probing Nietzsche's discourse as a potential can opener—a device to open a space for critical reflection.[51] In the final, tenth section of his introduction, Foucault "returns to the initial problem" of the relationship between critique and anthropology in order to highlight the problem of illusions—the transcendental and then anthropological illusions. The word *illusion* permeates Foucault's pages. Foucault protests that it is practically impossible to mount a "real" critique of these anthropological illusions; there is nothing but a constant and permanent circulation of the illusions in all of social science and philosophy such that, in the end, philosophers are incapable of exercising a real critique.[52]

It is here that Foucault's introduction deploys Nietzsche's writings to pry open a possible path forward. Here, Nietzsche stands not only for the death of God, but with it, the death of man. "Nietzsche's enterprise," Foucault writes, "could be understood as the end point to the proliferation of interrogations on man." He concludes his introduction with Nietzsche and these words: "La trajectoire de la question: *Was ist der Mensch?* dans le champ de la philosophie s'achève dans la réponse qui la récuse et la désarme: *der Übermensch*."[53] The *Übermensch*, for Foucault, may allow critical philosophy to get past man and the anthropological illusion. By killing God and, with him, man, by getting beyond man, not to a superman but to some place beyond humanity and humanism, Foucault suggests, it may be possible to get past the naturalized idea of man that always lurks in the background. Foucault experiments with Nietzsche's *Übermensch* to create a space, an opening. Looking back, it is not entirely surprising that Foucault apparently did not want his introduction published at the time.[54] It was indeed an experiment with Nietzsche, very much like his earlier essays: an experiment in the critical deployment of Nietzsche's writings as a way to denaturalize man.

A few years later, in July 1964, Foucault delivered a paper, "Nietzsche, Freud, Marx," that builds on these critical investigations to elaborate an epistemic theory of infinite interpretation—a theory that challenges head-on the possibility of epistemological foundations.[55] Foucault was, at the time, immersed in thinking and writing *The Order of Things*, which would be published nineteen months later, in April 1966. Foucault had already finished a first version of the book manuscript by December 1964, and thus he was at the tail end of the composition of this first version when he gave his conference paper in Royaumont. Shortly after the conference, in April 1965, Foucault rewrote another 300-page version of *The Order of Things*. It is here that Foucault tackles Nietzsche's writings to develop the idea of an epistemic condition of infinite interpretation.

Nietzsche's discourse becomes the paradigm of a particular mindset and logic. It becomes a specimen, an archaeological layer. It represents a system of interpretation, certain techniques, methods, and modes of interpretation, the purpose of which was to resolve age-old suspicions on the subject of language and the effects of language. These suspicions, Foucault suggests, had always existed. Two great suspicions, in fact: first, the suspicion that language does not work the way it is supposed to, that it does not say exactly what it is supposed to say; and second, that there are things in the world that speak in ways we had not previously suspected.[56] Foucault argues that in different ways, systems of interpretation had always targeted these great suspicions. The *episteme* of the Renaissance from the sixteenth century, based on resemblance, took aim at similar suspicions regarding language. Foucault's discussion of convention, of emulation, of analogy, of techniques of identity and resemblance in "The Prose of the World," the chapter on the *episteme* of the Renaissance in *The Order of Things*, was precisely an analysis of the techniques used to address these suspicions.[57] The system of interpretation from the Age of Reason—the relationship between identity and difference, the application of a certain order, and the categorizations and taxonomies that are characteristic of that age—was as well.

But it is in a third period, the modern age, that Foucault deciphers what he calls a "new possibility of interpretation." The writings of Nietzsche found anew, he claims, the possibility of a hermeneutics, a system of interpretation, and techniques of interpretation.[58] In his 1964 paper more directly, and more subtly in *The Order of Things*, Foucault proposes that Nietzsche's discourse modified the space of distribution within which signs operate. Nietzsche changed the spatial relations inherent in the interpretations of signs. Nietzsche's writings reveal that the work of interpretation goes into great depth. He shows that there is a verticality of metaphors and analogies. There is a depth perhaps, but also the realization that all depth leads us back to the surface, to the awareness that what exists deep down is simply another game, another interpretation. In fact, depth is no more than a fold in the surface.[59] Hence, there is a certain aporia: we are always attempting to go deeper in our search—as a technique of interpretation—but we find ourselves always, in fact, at the surface.

Interpretation becomes, then, an infinite task: every sign is but an interpretation of another sign. Foucault writes: "There is nothing absolutely primary to interpret, for after all everything is already interpretation, each sign is in itself not the thing that offers itself to interpretation but an interpretation of other signs."[60] In other words, there is no originary source, there is no original signified to which one can return. There are only acts of interpretation. "There is no original signified for Nietzsche," Foucault writes, and everything that one must interpret is always already an interpretation of signs imposed by a will. We find impositions of interpretation, but no original sources.[61]

"There is never, if you like, an *interpretandum* that is not already *interpretans*, so that it is as much a relationship of violence as of elucidation that is established in interpretation," Foucault declares.[62] This violence arises from the obligation to reinterpret everything, to test everything. There is only interpretation, and every interpretation "must overthrow, upset, shatter with the blow of a hammer."[63]

What is this violence, you may ask? It is the violence of never arriving at anything solid or reliable, of never achieving the original sign but of constantly reinterpreting interpretations—and contesting even those. In *Twilight of the Idols*, it is the violence of Nietzsche confronting Socrates, Plato, Kant, and Christianity. Nietzsche attacks Rousseau, Sand, Zola—so many respectable figures—and by contrast, and this is surely violent, he applauds Caesar, Napoleon, Dostoyevsky, and Goethe, as men of stronger, healthier character.

The violence consists of attacking interpretations, but also of posing the question: do these new interpretations hold? One way of thinking about philosophizing with a hammer is precisely to think of the physician's percussion tool used to sound the abdomen, to listen and to diagnose abdominal tympanism. The percussion hammer is used to hit an interpretation in order to hear if it is hollow or if there is a void behind it. This exact notion of verifying the tenability, the durability of an interpretation also was taken up in Deleuze's *Nietzsche and Philosophy*, in which he wrote: "The philosophy of values as envisaged and established by [Nietzsche], is the true realization of critique and the only way in which a total critique may be realized, the only way to 'philosophize with a hammer.'"[64] In Foucault's hands, philosophizing with a hammer consists of ceaselessly posing the question of interpretation.

The last paragraph of the 1964 paper ends with a comparison between semiology, Marxism, and Nietzsche's writings, and there, Foucault takes us back to the present. He emphasizes that semiology is completely different than these nineteenth-century hermeneutics: "It seems to me necessary to understand what too many of our contemporaries forget, that hermeneutics and semiology are two fierce enemies."[65] Foucault argues that his contemporaries, both semiologists and Marxists, put too much stock in the interpretations they apply. They ceaselessly deploy ready-made interpretations and have too much faith in the force of their own theories. They have stopped applying percussion on their own methods of semiology or dialectical materialism. They are too comfortable that their means of interpretation can operate in all contexts—that theirs is an originary sign that works.

One can hear, right there, Foucault's direct challenge to foundations. The text is now situated in the political debates of the mid-1960s. Foucault marshals the hermeneutics of Nietzsche—as well as the original writings of Freud and Marx—to contest contemporary methods that do not appreciate or understand the infiniteness of interpretation. The final word in the 1964 paper is "Nietzsche"—a word that stands precisely for that endlessness of interpretation. Two years later, in *The Order of Things*, Foucault boiled this down to a single passage. Nietzsche's writings open a critical space for contemporary thought and "marks the threshold beyond which contemporary philosophy can begin thinking again."[66] This is the Nietzsche of the death of God, and through the death of God, the death of man as well. As you know, that is where *The Order of Things* will end.

Foucault's work from the mid-1960s does more than discern in Nietzsche's writings a way of thinking that is proper to the nineteenth century. It opens a space for critical philosophy at the furthest limits of the imagination—where the infinite task of interpretation may produce a point of rupture, or even drive us mad. It is a space that comes closest to the experience of madness.[67] In this gesture, the 1964 essay returns to reinterpret, once again, that fragment from §39 of Nietzsche's *Beyond Good and Evil*, a fragment that Foucault had labored as early as 1953 and to which he would return again and again. Perhaps it makes more sense now: "To perish from absolute knowledge could well form part of the basis of being."[68]

From the Will to Know to the Will to Truth

Foucault plunges back into Nietzsche's writings in the period 1967–1973, around the time of the student uprisings and their aftermath, with the intent to distance himself from Marxism once again. In an essay "Nietzsche, Genealogy, History," published in 1971, as well as in his first lectures at the Collège de France in 1970–1971, originally named *The Will to Know* and published in 2011 under the title *Lectures on the Will to Know* (in order to differentiate it from the first volume of *The History of Sexuality*), Foucault reorients his approach to critical philosophy. Foucault develops a theory that he would call *vouloir-savoir*, or the will to know, that challenges normative foundationalism from a different angle.[69] It was the product, Daniel Defert notes, of a rereading of Nietzsche that Foucault began to undertake in the summer of 1967.[70]

In his indispensable chronology of Foucault's life, Defert writes: "July 1967: return to Vendeuvre [from Tunis]," followed by the following entry from a letter Foucault wrote to Defert on July 16, 1967:

> I am lizarding Nietzsche [*Je lizarde Nietzsche*]; I think I am beginning to see why his work always fascinated me. A morphology of the will to know in European civilization that we left to the side in favor of an analysis of the will to power.[71]

So in the summer of 1967, Foucault returned to Nietzsche's writings, but this time Foucault will work the texts in a different direction: "a morphology of the will to knowledge."

Morphology is a study of forms. In biology, *morphology* is the study of the external forms and of the structure of living beings; in linguistics, the term refers to the study of different categories of words and forms that are present in a language. Here, then, morphology would be the study of the forms that the will to know might take, and, Foucault's letter suggests, it is in fact this very study that others had set aside in favor of the study of the will to power. The notion of the will to know is perhaps more important, Foucault suggests—at least he did so in July 1967, while he was finishing writing *The Archaeology of Knowledge*. Immersed in the final stages of drafting that book, Foucault seemed to have found, in Nietzsche's writings, what had fascinated him for so long: the words *origin, birth*, and *beginning* used in relation to knowledge and truth.

Foucault's essay, "Nietzsche, Genealogy, History," plays with those words from Nietzsche's pen to develop the argument that knowledge is ultimately invented. He had already used (and would again use) those words in the titles of his books: *The Birth of the Clinic* in 1963, and *The Birth of the Prison* in 1975. But the words *birth* and *origin* raised more questions than they resolved. It turns out that language here is only partly helpful; there are so many words to reference "origins" in French, German, and English. In French, for instance, they include *origine, provenance, commencement, souche, cause, naissance.* There is an entire word cloud in linguistics, a large cluster of words that can be used to designate the word *origin* and that may be of interest to critical thinkers. So Foucault goes back to all the German terms used by Nietzsche:

- *Ursprung*, in a sense closest to the word *origin*, but which must be distinguished from the word *Herkunft*, signifying provenance
- *Entstehung*—creation, emergence, birth, apparition
- *Herkunft*—origin, provenance, filiation, stem
- *Abkunft*—familial origin
- *Geburt*—birth, childbirth
- *Erfindung*—invention, a word to which Foucault's writings return to at length in this 1971 essay, as well as in his 1971 McGill lecture on Nietzsche
- *Kunststück*—artifice
- *Erbschaft*—heritage, succession, legacy

Nietzsche's language is Foucault's laboratory, this time as the setting to analyze the "origin" of knowledge.

Foucault shows that Nietzsche sometimes—but not always—used the notion of origin, *Ursprung*, in an unmarked sense, without trying to distinguish one usage from the other.[72] His usage is a puzzle. But from it, Foucault ultimately privileges one connotation: invention, *Erfindung*, which is captured so powerfully in the opening allegory of Nietzsche's "On Truth and Lie in a Nonmoral Sense": recall that little star in a remote corner of the universe "on which some clever animals invented *knowledge*."[73] Foucault uses that as the opening to his 1971 McGill lectures.[74] The origin of knowledge, it turns out, is invention. In this sense, it is a disruption. It is happenstance. It has a strong element of contingency. And it is this notion of the invention of knowledge that will run through, not only Foucault's epistemological writings on the will to know, but also his later writings on subjectivity and care of self—what commentators used to refer to as Foucault's third period or his ethical writings—where Nietzsche is sometimes less present. The notion of invention is tied there to that of *peripeteia*, or the reversal of fortune. Peripeteia will become central to Foucault's interpretations of *Oedipus* and of the different ways in which truth is said and produced there. Peripeteia is at the source of Foucault's reflections on the way in which avowal can produce truth. It is at the very heart of his lectures at Louvain in 1981, and of the final courses at the Collège de France, on the relationship between jurisdiction and veridiction, and on *parrhesia*.

Foucault mines other connotations of origin as well, especially the notion of *provenance*, of descent, the word *Herkunft*, because the idea of provenance comprises and contains in part elements of social conflict, relations of power, and racial struggle. By deploying this connotation, Foucault pushes the reader to reflect on the context of social and racial struggle. He begins using the words *heritage, succession*, and, in German, *Erbschaft*. Once again, the notion of heritage is something that comes with a sense of contestation over the distributions of wealth and familial disputes over succession.

A third set of terms that Foucault uses frequently includes *emergence, apparition*, in German, *Entstehung*. This notion of emergence, of irruption even, points the reader toward force and struggle—toward an emerging notion of power struggles.[75] It points toward the will to power. But for now, though, Foucault is still immersed in the concept of the will to know: "The analysis of this great *vouloir-savoir* that runs through humanity."[76] Foucault's 1971 essay ends once more on these themes: first, the notion of the dangerousness of the will to know, and of its companion, the will to truth. This is the danger, the peril of absolute knowledge—the idea that the infiniteness of interpretation may lead us into madness. And second, the notion of critique—so central to Foucault's critical philosophy and so important to Deleuze's writings on Nietzsche.

Then, Foucault's "Lesson on Nietzsche," delivered at McGill University in April 1971, pushes his analysis further, from the will to know to the larger thesis of the will to truth.[77] The 1971 lectures begin with the famous passage from Nietzsche's "On Truth and Lie in a Nonmoral Sense." They begin with the language of *Erfindung*, of invention. But Foucault will rework this passage, during the lectures, from his earlier interpretation to a broader idea of the invention of truth. In a section of four to five pages, approximately a third of the way into the first McGill lecture, Foucault begins to explore the difference between the invention and emergence of knowledge on the one hand and the invention of truth on the other. This represents a double movement: "Knowledge was invented, but truth was invented later still," Foucault observes.[78] The conception of peripeteia, of reversal, becomes central again: at the heart of the notion of truth, there is not just a historical unfolding that emerges from knowledge, but a will—in this case, a will to truth.

This represents a radical and violent break with philosophical tradition because the will to truth is not the will to follow knowledge wherever it leads one, but rather the will to fight in a struggle for the production of truth. If the will to truth had always been important in the philosophical tradition, Foucault changes its character completely here. He delivers his lessons on Nietzsche almost at the same time that he delivers his first set of lectures at the Collège de France, but the whole project of those lectures at the Collège is almost audible at McGill. Foucault declares at McGill, "From there, we see the Nietzschean task to think the history of truth without relying on truth. In a context in which truth does not exist: the context of appearance."[79]

Knowledge-Power

In the period 1972–1975, Foucault pushes the concept of *vouloir-savoir* still further, elaborating a theory of *savoir-pouvoir* (knowledge-power) and a new critical method of genealogy. In a series of lectures on *Penal Theories and Institutions* and *The Punitive Society* in 1972 and 1973 at the Collège de France, in "Truth and

Juridical Forms" at PUC Rio in 1973, and culminating in the publication in 1975 of *Discipline and Punish*, Foucault harnesses all the epistemological strands he had experimented with and combines them into one coherent theoretical framework centered on the idea that the human condition is constantly reshaped by beliefs and practices that are the product of struggles of power. Power is to be understood here not as something that one possesses or can deploy against another. It is instead the medium within which individuals interact and struggle. It is not an object, but rather a relation of power and resistance. It entails a human struggle that shapes and manufactures knowledge and truth, and in the process, deploys those manufactured truths to shape practices and institutions in an ongoing material struggle. Knowledge and power are coconstitutive and inseparable. There cannot be any knowledge that is not produced by and not thoroughly traversed by relations of power; conversely, relations of power are infused by knowledge.

This fusion of knowledge and power is what ignites the genealogical method: genealogy is the search for the contingent twists and turns in history that give rise to systems of belief and modes of social practice in an ongoing power struggle. Genealogy traces those contingent moments of the invention of knowledge and explores the resulting effects of reality on the distribution of material well-being, on the creation of marginality, on the social condition. The contingency of knowledge and power and history does not exclude path dependence and lasting effects, but it does underscore the unexpected twists and turns. And it is those contingencies that shape the present.

By contrast to early critical theory, the genealogical method does not assume any necessity of or direction to history. As Colin Koopman emphasizes, "genealogy is concerned with conditions of possibility insofar as these conditions are contingent, rather than necessary."[80] There is never a solid or reliable normative foundation to be discovered, but rather an endless production of new knowledge and power. The genealogical method does not clear the way to a place from which the critic can understand the world as it is. Rather, it produces another space that is infused with relations of power and calls for more genealogical work.

Foucault develops his own unique method of genealogy. It is not merely the debunking method, generally associated with Nietzsche, nor is it the vindicatory approach of Bernard Williams. It has been called "problematizing" by some—I will get to this in the next chapter—and "possibilising" by others.[81] But in order not to confuse matters any more than necessary, I would simply call the method *knowledge-power genealogy* because that theory is what fuels the method. Foucault's genealogical method is the search for those moments when knowledge is invented during the struggle in relations of power. It is those moments that are the conditions of possibility of the present, that foreclose other understandings and possibilities, that give rise to entire regimes of truth, that distribute resources and material well-being, and that produce truth.

Foucault's conception of power lies at its heart. In the March 28, 1973, lecture in *The Punitive Society*, and in certain passages of *Discipline and Punish*, he carefully delineates the four key methodological aspects of his approach to theorizing power. First, power is not something that can be appropriated or possessed. It does not belong to any dominant social class, and it cannot be possessed because it is something that is exercised. It is never monolithic, he says; it is not controlled by anyone. It is always and constantly at play, always in struggle, producing momentary, local victories and defeats at a micro level.[82] Second, power cannot be understood as localized in the state or in "*les appareils d'États*," a direct reference to Louis Althusser. As Foucault explains in *The Punitive Society*, "State apparatuses are a concentrated form, or rather a structure of support for a system of power that goes well beyond it and much deeper."[83] It is, therefore, crucial to explore how power circulates in the realms of family, work, and private associations—all the realms that Foucault, Arlette Farge,[84] Jacques Donzelot,[85] and so many others explored. Third, power is not the guarantor of a mode of production; it is not subordinated to and does not simply maintain or reproduce certain social relations. Rather, as Foucault said in 1973, "power is in fact one of the constitutive elements of the mode of production, it is what makes it possible to constitute a mode of production."[86] Foucault would develop this theme, both in his 1973 Rio lectures "Truth and Juridical Forms" and in *Discipline and Punish*, into the idea that the accumulation of men—the accumulation of docile bodies—was just as necessary as the accumulation of capital for producing industrialization; that the two accumulations went together; and that the essence of human beings was not work, that it had to be made so.[87] Finally—and this is where it intersects so closely with knowledge—power cannot be mapped onto the logic of ideology: it simply cannot be the case that power works either through coercion and violence or through hidden forms of ideology—here too, he rejects Althusser's notion of the "state ideological apparatus."[88] There cannot be a simple opposition between being forced to do something and being indoctrinated to want to do it. Instead, Foucault argues, "we need to show how knowledge (*savoir*) and power are effectively linked one to the other, not at all on the mode of identity—knowledge is power or vice versa—but in an absolutely specific manner and according to a complex game." To study power, then, one must explore the struggles and strategies, the complex ways in which it is exercised, the way it is played, and all "the strategies, the calculations, the defeats, the victories"—in short, what Foucault refers to as "relations of power."[89] This is a multidimensional approach to thinking about power that grounds his theory of knowledge-power and genealogical method.

Over the trajectory of his genealogical research, Foucault's method would differ in many ways from Nietzsche's. Foucault paid far more attention to the archive, to the actual discourse and words of his subjects. He did not tell metastories about Jews, Christians, and Germans as Nietzsche did—no matter how brilliant they actually were. But as he developed his own method, Foucault confronted and engaged Nietzsche, as evidenced most clearly in the Rio lectures. "In Nietzsche," Foucault states there, "one finds a type of discourse that undertakes a historical analysis of the formation of the subject itself, a historical analysis of the birth of a certain type of knowledge—without ever granting the preexistence of a subject of knowledge." Subjectivity, Foucault understood, is shaped by the interpretations that subjects embrace and impose in a vertiginous cycle of meaning-making, one in which there is no preexisting subject. This, Foucault says, "can serve as a model for us in our analyses."[90]

I have written extensively about the steps and progression in Foucault's thought, in introductions to the 1972 and 1973 lectures and the French Pléiade edition of *Surveiller et punir*, and will not rehearse those again.[91] Instead, let me review the argument from the Rio lectures, which more directly engage Nietzsche's writings. In Rio, Foucault essentially developed his argument in five points. The first is that knowledge is invented. This follows directly from the linguistic analysis of the origin and source of knowledge discussed earlier. Here again, there is no single origin. Knowledge is not part of human nature, and it is not about instincts either; rather, it is a struggle. This leads to the second point—namely, the philosophically radical conclusion that, as a result, knowledge possesses no relation of similitude, representation, and affinity: it has no resemblance to things. There is a complete rupture between knowledge and things. As Foucault explains in Rio, "Knowledge has no affinity with the world to be known."[92] So we are in a world in which our knowledge is invented and completely separated from things in the world—a radical vision of the human condition that constitutes a sharp break with philosophical tradition. Foucault explains why in his third point: because the philosophical tradition has always needed a conception of the divine, an idea of God, to make the connection between knowledge and the world, things, the world that we perceive. If one returns to Descartes, or even to Kant, one sees the need for a conception of the divine in order for there to be such an affinity between knowledge and the perceived world. But given this rupture between knowledge and the world, we no longer need God. Hence, the death of God, and not only the death of God—and this is the fourth point—but also the death (or at least the possible death) of the subject. Now, in the breach, there is no longer any need for a unified and sovereign subject. The subject can thus disappear, or at least we are faced with a situation in which it could well be that the subject no longer exists. This leads to the fifth and final point: we are left in a situation in which "at the root of knowledge, Nietzsche places something like hatred, struggle, power relations."[93] At the end of the analysis, then, the subject is immersed in relations of power, which places the subject in relations of struggle rather than relations of science. Foucault concludes: "What we need then, is not to turn to the philosophers who think that the production of knowledge can be harmonious, pacific, or something of the sort; politicians know full well that what is needed is civil war."[94]

Foucault's theory of knowledge-power, in this sense, drives his genealogical method. It represents a frontal assault on the idea (or the possibility) of pristine knowledge or of epistemological foundations. And it is precisely here that Foucault most directly confronts Marx and the early Frankfurt School. It is at this point, following his discussion of Sophocles' *Oedipus Rex*, that Foucault performs the critique of Marx's notion of labor and alienation with which I started this chapter. Foucault emphasizes, in Rio, that the source of real critical philosophy is Nietzsche:

> It would have been possible, and perhaps more honest, to cite only one name, that of Nietzsche, because what I say here won't mean anything if it isn't connected to Nietzsche's work, which seems to me to be the best, the most effective, the most pertinent of the models that one can draw upon.[95]

With those words, Foucault has thrown down a gauntlet. Knowledge is inextricably tied to relations of power. There is no way to escape, no way to reach any firm epistemological or normative grounding. Critical philosophy is now far down the epistemological detour—far indeed, very far from praxis.

An Explosion of Critical Challenges

These epistemological challenges within critical philosophy during the 1960s fractured any possible coherence that Marxism had originally lent to the enterprise. Radically different conceptions of power, of desire, of subjectivity tested any possible cohesion. For the most part, the challenges originated from within the critical framework, which is what made them so powerful. Critical theorists were now drawing on a range of sources—not just the Kant-Hegel-Marx lineage, but Nietzsche and his genealogical approach, Freud and psychoanalysis, Saussure and linguistics.[96] The competing approaches further splintered the field of critical philosophy, even though, as a philosophical matter, it mostly retained its unity and identity as a predominantly European and Eurocentric discourse of men. But even that would begin to fracture with postcolonial and critical race, feminist, and queer challenges to its European patriarchal and imperialist character.

Some critical theorists, naturally, resisted and returned to Marxian or other foundations to rebuild and enrich the earlier generations of critical theory. Louis Althusser supplemented his earlier scientific interpretation of Marx, which he had set forth in *Reading Capital* (1965), with concepts of ideology and ideological state apparatuses in his *Notes Towards an Investigation*, published in 1970.[97] Jürgen Habermas reworked Marxian legitimation theory to offer a new diagnosis of crisis tendencies specific to advanced capitalism in *Legitimation Crisis*, published in 1973.[98] Paulo Freire returned to the foundational concept of class struggle to develop a revolutionary liberation theory of education in *Pedagogy of the Oppressed* (1968).[99] Others returned to Marx as well, such as Frederic Jameson in *Marxism and Form* (1971), Silvia Federici in *Wages Against Housework* (1975), Perry Anderson in *Considerations on Western Marxism* (1976), Mario Tronti in *On the Autonomy of the Political* (1977), Stuart Hall and colleagues in *Policing the Crisis* (1978), and Nicos Poulantzas in *State, Power, Socialism* (1978). Others continued to engage but disobey Marx, such as Cornelius Castoriadis in *The Imaginary Institution of Society* (1975). Still others deeply challenged the early reliance on Marxian categories and logics, pushing in different directions, including Jean Baudrillard in *The Mirror of Production* (1973), Hayden White in *Metahistory* (1973), and Luce Irigaray in *This Sex Which Is Not One* (1977). The critical production from the 1970s was truly remarkable—stimulated by a period of global political upheaval—but it substantially fractured the coherence of early critical thought.

At the core of the contestation, there was an epistemological disagreement about foundations that kept pushing the controversies and debates further down the epistemological detour: whether and how critical theory could ground itself in truth, such as through notions of progress, reason and rationality, learning processes, or communication and discourse; whether and how critical theory needed to be correct and objective; whether and how it needed to resemble a sociology and incorporate empirical research, or achieve something that could be thought of as objectively right; whether and how it could ever achieve anything like a ground to stand on when it was itself wracked by the forces of Eurocentrism, colonialism and imperialism, and patriarchy—and so often blind to those very forces. Of course, critical theory would always remain reflexive, and in that sense postpositivist; but the antifoundational contestation kept raising epistemological questions that challenged the foundations of critical theory.

The various epistemological sensibilities of the 1970s fragmented the critical project. The contrast, even with a more literary and aesthetic thinker like Walter Benjamin, was deep. In his notes from the time of *Krise und Kritik* in 1930, under the telling header "Some Remarks on Theoretical Foundations," Benjamin underscored his "thesis," in his own words, that "true validity," "fruitful validity," and "genuine validity" are only "guaranteed by the closest possible connection with social reality." This was because, he said, "Truth cannot be established by digression, by the collection and addition of all that's thinkable, above all by arbitrary flight from its consequences. Rather must it repeatedly be confronted with reality at every stage and point."[100] The contrast with the antifoundational approaches of the 1960s and 1970s could hardly have been greater. And the resistance was continuous. Each challenge upped the ante—now taking on not only traditional philosophy and Marxism, but the Western tradition of critical theory itself.

Postcolonial Critique :: Edward Said

In a series of writings culminating in the publication in 1978 of his masterwork, *Orientalism*, Edward Said refocused the critical challenge on the Eurocentrism and ethnocentrism of Western thought, in the process opening the way to a critique even of poststructuralist theory. Concern had often been voiced within critical quarters that critical theory itself had paid insufficient attention to colonialism and imperialism, was overly Eurocentric, and ignored the voices of the colonized subject and the subaltern. Said's writings on Orientalism provided critical tools to nourish a critique of Western critical theory, drawing precisely on a knowledge-power framework.

Said picked up where Foucault had left off—with Nietzsche. His book, *Orientalism*, represents, if anything, a radicalization of the argument that there is no possibility of powerless knowledge. All the Western knowledge and expertise about the Orient—all the scholarship, bureaucratic knowhow, and writings by what were called *Orientalists* (experts on the Orient)—were the product, Said shows, of relations of power. They were inextricably political. The imaginary of the Orient performed wide-ranging cultural, social, and identitarian work, and all of it was deeply political: it allowed the Orientalists and Western subjects to cultivate an identity for the West and Westerners as a foil to its "Other," to govern the Orient during colonial times, and to master the Arab world now. Writing in direct continuity with that formative passage from the 1973 Rio lectures, Said states:

> What I am interested in doing now is suggesting how the general liberal consensus that "true" knowledge is fundamentally non-political (and conversely, that overtly political knowledge is not "true" knowledge) obscures the highly if obscurely organized political circumstances obtaining when knowledge is produced. No one is helped in understanding this today when the adjective "political" is used as a label to discredit any work for daring to violate the protocol of pretended suprapolitical objectivity.[101]

Knowledge is political, and there is no escaping it. Knowledge is never objective in a nonpolitical way. "Orientalism calls in question," Said declares, "the possibility of nonpolitical scholarship."[102]

Said wrote in the furrow of Nietzsche, and did so explicitly. He quotes the famous passage from Nietzsche's essay "On Truth and Lie in a Nonmoral Sense"—"truths are illusions about which one has forgotten that this is what they are"—and then follows that up with what, surely, was one of the most explicit recognitions of the fabrication of truth: "Orientalism was such a system of truths, truths in Nietzsche's sense of the word."[103] Orientalism was a fabricated truth—an illusion in the fullest sense of the term—with devastating consequences for the Orient, and for the Arab world to this day.

Said's *Orientalism* is a rich analysis of the way in which the scholars, writers, and specialists of the Orient created an imaginary of "the Oriental," and later "the Arab," which served manifold purposes and worked in many ways: to help shape their own identity as Westerners, to render themselves superior, to justify their imperial conquests in the East, and to help them control and dominate their colonies. The book studies the way that knowledge operates as a cultural tool and a political weapon. Knowledge, Said argues, has material effects of reality. It shapes the conception of self and of the "other"—and it does so through a back-and-forth: by constructing an idea of the other that shapes a conception of the self in relation to the other, that at the same time shapes the other. It is a mutually constitutive act.

Said gives the example of Gustave Flaubert's projection of promiscuous sexuality onto the Oriental woman, whom he describes in his letters and novels as a machine: "the oriental woman is no more than a machine," Flaubert wrote, "she makes no distinction between one man and another man."[104] Said demonstrates how that imaginary inflected Western ideas of the Orient, Western conceptions of its own sexual restraint, and also Western fantasies, like those of Madame Bovary, of an Oriental world of liberated sexuality, of harems and belly dancers.[105] The imaginary of the Orient served in this manner to construct and to bolster Western identities and conceptions of self, while at the same time othering the Orientals and justifying Western imperialism.

Said studies ideas, imaginaries, and ways of thinking the "other" in the specific context of Western belief in its moral superiority and strength over the East. The core of his intervention is to demonstrate that this knowledge of the Orient was never pure, apolitical, or objective. Moreover, it is impossible to imagine knowledge that is not inflected by a political project—and an oppressive or dominating one at that. And lifting the veil of this Orientalism does not produce truth, but another space that would need to be investigated. This is no easy task because, as Said emphasizes, these ideas and imaginaries are not mere ideologies that can easily be lifted. They are deeply embedded. They become true, in the deepest sense of the word. They become naturalized in such a deep way that they resist unmasking. Said is describing ways of thinking that have lasted centuries.

This is an epistemological project. Said emphasizes this throughout—from start to finish. From the get-go, in defining the very term and articulating its meanings, Said underscores that Orientalism is a way of thinking and knowing the other. It is, in his words, "a style of thought based upon an ontological and epistemological distinction made between 'the Orient' and (most of the time) 'the Occident.'"

It is a form of discourse, Said writes, explicitly indexing Foucault's *Archaeology of Knowledge* and *Discipline and Punish.* Said is describing systems of representation, language, grammar, styles of thought, mentalities, and ideas about the Orient. And these epistemes have effects of power. As knowledge-power, they have deep implications and material effects. They have effects of reality, not just ideational effects. "European culture gained in strength and identity," Said emphasizes, "by setting itself off against the Orient as a sort of surrogate and even underground self."[106]

Said demonstrates the work of ideas—not just through cultural analysis, but through concrete political demonstration. He details, for instance, how Napoleon used his army of scholars to befriend and master local imams, muftis, and ulemas during his conquest of Egypt. Napoleon deployed his knowledge of the Qur'an and the vast expertise of his Orientalists as his "business card" to cloak his imperial project under the veil of the arts and sciences. Said documents how, upon leaving Egypt in the hands of his deputy, Jean-Baptiste Kleber, Napoleon gave him "strict instructions after he left always to administer Egypt through the Orientalists and the religious Islamic leaders whom they could win over; any other politics was too expensive and foolish."[107] Said's point is that these fabricated truths shape everything from Western identities to world geopolitics. He argues about how common these ways of knowledge are and that we must constantly guard against them. "If this book has any future use," Said writes, "it will be as a modest contribution to that challenge, and as a warning: that systems of thought like Orientalism, discourses of power, ideological fictions—mind-forg'd manacles—are all too easily made, applied, and guarded."[108]

Said is engaged in the critique of knowledge-power, but notice that he does not unveil in order to discover truth. He unveils to warn us about the dangers of truth, to put us on guard, to encourage us to unveil again. Said challenges the Western normative order and Eurocentrism, and he exposes the effects of ideas, the hold of ideas; but he does not seek to displace those with others or to unveil a truth. He reveals illusions; he does not expose the truth. This is knowledge work, epistemological work, which does not lead to solid ground, but rather to caution. Said closes his book in the following terms: "My project has been to describe a particular system of ideas, not by any means to displace the system with a new one."[109]

Ultimately, Said leaves the reader with a set of questions rather than answers. This is a reflexive set of questions that underscores the intractability of the problems of truth and the importance of critique: "How do ideas acquire authority, 'normality,' and even the status of 'natural' truth? What is the role of the intellectual?

Is he there to validate the culture and state of which he is a part? What importance must he give to an independent critical consciousness, an *oppositional* critical consciousness?"[110] Indeed, the questions become increasingly reflexive as Said moves from truth to power, to the role of the intellectual, to the role of the critical theorist. By the end, critical theory is in a position to question its own production of knowledge, its own potential ethnocentrism, and its own naturalization of truth. Said has turned knowledge-power critique onto the potential Eurocentrism of critical theory itself and opened a line of criticism that would then be developed by brilliant postcolonial scholars such as Gayatri Chakravorty Spivak, Homi Bhabha, Dipesh Chakrabarty, and Partha Chatterjee.[111]

Can the Subaltern Speak? :: Gayatri Chakravorty Spivak

Gayatri Chakravorty Spivak pushed the critique even further in an essay published under the title "Can the Subaltern Speak? Speculations on Widow Sacrifice" in 1985. Spivak's critique continues down the epistemological path, but if anything, is even more searing.[112] At one level, Spivak directly challenges the established European critical theorists, especially targeting Gilles Deleuze and Michel Foucault in their famous debate over power, intellectuals, and Maoism. "Deleuze and Foucault ignored both the epistemic violence of imperialism and the international division of labor," Spivak declares. But even worse, they relegated the subaltern and what was referred to then as the "*tiers monde*" (the Third World) to a purely instrumental afterthought. The existence of the subaltern was a mere codicil to their discussion. It entered the conversation only insofar as it was visible and useful to Western political struggles. There was no genuine effort to think through the situatedness of the subaltern. "This benevolent first-world appropriation and reinscription of the Third World as an Other," Spivak notes, "is the founding characteristic of much third-worldism in the U.S. human sciences today."[113]

Spivak underscores how Foucault himself failed to discuss or critique properly the territorial imperialism that was inscribed at the heart of the injustices and forms of domination that he challenged. He failed to show how the Western relations of power that he himself critiqued were the product of stages of exploitation that were inextricably linked to territorial imperialism. All his writings, and the tools he developed, were perfectly applicable to the problem of colonialism and imperialism, but instead of seeing and addressing the object itself, Foucault used it as a spectral mirror for European practices and institutions. Spivak writes:

> Sometimes it seems as if the very brilliance of Foucault's analysis of the centuries of European imperialism produces a miniature version of that heterogeneous phenomenon: management of space—but by doctors; development of administrations—but in asylums; considerations of the periphery—but in terms of the insane, prisoners, and children. The clinic, the asylum, the prison, the university—all seem to be screen-allegories that foreclose a reading of the broader narratives of imperialism. (One could open a similar discussion of the ferocious motif of "deterritorialization" in Deleuze and Guattari.) "One can perfectly well not talk about something because one doesn't know about it," Foucault might murmur. Yet we have already spoken of the sanctioned ignorance that every critic of imperialism must chart.[114]

Spivak's searing critique of these Western critical intellectuals raised fundamental challenges to the project of critical theory. It also threw an additional wrench in the internecine battles within critical theory—between, for instance, Derridians and Foucaultians.[115]

But Spivak goes even further with her critique, taking aim not only at established Western critical theorists, but also at subaltern scholars who themselves have difficulty hearing or deciphering the voice of the subaltern. Spivak writes of her grandmother's sister, Bhubaneswari Bhaduri, who, at the young age of sixteen or seventeen, took her life in a self-declared political act in North Calcutta in 1926.[116] Bhaduri wrote, in a letter she left for her sister, that she was taking her life because she had failed to carry out an assassination that she had been assigned as a member of an insurrectional group for Indian independence, and she felt that she needed to sacrifice her own life to maintain trust. Aware of the gender stereotypes, Bhaduri waited until she was menstruating to commit suicide, so as not to let anyone infer that she had done so because she was pregnant from an illicit sexual relation.

Spivak began exploring Bhaduri's suicide in relation to the ritual of sati-suicide, according to which a widow must await the end of her menstruation, as a matter of purity, in order to immolate herself following the death of her husband. During the course of her investigation, Spivak addressed herself to a peer scholar, someone she describes as having the same intellectual pedigree and production as herself, a woman philosopher and Sanskritist of Bengali origin. To her surprise, Spivak recounts, she received the following response from her colleague: "(a) Why, when her two sisters, Saileswari and Raseswari, led such full and wonderful lives, are you interested in the hapless Bhubaneswari? (b) I asked her nieces. It appears that it was a case of illicit love."[117]

That response, and their exchange, stunned Spivak, leading her to wonder aloud whether the subaltern can *ever* speak.[118] Spivak later clarified this, saying that she never intended to say that the subaltern could *not* speak, though she had, by her own admission infelicitously, written, "the subaltern cannot speak!" in her original essay—prompting others, such as Edward Said, in his 1994 Afterword to *Orientalism*, to protest that "the subaltern *can* speak, as the history of liberation movements in the twentieth century eloquently attests."[119] Spivak corrects that, emphasizing that "it was an inadvisable remark."[120] But as an open question, the interrogation mark lingers to the present day.

Ultimately, Spivak uses the incident to raise the question of the difficulty for the subaltern to be heard even by those closest to them. The critique posed a deep challenge not just to critical theory, but also to the field of subaltern studies that was emerging at the time in the work of Partha Chatterjee, Ranajit Guha, and others. As Chatterjee recounts, it was at the time of the publication of the first volume of *Subaltern Studies* in the early 1980s that he, Gyan Pandey, and Shahid Amin first encountered and conversed with Spivak, but only a few years later that he read and absorbed her critique published in 1985. Chatterjee recounts how "the impact of Spivak's critique of the early *Subaltern Studies* filtered through our work and changed the contents and direction of our project."[121]

Spivak's work triggered, even within subaltern studies, the type of reflexivity that was the very impetus for critical theory. It intensified, exponentially, the epistemological problem of foundations. It challenged not only traditional theory, nor simply European critical theory, but also the very possibility of postcolonial and subaltern studies as powerless knowledge. With Spivak, critical theory had gone all the way down the epistemological path.

Theories of Performativity :: Judith Butler

It would be possible to trace the various paths that these ideas and critiques took in critical legal studies, critical race theory, critical feminism, anarchism, and elsewhere, but I will end this chapter with their emanations in queer theory, focusing primarily on one of the original impetuses, Judith Butler's *Gender Trouble*, published in 1990.[122] In that work, Butler weds the theory of knowledge-power with the philosophy of language, especially the book by J. L. Austin, *How to Do Things with Words*, as developed further, she expressly notes, in the critical theoretic work of Derrida, Pierre Bourdieu, and Eve Kosofsky Sedgwick.[123] The identification of these critics is significant because Butler is indexing here certain strands of critical theory.

Austin's central idea, well known now, is that words at times can perform. Under certain conditions, utterances have material effects on reality and produce real outcomes—such as when a judge sentences someone to prison. As Butler explains, "Performativity characterizes first and foremost that characteristic of linguistic utterances that in the moment of making the utterance makes something happen or brings some phenomenon into being."[124]

In *Gender Trouble*, Butler extends the framework of performativity theory to gender, arguing that gender is performative insofar as, at the very moment of enacting gender, we make things happen, we affect relations of power in our immediate vicinity and beyond. As a simple illustration, Butler mentions the initial moment of gender assignment—corresponding to an utterance by a doctor or nurse—as identifying an individual with lifelong effects.[125] At a more complex level, what Butler does in *Gender Trouble* is, first, to trouble the distinction between sex and gender (in other words, it is not only gender that is constructed—biological sex is as well); second, challenge the notion of a "woman" identity (challenging the essentializing remainders in the work of first wave feminism); and third, argue that gender itself is performative: namely, that because there is no fixed identity behind the ways of being that are supposedly gendered, because these identities make up illusions of stable identities, and because gender is culturally constructed, gender is contingent, open to transformation, and can be resignified. Thus, it is possible to challenge gender, to be subversive of gender, and to trouble gender through performance. The performance of gender—and its performative effects—can be seized, played with, reversed, challenged, troubled, and transformed. It can be a locus of political struggle. It can challenge fixed hierarchies and inequalities.

In other words, Butler layers on top of the *constructed* nature of gender the *performative* nature of gender in order to explore how others can then work with the performativity of gender to challenge their political condition. In this, Butler is unveiling earlier conceptions of gender. In fact, her writings on gender up the ante on an earlier feminist unmasking. The first waves of feminism revealed that the common sense of an earlier, liberal way of thinking (namely, that sex and sexuality are defined naturally) was misleading because even if sex is biological, gender is constructed and can be reconstructed to equalize politics. Butler's theory of gender trouble, by contrast, argues that both sex and gender are constructed and performative, and thus can be troubled in order to more fundamentally challenge relations of power in society.

Butler's theoretical practice builds on the framework of knowledge-power but does not embrace any necessity or unveil any truth. There is a potential transformation on the basis of an emancipatory project, but it will not necessarily happen unless there is active, intentional praxis. There is simply an analysis of knowledge-power that can be deployed (or not) toward a critical horizon. In this respect, there is a deep parallel between Butler's relation to feminism and Foucault's relation to Marxism: recall that for Foucault, the central intervention is to displace the model of class struggle (i.e., of a somewhat fixed social mapping and struggle between the bourgeoisie and the proletariat) with the model of civil war (i.e., of a war of individuals and groups and constant regroupings). Foucault's intervention was to demonstrate that the imposition of a binary opposition itself produces crystallizations of power and affects relations of power. We might think here, for instance, of the tensions between the workers and the students during May 1968 as a reflection of power relations that ultimately hindered the revolutionary movement. Butler intervenes in a similar way with regard to feminism: the imposition of a binary opposition based on fixed identities (i.e., women and men) needs to be displaced by a more fluid conception that challenges gender. It is not the duality of woman versus man, but rather the whole woman-man construct that needs to be dismantled, in order to challenge not only patriarchy and phallocentric power, but also heteronormativity and conventional family relations. As Butler writes, "The point was precisely to relax the coercive hold of norms on gendered life—which is not the same as transcending or abolishing all norms—for the purposes of living a more livable life."[126] This requires praxis on our part, but it may lead in very different directions depending on how exactly we trouble gender.

In Butler's work, the practice of unveiling illusions does not expose the truth, but rather places the critic in a new position to act politically. It does not dictate which way to act, nor does it leave the critic in a space where power no longer operates. Rather, it creates space to continue the critical project. In a subtle and analytic intervention against the imposition of epistemological and normative foundations, in a set of debates in the 1990s over the clash between feminism and poststructuralism, Butler formulated very precisely the core of the critical challenge to earlier critical theory. The problem, she noted, is the work that it does, politically, to make a claim to epistemological and normative foundations. Let me close this chapter, then, with Butler's words:

> To establish a set of norms that are beyond power or force is itself a powerful and forceful conceptual practice that sublimates, disguises, and extends its own power play though recourse to tropes of normative universality. And . . . the task is to interrogate what the theoretical move that establishes foundations *authorizes*, and what precisely it excludes or forecloses.[127]

CHAPTER 3

Michel Foucault and the History of Truth-Making

At the turn of the 1980s, freed from the specter of Marx and, as a result, free to leave Nietzsche behind as well, Foucault traced a different genealogy for critical philosophy. He located it elsewhere. In his last years, Foucault traced critical philosophy back to the end of the fifth century BCE and the birth of the philosophical problem of truth-telling—a very different place than Marx, Hegel, or Kant, to whom we usually trace critical philosophy, or Nietzsche for that matter. By contrast to the Kantian task of determining the limits of reason or the question of assessing the criteria for the truth-value of statements, Foucault focused his attention on the activity of telling truth and its relation to the exercise of power. He asked a different set of questions: How has truth been produced, historically? What techniques and what forms have been used to make truth? Who gets to speak truth, about what, and with what consequences? He was not interested in truth-value—whether and by what criteria something is true—but in the history of who has been able to speak truth, how, and with what effect. And he traced this to the philosophical tradition following Socrates.

The contrast with Kant—and with certain texts of Frankfurt School critical theory—could not have been greater. Foucault posed orthogonal questions. He approached truth from a different perspective. Rather than identify the criteria to determine truth, Foucault's project was to write a history of truth production, of truth-telling, of truth-making. He was forging a historical account of how truth comes into existence: what techniques and methods, and what modes and forms, shaped the production of truth. This was not so much a history of what people believed, as he had done for instance in *History of Madness*, but more a history of the techniques to produce truth—the *technē* of truth-making. His approach was constructivist, and in that sense, it was close to the animating element of historical constructivism that was embedded in Horkheimer's original project, but it was worlds apart from the type of critical theory that emerged from the early, or even more from the late Frankfurt School.

Critical philosophy, Foucault explained, can give rise to two very different projects. One is the project, essentially inspired by Kant, to determine the limits of reason and the criteria of truth—to determine the internal or external rules by which certain statements can be deemed true or false. The other, which Foucault became interested in, is to explore how claims to truth get infused with truth-value and how truth-telling succeeds. This latter project provides the basis for a history of truth production and truth-telling: an analysis of the historical sequence of the methods by means of which the claim to speak truth (what Foucault referred to as *veridiction*, the diction or telling of truth, or *veritas*) achieves success and is performative.

Foucault explained the sharp difference between these two projects with great precision in his inaugural lecture at Louvain on April 2, 1981, and it is worth quoting extensively from that lecture to understand the chasm that separated Foucault from the Frankfurt School as both headed down an epistemological path:

> If critical philosophy is a philosophy that starts not from the wonderment that there is being, but from the surprise that there is truth, then we can clearly see that there are two forms of critical philosophy. On the one hand, there is that which asks under what conditions—formal or transcendental—there can be true statements. And on the other, there is that which investigates the forms of veridiction, the different forms of truth-telling. In the case of a critical philosophy that investigates veridiction, the problem is that of knowing not under what conditions a statement is true, but rather what are the different games of truth and falsehood that are established, and according to what forms they are established. In the case of a critical philosophy of veridictions, the problem is not that of knowing how a subject in general may understand an object in general. The problem is that of knowing how subjects are effectively tied within and by the forms of veridiction in which they engage.... In a word, in this critical philosophy it is not a question of a general economy of the true, but rather of a historical politics, or a political history of veridictions.[1]

It is this political history of truth that Foucault elaborated in his writings and lectures—one that he placed under the rubrics of critique and of *alethurgy*. It represented a very different genealogy for critical philosophy.

To be sure, like the Frankfurt School, Foucault traced it in part back to Kant, who figured prominently throughout his work, with crescendos in 1960, 1978, and 1984. Foucault began his academic career with the translation of and introduction to Kant's *Anthropology*, which served as his habilitation in 1961, and he would end it with recurring exegeses of Kant's essay on Enlightenment. In fact, when Foucault delivered his lecture "What Is Critique?" to the French Society of Philosophy on May 27, 1978, the "indecent" title that he would have given his lecture, had it not already been used, was "What Is Enlightenment?"[2] For Foucault, critique could not be disassociated from Kant; and the genealogical method that he developed had Kantian roots too, insofar as it sought to trace the conditions of possibility of belief systems.[3]

But Foucault would trace at Louvain a very different genealogy of critical philosophy that would reach, first, to the Christian pastoral and the modes of governing from the fourteenth to the sixteenth centuries—with reference to the Calvinist philosopher Pierre Bayle (1647–1706) and the English theologian, priest, and Oxford professor John Wycliffe (1330–1384)—and to the critical reaction against all these modes of governing (religious, state, familial, etc.) and then back to the fifth century BCE and the origins of truth-telling.[4]

Foucault first tied critique back to the arts of governing and, conversely, the arts of not being governed in those ways. Hegel and Marx do not figure prominently at all, and the Frankfurt School receives only a few mentions—mostly the *Dialectic of Enlightenment* as an illustration of skepticism and suspicion concerning the excesses of reason and of the inability of humans to respect the Kantian limits of reason, and as a kinship interest in questions of ideology. The philosophical tradition in France, Foucault argued, had a different relationship to rationalization as a result of the French Revolution, such that critique developed through different pathways in France than in Germany. This allowed Foucault to introduce the question of power and tie critique to his methods of archaeology and genealogy.[5] Then, Foucault reached back to antiquity. In the inaugural lesson at Louvain, Foucault distinguished his version of critical philosophy, which he placed under the label of "alethurgy" (a term Foucault coined using the ancient Greek root *alēthes*, that which is true),[6] from the analytic determination of truth, the Kantian critical philosophy of reason and its limits. Critique here involved the history of truth-making, the power of truth, and governing through truth production.

In other words—and this is perhaps the most important point—instead of addressing truth on the terrain of truth and the criteria of truth, Foucault entirely displaces the analysis to the history of the production of truth and methods for truth-making. He displaces the conversation completely to the orthogonal question of tracing histories of the forms of truth. That is radically different from seeking normative foundations. It is an entirely different enterprise that is, in effect, no longer even in conversation with anyone trying to argue about the validity or justifiability of a political or moral principle. From this point on, Foucault has essentially given up on the question of normative justification and grounding; he is proceeding on a different track: not to judge the validity or justification or truth of claims, norms, or normative orders, but instead to trace histories of how people manufacture truth.

With hindsight, from his clarifying propositions at Louvain in 1981, or at Berkeley in 1978, it is now possible to fully understand the work that Foucault was doing at the Collège de France and the full arc of his critical project. The clarifications place the earlier work in a new light. Liberated from the earlier contestations with Marxism and freed of the recourse to Nietzsche, Foucault visualized his project in a new light—one that may constitute the best lens through which to read all of Foucault's Collège de France lectures. In effect, over the course of his time at the Collège, Foucault attempted to write a history of forms of truth, of methods of truth production, or, more simply, a history of truth itself. Indeed, Foucault's lectures, and the books that were birthed from them—especially *Discipline and Punish* in 1975 and *The Will to Know* in 1976—can be understood as an inquiry into the production of truth through different modes of discourse—legal, historical, political economic, and, finally, *parrhesiastic*. Let me rapidly trace that history in this chapter in order to visualize Foucault's alternative way of doing critical philosophy.

By way of background, it is important to situate Foucault's Collège de France lectures within the arc of his work. Foucault began his thirteen years of lectures at the Collège in 1970, at the midpoint of his most productive years. The 1960s had been an incredibly productive decade for him: he had started out with his history of madness, turned to the clinic, and then shifted to a more philosophical orientation by analyzing the social sciences and humanities in *The Order of Things*. He concluded the decade with *The Archaeology of Knowledge*, his effort to systematize the work that had preceded it, especially the method of discourse analysis. At the Collège, Foucault would often resituate himself in terms of the larger arc of his work and the series that he so often reimagined: madness, the prison, and sexuality, or, at other times, madness, the clinic, the social sciences, the prison, and finally sexuality. By the end of the 1960s, Foucault had not only addressed the themes of madness, the clinic, and the social sciences, but also had already returned to his interest in the study of sexuality, specifically in his inaugural lecture at the Collège, *The Order of Discourse*.[7] At that time as well, in 1970, Foucault was pivoting toward penal institutions and the prison. This was the period in which he was actively involved in the *Groupe d'information sur les prisons* (GIP).

In reassessing his own work, Foucault always insisted that the heart of his interests remained unchanged, shaped by the triad of knowledge, power, and subjectivity; and with the publication of the full set of lectures at the Collège, this becomes even more clear, given that, for instance, the question of the subject was at the heart of his first lectures, *Lectures on the Will to Know*, in 1970. Foucault's project for a history of truth encompassed all three of these core interests—knowledge, power, and the subject. He often spoke about the idea of a history of truth in interviews, but with the full publication of his lectures, this becomes far clearer.[8] The critical project throughout, in the lectures and in the books that came from those lectures, was a history of truth-making, by which I mean an inquiry into the production of truth through various forms and discourses: first legal, then historical, then political-economic, and finally parrhesiastic.

Truth and Legal Forms

Foucault's history of truth-making begins in 1970 and extends through at least 1976 with an analysis of the legal procedures that produce truth. This first stage is probably most succinctly summarized in the title of his Rio lectures of 1973: "Truth and Juridical Forms." At the time leading up to the Rio lectures, Foucault labored at the Bibliothèque nationale de France (BnF), poring over legal texts and researching the history of law from the Roman period to the nineteenth century.[9] This would be the archive that he would mine: a treasure trove of legal history.

Foucault began his 1970–1971 course at the Collège, *Lectures on the Will to Know*, with the study of measurement and money as forms of truth-making, but then he turned rapidly to the legal form of the *épreuve* (test or ordeal), which he analyzed through a scene in the *Iliad* in which the Greek heroes Menelaus and Antilochus come into conflict over the results of a chariot race.[10] Rather than resolve the dispute by means of a trial of their peers, as Menelaus had originally suggested, Menelaus challenges Antilochus to take an oath to Zeus and swear that he is the better hero.

Faced with that test, Antilochus confesses that he was carried away by his youth, and he concedes the prize. In that action, Antilochus not only reconstructs his own identity, but he also reestablishes the social order and hierarchy of ancient Greece by putting the more senior hero, Menelaus, back in his rightful place. The truth of Greek society is returned to firm ground through the quasi-avowal of Antilochus. Truth is produced through the ordeal.

From there, Foucault shifts to Germanic law, in which truth is established by way of the sermon or through individual acts of courage or social standing. One of the most striking illustrations is the Germanic practice, in feudal law, of testing adversaries in litigation through forms of oath-taking in which the parties had to assemble around them witnesses who were willing to swear on oath. The resolution of the conflict turned on the relative social prominence of those witnesses, and thus of the parties: having witnesses who swore on your behalf "showed the solidarity that a particular individual could obtain, his weight, his influence, the importance of the group to which he belonged and of the persons ready to support him in a battle or a conflict." It was, in other words, the imposition of truth through social convention rather than as a form of truth-seeking. The ordeals were also a form of warlike resolution. There, Foucault emphasizes, justice is conceived on the model of the battle. It is what he called a "regulated way of conducting war between individuals."[11]

From the *épreuve*, Foucault then moves to the legal form of the *enquête* (inquiry or investigation), which he first traces to Sophocles' *Oedipus Rex*. Oedipus was, Foucault reminds us, the individual who inquired into and investigated his own act of murder. Foucault interprets that inquiry through a juridical lens, drawing parallels between the chorus and a jury, the presentation of evidence, persuasion, and—as he will develop later at Louvain in 1981—torture as a means of interrogation and truth-telling.[12] What is important here, for Foucault, is that Sophocles' *Oedipus* represents a significant shift in the history of truth-making. As Foucault describes it, "This dramatization of the history of Greek law offers us a summary of one of the great conquests of Athenian democracy: the story of the process through which the people took possession of the right to judge, of the right to tell the truth, to set the truth against their own masters, to judge those who governed them." Here, truth is no longer understood on the model of war, but rather of inquisition. It partakes of an inquisitorial model characterized by empirical proof, testimony, interrogation, and collective deliberation. Unlike the ordeal that Antilochus was put through, which entirely ignored the testimony of the witness who had been placed at the distance marker to see what actually happened, everything here turns on eyewitness testimony and evidence. It is on the basis of this model of inquiry that philosophy, rhetoric, and natural science emerged, Foucault suggests, including fields like geography, astronomy, and climatology.[13]

Foucault adds an additional dimension in 1973 in his lectures on *The Punitive Society*, which turn to the nineteenth-century penal sphere and the production of a new legal form: detention and imprisonment. The prison, as a legal form, becomes important because it produces a truth about the delinquent. It tells us something about delinquents and who they are, not just about their acts. But it does so, in part, through another juridical form, namely the examination. *Discipline and Punish* can be understood, in this light, as a case study into the legal procedure of the examination. Much like Foucault's earlier analyses of the ordeal or the inquiry, the book *Discipline and Punish*, on this reading, becomes an in-depth analysis of the ways in which the examination operates as a legal form that produces truth.

In the period that extends through 1975, Foucault explored the various ways in which different juridical forms—from the test or ordeal, to the inquiry, to the examination, detention, and prison—function as ways of producing the truth of events and of subjects. It is, incidentally, in this juridical context that avowal would become so important, leading Foucault to explore the function of avowal in criminal justice in his 1981 Louvain lectures.[14]

Truth and Historical Forms

These early explorations eventually led Foucault to discover other modes of truth production. Following this initial period, which culminated with *Discipline and Punish*, Foucault turned to what could be called the method of "truth and historical forms." This began with the 1976 lectures "*Society Must Be Defended*," in which Foucault suggests that the historiography of race wars, which erupted in the seventeenth century, constitutes what he calls a historical-political discourse or a counterhistory to earlier Roman history and philosophical-juridical discourse. The history of race wars, then, represents a new historical form with a unique relationship to truth. It produces truth in a uniquely new way—one that is marked by a "de-universalization."[15] Foucault takes this to be representative of a new historical method of truth-making.

By way of analogy or illustration, one could take realist thought in the study of international relations. Realism captures this decentering well. In this case, it is a decentering from universality, from the idea that one can determine what is true based on the ability to universalize. Universality is replaced by particularity: what is true and certain now turns on personal self-interests or the nation's specific interests. In realism, the one who is biased, who has real interests, is the guardian of truth.[16] This is a completely different way of producing truth, and it is based on a different type of historical sensibility—one that decenters universality. This is what Foucault refers to in "*Society Must Be Defended*" as a historical discourse that functions as a "truth weapon," or what he calls "a truth bound up with a relationship of force." It is "a discourse in which truth functions exclusively as a weapon that is used to win an exclusively partisan victory."[17] Here, it is no longer a juridical form, but a historical form that is doing the work of truth-making.[18]

Truth and Political Economic Forms

Following the shift from legal to historical forms of truth-making, Foucault turns toward political economy as a source for producing truth. It is a shift, one might say, from "truth and historical forms" to "truth and economic forms." Specifically, in *Security, Territory, Population* in 1978 and *The Birth of Biopolitics* in 1979, Foucault analyzes neoliberalism as a regime of truth. More specifically, he considers the market as the basis for the validation of political action. The market becomes the measure of truth. This is captured neatly in *The Birth of Biopolitics*, where Foucault states:

> The market must be that which reveals something like a truth . . . Inasmuch as prices are determined in accordance with the natural mechanisms of the market, they constitute a standard of truth which enables us to discern which governmental practices are correct and which are erroneous. . . . The market constitutes a site of veridiction.[19]

We are here at the juncture of truth and economic forms, where economic mechanisms, like the market, form the basis of veridiction.

This represents the heart of Foucault's intervention on neoliberalism, which is directly in continuity with his nominalist method: to explore the real effects of the category of the market and even more of our naming the category of the market.

As Foucault suggests in *The Birth of Biopolitics*, this analysis is perfectly in line with his nominalist critiques of madness, delinquency, and sexuality. It is also what grounds his truly insightful analysis of contemporary German governmentality: the idea that after the defeat of the Third Reich, the truth production of German sovereignty had to evacuate the space of war and military power, and instead focus purely on economic productivity—which is prescient because it feels as if his argument that "in contemporary Germany, the economy, economic development and economic growth, produces sovereignty" could have been written in the wake of the Greek debt crisis and the conflict in the Euro zone in the twenty-first century.[20]

Truth and Subjectivity

Foucault's thirteen years of lectures at the Collège de France thus span a series of analyses of the methods of truth production through its various modalities: beginning with legal procedures (the ordeal, the inquiry, the examination, and leading to the study of the prison form), Foucault then moves on to the historical forms, and then to economic forms as the market becomes the ultimate measure of truth. In his final lectures, Foucault then turns to truth and its various subjective forms, specifically to the practices of the self, to care of self, to truth-telling and truthful speech as a form of the care of the self that is intended to have effects on oneself and others. These subjective practices are meant not only to change the views of others, but also to serve as forms of autocritique meant to shape oneself. This final transition to truth and subjectivity is perhaps more obscure; however, there is perfect continuity between the earlier forms of truth-making and the later analyses of parrhesia and the emphasis on subjectivity. These latter become the principal basis on which truth is produced.

Understanding this final transition requires a bit more background, in part because of some confusion surrounding the naming of those final lectures.[21] Following his study of the emergence of disciplinary power in the nineteenth century in *The Punitive Society* (1972–1973), *Psychiatric Power* (1973–1974), and *Discipline and Punish* (1975), Foucault turned his attention to more contemporary forms of governmentality—namely, biopower and the neoliberal management of populations—in *The History of Sexuality, Volume I* and "*Society Must Be Defended*" (both in 1976). But in order to understand contemporary forms of governmental reason, Foucault had to trace a genealogy of neoliberal forms of rationality, starting with *Security, Territory, Population* in 1978—a genealogy that ran through pastoral power, *raison d'État,* the police, and liberal and neoliberal thought. As he explained in 1979 in *The Birth of Biopolitics*, understanding neoliberal rationality was an essential building block to analyzing the concepts of population and biopower.[22] As this research evolved, though, Foucault began to see that he needed to go even further back in history in order to trace the genealogy of our contemporary arts of governing. Foucault returned then to an earlier archive—namely, Sophocles, the Stoics, and the early Christian pastoral—to reexamine the history of contemporary neoliberal forms of rationality.

A few years earlier, in *Security, Territory, Population*, Foucault had stated that he did not think that there was an origin in ancient Greece or in Rome to the arts of governing, and that instead, the place to start was the pastoral.[23] By 1980, however, he realized that there was indeed an art of governing before that, and he needed to go back to those arts of governing from antiquity. So, in his lectures *On the Government of the Living* in 1980, Foucault returned to *Oedipus Rex* and reinterpreted it through the lens of the manifestation of one's truth, reorienting the project toward "the notion of the government of men by the truth." This pushed the inquiry past the market as the measure of truth, legal processes, and historical narratives, to the central place of the self—the "I," the avowal in the "ritual of manifestation of truth."[24] This reorientation ultimately led Foucault toward the examination of self, the direction of others, forms of truth-telling, avowal, the work on subjectivity, and eventually parrhesia. The trajectory would later lead to a displacement from the arts of governing to the arts of living, which would give birth to the final volumes of *The History of Sexuality*, including the fourth volume, *The Confessions of the Flesh.*

In the 1981 lecture series, *Subjectivity and Truth,* Foucault explicitly pursued this line of research, focusing specifically on the domain of ancient Greek and Roman sexuality, or rather, *aphrodisia* (because, as he explained, the term *sexuality* is a modern one and therefore anachronistic). The central question of the 1981 lectures is: "How to 'govern oneself' through actions of which one is oneself the objective, the domain on which they apply, the instrument that they use, and the subject that acts?"[25] To address this question, Foucault returned to texts from the period of Greek and Roman antiquity, and late antiquity, ranging from the *First Alcibiades* and Aristotle's *Nicomachean Ethics,* to Hippocrates and Xenophon, to Cicero's *De finibus,* to works of Plutarch, Pliny the Elder, and Hierocles, to Artemidorus' *The Interpretation of Dreams* and the *Physiologus* (both c.200 CE), in order to study the modes of ancient living through detailed analyses of marriage, marital life, and marital sex, and the questions of sexual penetration, pederasty, monogamy, and incest, among others.

As this research unfolds, it becomes increasingly clear that while Foucault was pursuing the line of inquiry that he had begun the year before, we begin to witness an important displacement in his thought from an earlier focus on the "arts of governing," beginning in 1977 and extending to 1980, to a more concerted focus on the "arts of living." In other words, there is an increasing interiority to the object of these arts, of these *technē*. While much of the earlier work on madness, the clinic, and the prison—and even, to a certain extent, the first volume on sexuality—examined the conduct of conduct by others, Foucault's deepening attention to subjectivity begins to produce a shift toward the conduct of conduct by oneself. What has not changed, however, is that even these *technē* are forms of truth-making in the very same way that the prison or the market created truth. Much like those other domains, these ways of conducting oneself, modes of life, manners of being, the arts of living, the arts of conducting oneself, *des consignes d'existence*, are, at the core, discourses and practices that produce the truth of the self and of one's relationship to others.

In the case of madness, or the clinic, or the prison, Foucault maintains, "the core of truthful discourse regarding the self was held from the outside, by an other"—by the psychiatrist, doctor, social worker, actuarian, or warden. By contrast, in the domain of aphrodesia, the truthful discourse on the self is institutionalized in an entirely different way: by the subject reflecting on oneself. "That is to say," Foucault explains, "it is not organized on the basis of an observation or examination, or of objective rules, but rather around the practice of avowal."[26] Truth is organized on the basis of a more internal or internalized reflection, on the basis of something that we, ourselves, tell ourselves about ourselves. It is not like the doctor who tells us we are mad, nor the psychiatrist who tells us we are dangerous; rather, it is we ourselves who talk about our own desires, about what *we* desire, what we *really* desire.

Knowledge-Power-Subjectivity

Foucault's trajectory at the Collège de France constituted a history of forms of truth-making. It would be particularly important to connect all the pieces back to each other—and to knowledge-power. This is precisely what Foucault himself suggests in 1984, shortly before his death, in the first chapter, titled "Modifications," of *The History of Sexuality, Volume 2*. Foucault maintains there that it would be an impoverished understanding of his writings on truth and subjectivity to see them as a displacement of his earlier problematics. The work on subjectivity complements his earlier investigations, adding a necessary dimension, without breaking from them. In his lectures in 1984, *The Courage of Truth*, Foucault puts it this way: "To depict this kind of research as an attempt to reduce knowledge (*savoir*) to power, to make it the mask of power and structures, where there is no place for a subject, is purely and simply a caricature"[27] and would represent an impoverished reading of his work. In a similar way, it would be an impoverishment of Foucault's work on truth and subjectivity not to integrate it back into the study of politics, epistemology, and power—back, that is, into the full theory of knowledge-power. For the study of sexuality, for instance, it would be essential to read the second and third volumes of *The History of Sexuality* back into the first. This is the only way to make sense of Foucault's critical project.

The task of integrating Foucault's work on truth and subjectivity back into the study of politics, knowledge, and power was cut short by his untimely death at the age of fifty-seven. However, with the posthumous publication in 2018 of the fourth and final volume of *The History of Sexuality*, titled *Les Aveux de la chair* ("Confessions of the Flesh"), it is now possible to see what that process of integration would have looked like. In that final Volume 4, Foucault began to connect his long history of the desiring subject since antiquity to the modern knowledge-power formations and to his critique of modern Western societies.

The link occurs in the final pages of Volume 4, dedicated to Augustine's treatment of marital sexual relations. There, Foucault discovers the moment of the birth of the modern legal subject and of the juridification of social relations, which would ultimately succumb to the knowledge-power formation of neoliberalism. Foucault identifies the moment when, in Western Christian societies, the mechanisms of social ordering in the single-most fraught domain of human interaction (namely, sexual relations) gave rise to what Foucault calls "the subject of law" (*« le sujet de droit »*) and which he describes as the modern rights-bearing and responsible individual inscribed in a legal framework of accountability, responsibility, and autonomy.[28] The appearance of the modern legal subject makes it possible to fully articulate Foucault's critique of our contemporary neoliberal forms of governing in the full three-dimensionality that Foucault had promised—the three-dimensionality of knowledge, power, and subjectivity.

The modern legal subject—*le sujet de droit*—begins to appear in Augustine's emphasis on consent, will, responsibility, accountability, and autonomy in the context of marital sexual relations in his writings such as *De bono conjugali* and *De nuptiis et concupiscentia.* The legal subject is born at that time and flourishes in the modern political theory of sovereignty of the sixteenth and seventeenth centuries. The modern political theory of individualism—from the Lockean notion of individual rights, through C. B. MacPherson's theory of possessive individualism, to Gary Becker's conception of human capital—depends on and derives from Augustine's juridification of marital sexual relations. And the emergence of the modern legal subject ends up placing certain limits on sovereign power and gives rise to ideas of checks and balances, of divided power, of limits on governing, and ultimately to the paradigm of mid-twentieth-century liberal democracy.

However, as against that regime of liberal democratic governance, there emerged a competing figure of *homo œconomicus*, first in the work of the Physiocrats and liberal economists of the eighteenth century, but then in more concentrated form in the writings of neoliberal economists after World War II. As the experience, practices, and very subjectivity of *homo œconomicus* begin to supplant that of the modern legal subject, the modern economic subject gradually deposes and delegitimizes the state in a far more radical way. It strips the state of all possible knowledge, rendering government entirely impotent: it is only the neoliberal subject who can know his own interests; the government and the collectivity, by contrast, have no access and no way to know any individual subject's self-interest. As a result, the collectivity is stripped of all knowledge, is ignorant and helpless. Whereas the modern legal subject only placed limits on the state, *homo œconomicus* divests the state of all knowledge and legitimacy, and thereby does away with it entirely.

But—and this is the locus of Foucault's critique of neoliberalism—the premise that *homo œconomicus* knows his self-interest best and that the collectivity or the government is ignorant on this score, is itself simply an assumption, a product of knowledge-power. It is an unfounded belief, a mere assertion of truth. It is, however, baked into the theory of neoclassical economics, from François Quesnay and Adam Smith to Friedrich Hayek and Gary Becker. As a result, the entire framework of neoliberal governance rests on an illusion, a sleight of hand: all of the outcomes, whether practices or institutions, are essentially baked into the cake via the initial imagination of an all-knowing *homo œconomicus.*

This is Foucault's central critique of neoliberalism in his lecture of March 28, 1979 in *The Birth of Biopolitics*: the very ideal of a deregulated government is baked into the cake of neoliberalism because of the underlying theory of the subject in the rational actor model. In other words, the political outcomes are themselves inscribed in the notion of the rational, self-interested subject that founds liberal economic thought. The original theory of the self-interested and self-knowing subject simply disqualifies the political sovereign or the collectivity; it assumes from the outset a subject who alone is the knowing subject, and as a result, the political body is automatically disqualified. Foucault had articulated this in *The Birth of Biopolitics*:

> Economic rationality is not only surrounded by, but founded on the unknowability of the totality of the process. *Homo œconomicus* is the one island of rationality possible within an economic process whose uncontrollable nature does not challenge, but instead founds the rationality of the atomistic behavior of *homo œconomicus*. Thus the economic world is naturally opaque and naturally non-totalizable. . . .
>
> *Homo œconomicus* is someone who can say to the juridical sovereign, to the sovereign possessor of rights and founder of positive law on the basis of the natural right of individuals: You must not. But he does not say: You must not, because I have rights and you must not touch them. This is what the man of right, *homo juridicus*, says to the sovereign: I have rights, I have entrusted some of them to you, the others you must not touch, or: I have entrusted you with my rights for a particular end. *Homo œconomicus* does not say this. He also tells the sovereign: You must not. But why must he not? You must not because you cannot. And you cannot in the sense that "you are powerless." And why are you powerless, why can't you? You cannot because you do not know, and you do not know because you cannot know. . . .
>
> The basic function or role of the theory of the invisible hand is to disqualify the political sovereign.[29]

In effect, the epistemological assumptions regarding the economic subject are entirely responsible for the theoretical outcomes: neoliberal economic theory rests on an illusion, an unfounded belief.

As Foucault emphasized in those 1979 lectures, in order to understand the contemporary moment, the neoliberal economic subject must be distinguished from the modern subject of law. "In the eighteenth century," Foucault emphasized, "the figure of *homo œconomicus* and the figure of what we would call *homo juridicus* or *homo legalis* are absolutely heterogeneous and cannot be superimposed on each other."[30] But to understand *homo œconomicus*, Foucault had to trace the history of subjectivity—the history of the desiring subject—from ancient Greece, through the Greco-Roman philosophers and practices of the first centuries, to the patristic period, in order to discover the birth and genetic make-up of the modern legal subject in Augustine's writings. *Les Aveux de la chair*, in this sense, ties together the long history of the subject with Foucault's critique of modern Western societies. It is the keystone in the full arc of Foucault's three-dimensional critique.

Foucault drafted Volume 4 sometime between 1980 and 1982, and put it aside after having sent the manuscript to his editor at Gallimard in the Fall of 1982. He then proceeded to draft Volumes 2 and 3 (which were intended to be a single volume on the ancients) and published them in April and May 1984, shortly before his untimely death in June of that year.[31] Foucault did not, however, have the time, given his illness, to reframe Volume 4. But its posthumous publication gives us a blueprint of how to fold the study of subject creation and subjectification into the knowledge-power-subject framework.

Many readers of Foucault complain that the turn to subjectivity, to care of the self, and to truth-telling at the end of Foucault's intellectual journey undermines the political force of his philosophy. Ella Myers argues, for instance, in her book *Worldly Ethics: Democratic Politics and Care for the World*, that Foucault's turn in the early 1980s away from the study of power and toward the practices of the self is ultimately depoliticizing and undemocratic.[32] This reading of *Les Aveux de la chair* should dispel that argument and open the way to fully integrate Foucault's critical projects. We find the blueprint in Volume 4.

In the end, our challenge, not only in reading Foucault but in pursuing our own critical projects, remains to integrate the analysis of knowledge-power with the work on subjectivity, such that the subject is fully part of the analysis of epistemes and relations of power and that the fully integrated project returns us to the question of praxis. Our task is to reintegrate the work on the history of truth-making back into the theory of knowledge-power and the struggle over relations of power, and then forward to praxis. We need, in effect, to exit the epistemological detour and get back to praxis. Before showing how to do that, though, let me finish the historical account.

CHAPTER 4

The Return to Foundations

The successive challenges came in wave after wave, pounding the solid ground of the epistemological and normative foundations of early critical thought. And, over time, it was not so much the figure of man, as Foucault had imagined or hoped at one time, but rather the figure of Marx that began to be wiped away, like an image drawn in the sand at the edge of the sea. Man was there, perhaps more than ever, especially with the renewed attention to practices of the self, the care of self, and the techniques of truth-telling. The anthropological illusion remained strong—threatened only now, perhaps, not by theory but by global climate change. Man was still present, too, in a field that remained dominated by men.

But it was the figure of Marx that began to be erased under the waves. Fewer and fewer critical theorists pledged allegiance to his philosophy of history or to dialectical materialism. Some continued to, of course, remaining communalist or at least retaining hope in the idea of communism or a communist hypothesis or horizon.[1] But they were few. For the most part, those critical thinkers who adversely experienced the loss of Marxian foundations turned elsewhere to find solid ground again—pushing the critical debate even further down an epistemological path, even further from praxis.

With Marx fading, the later generations of the Frankfurt School mostly turned back to Kant and Hegel. Some, such as Jürgen Habermas, Seyla Benhabib, and Rainer Forst, found their grounding more solidly in Kantian notions of universality, cosmopolitanism, and public discourse in the public sphere—so much so, in fact, that thinkers like Habermas and Forst began to sound more liberal than critical. Others, such as Axel Honneth and Rahel Jaeggi, found their grounding in a reborn Hegelianism: a thinner, but nonetheless distinctly Hegelian notion of a historical learning process as the foundation of a humbler claim to progress.

Others turned to Spinoza, some even Nietzsche, Wittgenstein, and Foucault, such as Martin Saar and Frieder Vogelmann. But for most of the second and third generations of the Frankfurt School, Kant and Hegel stepped in where Marx began to fade. And paradoxically, the erasure of Marx had the effect of widening the gap between the later generations of the Frankfurt School and those challenging foundations, rather than contracting it. It pushed the debate even further down an epistemological detour. Critical theory became even more contemplative as it struggled over the questions of epistemology and foundations. And with Marx effacing, his modern practical attitude seemed to fade as well. Critical theory became a debate over epistemological and normative foundations. It reverted, more and more, to the contemplative realm.

In the midst of those very first challenges to critical theory, and at the height of the controversy over *Eichmann in Jerusalem*, Hannah Arendt prefigured the return to solid foundations and to contemplation. In an essay published in the *New Yorker* in 1967 under the title "Truth and Politics," Arendt traced the genealogy of the conflict between truth and power directly back to the contest between theory and praxis—directly back, that is, to the original contest between those two ways of living life, the contemplative and the political. In the face of critical challenges, Arendt resoundingly sided with *theoria* over *praxis*. Her essay prefigured, I would argue, what was to come.

Truth and Politics :: Hannah Arendt

At the time, in the aftermath of the Eichmann trial and her reporting of it in the *New Yorker*, immersed in the controversy that followed, Arendt sounded disillusioned by political discourse and the lies that, she felt, were revolving around her. The problem was a question of truth and falsity—not just defects in reason or reasoning, but factual lies and misrepresentations. Today, some would describe this as the problem of a posttruth era. That, Arendt emphasized at the time, was far worse than what preceded it.

Arendt's 1967 article, "Truth and Politics," is grounded on the distinction between rational and factual truths—drawing, as she does, from Leibniz. Rational truths are the axioms, discoveries, and theories of the mathematical, scientific, and philosophical realms. They are theoretical truths. Factual truths, by contrast, are the facts and events of the world—Arendt's example: the role of Trotsky during the Russian Revolution, "who appears in none of the Soviet Russian history books." By factual truths, Arendt means to identify hard facts, like the fact that Germany invaded Belgium on the night of August 4, 1914; and to insulate those hard facts from interpretation and opinion. She argues that factual truths are even more fragile than rational truths and theorems. Once factual truths disappear or are crushed, they have little hope of returning.[2]

In her article, Arendt traces the conflict between truth (in either form, rational or factual) and the political sphere back to the tension between *theoria* and praxis—in her words, back to "two diametrically opposed ways of life—the life of the philosopher . . . and the way of life of the citizen." In antiquity, the conflict between theory and praxis presented as the conflict between the philosopher seeking to ascertain theoretical truths in mathematics, science, and philosophy, versus those who were "doing," the men of politics and of the *polis*. It is precisely the contest between theory and praxis that gives birth to Arendt's opposition between truth and politics. The opposition traces back, historically, to the contest between the dialogic form of the philosopher and the rhetorical form of the politician. It traces back to the contest between philosophical truth and mere opinion—between everlasting truth and illusions, between Socrates and the Sophists and rhetoricians, or later in Thomas Hobbes, between "solid reasoning" and "powerful eloquence." Today's conflict between factual truths and politics started as the conflict between rational truths and opinion—between philosophers and statesmen.[3]

Arendt argues that the historical clash between rational truths and opinion had been eclipsed and replaced in contemporary life by the clash between factual truths and politics. For Arendt, this was far worse because, at least back then, the rational truths could reemerge, rise from the ashes, whereas today, the crushing of factual truths leaves truth entirely impotent: "factual truth, if it happens to oppose a given group's profit or pleasure, is greeted today with greater hostility than ever before." What makes it more precarious is that factual truths are never self-evident. They depend on witnesses, testimony, and documents that are subject to forgery and misrepresentation—or worse, deliberate campaigns of lies. "Factual truth is no more self-evident than opinion, and this may be among the reasons that opinion-holders find it relatively easy to discredit factual truth as just another opinion." Factual truths are just as vulnerable, if not more, than rational truths, especially when opposed and challenged by throngs of biased, opinionated people.[4]

For Arendt, the heart of the problem of factual truth in politics stems precisely from the distinction between *theoria* and praxis. For Arendt, it is praxis, as a mode of being, that defeats truth. Arendt is stunningly clear about this in her *New Yorker* article:

> To the philosopher—or, rather, to man insofar as he is a thinking being—this ethical proposition about doing and suffering wrong [namely, that "it is better to suffer wrong than to do wrong"] is no less compelling than mathematical truth. But to man insofar as he is a citizen, an acting being concerned with the world and the public welfare rather than with his own well-being—including, for instance, his "immortal soul" whose "health" should have precedence over the needs of a perishable body—the Socratic statement [of the philosophical proposition that "it is better to suffer wrong than to do wrong"] is not true at all. The disastrous consequences for any community that began in all earnest to follow ethical precepts derived from man in the singular—be they Socratic or Platonic or Christian—have been frequently pointed out. Long before Machiavelli . . . , Aristotle warned against giving philosophers any say in political matters."[5]

It is precisely the tension between *theoria* and praxis that leads to the problem of untruth or posttruth in politics. The two ways of being collide—and in that context, Arendt squarely places herself on the side of philosophy, of contemplation.

Arendt embraces the figure of the truth-teller, whom she characterizes as being outside politics. The only place for truth-seeking, she argues, is outside politics. By contrast to Foucault, for whom the *parrhesiast* can be anyone steeped in practices of the self, Arendt's truth-teller is the isolated philosopher: the truth-seeking scholar in the academy, the judge reaching a decision alone, or possibly even the truthful journalist, as Arendt gestures to the press as another bastion of truth. All the paradigms for the truth-seeker come from the space of philosophy and *theoria* as a way of life.

By bringing truth into the realm of theory and placing truth on the side of philosophy—or at least, opposing it to politics and practice—Arendt places a heavy weight on the scale. She places herself, as a truth-teller, outside of politics—*necessarily* outside of politics: "To look upon politics from the perspective of truth, as I have done here," Arendt writes, "means to take one's stand outside the political realm." It is outside the political realm because that realm, at least in its quotidian politics, is debased by opinion and mass manipulation. As opposed to that realm,

Arendt seeks refuge in the attitude of the philosopher and "the various modes of being alone." She emphasizes the "anti-political nature of truth."[6] She weaponizes truth and philosophy. They become, for her, the answer to the question, "What is to be done?"[7]

To be sure, in the final paragraph, Arendt gestures to the greatness and dignity of politics—to the nobility of political life, "the joy and the gratification that arise out of being in company with our peers, out of acting together and appearing in public, and out of inserting ourselves into the world by word and deed."[8] Those are the high ideals of the political life in the *polis*. But those ideals are a weak nod at the end of a long essay that fundamentally has depicted a chasm between truth and politics, between theory and practice—and has sung the virtues of one at the expense of the other.

Arendt ends in the realm of contemplation as opposed to politics. Truth, by contrast to politics, she declares, is "the ground on which we stand and the sky that stretches above us."[9] Those are the final words of Arendt's essay. They call, mostly, for that way of life that is captured by the philosopher and the scholar—by the independence and solitude of those functions. In the end, truth, the highest value, is tied to the theoretical life. If anything, Arendt was pushing critical theory even further from praxis, a gesture that would return in wave after wave of reconstituted critical theory, beginning with Habermas.

Habermas Confronts Foucault

One of the first direct engagements with poststructuralism by the Frankfurt School occurred shortly after Foucault's death in 1984. A few years earlier, in 1981, Jürgen Habermas published the two volumes of his magnum opus, *The Theory of Communicative Action*. Foucault and Habermas met at the Collège de France shortly thereafter, in March 1983, when Habermas was giving a series of lectures at the invitation of Paul Veyne, and the two exchanged views and vaguely discussed the idea of a more formal debate.[10] That debate never occurred due to Foucault's untimely death a year later, but thereafter, Habermas published three essays on Foucault, principally within the context of his criticism of the critique of reason and attempt to rehabilitate an immanent critique of modernity.

Habermas's two chapters on Foucault in *The Philosophical Discourse of Modernity*, published in 1985, paint Foucault's turn to knowledge-power in the early 1970s as the product of both a political and an intellectual biographical accident. Habermas portrays the turn to power as the result, politically, of Foucault's disenchantment with the failure of the student revolution of May 1968, and intellectually, of his embarrassment at the static nature of the archeological enterprise.[11] Habermas argues that Foucault's theory of power lacks any sociological basis. It is authorized or justified by reference to Nietzsche, Habermas suggests, but neither the use of Nietzsche nor the concept of power works in Foucault's philosophy. "Nietzsche's authority, from which this utterly unsociological concept of power is borrowed, is not enough to justify its systematic usage," Habermas writes. Foucault's deployment of the concept of power, though biographically coherent, ultimately remains, in Habermas's words, a "paradoxical undertaking."[12] Habermas effectively rejects Foucault's challenge out of hand.

In a later essay titled "Taking Aim at the Heart of the Present," Habermas takes a slightly different tack. Having read Foucault's essay "What Is Enlightenment?"[13] Habermas argues instead for a different interpretation of Foucault in continuity with the Enlightenment. Habermas argues that, in the last sentence of his essay, Foucault places himself and understands himself "as a thinker in the tradition of the Enlightenment." Having thus tamed Foucault, Habermas then asks how Foucault could reconcile that with his own radical critique of reason—in which there is "power and nothing but power," "an insidious disciplinary force at work," and a "bottomless will to knowledge." Habermas claims that Foucault reconciles all this by ultimately privileging the will to know as the fundamental critical impulse—one that must be preserved and that actually traces back to Kant. Habermas maintains that in this way, by sorting out these internal contradictions that entangled him, Foucault ultimately placed himself in "the philosophical discourse of modernity."[14] Thus, Foucault's challenge is again tamed.

Through both of these strategies, Habermas tries to pry the theory of knowledge-power out of Foucault's work. He aims for and targets the element of conflict, of civil war, or relations of power that Foucault placed at the heart of social relations in the early 1970s. He does this first by arguing that it is a particularly "unsociological" theory that does not function; and second by defanging the idea and associating it with a critical impulse tied to the Enlightenment project. In both cases, Habermas is trying to protect the project of reason and communicative ethics from the threat of a model of social relations based on civil war.

In this, Habermas's encounter with Foucault was entirely prefigured in Habermas's 1962 book *The Structural Transformation of the Public Sphere: An Inquiry into a Category of Bourgeois Society*. There, even before any possible encounter with Foucault's theory of knowledge-power, Habermas analyzed the rise and fall of the bourgeois public sphere, infusing that category with the attributes that Habermas would later aspire to, normatively: a sphere of equals who decide on the basis of reason and the better argument alone; a social grouping that "disregarded status altogether," that is based on a principle of inclusiveness, and that "knew of no authority beside that of the better argument and because they felt themselves at one with all who were willing to let themselves be convinced by arguments."[15] This idealized vision of a public sphere is precisely what Habermas ultimately aspires to—and, of course, it requires extracting power and conflict from the mix. It requires removing Foucault even before he was there.

In *The Structural Transformation of the Public Sphere*, Habermas describes the rise of the bourgeois public sphere through a history of commercial exchange and early capitalism—how it emerged hand in hand with long-distance trading interests, the need for information, and news about markets; and how it developed, as the press and journals embraced criticism, literary reviews, and scholarly interests, in salons in France, coffeehouses in England, and table societies in Germany. Habermas argues that it depended on the separation of a private realm or civil society from the state. And he idealizes this public sphere, giving it the aura of the Greek *polis*. Habermas writes:

> Bourgeois culture was not mere ideology. The rational-critical debate of private people in the *salons*, clubs, and reading societies was not directly subject to the cycle of production and consumption, that is, to the dictates of life's necessities. Even in its merely literary form (of self-elucidation of the novel experiences of subjectivity) it possessed instead a "political" character in the Greek sense of being emancipated from the constraints of survival requirements.[16]

Surprisingly, Habermas traces the fall of this idealized public sphere to universal suffrage and the introduction of the popular classes into the public sphere, which effectively deconstructed the separation of civil society and state. With the "dialectic of a progressive 'societalization' of the state simultaneously with an increasing 'stateification' of society," we could observe the gradual destruction of the very "basis of the bourgeois public sphere," Habermas writes. Marx is already fading at this time. Contra Marx, Habermas argues, this collapse of the civil society/state separation destroyed the possibility of a robust public sphere. "In reality," Habermas writes after discussing Marx, "the occupation of the political public sphere by the unpropertied masses led to an interlocking of state and society which removed from the public sphere its former basis without supplying a new one. For the integration of the public and private realms entailed a corresponding disorganization of the public sphere that once was the go-between linking state and society."[17] The fall of the public sphere happens when it becomes pure consumption and consumerism, when it is nothing more than publicity and advertising, when it simply "assumes advertising functions." Consumption and consumerism now become merely a business: from "a public critically reflecting on its culture" to "one that merely consumes it." In this public sphere, there is nothing but sham public opinion. This is the model of what Habermas calls "public relations." And it is devoid of reason: "the criteria of rationality are completely lacking in a consensus created by sophisticated opinion-molding services under the aegis of a sham public interest."[18]

In between the lines, and at times explicitly, Habermas argues for a revival of an idealized public sphere as a way to enable democratic processes and make possible "social democracy." His vision is extremely Kantian: it is a "public sphere constituted by private people putting reason to use." In these words, one can hear, loudly, Kant's essay from 1784. Habermas is interested in what he calls "the *liberal* model of the bourgeois public sphere," not "the *plebian* public sphere," like that of the French Revolution. (He is explicit about that; those are his italics in the quotes.)[19]

But the only way to make that possible and revive that public sphere today is to carve out the Foucault of the 1970s—to eliminate power struggles and civil war as the model of social relations. This is most evident in the concluding paragraphs of the last two chapters of *The Structural Transformation of the Public Sphere*. At the close of Chapter VI, Habermas takes on the present—"our day," as he writes. Two features mark present times: first, the possibility of an end to scarcity, given that Europe at least constitutes affluent societies; and second, the risk for self-annihilation, given the nuclear arms buildup. Given those two features, the possibility of an effective public sphere becomes possible, Habermas argues. It is no longer simply a utopian dream; however, it depends on dissolving the idea, or the reality, of "irrational relations of social power and political domination."[20] It is almost as if Habermas were addressing the future Foucault.

How, then, can this be done? Habermas responds in the final paragraph of his book: by understanding that the very categories of conflict, power, and domination—Foucault's categories—are social categories that can change historically. They can be tamed in history. They are neither eternal nor universal. Habermas writes, closing his book in 1962:

> Conflict and consensus (like domination itself and like the coercive power whose degree of stability they indicate analytically) are not categories that remain untouched by the historical development of society. In the case of the structural transformation of the bourgeois public sphere, we can study the extent to which, and manner in which, the latter's ability to assume *its* proper function determines whether the exercise of domination and power persists as a negative constant, as it were, of history—or whether as a historical category itself, it is open to substantive change.[21]

In other words, the possibility of a robust public sphere for social democracy depends on whether we can extricate domination and power from the public sphere. It depends on whether we can erase Foucault.

Even before he had encountered Foucault's theory of knowledge-power (or for that matter probably any of Foucault's writings) in 1962, Habermas already had formulated a response to Foucault and the challenge of knowledge-power: it had to be erased. Habermas's political project already was the creation of a reason-based, egalitarian public sphere, guided by a Kantian ideal of Enlightenment. The main nemeses were power, conflict, and irrationality. The main threat to the realization of this ideal was if social relations were based on power. The main threat, in other words, was the Foucault of the 1970s and his challenge to now Kantian, no longer Marxian, normative foundations.

The later confrontation with Foucault and poststructuralism in 1985 was, in this sense, prefigured in Habermas's 1962 book. The actual confrontation with Foucault's writings in the mid-1980s simply rehearsed the argument and widened the gap. Habermas's future trajectory would create an unbridgeable divide between his theory of communicative action and poststructuralism, as Habermas veered further and further away from critical theory and toward liberal political philosophy. The epistemological confrontation had turned into a veritable chasm that now separated the second generation of the Frankfurt School not only from Foucault and his theory of knowledge-power, but more broadly from the way of being of praxis.

Habermas & Rawls

Jürgen Habermas's subsequent trajectory, if anything, reified his Kantianism—further widening the epistemological differences with poststructuralist and later postcolonial, critical race, and queer theories. The publication in 1996 of *Between Facts and Norms*, and especially his debate with John Rawls, cemented this passage from critical to liberal political philosophy.[22] Even more than that, it revealed, by contrast even to Rawls's pragmatism, a will to truth in Habermas: a deep-seated drive to ground his discourse theory in a way that could best approximate truth. His exchange with John Rawls in the *Journal of Philosophy* in 1995 and its subsequent emanations were particularly revealing.

From the outset of the exchange, from his first intervention, it is clear that Habermas enjoyed an entirely different relationship with Rawls than he did with Foucault: with Rawls, Habermas is engaged in a "familial dispute," in his own words. "I admire this project," he emphasizes, "share its intentions, and regard its essential results as correct."[23] This familial dispute is within liberal political theory, not critical theory. As Habermas wrote later, in a final reply to his critics, he "shared" with Rawls "the principle of the priority of the right over the good."[24] In fact, perhaps the term *family* is even stretching it here: in the exchange, Rawls appears far more pragmatic, behavioral, even skeptical of truth, whereas Habermas presents as far more anchored, comprehensive, and grounded in truth claims. By contrast even to Rawls, Habermas becomes a foundationalist.

If anything, the exchange with Rawls pushes Habermas, paradoxically, toward a certain illiberalism of truth. He ends up appearing far more rigid on norms and on truth, by contrast to Rawls's political pragmatism. "The philosophical enterprise is institutionally framed in terms of a cooperative search for the truth," Habermas writes in his second reply.[25] "I cannot think of any serious philosophical study, in whatever subdiscipline, that would and could not seriously make truth claims," Habermas concludes in his last one.[26] While both philosophers pursue a form of political liberalism that allows universalization and provides moral and political guidance, in the end Habermas presents as far more wedded to concepts of rationality and truth, Rawls to reasonableness and pragmatism.

Habermas's principal criticism of Rawls derives from the difference between their two methods—on the one hand, Rawls's framework of political liberalism and his device of the original position behind the veil of ignorance as the grounds for achieving an overlapping consensus on principles of justice among people having different worldviews; and, on the other hand, Habermas's social democratic communicative action theory and his refined use of a universalization principle, according to which a shared norm would be valid only if, knowing its consequences and effects, it could be freely accepted jointly by everyone concerned. On Habermas's view, his own universalization principle operates through substantive ethical debate about the welfare of everyone in a deliberative manner that takes the world as it presently is, whereas Rawls's device functions in a rational-choice manner to incentivize actors to pursue their own interests as a way to protect the interests of others without drawing on their ethical selves.

This is the difference, in essence, between a normative theory and a rational-choice model, and, according to Habermas, it has significant political and philosophical implications. Rawls's method ends up privileging rights over the democratic process and does not allow for grounded normativity. Rights and rights-bearing individuals become more important than democracy and agreed-upon norms. As Habermas explains, Rawls's approach results "in a construction of the constitutional state that accords liberal basic rights primacy over the democratic principle of legitimation. Rawls thereby fails to achieve his goal of bringing the liberties of the moderns into harmony with the liberties of the ancients."[27]

The disagreement, then, centers on the advantages and drawbacks of the two devices—universalization principle versus original position. The horizon of political liberalism is not that different, but what the exchange reveals is that Rawls is more of an American constitutional liberal, and Habermas more of a deliberative social democrat or Kantian republican.[28] And this has significant effects on their debate. Habermas espouses a practice of open, intersubjective argumentation and the use of public reason that does not set aside worldviews and convictions, but instead leads to forms of cooperation that can be judged as rational and correct.[29] These have effects of truth that, for Habermas, are productive. For him, the inquiry cannot escape truth and validity.

In other words, the exchange with Rawls pushes Habermas onto even more grounded epistemological foundations, further and further from poststructuralism, postcolonial and other critical theories. Habermas embraces an even thicker conception of the normative and of deliberation versus Rawls's thinner conception of the political as just the overlapping of self-interested agents. Habermas does not think that Rawls can get away with this thinner rational-choice overlap. He argues that Rawls has to deal with the issues of rationality and truth that he wants to avoid. Habermas says this explicitly in closing his first exchange:

> Rawls insists on a modesty of a different kind. He wants to extend the "method of avoidance," which is intended to lead to an overlapping consensus on questions of political justice, to the philosophical enterprise. . . . But even Rawls cannot develop his theory in as freestanding a fashion as he would like. As we have seen, his "political constructivism" draws him willy-nilly into the dispute concerning concepts of rationality and truth. His concept of the person also oversteps the boundaries of political philosophy. These and other preliminary theoretical decisions involve him in as many long-running and still unresolved debates. The subject matter itself, it seems to me, makes a presumptuous encroachment on neighboring fields often unavoidable and at times even fruitful.[30]

Rather than speak about the reasonableness of the overlapping consensus, Habermas wants to speak about truth: the premises must be recognized as true. The proper predicate to use is not merely reasonableness—it is truth.[31]

Habermas scolds Rawls for compromising the epistemic status of justice in his first exchange.[32] And this becomes, essentially, the focus of the subsequent exchanges. Rawls's principal response to Habermas is that the methods and principles of political liberalism should not use moral truth, but instead just reasonableness. Rawls advocates a thin conception of politics and accuses Habermas of being far too comprehensive.[33] In a second response, Habermas argues that Rawls mistakenly attempts to keep the political consensus thin to avoid hard philosophical questions, but again, he cannot avoid them. Although Habermas claims to reject both moral realism and modern value-skepticism, like Rawls, he nevertheless draws an analogy, in his words, "between truth and normative rightness."[34] And in his final reply to his critics, Habermas lays down his Kantian cards, face up: "For my part, I follow Kant in assuming that, with the concept of autonomy, the practical reason shared by all persons offers a reliable guide both for morally justifying individual actions and for the rational construction of a legitimate political constitution for society."[35] Habermas refers to this as "individualistic and egalitarian universalism." And he associates it with a position of moral rightness: "Valid norms are 'right' in the sense that they deserve the agreement of their addressees because they coordinate actions in the equal interest of all concerned."[36]

Habermas, by the end, is at the opposite pole from Foucault, Deleuze, Said, Spivak, and the other postfoundational challengers. If anything, the gap has widened and is now unbridgeable. One could even argue that at this point, Habermas is no longer even working in critical theory, but in liberal political philosophy. He pays lip service to critical theory when he starts his first response to Rawls by indexing "critique" and "immanence." He proposes, on the second page of his first intervention, "My critique is a constructive and immanent one." But this is not critique in the early critical theory sense, nor is it really immanent critique. It surely does not take an inherent and internal contradiction in Rawls to demonstrate how it could sublate and resolve. It is internal, insofar as it accepts the framework of political liberalism, but no real contradiction is driving the analysis. Habermas uses the word *contradiction* once—but not in a way that motivates a resolution to his discourse ethics. He posits his discourse ethics. In another passage, he mentions contradiction, but if anything, it is an external contradiction.[37]

At this point, Habermas's analysis is not critical in the way that I have been discussing critical philosophy—I will come back to this in chapter 5. Instead, it is liberal and Kantian in a universalizing way. It is solidly grounded anew on Kantian normative foundations. Marx has essentially disappeared, but not the foundationalism, by any means. On the contrary, if anything, the foundations have solidified. Several generations of the Frankfurt School followed Habermas along this trajectory, with important differences, but nevertheless creating a growing distance from other critical approaches. The first of these scholars was Seyla Benhabib.

Cosmopolitanism and Human Rights ▪ Seyla Benhabib

In 1986, Seyla Benhabib published *Critique, Norm, and Utopia: A Study of the Foundations of Critical Theory* with Columbia University Press. In this work squarely located in the field of critical social theory and in the lineage of the Frankfurt School, Benhabib set out to establish, in her words, "an alternative normative foundation for critical theory"—alternative, that is, to Jürgen Habermas's theory of communicative action. *Foundations* are in the very title of the book, and they constitute the central question presented, a question triggered precisely by the antifoundational challenges coming from both contextual pragmatists like Richard Rorty and poststructuralists like Foucault and Lyotard.[38]

Benhabib approaches the task systematically, tracing the normative foundations of critical theory in Hegel, Marx, Horkheimer and Adorno, and ultimately Habermas. She demonstrates how the original normative foundation in Hegel and Marx rested on what she calls a "philosophy of the subject," a subject who achieves emancipation through work and labor. This model of normative development of human agents gaining autonomy through their labor—which we can recognize well in Hegel's master-slave dialectic in *The Phenomenology of Spirit* and Marx's theory of alienation—Benhabib calls the "work model of activity," and she locates it as well in the early writings of Horkheimer, especially his 1937 article, "Traditional and Critical Theory."[39] The normative foundations begin to shift in Horkheimer and Adorno's collaborative work, which highlights the dimension of man's "non-dominating relation to nature," and then, more dramatically, in Habermas's communicative ethics. Habermas effectively shifts the normative foundations from the subject's relation to an object (labor or nature) to a subject-subject relation: this is the linguistically mediated relation of subject to subject through communicative action. Ultimately, Benhabib does not locate an alternative normative foundation for critical social theory and instead embraces, for the most part, Habermas's communicative ethics. As she writes, "Constructing a social theory adequate to the task of elucidating late-capitalist societies, I argue, involves methodologically and empirically developing a concept of social action based on the model of communication. This entails nothing less than a paradigm shift in critical theory from production to communicative action, from the politics of the philosophy of the subject to the politics of radical intersubjectivity."[40] The Habermasian elements are clear.

In *Critique, Norm, and Utopia*, Benhabib does not directly address, but rather comments on Foucault and the poststructuralist critiques. She distinguishes her position—specifically, her critique of the philosophy of the subject—from "the currently fashionable structuralist and post-structuralist searches for a philosophy without the subject." Benhabib compares Foucault unfavorably to Habermas, noting that for Foucault, modernity means nothing but an "increase in the power of domination." She associates Foucault with Nietzsche and Adorno, who, as opposed to Habermas's progressive account of the development of modern rationality, "view this same process as one of forgetting, repressing, and sublimating."[41]

Here, too, one gets the sense that, like Habermas, Benhabib is closer to Rawls than to Foucault. She notes that her approach, in her words, "shar[es] with Rawls's theory the vision of a community of rights and entitlements," but it must be oriented more centrally to the norm and utopia of "a community of needs and solidarity."

Here too, the normative anchor pushes Benhabib's version of communicative ethics toward rights and entitlements, toward liberal political philosophy, and away from critical poststructuralist interventions that seek to unmoor those very foundations. Benhabib's work ultimately orients itself in a universalist direction: it adopts a universalist standpoint and acts on that basis. It seeks to ground criteria of validity, not in external values or external foundational arguments, but rather in the immanence of critique and intersubjectivity. It involves creating normative legitimacy through "the generation of norms under conditions of communicatively achieved, and rationally motivated, arguments." Benhabib emphasizes: "Insofar as contextualism and post-modernism, however, reject that criteria of validity and legitimacy can be formulated, and transform philosophy into literary criticism, aphorism, or poetry, critical social theory dissents from this result." Benhabib's approach, in reaction to the Foucaultian challenge, is to press harder on normative grounding, on the bases of validity, on universalism, and on rationality. Although she would eventually call this a nonfoundational approach, it unquestionably ups the ante on the normative grounding of critical social theory.[42]

A few years later, in 1990, in a philosophical exchange with Judith Butler, Drucilla Cornell, and Nancy Fraser called *Feminist Contentions*, Benhabib confronts poststructuralism more directly.[43] If anything, the encounter reinforces her commitment to normative foundations. Benhabib approaches the exchange from the intersectional perspective of a critical social theorist and feminist. As such, she situates herself, in part, as a feminist critic of Habermas's communicative action theory. (She would do so more forcefully in *Situating the Self* and other writings that focused on dissent and social movements.)[44] Here, though, and more important, Benhabib distances herself dramatically from Foucault and Butler. While feminism could serve to tweak communicative ethics, it needs to resist and oppose poststructuralism strenuously, because, in Benhabib's words, it "place[s] in question the very emancipatory ideals of the women's movements altogether."[45]

Poststructuralism simply goes too far, Benhabib argues, and it undermines the possibility of validity, universalism, hope, and feminist utopia. To be sure, poststructuralism usefully highlights the linguistic and cultural construction of subjectivity, which Benhabib embraces (up to a point) through her own discourse ethics. It would be impossible today not to imagine the subject as caught in symbolic webs of meaning, she admits. But poststructuralism goes too far in proposing a radical antifoundationalism that does away, on Benhabib's reading, with agency, authorship, autonomy, and selfhood. In embracing the Nietzschean idea that there is no "doer behind the deed," poststructuralism is self-defeating and leads only to "self-incoherence," in Benhabib's words.[46]

The reason that poststructuralism fails, according to Benhabib—and this is the key point for the purposes of our discussion—is that it repudiates the epistemological project of philosophy, namely the project to articulate the bases of validity claims. This was the path that Foucault explicitly avoided. In this sense, Benhabib pushes the conflict even further or deeper into the epistemological gulf. In conversation with Richard Rorty's *Philosophy and the Mirror of Nature*, Benhabib argues that the philosophical project of epistemology—as "a meta-discourse of legitimation, articulating the criteria of validity presupposed by all other discourses"—is absolutely essential to any critical project, including the feminist critical enterprise. Criticism, and feminist criticism especially, cannot function without philosophy understood as epistemology. As Benhabib says, "Social criticism without philosophy is not possible, and without social criticism the project of a feminist theory, which is committed at once to knowledge and to the emancipatory interests of women is inconceivable."[47]

It is essential to unpack this move: as against a Foucaultian genealogical method or, for that matter, Foucault's long history of truth-making, Benhabib argues specifically for a return to the more traditional *epistemological* project of philosophy that has, at its core, the question of the "validity of right knowledge and correct action." These are the normative foundations—questions of validity, correctness, rightness, and truth, essentially—that are specifically challenged by the antifoundational critics, such as Foucault, Deleuze, Derrida, Said, or Spivak. And it is here that Benhabib draws the line—or rather, reinforces the return to epistemology and philosophy. She rejects even situated criticism, which would anchor normativity in particular intellectual traditions and immanent social criticism. Situated criticism, Benhabib argues, assumes a monism to interpretation and meaning that is too facile.[48]

Overall, Benhabib criticizes poststructuralism for causing "a retreat from utopia within feminism" and a loss of hope.[49] Confronted with the challenge of the antifoundationalist critics, Benhabib proposes reinforcing the normative path: the only way forward, she writes, is "by articulating the normative principles of democratic action and organization in the present." She concludes by asking: "Will the postmodernists join us in this task or will they be content with singing the swan song of normative thinking in general?"[50]

Coming back to the debate with Butler and Cornell a few years later, Benhabib ups the ante again—this time aiming her critique more directly at Butler's theory of gender performativity. The central problem with Butler's approach is her lack of a normative conception of agency. This produces, in Benhabib's view, a void, an absence of a normative grounding for resistance. And without that normative foundation, there is no way to properly understand and evaluate women's struggles and actions. As Benhabib writes, the "views of selfhood and agency which follow from certain contemporary French philosophies render incoherent, problematic, conceptually confused, women's own struggles for autonomy, agency, and equality."[51] Benhabib concludes her second intervention in the *Feminist Contentions* debate in the following terms:

> By "normative foundations" of social criticism I mean exactly the conceptual possibility of justifying the norms of universal moral respect and egalitarian reciprocity on rational grounds; no more and no less. Whereas most of my colleagues in this volume seem to think that even this is in some sense too much, I think that to want to deny this point is like wanting to jump over our own shadow.[52]

Benhabib would label her position "nonfoundationalist," but I think that is somewhat inexact. Her position is firmly normatively grounded and achieves claims of validity, of correctness, of rightness. In that sense, it has a solid foundational element.

Drawing on Hannah Arendt's framework of the "right to have rights," Benhabib would later combine critical social theory, from a feminist communicative ethics perspective, with a transnational human rights approach in order to argue in favor of universalistic human rights, especially in the context of immigration and asylum, but also in the European controversy over the wearing of headscarves, in other words, in the area of gender and human rights.[53] Here, Benhabib argues that international human rights regimes, treaties, and institutions are normatively valuable, not so much because of their enforcement or effectiveness at the empirical level, but because they generate discursive possibilities and open communicative avenues that can be deployed in the public sphere by women, immigrants, and marginalized persons to resist forms of domination. They create language, expressions, and arguments that can then be used toward emancipatory efforts.

In this, Benhabib opposes an array of international human rights skeptics, including those like Samuel Moyn, who argue that human rights discourse has displaced other emancipatory alternatives; like Mahmood Mamdani, who claim that it is merely an imperial and neocolonialist project of domination; and like Thomas Nagel or Michael Walzer, who believe that it infringes on the national debate over justice. Benhabib's response is not that human rights regimes are necessarily effective at protecting vulnerable individuals, but rather that they create arguments and discourse that can then be deployed by the vulnerable as tools in political debate. This is the jurisgenerative aspect of law, to borrow Robert Cover's term. And it is, Benhabib argues, internal to the democratic conversation, and in that sense, it is a form of self-governing, not an external imposition. Benhabib argues that the process of internalization necessary to the realization, enactment, and deployment of human rights discourse is one that requires local buy-in, local interpretation and contextualization, and local verbalization or vernacularization by local self-governing peoples—and in that sense, it is not imposed on them as an imperial project. What it enables, ultimately, according to Benhabib, is the possibility of new social movements using these discourses "to empower themselves by introducing new subjectivities into the public sphere, by articulating new vocabularies of claim-making, and by anticipating new forms of togetherness."[54]

In other respects, Benhabib today takes more of an institutionalist approach that defends international human rights norms on substantive grounds—not just as jurisgenerative. As she writes in 2019, "The left critique of neo-liberal globalization must be accompanied by envisaging new forms of global institutions for controlling capitalism, rebuilding institutions of sustainable and ecological planetary growth among peoples, and supporting the international human rights system in limiting the sovereignty of states such as to respect and further these rights."[55] These positions naturally present risks and uncertainties, as well as some concerns, as Benhabib acknowledges. But, she maintains, these are outweighed by the hope of jurisgenerative norms. She concludes: "Call this loyalty to an old-fashioned Enlightenment ideal!"[56]

Indeed, Benhabib's loyalty, in the end, is to Kantian normative foundations, and the years (or even decades) of confrontation with poststructuralism and other critical challenges have, if anything, entrenched those foundations. By contrast, some other Frankfurt School critical theorists turned back more to Hegel than to Kant, but that too set them further apart from their postfoundational critics. The first here was Axel Honneth, now at Columbia University.

Critiquing Power ∷ Axel Honneth

In 1985, at about the same time as the publication of Benhabib's *Critique, Norm, and Utopia,* Axel Honneth published *The Critique of Power: Reflective Stages in a Critical Social Theory.* There, Honneth directly engages Foucault, as well as Habermas, in his own effort to reconstruct the normative foundations of critical social theory.[57] Honneth's reintroduction and emphasis of the term *social* into "critical *social* theory" are not accidental; they are the core of his intervention for and against Foucault.

Honneth turns to both Foucault and Habermas to remedy the sociological deficit left by Horkheimer and Adorno: the fact that they ignored the broader social and cultural dimensions of human interaction and focused exclusively on labor, production, and economic exchange in analyzing social conflict, leaving critical theory with few or no tools to determine how social groups participate in rebuilding and integrating society. In Foucault and Habermas, Honneth identifies resources that can be used to comprehend the organization of societies—in Foucault, a model of power struggle and strategic systems–theoretic action without normative direction; and in Habermas, a model of communication with the potential for moral development. Honneth ultimately discards Foucault's model because it offers only a description of social conflict; instead he embraces a reconstructed Habermasian model that allows a justified normative critique of forms of social organization. Placing Adorno on the side of Foucault and might-makes-right politics, Honneth proposes a critical social communicative theory that "would make it possible to understand the social organizations that Adorno and Foucault mistook as power complexes functioning in a totalitarian manner as fragile constructions that remain dependent for their existence on the moral consensus of all participants."[58]

Honneth's dialogue with Habermas ultimately focuses on the epistemological dimensions of his work, or what Honneth refers to as "Habermas' Anthropology of Knowledge," in conversation with the epistemological debate between Karl Popper and Adorno, hermeneutic philosophy, and American pragmatism. In this sense, it represents a continuation of what I have called the epistemological diversion in critical theory.[59] Honneth's engagement with Foucault, though, focuses more on the question of power, as had Habermas's chapters in *The Philosophical Discourse of Modernity.*

Insofar as the encounter with Foucault pushes Honneth toward communicative theory, and given where Habermas would evolve in his debate with Rawls, it becomes clear that the poststructuralist critiques of the 1960s and 1970s pushed the later generations of the Frankfurt School in even more of a normative and epistemological direction and away from critical praxis, understood as revolt and active resistance. Or, to put this another way, insofar as communicative action is a form of discursive practice, and thus itself a praxis, the encounter with Foucault and other critics in the 1960–1970s pushed these Frankfurt School thinkers toward a model of social reform (akin to Eduard Bernstein's in his debate with Luxemburg) without much of an accent on the praxis questions. In most of these writings, there is little to no attempt to draw connections to political constellations or possibilities for action.

Honneth's *Critique of Power*, then, represents the first full-fledged effort to reconcile, but ultimately confront, Foucault with early Frankfurt School critical social theory. The effort did not draw Honneth closer to Foucault, nor did it narrow the epistemological divide. On the contrary, it may well have marked the apex of Honneth's hope of recuperating Foucault (which essentially he has lost since then). Over the course of his subsequent intellectual journeys, Honneth became far more Hegelian, as I will show. The Hegelian elements were already pronounced in *The Critique of Power*, insofar as Honneth viewed the entire dialogue between these philosophers as a learning process that leads to theoretical improvement and ultimately progress. But in the end, Honneth's encounter with Foucault only widened the epistemological gap.

It is interesting to note here one missed opportunity. An important dimension of Honneth's critique of Horkheimer and Adorno is that they failed to pay sufficient attention to questions of subjectivity. They ignored the ways in which individuals, as part of social groups, participate in the creation of social order.[60] Foucault's research during the 1980s, especially in his 1981 Louvain lectures on the function of avowal, evolved in this precise direction; but the work was not yet available and would really become part of philosophical discourse only with the publication of the later Collège de France lectures in the early twenty-first century. There is a lot of material there for a theory of ethical development, and there is a real conversation to be had with Honneth's communicative theory of moral development. Amy Allen takes precisely this position in her reconsideration of the Foucault/Habermas debate, suggesting that their potential encounter was a missed opportunity to put in conversation their respective accounts of subjectivation. Had there been such an encounter, Allen suggests, there may have been the opportunity to find some middle ground between rationality and power.[61]

In any event, Honneth's rejection of Foucault only widened the gap. This is evident from a close reading of the exchange. In an interesting way—consonant with chapter 1 of this book—Honneth's *Critique of Power* functions as a critique of the first generation of the Frankfurt School. Honneth criticizes Horkheimer especially for remaining too wedded to a Marxian philosophy of history and unable to imagine or focus properly on the broader social sphere of contestation over needs, resources, and distribution. It is a searing critique of Horkheimer's 1937 article and his wholesale adoption of Marxian theories of class struggle and proletarian revolution. Honneth's take is that Horkheimer failed to genuinely engage in the sociological work that would have been necessary to push social actors past the impasse of social conflict. Later, he would accuse Foucault of doing the same.

In this sense, Honneth develops in *The Critique of Power* a critical social theory as a critique not just of Marx, but of early critical theory. If, as I was suggesting earlier, there emerged two variations on the theme of critical theory in the Frankfurt School lineage, Honneth is taking the road of *critical theory as a critique of Marx*, but he ups the ante to make it as well *a critique of critical theory*. In charting this path, though, Honneth is not moving in the direction of a postfoundational constructivism—as that path could have led to—instead, he is trying to find another normative foundation for a socialist project.

The error of Horkheimer and Adorno, in Honneth's view, was to impose class struggle as a universal. Horkheimer especially neglected any analysis of everyday life struggle. He focused too exclusively on the dimension of social labor and ignored the other realms of cultural interaction. He imposed a model of "social praxis," defined as praxis of the working class in the labor context, instead of looking more granularly at social conflict writ large.[62] This produced a "sociological deficit," in Honneth's words. It represented an *aporia*, insofar as the early Frankfurt School wanted to be interdisciplinary and turned to psychoanalysis and economics to address the question of ideology, but ended up missing the sociological dimension. This then led to the "unexpectedly pessimistic diagnosis" from the 1940s of mass culture and the end of reason. The problem with all this is that it rendered their vision of the oppressed subject a completely passive and intentionless victim. It led to resignation—or what Honneth refers to as "this resignative turn . . . reflected in the methodological structure that critical theory assumes in Adorno writings after the war."[63]

Honneth interprets Adorno as pushing critical theory then into an aesthetic direction that assigned only to art any normative task and possibility, displacing social scientific inquiry or the possibility of a sociological exploration of social conflict. This leads to a dead end for Honneth. "In the end," he writes, "critical theory seems to have renounced the theoretical possibility of determining whether, and to what degree, social groups actively participate in the integration of society." *The Critique of Power* operates as a critique of the first generation of the Frankfurt School, but Honneth is particularly sour on Adorno. Honneth remarks that he is "surprised" by the current return to Adorno. He speaks of Adorno's work still being "relevant" today "despite its many weaknesses." He makes no bones of his own distaste for Adorno's writings, which he views as negative only and unsystematic. He writes of his "negativism"—in a pejorative sense, and of his "resignative philosophy." He speaks of "the philosophical-historical dead end into which critical theory was led with Adorno's negativism."[64] It is clear that, sensibility-wise, Honneth places himself on the side of the constructivism of both Horkheimer and Habermas. And, naturally, it comes out in his conclusions.

Very schematically, then, Honneth argues that Horkheimer failed because he was too wedded to Marx and the dimension of social labor, and he did not see the sociocultural dimension of social conflict; that Adorno saw domination everywhere and therefore offered no way forward; that Foucault helped us focus on social conflict but offered no basis for normative agreement and therefore provided only a description of systems of domination. On the other hand, Honneth argues that Habermas provides, with communicative theory, a way to understand domination, as well as a way forward: "a dynamic of social struggle that is structurally located within the moral space of social interactions."[65] In both Foucault and Habermas, Honneth originally identifies resources to develop a thicker sociology of social organization, and therefore to overcome Horkheimer's theory of ideology, but in two very different ways: Foucault by means of a theory of power that, in Honneth's opinion, reduces social conflict to warlike strategic action, and ultimately to the law of the stronger; Habermas by means of a discourse ethics that, in Honneth's opinion, is more promising, normatively, to resolve social conflict. Ultimately, Honneth casts off Foucault as overly focused on power and strategic action—and in this, one can hear an echo of Habermas's critique of Foucault as well. Foucault fails to offer Honneth a way to normatively ground social reconciliation.

The sociological deficit is what motivates Honneth's intervention and pushes him to read and engage Foucault. Honneth does his best to bring Foucault into conversation with the Frankfurt School, but ultimately he misidentifies him as developing a theory of the "social"—a term and a concept that would have been foreign to Foucault, an object for genealogy rather than analytic study—and then reads him as a systems-analytic thinker. Honneth criticizes Foucault for "a crude behaviorism," for a "fundamentally mechanistic conception," and for developing a one-sided systems theory.[66] Now, while Foucault did deploy a conception of society at times (as in his lectures on *The Punitive Society*) and sometimes displayed a functionalist approach as well, the characterization of his work as systems theory does not ring true, especially in light of all of the additional writings that have been published since Honneth's book. It is clear today, especially since the publication of *The Birth of Biopolitics*, that the category of civil society is something that Foucault would genealogize—like the category of the state itself.

In any event, Honneth turns instead to Habermas's communicative ethics as a way to explore the realm of social contestation and to ground the normative basis to resolve it. Here, Honneth takes a full-fledged turn to epistemological questions and the positivist dispute, in conversation with Edmund Husserl's *The Crisis of European Science and Transcendental Phenomenology*, Popper's *The Logic of Scientific Discovery*, Hans-Georg Gadamer and hermeneutics, and American pragmatism—by contrast to Foucault's epistemological understanding of interpretation in his most epistemological work, *The Archaeology of Knowledge*.[67] By means of a Hegelian learning process, Honneth ultimately reaches a normative foundation that is centered around Habermas's communicative action theory. If anything, Honneth's attempt to embrace Foucault once again widens the distance in the end.

Reborn Hegelianism :: Honneth on Socialism

The later iterations of the Frankfurt School came in different variations. Almost everyone gave up on Marxism and dialectical materialism, so those normative foundations were mostly off the table. Some turned to critical theory as a critique of Marxism and in the process gravitated toward the ideal of socialism. Others sought to rehabilitate ideology critique, in effect turning critical theory into a corrective to Marxism. Along these lines, the effort was to put the epistemological work in service of a leftist politics. Two books published in the late 2010s illustrate these paths:

Axel Honneth's *The Idea of Socialism* reflects the former, and Rahel Jaeggi's *Critique of Forms of Life* the latter. Let me turn to these works now.

In *The Idea of Socialism*, Axel Honneth gravitates toward critical social theory as a critique of Marxism, but one that retains normative grounding of another kind. His project there is to exorcise the Marxism and the context of industrialization from the idea of socialism. Honneth abandons a Marxian philosophy of history—he severs the core historical tenets of Marx's writings—in order to develop an experimentalist version of socialism that seeks emancipation not only in the economic sphere, but also in the public sphere of democratic deliberation. Honneth proposes a clear break from Marx and an embrace of Habermasian notions of publicity, the public sphere, and reasonable deliberation, but he does this in a Hegelian manner: through a learning process. History, in Honneth's hands, does not so much have a direction as it teaches us lessons. There is a Hegelian learning process and moral evolution in history. Ultimately, Honneth embraces a vision of what he calls experimental socialism, as opposed to the traditional options of reformist or revolutionary socialism: rather than opt simply for reform, having severed the Gordian knot of Marxism and overcome proletarian revolution, Honneth proposes an experimentalism tied principally to parliamentary and public policy approaches.

What motivates Honneth's project is the puzzle as to why the idea of socialism has become unthinkable today. Honneth sets out to demonstrate that the idea of socialism remains vibrant or, in his words, "still contains a vital spark," but he argues, this is possible only if we reframe the idea of socialism, extracting it from its early industrialist historical context, and placing it in what he calls "a new socio-theoretical framework."[68] That new sociotheoretical framework has several dimensions. First, it abandons the Marxian philosophy of history (in other words, the expectation that capitalism will collapse from its own internal contradictions and lead to the withering of the state) and also abandons the idea that the working class or proletariat is the already-existing embodiment of the ideals of socialism; second, it expands the notion of social freedom (the core concept of socialism according to Honneth) to include not just economic organization and production, but also the democratic political sphere.

According to Honneth, the early socialists were concerned principally with the question of freedom. In a very telling passage, he writes that the idea of socialism was itself an immanent critique of postrevolutionary bourgeois society and the modern, capitalist social order. It basically accepted the ideals of postrevolutionary France (namely, the trinity of liberty-equality-fraternity), but argued, in Honneth's words, that "these values cannot be fully reconciled with each other as long as liberty is not interpreted in a less individualistic and more intersubjective manner."[69]

The notion of immanent critique is key to the structure of Honneth's argument. Honneth contends that the young Karl Marx also developed the idea of socialism immanently—or, as he writes, "on the basis of the contradictory aims of the liberal social order." According to Honneth, Marx offered a version of social freedom that was linked to solidarity by means of the mutual recognition of each other's aims and needs. Honneth, following Habermas, criticizes the early socialist writings, from the first ones to those of Marx, for focusing exclusively on the economic sphere of production and setting aside the question of social freedom in the context of political democracy. He calls this the "congenital defect of the socialist project": the failure to investigate questions of freedom in the political sphere, the questions of political democracy and public deliberation.[70]

The heart of the idea of *social freedom*—the term that Honneth coins and embraces as representing the core concept of socialism as originally defined by the early socialists—involves a mutual recognition as members of a shared community with solidarity. In Honneth's words, "social freedom therefore means taking part in the social life of a community whose members are so sympathetic to each other that they support the realization of each other's justified needs for each other's sake."[71] At the heart of this concept is a notion of community, collectivity, and solidarity, embedded in the idea of freedom. It is a holistic notion, involving a community in solidarity that enables social freedom. Honneth proposes a reconstructive project—an experimental approach that allows improvement, without a philosophy of history, by means of a turn to democratic politics. He discusses the various kinds of socialist interventions after World War II that tried to rehabilitate the idea of socialism. One was "analytical Marxism" of the type of G. A. Cohen (or perhaps even Jon Elster): this approach basically tried to argue for socialism as a type of political theory, just another normative theory, an alternative to liberal political theory and the liberal theories of justice. The other approach is that of Castoriadis and Habermas, which Honneth is more comfortable with because they retain "the thought that socialism must reflect on its own conditions of possibility and aim to bring about an alternative life-form." Honneth insists that he wants a theory that brings about actual practical change. He writes that, "if socialism is to have a future, it must be revived in a post-Marxist form."[72]

Ultimately, Honneth focuses on the central issue of democratic will-formation. Marxism had dispensed with the notion of citizenship and political rights, imagining that economic cooperation would produce a world of equal producers, who would be emancipated and no longer need the liberal state for purposes of citizenship. Honneth is adamant about removing that limitation, in part because it is based on the exclusive economic focus of socialism. He wants to add the process of democratic decision-making as a central element of social freedom. This is the central political dimension of socialism that has been lacking since the start, according to Honneth. Socialism never understood the importance of the political or civil society because, from its inception, it failed to appreciate or recognize the functional differentiation of the various spheres of life—such as the family, civil society, and democratic spaces. This also produced a certain disregard for the importance of rights, and, he writes, "This in turn meant that they necessarily lost sight of the emancipatory role these liberties play in the entirely different sphere of political will-formation."[73]

This then raises two important questions: first, the question of which institution or authority should manage the complexity of the different social spheres and differentiated functions of family and civil society; and second, the geopolitical unit that should be considered to ease the transformational process, whether the nation-state or something larger. With regard to the first question, Honneth turns to John Dewey and to the notion of a "public sphere," where citizens participate as freely and equally as possible. It is the public sphere, he argues, that should serve as the social organ to steer society. The resemblance to Habermas's *The Structural Transformation of the Public Sphere* is evident; Honneth says in *The Idea of Socialism*, "There can be no doubt that the democratic public sphere, occupied by deliberating citizens, must take over the role of supervising the functioning of the entire organic structure and making the requisite adjustments."[74] We are in the realm here of democratic politics and a democratic form of life. With regard to the second question, Honneth sees value in both the internationalist project and the nation-state, and he argues for a dual approach that recognizes both the advantages of internationalism and the importance of local traditions.

Honneth concludes by describing his entire effort as an attempt "to free socialism from the shackles of nineteenth-century thought and give it a form that is more appropriate to the present."[75] He confidently disposes of old socialist dogmas, especially the inevitability of revolution and the paradigmatic nature of the working class. He calls these in fact "illusions"[76] and says that they are the greatest roadblock to possibly realizing the socialist project today. That project includes, at its core, not just economic experimentation, but also the introduction of social freedom in every sphere of society—not just the economic sphere, but also politics and personal relations. In part, Honneth is responding to the critique that Amy Allen leveled at the Frankfurt School in *The End of Progress.* In his turn to the public sphere and democratic politics, he is explicitly broaching the topics of gender, race, and sexuality, especially when he places the issues (e.g., same-sex marriage) within the sphere of democratic politics that can afford us emancipatory potential. But Honneth does not talk about the practical implications of these concepts. Although the work is deeply pragmatic and he is formulating a vision for socialism, he does not engage the question of praxis. As I noted in the introduction to this book, he explicitly starts off by disclaiming any practical implications. "I make no attempt to draw connections to current political constellations and possibilities for action," Honneth emphasizes.[77]

In effect, Honneth has refounded his project and placed it on new normative foundations, using a Hegelian learning process theory. But in the process of freeing himself from Marx, he has also distanced his project from the modern practical attitude that inaugurated critical philosophy. Here too, there is no bridge to the postfoundational challenges.

Critiquing Forms of Life ∷ Rahel Jaeggi

Rahel Jaeggi gravitates closer to the second version of critical theory in her book published in 2014, *Critique of Forms of Life*: critical theory as a corrective to Marxism.[78] There, Jaeggi reformulates Hegelian immanent critique and Marxian ideology critique in an effort to ground normative judgments about what she calls forms of life. Some forms of life will be deemed rational and correct, as good problem-solving tools; others, irrational and to be discarded. The critical project here is to make possible judgments about ways of living. With Jaeggi, we are back to a solid normative foundation, at odds with the 1960–1970s antifoundational critiques. It is a Hegelian approach, insofar as the metric to assess rationality and problem-solving involves a learning process. It retains a conception of progress, in a weak form. There is no Marxian philosophy of history, but the Marxian element of ideology critique is maintained, in fact strengthened.

It is a critique of ideology that rehabilitates not a Marxist vision, but a leftist (Hegelian) vision.

Jaeggi's book is a contemplative philosophical text that addresses the question of whether critical thinkers can judge forms of life, understood as ways of living, such as gay marriage or arranged marriages; public support for child care; the privatization of education or health; particular designs of urban spaces; or the understanding of society as being a work-oriented society. She suggests that her idea of forms of life is similar to Hegel's notion of "ethical life." In this sense, Jaeggi is in conversation, most directly, with the Hegelian tradition of critique, supplemented by John Dewey and Hilary Putnam. Her work is in the tradition of the Hegelian dialectic, especially *The Phenomenology of Spirit*, where progress is identified as a learning process. In the same way in which Hegel described the development of consciousness there as a learning process, and in the same way in which Honneth described the history of critical theory as a learning process in *The Critique of Power*, Jaeggi embraces a concept of a learning process as the very foundation of the form of criticism that she develops in her book. As Jaeggi writes, "it is precisely the fact that forms of life can be understood as historically developing learning processes endowed with normative claims to validity that is the key to their evaluation."[79]

The book proceeds at a high philosophical level, and the central philosophical question presented is whether visions of the good life can be criticized and judged. The traditional position of liberal political theory, as developed in John Rawls's work, is that competing visions of the good life cannot be judged and must not be evaluated, but instead should be allowed to flourish. The state's action is limited to guaranteeing rights that allow each individual to pursue their own vision of the good life. This is known as "the priority of the right over the good," and it has become the classic statement of liberalism—embraced even, as I discussed earlier, by philosophers such as Jürgen Habermas. Jaeggi captures the idea neatly in the opening pages of her book, where she writes that "the political order of the liberal constitutional state is represented accordingly as an attempt to organize this cohabitation so that it remains neutral between forms of life."[80]

The central intervention of Jaeggi's book, then, is to contest this liberal thesis. Jaeggi argues that forms of life *can* and *must* be criticized. They can be evaluated on whether they are successful at their task. They can be determined to be rational, as forms of life. Jaeggi does not believe that critical judgment of forms of life could or would lead to consensus on one single form of the good life. She does not espouse or propose agreement on a form of life and would not impose one form on others. The thrust of her project, instead, is negative critique: not so much to identify good forms of life, but rather to judge the weaknesses and irrationalities of particular forms of life. Jaeggi's project is not intended to dictate one good way of living, or even to narrow it down to a handful of ways, but rather to identify a mode of critique that can show when modes of life are not living up to the problems that they are intended to address.

This point is very important: Jaeggi describes modes of life as problem-solving devices. Insofar as they are intended to solve a problem, it becomes possible to evaluate whether they are successful at doing that, and whether they are rationally oriented toward solving the problem. Jaeggi describes forms of life as clusters of social practices that are constructed by humans and therefore can be changed. This is the first precondition for criticizing forms of life. As Jaeggi writes, she has developed "an understanding of forms of life as ensembles of social practices in which these ensembles—notwithstanding all moments of inertia—were shown to be human constructs and hence to be *open to change in principle.*" These forms of life are located at some intermediate level between mere taste and clearly morally justified proscriptions, like spanking children (although that seems to be somewhat culturally determined, at least in the United States). Examples of forms of life include polyandry versus monogamy; using the television as a babysitter; the spread of shopping malls; watching television; surrogate motherhood; or market ties to health care. Insofar as these forms of life are problem-solving devices, Jaeggi proposes a way to judge them.[81] It is ultimately a pragmatic vision, which explains Jaeggi's heavy engagement with Dewey.

It is in this intermediate space between tastes and morally justified proscriptions that Jaeggi tries to theorize arguments about whether a form of life is "sterile, lifeless, tawdry, bleak, or regressive," or "cool, original, enthralling, fascinating, or progressive." This is the space of what Bernard Williams called "thick ethical concepts," as Jaeggi remarks. The purpose of the intervention is to "spell out systematically the intermediate level between prohibition and individual whim, a level that seems to have argumentatively dried up to a certain extent in the face of the dominant currents in political liberalism and Kantian moral philosophy."[82]

The project, then, is to formulate normative grounds for judging whether forms of life succeed or fail. The project is unabashedly normative; and the model that Jaeggi develops is a strong form of immanent critique inspired by Hegel and Marx, which neither depends on external standards nor is merely internal critique.

It involves a type of overcoming or transformative process that Jaeggi describes as "an ethical learning process or, in more old-fashioned terminology, as an emancipation process."[83] Jaeggi wants to avoid criticism of forms of life from an Archimedean viewpoint, but she does not merely want to criticize internally, and so she reconstructs a full theory of immanent critique (which I will discuss in chapter 5).

Jaeggi introduces an element of rationality into her theory of immanent criticism, which is what allows firm criticism of forms of life. She writes that "the possibility of establishing a critical standard for evaluating forms of life depends on being able to describe something like a *rational learning process*." It is the rationality of that learning process that makes it possible to argue either that a form of life is not rational and not successful or that it offers a correct or incorrect solution to a problem or to a crisis. In her words, it makes it possible to talk about validity as measured by a "historical index." Forms of life form part of historical transformations, meaning that they are embedded in a historical sequence of failures and successes of forms of life. There are constant historical transformations of ways of life, as they encounter problems and crises and make changes to solve them. What becomes subject to judgment is the way in which these historical dynamics take place: the way in which forms of life respond to crises that arise as a result of previous forms of life. "It is no longer the individual solution to a problem that can prove to be appropriate or inappropriate, rational or irrational, good or bad, but the historical dynamic of the transformation process that it sets in motion," Jaeggi writes. So the measure of the success of life forms is the rationality of the solution to problems arising. In this way, "a successful form of life is something that can be understood as the result of a successful dynamic of transformation."[84]

On the other hand, bad forms of life are those that are blocked or disruptive, fail to solve problems, and reduce the transformative process. This allows Jaeggi to displace the question from a mere evaluation of the content of a form of life, shifting it to the process and dynamics of the development—in other words, to the question of social learning processes. The question is not simply whether a form of life is good, but the larger issue of whether there have been successful processes of social transformation. There is a developmental logic here that becomes central, which Jaeggi wants to describe as a genuine learning process. Jaeggi writes, in conclusion: "If we follow my investigation, there is no positive answer to the question of what makes a form of life a good or adequate form of life. However, there is a negative, indirect answer: failing forms of life suffer from a collective practical reflexive deficit, from a blockage to learning. In other words, they are not able to solve the problems they face or to perceive the crisis experiences to which they are exposed in appropriate ways as experiences and to transform themselves accordingly."[85]

"A critical theory of criticism of forms of life":[86] Jaeggi's project grounds normative judgment in a Hegelian learning process theory. In the end, what is wrong with liberal political theory and its bracketing of ethical life is that they stunt the potential for more learning. They stop in its tracks the process of development of forms of life. That is where Jaeggi ends her book.

Jaeggi directly challenges liberal political philosophy. As noted earlier, both Rawls and Habermas took the position during their exchange that we should not evaluate visions of the good life, in order to avoid forms of illiberalism and paternalism. Both agreed that we should abstain from debating the ethics of ways of living. Jaeggi argues, by contrast, that in contemporary society, the conditions of modernity create an even greater need to avoid what she calls "ethical abstinence." Drawing on the logic of Hegel's *Elements of the Philosophy of Right*, Jaeggi suggests that in modern society, the greater dependence of individuals creates an enhanced need for us to judge manners of living. While Jaeggi is careful not to embrace an "illiberal moral dictatorship" and wants to avoid any notion of policing, she nevertheless pushes against the agnosticism of liberalism.[87]

In an odd way, then, Jaeggi ends up in a more foundational place than most liberal political theorists—and in that sense, even further from the poststructuralist, postcolonial, queer, and other postfoundational critics. Although very different from the Kantian project of Habermas, Jaeggi embraces a notion of reasonableness and rationality as a way to judge the problem-solving nature of new forms of life, which is diametrically opposed to the antifoundationalists who challenged early critical theory. This is clear when Jaeggi reduces her thesis to a succinct formula:

> Forms of life are complex bundles (or ensembles) of social practices geared to solving problems that for their part are historically contextualized and normatively constituted. The question of the rationality of forms of life can then be formulated from a context-transcending perspective as one about the rationality of the dynamics of development of the respective form of life. Such a perspective adopts as its criterion of success *[Gelingen]* not so much substantive aspects of content but rather formal criteria relating to the rationality and success of the process thus described as an ethical and social learning process.[88]

Judgment thus turns on the rationality and success of forms of life in solving problems that we encounter. Jaeggi's argument takes the form of a negative critique as a means to justify validity claims. She does not call for a single right form of life, and she does not believe that her critique would give rise to a single right form. But her method of critique does rest on the articulation of reasons, justifications, and rationality, and therefore it gives rise to validity claims. In the end, Jaeggi writes, "Forms of life imply validity claims."[89]

Insofar as those validity claims hold not only for oneself, but for others, and participate not just in practices of the self, but in conducting the conduct of others, Jaeggi's critique has widened, not bridged, the epistemological and normative gap.

Rational Foundations :: Rainer Forst

At the furthest extreme perhaps, at least within the late Frankfurt School, is Rainer Forst's project of developing a theory of justification. Building on Habermas's discourse ethics and returning to Kant, Forst has focused his research on normative grounding and normative order. Alongside Habermas, Forst is perhaps furthest from the postfoundationalists.

Forst's extensive research and writings—and institution building, as reflected in "The Formation of Normative Orders" research cluster at the Goethe-Universität Frankfurt—are all geared toward developing a critical theory of political justification, that is, principles of just and legitimate political action. His starting point, and in his own words, the "guiding idea," is reflexivity—which, you will recall, was also the starting point for Horkheimer. Forst launches his inquiry into political justification with a reflexive move: the question of justification must begin by asking *who* is the subject or object of justification, *who* gets to decide, or in his own words, "Who actually poses this question and who has the authority to answer it?"[90]

But Forst's notion of reflexivity, although historicized and contextualized, pushes in the direction of an abstract subject and then, almost immediately, toward a notion of universalizability. After introducing the core concept of reflexivity, Forst pivots to the universal: "From the perspective of those who raise this question as a question of justice," he writes—in other words, from the reflexive position of the political actors themselves, *for* themselves—"the justification on which everything turns is one which they can accept individually and jointly as free and equal persons, where their acceptance or rejection are themselves in turn governed by specific norms."[91]

Forst pivots quickly from the reflexivity of the subject to that of joint agreement on specified norms, which recalls Kant, Habermas, and Rawls. In rapid succession, the question of justification turns into "the thesis that such a justification must be 'reasonable,' 'acceptable,' or 'just.'"[92] This in turn poses the central challenge of rationally justifying a normative order, and this, Forst tells us, "presupposes a concept of fundamental justice as *discursive justice*."[93] On the basis of this theory of justification and discursive justice, Forst then develops a theory of power, which he calls "noumenal power."[94] He uses the concept of power in a nonnormative way. He does not inflect it with value, but rather deploys it as a way to articulate justification. As he explains, "Power is the art of binding others through reasons; it is a core phenomenon of normativity."[95]

Reason and reasonableness: we are back at square one, facing an epistemological gulf that has only grown with the erasure of Marx and the return to Kantian foundations. In returning so forcefully to Kant and notions of universalizability, Forst, and Habermas before him, have put extreme pressure on the concept of critical theory.

Critical philosophy was, at its origin, a challenge to the universalizing claims of reason—a challenge to the Hegelian privilege of reason over materiality; a challenge to the privilege of theory over praxis; a challenge to the purported neutrality and objectivity of reason and universalizing principles; a challenge to being governed in this reasonable way, to being governed like this; a challenge to the Eurocentrism, imperialism, heteronormativity, and patriarchy of the idea of the reasonable throughout history. And yet, we are right back there, and in this, the writings of Forst and Habermas reveal that the Kantian notion of critique itself may also be at the root of the epistemological conflict that has wracked critical theory.

There are in effect two radically different ways in which Kantian critique has inflected critical theory: as a search for truth and as a condition of possibility. On the one hand, Kantian critique was born of the ancient drive to separate truth from falsity. Kant's critical project and the Enlightenment search for the limits of reason trace back to the notions of discrimination and adjudication at the heart of the Greek root *kri-* in *krinein* (to judge) and *krisis* (to dispute and discriminate). To parse, separate, distinguish, differentiate, and ultimately to decide and judge—those actions are at the very root of the critical task, whether in medicine at the acute moment of a critical condition, in classical tragedy at the turning point of a peripeteia, in aesthetics and art criticism at the point of critique, or in law at the final moment of judgment. As both Habermas and Foucault emphasized, and as Koselleck, Benhabib, and others demonstrated as well, parsing and separating truth from illusion lie at the root of our contemporary usage of terms like *critique* and *crisis*.[96] Kant's *Critique of Pure Reason* provided that nomenclature and inaugurated the strand of critical philosophy associated with the project of distinguishing what we can know about the world from illusions. Kant's project, in part, was to determine the a priori concepts that were the condition of all possible knowledge, in order to identify what we can truthfully know and what, by contrast, qualifies as illusions or the exercise of our faculties beyond the limits of reason. This traced far back in history. In antiquity already, the concept of judging had been twined to that of truth. With Greek poetry and philosophy already, there had emerged, as Foucault reminds us in *Wrong-Doing, Truth-Telling*, a "direct link between this *dikaion* and this *alēthes*, between the just and the true, which would become the problem, one could argue the constant problem, of the Western world."[97]

On the other hand, Kant's critical project gave birth to the notion of "conditions of possibility" that would serve as the main conceptual tool for constructivism and the genealogical enterprise. This would push critical philosophy in the direction of searching not for truth, but for the contingent conditions of possibility that naturalize certain ways of thinking, that shape the world we live in, and that foreclose other possible worlds. This is the sense in which, as Colin Koopman reminds us, Foucault and Deleuze are Kantian as well. In asking the question of conditions of possibility, Foucault and Deleuze are at the heart of Kantian critical philosophy as "a philosophy that asks of its objects of inquiry, 'What makes this possible?' "[98] The genealogical method is precisely about conditions of possibility. It is, again in Koopman's words, "concerned with the conditions of possibility that define the present in such a way that certain actions simply are not possible for us."[99] For those working in this Kantian tradition, the conditions of possibility are not just the Kantian categories of space, time, or cause and effect, but instead the contingent historical events that shape the way that subjects see the world and understand themselves, that produce regimes of truth, and that determine the way that power circulates throughout society.

These two dimensions of Kantian critique are radically at odds, as an epistemological matter. And one can trace right there, as well, the tension at the heart of critical philosophy. It is similar to the tension between the methods of strong immanent critique and thin defetishizing critique, which I will turn to next. It is similar to the tension that was at the core of Horkheimer's 1937 article setting forth a vision for critical theory. And it explains much of the contestation over the very term *critical philosophy*. In what may have been at the time an enigmatic first endnote to this book, I mentioned that the term *critical philosophy* is most often associated with Kant and his three critiques, but that other critical theorists understand the term differently. Deleuze traced true critical philosophy back to Nietzsche. Honneth and Jaeggi point elsewhere, toward Hegel. Foucault went further back, to Socrates and the ancients. Many, of course, trace critical philosophy to Marx. In this book, I trace critical philosophy to the modern practical attitude, captured so brilliantly by the ambition to change the world, not just interpret it. That, I would argue, is critical philosophy, and it need not be qualified as "radical." Critical philosophy, I believe, begins with the praxis imperative. But the conflicts that have wracked it ever since trace back to these two conflicting dimensions of Kantian critique. I believe that the early critical impulse and the postfoundational challenges have always targeted, precisely, the problematic link between judgment and truth. To date, the field of critical theory has not been able to reconcile that chasm.

I interrupt the historical account here to turn, now, directly to the theoretical problem. In doing so, I jump over many other important critical contributions that proliferated in reaction to the different challenges already discussed. Critical theorists such as Philippe Lacoue-Labarthe and Jean-Luc Nancy, Claude Lefort, Jacques Rancière, and others, inserted a wedge between the concepts of *politics* and *the political* as a way to emphasize "the collapse of certainties" and develop what Oliver Marchart has called postfoundational political thought.[100] Others, such as Dipesh Chakrabarty and Bruno Latour, turned to the concept of the Anthropocene to capture humankind's effect on the Earth and to historicize the phenomenon of global climate change[101]—with some even extending this into the domains of surveillance and digital technologies.[102] Others turned to the framework of neoliberalism and biopolitics to capture the globalization of a new political economy of profiteering, financialization, and consumerism.[103] Some looked for new definitions of populism in order to capture the rise of right-wing political movements and parties in Hungary, Poland, or the Philippines. Still others crafted new concepts of precarity, necropolitics, racialized assemblages, critical fabulation, intersectionality, critical anthropology, decolonizing, and other theoretical frameworks to make sense of our present time.[104] Many or most of these continued to challenge the epistemological and normative foundations of the later Frankfurt School.

As for the Frankfurt School itself and where it is headed, that remains to be seen—or, in Martin Saar's words, "We shall see."[105] Saar, the philosopher who succeeded Habermas and Honneth in the chair of social philosophy at the Goethe-Universität Frankfurt, is far more accommodating to Foucault's genealogical method and attention to subjectivation than his predecessors.[106] His first book, *Genealogy as Critique*, analyzed the continuities and differences between the genealogical methods of Nietzsche and Foucault, and, although Saar underscores in his reading the multiple (and at times inconsistent) dimensions of genealogy in Foucault, Saar proposes what he considers to be a rehabilitated reading of Foucault that ultimately puts him in productive conversation with the Frankfurt School.[107]

Drawing on the Frankfurt tradition, from Adorno and Horkheimer to Honneth and Jaeggi, as well as on Foucault, Castoriadis, Lefort, Balibar, and Butler, Saar is developing a new orientation for social philosophy as, what he calls tellingly, "a critique of power." But by contrast to Honneth's book of that name, or Forst's theory of noumenal power, Saar is trying to reconcile and incorporate Foucault. His critique of power, he writes, again tellingly, is "an analysis that describes and assesses the effects of power while at the same time thinking about the costs, the price, and even the victims of a given constellation of power." Saar is particularly open to the dimensions of subjectivation and self-transformation that are classically associated with Foucault.[108] In reconciling the Frankfurt School with poststructuralism more broadly, he offers a promising alternative way forward out of the epistemological detour—one that will, I suspect, have a strong Spinozist character and draw inspiration from Adorno. But again, we shall see.

In the meantime, contemporary critical theory is caught in acrimonious debates over epistemology and normative foundations—leaving contemporary critical thinkers and practitioners disarmed before the crises that have come, in wave after wave. There is no time to wait and see. It is time now to exit the epistemological detour and return critical philosophy to its mission: to change the world. Let me now turn to the conceptual core of the problem (in chapter 5) and to the way forward (in chapters 6 and 7).

CHAPTER 5

The Crux of the Problem

The historical trajectory of critical philosophy reflects a widening epistemological gap between, on the one hand, the heirs of Left Hegelianism, the later generations of the Frankfurt School, neo-Kantians, and neo-Marxians, and, on the other hand, those we might broadly call postfoundationalist, such as poststructuralists, postcolonial and queer theorists, critical race and trans* theorists. Within each pole, naturally, there remain significant epistemological differences and oppositions. Some neo-Marxians, such as Joshua Clover, still deploy elements of a Marxian philosophy of history and consider themselves adamantly opposed to the critical theory of the Frankfurt School; some postcolonial, subaltern scholars and queer theorists, such as Ann Stoler, Anupama Rao, and Sharon Marcus, remain deeply critical of the blind spots of poststructuralism. These are by no means two coherent poles, internally. But they reflect a deep chasm as well as gradations along a central fault line: epistemologies and normative foundations. The root of the problem and what pushed critical theory down the epistemological detour are larger than the belief of some in historical progress. It can be traced, instead, to the broader problem of foundationalism. And this problem plagues critical theory at a number of levels—both methodological and theoretical.

At the methodological level, the core problem is that the two principal methods of critical philosophy—immanent critique and defetishizing critique—are in deep tension with each other and point in potentially different epistemological directions. Immanent critique contains at its core a notion of necessity and a distinction (internal versus external values) that operate at a quasi-scientific level: in immanent critique, generally, an inherent internal contradiction necessarily produces an overcoming that results in the favorable transformation of those internal values. So, for instance, very schematically, the inherent contradiction in capitalism between the values of freedom and equality produces crises that will eventually lead to the transformation of these values and an overcoming of capitalism. Both the necessity of the inherent internal contradiction, which serves as the motor of historical transformation, and the ability to clearly distinguish internal from external values constitute the rigor of immanent critique.

By contrast, the method of defetishizing (also called *unveiling* or *unmasking*) critique is generally an unmasking of an illusion and can point in two diametrically opposed directions: either back toward immanent critique, in what is often called *ideology critique*; or toward a deeply antifoundational method that does no more than clear the ground of illusions without revealing what might be called real interests or valid normative grounding. As a result, there are different ways of doing critical philosophy that point in radically different epistemological directions.

The classical expressions of immanent critique, from Hegel and Marx to Horkeimer and more contemporary philosophers like Rahel Jaeggi, distinctly reflect the proto-scientific elements of necessity and classification. In contrast to mere internal criticism, which identifies connections and establishes discrepancies, immanent criticism argues that the internal contradictions are inherent to the object critiqued, that the transformations resulting from the contradictions are the product or "ferment" of that necessary relation, and that the transformed values, norms, and practices remain "internal" to the original object of critique. As Jaeggi suggests in her chapter on immanent criticism in her book *Critique of Forms of Life*—which offers one of the most rigorous recent reconstructions of the method of immanent critique—the model of immanent critique depends on there being a dialectical contradiction within the object that itself produces a transformation that is a rational learning process necessarily bringing about a resolution (in the Hegelian sense of an overcoming or sublation) of the contradiction: "the results of immanent criticism—the transformation that it has initiated—represent in each case the *correct* (and *unavoidable*) solution to a problem or a crisis to which a particular situation (a social practice or institution) has succumbed," in Jaeggi's words. The value or practice that is transformed through this method remains "within" the original object: although it has been substantially transformed, it is not, at the end, a foreign or external value that one would have to argue for from the outside. It remains a value that is internal to the original formulation. All of this has a positivist or scientistic sensibility, as evidenced by the way that Jaeggi ends her discussion of immanent critique: "Normative rightness (like epistemic truth) is not something 'out there' but is the result of engagement in the process of criticism." And she adds:

"Thus, the plausibility and applicability of the model of immanent criticism depend on the possibility of demonstrating that such a process is *rational*."[1]

Insofar as the method of defetishizing critique approximates immanent critique, it too can take on this quasi-scientific nature. For Jaeggi, the critique of ideology as a method is "a specific type of immanent critique."[2] Her reconstructed version of immanent critique is, in her words, "the foundation of the critique of ideology." As a result, ideology critique, as a form of defetishizing critique, has five traits for Jaeggi: first, it takes up norms that are "constitutive" and "inherent" (or, I would say, "necessary"); second, it views the norms as inherently "inverted" or "turned" on themselves and inconsistent or deficient; third, it considers this "not a contingent contradiction, but instead one that is somehow stringent, a *necessary contradiction*"; fourth, it understands the contradiction as necessarily transformed and overcome; and fifth, "this necessary transformation" extends to "*both reality and the norms*." In the process—a process that is viewed as "a *process of evolution and learning*"—the new norms remain integral to the original setting and thus are not a matter of external critique. As she writes, "The 'new' is always already a result of the transformation of the 'old' which is 'sublated' in it (in the three senses of the term—negated, preserved, and transposed) to a higher level."[3] As a form of immanent critique, Jaeggi's version of ideology critique retains all the rigor and quasi-scientific elements that push it in a positivist epistemological direction. And, of course, Marx's style of defetishizing or unmasking critique, which as Peter Baehr notes has been perhaps the most influential, was intimately tied to dialectical materialism.[4]

But other forms of defetishizing critique, such as Foucault's theory of knowledge-power, or later, of regimes of truth, or even certain later Adorno-Horkheimer writings, perform the act of unveiling in a dramatically different manner—one that pushes in a postfoundational epistemological direction. These types of unmasking do not depend on anything like a rational learning process, do not require a concept of the rational or of progress (no matter how limited), and do not incorporate requirements of necessity or inherent internal contradictions. They act instead to clear ground, revealing the illusory nature of belief systems that mediate domination and oppression, without arguing for the correctness of a resolution, the suggestion of an overcoming, or the validity of transformed values, norms, or practices. They leave us in a bare or naked situation where we realize that we have been operating on the basis of an illusion (such as, in *Discipline and Punish* for instance, the naturalness of disciplinary techniques), or falsely believing in a notion of progress (such as, for instance, that the prison is more humane than corporal punishment). In unmasking those beliefs, these forms of defetishizing critique do not claim that another way of seeing the world is correct, nor do they claim that the unmasking is the necessary product of an inherent internal contradiction. As critical theorists, we may, in our impulsiveness, substitute a new way of being for the old, but the critical method itself does not impose any. It chips away at foundations; it does not replace them.

There is, in other words, a deep tension between the two methodological extremes: strong immanent critique on the one hand, and defetishizing critique on the other. At the extremes, those two methods are at odds, mutually exclusive. They rest on different epistemologies. They are in conflict. At the very core of critical philosophy as a method, then, there is a clash between immanent and defetishizing critique—between the scientism of the first and the endless constructivism or antifoundationalism of the second. This is very similar to the theoretical conflict that was inscribed in Horkheimer's original vision for critical theory in 1937 and that I highlighted, historically, through all these stages of critical challenges, reactions, and responses. The history that I have traced is one of constant epistemological tension that effectively pushed the different critical theorists further and further apart.

The tension, in fact, at times, is so great that one may wonder whether it even makes sense to assemble the various strands of critical philosophy under one single rubric. The temptation, for instance, to recategorize the late Habermas into liberal political philosophy reflects that. Should we even retain the single label of *critical philosophy* for all these critical interventions? Or is it too problematic, or even imperialist? Those are difficult questions, especially given the widening gap over time, as Marx receded and was replaced, for some, by Kant or Hegel or even Nietzsche.

But the fact is that all the different versions of critical philosophy that I have discussed share a number of essential common elements—even if some of those elements need to be adjusted. They share too much not to be conceptualized together. They have too much in common and, most important, they have a similar emancipatory ambition to make the world more equal, solidary, and socially just. In the end, the reason that it is essential to group these strands of critical theory together under one rubric, critical philosophy, is that they share central theoretical features that set them apart from the other dominant traditions of progressive contemporary thought (namely, liberal political theory, analytic philosophy, positivist social science, and even postpositivist social science). Obviously, the various critical strands all differ from Burkean and conservative thought and the

New Right—that goes without saying. But they also differ in essential and important ways from other progressive or liberal theories. This is due to the common features they share—despite the points of friction.

The Elements of a Critical Theory

Brilliant critical philosophers such as Amy Allen, Seyla Benhabib, and Rahel Jaeggi, as well as more analytic philosophers such as Raymond Geuss, have clearly articulated major common elements of critical philosophy.[5] Taking a step back from their analyses and reflecting on the long tradition of critical philosophy from before Marx and Nietzsche to the present, I would identify six dimensions that run through most, if not all critical theoretic work. I have, naturally, already touched on them at various points in this discussion. For the purposes of this theoretical analysis, I would group them under the following six headings:

1. The reflexivity of the critical theorist
2. The importance of mental categories and constructs
3. The method of immanent critique
4. The method of defetishizing critique
5. The essential relation between theory and praxis
6. The goal of human emancipation

These six dimensions are central to most, if not all of the critical interventions that I have discussed thus far. The order in which I list them is not essential, though it does reflect a certain logic. Some of these dimensions are not in dispute, I would argue, and do not cause friction. The first, second, fifth, and sixth dimensions, for instance, at a general level, are not in doubt and are not at the root of the theoretical and methodological problems. So let's begin with those.

The first, the reflexivity of critical theorists, is a quintessential element that distinguishes critical theory from positivist and postpositivist social science (insofar as the latter is understood as attempting to achieve objectivity through minor empirical tweaks and self-awareness of the researcher) and analytic philosophy. It was just as central to the birth of the Frankfurt School as to the genealogical method from Nietzsche to Foucault and Butler, as Martin Saar demonstrates well.[6] It is equally central to the situated self and self in context in Seyla Benhabib's writings as it is to Rainer Forst's theory of justification.[7] It is at the core of Jaeggi's critique when she emphasizes that "in so far as crises and problems not only exist objectively but are produced by subjects, criticism is at the same time a component of the crisis—and as such is part of what constitutes the dynamics of forms of life."[8] The act of criticism is historically interrelated with the crises that are produced by human subjects. Reflexivity is at the heart as well of Edward Said's study of Orientalism. "We must take seriously," Said writes, "Vico's great observation that men make their own history, that what they can know is what they have made."[9] It reflects an understanding that critical theorists inevitably and necessarily affect their object of study and are simultaneously shaped by it, so that critical theorists can never speak in universal or transhistorical terms that do not reflect the relations of power that shape the contemporary moment. The minute critical theorists speak of universal norms or transhistorical rights or transcendent values, they speak in liberal political theory, no longer critical theory. I would argue that most (if not all) critical theorists would agree with this, although it may have slightly different implications and meaning depending on different conceptions of history.

The second dimension, the importance of ideas and ways of thinking and seeing the world, also runs through most (if not all) critical interventions. Most critical theorists agree that domination today is mediated by mental constructs, whether one calls this ideology, knowledge-power, regimes of truth, Orientalism, othering, heteronormativity, or something else. Domination does not happen directly or materially alone; it is mediated by systems of belief. The specific schema of the ideational varies widely, but most reject the idea, in Jaeggi's words, "that domination today has an immediate effect or impact."[10] Even the most materialist critical theorists tend to retain some role for the phantasmagoria of the human mind. Most critical theorists are focused on mental constructs, which is what accounts, in fact, for the epistemological detour I have been describing and decrying.

The fifth dimension, the relation of theory and praxis, is at the core of critical philosophy as well. It is what animates the critical enterprise. The interpretation of that relation, though, varies. It is tempting to call this element the "unity" of theory and praxis, but that is precisely where the disagreements lie, at least in interpreting the notion of unity. Despite that, there is no question that today, critical theory retains at its core an interrogation of the essential relationship between theory and practice. It is that relationship that I will return to in part III of this work.

The sixth dimension, the goal of emancipation, is also not in question—though it too is subject to different interpretations, as I will discuss in part II. But the ambition of emancipation has been part of critical philosophy since its inception. An ideal of emancipation was at the heart of Kant's definition of Enlightenment as a coming of age and maturity. It was at the core of Hegel's idea of spirit actualizing itself. Critical philosophy in the nineteenth century reoriented this emancipatory ideal to the ends of equality, solidarity, autonomy, and social justice. These critical values were at the root of Marx's theory of human emancipation, and they continue to infuse critical theories today. They are what inspire Seyla Benhabib in her writings on utopia and emancipation.[11] They run through Honneth and Forst, and Jaeggi, and Saar.[12] They are why Luc Boltanski, a critical theorist who is critical of critical theory, gives his book *De la critique*, published in 2009, the following subtitle: *Précis de sociologie de l'émancipation* (a sociology of emancipation). The critical project, Boltanski writes, is "an intervention aimed at the emancipation of the dominated classes, until now coerced into compliance."[13] As we saw earlier, emancipation was at the heart of Horkheimer's project, of Foucault's turn to practices of the self, of Spivak's interventions in subaltern studies. It is identified as a core element even in the analytic treatment of critical theory in Raymond Geuss's succinct definition of critical theory as "a reflective theory which gives agents a kind of knowledge inherently productive of enlightenment and emancipation." As Geuss emphasizes, critical theories "are inherently emancipatory, i.e. they free agents from a kind of coercion which is at least partly self-imposed, from self-frustration of conscious human action."[14]

Immanent and Defetishizing Critique

At a theoretical level, then, it is the potential clash between the remaining two common elements of critical theory—the methods of immanent and defetishizing critique—that sparks the epistemological tension. Benhabib and Jaeggi provide rigorous philosophical treatments of immanent critique and ideology critique in the Hegelian tradition in their treatises *Critique, Norm, and Utopia* and *Critique of Forms of Life*.[15] Let me offer here a contemporary version of these critical methods that is shorn, as much as possible, of the Hegelian jargon. The fact is, these methods are central to critical interventions that do not all embrace Hegel's philosophical system. So let me reformulate the methods—and the conflict—in a more general manner.

The first method, immanent critique, is often considered the crown of critical theory. For some, it is the single most characteristic method that defines critical theory.[16] For others, it is the genus that produces, as a subset, ideology critique.[17] The idea of immanence is to accept and examine the inner workings (premises, norms, values, practices, aspirations) of the object of critique in order to reveal internal contradictions that serve as the motor of a transformation to improve those norms or values or practices. In this sense, it is a specific type of internal critique that enters its object in order to avoid immediate resistance.[18] What has always been powerful about the method of immanent critique is precisely that it formulates criticism on the basis of the values of its object. So it does not have to reach outside its object or convince others of different values. It starts within its object of critique and accepts its values. That is far easier or more seamless than to have to impose other values or outside values on someone else. Formally, immanent critique differs, in this way, from external critique; but it also is not merely internal critique. It differs from simple internal critique, such as a *reductio ad absurdum* argument, for instance, that would demonstrate the internal incoherence of a position; immanent critique, by contrast, is an evolved form that utilizes an internal contradiction not to demonstrate the impossibility of the proposition (e.g., "if you believe nothing is true, that cannot possibly be true"), but to lead us forward toward something else that is better. In immanent critique, the critic excavates contradictions that lead forward. In effect, the social contradictions lead toward social emancipation. David Harvey explains this in a synthetic way:

> Critical theory at its most abstract and general level... begins as a formal "negativity." As a dissenting motif, it selects some tradition, ideological premise, or institutionalized orthodoxy for analysis. As immanent critique, it then "enters its object," so to speak, "boring from within." Provisionally accepting the methodological presuppositions, substantive premises, and truth-claims of orthodoxy as its own, immanent critique tests the postulates of orthodoxy by the latter's own standards of proof and accuracy. Upon "entering" the theory, orthodoxy's premises and assertions are registered and certain strategic contradictions located. These contradictions are then developed according to their own logic, and at some point in this process of internal expansion, the one-sided proclamations of orthodoxy collapse as material instances and their contradictions are allowed to develop "naturally."[19]

The idea is to find the internal contradictions within, say, capitalism that will necessarily push us beyond capitalism. These contradictions include, for instance, crises of capital accumulation, profit maximizing that leads to machines replacing human labor, and tendencies toward inequality—that themselves necessarily produce an internal process of evolution that pushes us toward emancipation.

Here is a modern example: In Thomas Piketty's early work on capitalism and also in his *Capital in the Twenty-First Century*, he developed the thesis known as "R > G." This thesis holds that, in the long term, the average return on capital (R) tends to be greater than the rate of economic growth (G), resulting in an economic law that the holders of capital will gradually become wealthier than the rest of the population. This imbalance, in essence, represents an internal contradiction in capital that would necessarily lead to greater and greater inequality and, ultimately, to the demise of capitalism. Piketty has abandoned the hypothesis since the publication of *Capital*; but notice that it represents a strong version of immanent critique: an inherent contradiction in capital that would necessarily undermine capitalism.[20]

There are stronger and weaker versions of the method of immanent critique. When Max Horkheimer writes, for instance, in *Eclipse of Reason* that "the contradiction between the existent and ideology [is] a contradiction that spurs all historical progress," he is offering a strong, transhistorical version. Horkheimer there speaks of necessity and inevitable processes. "Again and again in history," he emphasizes, "ideas have cast off their swaddling clothes and struck out against the social systems that bore them."[21] In his 1937 article, Horkheimer repeatedly proposes strong versions of necessary contradictions. For Horkheimer, bourgeois society produces contradictions and excessive friction that make men feel alienated from their work and produce wars and wretchedness. He writes that in "the bourgeois type of economy," "the life of society as a whole proceeds from this economy only at the cost of excessive friction, in a stunted form." He discusses "the contradiction-filled form of human activity in the modern period." These inherent contradictions produce a situation where "their work and its results are alienated from them, and the whole process with all its waste of work-power and human life, and with its wars and all its senseless wretchedness, seems to be an unchangeable force of nature, a fate beyond man's control." In critical theory, Horkheimer argues, those who adopt the critical attitude are conscious of the contradiction at the heart of society between the willed totality of society and all the "war and oppression." This is the "world of capital": People have come to "recognize the contradiction that marks their existence," and this will lead to emancipation. This contradiction is what Horkheimer refers to as the "whole condition of the masses," namely, "unemployment, economic crises, militarization, terrorist regimes" that are all due to capitalist modes of production, to "circumstances of production which are no longer suitable to our time," and to selfishness, private property, and the ideal of private interests.[22] In perhaps a perfect articulation of the strong version of immanent critique, Horkheimer writes:

> If we take seriously the ideas by which the bourgeoisie explains its own order—free exchange, free competition, harmony of interests, and so on—and if we follow them to their logical conclusion, they manifest their inner contradiction and therewith their real opposition to the bourgeois order.[23]

This is a pristine version of strong immanent critique.

The strongest versions tend to derive from Hegel and Marx. They are modeled on the necessary evolution of reason and consciousness in Hegel's *Phenomenology of Spirit*, as well as on Marx's inversion of that dialectic into historical materialism. But not all internal critique is of this strong version. There are also thinner versions that do not embrace the absolute necessity of internal contradictions and allow greater historical contingency, but nevertheless enter the object of critique and use the internal values and norms as the best way to argue for change. Deleuze, for instance, can be interpreted to have used, at times, a more experimental version of immanent critique, as Colin Koopman shows. On this mode, "philosophy is a pursuit in the modality of a critical experimentation *from within*, and takes as its basic focus the conditions of indeterminacy that enable experimentation."[24] John Rajchman explains this well in his introduction to *Pure Immanence*, a collection that includes Deleuze's own essay by that name, "Immanence: A Life."[25]

The same is true of defetishizing critique: there are stronger, more scientistic versions and epistemologically thinner versions as well. Defetishizing critique comes in different variations, from ideology critique to regimes of truth. The first, again, tends to trace to German idealism; the latter has been shorn of that heavy luggage. Regardless, it is fair to say that it is a common method that threads through most critical theory work. Defetishizing critique is, in essence, "a procedure of analysis whereby the given is shown to be not a natural fact but a socially and historically constituted, and thus changeable, reality."[26] Let me begin this time from the other end and discuss first thinner versions of defetishizing critique.

A good illustration is François Ewald's analysis of liberalism in his book *The Birth of Solidarity.* In that work, originally published in 1986, Ewald unveils liberal ideas regarding poverty in the legal domain in early nineteenth-century France. There was a particular way of conceiving of poverty that shaped judicial decision-making at the time and produced a legal regime of individualized responsibility. That way of thinking, or what Ewald himself refers to as "the rule of liberal judgment," essentially provided as follows: "The causes of poverty are not to be found anywhere other than in the poor themselves, in their moral dispositions, in their will. *Poverty is a way of behaving.* It must be analyzed and combatted as such. The poor alone are responsible for a state from which they alone can remove themselves." This liberal ideology gave way, over the course of the nineteenth century, to the necessity of industrialization, which resulted, as Ewald demonstrates, in the replacement of civil law tort remedies by a worker's compensation system of insurance, or what he calls social law, that ultimately gave birth at the turn of the twentieth century to the welfare state. Ewald's argument is that these ways of thinking invisibly shape juridical decision-making and have real effects on the way we organize society. In this case, the transformation of these rules of judgment gave birth to what Ewald describes as "a society that would be called, for better or worse, insurantial."[27]

In this work, Ewald is demonstrating how ways of seeing the world change over time and how they have real material effects on legal regimes and societal outcomes. In this history of the French welfare state, he is unveiling how probability became politicized. He demonstrates how industrial power integrated French society by assuming the risk of work accidents, and in the process, unveils the birth of a twentieth-century insurantial society that, incidentally, is now itself at risk. But at no point does Ewald claim that the conflicts at the heart of the earlier ideological constructs, or of the ones that came into being with workman's compensation schemes, were necessary in any sense, nor that they were better or reflected a learning process, nor that there was a progressive evolution of the internal values and norms of the earlier regime. There are transformations and differences, but no necessity; moreover, the notion that the transformed values or norms or practices remain internal to the original earlier regime is beside the point and impossible to verify or test. Ewald offers a form of ideology critique that is shorn of the necessity and quasi-scientism of strong immanent critique.

Another illustration is Judith Butler's writings on performativity, which I discussed in chapter 2. In these writings, Butler unmasks naturalized conceptions of gender without replacing those with others, without reaching solid ground. She unmasks to reveal not the truth, but rather a space for ethical choice. These thinner styles of critique remain wedded to reflexivity and self-criticism—to the idea that one is always vulnerable to the next round of critical work. These critiques entail endless work on the self—or in Martin Saar's words, on "your own culture, your milieu, your family, your *genus*"—and this self-criticism, central to these more genealogical approaches, resists the temptation to reach an objective or neutral ground, the ground of truth. As Saar writes, "this seems to be one of Foucault's implicit objections to ideology critique in the neomarxist sense, on the basis that the more classical modes of social critique miss this point and try to take a view from the outside or form an allegedly anthropological neutral ground."[28]

In contrast to these thinner styles of defetishizing critique, other critical theorists propose a version of ideology critique that maps onto the strongest version of immanent critique. Rahel Jaeggi, for instance, argues for the return, reconstruction, and revitalization of a form of ideology critique as a form of immanent critique and "as a form of social critique."[29] To begin with, Jaeggi defines ideology as a systematic set of beliefs that have real-world effects and consequences, but that are mistaken or wrong—notice the use already of a more determinate language of right and wrong, and error. Ideologies represent, in her words, "a false interpretation of this state of affairs."[30] When Jaeggi speaks about a person having an ideology, she has in mind the fact of someone being caught or held in the grip of that false interpretation. It is important to emphasize that Jaeggi does not have a merely sociological understanding of ideology, like Karl Mannheim; rather, she infuses the notion of ideology with the idea of falsity and error.[31] The term *ideology* is not reduceable to error or mistake, but those dimensions are integral parts of her idea of ideology. In addition, there has to be the fact that persons are caught in the grip of this systematic set of beliefs. Jaeggi's conception of ideology has these two central elements: error and stickiness. And on the basis of this definition of ideology, Jaeggi articulates four key dimensions to a reconstructed and robust critique of ideology. First, it represents a critique of domination understood as a critique of the naturalization of processes of domination. Second, it reveals the inherent internal contradictions and inner inconsistencies of the situation. Third, it is always a hermeneutic of suspicion, and in this sense is dubious or skeptical of individuals' own interpretations and of their stated self-interests. Fourth and finally, it brings together analysis and critique in the sense that analyzing a state of affairs is part of, not a precondition to, the critical process.[32]

Ideology critique, for Jaeggi, represents an unmasking that reveals the normative character of certain understandings and interpretations. In this sense, it has what she calls "*second order* normativity": it exposes the hidden normativity of positions, and in that sense is normatively significant. But it is more than that too, she claims. Jaeggi argues that critique of ideology develops "standards based on the very situation it criticizes." It does this in a dialectical manner. Jaeggi writes that "it does this following a pattern of determinate negation (or of a 'dialectic process of development'), or, in other words, according to a principle that is crucial for the Hegelian variant of immanent critique: the right follows from a 'sublating' overcoming of the wrong."[33]

For Jaeggi, it is not just a question of extricating an ideal from within a situation or confronting it with a prefabricated ideal, but rather of developing the normativity from the internal contradictions and the contradictory dynamic of reality. Ideology critique then functions along the following lines. First, it takes norms inherent to the social situation, and in that sense, it is internal. Jaeggi views these as justified and reasonable norms, not just matters of fact. Second, it sees these norms as inverted or turned on themselves—not just weak, but internally inconsistent. Third, it focuses on these internal inconsistencies and views them as necessary, not merely contingent contradictions. There is something about the norms themselves, about the very character of the norms, that produces the deficiency. Fourth, it is transformative. It seeks to overcome the contradiction and turn it into something new and positive. The idea is not simply to return to the original state or to reestablish the previous order, but to move us forward. Fifth, it argues that the deficiency is in the norms themselves, and that our understanding of those norms needs to be transformed as well. It's not just that there is a contradiction in the situation, but that there are deficiencies in the norms that require "*a transformation of both reality and the norms*," Jaeggi emphasizes.[34] The result is that ideology critique produces a new reality, but in the course of creating that new reality, the norms themselves are transformed toward a fuller or more comprehensive understanding of those norms themselves.

In sum, Jaeggi's strong version of ideology critique has a conception of progress that depends on a necessary internal contradiction, a Hegelian notion of sublation, and an idea that the transformed values or practices remain internal to the object of critique and can lead to a correct or normatively right form of life. Those are far more demanding criteria, and they point in the direction of a much more solid or foundational epistemic sensibility.

Steven Lukes, like Jaeggi, rehabilitates and reconstitutes a strong version of ideology critique. In an article in 2011 titled "In Defense of False Consciousness," Lukes argues for the workability of the Marxian concept of false consciousness. As opposed to those who deride the term as vulgar Marxism, he believes that the idea of false consciousness functions well. Drawing on his brilliant earlier book, *Power: A Radical View*, Lukes offers a step-by-step defense of the idea of false consciousness, which he compared negatively to Foucault's framework of knowledge-power and regimes of truth. In contrast to Foucault, Lukes argued that the concept of false consciousness allows the unveiling of erroneous ideologies that ultimately permit an accurate analysis of people's real interests. Lukes emphasizes that, *contra* poststructuralists, "there is truth to be attained."[35] For Foucault, by contrast, Lukes writes that "there can be no liberation from power, either within a given context or across contexts; and there is no way of judging between ways of life, since each imposes its own 'regime of truth.'"[36] The contrast, here, to thinner notions of defetishizing critique could not be clearer.

The Crux of the Problem

The problem is that the two extremes represented by these critical methods—on the one end, the stronger version of immanent critique and at the other, the thinner version of defetishizing critique—are incompatible and irreconcilably in tension. Critical theorists who deploy a genealogical method of unmasking reject the necessity and quasi-scientific dimensions of a strong version of immanent critique, and those who deploy the latter are simply unsatisfied with the former.

The problem is not just taste or preference for one method over the other. The problem cannot be resolved simply by giving critical theorists the option to go one way or the other. It cannot be resolved simply by going à la carte on a methods menu. Critical theorists cannot choose to deploy strong immanent critique at some times and thinner genealogical unmasking at others. The reason is that the two methods are epistemologically contradictory. One is grounded on the notion that the critique produces a normative order that is correct and can serve to justify practices and institutions. This first approach achieves a form of correctness or truth. The second defies that very idea. It is based instead on the idea that an unmasking only clears the ground of an illusion, but is subject to further unmasking. It does not reveal a truth. It leads to a place that calls for an ethical or aesthetic form of judgment. In other words, the two methods lead to radically different places: one that allows claims of truth and validity, the other that calls for an entirely different type of judgment. One authorizes the critic to say that a way of life is bad or that a political choice is right; the other gives the critic no ground to say such things, but just lands the critic in a temporary, disillusioned place to act.

The epistemological chasm between the two cannot be bridged. There is simply a gulf between them—an epistemological gulf. Many critical thinkers have tried to soften the tension (and I would include myself here, regretfully, though I am certainly not alone).[37] But in the end, none of those efforts can truly bridge the epistemological breach, for two central reasons: the first having to do with the unfounded scientism of strong immanent critique, the second with the problem of rationality.

The Unfounded Scientism of Strong Immanent Critique

The first reason is that the scientism of strong immanent critique does not withstand scrutiny. Just like the Marxian philosophy of history in early critical theory, the scientism here does not hold up. It offers only unstable foundations that cannot withstand the test of time or analysis or critique.

To demonstrate this, let me return to Marx's critique of capitalism, specifically his analysis of capitalist civil society, drawing on the interpretation that Jaeggi offers in her reconstruction of the critique of ideology. Marx had critiqued capitalist ideology on the grounds that the internal ideas of freedom and equality are not realized but are internally contradictory. As Jaeggi shows, in his view, there is, on the one hand, the natural law idea of freedom and equality that posits the formal or legal parity of the participants, capitalist owners and workers. As independent contracting parties, they all supposedly should be able to act freely and equally. But the reality, on the other hand, is that there is coercion, and the coercion undermines both the freedom of the exchange, which is in truth forced because of the dearth of alternatives, and the possibility of equality, as material inequality becomes systematic. According to Marx, the ideology of freedom and equality is not just a factual matter; it is also part of what produces the coercive and unequal position of the parties. In this sense, they have a real impact on the social situation.[38]

Marxian critique challenges the idea of free and equal exchange, showing that it systematically produces inequality. Marx decodes the mechanism of surplus-value production, which necessarily causes the problem. The necessary internal contradictions of capitalism, thus, produce the resolution and a sublation of the inherent tension: as Jaeggi writes, "the contradictions between the natural law norms of equality and social reality can be solved only through a new economic and social organizational structure, but in the course of this solution, the concepts of freedom and equality are transformed towards (in this case) a fuller and more comprehensive understanding of freedom as 'positive freedom' and as a 'material understanding of equality.' Thus, the critical standard is changed in the course of the critique (or better, it both changes and stays the same)."[39] This is the process of normative transformation of the internal values of freedom and equality—internal, that is, to capitalist ideology.

There is, however, a real problem with this more scientistic approach to critique—one that, I argue, is ultimately fatal to the more foundational approach to critical theory. The problem is that there is no way to determine whether what emerges from the normative transformation is really the same as, or even a modified version of, the original values of freedom and equality, or if we face different values entirely—in other words, external values that would call for an external critique. In this illustration, it is simply unclear whether the question of internal versus external is helpful, or operative, or can guide us. The values at the end are so fundamentally different. The modified notions of freedom and equality are so foreign to the original capitalist ideology. They may have the same label, but they are simply foreign. It is not clear that one really emerges organically from the other, and it requires a nineteenth-century taxonomy or nosology to parse whether these hybrids belong to the original family or are now their own genus. But that exercise is pointless because, in this situation, the person trapped in capitalist ideology will say that those new versions of liberty and equality are simply foreign to capitalism.

The values of positive freedom and the material understanding of equality do not speak for themselves. Their reattachment to earlier capitalist ideas—illusions, actually—of free markets, meritocracy, and just distributions does not work at legitimating them or convincing others. All the work will have to be done through more modern forms of persuasion and politics. The elements of "necessity," of "inherence," of "internal contradiction," and of "a rational learning process" are nineteenth-century clutter that is superfluous to contemporary politics and political discourse. They reflect a will to truth that is out of step with reality, with contemporary society, with present-day politics, and paradoxically, with the original impetus of critical philosophy. This misplaced scientism has plagued critical philosophy since its inception, resurfaced throughout the history of critical theory, and produces endless epistemological detours, distractions, and internecine battles.

The proto-scientific tendencies of immanent critique, just like the Marxian philosophy of history, is indefensible today and undermines critical praxis. We need to let go of it. That is what I recognize as valuable in Amy Allen's intervention. It is also what I see in part, at a theoretical level, in Axel Honneth's theoretical work in *The Idea of Socialism*—where he abandons a Marxian philosophy of history and advocates a form of experimentalism. It is what I sense even in Jaeggi's constant effort to minimize the notion of progress by always qualifying it as "not in a very strong sense"[40]—even if she retains a problematic faith in rationalism, I would argue. Once and for all, though, critical philosophy has to let go of its misplaced scientism.

The Problem of Rationality

The second reason is that immanent critique—and, for that matter, a critical theory of justification—cannot ground itself on a claim to rationality, to the reasonable, or to reasonableness. The idea that a political, moral, or legal judgment could be "reasonable" or "rational" (or, for that matter, in any way true and correct) is nothing more than a vain attempt to achieve consensus or resolution in a manner that masks the relations of power that make it possible to believe that a part stands for the whole. The idea of reasonableness is an artifact of a time and a maneuver that we, critical theorists, should have gotten over by now. It is an illusion that masks the imposition of the partial for the whole.

As a historical matter, the idea of reasonableness was a valiant attempt of the Enlightenment to rid itself of religious dogma, but, like every unveiling of an illusion, it too produced a temporary resolution that later proved itself to be just another illusion. It did not achieve the universality that it hoped for, but showed itself, again and again, to impose the partial as the whole—as, for instance, when our enlightened founders declared all men to be equal while they enslaved African men, women, and children; or when our enlightened justices declared that equal protection of the law justified racial segregation or the internment of American citizens of Japanese descent; or when our best jurists declared that due process allows the summary execution of American citizens abroad. Again and again, the claim to reason had to be revised and corrected because it always was, and is, an imposition of a partial understanding on the whole, an imposition of consensus where there is none—or when there should not be.

As an empirical matter, the idea of reasonableness is no more than an attempt to achieve consensual agreement in a context where, as a factual matter, there will never be consensus. It necessarily imposes a partial judgment on the whole, and insofar as it makes a claim to correctness or neutrality or objectivity, it effectively infuses that partial resolution with authority. And as a philosophical matter, even if everyone hypothetically agreed, the claim to reasonableness elides the social order and hierarchies that produce that agreement, and in that sense, it elides the relations of power in society that makes possible the hypothetical universal agreement.

When people claim reasonableness in politics, they are trying to achieve agreement between everyone so that the rules of politics can be perceived as consensual. They are trying to reconcile differences, negotiate disagreements, and reach a plane where most everyone, individually and together, agree on the political choice or outcome. They aspire to achieve both equality (in the sense that everyone must equally agree and is entitled to a voice in the decision-making) and autonomy (in the sense that everyone is freely giving their own agreement to the political thing). This is captured well in Rainer Forst's formulation that "the justification on which everything turns is one which they [subjects] can accept individually and jointly as free and equal persons, where their acceptance or rejection are themselves in turn governed by specific norms."[41] But for anyone who has seen closely how justice is meted out or how political compromises are reached, the idea that subjects individually and together reach agreement on politics, law, or morality is a figment of the imagination; and when that wishful thinking becomes a claim to justification, it is a dangerous illusion that masks all the relations of power that make it possible, at that time, to believe that a partial resolution is actually the voice of the whole, or that the voice of the whole does not rest on social hierarchies that some would contest if they saw them in the light of day.

In the juridical domain, the idea of reasonableness—historically associated in the common law, tellingly, with the "reasonable man" or what English judges referred to as "the man on the Clapham omnibus"—is nothing more than a judicial will that is masquerading as neutral or correct determination. In the political domain, we never reach agreement on the reasonableness or justifiability of a decision or outcome. There is never quasi-universal or consensus reasonableness. We use voting mechanisms, we try to exclude people, we use a little coercion, we seduce, we threaten, or we use all kinds of ploys to achieve a majority. But that resolution does not embody reasonableness and should never be defined as the reasonable, even under good conditions of deliberation. In our discursive practices and in the public sphere, we never come close to achieving the type of quasi-universality that reason aspires to. In the moral domain as well, we are hardly ever close to the kind of consensus that could be called near-universal. We are not even in agreement as to the method or philosophical approach to take to morality—whether utilitarian or deontological, for instance. To impose any lesser degree of agreement as reasonableness is to impose criteria that, by definition, not everyone has agreed to. That is what we do when we call something reasonable, and that is precisely imposing the partial for the whole, by means of relations of power. To believe that the result is in fact reasonable is precisely the illusion. It is the illusion of reason that hides the relations of power at play.

In the halls of justice, the reasonable and the justified are never even close to being universal, or "individually and jointly" acceptable, or interpretable through a universalizable norm. It is always a partial judgment that is the product of power struggles. When anyone calls it reasonable or justified, they are simply trying to impose their will as the will of everyone. If they claim reasonableness, they are simply trying to hide the relations of power. They are using reason as an illusion.

The point is not that reason always leads us down a dark path, nor that there is a negative dialectic of reason. Sometimes it may lead in a direction that many of us fully sympathize with—for instance, desegregated schools or same-sex marriage as a form of life. But to suggest that that is reasonable is blinking reality. It is the product of shifting relations of power in society—and it is fragile. Reason is in no sense unidirectional, bad or good for that matter. But the advent of reason did not historically, and does not actually, bring us to a place where power no longer circulates; it just circulates differently. Different individuals and groups have a privileged position with reason, as opposed to religious dogma for instance. The civilian judges, academics, philosophers, and lay experts have the authority now—not the popes and priests any longer. But that has by no means produced a condition that could be called rational, reasonable, valid, or correct.

The Problem of Truth

This brings us, then, to the very heart of the dispute: the problem of foundations and normative order, which, in the end, is just a delicate way of speaking about the problem of truth. The source of the tension that pushed critical theory down its epistemic detour is precisely the question of truth. Truth is what has wracked critical philosophy since its inception. Foundations and truth, as well as their cognate concepts of validity, justification, objectivity, correctness, rightness, and notions of reasonableness, universality, and universalizability, are at the bottom of the disagreements and contestations between the various strands of critical theory.

Here is the nub of the problem. The fields of philosophy can be ordered on a descending scale with respect to the level of certainty that most sophisticated thinkers are willing to consider appropriate for any distinct realm. The rank ordering, from highest to lowest, tends to go something like the following: ontology, epistemology, jurisprudence, politics, morality, ethics, and aesthetics. Most sophisticated thinkers likely would discuss ontology in terms of the existence or being of objects; epistemology in terms of knowledge or certainty; jurisprudence in terms of correctness or authority; politics in terms of justifiability; morality, in terms of validity; ethics, in terms of virtue or good ways of life; and aesthetics, in terms of taste or judgment. For this reason, sophisticated thinkers tend to use terms such as *fact, facticity, factual, existence,* and *reality,* in the ontological realm; *justified, valid,* and *compelling* in the normative and political realm; and a good or virtuous way of life or a sublime or stunning object in the ethical and aesthetic realms.

Along this conventional spectrum, the strong version of immanent critique pushes political and moral judgment toward the former, the greater levels of certainty—toward the fields that are more likely to make a claim to truth—whereas the thinner versions of defetishizing critique push political and moral judgment toward the latter, the realm of ethical or even aesthetic judgment. And that is what causes the fundamental and recurring clash over foundations in critical theory.

To be sure, most sophisticated thinkers today, whether they are critical or analytic, prefer to cabin the term *truth* to the ontological or epistemological fields. Sophisticated philosophers understand that there may be parallels between an assertion of truth in the context of a statement of fact and in the context of a moral judgment;[42] but they try to maintain those distinctions carefully. That is less the case in ordinary parlance and in political debate. In ordinary life, in politics and law, the concept of truth slips and slides and qualifies judgments across the spectrum. Most of us use the concept of truth not only to describe the existence of objects from an ontological perspective (e.g., "It's true that there is an ozone layer around the Earth"); and to qualify the certainty of knowledge (e.g., "I know that climate change is true"); but also to qualify the correctness of statements of law (e.g., "It's true that the states have legal authority over automobile emission standards"); the justifiability of positions in the political domain (e.g., "We hold these truths to be self-evident, that all men are created equal"); and the validity of normative judgments in the moral domain (e.g., "You truly need to recycle that plastic"); as well as, even, to state whether ethical judgments are good (e.g., "It's true that we should live a far less consumerist life"); or to qualify aesthetic judgments (e.g., "That is truly the most beautiful sunset I have ever seen"). In each of the previous examples, there are more precise and technically correct terms to use than *true*: existence for being in ontology, certainty for knowledge in epistemology, correctness for law, justifiability for political judgment, validity for moral precepts, virtue for ethics, and taste for aesthetics. But in our ordinary and political conversations, most of us tend to deploy the term *truth* across the board.

This is not the case among sophisticated thinkers, who try to maintain the distinctions for the most part. But even though sophisticated thinkers try hard, they too often slip back into claims of truth—or push their normative analysis too far toward claims of normative rightness or correctness. And this, in effect, simply replicates, like a crystalline structure, the problem of truth. Surprisingly, even sophisticated critical theorists sometimes elide the subfield distinctions and end up, at the bitter end, arguing about truth in the context of politics and morality. There seems to be, in effect, even among the most sophisticated philosophers, the same will to truth as in ordinary parlance: high-level philosophical debate on matters of politics, justice, and morality, even ethics, often devolves into a question of truth, even among progressive thinkers, and even on the most sophisticated level in political and moral philosophy, where everyone agrees that the questions revolve around the validity and justification of normative arguments and not their truth. Even there, the controversy often boils down to a claim of truth and often to an accusation that one's interlocutor is not sufficiently attentive to truth. This problem does not just plague weak philosophical fields. It strikes at the heart even of the most sophisticated debates in the field of critical philosophy. Let me give three illustrations.

The Habermas-Rawls Debate

The philosophical exchange between Jürgen Habermas and John Rawls, discussed earlier in chapter 4, is a perfect illustration.[43] Both Rawls and Habermas understood perfectly that their debate was a contest in political and moral philosophy only, between, on the one hand, Rawls's framework of political liberalism and his device of the original position (OP), and, on the other hand, Habermas's social democratic communicative action theory and his use of a universalization principle. This was clear from Habermas's first intervention in the debate, where Habermas focused on the negative consequences of the rational-choice underpinnings of the OP method on democracy.[44] It was equally clear from Rawls's handwritten notes, in which he jotted down, referring to Habermas's universalization principle, "Analogue or substitute for OP?"[45]

Both philosophers understood their contest to be a question of the validity or justifiability of the resulting norms. They mutually understood this to be a matter of political and moral philosophy, not of epistemology—a question of validity and justification, not a question of truth in the epistemological sense. Rawls had been very clear in his earlier writings that his theories of justice and of political liberalism were in practical philosophy and not in metaphysics or epistemology. As Rawls had written (and as Habermas quoted in his first essay): "The aim of justice as fairness as a political conception is practical, and not metaphysical or epistemological. That is, it presents itself not as a conception of justice that is true, but one that can serve as a basis of informed and willing political agreement between citizens viewed as free and equal persons."[46] This was not a question of truth.

In his first intervention, Habermas remains mostly in the realm of questions of validity and justification. His critique, you will recall, is that Rawls's political liberalism achieves only acceptance, in other words, a form of social stability, and not acceptability as a form of validity. The problem with Rawls's approach, put succinctly, is "the assimilation of questions of validity to those of acceptance." For Habermas, the difference between acceptance and acceptability has an epistemic character, and there is at the very least an analogy between acceptability and truth—one that Habermas accuses Rawls of eliding by his use of the term *reasonable*. But still, in this first intervention, Habermas remains on the terrain of normative validity and justifiability, for the simple reason that moral questions—by contrast to ethics, Habermas underlines—are susceptible to a validity check: "Questions of justice or *moral* questions admit of justifiable answers—justifiable in the sense of rational acceptability—because they are concerned with what, from an ideally expanded perspective, is in the equal interest of all."[47]

In his lengthy reply to Habermas, Rawls emphasizes that his own understanding of political liberalism is that it does not make a claim to truth and does not raise questions of epistemology; rather, it is only a practical political theory that "falls under the category of the political." Rawls specifically distinguishes Habermas's approach, which he qualifies as a comprehensive doctrine, as one that elides the difference between moral validity and truth.[48] In contrast to Habermas, Rawls stays on the terrain of "reasonableness," not truth. He emphasizes: "Political liberalism does not use the concept of moral truth applied to its own political (always moral) judgments. Here it says that political judgments are reasonable or unreasonable; and it lays out political ideals, principles, and standards as criteria of the reasonable."[49]

Habermas would write two further rebuttals to Rawls, each of which got somewhat more heated on the question of truth. In each of those, Habermas tried to maintain the distinction and to not simply claim truth, but this evidently got increasingly difficult for him. Habermas's first rebuttal actually has truth in its title: "'Reasonable' Versus 'True,' or the Morality of Worldviews."[50] There, Habermas responds to Rawls that his effort to remain within the practical domain necessarily fails and that it is impossible to avoid entirely the epistemological dimensions even in practical philosophy. But by his last rebuttal, "Reply to My Critics," Habermas lets his guard down and embraces the centrality of truth to *all* philosophical domains—not just epistemology, but politics, morality, and even ethics: "I cannot think of any serious philosophical study, in whatever subdiscipline, that would and could not seriously make truth claims," Habermas declares.[51] Even ethics, which he had earlier carefully distinguished from moral judgments, is not exempt.[52] "Ethical statements about what is good 'for me' or 'for us,' for instance, remain captive to the perspective of a particular understanding of oneself and the world, but we claim (with this relativizing qualification) validity for them, too. Otherwise ethical advice would be pointless."[53] At this point, though, the relativizing qualification is hardly relevant or convincing. It is just a mere parenthesis. By this point, it is clear that truth operates across the board—in politics, morality, and even ethics—it is just a question of how forcefully we make the claim to truth. In *every* subdiscipline, *serious* philosophers apparently claim truth.

So in the end, according to Habermas, the central defect with Rawls's political liberalism is that it does not allow a measure of truth to attach to the agreed-upon norms. It lacks that solid foundation on which we could say that this is true, or what others should do. It cannot make a claim to truth. In the end, all the sophistication and analytic distinctions tend to fall by the wayside, and we are left with a claim to truth even on normative and ethical questions. We are back to square one: truth and foundations.[54]

Steven Lukes on False Consciousness

The second context is my ongoing debate with Steven Lukes on the question of ideology versus regimes of truth. As you will recall, in an article titled "In Defense of False Consciousness" published in the *University of Chicago Legal Forum* in 2011, Lukes originally mounted a defense of false consciousness as a method that reveals real interests and allows critics to judge ways of life. It allows what Lukes calls a "correct view that is not itself imposed by power," in sharp contrast to Foucaultian critique.[55]

In a first reply, also published in the *University of Chicago Legal Forum* in 2011, I emphasized the common genealogy of the two frameworks—the Marxian and the Foucaultian. I underscored that both were born as forms of resistance to a more traditional epistemological model holding that an individual's stated interests should be considered accurate when they can articulate good reasons that represent the basis for their actions, what is commonly referred to as the "justified true belief model of knowledge."[56] This led me to suggest that, rather than viewing the two critical perspectives as mutually exclusive, it might be more productive to explore instead how they complement each other. As Foucault himself remarked in an interview in *Telos* in 1983, referring to the Frankfurt School, "nothing is better at hiding the common nature of a problem than two relatively close ways of approaching it."[57] Our mutual effort, I suggested, should be to explore how the commonalities and distinctions can move our critical projects forward.

I then advanced three theses. The first was that Lukes, by demanding some Archimedean point of pure knowledge, was rehearsing the problem of infinite regress—the question of whether it is "turtles all the way down" or, here, "power all the way down." This, I suggested, may not be the most constructive direction in which to push the conversation. Second, I suggested that Lukes's charge—namely, that for Foucault, "there is no way of judging between ways of life"—is not entirely correct. Foucault's genealogical (and later alethurgical) critique denaturalizes our dominant categories in a way that allows us to see, quite well, the consequences of belief systems. Showing how the idea of the delinquent or of the criminal or the madman is born, emerges, and evolves—how these truths are produced and change over different periods—denaturalizes the resulting rationalities within which they are embedded (e.g., the actuarial criminology perspective, the theory of social defense, or even the use of asylums and prisons). It creates the condition of possibility for critique. Third, and finally, I proposed that it may be productive for critical theory to explore the various sets of questions that the two approaches ask. The focus on a robust notion of falsity, I suggested, pushes the inquiry toward identifying false reasoning and revealing the incompatibility of ideological beliefs with true interests. By contrast, the focus on regimes of truth orients the inquiry on how beliefs evolve over time and how individuals participate in the processes that turn them into subjects of knowledge. The shift in focus, I argued, is productive for contemporary critical theory because the truth of ideological beliefs is actually far more complex than the simple notion of falsity conveys. Ultimately, I concluded the exchange with Lukes on a paradoxical note: it might not be Foucault's insistence on power that impedes the critique of ideology and the argument of false consciousness, but rather the concepts of truth embedded in the argument of false consciousness that impede future critical interventions down the road.

At a subsequent conference at Princeton University in April 2012, Lukes and I were invited to elaborate on our earlier exchange and reflect on our points of disagreement. By that time, having returned to Foucault's critique of Marx, I took the view that my first response may have been too facile. I argued that it may not have done justice to the real tension between the Frankfurt School's notion of falsity and Foucault's exploration of an aesthetic of existence. The turn to a notion of aesthetic judgment in the later Foucault represents a significant departure from a traditional model of truth or validity in politics and morality. Foucault's questioning of whether the discourse of good and bad is "no more than an aesthetic discourse that can only be based on choices of an aesthetic order"[58]—and his embrace of an aesthetics of existence in a later interview with Alessandro Fontana in 1984[59]—offered a pointed contrast to the Frankfurt School. The contrast, I argued, could not so smoothly be papered over, even if both traditions originate from a rejection of the justified true belief model of knowledge.

In concluding, then, what was my second reply, I emphasized that in both critical approaches, there is ultimately a form of enlightenment, but that it happens in different ways.[60] The tension, I argued, is productive. In the first view, when we shed ideological beliefs, we stand on firm ground. We have achieved and can articulate a correct state of affairs—and this, of course, places us in a righteous position. In the second view, that never fully happens. When we shed ideological beliefs, when regimes of truth shift, we are merely in another place that needs to be reexamined—a new space, where relations of power are at play, may become entrenched, may turn problematic. This is another place where we need to exercise judgment and critique.

Lukes's final rebuttal at Princeton surprised me. He was not satisfied with the temporary nature of the resolution in Foucault's view. Even if it had succeeded in lifting the veil of a noxious illusion, the fact that it had not revealed truth, but just another place where illusions might operate, did not satisfy him. What I recall most vividly, as Lukes gave his closing statement and finished our debate, is that he stressed that what we need, in the end, "is truth." I fell off my chair, literally. After all the careful work Lukes and I had done to distinguish aesthetic from moral and from political judgments, to find ways to put Marx and Foucault in genuine conversation, to be careful about validity and justification, it all boiled down to a claim to truth. All our fancy theorizing came to naught. Truth was the only issue.

Rahel Jaeggi on Ideology Critique

The third example returns to Rahel Jaeggi on ideology critique. As I have shown, for Jaeggi, the process of ideology critique as a strong form of immanent critique can ground correct norms. A rational learning process is at the heart of her ability to judge forms of life. Getting beyond social problems is a constructive process that transforms the situation on the model of Hegelian sublation. There are all three moments of sublation: negation, preservation, and transposition to a more firm position. And it is this sublation that represents the moment of progress: "The experience of crises and their overcoming is sublated in this process of experience, and that is exactly why such a *process of experience* can be understood as *progress*—as a process of change for the better (although, at this point, not in a very strong sense)." The caveat—"not in a very strong sense" of progress—reflects the fact that Jaeggi rejects a pure Hegelian philosophy of history with an internal teleology. As a result, progress needs to be understood in a weaker historical sense as a process that ends up "'doing a good job' in both a functional and an ethical sense."[61] For Jaeggi, the notion of doing a good job is one that is able to solve *more* of the problems and crises that arise or may arise.

But that caveat—a learning process as progress "not in a very strong sense"—still does not undermine the fact that Jaeggi retains a notion of normative rightness that pushes her critical theory in the direction of truth rather than ethics or aesthetics. It pushes her critical theory in the direction of ontology rather than aesthetics.

In the end, Jaeggi writes, "one criterion for judging something to be 'better than a given situation' is its capability to help solve the problems and crises that came up. A solution includes (to take up a thought of A. MacIntyre) a way to understand how the crisis in question came about and a plausible story or interpretation that manages to make the solution understandable as a solution of the problem."[62] To be sure, this is weaker than Hegel or Marx, but it retains a way of parsing normative rightness from wrong. It retains a valence of normative truth. It allows the critical theorist to tranche right from wrong in the normative space of ways of living. In this view, ideology critique is ultimately a cognitive enterprise that produces a kind of knowledge intended to lead to normative judgment.[63] It is diametrically opposed to Foucault's theory of knowledge-power, which amounted to a radical critique of knowledge and aimed to unmask precisely the illusion that it is possible to sever knowledge from power.

Getting Beyond Truth

I would argue that in these exchanges, and more generally, the claim to truth is an unnecessary and deceptive move in the end. When a sophisticated thinker, especially a critical theorist, is claiming truth in the political realm, they are overplaying their hand. They are overdoing it. They are, essentially, abusing truth. Moreover, by trying to claim the solid ground of truth, the sophisticated critic elides the relations of power that shape the institutions and practices that affect our beliefs. The imposition of a true foundation as if it were true and sure, as if it were beyond power relations—as if, in Lukes's terms, there were a "correct view that is not itself imposed by power"—hides all kinds of relations of power. The imposition of a foundation, the claim to truth, is itself a power play. Critical philosophy must avoid that.

To date, the discussion of this fundamental problem of truth in critical philosophy has been shrouded in jargon and mystification. The problems of foundations have recurred, over and over, because critical theorists have constantly reconstructed intricate, ornate systems of thought that mask the fact that they are basically dealing with the same question of truth-value and certainty. It is essential to cut through the jargon and pare down these baroque systems, in order, once and for all, to get out of this epistemological quagmire. It is vital to take a step back and honestly consider the matter.

The claim to truth, validity, and certainty in political, legal, and moral philosophy is nothing more than the quest for a solid foundation on which to ground oneself or to convince others—to assure oneself that one is living a good life, to persuade others that one is right, to convince others that one's way of living is good or better, to induce others to do as one says. It has a long and tortured history. Throughout human history, God, gods, and divine forces such as oracles provided the most solid basis for claiming correct beliefs and just actions. For Enlightenment thinkers, human reason rather than religious belief operated as that firm grounding; enlightened moral philosophers grounded right action on rules of reason, such as the universalizability or reasonableness of one's maxim. For positivist thinkers, since the nineteenth century at least, science and empirical evidence serve as the foundation on which to ground one's certitude. God, reason, science, these have constituted, throughout history, the main grounds of truth—alongside others, such as nature, might, or human nature. In ordinary life, when we seek to assure ourselves or convince others of the truth, many of us often return to one or another of these solid foundations. That was, of course, Descartes's method: to start from scratch and find the most bedrock first truth—*cogito, ergo sum*—and on the basis of that foundation, to build a series of equally solid arguments that showed us the truth and told us what to believe and how to act.

In ordinary life and politics, most of us know what truth feels or looks like. Truth is that certainty about the object I hold in my hand. Truth is the fact that each one of us someday will die. Knowing what these truths feel and look like, many of us try to mimic and extend that level of certainty to politics, law, morality, in our romantic lives, in friendships, and elsewhere. Many of us want to have the same feeling that, just as I can point to this book and say, "It is true that this is a book that I am reading," we can point to scientific studies and say, "Global climate is changing and unless we do something about it, human life on Earth will cease to exist." Many of us want to say, with the same feeling of certainty that we will someday die, that "inequality has increased in the United States over the past four decades as a result of deliberate political decisions that have benefited the wealthiest 1 percent." To achieve that level of certainty, for ourselves and to convince others, many of us make claims to truth: some marshal scientific studies, others craft reasoned arguments, and some try to enthrall others with their winsome oratory or their charisma. At other times, people refer back to human nature, especially when they discuss sexuality; others turn to Scripture; still others to sentiments, affect, or universal principles. And in disagreement, many of us turn to truth. We often start our political arguments with "The truth is" or "The fact of the matter is." On those occasions, the speaker is claiming truth to lay a foundation for himself or herself or to convince others, to seek solid ground or stable footing—to seek a foundation, rather than simply saying, "That's my opinion, you are entitled to yours." The speaker is claiming that those political or normative judgments are as solid as the truth of this book I am reading—that there is something objective or valid about them, or right, not just for the speaker, but for the listener as well.

It is precisely at those moments, when we claim truth, when we claim validity for others, that we have exceeded the bounds. We have borrowed from metaphysics a type of certainty that does not belong in politics or law or morality. And it is precisely here that we need to be more careful and honest about the noun *truth* and the adjective *true.* This is especially the case for critical philosophers who know that they should limit truth to ontology and epistemology at most, and yet they extend it or its cognate family of terms (reality, certainty, rightness, correctness) to the political and moral realms, and even the ethical realm. Critical philosophers claim to understand the family kinship and parallels, the differences between an assertion of truth in the context of a statement of fact and in the context of a moral judgment[64]; but as evidenced above, so often they simply elide the differences and call for truth in politics. When they deploy that term, they gesture toward a more permanent or universal statement about the human condition. But that is actually unnecessary. At most, they may have temporary, punctual determinations about what all the best evidence suggests right now, which they should call their better interpretation.

When we have to act, of course, we need to decide on the better interpretation. We may engage in the epistemological work of unmasking to try to rid ourselves of an illusion. But at some point, when we must act, we do, and the model we use, most often, is a rough-and-ready juridical model: we review the evidence and decide based on a burden and a standard of proof. Someone has the burden of proving. There may be a presumption one way or the other. And proof has to be established to a certain degree—whether it is just an iota of evidence, or more than

50 percent, or practical certainty. We decide on a standard and who carries the burden, and then we let the chips fall where they will. Using effectively a juridical model, we often reach a temporary judgment. But that does not mean the judgment is true. It means that it is a temporary assessment of the evidence and arguments.

This is precisely what we do in an American criminal or civil trial: the jury and judge, or attorneys in negotiation, determine whether there is sufficient evidence that satisfies the burden and standard of proof. When an American jury returns a guilty verdict in a criminal case, it is not telling the truth—although that is a common perception. The verdict is just a temporary assessment of the weight of the evidence, and it is open to later reassessment on a motion for new trial or postconviction proceeding. The verdict does not mean, by any means, that the convicted person actually, in truth, committed the crime, but just that the prosecutor, who bears the burden of proof, has marshaled sufficient evidence to satisfy the standard of proof (namely, beyond a reasonable doubt). Of course, our contemporaries project all kinds of biases and misleading interpretations and judgments into and onto the process—including racial and ethnic bias, class stereotypes, and moral panics that distort their interpretation of the evidence and reinforce their false perception that the verdict is the truth. But if we are being careful about what is going on and attentive to how best to describe the situation, a criminal verdict is no more than a temporary assessment of the evidence in relation to a burden and standard of proof. It is not *the* truth.

The term true, it turns out, is too unstable in the sense that it can only be proven wrong. Truth is never for always, or universal, or preclusive. What we ordinarily call truth is just a temporary, punctual evaluation of evidence or reasons. And once we have cut truth down to size, then we realize that it hardly makes sense to speak of truth in the political context, and it never makes sense to speak of Truth with a capital T. If we were more careful in critical philosophy, we would use the word truth much more sparingly. We might not even use it at all. It tends, misleadingly, to connote a level of certainty associated with the existence of things-in-themselves that gets improperly projected onto the validity of normative arguments or predictions about the future. Strategically, it actually weakens arguments because it allows the other side to seize on any bit of uncertainty and use that differential to demonstrate that we are making truth up. It also distracts from the larger political question of the kind of world we want to live in and of what we believe in—whether it is God, or reason, or science, or ethics.

Inevitably, at certain historical junctures, the solid foundations shift. The Enlightenment in Europe in the eighteenth century was just such a moment. At that time, the religious foundation began to crumble and was displaced by reason and rationality. A new discourse came to dominate: new words, a new language and new grammar, and new arguments, all shorn of Scriptural references and authority, became omnipresent. These paradigmatic shifts in foundations are often accompanied by fear and insecurity. Many religious thinkers viewed the Enlightenment as a deep menace, although many of us today do not believe that it led to an increase in immorality in Western society. Some, like Steven Pinker, argue that Western societies actually became less violent and that well-being increased.[65] Others contend that the scale of barbarity associated with modern slavery, imperialism and colonialism, and the world wars of the twentieth century and the Holocaust, suggest otherwise—some, like Homi Bhabha, suggest these may actually be the *consequence* of Enlightenment ideas.[66] Others remain agnostic or adhere to Richard Rorty's more reserved assessment: "When the thinkers of the Enlightenment dissociated moral deliberation from divine commands, their writings did not provoke any notable increase in the amount of immorality."[67]

Hannah Arendt voiced that worry and concern in her *New Yorker* essay "Truth and Politics," discussed in the last chapter. She feared that we had entered a time where factual truth no longer held. Many thinkers today, especially progressive thinkers, believe that we are at risk of another paradigmatic change in foundations, associated with the advent of the digital age, the birth of social media, the growth of cable news networks, and the development of accessible and cheap technology to easily alter digital evidence. The fear is that we have entered a "post-truth" age or a "post-truth" society—to borrow the Oxford Dictionary word of the year for 2016.[68] Many progressive thinkers believe that this new post-truth society is one in which alternative facts, pseudofacts, and "fake news"—to borrow the Collins Dictionary word of the year for 2017[69]—will masquerade as actual evidence, and propaganda and political spin will replace public discourse.[70] Elsewhere, I have argued that the post-truth argument may not be the best argument to make in these times, as a purely strategic or political matter.[71] But it is indeed a symptom of the epistemological chasm that has engulfed critical theory.[72] And it underscores the careful work that needs to be done to honestly address and resolve the problem of truth.

When I look back over the history of critical philosophy, it feels almost inevitable that theorists will continue to claim truth in politics. The will to truth has been with us for too long; it seems unlikely to evaporate, even after careful reflection.

Nevertheless, it is worth investigating more productive ways forward—more productive, that is, than to claim the truth. As I showed in chapter 3, Foucault offered one such approach: instead of dedicating oneself to the infinite task of distinguishing truth from falsity, especially in those domains where truth should not govern, Foucault proposed the orthogonal project of documenting the historical ways in which truth has been produced, the history of truth-telling, and the power of truth in human history.

In the next two chapters, I will articulate another approach: to take seriously the idea of unmasking and develop a radical critical philosophy of illusions. I argue that our understanding of the world and social relations are indeed mediated by mental constructs and interpretations that have effects of reality and redistribute material resources, wealth, and well-being. So many of the leading and most significant beliefs—in the benefits of natural order, the efficiency of free markets, or the threat of internal enemies—are in fact illusions that have significant consequences in terms of material distributions. I will propose an approach that lifts the veil of illusions, but not in order to discover the truth; rather, to reposition us to interpret again, but also to act. I concede that those new interpretations will eventually themselves need to be unveiled in the future, but—somewhat on that juridical model that I described earlier—I accept that we must act on them while simultaneously challenging them. I do not unmask illusions to claim truth, but rather to act and propose other interpretations that surely will need to be critiqued.

I will prefigure this unending cycle of critique, or what I call a radical critical philosophy of illusions, with a simple illustration. Simone de Beauvoir's groundbreaking writings in *The Second Sex* represented a crucial and necessary critique, a step forward that unveiled many of the illusions of patriarchy and male superiority. Beauvoir brilliantly disentangled gender (man/woman) from sex (male/female), and that conceptual move of decoupling gender from sex had dramatic ramifications for gender equality. In the process, Beauvoir's writings opened the space of praxis.[73] But they nevertheless reinforced notions of binary gender and a certain essentialism that would later be unveiled and critiqued by queer theory—which in turn would then be critiqued by trans* and other more contemporary theories. Beauvoir moved us forward and unveiled illusions, but she did not reveal truth, real interests, or, in Steven Lukes's terms, a "correct view that is not itself imposed by power." It was just a better interpretation at the time that would enable praxis and call for more critical work.

Judith Butler showed, for instance, how Beauvoir's original critique was the condition of possibility to later denaturalize gender entirely, so that all gender becomes "by definition, unnatural." By denaturalizing gender, especially the binary nature of gender, it becomes possible to imagine multiplicities of gender or a gender continuum. "Not only is gender no longer dictated by anatomy," Butler wrote, "but anatomy does not seem to pose any necessary limits to the possibilities of gender." And this would later problematize the independence of biological sex and make it possible to question the binary nature of sex as well. In effect, Beauvoir's initial intervention serves as a catalyst for later unveilings. Her initial unsuturing—the cutting of the first seam—unravels other threads and undoes a number of related knots in ways that, as Butler suggests, "Beauvoir probably did not imagine."[74]

The same could be said of Foucault's writings: his analysis in *The Punitive Society* and *Discipline and Punish* exposed the illusion of Western Enlightenment thinking in the field of punishment and social control. It revealed that, instead of punishing less, French practitioners in the nineteenth century learned to punish better, using mechanisms of discipline that included normalization, regimentation, and panopticism. Foucault's interpretations of the punitive society and of disciplinary power were productive at the time (in the early 1970s) to challenge liberal democratic forms of government and the carceral archipelagoes of the West, as opposed to those of the East. But even Foucault himself, by 1979, would critique his own interpretations for having still placed too much emphasis on the coercive dimensions, for failing to highlight the pastoral elements of governing, for inadequately theorizing our own role in our subjectivation—indeed, for somewhat ignoring the full dimension of subjectivity. Foucault was actually one of the first to point out these deficiencies and to critique his own productive interpretations at the time.

That is the work of a radical critical philosophy of illusions: it unveils not to discover truth, rather to offer a productive interpretation that can animate praxis, but that will quickly need to be critiqued. Let me spell out in the next two chapters how to breathe life into this approach and show how it works.

CHAPTER 6

Reconstructing Critical Theory

The epistemological impasse cannot easily be bridged. Instead, critical theory must be reconstructed. And it can be, as I intend to show, with the help of a conceptual device, a type of conceptual can opener that I will call the *counter*-move. Specifically, in the context of critical philosophy, the epistemological chasm can be overcome by conceptualizing, at least for a brief moment, what could be called "counter-foundational critical theory."

Counter-foundational critical theory is by no means *anti*-critical theory; rather, it is a form of contemporary critical thought that goes beyond the recurring epistemological disputes in contemporary critical theory. It operates what I would characterize as a counter-move. The conceptual prefix *counter* in *counter*-foundational critical theory indexes the resistance to positivism in early critical thought. It indexes the element of reflexivity that was there from the beginning. It aspires to overcome the recurring foundationalism and scientism in order to generate a fully autonomous critical approach. Counter-foundational critical theory becomes autonomous, in this way, when it becomes a radical theory of illusions—a theory of relations of power in flux, such that every critical unmasking forces us to reexamine the resulting redistributions of power. At that point, it continues to index, but it no longer needs to concern itself with, or argue against, recurring foundations. At that point, the original critical insight no longer needs to refer back to the object challenged. At that point, counter-foundational critical theory develops fully into its own independent way of thinking. This is an ambitious project, I believe, but it is realizable.

The Idea of a Counter-Foundational Critical Theory

A similar conceptual movement runs through Foucault's writings and method at times. A good illustration comes from Foucault's inaugural lesson to his 1981 Louvain lectures, *Wrong-Doing, Truth-Telling: The Function of Avowal in Justice.* At the close of that inaugural lesson, Foucault offers, as the overarching framework of his intervention, the notion of a *counter-positivism,* which, he explains, "is not the opposite of positivism, but rather its counterpoint."[1] The full passage is as follows:

> We often speak of the recent domination of science or of the technical uniformity of the modern world. Let's say that this is the question of "positivism" in the Comtian sense, or perhaps it would be better to associate the name of Saint-Simon to this theme. In order to situate my analysis, *I would like to evoke here a counter-positivism that is not the opposite of positivism, but rather its counterpoint.* It would be characterized by astonishment before the very ancient multiplication and proliferation of truth-telling, and the dispersal of regimes of veridiction in societies such as ours.[2]

This notion of "counter-positivism," in fact, provides the key to the Louvain lectures. The notion conveys more than merely an opposition to positivism because Foucault is admitting that he is embracing something akin to a positivistic view of the history of shifting truth-telling forms. There is, in fact, a history in the lectures. Foucault traces a series of truth-telling forms. It is a history of regimes of truth—more specifically, of regimes of veridiction and of speaking truth, which fits neatly into the broader arc of his research and lectures at the Collège de France as discussed earlier in chapter 3.

Foucault's method, both at Louvain and at the Collège, is not *anti*-positivist, but instead is a counterpoint, deploying positivistic sensibilities against narrow positivism. And the central point is that Foucault's counter-positivist method culminates in a philosophical intervention that is independent of both positivism and of anti-positivism, that does not depend on either, and that no longer merely responds to the opposition, but rather becomes its own autonomous method: a pure philosophical method, a way of seeing the world. In fact, it is perhaps the most important compass to decipher the Louvain lectures—which is why, incidentally, the passage ended up on the back cover of the original French edition, where it remains the most significant part of those lectures. It is the height of the philosophical intervention. A similar move can often be found in Étienne Balibar's writings as well, as for instance when he writes, in *Equaliberty*, "It is necessary to institute a counter-city or a counterpower in the face of legitimate power that has become the mere property of those who exercise it or the expression of governmental or administrative routine."[3]

In a similar way, it would be possible to imagine a counter-foundational critical theory—distinct from this counter-positivism—that is not anti-critical, but instead overcomes the return to foundations of critical philosophy. It indexes the original impulse of critical theory and its core insight, but it eventually gets beyond it. At its core, critical philosophy has always prized the notion of illusions: the world that we find ourselves in, rife with inequalities, injustice, and prejudice, is made tolerable by a series of illusions—the myths of individual responsibility and merit, the illusions of liberalism and free markets, the fantasy of upward social mobility, and so on. These illusions are what make our unequal world tolerable to too many of us. And they are what critical theory unmasks, unveils, reveals. But not to give way to a truth underlying those illusions—not to reveal real interests, or genuine class interests. The illusions instead give way to another set of ambitions that we will need to unmask again eventually. In this sense, counter-foundational critical thought becomes *a radical theory of illusions.*

Overcoming the Epistemological Detour

The concept of counter-critique is precisely to get beyond the original opposition from which it is born—the reflexive challenge to the idea of objectivity and foundationalism—and to generate an autonomous conceptual form. Again, this would not be in the Kantian or Hegelian sense (for a number of reasons, not the least of which is that the prefix *counter-* functions differently from the prefix *anti-*), but rather as an original counterpoint that itself becomes so powerful as to liberate itself from the oppositional relationship and transform itself into a freestanding concept, intervention, or mode of critique. Such a counter-critique would have to present more than simple resistance to the recurring foundationalism of critical theory. For it to achieve its full potential, it would need to liberate itself from its original opposition and transform itself into an autonomous, self-referential, fully articulated form of critique. This alone could guarantee that the *counter*-foundational move would develop into its own independent mode of critical philosophy.

A model for this can be found in Joseph Conrad's novel *The Secret Agent.* The character of the Professor had a flask of explosives strapped on him at all times and carried a small detonator in his hand—ready to blow himself and everyone around him to bits at any moment. By means of this device, he claimed to have gotten past the conventional opposition between revolutionaries and the police. He claimed to have overcome the mere "game" of moves and counter-moves and reached a higher—and more threatening—stage. He claimed to have transformed his reactivity into a pure force, into a form of perfection. The Professor says: "The terrorist and the policeman both come from the same basket. Revolution, legality—counter moves in the same game; forms of idleness at bottom identical. He plays his little game—so do you propagandists. But I don't play."[4]

Conrad, who always labels his characters for us, refers to the Professor as "the perfect anarchist." You will recall that it was the figure of the Professor, more than Conrad's other characters, who inspired later anarchists. What exactly, you may ask, is the ambition of this "perfect anarchist"? "What is it you are after yourself?" the Professor's comrade, Ossipon, asks him with indignation. "'A perfect detonator,'" the Professor says, in a response that Conrad describes as "the peremptory answer."[5] One can infer from Conrad's novel that the Professor himself had begun as an anarchist caught in the counter-moves that he himself disparaged—caught in the play, in the game, in the parry. And one can assume that he was originally part of that dance, that judo of counter-moves. But the implication is clear: the Professor is going beyond the mere tit-for-tat, beyond the mere back and forth, the constant parrying, and achieves instead a more *perfect* form of anarchism.

What made this the most perfect or peremptory anarchist state was precisely getting beyond the counter-move to another level—a level that was autonomous of the opposition itself. It was a pure state, independent of the back and forth between the revolutionaries and the police. Precisely because of the explosives he has strapped on himself at all times, the Professor remarks, "They know . . . I shall never be arrested. The game isn't good enough for any policeman of them all. To deal with a man like me you require sheer, naked, inglorious heroism."[6] The Professor may sound almost delirious, and self-aggrandizing for sure, but he has achieved something unique: He has moved beyond the ordinary relation of opposition.

The Professor ultimately has the last word in *The Secret Agent.* After the counterintelligence and counterespionage is all over—after Winnie Verloc's story has reached, in Conrad's words, "its anarchistic end of utter desolation, madness, and despair,"[7] after her brother's accidental explosion at Greenwich Station, her own murder of her husband, and her suicide—it is the Professor who closes the book, "the incorruptible Professor," as Conrad adds. Conrad ends:

> He was a force. His thoughts caressed the images of ruin and destruction. He walked frail, insignificant, shabby, miserable—and terrible in the simplicity of his idea calling madness and despair to the regeneration of the world. Nobody looked at him. He passed on unsuspected and deadly, like a pest in the street full of men.[8]

The Professor has become sheer force, ruin, and destruction. He has overcome his opposition to the system to become something as deadly as the pest. He has achieved the full effect of the counter-move. This overcoming is not very attractive here, but we do not always have control over the consequences of our conceptual moves.

In a parallel way, Foucault's counter-positivism in the Louvain lectures becomes a full-fledged method, completely detached from any dispute with positivism. Foucault used the counter-move extensively—in fact, one could argue that it was one of his most productive devices, a veritable conceptual-production technique. Nietzsche did as well, referring, for instance, to "art" as the "countermovement" against nihilism; and he coincidentally adds, in *Twilight of the Idols*, that "in art, man takes delight in himself as perfection."[9]

In conversation with Étienne Balibar, during his seminar on Foucault at Columbia University in the fall of 2015, we began to identify and catalogue the occurrences of the counter-move in Foucault's work. This includes the concept of "*contre-pouvoir*" in his debate with Maoists;[10] the concept of "counter-history" in "*Society Must Be Defended*";[11] the concept of "counter-conduct" in *Security, Territory, Population*, or in the same lectures, the concept of "counter-society": "In some of these communities there was a counter-society aspect, a carnival aspect, overturning social relations and hierarchy";[12] or the concept of "counter-justice" again in his debate with Maoists,[13] of the "counter-weight" to governmentality in the *Birth of Biopolitics*,[14] and of the idea of psychoanalysis as a "counter-science" in *The Order of Things*.[15] Throughout his writings, his lectures, and his interviews, Foucault constantly returned to the prefix *contre-* to create concepts, to fashion new and autonomous ideas.

The counter-move—by which I mean, to be clear, the movement of thought and practice, the action that is captured by adding the prefix *contre-* or *counter-* to another concept—is itself a conceptual factory. Its generative power is remarkable. It is not so much a concept itself, but instead the creator, the producer of concepts. The counter-move produces rich constructs. It practically defines the distinction between concept and notion: nothing here is intuitive and immediate, as are notions; on the contrary, the counter-move is complex, constructed, and stabilized over time. It is intellectual work product. It is the infrastructure to myriad new concepts. In fact, if one looks in the *Oxford English Dictionary*, for instance, the entry for "counter-" becomes a litany, a catalogue, an enumeration of *counter-* concepts: "Counter-address; counter-advise; counter-affirm; counter-ambush; counter-avouch; counter-beat; counter-bid; counter-bore,"[16] and I am still only at the beginning of the *B*s. Each term has its own early etymological use and history.

The counter-move is of central importance in reading and understanding Étienne Balibar's writings as well. There are, in his *Equaliberty* essays and many other brilliant writings, multiple deployments of the counter-move: Balibar speaks of "counter-racism" and of "counter-populism"; there is the "counter-city" and the "counterpower."[17] Then, there is also this important counter-move, which falls on the darker side of the ledger:

> The crisis of the national-social state correlative to globalization and the re-proletarianization that constitutes both its result and one of its objects from the side of the dominant classes (of financial capitalism) gives rise to a whole series of national or international political initiatives that relate to what could be called a *preventative counterrevolution*, even more than neoimperialism.[18]

There is also the counter-move that counters the counter-revolution with a "counter-counterrevolution," setting things somewhat more straight for the resisters and the disobedients among us:

> The whole question is whether a policy of this kind, more or less deliberate but perfectly observable in its effects, which combines financial, military, and humanitarian aspects and which I believe can be characterized as preventive counterrevolution, elicits a revolutionary response, or, if you like, a counter-counterrevolution, according to the schema of "going to extremes" that was largely shared among Marxist and Leninist representations of the socialist transition after the experience of the insurrections of the nineteenth century.[19]

In his culminating seminar at Columbia University in the fall of 2015, Étienne Balibar proposed that Foucault had developed a "counter-politics"—in contrast to the political, the apolitical, or even the unpolitical. Following that, at a conference at the University of Paris—Créteil on June 1, 2016, Balibar further developed this counter-move, suggesting that the central element of truth-telling in Foucault's work—of *parrhesia*, veridiction, and all its associated forms of diction—is a form of "*contre*-diction" and "*contre-conduite*," effectively placing the element of the counter-move at the very center of Foucault's thought. Balibar pointed in particular to the back covers of Volumes 2 and 3 (and now 4) of the *History of Sexuality*, which reproduce the following quote by René Char:

> *L'histoire des hommes est la longue succession des synonymes d'un même vocable. Y contredire est un devoir.*

To *contre*-dict is a duty: for Balibar, this notion of parrhesiastic contradiction has within it the seeds of a counterdemocratic principle—not in Pierre Rosanvallon's sense, but as was exercised by certain parrhesiasts such as Socrates or Diogenes. This reflects an element of the counter-majoritarian in Foucault's work. And by means of the counter-move, Foucault's intervention and turn to parrhesia become an autonomous, independent theory based on a "contra-diction" that is indexed, but that we barely see.[20]

In an article titled "In Praise of Counter-conduct," Arnold Davidson underscores how so many of the forms of resistance that we admire in Foucault's writings return to the concept of "counter-conduct":

> In a series of remarkable formulas concerning freedom, Foucault speaks of the "insubordination of freedom," the "rebelliousness of the will and the intransitivity of freedom," the "art of voluntary inservitude" and of "deliberative indocility." All of these phrases belong to the semantic field of counter-conduct and make evident the double ethical and political scope of this counter-conduct.[21]

One can sense, in Davidson's article, a kind of admiration for the concept of counter-conduct. But it is important to emphasize that the counter-move is not always or necessarily progressive. As with concepts such as solidarity[22] or internal frontiers,[23] there is an equivocal nature to counter-concepts. They too can go a bit all over the place and be deployed against the interests of a progressive agenda.

This is reflected in what Robespierre referred to as the "counter-revolutionary";[24] or, depending on your political interpretation, what Pierre Rosanvallon referred to as "Counter-Democracy." I am here again in Balibar's *Equaliberty*—or, rather, in his footnotes.

Many of us bear an almost romantic attachment to the *counter-* practice itself. It feels so intimately linked to notions of disobedience, resistance, and countering power. But it is important not to get carried away.

Counter-Foundationalism

Let me set forth as systematically as possible this concept of counter-critique, then. There is a particularity to the counter-move that distinguishes it from other political devices or mechanisms. It does not function like a dialectic. It is not an opposition that leads to a synthesis, but rather to a stage of "perfection," in Conrad's terms, that, first, merely indexes its former opposition, and, second, becomes a fully independent force, all in itself, that does not incorporate its opposition and is no longer a reaction against it. This is very different from the way that concepts generally work. It is markedly different, for instance, from the Nietzschean idea that concepts are the cumulative effect of dead metaphors, and that only when its history is forgotten can something become a concept. It may be useful, then, to delineate three dimensions of the counter-move.

The first dimension distinguishes it from the more classic or simple opposition associated with the prefix *anti-*. Adding the prefix *anti-* serves only to defeat or eradicate its object, directly. For instance, antiterrorism aims to eliminate terrorism by stamping it out, in contrast to counterterrorism, which uses the logic and strategies of terrorism to undermine it. The counter-move is more internal: it engages in a play, a movement, a dance with its object, using the force of the object against itself, in order to get beyond that game. It uses the energy of the object, as well as the internal logic of the object, to defeat it. It starts in a game with the object—as in chess, or fencing, or martial arts—but then transcends it. There is, in this sense, some proximity between the counter-move and the term *against*—as in Paul Feyerabend's *Against Method*, or in my book *Against Prediction*. *Against* is closer to *counter-* than to *anti-*, insofar as it attempts to develop a new method in the oppositional work rather than simply defeat its object.

In any event, the counter-move is different than the anti-move.[25] Returning to the example of security, specifically of counterinsurgency: Counterinsurgency uses the internal logic of Maoist insurgency to defeat an insurrection. It adopts and accepts the logic—in fact, it fully embraces it—but it tries to do it better, to reappropriate it, to redeploy it even more aggressively. It does not rest on the idea that there would be two opposing views that are contrary to each other in a dialectical confrontation. Instead, it burrows into the logic and deploys it against its opponent.

The counter-move differs as well from the Socratic dialectic (the testing of an opposing view), the Kantian model of dialectics (thesis-antithesis-synthesis), and the Hegelian method (abstract-negative-concrete). It differs, in its very foundation, from Adornian negative dialectics. It differs as well from Marx's dialectical materialism—which rests on a notion of direct opposition, as expressed in *Capital*:

> My dialectic method is not only different from the Hegelian, but is its direct opposite. To Hegel, the life-process of the human brain, i.e. the process of thinking, which, under the name of "the Idea," he even transforms into an independent subject, is the demiurgos of the real world, and the real world is only the external, phenomenal form of "the Idea." With me, on the contrary, the ideal is nothing else than the material world reflected by the human mind, and translated into forms of thought.[26]

To be sure, of course, there is a family resemblance between all these forms of opposition. Foucault was keenly aware of this, and in fact, he suggested as much in an interview, discussing what he called "countereffects," where he added: "I dare not use the word *dialectics*—but this comes rather close to it."[27] The counter-move "comes rather close" to a dialectic, but is not the same thing. It also comes close to the anti-move, but again differs. One can hear that as well in Foucault's writing, with passages for instance in *Security, Territory, Population* that read as follows: "the first element of anti-pastoral or pastoral counter-conduct is asceticism." Here and elsewhere, Foucault is struggling to pin down the conceptual move, using the term "anti-pastoral struggles" interchangeably with "pastoral counter-conducts," but trying to correct and replace the first with the second.[28]

A second dimension concerns the *internal* logic of the counter-move. It is almost an immanent form of critique, in a thin sense: The object that is being opposed is taken as such, it already exists fully, and the counter-move effectively goes into the object to oppose it. Notice how the *Oxford English Dictionary* defines the term:

"Done, directed, or acting against, in opposition to, as a rejoinder or reply to another thing of the same kind *already made or in existence*."[29]

Arnold Davidson points directly to this notion of immanence in his article "In Praise of Counter-conduct," where he writes that, as in the interiority of the relationship between points of resistance and relations of power,

> In *Security, Territory, Population*, Foucault also emphasizes the nonexteriority, the immanent relation, of conduct and counter-conduct. The fundamental elements of the counter-conduct analysed by Foucault are not absolutely external to the conduct imposed by Christian pastoral power. Conduct and counter-conduct share a series of elements that can be utilized and reutilized, reimplanted, reinserted, taken up in the direction of reinforcing a certain mode of conduct or of creating and recreating a type of counter-conduct.[30]

There is, Davidson explains, a "tactical immanence" of counter-conduct to conduct. Counter-conduct is not "simply a passive underside, a merely negative or reactive phenomenon, a kind of disappointing after-effect." In the words of Foucault, counter-conducts are not "*les phénomènes en creux*." There is a "productivity of counter-conduct which goes beyond the purely negative act of disobedience." It is in this sense that, for Davidson, "the notion of counter-conduct adds an explicitly ethical component to the notion of resistance." As a methodological matter, the *counter-* element of *counter-conduct* works in a similar way as resistance to power—as something internal, that does not reach beyond, that is not a gap or absence. Foucault talks about counter-conduct that is "used against and to short-circuit, as it were, the pastorate."[31] Notice the use of the term *against* and the idea of short-circuiting. The short circuit is tied to the internal dimension of the counter-move. It uses the circuit, the flow of electricity, against itself. Davidson comes back to this in regard to homosexuality:

> Foucault describes these relations with the same expression, *court-circuit*, that he had used to describe religious counter-conduct: "these relations create a short-circuit, and introduce love where there should be law, rule, habit."[32]

A third dimension, and perhaps the most important, is the ultimate emancipation of the counter-move, which goes beyond its oppositional object, is liberated from it, and becomes autonomous. At that point, it is no longer *counter-*. It is more like the

Professor in Conrad's *The Secret Agent*: outside the game, outside the dance, beyond the counter-moves in the same game. But it always indexes the original opposing object. The Professor is perhaps the "perfect anarchist," but he is still an *anarchist*.

When the counter-move works, it gives rise to something that is not the opposite, nor even the dance partner, but instead is perfectly autonomous and self-sufficient—a concept that functions all on its own. Counter-conduct is no longer conduct that resists something, but conduct that has become its own form, a pure form of force, disobedience, or resistance.

Let me offer a more tangible or concrete illustration: the example of jujutsu, a form of judo. As I see it, jujutsu is the perfect illustration of the counter-move. *Ju* means pliable or yielding to another, and *Jutsu* means *technē*, or art. Together, these fragments create a term signifying the art of yielding to the other's force. "The word jujutsu may be translated freely as 'the art of gaining victory by yielding or pliancy.'"[33] The central idea of jujutsu is to use the opponent's own force against them. Rather than confront the other with one's force, the idea is to turn the force of the opponent into your own weapon—in other words, to turn one's opponent's energy against them, rather than trying to oppose that energy directly. In an article from 1887, "Jujutsu and the Origins of Judo," Kano and Lindsay explain that "its main principle [is] not to match strength with strength, but to gain victory by yielding to strength." And the first principle of the art is expressed as follows: "Not to resist an opponent, but to gain victory by pliancy."[34]

I would identify this as that first moment of the counter-move: to parry, to block, to ward off by a corresponding move. But what I would suggest is that forms of jujutsu as judo transcend that parry. The philosophy of jujutsu is that of the counter-move: to use the force of the attack and transform it into something else, something that is neither an attack nor a block. When the counter-move can exist on its own, without responding to its counter, always perhaps indexing it, but fully unmoored, detached, independent, above its counter, doing what it does without responding to its counter, countering without reference to its counter—that, I take it, is the final productive moment of the counter-move.

The darkest illustration of the counter-move—one that, paradoxically, demonstrates well its fullest potential—lies right before our own eyes: the American Counterrevolution. As I demonstrate in *The Counterrevolution: How Our Government Went to War Against Its Own Citizens*, a new form of governmentality characterized by counterinsurgency strategies has come to dominate American government. Developed as a counter-move to insurgencies that drew extensively on Maoist theories of insurrection, this new form of governmentality has liberated itself from its oppositional object and become a form of governing *despite the absence of any domestic insurgency*. It has become an autonomous form of government.[35]

Since the attacks of 9/11, the United States has undergone a dramatic transformation in the way that it carries itself abroad and governs itself at home. Long in the making—at least since the colonial wars abroad and the domestic turmoil of the 1960s—this historic transformation has come about in three waves. First, militarily in Vietnam, and now in Afghanistan and Iraq: U.S. military strategy has shifted importantly from a conventional model of large-scale battlefield warfare to unconventional forms of counterinsurgency warfare. Second, in foreign affairs: as the counterinsurgency paradigm took hold militarily, U.S. foreign policy began to mirror the core principles of unconventional warfare—total information awareness, targeted eradication of the radical minority, and psychological pacification of the masses. Third, at home: with the increased militarization of police forces, irrational fear of Muslims, and overenforcement of antiterrorism laws, the United States has begun to domesticate the counterinsurgency and to apply it to its own population. The result has been radical: the emergence of a domestic counterinsurgency model of government, imposed on American soil, in the absence of any domestic insurgency. The counterinsurgency has liberated itself from its oppositional object to become a new and radical form of government. It is a *counter*insurgency without an insurgency, an autonomous form of unconventional warfare unmoored from reality.

This illustrates perfectly the counter-move: born in an opposition, it soon exceeds it. Neither inherently good nor bad, it can go in multiple directions. It is not thesis, antithesis, synthesis. It is not anti-. There is no inherent necessity to these logical steps, nor with the counter-move. *Counter* can fail. But when the counter-move succeeds, it tends to be a powerful device, born of contestation. It has worked powerfully on the other side.

It is time to reappropriate the counter-move to push critical philosophy forward. And having done so, having appropriated it, and used it here, I think we can then discard it. I hope to have shown that the *counter*-move is a useful device to push forward. I hope to have convinced you that it is sharp and suitable to a critical project. But I fear that retaining it leaves a residual. It leaves the idea of constantly being in *counter*-position to a recurring proto-scientism or foundationalism. I believe we can now get beyond that. So rather than speak of a counter-foundational critical theory, let me use another term from now on: *a radical critical philosophy of illusions*.

CHAPTER 7

A Radical Critical Philosophy of Illusions

In proposing a radical critical philosophy of illusions, I use the term *illusion* advisedly—despite, or perhaps over the objection of Foucault, the Frankfurt School, and others. I understand fully their opposition to the term and preference for expressions such as knowledge-power, regimes of truth, ideology, false consciousness, phantasmagoria, and others. The struggle over proper terminology reflects deep disagreement over the very existence of truth, the stickiness of belief systems, the origin and nature of ideational constructs, and how or whether it is even possible to displace them. And yet, along all these dimensions, the simple and common word *illusion* is far more serviceable and appropriate than the other terms and functions best across different situations and different times.

Illusions, Ideologies, and Regimes of Truth

Of all the critical theorists, surprisingly, it was Sigmund Freud who was most comfortable using the term *illusion*; however, he inflected its meaning with the notion of wish fulfillment, pushing it in a slightly different direction than I would. Because of that central dimension of desire, Freud and later psychoanalytic theorists, as well as critical thinkers like Slavoj Žižek, twined a dimension of fantasy to the notion of illusion.[1] Freud's careful analysis of the term is nevertheless instructive.

In his book, *The Future of an Illusion*, which addressed religion and religious beliefs, Freud offered a taxonomy of terms, settling at the time, for his purposes, on the word *illusion*. For Freud, writing in 1927, the term *illusion* captured the notion of a desired set of beliefs. The guiding meaning was the fulfillment of a wish or desire, or as he wrote, "fulfilments of the oldest, strongest, and most urgent wishes of mankind."[2] The German term that Freud used was "*einer Illusion*,"[3] a term intended to connote the strength of the beliefs. "The secret of their strength lies in the strength of those wishes," Freud explained. Religious belief, which he defined as "teachings and assertions about facts and conditions of external (or internal) reality which tell one something one has not discovered for oneself and which lay claim to one's belief," are illusions in Freud's sense; but as illusions, they are not the same thing as errors, nor are they necessarily erroneous. "Illusions need not necessarily be false—that is to say, unrealizable or in contradiction to reality," he wrote. Similarly, they also are not the same as delusions for Freud, for whom the essential character of a delusion is to be "in contradiction with reality." Thus, Freud gave the term *illusion* the following specific meaning: "we call a belief an illusion when a wish-fulfilment is a prominent factor in its motivation, and in doing so we disregard its relations to reality, just as the illusion itself sets no store by verification."[4]

Freud distinguished, then, three terms: *illusion* ("*Illusion*"), *error* ("*Irrtum*"), and *delusion* ("*Wahnidee*"). The first, *illusion*, is not necessarily true or false for Freud. Falsity, being in contradiction with reality, is not the central element of an illusion, as opposed to a delusion. An illusion can be realized and, in that sense, can become factual, in Freud's view. The two others, by contrast, are falsities by definition. An error is a false factual belief; a delusion, as well, is necessarily in contradiction with reality—that is its essence for Freud. As Raymond Geuss notes, the Freudian "error" consists of no more than "a normal, everyday, false factual belief, e.g., the belief that Sigmund Freud was born in Vienna." (Actually, he was born in Freiberg in Mähren, Moravia, in the former Austrian Empire.) Freud gives the example of the Aristotelian belief that vermin come from dung as an error. The delusion is necessarily false and held, as Geuss notes, "*because* holding this belief satisfies some wish the agent has." The example that Geuss gives is of "a man who falsely believes that he is Charlemagne because this belief satisfies his wish to be an important historical personage."[5]

By contrast, the Freudian illusion may or may not be false or in error, but it fulfills a wish. It can be an error that satisfies a wish. Freud gives the example of Columbus believing that he had discovered a route to the Indies: that was false, but he wanted it to be true. Or it can be a belief that has not yet been falsified. It is too early to tell, Freud says, whether religious beliefs are true or false. "The riddles of the universe reveal themselves only slowly to our investigation," Freud writes, and for that reason, he qualifies them as illusions. Freud also gives the example of a middle-class girl who believes—or, rather, has the "illusion"—that a prince will come sweep her off her feet. As Freud notes, this is improbable, but not untrue, "a few such cases have occurred."[6] It remains an illusion because it is a quintessential wish fulfillment. This is what rendered the term *illusion* so serviceable for Freud.

In contrast to Freud, Marx, Foucault, and those who followed in their wake leaned toward different terms to capture the idea of epistemic systems or beliefs that have effects of reality and that we need to overcome. Marx did occasionally use the term *illusion* and other visual allusions. He referred to the monetary system, for instance, explicitly as "the illusions of the Monetary System."[7] In 1867, Marx famously used the metaphor of the "phantasmagoria"—the theatrical use of a *laterna magica* to project images on a screen—to describe commodity fetishism. Here, as with Freud, religion played an important role as a central analogy for this form of mystification, but wish fulfillment was less evident. "In order . . . to find an analogy we must take flight into the misty realm of religion," Marx claimed. "There, the products of the human brain appear as autonomous figures endowed with a life of their own, which enter into relations both with each other and with the human race."[8] The same is true with things *qua* commodities, Marx explained: "It is nothing but the definite social relation between men themselves which assumes here, for them, the [phantasmagoric][9] form of a relation between things."[10]

Marx's idea drew on the optical illusion. He used the notion of perception, of the optic nerve, of sight, as a way to explain the relation to commodities:

> In the same way, the impression made by a thing on the optic nerve is perceived not as a subjective excitation of that nerve but as the objective form of a thing outside the eye. In the act of seeing, of course, light is really transmitted from one thing, the external object, to another thing, the eye. It is a physical relation between physical things. As against this, the commodity-form, and the value-relation of the products of labour within which it appears, have absolutely no connection with the physical nature of the commodity and the material [*dinglich*] relations arising out of this.[11]

Marx's discussion of commodity fetishism is steeped in visual allegories—that is, in sight and optics. The phantasmal dimension of Marx was pronounced at that time.

Eventually, however, Marx's preferred term became *ideology*. As Peter Baehr documents in *The Unmasking Style in Social Theory*, Marx and the Marxist tradition used various names, including *false consciousness, motivated mistake, hegemony,* and others, but, in Baehr's words, "Marx prefers *ideology*."[12] The Frankfurt School, as the earlier discussion reveals, also embraced the term *ideology* and *Ideologiekritik*, as did the Marxist critical philosopher, Louis Althusser.[13]

Foucault started out more favorable toward the word *illusion*, but then he turned against the term. During the 1960s and early 1970s, he used the term *illusion* freely. As noted in chapter 2, the word *illusion* permeated Foucault's introduction to Kant's *Anthropology* in 1961.[14] His use of the term continued steadily through the early 1970s. In fact, in his 1974 lectures on *Psychiatric Power*, Foucault would use the term to pinpoint one of his most important interventions—his claim about the illusion of Man:

> What I call Man, in the nineteenth and twentieth centuries, is nothing other than the kind of after-image [*image rémanente*] of this oscillation between the juridical individual . . . and the disciplinary individual. . . . [And] from this oscillation between the power claimed and the power exercised, were born the *illusion* and the reality of what we call Man.[15]

In those lectures, and especially in 1975, in *Discipline and Punish*, Foucault drew importantly on the notion of optics and optical illusions to discuss the *panopticon* prison.[16] The very idea of the architectural inversion of the spectacle into surveillance was centered on a visual metaphor: in antiquity, the spectators amassed in arenas, all there to watch one or two gladiators; in modern times, the single guard in the watchtower of the panoptic prison has the ability to watch all the prisoners in their cells. This becomes an illusion when the guard no longer even needs to be in the watchtower for the prisoners to internalize his gaze. The gaze and the role of visualization are central to Foucault's thought, especially in the 1960s and early 1970s. His book *The Birth of the Clinic* centered on the way in which the visual changed medical science. That is, of course, how he opened this text, referring to eighteenth-century medicine as "the language of fantasy."[17] The word that Foucault uses, in the original, is "*fantasmes*,"[18] the form of the common genus that privileges sight. The term carries a visual, hallucinatory element.[19] *Vision, allusion, illusion*, and *hallucinations* worked, for Foucault at the time, to project the meaning of legibility.

However, a few years later, Foucault would strongly reject the term *illusion*—as well as, for that matter, the word *error*, and, of course, *ideology*. In fact, Foucault was consistent in always resisting the latter term.[20] He gravitated instead toward words with a more pronounced epistemological meaning. Illusions, errors, and even ideologies, for Foucault, did not capture properly the depth of the epistemological layers. They did not project the meaning and thickness of *epistemes*: of ways of thinking that shaped entire disciplines over the centuries. Foucault reached for terms like *knowledge-power* or *regimes of truth* to convey the idea that these were not mere veils or ideas that could easily be lifted.

For Foucault, regimes of truth are by no means a mere illusion, even though they are made to appear and eventually disappear. Conceptions of madness, delinquency, and sexuality are not illusions, even if they are the product of a whole series of practices that give birth to something that did not exist beforehand and continues not to exist. Foucault's project, he himself would emphasize, did *not* seek to demonstrate that these things are no more than "villainous illusions or ideological products that must be dissipated in the light of reason." Instead, as Foucault explained in his lectures on *The Birth of Biopolitics* in 1979, "The goal of these studies is to demonstrate how the pairing of series of practices and regimes of truth forms an apparatus of knowledge-power that marks effectively in reality that which does not exist and submits it to the exclusion of truth and falsity." As a theoretical matter, Foucault insisted, these are not mere illusions: "They are not an illusion since it is precisely a set of practices, of real practices, that have established them and mark them imperiously in the real."[21]

What bothered Foucault most about the term *illusion*, in his later work, was that it signaled (to him at least) that beliefs could be easily dismissed as false or did not have "real" effects.[22] Many poststructuralist or postcolonial thinkers felt the same way, emphasizing how durable, thick, and resilient these mental constructs could be. Edward Said emphasized the same thing at about the same time: "One ought never to assume that the structure of Orientalism is nothing more than a structure of lies or of myths which, were the truth about them to be told, would simply blow away," he wrote.[23] He continued:

> After all, any system of ideas that can remain unchanged as teachable wisdom (in academies, books, congresses, universities, foreign-service institutes) from the period of Ernest Renan in the late 1840s until the present in the United States must be something more formidable than a mere collection of lies. Orientalism, therefore, is not an airy European fantasy about the Orient, but a created body of theory and practice in which, for many generations, there has been a considerable material investment.[24]

These systems of ideas, Said emphasized, are neither simply errors, nor lies, nor thin illusions; rather, they are thick epistemological layers that last centuries. They cannot easily be dispelled or blown away. They cannot easily be liquidated.

And of course, Foucault and Said put their finger on an important aspect of these belief systems. They challenged, in a way, psychoanalysis itself. Freud, for instance, did believe that psychoanalysis could dispel illusions. He expressly said, for instance, regarding the illusion that children are without sexuality, that the belief could be "destroyed by psycho-analysis."[25] Some might argue, naturally, that the full psychoanalytic method is extremely demanding. No doubt, it is. But it is important to recognize how these imaginaries—illusions, fantasies, ideologies, regimes of truth, whatever name you give them—have truthful effects that are long-lasting and thick, that may last centuries in fact. And it is important to emphasize that they have *real* effects—real effects of truth—that can be unforgiving and resilient over the ages.

But that does not mean that we need to invent jargon and infuse that jargon with intricate theoretical moves that few critical philosophers even agree on—and no layperson understands. Illusions can last for centuries, and they can be extremely thick epistemologically, as well as resilient. For these reasons, I would retain the terminology of illusions because it captures best, in more accessible language, the idea of a misleading solid belief that masquerades as truth, but through critique and a lot of work, over perhaps decades or centuries, can ultimately be unveiled, not to arrive at truth but instead at another space that will eventually itself become an illusion, need to be critiqued, and once again be unveiled. I do not contend that truth traverses any of this, nor that we can get beyond power in analyzing these illusions.

It is, after all, truths that we reveal to be illusions. In that sense, the term *illusion* is directly related to its object of critique. A theory of illusions attacks purported truths. It counters truth-making. The terminology of *regimes of truth*, by contrast, is an ironic use of the term *truth*, and it does not convey the critique. For our purposes, the openly derogatory or tendentious valence of illusions, which some theorists such as Peter Baehr criticize, is useful.[26] I am not using *illusions* in a nonderogatory sense. I am not doing a sociology of ideology. Beliefs are illusions precisely when they have detrimental effects of reality—detrimental, that is, to the ambition of critical philosophy: an equal, solidary, and socially just society. The term *illusion* conveys that. And it also frees us from all the baggage of strong immanent critique that can infuse the term *ideology* in an unconvincing way, as I showed earlier in chapter 5. Illusions have genealogies and elements of contingency that resist the strong claims of necessity and sublation associated with ideology critique. In the end, it is the close relation between illusions and claims of truth—and the way in which a theory of illusions constantly challenges claims of truth—that infuse the term *illusion* with its importance.

The Illusion of Free Markets

Let me provide here the most precise articulation of the concept of *illusion* that I embrace, using as an illustration what I have called previously the "illusion of free markets."

The illusion of free markets is a widely shared belief in the United States that free markets are better and more efficient than government regulation. In my research, I trace the origins of this shared belief back to the first French economists known as the Physiocrats, to Adam Smith, and to the eighteenth-century debates over public economy. More specifically, I trace the contemporary idea of the efficiency of competitive markets back to the introduction of the idea of "natural order" into economic thought in the writings of François Quesnay, Mirabeau, and Le Mercier de la Rivière—back to Quesnay's famous *Tableau économique*, which was one of the first conceptualizations and visualizations of a space of economic exchange that could thrive best without governmental interference.[27] Others trace it even further back—as far back, some critical theorists such as Dotan Leshem suggest, to Late Antiquity.[28]

This belief, I argue, is an *illusion* because a free market does not really exist. The categorical distinction between free and regulated economies—or the spectrum, if you prefer, between less and more regulated markets—is misleading. There is no such thing as a free market: all markets, all forms and venues of economic exchange, are artificial, constructed, regulated, and administered by often complex mechanisms that necessarily distribute wealth in large and small ways. The state is always present in the market. In a purportedly free market, the state is just as present, enforcing private contracts; preventing and punishing trespass on private property; overseeing, regulating, policing, and enforcing through criminal, administrative, and civil sanctions the market transactions themselves; and distributing wealth through the tax code, military spending, bureaucratic governance, and myriad other means. The state creates, maintains, and regulates free markets extensively—criminalizing market bypassing, fraud, misrepresentation, and other deviations from the purportedly orderly course of human affairs; and policing private property and social relations. Whenever the state is not explicitly directing economic behavior or setting prices, it is nevertheless present in equal magnitude, enforcing breaches of contract; criminalizing insider trading, cornering the market, and unfair trade practices; defining and protecting private property; and punishing black-market activity.

The complex mechanisms necessary for a colossal late-modern Western economy regulate in large and small ways. Tax incentives for domestic oil production and lower capital gains rates are obvious illustrations. But there are all kinds of more minute rules surrounding wheat pits, stock markets, and economic exchanges that amount to complex regulation: limits on the ability of retail buyers to flip shares after an initial public offering (IPO); rulings allowing exchanges to cut communication to nonmember dealers; fixed prices in extended, after-hour trading; even the creation of options markets. The mere existence of a privately chartered organization like the Chicago Board of Trade, which required the state of Illinois to criminalize and forcibly shut down competing bucket shops, represents complex state intervention that has effects on farmers and consumers, bankers, brokers, and dealers.[29] In the end, the categories of free and regulated markets are misleading heuristic devices.

These misleading categories are deeply entrenched in our systems of belief, and they have real, material effects. Even though they are not themselves correct or accurate, they have effects of truth on the real world. They are not mere mistakes that can easily be corrected. They endure for centuries. They are resilient. And they have wide-ranging effects. The belief in free markets has produced a significant redistribution of wealth in American society. For instance, since the 1970s, it has legitimized public policies that are euphemistically called *deregulation*. These policies have masked massive redistribution of wealth by claiming that they are *deregulating* the economy, when all along they were actually *reregulating* economic and social relations for the benefit of wealthier citizens. This reregulation of the economy has had tangible effects on distributions of wealth. As the sociologist Douglas Massey minutely documents in his book *Categorically Unequal*, and as Thomas Piketty does in his research, following decades of improvement, the income gap between the richest and poorest in this country has dramatically widened since the 1970s, resulting in what social scientists now refer to as a "U-curve" of increasing inequality.[30]

The illusion of free markets has lasted for centuries. As I show in my research, the notion of efficient markets is merely an updated version of a concept of natural order in economic thought from the eighteenth century. In this sense, it is extremely resilient. It is not easily unveiled. It is epistemologically thick—as thick, for instance, as Orientalism, although the two operate in different ways.

It bears many of the attributes of the other competing terms. There is probably an element of wish fulfillment, although I would not prioritize this dimension. But it exists. As a factual matter, I believe, it could be shown that the wealthier in American society have indeed benefited during the recent period of renewed faith in free markets since the 1970s, so the belief does satisfy the desires of the wealthy. It may not have served the economic interests of the middle and lower classes. But even for the latter, it may satisfy a desire without them necessarily realizing it. For the mass of Americans who do not benefit materially from the belief in free markets, though, there is often an intimate connection between the belief in the free market and the wish for freedom and individual liberty. Often, there is also a connection between believing in the free market and being American, being a patriot, or feeling superior to other nationalities and cultures. In other words, it can satisfy wishes or desires without benefiting people materially. The appeal of liberty is indeed a powerful motivator—especially when it is tied, as it has been since the Physiocrats, to the notion of orderliness and economic freedom. Friedrich Hayek recognized this well.[31]

The illusion of free markets, however, is not simply a delusion. It is not just *self*-deception. There are people who have aggressively promoted the illusion, including thinkers such as Friedrich Hayek, Milton Friedman, Richard Posner, and Richard Epstein, and politicians such as Ronald Reagan and Margaret Thatcher. There are foundations and wealthy individuals who endow institutions and professorships that promoted the ideas of free markets. Hayek, in fact, went to the University of Chicago in 1950 thanks to funding from the Volker Fund, a conservative foundation that helped establish the law-and-economics movement at the University of Chicago; and the John M. Olin Foundation, another conservative grant-making foundation, essentially bankrolled law-and-economics in United States law faculties for decades.[32] It is, of course, important to explore the subjective dimension of these beliefs. It is a bit too easy to always point fingers at neoconservative thinkers and absolve others of any responsibility. But there is far more than just self-delusion here. These ideas have been bankrolled for centuries by wealthy, conservative institutions.

The illusion of free markets, also, is not simply an error. It cannot simply be demonstrated to be false and then corrected. There may be factual errors in this illusion (e.g., that an unregulated or less regulated market can even exist), but that does not mean that we can say that the illusion is wrong. There are investments in the illusion that are too thick and complex for us to say that they are errors. For instance, the attachment to a self-image of rugged individualism includes sexual, social, and personal desires that cannot simply be reduced to error. The illusion of free markets is an imaginary about liberty and governance as well—namely, that individual responsibility and a limited state are better for everyone in the long run.

This latter claim is not subject to the same type of empirical falsification as an error. In other words, the political belief in the advantages of limited government has different truth-value than an erroneous assertion about, for example, whether poor Americans would benefit from the elimination of the estate tax. It is easy to demonstrate that the latter assertion is false and that the opposite is true. It calls for a binary "true or false" judgment. But the former claim is not of that type. It is not possible to say that the attachment to limited government and rugged individualism is false and its opposite, the belief in a welfare state, is true.

As for the analogy to religion, Renata Salecl provocatively writes in her book *Choice*, "Following Walter Benjamin's prediction that capitalism would function as a new form of religion, some today argue that the market has become God: until the recent financial crisis anyone opposed to the dogma of the free market economy was labelled a heretic."[33] It is amusing to discover, in light of this, that a survey of religious attitudes reveals that an unexpectedly large percentage of Americans associate the free market with God. According to the 2011 Baylor Religion Survey of 1,714 American adults, about 20 percent of Americans "combine a view of God as actively engaged in daily workings of the world with an economic conservative view that opposes government regulation and champions the free market as a matter of faith."[34] As sociologist Paul Froese, coauthor of the survey, suggests, "they say the invisible hand of the free market is really God at work." "They think the economy works because God wants it to work. It's a new religious economic idealism," Froese explains.[35] It is interesting to see reality mimic theory. The concepts of fantasy, illusion, and phantasmagoria were, from the start, closely associated with the religious sphere. Recall that Marx drew on religion as the best analogy for the mystification of commodities, and Freud explored the future of religion as a form of illusion. Still today, the religious dimension remains enlightening, especially insofar as it reveals how beliefs that are nonevidentiary can become "truthful" and gain traction.

Infinite Interpretation

In the end, the term *illusion* is the most serviceable. It avoids unnecessary jargon and indexes perfectly the recurring claims to truth and foundationalism that need to be countered. There is a way in which Nietzsche set us on this terminological path, with his own challenge to the value of truth. He too privileged the term *illusion*, provoking us with those infamous words: "Truths are illusions that we have forgotten are illusions."[36] Nietzsche represented that break in the nineteenth century, which challenged critical thinkers to a new hermeneutic: the interpretation of a world made of interpretations that have effects of reality—a world of infinite regress of interpretations, going down vertically.

A radical critical philosophy of illusions calls for infinite interpretation as well. It calls for constant and better interpretations that do away with illusions, again and again. The political struggle today demands trenchant and forceful resignifications, along with an unbending commitment to resist the recurring shadows.

You will recall Foucault's essay, "Nietzsche, Freud, Marx," where he identified that modern hermeneutic: a different style or system of interpretation with its own devices, techniques, strategies, and methods. It was a hermeneutic in which interpretation always precedes the sign. Interpretations do not escape interpretation, but rather fold back on them. Signs are deceptive, and all that we are left with is an endless series of meaning-making. "Interpretation finds itself with the obligation to interpret itself to infinity," Foucault wrote, "always to resume . . . Interpretation must always interpret itself."[37]

This is a world in which we never get to the original meaning or first source. We never get to truth in politics. Instead, we unveil, and act, and continue to unveil more. But we do not get to solid ground. Take, for instance, the question "Why do we punish?" that Didier Fassin asks in his lectures *The Will to Punish*. In response, we can offer an interpretation: you are familiar with them, so to get beneath the obvious first answers—deterrence, retribution, incapacitation, rehabilitation—we could say that we punish to maintain a social order, one that is characterized by white supremacy and capitalist consumption. We punish to control the poor by imposing small fines and attaching their wages, if they have any—or adding their fines to their water bills in municipalities across the United States. But where does that come from? Well, perhaps from earlier forms of social ordering, such as the debt prisons and the relation between debtors and creditors, as Fassin discusses.

And that? Well, it might trace back earlier, to forms of indentured service, of owing work for one's freedom . . . and so on, and so on . . . But one never gets to the original meaning. And in the end, we do not know anymore why we punish: we just punish. Or, as Nietzsche said so eloquently in *The Genealogy of Morals* in 1887: "Today it is impossible to say for certain *why* people are really punished: all concepts in which an entire process is semiotically concentrated elude definition; only that which has no history is definable."[38] There is, then, no first origin and no resting place. There is no omega. The interpretations do not end. We do not get to a place of truth or a place where there is no power. As Foucault wrote, "There is nothing absolutely primary to interpret, for after all everything is already interpretation, each sign is in itself not the thing that offers itself to interpretation but an interpretation of other signs."[39]

To properly address our political situation today and get beyond it, then, we need to return to these insights, to remember what a struggle there is in interpretation and how much is at stake, and to recognize how violent the process can be. As Nietzsche emphasized, again in the *Genealogy*, meanings "are only *signs* that a will to power has become master of something less powerful and imposed upon it the character of a function." As Foucault reminded us as well, these acts of interpretation are "as much a relationship of violence as of elucidation." As Adorno acknowledged already in 1931, we have no choice but to "proceed interpretively without ever possessing a sure key to interpretation," because—as he wrote three decades later in *Negative Dialectics*—"objects do not go into their concepts without leaving a remainder," and this "indicates the untruth of identity, the fact that the concept does not exhaust the thing conceived."[40]

Indeed, within the Frankfurt School tradition, it is likely Adorno who serves as an interpretive bridge with postfoundational thought. Adorno reacted against the systematicity of Hegel's dialectic and searched for the gaps and ambiguities, the places of non-identity that disrupted the closed system and the necessity of an overcoming. In this sense, Adorno was looking to trouble the relation between concepts and reality, between words and things. He shared this sensibility with Deleuze and Foucault—perhaps even with deconstructionists like Derrida. The aporetic condition is close to the negative dialectic, as is Deleuze's *Difference and Repetition*. They share an anti-Hegelianism and an insistence on the moment of non-identity. Adorno's negative dialectic, in effect, fits in that narrow space between pure negativity (as a corrective to German idealism) and nihilism (as an abandonment of the action imperative). As such, Adorno's thought can serve to fend off the slide of Frankfurt critical theory back to Kant or Hegel—back to the illusion of reason and progress. Adorno's negative dialectic serves as an internal voice of skepticism within the Frankfurt School, an authentic and in that sense fully legitimate voice, internal to the discourse of the Frankfurt School, that returns us to pure interpretation in the continuing confrontation and struggle with reality.

But we must push further than this. We must also get beyond Nietzsche and Foucault and Adorno. To move forward, from the perspective of a radical critical philosophy of illusions, we need not simply to *understand*, but to *deploy* the infinite regress of interpretations—knowing that even we do not preexist the meanings that we impose on the world, that our subjectivity is shaped by those infinite interpretations, and that the struggle, in the end, is a struggle over life and death, a struggle over our subjectivity, a battle over the imposition of those interpretations.

In such a world of interpretations, we must struggle by means of resignification. In a world in which we never get to the original meaning or first source, we must learn to interpret and interpret better. Today, more than ever, we need to go on the offensive with our critical theory, both in the sense of offering better and more compelling interpretations and in the sense of exceeding the illusions we counter. This is what happens when, for instance, counterpositivism becomes a philosophical method that no longer refers back to positivism. It is what happens when, here, counter-foundational critical theory becomes a radical theory of illusions—autonomous, and no longer tied to the rejection of the recurring foundationalism in critical philosophy.

The Critical Method

There is another sense in which we need to get beyond Nietzsche, beyond Marx and Freud as well, and also beyond Horkheimer, Adorno, and Foucault: as critical theorists, we cannot and must not understand ourselves as spellbound by these critical thinkers. At all times, we interpret them, we interpret their words, and those interpretations are our own, not theirs. In critical theory, there is no room for influence or for followers. Instead critical theorists must use and *deploy* critical texts to their own critical ends. In this way, critical theorists first *interpret* interpretations and then *deploy* them in order to change the world. And in this manner, contemporary critical thinkers can get beyond the epistemological impasse to a radical critical philosophy of illusions.

It is often said that Foucault himself was "influenced" by Nietzsche. Many say that he was "Nietzschean."[41] But that precisely gets it all wrong. It fails to grasp the core of the critical method. The relationship was entirely other: Foucault plied his critical method on Nietzsche's writings in a similar way that he interpreted the discourse of madness, of clinical medicine, of the human sciences, or of the practice of discipline and experience of sexuality. Foucault treated Nietzsche's texts as objects of interpretation—at times an epistemological object, at other times a linguistic, alethurgic, or directly political object of study. He worked Nietzsche's written words to better understand how to think and how to act. Foucault was often keen to say—at those junctures when he would reframe his intellectual project—that he had worked on madness, the prison, and sexuality, sometimes adding to the series clinical medicine or the human sciences. But it would be far more accurate to say that throughout his own intellectual life, Foucault worked on *Nietzsche*, and madness, the prison, and sexuality—perhaps in that order. Nietzsche's writings were just as productive an object of interpretation for Foucault as those other three discourses.

It is not only reductionist, but deeply misleading to portray the relationship as one of influence or borrowing—even for the most direct overlaps, such as the use of the term *genealogy*. Not just because Foucault's genealogical method is markedly different from Nietzsche's—as Amy Allen, Colin Koopman, Daniele Lorenzini, Martin Saar, and others demonstrate well.[42] But because his critical method was to treat Nietzsche's discourse as an *object of interpretation* no different than any other discourse. That has deep implications for our own work and our own critical method.

Foucault worked Nietzsche's writings as a critical, epistemological, linguistic, alethurgic, and political object of interpretation. In the introduction to his translation of Kant's *Anthropology*, Foucault used Nietzsche's discourse as a critical object of study and a device to open a space beyond the recurring anthropological illusions that plague phenomenology, and especially existential phenomenology. In his 1964 essay "Nietzsche, Freud, Marx," Foucault treats Nietzsche's writings as an epistemological object of study in his archaeology of knowledge. In his 1971 essay "Nietzsche, Genealogy, History," Foucault uses Nietzsche as a linguistic object of study, as a laboratory to develop his theory of the will to know. In his Rio lectures, "Truth and Juridical Form," Foucault treats Nietzsche's writings as a political object of study and model for a critique of knowledge-power and of the subject.

In effect, at each of these stages, Foucault takes Nietzsche's writings to interpret them from a different angle, plying Nietzsche's discourse to his intellectual pursuits as they develop over time from an epistemology, to a politics, to an alethurgy. Foucault was not merely discovering ideas in Nietzsche's writings or borrowing his concepts; rather, he was projecting his own thinking, playing with Nietzsche's words as a way to make progress on his philosophical investigations. At the end of his discussion of Nietzsche in Rio, Foucault declares that he is studying certain passages of Nietzsche, but not Nietzscheanism. He responds to his critics—who accuse him of cherry-picking passages that relate to power simply because he wants to find relations of power everywhere—in the following way: "First, I took up this text in function of my interests, not to show that this was the Nietzschean conception of knowledge;" nor because Foucault wants to say that this is a systematic and coherent conception of Nietzsche "since there are innumerable and often mutually contradictory texts on this topic."[43] Foucault is not interested in discovering the true Nietzsche: among mutually contradictory texts, he sets aside those that are of no interest to him; he turns to those that interest him and finds there, and only there, something that is useful to him in Nietzsche: "A certain number of elements which provide us with a model for a historical analysis of what I would call the politics of truth. It is a model that one does find in Nietzsche, and I even think that it is one of the most important models to be found in Nietzsche's work, in order to understand some apparently contradictory elements in his conception of knowledge."[44]

Foucault interpreted Nietzsche's texts, selecting, finding those that allowed him to discern a model that worked for his critical political project. The model may be only one of many possible Nietzschean models, but for Foucault, it was the one, the use of which would make it possible to construct his history of truth-making. Foucault himself admitted as much in an interview in 1977—although we should be wary of attributing too much to his own self-assessments. Foucault remarked, "For myself, I prefer to utilise the writers I like. The only valid tribute to thought such as Nietzsche's is precisely to use it, to deform it, to make it groan and protest. And if commentators then say that I am being faithful or unfaithful to Nietzsche, that is of absolutely no interest."[45]

And let me emphasize: This is precisely how we should treat Foucault's writings and, more generally, critical philosophical discourse: as objects of experimentation, of interpretation, of study in furtherance of our own intellectual and political projects. I am not here merely rehearsing Roland Barthes's thesis on the death of the author. What I am suggesting reaches further. As critical thinkers, we need to treat these past critical texts actively, as objects for experimentation, for interpretation, for intervention, for critical praxis. Critical philosophical discourse, in effect, is hardly different from those other objects—the discourse of madness, of the prison, of sexuality, or, perhaps, of natural order, of neoliberalism, of counterinsurgency. For the critical actor, it never lends itself to borrowing or influence. Those very concepts of borrowing and influence are incongruous. What we do, as critical theorists and practitioners, is always to ply the written traces to our work: to put critical philosophical texts to work to further our own political projects.

The broader point is this: if we approach critical philosophical discourse critically, there is no such thing as "Nietzsche"—no "Nietzsche" to whom one could be faithful. "Nietzsche" does not constitute a coherent whole, so one could not even be "Nietzschean" if one tried. The same is true of "Foucault." There are written fragments, essays, and books that collide and confront each other. We use the terms Nietzsche, Marx, or Foucault in shorthand. We anthropomorphize the texts or the *oeuvre*, when all there is, in fact, are written words on which we project meaning and which we deploy for our political purposes.[46] As critical theorists, we should not deny that, or be embarrassed by it; rather, we should embrace it. It forms the heart of the critical method: critical philosophical texts are just written traces that lend themselves to interpretation—to infinite interpretation. In other methodological traditions, to be sure, writers may conceive of themselves as inscribed and influenced by a thinker. They may even self-identify as, say, "Rawlsian" or even perhaps "Marxist."[47] But to speak of being "Nietzschean," or "Foucaultian" for that matter, should make no sense.

This raises an interesting question: Did Foucault need Nietzsche? Or, more relevant to us, do we, critical thinkers, need Nietzsche—or, for that matter, Foucault? Some have already responded no—as evidenced by a book published by Grasset in 1991 under the title *Why We Are Not Nietzscheans*. The volume includes a number of French philosophers, including Vincent Descombes, Luc Ferry, Philippe Raynaut, Alain Renaut, and others—it was a collective effort to repudiate Nietzsche, as so many had done before and will no doubt continue to do. Nietzsche's way of thinking, they tell us, relativizes values, glorifies a deconstruction of discourse, and can lead, ultimately, to nihilism. Others disagree and claim Nietzsche. Most recently, Dorian Astor, a biographer of Nietzsche, and Alain Jugnon edited a collection published in 2016 entitled *Why We Are Nietzscheans*.

But the question itself is not the right one to ask. It has little meaning and is methodologically demeaning. What we do with texts and ideas, as critical theorists and practitioners, is not to follow or apply them, but to interpret, test, and deploy them in pursuit of our own political projects. We often refer to "Nietzsche" or "Foucault," but those terms do not have coherent meaning. They are shorthand for written traces. Again, it may well be that we anthropomorphize philosophers, books, and their *oeuvre*; but that is just our human weakness, not a critical method. The only way to do justice to our critical task of writing, theorizing, and (again, more important) engaging in critical praxis, is precisely to put these critical traces to work to further our own political project—to get beyond them in pursuit of the ambition of critical philosophy: to change the world.

Resisting the Shadows

The original project of critical philosophy was to analyze contemporary society with the ambition of contributing to a radical transformation of society. The goal was the emancipation of contemporary women and men from the oppression, barbarity, and wars produced by advanced capitalism. Yet critical philosophy took an epistemological detour.

Critical theory, as spelled out at the origin of the Frankfurt School, especially by Max Horkheimer, was modeled on Marx's critique of political economy, but through historical happenstance, it had to address the failures, the ideological distortions that plagued the working class. The prevailing ideologies at the time were masking the internal contradictions of advanced capitalism, supposedly, such that the workers themselves—the proletariat—were not experiencing the tensions and contradictions of capitalism as a motivating force toward social transformation. As such, critical theorists had the task of helping to foster the awareness and activism of workers. Critical theory had to take another path: epistemology.

Critical theory was originally sensitive to the importance of history and conscious of the implication of the theorist in social reality: the theorist was necessarily part of the movement of history, shaped by his historical circumstances, and limited by the conditions of possibility of the existing political economy. A theorist in feudal times may have had their field of vision limited to bourgeois reform; a theorist in late-modern capitalism may have had their field of vision limited to overcoming those contradictions. This required constant self-reflection on the part of the theorist. Yet the Frankfurt School gravitated toward quasi-universal notions of truth and reasonableness.

Critical theory was opposed to the universal and ahistorical claims of traditional social scientific research. It was opposed to formal positivism. Yet, in continuing to embrace Marxian concepts and logics, it reinstantiated a certain form of proto-scientism and foundationalism—one that went directly against the idea of historical constructivism. Recall from chapters 1 and 2 the sharp difference between what Foucault does with Homer, in Book 23 of the *Iliad*, and what Horkheimer and Adorno do with Homer, in Book 12 of the *Odyssey*. Horkheimer and Adorno impose a Marxian framework on the myth of Odysseus and the Sirens. Everything becomes the domination of the master, Odysseus as captain of industry, over the oarsmen, who become factory workers. The myth serves to make their point about enlightenment and man's domination over nature—but it does so by imposing the prefabricated Marxian framework on the myth. By contrast, in *Wrong-Doing, Truth-Telling*, Foucault tells the story of Antilochus and Menelaus as a way to show how Antilochus' quasi-avowal reconstitutes the truth of the social order of ancient Greece. This was a very different project: this one geared toward unearthing the ways in which truth-telling establishes or reestablishes an order of truth, the hierarchy of ancient Greek society. The same work could have been done with the myth of the Sirens to show how it reestablished a gendered ideology where women are portrayed as the temptresses, as the monsters, as killers and eaters of men; where women seduce men and destroy them; and how Odysseus inscribes himself in this social order. His actions ultimately defeat the Sirens, in the end. He is master of them. He does not succumb. But in triumphing over them, he further reinforces gender hierarchies. A different set of questions produces different theories. Here, the Frankfurt School merely laid the Marxian concept over the myth—despite being so antipositivist.

It was Nietzsche's idea that humans killed God, but are always seeing his shadow. As Nietzsche wrote, "After Buddha was dead, they still showed his shadow in a cave for centuries—a tremendous, gruesome shadow. God is dead; but given the way people are, there may still for millenia be caves in which they show his shadow. — And we—we must still defeat his shadow as well!"[48] The foundationalism, the claims to truth always come back. And we, critical theorists, constantly have to resist them. It is like bread that crusts. It is like silver that tarnishes. Our task is to constantly polish the silver, or cut the crusty part off the bread, in order to do the genuinely critical work. In the end, a reconstructed critical theory must bring us to the heart of revolt and disobedience as well. Critical theory starts from a radical theory of illusions but moves directly into a theory of action. It needs to be about praxis. It needs to *be* praxis.

Exiting the Epistemological Detour

In the epistemological debates, most often between critical theorists of the Frankfurt School or post-Marxists and those who might be called poststructuralist or postcolonial or queer, the former often return to truth. Arendt foreshadowed this in her essay "Truth and Politics," which ends, you will recall, by claiming truth as "the ground on which we stand and the sky that stretches above us."[49] Benhabib instantiates this in her response to the *Feminist Contentions* debate, when she argued that denying moral and political foundations "is like wanting to jump over our own shadow."[50] Steven Lukes rehearsed it in his debate with me when he argued that "there is truth to be attained."[51] But these are, I would argue, nothing more than power plays that call out for a radical theory of illusions. They highlight the exact location of the problem: the problem of truth. It is exactly where and when we slip, as we so often seem to, from the ontological certainty of existence to political, moral, or ethical judgments that are orthogonal to truth, that we get in trouble. The resort to truth in politics and morality responds to the fear that if we cannot parse truth from falsity and right from wrong, then there is no way to convince others and no path forward. If we cannot claim truth, we are lost.

Well, I am not. My political positions and political actions are not determined by a claim to truth, but by temporary assessments of how, after critically unmasking illusions like the myth of the free market, practices and institutions interpreted through a next-best theory are likely to redistribute resources in society. I know that even better interpretations will need to be revisited—that I will undoubtedly be wrong. What is that notion of better, you may ask? It is not truth. It is an assessment, based on the best available evidence, of the effects of reality of that new interpretation and how it is likely to affect material distributions. These are judgments that are ultimately more in the ethical realm. They concern a way of being and decisions on how to act politically, and they are not intended to tell others what to do. They are not in the realm of morality—they are not about deciding on a rule of action for others. They are about the way that I lead my political and ethical life. At most, I imagine that my political acts may serve as an illustration of an ethical way of thinking and of being that might constitute one possible approach to politics. By acting in this way, I do not aspire to lead by example, nor do I claim truth for others. When one is on solid ground, one does not need to claim truth. Claiming truth, in fact, often is an indication of weakness. It is necessary only when one has failed to persuade.

In the end, for the very same reasons that we need to chasten truth, I believe that it is crucial to limit the construction of foundations. Foundations are just metaphors for truth, metaphors that claim more than they should. They construct positions that sound universal or permanent, or beyond power relations, but in reality are temporary and fallible. It is not clear that laying foundations is even the most effective or expedient political strategy. Just as we do not need a solid idea of truth when we can use better interpretations, we should dispense with foundations. And in the meantime, when we need to decide, we can use a workmanlike juridical model. We decide, at a moment in time, what is most probably accurate and the better theory, stating precisely the standards and burdens of proof we have used. It is no more than a census—what we believe today. It can change. But it is a necessary basis for action. And those decisions are only a temporary placeholder, not truth. They can never be universal or forever. Judith Butler again captures this well: "Indeed, I would suggest that a fundamental mistake is made when we think that we must sort out philosophically or epistemologically our 'grounds' before we can take stock of the world politically or engage in its affairs actively with the aim of transformation."[52] Yes, we must act, and when we do so, I propose that we use a rough-and-ready juridical model. That does not mean that we make a claim to truth.

Onward to the Ambition of Critical Philosophy

In his last years, you will recall, Foucault traced critical philosophy back to the end of the fifth century BCE and the birth of the philosophical problems of truth-telling. Although his work was different from ideology critique, he was in the same epistemological space, relating questions of power to truth-making: who has the ability to make truth, how do they produce truth, with what methods and forms, with what consequences, and how is this done in relation to power? His investigation formed part of the epistemological detour. Referring to these questions—"what is the importance of telling the truth, who is able to tell the truth, and why should we tell the truth, know the truth, and recognize who is able to tell the truth?"—Foucault declared: "I think that is at the root, at the foundation of what we could call the critical tradition of philosophy in our society." He then added: "From this point of view, you recognize one of my aims since the beginning of this seminar: to fashion a kind of genealogy of the critical attitude in philosophy."[53] Notice that the critical attitude was not directly "to change the world," but if the latter remained part of the project, it was to do so *through* the epistemological detour of understanding: One cannot change the world unless one changes beliefs and belief systems. But the questions then become: How are we going to go about changing belief systems? How do we go about changing beliefs?

In his lectures, *Discourse and Truth*, in 1983 at Berkeley, where he traced critical philosophy back to Socrates, Foucault had an idea, though he did not reveal it to his audience. It had to do with the idea of turning something into a problem. Foucault explained that throughout his philosophical work he sought to analyze how his objects of study became a problem: how madness or delinquency or sexuality became understood as a problem that society needed to deal with. He said, "What I have tried to do from the beginning was to analyze 'problematization,' that is, how and why certain things, conducts, phenomena, processes, become a problem."[54]

Now this question of "problematization" asks how things become known—which ties back to that critical attitude. It is about how we come to view a particular thing, conduct, phenomena in a particular way. Colin Koopman describes this method of problematization in Foucault as "a mode of experimental immanent critique."[55] For Foucault, there is a lot of contingency in this—meaning that it is hard to predict. We can never really know, according to Foucault, how things will emerge and develop. "The problematization is in a way always a kind of creation," Foucault observes, "but it is a creation in that sense that, given a certain situation, you can never infer that *this* kind of problematization will follow."[56] We can never know how any particular problem emerges or in what shape it will emerge.

This assigns, then, a key function to historians to trace how particular kinds of problematization arise. This is the task that Foucault assumed: "That's the task of the historian when he tries to analyze problematizations: the task of the historian is to make comprehensible why this form of problematization has been put into operation, why it appears as an answer to certain elements of reality."[57] This task is that of the historian, or better, the genealogist.

But the contingency makes it difficult to imagine how we might, in a forward-looking way, intentionally deploy problematization as a way to reshape beliefs and, eventually, our world, our reality. Foucault is cognizant of that reality—he is by no means an idealist only. He specifies here, at Berkeley, that the challenge is precisely to see how "thought and reality," or "truth and reality," are related in these moments of problematization; to discover how answers are formulated in response to certain concrete facts and situations we confront. It is not all made up. There are material conditions to which problem-making responds. Yet historical contingencies and unforeseeable relations of power make those difficult to predict.

At Berkeley, on November 30, 1983, Foucault did not deliver the last few sentences of his manuscript to his audience at his lecture. But they are telling—and they offer perhaps the best clue to his praxis at that moment. After closing the public lecture by explaining that his analyses of problematization aim to explore, precisely, the ways in which truth claims emerge in confrontation with reality, Foucault had written in his notes, but did not deliver:

> And then we can come back to the problem of critics. The aim of critics is to change the problematization. There is no diatribe, no deconstruction. But a task of permanent reproblematization.[58]

"Permanent reproblematization": that is Foucault's praxis, or advice on praxis. It is buried in the manuscript—not delivered.

I would have wanted to know *what to reproblematize today*? And how should I do it? Those are the key questions. Those are the ways to reformulate the imperative: "What is to be done?" and to reformulate it in such a way that it is not a demand to show your papers, but an invitation to help address the single most important issue before us today.

A reconstructed critical theory must begin here, at the end of the epistemological detour, at the point at which we go back to the project of changing the world. It must begin in those last paragraphs or last sentences or last provocative thoughts of our critical thinking. Have you ever noticed that critical philosophy so often spends all of its time getting warmed up, and then only gestures at the end of the text to the heart of the matter—and only does so in a provocative but allusive way?

Rather than always end there, we need to *start* there. In other words, we need to do the work of unveiling illusions, but we need not fear proposing—and we need to start working where the unveiling ends. From *Discipline and Punish*, for instance, which does the work of unveiling the disciplinary society, the punitive society—work that is essential—we need to start at the end now: *le grondement de la bataille*. Foucault closed his book by emphasizing that, in relations of power, "we must hear the distant roar of battle." He then abruptly interrupted the text, indicating work to be done (although he pointed, predominantly, to further epistemological studies—in his words, "studies of the power of normalization and the formation of knowledge in modern society.")[59] I would argue instead that right then, in 1975, what needed to follow was to directly address *le grondement de la bataille* that Foucault had unveiled: how to lead that battle, how to reform knowledge, how to reshape society so that it is no longer the punitive society, but one that nurtures every woman and man.

We need to start from the end now—from the recognition of historical constructivism, which entails an endless, recurring unveiling of illusions, one that serves to denaturalize the present and expose the distributional consequences of those illusions. Critical theory must now start from the end point that demonstrates how the myths in which we believe so deeply distribute resources and power in society—knowing that, as we unveil one set of illusions and allow others to take their place, we will need immediately, once again, to unpack the next set of myths. This constant unveiling and demonstration of its distributional effects may be an infinite regress, but that must not intimidate or stop us.

Reconstructed critical theory must springboard off an unapologetic and radical theory of illusions. It must accept the constant retracing, over and over, endlessly, of the real effects—*les effets de réalité*—of our belief systems. Performing this unveiling means, at all times, challenging interpretations and offering new ones, and not being intimidated by what is to come. It means engaging in an endless form of reinterpretation, fully cognizant of the fact that there is no end to interpretation—and that our next interpretation will get things wrong, will have negative effects, will need to be reinterpreted. This should not stop, instead it should encourage reinterpretation. As Olivier Marchart suggests in outlining one version of a postfoundational philosophy, "the impossibility of a *final* ground" does not entail the absence of offering interpretations; it implies instead awareness of the need to reinterpret and of the political nature of this work.[60] It is interpretations all the way down and the task is to ceaselessly explore how the next set of interpretations—which we ourselves will be accountable for—produce a new social order and trigger distributional consequences that we ourselves must then reevaluate.

The epistemological detour in critical philosophy, no doubt, has taught us necessary lessons about the mediating forces of domination. But it has now created irreparable tensions concerning the problem of truth. The detrimental effects on critical theory are especially acute today. Critical philosophy is mired in tribal politics and internecine struggles for influence among its offshoots.

With class struggle no longer a unifying theme, and the prospect of a proletarian revolution faded, the old glue of critical theory has worn down. It is time to get out of the epistemological detour and back to the original impulse that animated critical philosophy: how to change the world. The place to start is by reimagining the critical ambition itself.

PART II

Reimagining the Critical Horizon

For much of its history, critical philosophy was wedded to a socialist or communist vision, tied either to the withering of the state (for Marxists, but also for some libertarian or anarchist deconstructionists and poststructuralists) or to a solidaristic state (for socialists and social democrats). But in the same way in which a reconstructed critical theory along the lines of a radical critical philosophy of illusions liberates us from unfounded epistemological foundations and scientism, it also calls for a reimagining of these critical utopias.

A reconstructed critical theory challenges the illusions that underlie political and economic utopias, whether they are conservative and reactionary, liberal, or even far Left. It not only unveils the myth of natural order of the early Physiocrats and the illusion of free markets of Hayek and the Chicago School, but it also unmasks the converse: the myths surrounding planned economies, worker cooperatives, and the proletarian control of the modes of production. These broad beliefs—whether of the efficiency of deregulated markets or the superiority of planned economies—are illusions that have significant effects of reality and major distributional consequences. But once they have been unmasked as illusions, it is impossible to know ahead of time, in a general and abstract way, which political economic regime will more fairly distribute wealth and resources or best achieve our emancipatory ambitions.

All political economic regimes are regulated and distribute wealth and resources based on intricate second-order or lower-level rules and regulations that operate below the surface of the abstract regime type. In a complex economy, the real distributional effects are the result of infinite and minute regulatory mechanisms, not of the overarching economic categories. The outcomes are the product of specific organizing rules and principles in operation—not just whether the regime is based on private property, communal ownership, or a nationalized economy. As a result, it is not possible to judge a political economic regime on the basis of its label or to idealize any abstract regime type. Everything is in the details of the minute second-order regulatory apparatus that distributes resources and adjudicates disputes. To give just one quick illustration, state-controlled enterprises that distribute disproportionally to elites, such as ruling party members, may be far less equitable than privately owned corporations that distribute primarily to their workers. Everything turns on the intricate details of the internal distributional mechanisms and the techniques of dispute resolution. For a reconstructed critical theory, this means that the older utopias of socialism or communism need to be placed in a museum and replaced with a far more nuanced assessment of the mechanisms that really produce distributional outcomes.

Although the early Frankfurt School was broadly committed to Marxian concepts, there are indications that Horkheimer appreciated these distinctions. In a postscript to his 1937 article, Horkheimer underscored the importance of scratching beneath the surface of labels and focusing on real distributions. He emphasized the need to investigate, on a case-by-case basis, the exact social implications of any economic arrangement. Horkheimer wrote:

> If industrial production is under state control, this is a historical fact the significance of which in the critical theory would have to be analyzed for each state. Whether a real socialization is going on, that is, whether a higher principle of economic life is actually being developed, does not depend simply on, for example, a change in certain property relations or on increased productivity in new forms of social collaboration. It depends just as much on the nature and development of the society in which all these particular developments are taking place. The issue, then, is the real nature of the new relations of production.[1]

Horkheimer's point was that one could not trust or limit the analysis to formal categories and official labels. One cannot judge a political-economic regime on the basis of its putative property relations. It is necessary, instead, to examine "the real nature of the new relations of production." The labels may be deceptive; what matters are the real relations and distributions. For legal scholars, there is a well-worn distinction between the law on the books and the law in action. The point here is similar: it is the difference between the formal, abstract type of political economy (capitalist or socialist) and the actual second-order regulations and practices that ultimately distribute wealth and resources.

For Horkheimer, this distinction was especially important, given that his native country was formally a socialist economy. Germany was under the control of a party that called itself National Socialist. Horkheimer specifically discussed this, emphasizing that those labels could not be trusted. Regarding the case of Nazi Germany, Horkheimer wrote: "When a totalitarian State proceeds to a partial nationalization of property, it justifies itself by appeals to community and collectivist practices. Here the falsehood is obvious."[2] The case of Germany under Hitler was an easy one for Horkheimer. The Third Reich may well have called itself socialist, but it was not really socialist in operation. That was palpable.

The "falsehood" under the Third Reich was evident. Nevertheless, Horkheimer generalized the point: "even where steps are honestly taken," he wrote, "the critical theory has the dialectical function of measuring every historical stage in the light not only of isolated data and concepts, but of its primary and total content, and of being concerned that this content be vitally operative."[3] A critical analysis must probe beneath formal labels and challenge dogmas, even honest ones. Now, despite this, Horkheimer's commitment to Marxian categories blinded him to his own dogmatism. In the end, he was not willing to fully question his own abstract formulations of Marxian analysis. So, for instance, he wrote, uncritically, that late capitalism "contains in itself the internal and external tensions of the modern era," and that this internal contradiction "hinders further development and drives humanity into a new barbarism."[4] In other words, capitalism necessarily leads to barbarism. Horkheimer was not willing to draw his own critical analysis to its logical conclusion. But we must.

A reconstructed critical theory must get beyond mere labels, formal categories, and regime types in order to critically interrogate actually existing political economic arrangements and dissect their material distributions. It cannot have, as its utopia, an abstract political economic category. What must guide the critical analysis and its vision for the future—the new critical horizon—is how well the really existing regime within which it finds itself achieves or approximates the values that it holds dear. From its inception, critical philosophy has valued equality, compassion, respect, solidarity, social justice, and autonomy in assessing social forms and distributional outcomes. The task of a reconstructed critical theory, then, is to reorient the critical horizon toward a situated and contextualized evaluation of actually existing political economic regimes along the lines of these critical values.

This is particularly significant today because it means that a reconstructed critical theory can operate—and should operate—within *any* political economic regime. Naturally, it must operate under the dominant conditions of neoliberalism. But it must be equally vocal in the context of state-controlled economies, socialist countries, or communist regimes. A reconstructed critical theory must offer robust critique, regardless of the putative political economic regime in which it finds itself.

In this, a reconstructed critical theory must be guided by the values that critical philosophy has always placed front and center: equality, solidarity, social justice, and autonomy. These values must be understood not as epistemologically foundational or normatively grounded in reason or rationality or science or God, but instead as arising historically in tandem with critical philosophy and as requiring contextual elaboration. So, for instance, in liberal democratic postindustrial societies, there is a greater need to emphasize equality and solidarity than autonomy, insofar as one of the greatest impediments to autonomy is unequal opportunity and resources; by contrast, in strictly autocratic regimes, there may be more of a need to work simultaneously on equality and autonomy. In these analyses, it is helpful to draw on a framework of contextualism, such as the one that Amy Allen develops in *The End of Progress*.[5] Rather than being foundational in an epistemic or normative sense, these contextual values are associated with an intellectual and political tradition of critical philosophy that is historically and geographically situated. There is no universality or epistemic grounding. The weighing of the values is situated and contextual. As such, they guide the normative analysis of really existing mechanisms of economic distribution. They are, in fact, the only measures that can provide normative direction. For this reason, a reconstructed critical theory calls for *a radical critical theory of values.*

CHAPTER 8

The Transformation of Critical Utopias

I have already written about the illusion of free markets and the myth of natural order—the illusion that supposedly less regulated political economies are more efficient, or, for that matter, that there could even exist such a thing as a "less regulated" or an "unregulated" market.[1] All political economies are fully regulated, and the peculiarity of specific regulatory mechanisms is what produces the unique redistribution of wealth and resources in each regime. Political economies that are labeled "free markets" produce the redistribution predominantly through a complex, second-order enforcement mechanism involving private property rights and the legal enforcement of property interests that range from liens and intricate bankruptcy rules to street policing and the use of lethal force by law enforcement. Free-market regimes are just as regulated as state-controlled economies, only in a different way.

The upshot of this earlier work is that the formal type or abstract category of political economic regime does not determine distributional outcomes or equity. It is the minutiae of the second-order rules, regulations, procedures, and policing that do so. A nationalized or state-controlled economy can redistribute wealth in a hideously unequal manner, by privileging a central party apparatchik, for instance. On the other hand, a privately owned corporation can distribute most of its wealth to its workers, or to charity, if the property owners or managers are so inclined. It can distribute its equity to workers, and vice versa. State-owned enterprises can distribute more equitably to the public or to workers, and private corporations can distribute primarily to shareholders, executive officers, and managers—as is so often the case.

But the fact is, capital itself does not have an inherent redistributional tilt, nor does it contain necessary internal contradictions that lead to the demise of capitalism. Capital—as accumulated wealth, equity, machinery, or even human potential—exists in both state-controlled and privatized economies. Capital itself does not dictate distribution; human judgment and decisions do. Everything turns on the regulation of capital. It is only the advanced capitalist form, tied to particular values of self-interest, that increases the disparity between worker and executive compensation. None of this is natural or inevitable. It is chosen. There can be path dependencies, but those are not inevitable or unchangeable either. Often, the inequalities are sustained and justified by certain myths about the free market that naturalize the political economic regimes. When we expose these myths, though, it becomes clear that every political economy is regulated in unique ways, and what we can and must do is judge the distributional outcomes that result from their second-order operating rules, mechanisms, and policing.

The result is that critical theorists simply cannot say ex ante that one type of political economic regime—centralized, nationalized, socialist, syndicalized, private, or anarchist—is more favorable to critical values than another. We, critical theorists, cannot espouse or promote, in the abstract, a socialist state or a communist regime. We can only judge the distributional outcomes of already existing political economies, and we can only judge them based on the values that are at the heart of critical philosophy. This represents a fundamental break from early critical theory, which tended to orient itself around a specific utopian vision, generally the idea of socialism or communism. (I should emphasize that I am using the term *utopia* here to signify the normative dimension and vision of critical theory. I am keenly aware that there has been intense disagreement within the Left over the very idea of utopianism—with Marx, for instance, rejecting utopianism as a form of postponement, and others embracing it as a necessary element, along with hope, of any progressive movement.[2] I do not mean to enter those debates, which I do not find particularly fruitful. Instead, I am using the word *utopia* to capture critical philosophy's normative direction and horizon.)

Now, to be sure, there remain critical theorists, such as Alain Badiou, Jodi Dean, or Slavoj Žižek, who call for the idea of communism, a communist horizon, or the communist hypothesis—all relatively close to the more traditional Marxist vision.[3] There are other critical theorists who continue to imagine the possibility of communist insurrections, or even revolutions. Étienne Balibar remarks, suggestively, that "civic and democratic insurrections, with a central communist component against ultra-individualism, also involving an 'intellectual and moral reform' of the common sense itself (as Gramsci explained), are probably not destructible."[4]

Even more provocatively, he still imagines a revolution along those lines. "Call 'revolution' the indestructible? I would suggest that possibility," Balibar declares.[5]

But the realistic prospect of a proletarian revolution in liberal democratic regimes, or a proletarian dictatorship (in the sense of rule), has faded, especially given the absence today of a leftist self-consciousness among many workers, at least in the West. The belief in a Marxian philosophy of history and the inevitability of revolution has faded. In an earlier time, certainly, it would have been much easier to talk about a critical utopia. Dialectical materialism remained more central to critical theory, either as an animating force (for instance, in much of the critical thought and writings on Maoist insurgency, even in the 1970s), or as a foil and point of resistance, reconceptualization, or augmentation (for instance, in Foucault's or Deleuze's writings through the mid-1970s). But the geopolitical landscape by the twenty-first century, the dissipation of a Left-leaning working class—with the rise of far-right movements that have cannibalized the traditional base of socialist and communist parties—and the general fatigue with metahistories have all dramatically eroded the prospects for a workers's revolution. The result is that today, even the writings of the first generation of Frankfurt School authors feel out of touch with present critical sensibilities.

The reasons trace, in part as well, to the transformation of the very concept of revolution that was embedded in more classical critical theory. Reinhart Koselleck and Hannah Arendt famously traced the emergence of the modern concept of revolution to the eighteenth and nineteenth centuries. In contrast to ancient conceptions of revolution tied to astronomy and revolving cycles—to the cyclical returning to a point of origin, to the astronomical cycle of the stars, or to the cyclical progression of constitutions (from monarchy to its dark twin, tyranny, to aristocracy and then oligarchy, and finally democracy and ultimately ochlocracy, or mob rule)—the so-called modern concept of revolution signified a watershed social transformation or a binary break, a singular moment represented by the collective concept of "Revolution," with a capital R and in the singular. What characterized the modern concept of revolution was the passage from the idea of a political to a total social transformation: the idea that a revolution is about social change, about "the social emancipation of all men, [about] transforming the social structure."[6]

As the latter half of the twentieth century approached, this modern concept of revolution collapsed under the weight of its own exigency, leading to other late-modern or postmodern forms of uprising, insurgency, riots, and insurrection.

The breakdown was triggered, in part, by the anticipated failure of the Revolution, which nourished an expectation or fear of miscarriage—what Étienne Balibar refers to as an "accumulation of factors which make the failure of revolutions their only possible outcome, therefore depriving them of their historical meaning and their political effectivity."[7] The collapse was also due, in part, to the recurring idea that Revolution leads only to terror—or, in Simona Forti's words, that Revolution "hosts in its genetic code the mark of terror and totalitarianism,"[8] a thesis notoriously made famous by François Furet and other midcentury conservative historians. It was partly due, as well, to the omnipresent fear that the prospect of Revolution brings about a more powerful preemptive counterrevolution; and to the fact that words and things had become so intertwined that it became practically impossible to talk about Revolution without merely interpreting it. The result is that any prospect for transformation is better understood today through other rubrics than Revolution—such as through the various modalities of riots, uprisings, strikes, assemblies, occupations, or political disobedience.[9] And it is not entirely clear how or whether earlier critical theory tied to the earlier critical utopias could provide guidance regarding these modalities of revolt.

There has been a historical transformation of the critical horizon that has been accompanied by a structural reshuffling of the utopian imagination. A reconstructed critical theory, based on a radical theory of illusions, must take a break from the earlier critical utopias. The historical transformations pushed critical philosophy, especially the revolutionary side of critical theory, from its origins in Marxist class struggle, through a disruption associated with Maoist-inspired forms of insurrection, to more contemporary models of assemblies, occupations, riots, and hashtag movements, which have a completely different texture and offer different visions for the future. The move from Marxist revolution to Maoist insurrection, and ultimately to these new forms of prefigurative uprisings and occupations, has laid a new foundation for critical utopias. It was driven by historical forces that will have a lasting impact on critical philosophy—two in particular.

Loosening the Grip of History

The first is the loosening grip of the philosophy of history—especially among the more revolutionary factions of critical philosophy that I will focus on here.

This was a gradual process, first in Mao's ideas themselves, but more so in the later receptions of his writings, starting in the 1960s and 1970s. Mao started with a strongly Marxian philosophy of history, no doubt; but it slowly dissipated from his writings, and even more so from the reception of his writings. Today, even insurrectional writings that remain inspired by Maoist thought have a far less determinist historical tone.

Mao's early writings—or, at least, the official English translations produced by the Foreign Languages Press of the Chinese government in the late 1960s[10]—were heavily influenced by a Marxian philosophy of history. Mao's *Report on an Investigation of the Peasant Movement in Hunan* (March 1927) firmly embraced dialectical materialism, trumpeting the coming revolution in resolute terms, echoing the Marxist inevitability of social revolution.[11] Similarly, Mao's more philosophical writings from the period, such as his essay *On Contradiction* (1937), represented a vigorous appropriation of Marxist dialectical materialism in contrast to what Mao called the metaphysical or vulgar evolutionist worldview—what we might refer to today as the liberal progressive view of history. But even early on, Mao's emphasis on internal contradiction as the driving force of history, of social science, of physics—of in effect everything—already felt less historical than that of Marx, particularly the Marx of *The Eighteenth Brumaire of Louis Napoléon*. In Mao, there was already an almost mechanical feel to the notion of contradiction, as it passed from the human to the natural realm and back. Drawing on Lenin, Mao illustrated "the universality of contradiction" in the following terms:

> In mathematics: + and –. Differential and integral.
> In mechanics: action and reaction.
> In physics: positive and negative electricity.
> In chemistry: the combination and dissociation of atoms.
> In social science: the class struggle.
> In war, offence and defence, advance and retreat, victory and defeat are all mutually contradictory phenomena. One cannot exist without the other.[12]

This reflected a mechanical dimension to Mao's philosophy of contradiction that sounded more appropriate in natural science than in history. The problem may well be in the translation, but the imposition of a natural science framework and rhetoric on history and human affairs foreshadowed an eventual loosening of the grip of history.

By the time of the Cultural Revolution, the urgency of the laws of history had dissipated. In 1957, right after the uprisings in Hungary, Mao already began to acknowledge that the classical Marxist teachings and doctrines were no longer as compelling as they were before. "It seems as if Marxism, once all the rage, is currently not so much in fashion."[13] And by 1964, certainly, there had been a loosening of the hold of history. Class struggle remained key, but the call to churn society through a cultural revolution was presented more as a promising pragmatic idea than as a historical necessity. The universality, the necessity, and the mechanical were now muted, and instead there was more of a practical sense to politics. Almost a recommendation now, rather than a command of nature:

> You intellectuals sit every day in your government offices, eating well, dressing well, and not even doing any walking. That's why you fall ill. Clothing, food, housing and exercise are the four great factors causing disease. If, from enjoying good living conditions, you change to somewhat worse conditions, if you go down to participate in the class struggle, if you go into the midst of the "four clean-ups" and the "five antis," and undergo a spell of toughening, then you intellectuals will have a new look about you.[14]

Notice how the tone had changed, the relation to history, the form of argument. The grip of history loosened. There was now a certain pragmatism and softening to the discourse and to the argumentation (again, at least in the translation). There was cajoling, and reasoning, all of which sounded like a different nature.

The loosening of the grip of history became even more accentuated with the Western European reception of Mao in the 1960s and 1970s. When Maoism became a form of Dadaism, for instance, with the Mao-Dadaism of the 1970s in Italy and the publication of the review *A/traverso*, which pursued "a 'poetic of transformation' and invented a language called Mao-Dadaism, whose starting point was the idea that Mao's declarations, if read under the right light, are pure Dadaism";[15] or when Jean-Luc Godard portrayed Maoism in *La Chinoise* (1967) as a form of summer training camp for youngsters in love and distress—at that point, the siren call of determinist history was hard to hear.

Of course, the reception of Mao by young critical leftists in the 1960s and 1970s—as well as by more mature philosophers and activists, such as Simone de Beauvoir and Jean-Paul Sartre—was entirely situational, as I will discuss shortly.

They needed an alternative to Soviet-style communism, and the only demonstrable alternative available was their interpretation of Maoism. Mao became a mirror in which they projected their ideas and desires—and internecine conflicts. One can get a good sense of this by rereading a debate between Michel Foucault and two young Maoists, Benny Lévy and André Glucksmann, which took place in June 1971 and was transcribed in the exchange "On Popular Justice: A Debate with Maoists."[16]

But by the time we got to the twenty-first century, even the most Maoist-inspired insurrectional writings had lost their Marxian history. This is reflected, for instance, in the Maoist-inspired book of the Invisible Committee, *The Coming Insurrection* (2007). The grip of a determinist philosophy of history has been undone. Rather than a determinate future, the situation is described as a doomsday scenario. Dialectical materialism and theories of contradiction have been replaced by the powder keg. The insurrection is coming because everyone is sick, depressed, pushed to the limit. We are in a state, the Invisible Committee tells us, of "the most extreme alienations—from ourselves, from others, from worlds." Political representation is over. "The lid on the social kettle is shut triple-tight, and the pressure inside continues to build." There is no theory of institutional change here, but instead a movement from institutions to the personal, to the subjective. "Organizations are obstacles to organizing ourselves," the Committee writes. Instead of forming organizations, we need to turn inward to transform the self. There is little hope for social change and no use for traditional political means. "There will be no *social* solution to the present situation," the Committee states.[17] Instead of politics, there is, if anything, a negation of politics. Instead of history, there is a ticking time bomb.

The Soviet Conjuncture

The second factor is more conjunctural. The movement away from traditional Marxism and the reception of Maoist thought in the West and South in the 1960s was influenced by the historical conjuncture of, on the one hand, European communist parties that were still captured by the Soviet Union, with a Stalinist shadow, and, on the other hand, the absence of an attractive socialist alternative. Young militants projected onto Maoism their hope for a substitute for Soviet communism. This was true across the political Left—from the more hard-core Leninist or Jacobin or Bolshevik politics of someone like Alain Badiou and his *Union des communistes de France marxiste-léniniste* at one end, to the more aesthetic, libidinal, and subjective politics of the *Vive la revolution!* group in France at the other.[18] In this regard, the reception of Mao in the West and South has to be understood through the lens of Orientalism and of the projection of Western leftist desires onto China.[19]

From lengthy conversations with Daniel Defert and François Ewald, who were both Maoists in the late 1960s and early 1970s, it is clear that they turned to Maoism primarily as an alternative, as a way to avoid both the Stalinism of the *Parti communiste français* (PCF) and the dogmatism and top-down hierarchies of the French socialist party.[20] Maoism had available—or at least, it was perceived by these young militants as offering—an opening to a new Left politics and a new form of insurrection, a fresh alternative. For some, it offered a more creative and aesthetic politics; for others, a more dynamic and engaged politics; and for still others, a more extreme insurrectional politics. But it was a new horizon all around.

There is a passage from Simone de Beauvoir's memoir from the period, *All Said and Done*, that captures this dynamic perfectly:

> Despite several reservations—especially, my lack of blind faith in Mao's China—I sympathize with the Maoists. They present themselves as revolutionary socialists, in opposition to the Soviet Union's revisionism and the new bureaucracy created by the Trotskyists; I share their rejection of these approaches. I am not so naïve as to believe that they will bring about the revolution in the near future, and I find the "triumphalism" displayed by some of them puerile. But whereas the entirety of the traditional Left accepts the system, defining themselves as a force for renewal or the respectful opposition, the Maoists embody a genuinely radical form of contestation. In a country that has become sclerotic, lethargic, and resigned, they stir things up and arouse public opinion. They try to focus "fresh forces" in the proletariat—youth, women, foreigners, workers in the small provincial factories who are much less under the influence and control of the unions than those in the great industrial centers. They encourage action of a new kind—wildcat strikes and sequestrations—and sometimes they foment it from within . . . I shall never regret whatever I may have done to help them. I should rather try to help the young in their struggle, than to be the passive witness of a despair that has led some of them to the most hideous suicide.[21]

A Restructuring of the Utopian Landscape

These two forces brought about a structural transformation in the landscape of revolutionary critical utopias over the course of the twentieth century. The influence of Maoism on European militants during the late 1960s and 1970s represented a rejection of a more classical, unified, or coherent Marxist vision of proletarian revolution led by an organized, industrialized working class, guided by an intellectual vanguard, and determined by history.

The Maoist shift represented in part the replacement of the proletarian working class with agricultural workers or "peasants"—that was one important dimension. This mirrored a larger concern, in the anticolonial context, about the supposed universalism of the proletarian worker as the revolutionary actor.[22] Frantz Fanon, and other postcolonialist thinkers, challenged the Euro-centric notion of the proletariat.[23] As Fadi Bardawil notes, "In opposition to the colonized militants dabbling in 'abstract' slogans of power to the proletariat, Fanon elevate[d] the 'wretched of the earth,' who are not assimilated to the colonial world and whose bodies bear its brunt, to the role of the primary revolutionary agent."[24]

But an equally important shift was from a unitary notion of "Revolution" (with that capital R and in the singular, as Koselleck emphasized), as a tidal wave involving one class rising up against another, to the idea of microinsurrections by minority insurgents that would culminate in a massive movement of the people. This transformation entailed far more insurrectional strategies at the micro level, insurgent tactics, and game-theoretic strategizing—which influenced the movements of May 1968, the *groupuscules* and anarchist cells of the 1970s and 1980s, and the more strategic activism of the last decades of the twentieth century.

The evolution produced a fundamental shift in the map of revolutionary critical horizons. At first, for Marx and for the first generation of the Frankfurt School, the driving force of history was class struggle, imagined as a struggle between the bourgeoisie and the proletariat. It was a struggle between two classes, two entities, two enemies. By contrast, for Mao, the struggle involved three parties: the active insurgents, the active counterinsurgents (early on, the Kuomintang), and the peasant masses. The central Maoist strategy was for the small minority of active insurgents to gain the allegiance of the masses in order to seize power from the counterrevolutionary minority.[25] Mao's discourse was all about embracing the peasant masses—about striving to win over their hearts and minds. This was evident not only during the original insurgency that led to his victory over Chiang Kai-shek in 1949, but even as late as the end of the Cultural Revolution in 1968. One can still hear it when, in confronting the Red Guards—the young radical high school and university students empowered under the Cultural Revolution—Mao told them that their mission had been precisely to embrace all segments of society, to serve the people.[26]

In the following decades, the map of political struggle was essentially similar to Mao's, in the sense that there was a demarcation between the small minority of activists, the police state, and the general population; however, it seemed that the more radical activists viewed themselves as an embattled minority with little interest and even some disdain for the masses. The discourse of uprising became that of a pitched battle against the counterrevolutionary forces of the state, but at a distance from the majority of the population—masses that did not seem movable or winnable. The general population had become the consumerist, neoliberal bulk of individuals, more objects of disdain than a popular force to be won over.

The resulting revolutionary critical utopias were very different. They did not rest on a union of workers uniting to take power or end with the withering of the state; instead, they started with a small cell of activists disrupting and causing havoc, or an assembly prefiguring a new democratic form, without much of an end game. Although Mao insisted on the idea of winning the hearts and minds of the masses, it is not at all clear that later cellular uprisings hoped to bring the masses to their side. There was a far more separatist element to critical activism, a desire to live apart, in a commune, away from others. They envisaged cellular secessionist futures.

The shift from Marx to Mao and to later insurrectional visions can be characterized as a transformation from the Marxist theory of binary class struggle leading to revolutionary upheaval and communism as a necessary product of dialectical materialism, to a paradigm of tripartite warfare, in which a small minority of insurgents win over the masses through insurgent practices, to finally a microstrategic insurrectional strategy of an embattled minority in violent struggle against a police state, with little hope of gaining the allegiance of the neoliberal masses. The revolutionary critical utopias had structurally morphed and fragmented.

CHAPTER 9

The Problem of Liberalism

The fragmentation of the critical horizon reflected a deeper problem within critical philosophy—namely, its failure to come to terms with the antifoundational challenges of the late twentieth century. By their very nature, the post-1968 experiments in critical philosophy, especially of a poststructuralist or deconstructive nature, did not mobilize a critical utopia. Foucault engaged in political interventions on the basis of a subjective sense of self and developed what he called an aesthetics of existence. He viewed his life and deep political engagements more as a form of ethics and art, as a practice of the self, than as a normative matter of critical theory. He wrote of heterotopias, but mostly as a way to explode the notion of utopia and to ambiguate normativity.[1] Deleuze and Guattari gestured toward desire and vitalism as sources of political engagement and as possible critical horizons. Derrida was even more elusive, most often deconstructing his own critical vision at the very moment that he was articulating it.

Foucault explained his own position in frank terms and put these deep tensions into words. In an interview with Jean François and John De Wit on May 22, 1981, on the occasion of his Louvain lectures *Wrong-Doing, Truth-Telling*, in response to a question about the "coherence" of the various facets of his multiple political engagements, Foucault responded in these hesitant terms:

> I would say that I am not looking to establish any coherence. I would say that the coherence is the coherence of my life. I have fought for certain issues, it's true: these are fragments of my experience, fragments of my autobiography. I had a certain experience in psychiatric hospitals; I had, for other reasons, experiences with the police; and I have, in relation to sexuality, a certain experience as well. That is my biography.

> I try to fight when I perceive a logical connection, implication, or coherence between one element and another. But I do not understand myself as a universal combatant for a humanity suffering in all of its different forms and aspects. I also remain free with regard to the struggles with which I have associated myself.
>
> I would say that the coherence is strategic. If I am fighting for such and such an issue, it is because, indeed, it is important to me in my subjectivity. I completely realize that the foundation and coherence pass through there as well. But on the basis of these choices that are drawn from a subjective experience, one can move on to other things in such a way that there is a real coherence, a schema, or a point of rationality that does not take as its foundation a general theory of man.[2]

In this sense, Foucault had no political utopia, nor a desire for normative coherence. He had critical struggles. Throughout his life, he was politically engaged, and those political engagements reflect certain values that I would associate with critical philosophy. But they did not cohere into a utopian vision.

The subsequent wave of postcolonial theory would critique critical utopias even more, as the misguided (or worse, perverse and invidious) projects of imperial expansion and white European supremacy. Edward Said, Gayatri Chakravorty Spivak, and Ann Stoler criticized European critical theory for ignoring questions of colonialism, of racism, of imperialism.[3] Dipesh Chakrabarty called for the deprovincialization of critical theory.[4] Partha Chatterjee challenged the ideas spread by Western thinkers, and Homi Bhabha demonstrated how postcolonial theory superseded poststructuralism.[5] As Stoler would suggest later, Foucault chose only tangentially to discuss state racism, and when he did, "he chose not to target how it was 'made in France.'"[6] Spivak's critique was even more unsettling, insofar as it challenged not just the position of the European critical intellectuals such as Foucault and Deleuze, but even the ability of subaltern scholars to hear the voice of the subaltern.[7] If in fact even those intellectuals who are closest to subjects at the margin of society could not understand their struggles—or worse, distort their lives—then how could critical theory possibly hope to pursue its critical utopia?

Many critical theorists had difficulty reconciling with the newer forms of poststructuralist and postcolonial critique because of their cautiousness about (and in many cases rejection of) a positive political agenda. Few were willing to concede that there might not be a solid critical utopia, a fixed object on the horizon—that, for instance, there may be no singular type of political economic arrangement that guarantees equitable distributions, no single communalist idea that could ensure equality and a just society, no one utopic social arrangement on the critical horizon. Worse, perhaps the very discourse of critical projects and progress was hopelessly imperialist, colonialist, and fraught. In effect, the field of critical philosophy struggled to accept a reflexive, constructivist critical theory shorn of Marxian or Left foundations. Not surprisingly, the poststructuralists and deconstructionists, the postcolonialists, and later queer theorists were somewhat isolated on the Left, and often put on the defensive as well.

It is, after all, hard to accept the idea that, just as there is no institutional fix or charter of rights that would guarantee liberal democracy, there is no institutional or structural way to ensure a critical utopic future. It is difficult to concede that an equitable social outcome will depend on reconfiguring the specific minutia of second-order rules and principles that are instantiated in existing political economic arrangements. This is practically unbearable, especially among those who aspire to equality, social justice, fair distribution, and autonomy. The fact that a Leftist revolution could so easily lead to a terribly unjust society, the fact that the style, type, or form of economic and political organization is hardly relevant to the justness of the outcomes, the fact that what matters are the situated values that regulate production and distribution—these are all difficult to imagine, especially from within an earlier Marxian critical space.

The eclipse of a philosophy of history felt like a loss of mooring and destabilized critical philosophy throughout the late twentieth century. With the collapse of the Marxist horizon, the main alternative became the liberal Left.[8] This alternative was the political imaginary of liberalism, of neutral laws, of rules of the game, that supposedly allows citizens to pursue their personal interests without interfering with others.

Liberalism, and especially liberal legalism, became the most seductive alternative to critical theory. It is not so much the fragmentation of critical utopias, but rather the promise of a cease-fire that undermined critical theory: from the left liberal viewpoint, there is no need for an endless struggle over values because, under the rule of law, everyone could pursue their vision of a good life without encroaching on others. They do not need to impose their values on others; they could keep their values personal and pursue them respectfully by following the rules of the game, and ultimately everyone would be able to achieve their ideals in their lives. All we need to do, in this view, is enforce the rules of the game.

The power of the liberal view was the result, in part, of the fragmentation and all the internecine battles within critical theory. As the Marxian foundation began to erode—as the concept of class struggle and the vision of proletarian revolution began to be eclipsed—many critical theorists reoriented toward liberalism, even some of the most prominent Frankfurt School critical theorists such as Jürgen Habermas, as I discussed in chapter 4. Habermas may well have still claimed, in 1989, that he felt more like "the last Marxist," but his later exchange with Rawls presents a different portrait.[9] The development of communicative ethics and deliberative processes placed Habermas more in conversation with liberals than with the critical Left. Gradually, other Frankfurt School theorists also gravitated back to Kant and liberal theory. The result is that, today, the single greatest challenge to critical theory is liberal legalism: the idea that we should conform to the rule of law as a way to avoid political strife.

Liberal Legalism and the Rule of Law

The liberal view rests on a profound illusion, however, because there is simply no way to set up rules of the game that do not already have values and ideals inscribed in them. All legal frameworks—all systems of laws, all codifications, all laws, all rules of the game—necessarily instantiate a political structure that imposes a vision of the good society and the good life on the subjects of law. This occurs, first and foremost, in contemporary advanced capitalist societies through the legal definition of property and the resulting system of private property rights. The fact is that the supposedly neutral rules of the game are founded on definitions of property that necessarily and inevitably impose a vision of the preferred life on all subjects of law.

Now, as a historical matter, liberalism did not have to be coterminous with the heightened, almost absolute, protection of individual private property rights that effectively shapes the kind of society in which those of us in the West live. The rules of the game, for instance, could have been designed to cap individual possession at a certain point, prohibit inequality from going beyond a certain ratio, or require universal rights to shelter, employment, and food. But they could be (and more often were) designed to allow unlimited accumulation of private property and wealth, to allow unlimited inequality between the wealthiest and the poorest in society, and to require little to no mandatory assistance to the most destitute.

There are different ways of writing the rules of the game, and each entails different visions of the good society and facilitate or impede individuals' specific views of the good. They tranche the question of justice. These rules determine what is and is not possible in terms of the individual pursuit of a good life. They interfere—physically, concretely—with an individual's pursuit of happiness. In this sense, the rules of the game shape the vision of the good society and enable or disable individuals from pursuing their vision of the preferred life. They thus survive and function, in fact, based on a deep illusion.

Today, it is that illusion of liberal legalism, more than the fragmentation of critical theory (though in part reinforced by it), that threatens critical theory and obfuscates the critical horizon. Thus, that illusion is what we most need to unveil.

To be sure, it would be naive to suggest that liberalism does not embrace *any* values, or that it does not promote *any* vision of the good life. Most liberal theorists will concede that it does. It embraces a love of liberty, which is in its root etymology. It also incorporates, at its very core, an ideal of tolerance that is reflected in the notion that people should be free to pursue their own conception of the good, so long as it does not harm others. It is uncomfortable with state authority and has a strong distaste for authoritarianism. It privileges individual preferences over collective ones. It is not, and does not claim to be, entirely neutral.

But liberal theory does suggest that, within those bounds, it is possible to set up rules of the game that allow individuals to pursue their own self-interest without fundamentally imposing any specific vision of the good life on others—that the rules of the game are not rigged to a particular vision of the good. This liberal view purportedly puts an end to the endless political struggles: a legal-liberal rights regime, in this view, mostly solves the political quandary that we find ourselves in, halts the slippage into authoritarianism, and offers the most viable utopic vision. There is no need for endless political struggle, just for the implementation and enforcement of the rule of law.

Most people in advanced capitalist countries believe this. Most have faith in the rule of law and believe in its neutrality. And, to be honest, if I lived in an open autocracy or dictatorship, I too would argue for the advantages of rules and laws—I would clutch at any straw. But insofar as I am surrounded instead by excessive faith in the neutrality of the rule of law, that, I take it, is what I must challenge because it is the illusion of liberal legalism that renders too many, here and now—in the United States at least—docile subjects. It is what prevents people from seeing that they are engaged in political battle all the time. It is what encourages individuals to put politics aside, to not get involved, to let others decide their fate. It is what renders so many of us immature in the Kantian sense: servile to others.

The liberal illusion alone is not what entirely stifles political action. There is also desperation, depression, a growing sense of futility, and problems of collective action. For many, there is a feeling that nothing will change anyway. There is a sense of powerlessness. Indeed, there are many other forces dampening political engagement. But all of them are facilitated by the overarching sense that there are rules of the game that need to be followed and can be neutral. That is an illusion.

Law as Hedges :: Thomas Hobbes

The notion of the rule of law was born in antiquity, especially during the Roman republic, but it found its most solid footing during the emergence of modern political theory with Thomas Hobbes—a most illiberal progenitor of liberalism in other respects. On the question and definition of law, paradoxically, Hobbes was the most important precursor to contemporary liberal legalism. He articulated, in his *Leviathan* of 1651, a modern positivist conception of laws and justice that laid the foundation for liberal legalism.

For Hobbes, laws are what allow individuals to pursue their own interests without getting into each other's way. Laws, Hobbes wrote, are like "hedges": they are not intended to stop us from pursuing our ends, but rather to help us achieve those ends without going astray, without knocking into others, without harming others. They are not intended to shackle us, but rather to free us. They are not intended to "bind the People from all Voluntary actions," but instead "to direct and keep them in such a motion, as not to hurt themselves by their own impetuous desires, rashness, or indiscretion."[10] Hobbes then added, in what is perhaps the most important passage:

> as Hedges are set, not to stop Travellers, but to keep them in the way.[11]

This notion of "hedges" is absolutely crucial to understanding the premise of modern liberal thought: namely, that laws are intended to facilitate individuals' quest for their self-interest rather than impose upon them ideals or values; that laws are what render subjects free; that laws are what guarantee our liberty to pursue our private ends.

Laws function as rules of the game, allowing each individual, then, to play his or her own game and achieve his or her own objectives. Hobbes, in fact, helped coin the notion of laws as rules of the game. He explicitly compared the laws of a commonwealth to the "Lawes of Gaming," to underscore the idea that whatever the subjects of a commonwealth agree to, just as whatever the players of a game agree to, will necessarily be just to all players.[12]

Laws are also what ensure that the sovereign achieves its raison d'être—namely, to guarantee the people their "Contentments of life." Not just security or safety in a narrow sense, but their contentment writ large, "which every man by lawfull Industry, without danger, or hurt to the Common-wealth, shall acquire to himselfe." What is especially important, and telling, is that the core of this contentment is that every subject be secure in his possessions. At the heart of Hobbes's vision, justice consists in making sure that everyone remains in possession of their property—or, in Hobbes's words, it consists "in taking from no man what is his." Hobbes spelled this out, making clear that property and possession are at the very center of good laws: men must be taught, Hobbes declared, "not to deprive their Neighbours, by violence, or fraud, of any thing which by the Soveraign Authority is theirs."[13] Hobbes then added:

> Of things held in propriety, those that are dearest to a man are his own life, & limbs; and in the next degree, (in most men,) those that concern conjugall affection; and after them riches and means of living. Therefore the People are to be taught, to abstain from violence to one anothers person, by private revenges; from violation of conjugall honour; and from forcible rapine, and fraudulent surreption of one anothers goods.[14]

The emphasis on possessions and propriety is what led a scholar like C. B. Macpherson to place Hobbes at the fountainhead of a strain of liberal thought that he called, coining a term, "possessive individualism."[15] This is the idea that all subjects possess these things—life, limb, conjugal relations, riches, and possessions—on their own, that they owe nothing to others, and that they have full entitlement to them as a result. This would be the case, as if man's possessions were entirely the fruit of his own labor and he owed nothing to anyone else.

More important for us here, though: laws are what allow subjects to possess what is their own, to pursue their own possessive interests, to maintain their possessions. The law is what prevents others from interfering, through force or fraud, in another man's possessions and pursuits.

This is, in effect, the central thrust of laws as "hedges"—perhaps the single most important metaphor in modern political theory because it conveys perfectly the implicit assumptions undergirding the concept of the rule of law. The metaphor of a hedge conveys objectivity and neutrality: we agree on where we place the hedge, and *it* does not impose values or interests on us, *we* do all the work—within the limits of the agreed-upon rules.

The metaphor resurfaces in John Locke's *Second Treatise of Government* and becomes a central allegory for law. Laws, Locke wrote, as Hobbes had, are not confining or limiting of freedom. They are what allow us to pursue our interests; they enable us to be free. And for this reason, Locke emphasized, law should not be called "confinement": "that [the *Law*] ill deserves the Name of Confinement which hedges us in only from Bogs and Precipices." Locke's editor, Peter Laslett, notes in the margin after observing the similarity in language with Hobbes, "Presumably a verbal coincidence or an unconscious re-echo, though see Gough, 1950, 32."[16] Coincidence? Unconscious reecho? That seems inconceivable because the notion of "hedges" is so central to Hobbes's conception. It is so central to Locke's as well: laws are those hedges that make possible our pursuit of self-interest and our liberty. He spells this out as clear as day:

> For *Law*, in its true Notion, is not so much the Limitation as *the direction of a free and intelligent Agent* to his proper Interest. . . . So that, however it may be mistaken, *the end of Law* is not to abolish or restrain, but *to preserve and enlarge Freedom*. . . . For *Liberty* is to be free from restraint and violence from others which cannot be, where there is no Law.[17]

The central notion, here again, is that the legal hedges allow us to be free and to pursue our interests and our visions of the good life. They enlarge our liberty and do not restrict it: they do not shape who we are or what we want; they make it possible for us to achieve our vision of ourselves and the good life.

For Locke, as with Hobbes, this vision of legal hedges *is* intimately tied to a conception of the propertied self: what is foremost, after life and safety, are man's possessions, from the perspective of private property. Locke emphasized:

> Freedom is not, as we are told, *A Liberty for every Man to do what he lists*. . . . But a *Liberty* to dispose, and order, as he lists, his Person, Actions, Possessions, and his whole Property, within the Allowance of those Laws under which he is; and therein not to be subject to the arbitrary Will of another, but freely follow his own.[18]

This notion of man's independence to pursue his own will and interests, to dispose of his own possessions, to instantiate his own vision of a good life—so long as he does not do violence or fraud to another—is at the very heart of the liberal conception of the law as hedges. And it reappears in various other guises in Locke's analysis, as well as in that of later liberal thinkers. It appears through the image of the "Fence" in the *Second Treatise*. In discussing the right to use force against a robber—which, as Andrew Dilts suggests, paradoxically founds the ideal of liberty[19]—Locke refers to the framework of rights, specifically "the Right of my freedom," as the safeguard of his own preservation, using the term "Fence" to describe that safeguard.[20] Michael Walzer, in his article on "Liberalism and the Arts of Separation," added the image of the "wall," emphasizing in his words that "Liberalism is a world of walls."[21] Hedges, fences, walls: in liberal thought, laws represent these ostensibly neutral constructs that allow us to pursue our utopias without getting in each other's way.

A Radical Critique of Law

Many before me have critiqued this view, but not always for the same reason. More often than not, the critique challenged what it perceived as the *false* image of man embedded in these liberal assumptions. Man was, instead, by nature more compassionate, or empathetic, or solidaristic. In other words, the selfish possessive individual of liberalism did not reflect our true *species-being*—to borrow Marx's terminology.

These critiques were useful, insofar as they exposed the hidden assumptions of liberalism, but they did not go far enough. They too went off-track, giving way to new illusions about the real nature of subjectivity.

Marx offered a stinging critique of liberal legalism in his early essay "On the Jewish Question."[22] The model of civil and political rights, he argued, is premised on the notion of a liberal subject that is self-interested and self-centered and pursues only his private self-interest. On the basis of this atomistic subject, in his private space and pursuing his private interests, liberal theory envisages law as what protects one subject from the harm of another. The theory, however, assumes an atomistic subject who is not tied to a community and does not belong to a community—who depends in no way on others.

Marx argued that the liberal construct of civil and political rights rests on a particular view of man: "the egoistic man, man as he is, as a member of civil society." This conception of the subject is one of "an individual separated from the community, withdrawn into himself, wholly preoccupied with his private interest and acting in accordance with his private caprice." He pursues his own individual interests, and as such needs to be protected against others who are doing the same. The conception of law is that of "hedges," in Hobbes's terms; and liberty is conceived of as that which permits the pursuit of individual interests. "Liberty is, therefore, the right to do everything which does not harm others." The law—as in civil and political rights—is what serves to protect that: "The limits within which each individual can act without harming others are determined by law, just as the boundary between two fields is marked by a stake."[23]

What grounds this concept of law is that of the atomistic individual pursuing his own interests and needing to be protected from the pursuits of others, Marx emphasized. Political rights depend on the self-interested, isolated man. "The only bond between men is natural necessity, need and private interest, the preservation of their property and their egoistic persons." This is detrimental to how men view men. "It leads every man to see in other men, not the *realization*, but rather the *limitation* of his own liberty."[24]

Rights produce what Marx referred to, tellingly, as an "optical illusion": an inversion of collective interests for the protection of individual rights. They prevent us from seeing the true nature of man. The contrast, here, is to a vision of man as interconnected and interdependent. This is the notion of man as a "species-being" for Marx: drawing, as he does, on Rousseau, this is the notion of man as "*part* of something greater than himself, from which in a sense, he derives his life and his being."[25] And it is for this very reason that Marx would critique as insufficient civil and political rights. He would emphasize that they are great progress, of course, but not enough: "*Political* emancipation certainly represents a great progress," Marx underscores. "It is not, indeed, the final form of human emancipation, but it is the final form of human emancipation *within* the framework of the prevailing social order."[26] To get beyond that social order is the task of *human* emancipation: "Human emancipation will only be complete when the real, individual man has absorbed into himself the abstract citizen; when as an individual man, in his everyday life, in his work, and in his relationships, he has become a *species-being;* and when he has recognized and organized his own powers (*forces propres*) as *social* powers so that he no longer separates this social power from himself as *political* power."[27]

There is, then, an embedded conception of subjectivity hidden in liberal theory, Marx shows: there is already, baked into liberal theory, a biased view of the subject as a highly individual, self-centered, and self-interested, egotistical agent who is primarily focused on his own possessions and private property and feels neither solidarity with nor debt to others.

This critique of possessive individualism resurfaces throughout the history of political thought. Foucault, for instance, levels a similar critique against American neoliberalism in his discussion of Gary Becker's writings in *The Birth of Biopolitics*: a particular conception of the subject is already baked into the cake of human capital theory.[28] Similarly, Michael Sandel argues in *Liberalism and the Limits of Justice* that liberalism embeds a particular self-centered conception of the individual and a specific vision of the good life; so it does not ensure the priority of the right over the good because it assumes a propertied notion of rights. It has embedded within it a notion of the good as being linked to private property and the independence of subjects. It does not have an idea of human emancipation as the end or goal; it has already picked a vision of the good tied to private property. Here too, though, Sandel embraces a different conception of subjectivity, which is more communitarian—embedded in the community.

But these critiques rarely went far enough. They did not fully come to terms with their *own* illusions. They did not fully embrace a radical theory of illusions. The crux of the problem is not that the liberal conception of the subject is false but that another view of human nature is more exact. It is not that we are actually empathetic animals or inherently part of the collective, rather than individualistic. It is not that we are in truth social animals or political animals.

The problem is that all these claims about human nature are entirely constructed and, when they become naturalized, they are illusions that have political effects of reality.

The distinction is crucial: we will never accurately capture or synthesize human nature. The concept itself is deeply problematic. Hobbes was not necessarily right about our primordial fear of conflict and death; and Rousseau was not necessarily right about our empathy for each other, though he was surely right that assumptions about the self have subconsciously driven most political thought. We do not need an alternative conception of the self; rather, we have to critically understand that these conceptions of human nature are constructed, as are the political conditions that we build on top of them. The idea of individual merit is constructed. So is the idea of desert, or of responsibility—of what we owe each other, and so on.

The level of equality and freedom in society is constructed, and we have control over political outcomes. We can decide whether humans are generous and altruistic or not, selfish and self-centered or not, by setting up society in a certain way to be generous and altruistic—or not.

This is where Sartrian existentialism remains vibrant: we are *our* actions. We are *our* political decisions. It is the type of society that we construct that tells us who we are, not the other way around. We do not have inner qualities that dictate what kind of society will emerge and develop. We have control over the kind of society we make—with as much or as little equality, equity, and justice as we see fit. We are not predefined and have no fixed human nature. We are malleable constructs, shaped for the most part by our prevailing beliefs and material surroundings, deeply caught in language and ways of thinking and speaking—in our forms of rationality. And yes, we are even blinded at times by our ways of thinking—by our illusions.

The Illusion of Liberal Legalism

The crux of the problem, then, is the following: the naturalization of the liberal vision of man—the fact that this liberal vision of man is surreptitiously baked into liberal political theory—produces a series of illusions that then justify claims to objective truth (such as the belief in individual responsibility and individual merit), which then justify the ratcheting up of unequal social institutions and processes.

Now, nothing is wrong with individual striving and ambition. But the idea that politics can neutrally set up rules of the game that allow everyone equally to pursue their goals is a fiction. It is an illusion that has detrimental effects, specifically that facilitate particular individuals, well situated and well endowed, to achieve their own objectives and that allow them to impugn those individuals who are not well situated when, because of the ways the laws are set up, they fail to achieve their goals. The rules of the game are not neutral; rather, they distribute opportunity. Just as the height of the basketball hoop will statistically favor tall players, limitless inheritance will favor the children of wealthy parents.

The point is that there is no neutral notion of merit. There is no way to objectively speak about individual responsibility. A child who grows up in the inner city, with poor educational and work opportunities, is simply not on equal footing with a child who attends the best private schools and has unpaid internships throughout the adolescent years. Those differences are the direct product of the ways in which the rules of the game are established—they are a direct consequence of unlimited rights to property, tax laws, inheritance, and other advantages. The rules of the game create these differences and maintain them. As a statistical matter, as a question of probabilities, they reproduce social inequalities. To be sure, there will be exceptions, and some individuals will be able to transcend their likely outcomes—for better or for worse. Some will fall; others will rise. But those are the outliers. For the most part, the rules of the game heavily influence the fate of most individuals.

The central problem, then, is not the embedded idea of individual ambition and self-reliance, but rather the way in which the accompanying notion of laws and legal structures hides the reproduction of wealth and power; how it creates a fictitious idea of individual merit and responsibility; how it advantages some and disadvantages others; and how, ultimately, it facilitates an increasingly unequal social condition.

Let me emphasize an important point: There is nothing inherently wrong with individualism. In fact, Sartre may be right that "*l'enfer, c'est les autres*"— hell is other people. But despite that, our human condition requires forms of cohabitation that demand a modicum of justice and equality among us all. It requires that we live in solidarity, one with another. Our social condition and mutual interdependence force upon us the need for solidarity. And liberalism makes this difficult because historically it has been built on notions of private property that have facilitated the accumulation of wealth. Of course, it need not have been that way, and there were potential limits (for instance, in the Lockian notion of possession based on labor, on what can be used and consumed); but that is not the way in which the liberal tradition evolved. So today, liberalism facilitates rather than hinders the hoarding and grabbing of property. It masks selfish accumulation under the guise of individual merit and responsibility. And more and more—as we see in the research of Thomas Piketty and his colleagues—it is facilitating a grab for the public commons.[29] There were a few restraints during the twentieth century, such as world war and the threat of communism—the specter of Marx—which forced liberal democracies to redistribute; but those are (for the first, at least, hopefully) things of the past. Liberalism today faces no more competition, and as a result, capital accumulation is exceeding all bounds. This is now facilitated by the illusion of liberal legalism.

The crux of the problem today, then, is the myth of legal-liberalism. Let me emphasize here, though, the historically situated nature of my claim. This is the case for those, in the West, today, who live in putative liberal democratic regimes. There, it is the naturalization of liberalism that is most problematic. That is not necessarily the case in more autocratic regimes elsewhere. Moreover, liberalism is not the only political construct that produces illusions. For its part, communism carries its own illusions: the very idea that state institutions could wither away, for instance, is a myth. There will always be regulatory mechanisms, whether we call them the state or not. To speak of the withering of the state is a dangerous illusion that draws our attention away from the fact that regulatory mechanisms will necessarily distribute wealth, power, and opportunity. But in the West today, we are not facing a political condition in which communist mythology shapes us, and so that particular illusion is not relevant right now. By contrast, liberalism is dominant, hegemonic, and only increasing—and for that reason, it is the illusion of liberalism that is the most damaging today in the twenty-first century. In this, I agree with Slavoj Žižek. He uses slightly different language, but the underlying idea is the same. For Žižek, as for Badiou, the real problem today, the real hindrance to social transformation, is the illusion of liberal democratic reform:

> It is the "democratic illusion," the acceptance of democratic mechanisms as providing the only framework for all possible change, which prevents any radical transformation of society. In this precise sense, Badiou was right in his apparently weird claim: "Today, the enemy is not called Empire or Capital. It's called Democracy." It is the "democratic illusion," the acceptance of democratic mechanisms as the ultimate frame of every change, that prevents the radical transformation of capitalist relations.[30]

So what then are these "rules of the game" that tilt the playing field? you may ask. In a country like the United States, they are the protection of limitless private property, tax breaks and rates on income and capital gains, the lack of an inheritance tax, the privileging of civil and political rights at the expense of social and economic rights, the way we police communities, what we choose to criminalize and enforce, to name a few. These are the intricate legal rules—the rules of the game—that make possible capital accumulation and growing inequalities. Some liberal thinkers will argue that these are not the rules of the game, but the outcomes, and that the rules are the higher-order constitutional norms that determine how political decisions are made—in effect, that there are two (or perhaps even more) levels of laws, and that it is only the higher-order rules that qualify as the real rules of the game: so, for instance, federalism, the separation of executive, legislative, and judicial powers, bicameralism, the presidential veto power, freedom of the press and religion, and so on.[31] But those rules too are malleable and affect the tilt of the playing field. Redistricting after each Census has significant effects on our political condition. Voter eligibility and felon disenfranchisement laws have turned presidential and congressional elections in the United States in past years.[32] The Electoral College can trump the popular vote and, today, favors large-area, low-population rural states. All of these purportedly neutral institutions and rules have political consequences, and to suggest that they are neutral or objective is to mask, once again, the political struggles that underlie our political condition.

In the end, the illusion of liberal legalism—that laws are neutral rules of the game—favors certain political outcomes (for instance, capital accumulation and increased inequality) that should be the product of political contestation. It does this, first, by naturalizing the rules of the game, by convincing us that laws are neutral devices that promote our individual liberty. But second, and equally important, it favors certain political outcomes through the way in which it conceptualizes violence, a point that I will return to in chapter 12.

CHAPTER 10

A Radical Critical Theory of Values

What matters, then, is not the formality of law, nor the rule of law, but instead the values and ideals that underlie the interpretation and enforcement of legal norms. To be clear, liberal legalism cannot prevent the rise of authoritarianism, as we have witnessed in the United States since 9/11; more often than not, it is plied by able lawyers during perceived moments of threat and crisis. Moreover, the rule of law does not preclude despotism. The Third Reich, for instance, followed a strict rule of law. The problem was the values and ambitions of its political leaders. In discrete political situations—for instance, the investigation of Donald Trump by special counsel Robert Mueller and the House impeachment committees—the rule of law can serve as a potent weapon in the hands of liberals; but it is equally forceful in the hands of conservatives, especially in the battle over Supreme Court confirmations. In the end, the rule of law is almost infinitely malleable, and it can be reshaped easily by skilled lawyers on either side, particularly in times of crisis. It is not the formal structure of legal regimes that prevents a downward spiral toward tyranny. What matters are the values that infuse those structures and the ways in which they are interpreted and implemented.

This applies as well to the formality of political economic regimes. Here, too, there is no inherent tilt to either free markets or controlled economies. There are no *necessary* correlations between the formal structures of market regulation (e.g., private property regimes versus nationalized industries) and outcomes. As a result, we cannot say, as critical theorists, that any specific type of political economic regime will produce just outcomes. The horrors associated with former communist regimes bear this out: the gulag and the corruption of the Soviet Communist Party; the millions of deaths caused by the Great Famine in Maoist China; the killing fields of the Khmer Rouge leaders. Plus, consider the complete ineffectuality of certain Socialist governments, such as that of former French president François Hollande. State-directed and socialist political economies, and their derivatives, are no more likely to produce just outcomes than regimes built on private property. There is little room for discussion on this point. Here too, what matters is not a particular form or regime of political economy; rather, it is the minutia of second-order rules, regulations, policies, and decisions that determine distributions of resources, wealth, well-being, and life itself. It is the inevitable regulatory web and how it allocates materiality.

The Centrality of Critical Values

This has dramatic consequences regarding the question of critical utopias and normative visions. It means that the critical horizon can no longer be a collectivist state, a socialist government, a planned economy, or the withering of the state. None of these forms offers any guarantees. What matters, in terms of the vision for the future, is how an already existing set of political economic regulations shapes the production, distribution, and enjoyment of material wealth and well-being in society. What matters is how closely the resulting social reality approximates our political values—specifically, the values at the root of critical philosophy. In terms of a critical horizon, then, all that we can judge, as critical theorists, are the material effects, and we can do that only by assessing how closely they approximate critical values.

This explains why a reconstructed critical theory, a radical theory of illusions, has to focus, almost by default, on its core values and ideals. It needs to be idealist and materialist at the same time—entirely so—but then normatively assess on the basis of the values at the heart of critical philosophy: to shape a world of equal and compassionate citizens in solidarity and autonomy. When it unveils the illusions of the free market or of controlled economies, we are only left with an analysis of how the internal rules and regulations function and actually distribute resources, and we can only assess those distributions in relation to the critical values of equality and solidarity.

In the end, we come face to face with values—and *only* values. The effort to construct formal or procedural devices fails, whether in law, politics, or economics. Even the most venerable and popular devices, such as John Stuart Mill's "harm to others" principle, meet the same fate. Mill designed this as a neutral liberal principle that would prevent the state from imposing values on its citizens. Like Hobbes's notion of hedges, the harm principle was intended to allow each individual to pursue their conception of the good, unimpeded by others or by the state. But the notion of harm proved infinitely and inevitably malleable. In Mill's hands, the notion of harm ultimately was infused by an ideal of human self-development and perfection derived from von Humboldt's writings, which allowed massive regulation of alcohol, parenting, education, and other activities tied to human self-development.[1] The normative drift was inevitable because harm cannot be defined absent a vision of human well-being any more than the law can.

All these inventions lead to the same conclusion: in the end, political arrangements must be evaluated on the basis of substantive values, not merely the procedures or abstract regime categories. It all turns on an assessment of critical values, whether we label them internal or external to the procedures or regimes. As a result, the critical horizon cannot simply be an institutional design, a categorical principle, or an abstract political economic regime. Neither can it be a particular set of constitutional arrangements, nor for that matter a constitution itself. The British do not have a written constitution, but, as Richard Tuck argues, that may allow the United Kingdom to move Left;[2] by contrast, Hungary was given a liberal constitution, but that has not prevented it from drifting right. The critical utopia can never be simply structures, organizations, or institutions. It is, and can only be, a set of shared values.

The Source of Critical Values

Those shared values to critical philosophy do not come out of thin air. They derive from a historical tradition and shift over time. They are not spur of the moment, nor do they reflect individual or personal preferences. They are not a matter of simple taste, but rather of lengthy debate and discussion, disagreement and contestation, exchange, reading, and interpretations of Rousseau, Marx, Luxemburg, Horkheimer, Arendt, Adorno, Beauvoir, Fanon, Sartre, Foucault, Said, Spivak, Butler, Rorty, and others.

Richard Rorty is important in this genealogy because he too resisted foundations as he engaged and debated critical philosophy, and ended up in a similar political position as postfoundationalists, but he disparaged what he called the "Foucauldian Left." His polemics were sharp. "Foucauldian theoretical sophistication," he wrote, "is even more useless to leftist politics than was Engels' dialectical materialism."[3] Rorty wrote out of frustration, but he nevertheless contributed to this lengthy and ongoing debate over the values of the critical Left, which he viewed as the movement of hope and moral identity. He tried to push the critical Left away from its concern with stigma and identity and toward greater attention to matters of wealth, economics, and unionization.[4] Despite his polemics and theoretical disagreements, Rorty ended up in a similar space: debating core critical values of equality and solidarity.

These are the critical values that have motivated critical philosophy since its inception: to create a more equal, compassionate, and just society where there is less oppression, marginalization, and domination, a lower social differential, and a greater possibility for everyone to achieve their fullest potential and autonomy. These values reflect an emancipatory ideal that has infused all of critical thought.

In an important book, *Why America Needs a Left: An Historical Argument*, the historian Eli Zaretsky traces these values of the critical Left in the specific case of the United States.[5] Contrary to popular opinion, Zaretsky demonstrates a long tradition of the Left in America—one that evolved in three stages in response to three crisis moments: the abolitionist movement as a response to slavery, the socialist movement as a response to the Gilded Age and the Great Depression, and the New Left as a response to the Vietnam War and the concentration of wealth beginning in the 1960s. Zaretsky specifically and correctly refers to these as a "tradition": "Each crisis generated a left—first the abolitionists, then the socialists, and finally the New Left," he writes, "and together, *these lefts constitute a tradition*."[6] The central value of this tradition, he underscores, is the value of equality. Equality took on different shapes over time, but the value was and remains the touchstone of the critical Left. Zaretsky explains:

> At the core of each left was a challenge to the liberal understanding of equality—the formal equality of all citizens before the law. In place of that understanding, each left sought to install a deeper, more substantive idea of equality as a continuing project. In the first case, the abolitionists, the issue was political equality, specifically the abolitionist belief that a republic had to be founded on racial equality. In the second case, the socialists and communists, the issue was social equality, specifically the insistence that democracy required a minimum level of security in

> regard to basic necessities. In the third case, the New Left, the issue was equal participation in civil society, the public sphere, the family and personal life. Central to our history, then, is a struggle between liberalism and the left over the meaning of equality.[7]

This value of equality, naturally, is tied to the goal of emancipation from forms of oppression and domination. Zaretsky embraces this emancipatory vision, calling specifically for a reinvigorated fourth cycle of American leftism. What it would depend on, he suggests, is "a revival of the egalitarian traditions—racial equality, social equality, cultural and sexual equality, and equality between the peoples of the world."[8]

Zaretsky draws as well on the writings of Norberto Bobbio and Steven Lukes, who both trace the core values of the critical Left to equality.[9] Both of their work, naturally, reaches beyond America to discuss the unifying values of the Left across time and space—at a more global level. As Lukes suggests, equality stands at the center. Regarding the Left, Lukes writes, "Its distinctive core commitment is to a demanding answer to the question of what equality means and implies. It envisions a society of equals and takes this vision to require a searching diagnosis, on the widest scale, of sources of unjustifiable discrimination and dependency and a practical programme to abolish or diminish them."[10] Equality of resources, of well-being, of wealth and living conditions, of recognition, of respect, of opportunity, along all dimensions of class, gender, race, religion, sexuality, and sexual preference—these are the core values of critical philosophy.

These questions of values are not simply a matter of faith. There are texts to read, generational discussions and debates to have, and even, as evidenced with Rorty, deep disagreements, accusations, and sometimes excommunications. Like any other tradition, there are ruptures, breaks, and disagreements. This is true of practically all traditions. It is equally true of the Christian tradition, in which Franciscan values differ from Benedictine.[11] It is true within the Islamic tradition as well, which encompasses different ways of interpreting the sacred text, leading to more conservative, backward-looking branches like Salafism, others like Qutbism that are more radical, as well as an Islamic Left, and a progressive Left spiritualism, as evidenced by the life and writings of Ali Shariati.[12]

Within critical philosophy as well, there are differences and variations, disagreements and struggle. Nietzsche's writings are a case in point. Many critical philosophers would set Nietzsche's writings aside or exclude them from the critical conversation; but here too, it is a question of interpretation. There are, naturally, the Nietzsche writings of the noble and strong predator, of the Viking warrior, of the prophet Zarathustra, who leads a small band of chosen ones, of "men of knowledge," who know and can see, and can get beyond man to the *Übermensch*. Recall Nietzsche writing, through the voice of Zarathustra: "For thus, justice speaks *to me*: 'humans are not equal.' And they shouldn't become so either! What would my love for the overman be if I spoke otherwise?"[13] But if that may feel at odds with the left critical tradition, there is also the Nietzsche of §10 of the second essay of *On the Genealogy of Morals*, of that nobleness of spirit that comes from a consciousness of power, of that possibility of getting beyond punishment, of rising above *ressentiment* and petty rivalries with confidence and a sense of self. "It is not unthinkable that a society might attain such a *consciousness of power* that it could allow itself the noblest luxury possible to it," Nietzsche wrote: "letting those who harm it go *unpunished*. 'What are my parasites to me?' it might say. 'May they live and prosper: I am strong enough for that!'"[14] Those Nietzsche writings may well be at the heart of a reconstructed critical theory and of its critical values. It is, after all, Nietzsche's writings that raised the question of the value of values.

Situation and Contextualism

The task of identifying and interpreting critical values is necessarily situated and contextual. As critical theorists, we interrogate and pursue these values in confrontation with really existing political circumstances. We examine how the existing regulatory mechanisms—whether in a capitalist, socialist, or communist state—shape our material and spiritual world, how they distribute material wealth and well-being. We are temporally and spatially located and can only judge the political economic circumstances within which we find ourselves. Some of us may live in capitalist liberal democracies, others in socialist democracies, others in communist countries, and still others in openly authoritarian regimes. Each of us, critical theorists, may need to push those regimes in different directions in order to realize our shared critical values better. In this sense, the critical work is inescapably and deeply situated. We are always *en situation*, as Sartre maintained.

At the same time, the critical values need to be understood, normatively, from a contextualist perspective. Amy Allen advances a theory of metanormative contextualism in her book, *The End of Progress*, which provides a compelling philosophical framework to understand the counterfoundational normativity of a reconstructed critical theory.[15] Allen distinguishes between first-order normative values (say the substantive values of equality and autonomy) and second-order normative justification at the higher metanormative level. To avoid the poles of both relativism and absolutism, Allen proposes for the second-order metanormative level the kind of humility that she identifies in Adorno's writings. Humility calls for awareness of the dangers of normativity, a consciousness of the postcolonial critiques of European notions of progress, and, in this sense, great care and a willingness to reconsider. But, according to Allen, it does not thereby undermine the solidity of the first-order values.

Allen does not claim any transcendental or transhistorical basis at the metanormative level. She does not seek to render the normative analysis universal or transhistorical, but instead she wants to deeply contextualize the normative work, both in the present and in light of traditions of thought and practice. Allen writes: "On this view, we take the position that we are committed at a first-order, substantive level to these normative principles inasmuch as our form of life and sense of ourselves as practical moral agents depend on them, but that we simultaneously acknowledge, at a second-order, metanormative level, that those very ideals themselves demand of us an awareness of the violence inherent in them and also a fundamental modesty or humility regarding their status and authority."[16]

In this, Allen draws predominantly on Adorno and Foucault, while recognizing and criticizing their faults and tendencies toward Eurocentrism. From Adorno, Allen draws a type of epistemic and normative "modesty"—one that is akin, she notes, to the "humility" that Saba Mahmood embraced.[17] From Foucault, she draws mostly on the "problematizing" conception of genealogy that Colin Koopman develops in his work as well—a problematization that is reflexive and opens up a space for creating some distance from practices and institutions.[18] Both of these—humility and problematizing—allow the critical theorist to remember and emphasize that values can be dangerous, that we need to proceed with caution, that, in Allen's words, "the norms that we adhere to have their roots soaked thoroughly in blood, as Nietzsche would say."[19] Allen concludes:

> We could understand ourselves, at a first-order, substantive normative level, to be committed to the values of freedom, equality, and solidarity with the suffering of others, but understand these commitments, at the metanormative level, to be

> justified immanently and contextually, via an appeal to specific historical context rather than via an appeal to their putatively context-transcendent character. Such a metanormative contextualism offers a better way of instantiating the virtues of humility and modesty that are required for a genuine openness to otherness.... In other words, we advance our normative commitments with a fundamental modesty or humility about the justificatory status of those commitments; we recognize that such modesty or humility is necessary for realizing those very commitments, that is, for the possibility of finally becoming human.[20]

This leads Allen to embrace what she calls "contingent foundations": normative commitments that come from particular historical traditions that she can defend with humility and care, but that do not rest on any context-transcendent justification, transhistorical argument, or Archimedean point.[21]

Allen's metanormative contextualism offers a compelling philosophical framework to understand the normative position of this reconstructed critical theory. But I would add, there also needs to be historical and geopolitical contextualization of the first-order values themselves. Even if we agree on the historical tradition and contexts that we draw on for our critical values, those will need to shift and adjust over time and space. Historical changes and geopolitical forces will call for fine-tuning, for relative privileging, for slight tweaks.

Critical theorists themselves drift over time in their own balancing of values. This is evident if one looks closely and compares different writings over time. For instance, the emancipatory ambition of Horkheimer shifted slightly from a more collectivist vision represented in his earlier expressions regarding the goal of a just and equal society—recall the different formulations in chapter 1—to a more individualistic vision that privileged freedom over equality by the 1960s. The new preface to the reedition of *Dialectic of Enlightenment*, published in 1969, signals this shift in emphasis regarding emancipatory projects. Whereas in the late 1930s, the ambition was, as you will recall, "a reasonable organization of society that will meet the needs of the whole community,"[22] in 1969, it becomes instead the goal of "preserving freedom, and of extending and developing it."[23] Twice, in that short preface, Horkheimer and Adorno talk about "freedom," which they explicitly privilege over Horkheimer's earlier call for a more rationally administered world. This is no doubt the result of their experience with Nazi Germany and imposed conformity, which they specifically reference: "The horde which so assuredly appears in the organization of the Hitler Youth is not a return to barbarism but the triumph of repressive equality, the disclosure through peers of the parity of the right to injustice."[24] It may also reflect, not just the experience of the war, but the influence of Adorno on Horkheimer. That disgust with conformity permeates their chapter on the culture industry. The later writings highlight a strand of individualism that was less noticeable earlier, reflected in their discussion of mass culture and elsewhere. The lack of appreciation of the possible benefits of mass entertainment—of entertainment that becomes available to the masses through processes of a quasi-industrialization of culture—even, at times, bears a slight hint of elitism. The progression reflects a drift over time and differences with other critical theorists as well. The contrast with their colleague, Herbert Marcuse, could hardly have been greater. In his most famous work, *One-Dimensional Man*, published in 1964, Marcuse remained much closer to the collectivist vision of Marx and true to Marxian theory. Marcuse explicitly declared that Marx was right and his theories were true, in terms of the historical process they described. "Marxian theory was already true at the time of the Communist Manifesto," Marcuse wrote.[25] A few years later, in *Counterrevolution and Revolt*, published in 1972, he added that "Marxian theory remains the guide of practice, even in a non-revolutionary situation."[26] Marcuse clearly drew his first-order values more directly from Marx.

Amy Allen, by contrast, seems to draw her first-order values from the Enlightenment tradition and from advanced modernity. "For those of us situated in the context of late modernity," she writes, "those resources include Enlightenment notions of freedom, autonomy, reflexivity, inclusiveness, and equality."[27] Even while critiquing it, she references predominantly our "Enlightenment inheritance" when she discusses first-order values. That gives her discussion its emphasis on freedom and liberty. This may be because Allen draws mostly on Adorno and Foucault, who could be more closely associated with freedom and justice than with equality. But there is a slippage, and it is hard to always know whether she is talking about Enlightenment values, Adorno's and Foucault's values, or her own values. In any event, freedom and justice are privileged. Equality, when it appears, is usually in last place.[28]

The normative slippage in Horkheimer and Adorno foreshadowed the eventual abandonment of Marxism by later generations of the Frankfurt School and pushed them to search for a slightly different balance of values. With Marx out of the picture, Habermas would turn to democratic deliberation to infuse critical values; Foucault, late in life, to practices of the self; Honneth, to recognition, and then, more explicitly, to socialism; Butler, at times, to an ethic of love; Forst, to tolerance.

These all reflect different sources of inspiration and interpretation to infuse critical values.

It is crucial, then, to first identify properly the values that are central to critical philosophy, as Zaretsky, Lukes, and Bobbio do: critical theory draws on a Leftist tradition that values equality, compassion, respect, solidarity, social justice, and autonomy. It does not really draw more broadly on the Enlightenment, I would argue, not only because of what the postcolonial critique of Enlightenment ideals has shown us, nor just because of the nefarious directions that reason and rationality led in the twentieth century, but because the Enlightenment tradition is far too broad and includes thinkers as different as Locke and Rousseau. Instead, we need to look specifically at the Leftist critical tradition that places equality and solidarity and social justice at the front of the queue. The critical task is to pursue these values: equality, compassion, respect, solidarity, social justice, and autonomy—not a particular type of state organization or economic regime, but rather a social order that promotes those critical values.

It is important, second, that the calibration and balancing of these critical values depend on a punctual analysis of the historical and geopolitical circumstances. These first-order values must also be contextualized. If we are going to allow a reconstructed critical theory to operate not only in liberal democracies, but also in more authoritarian states, or in communist or socialist countries, then we have to allow a contextualization not only at the metanormative dimension, but also of the balancing of first-order values. Problems of inequality may be more pressing in certain postindustrial liberal democracies, whereas basic liberties of expression (or even of movement) may be more important in despotic autocracies.

Amy Allen's framework rests on a sharp distinction between the second-order metanormative contextualism and the more solid nature of the first-order values. She argues that the contextualism at the metalevel "need not entail relativism at the level of our first-order substantive normative commitments."[29] I am less concerned about this. I believe that the contextualization applies as well to our first-order normative commitments, insofar as we need to adjust them and their relative rankings based on shifting historical circumstances and geopolitical circumstances. To be clear, I would contextualize and calibrate the critical values differently during an Obama administration than during a Trump administration in the United States, and differently between a Trump administration, a Macron administration in France, a Putin administration in Russia, and an Erdoğan administration in Turkey. I would argue for slight recalibrations of the balancing and relative weighing of the core critical values of equality, compassion, respect, solidarity, social justice, and autonomy. That does not render the normative analysis relativistic. It means that the analysis calls for contextualization and good judgment.

The Value of Critical Values

But what is the value of these critical values, you may ask, especially insofar as they are external to liberalism or conservatism? Hegel demonstrated the importance of getting beyond the naiveté of simple evaluation. In Benhabib's words, the Hegelian dialectic was a rejection of the prescriptive nature of Kant's moral philosophy—an effort to "avoid the naïveté of openly evaluative and prescriptive inquiries."[30] The turn to immanent critique was intended to overcome the weakness of external forms of criticism. As Benhabib wrote, "Hegel develops the method of immanent critique in order to avoid the pitfalls of criteriological and foundationalist inquiries both in epistemology and in moral, political philosophy"—turning instead to internal contradictions as a way to proceed.[31] Nietzsche, for his part, fifty years later, would challenge the value of values. What, then, is the value of critical values, especially if they are external to legal liberalism or conservative thought?

The answer is: political. These critical values are explicitly political, in contrast to the religious or moral values that Nietzsche critiqued. Moreover, as I demonstrated in chapter 5, the distinction between internal and external values breaks down in the Hegelian dialectic. The strong form of immanent critique does not hold up, the internal-external dichotomy collapses under the weight of the dialectical transformation. We thus have no choice but to defend our values as if they are external, and for critical theory, on political grounds.

In this regard, then, both Nietzsche's and Hegel's challenges are answerable. Values are neither natural, nor neutral, nor simply true or correct. They are also neither divine nor categorical. Values are productive: they have political value. And in the case of critical philosophy, these explicitly political critical values have value insofar as they move society toward greater equality and justice. Their value is to change the world. These critical values are valuable insofar as they make critical horizons possible.

Naturally, Nietzsche's question was also intended to unearth hypocrisy—for example, the hypocrisy of Christian morality that, in his view, does not seek to protect the meek, but dethrone the powerful; or the hypocrisy of an ethic of charity that is nothing more than *ressentiment*; or of a vow of poverty that is nothing more than a will to power. Along these lines, naturally, we could ask ourselves whether these critical values, or the contextualist framework, are themselves nothing more than subterfuge that allows some privileged individuals to sleep well at night, to feel good about themselves, to deflect real social upheaval. We could ask ourselves whether, in effect, all this talk of critical values and a radical critical theory of values is a will to power and to personal advancement.

There is, in truth, no way to falsify this counterfactual. One could argue that, if those were one's goals, there would be many better ways to pursue them than to discuss philosophers like Foucault or Marx, who are hardly stepping-stones to popularity or success today—or to write theoretical treatises for limited audiences. But on this point, ultimately, there is no refutation. Even the most selfless service to others can always be portrayed cynically as satisfying an urge to feel good about oneself or to see oneself as virtuous. There will never be a way to disprove such cynical interpretations.

In Nietzsche's case, the interrogation of the value of values ultimately led him to a return to nature—a return to certain natural values. Nietzsche certainly did not leave us ungrounded. He was full of values—of health and personal nobility—he was just open about them and wove them into his genealogical description and vocabulary.[32] He inserted them in his own genealogies of good and evil. As Martin Saar notes, "the description and representation, for Nietzsche, already *are* the however implicit evaluations."[33] The value of those values is baked into the historical accounts. Questioning the value of values does not mean, in the end, that we do not *have* values. It means that we interrogate them and test them, with a hammer. That, I am prepared to do—and do on myself, as part IV of this work seeks to demonstrate, ruthlessly.

We live in a world of scarce resources—of scarcity, as Sartre emphasized—and even those resources are inequitably distributed. The concentration and accumulation of resources in the hands of a global elite are unjustified and unjustifiable, and they defy any possible ethical position. The fact that today, as Sam Moyn reminds us, "a mere eight men control[] more wealth than half the inhabitants of the planet—several billion people,"[34] is unconscionable. It is made possible by illusions: the illusions of legal-liberalism and free markets, the fantasy of individual responsibility and merit, the myth of upward social mobility. These illusions are what make our unequal world tolerable.

A reconstructed critical theory can and must unveil these myths and illusions, expose their consequences, evaluate them against critical values, and move on to praxis. In the end, critical theory has thrown its lot on the side of greater equality, compassion, respect, and justice in society, in a quest for individual autonomy. The notion of autonomy, though, is empty when citizens do not have equal access to education, health care, and good living conditions. Everyone should have equal educational opportunities—a first-rate public education, available to all. Quality health care should be provided to everyone in need. And everyone should have sustenance and shelter. Most important, there should no longer be gross disparities in wealth. These are critical values and aspirations. They have and must continue to guide critical philosophy.

CHAPTER 11

A Critical Horizon of Endless Struggle

The end of stable utopias, the need to contextualize critical values, the eclipse of a philosophy of history—these all underscore another central feature of critical philosophy today: namely, the idea that there is no end in sight to the political struggle and that, given the infinite political contestation, the ongoing struggle itself must form part of the critical horizon. This is a core insight of a reconstructed critical theory. The political struggle itself is both our condition and our future. Our critical horizon presents a constant and unending struggle that never reaches a stable equilibrium but endlessly redistributes wealth, well-being, freedom, and life itself through the organization and reorganization of political economies.

The Reality of Permanent Struggle

This is the core of a reconstructed critical theory as it concerns the normative horizon: the political condition is an endless struggle that does not terminate in a perfect situation or a utopian state, but rather goes on forever, so that in the end, the political struggle has to be itself part of the utopian vision and of what critical theory normatively embraces. The political reality is an ongoing struggle in which some seek solidarity, others self-interest, and still others supremacy and domination. The human condition is a relentless contest over resources, possessions, ideals and identity, and existence itself. It is not just a war, nor is it a civil war as Foucault suggested. The notion of a war has an end in sight—or at least, it used to. But our political condition of endless struggle does not. The concept of civil war is too binary. We face instead endless battles, in which alliances are fluid and shifting.[1]

Political economies are constructed, deconstructed, reconstructed, and constantly shifting as we pursue survival in times of scarcity and competition and under the shadow of the looming climatic crisis. The political condition is not merely a Hobbesian state of brutal, solitary, and short-lived existence in a natural condition of war of all against all that comes to an end in the mutual submission to sovereign authority. Neither fear of loss, nor death, nor hope, nor reason, nor even pragmatism propels us out of this predicament or puts an end to the never-ending power struggle. No, the political condition itself provides the weapons, tools, new strategies and tactics, new venues, and jurisdictions, as well as the space and time of combat. This occurs not just through parliamentary debate rules and executive orders, not only in electoral campaigns or in the drawing of district lines, but also in the very minutiae of locating a polling place, granting (or not) a protest permit, enforcing orderly conduct, infiltrating a political movement, or prosecuting—always selectively—an individual or organization or racial group.

Over the centuries, we rarely have had the strength or courage, or perhaps the stamina to confront this. Most often, instead, we found ways to mask our predicament by means of creative, but fanciful, illusions: liberalism and the rule of law, the myth of natural order, the imaginary of a general democratic will, the illusion of free markets, or even the fantasy of actually existing socialism. Our desperate desire for security and stability has blinded us, over the centuries, to our inescapable political condition—to the constancy of the recurring battles, the succession of confrontations and competitions, the instability of it all, even within established leftist regimes. We wish, we fantasize our way out of our political predicament—only to find ourselves engulfed in it, again, and again, and again.

Throughout history, political thinkers have merely played at the edges trying to avoid the depth of our political contestation. Even the most aware, like Machiavelli, perhaps earnestly believed that they could propose a set of tools, a bag of tricks to tame political providence—to domesticate *fortuna*. Hobbes imagined the towering sovereign as a means to steady the strife and enable civil society—terrorized, as Hobbes was, by the fear of war and death. He let us fantasize an end to the war of all against all, even if temporary, and the possibility of a civil condition. Locke hungered for a parliamentary solution to appease the sovereign's authoritarian impulses. Montesquieu made up checks and balances; Marx, a commune of like-minded workers and the withering of the state; and Rawls, procedural mechanisms to ensure justice. Even after the Holocaust, perhaps one of the most brutal forms of politics, with openly exterminatory, supremacist, eugenic effects, Western thinkers timidly placed their hopes in liberal legal mechanisms, legal process theory, and human and civil rights as safeguards against the recurrence of fascism first, and later, especially after the collapse of the Soviet Union, of communism. Some would even fancy liberal democracy as the end of history—in effect, an end to politics, to our endless condition of political struggle.

But these political pipe dreams have done nothing more than exacerbate the hold of illusions and obfuscate the lines of battle. They have diverted attention from our inescapable political condition: namely, there is no institutional fix or structural design or practical device that will stem the conflict or avoid political upheaval, let alone guarantee political stability. All forms of supposed political stability are nothing more than a moment of brutal consolidation of power, at the expense of others whose interests are not even acknowledged. It is always at the expense of others. There is no way to put in place a system of rights or of agencies, or of laws, of judges or ombudsmen, or even simply of men and women, that will protect against political struggle and its resulting harms—small or large, from mere corruption, to expropriation, to genocide. There is no procedural mechanism, no judicial review that can independently ensure justice. Neither are there any laws of economics, nor politics, nor human nature that push history forward—or backward. There is, in effect, no teleology and no possibility of a determinist philosophy of history.

Our political fate and our present circumstances are, and always will be, determined by *what we struggle for and how*. The individuals creating, operating, and manipulating the institutions, what they are made of—those individuals and their values—shape our political condition. It is what *we* do—each one of us, in terms of the justice and equity that each one of us fights for. Ultimately, our political circumstances depend on *our* actions: when and what we protest, whether we vote, whom we endorse, where we contribute, what we say, how we act, where we fight. Institutions are no safeguard. Rights are not self-enforcing. Political parties go astray. It is *what we are made of* and *what we fight for*—each and every one of us, individually, collectively, and severally—that shape our human condition and social and political relations.

Even within critical theory, these are difficult things to accept. Many critical theorists try to soften the blow. It is not warfare or struggle, many suggest, but the *agon*, a modern, updated version of the contest or competition, that now includes digital spaces. Chantal Mouffe, in *For a Left Populism*, retreats from any earlier proximity to Carl Schmitt and the friend-enemy distinction in order to embrace an agonistic view of social relations. She espouses agonism, not antagonism. She embraces Sheldon Wolin and Hannah Arendt, not Schmitt any longer.[2]

None of this acknowledges, though, that what the critical Left faces today in its opposition is a warfare paradigm based on counterinsurgency theory and practice, which has guided several terms of American executive power since 9/11. In this regard, Michael Hardt and Antonio Negri capture better our political condition today. They recognize the extent of the struggle.[3] They opt for, as Joshua Smeltzer underscores, "active counterpowers" and "antagonistic formations within and against the state."[4] They are willing and ready to consider extreme struggle and evaluate it from a strategic perspective.[5] These are more concrete engagements with the model of permanent warfare.

To avoid or ignore the permanence and degree of struggle is dangerous. It cedes too much to the warfare paradigm that the critical Left confronts today—at least in the United States.

Counterinsurgency Warfare on the Other Side

Today, as I demonstrate in *The Counterrevolution*, we face in the United States a new model of governing based on counterinsurgency warfare theory. Since 9/11 and the wars in Iraq and Afghanistan, the U.S. government has embraced a new way of governing abroad and at home that is modeled on counterinsurgency warfare. At its heart is the deliberate construction of internal enemies on domestic soil—a central tactic of counterinsurgency warfare—as a way to centralize and unleash unbounded executive power. We are now living through a new period that can only be properly described as the "American Counterrevolution." Few grasp the magnitude of this historical shift—or what it implies for social struggle and normative analysis.

The seeds of this new counterrevolutionary warfare paradigm were planted at the birth of the republic, when Black slaves and Indigenous peoples became the country's first internal enemies. The gestational period extended over decades, or even centuries—from the Trail of Tears to the demise of Reconstruction; through Jim Crow and the era of lynching; through the Asian Exclusion Act and quotas on Arabs, Italians, and Jews; to the Japanese internment camps and the Vietnam War.

But it was at that time specifically—in the 1960s—that this new mode of governing took shape: Counterinsurgency warfare emerged as a new way of pacifying populations abroad and citizens at home. Counterinsurgency strategies were honed during the brutal Western colonial wars in Indochina, Malaya, Algeria, and Vietnam, and were rapidly brought home to the United States to surveil and repress minorities. With the COINTELPRO program of the Federal Bureau of Investigation (FBI), its targeting of civil rights leaders, and the brutal repression of the Black Panther movement, counterinsurgency methods were domesticated.

Since 9/11, this warfare paradigm of government has been perfected, expanded, and turned into an art form. In a three-step movement of world historical proportions, American political leadership has brought home and now governs through the logic of counterinsurgency warfare. It started abroad, in the wars in Iraq and Afghanistan, when the U.S. military retooled counterinsurgency tactics from the colonial wars and embraced those very strategies—waterboarding and stress positions, indefinite detention, targeted assassinations, and other actions—but this time against Muslims in the war zone and at "black sites" and secret prisons around the world. The U.S. government then extended those counterinsurgency strategies more widely throughout its foreign policy in international affairs, using targeted drone strikes *outside* war zones, rendition of suspects for torture to complicit countries around the world, and total information awareness on *all* foreigners. American leaders then brought those techniques home. Covert operatives began infiltrating mosques and college student groups and surveilling Muslim businesses—without individualized suspicions to justify such actions. The National Security Agency (NSA) turned its total surveillance apparatus on ordinary Americans, bulk-collecting all their telephony metadata, social media, and digital traces. Local police forces became hypermilitarized, with excess counterinsurgency equipment and techniques—military-grade assault weapons, armored vehicles, tanks, night scopes, grenade launchers, and more.

The surprise Electoral College victory of Donald Trump in the 2016 presidential election, as well as the right-wing populist wave that ensued, crystalized this new mode of governing and propelled it to its ultimate and final stage: a perfected model of domestic government through a counterinsurgency warfare paradigm *despite the absence of an active insurgency at home*. This is a counterrevolutionary method of governing *without a revolution*, a counterinsurgency *without any insurgency*, through the creation out of whole cloth of internal enemies—transforming religious and ethnic minorities into dangerous threats.

And the U.S. Supreme Court placed its constitutional seal on this new and radical way of governing. The Court's decision to uphold the Muslim ban constitutionally whitewashed President Trump's explicit and open discriminatory animus. It placed the highest court's constitutional imprimatur on the historical transformation in how Americans govern themselves abroad and at home: America's political leaders now can rule through the willful demonization of minorities, through the deliberate construction of internal enemies, and, more broadly, through a counterinsurgency warfare paradigm of government. By failing to censure President Trump's hate-filled rhetoric or to pierce his administration's pretext and smokescreen, the Supreme Court pushed the country further down this extremely dangerous path. Justice Anthony Kennedy's retirement and replacement by Justice Brett Kavanaugh only made matters worse, paving the way for a solid, decades-long conservative majority on the Supreme Court that likely will entrench the immunity that it bestowed on our political leaders.

Behind this new and radical way of governing, a populist wave of social reforms is waiting in the wings: restrictions on women's reproductive choice, limits on health-care regulation, expanded religious exemptions to certain laws, the elimination of affirmative action in education, exclusionary policies against sexual minorities, and virulent law-and-order policies that will further target and destroy minority communities.

We are now facing the American Counterrevolution. The evidence is all around us. First, practices of terror integral to counterinsurgency strategy—torture, indefinite detention, and summary drone strikes—have become normalized. This is so much the case that President Trump could appoint to head the Central Intelligence Agency (CIA) a woman who personally oversaw a black-site prison in Thailand during the heyday of the torture program during the George W. Bush administration. We Americans now prize rather than revile the brutal excesses of the "war on terror." We reward, rather than penalize, those who carried them out.

Second, indefinite detention, which President Barack Obama had pledged to end during his administration, has now become entrenched. President Trump left vacant the position at the U.S. Department of Defense responsible for approving any transfers out of the Guantánamo Bay camp. As a result, even those men who were approved for transfer before Trump's inauguration remain indefinitely imprisoned.

Third, targeted drone assassinations have become so routine that Americans no longer pay attention to them—despite significant increases under the Trump administration. There has been a dramatic decrease in public information about drone strikes and less and less news reporting about civilian drone casualties. Soon we will no longer even recognize or acknowledge the summary executions and the innocent casualties.

Fourth, total information awareness—the cornerstone of counterinsurgency theory—has now been achieved on all the American population. The groundwork was laid in the immediate aftermath of 9/11, with the bulk collection of all telephony metadata of American citizens through programs such as Section 215 of the USA PATRIOT Act and the myriad NSA tools exposed by Edward Snowden. Those programs remained virtually unchanged since then.

Fifth, counterinsurgency tactics and logics now pervade policing and law enforcement across the United States. With the surveillance of mosques and Muslim businesses by the New York Police Department (NYPD), the targeting of Muslims for interrogations without suspicion by the Department of Justice (DOJ), the FBI crackdown on Pakistani neighborhoods in New York City, and hypermilitarized police forces, we now live the Counterrevolution on Main Street USA.

Sixth, President Donald Trump deliberately constructed phantom internal enemies on domestic soil—another core tactic of counterinsurgency warfare. With his campaign pledge for "a total and complete shutdown of Muslims entering the United States," his unambiguous Islamophobic propaganda, and his crystal-clear innuendos taking issue with "political correctness," Trump methodically turned Muslim Americans and Muslim immigrants into internal enemies who need to be contained and eliminated. The Muslim ban was the centerpiece of that strategy. "Islam hates us," Trump declared, "we can't allow people coming into this country who have this hatred of the United States . . . and of people that are not Muslim."[6] With his call for a database, or even worse, for the registration of Muslims and the renewed infiltration of mosques, Trump demonized Muslim Americans and turned them into a dangerous insurgency. Other groups were targeted as well. The FBI's designation of "Black Identity Extremists" converted ordinary African American and #BlackLivesMatter protesters into internal threats. Trump's derogatory remarks about Mexicans and Hispanics and about the approaching "caravans," and his persistent effort to build a wall on the southern U.S. border, turned Latinx into criminal social enemies.

The evidence is indeed overwhelming: Since 9/11, but especially under the presidency of Donald Trump, governing through counterinsurgency warfare has become entirely normalized. Our political leadership has embraced a counterinsurgency model of governing at home that operates through total information awareness, creating and targeting phantom internal enemies, and pacifying the general population—the three core strategies of unconventional warfare. We have brought home the mentalities and logics, the techniques and tactics, and all the equipment from the wars in Iraq and Afghanistan to use in domestic policing. And by failing to censure these discriminatory tactics, or to acknowledge President Trump's religious animus in words and language, or to cut through the pretextual charade that Trump himself mocked (in his own words, "We all know what that means!")—the Supreme Court constitutionally immunized this new warfare paradigm of governing.

With that new and radical form of governing, a populist wave of social conservatism blanketed the country. Trump seized unbounded executive power through a series of unconscionable executive orders discriminating not only against Muslims, but against all immigrants, Latinx, LGBTQ communities, and other minorities. Trump oversaw the dismantling of social structures and institutions—from the national parks, national service programs, and refugee resettlement to net neutrality and health care—in order to facilitate an even more aggressive grab on the public commons. Trump led a putsch of political norms—a coup d'état, not of the rule of law, which itself was moribund post 9/11, but rather of norms, from small to large. The fact that President Trump did not disclose his federal taxes, or that he so willingly flouted the norms surrounding conflicts of interest—ditching Camp David for Mar-a-Lago—or that he effectively enthroned a royal family and a storm of palace intrigues, all reflect a style of regal government of wealth accumulation and inequality. Trump and the richest Americans became, somehow, above the rest—a class unto themselves, as evidenced when Trump touted the unprecedented right to extend the presidential pardon to himself. From the moment he entered the White House, Trump converted, in a strange alchemy, wealth inequality into power, inching the country more and more toward an authoritarian and unbounded executive reign.

I was struck, in rereading Herbert Marcuse's 1972 book *Counterrevolution and Revolt*, by how prescient he was regarding our present political situation. Marcuse virtually predicted the protofascist turn and Donald Trump's embrace of what I have called a neofascist, white-supremacist, ultranationalist, American Counterrevolution.[7] Marcuse identified, at the turn of the 1970s, the beginnings of a counterrevolution marked by the global use of torture, of extreme militarization, and of the brutal repression of student movements. "The Western world has reached a new stage of development," Marcuse declared, opening his book on

Counterrevolution and Revolt by saying: "now, the defense of the capitalist system requires the organization of counterrevolution at home and abroad."[8] Marcuse emphasized the use of torture—"Torture has become a normal instrument of 'interrogation' around the world."[9] He stressed the massacres and persecutions by the dictatorships in Latin America and South East Asia, and also the repression of students "slaughtered, gassed, bombed, kept in jail."[10] He pointed to the killings at Kent State and the assassinations of Fred Hampton and George Jackson.

By focusing on Vietnam, torture, and summary executions, Marcuse also gave his notion of counterrevolution a counterinsurgency warfare character. He also spoke of the domestication of those counterinsurgency techniques. "The Nixon Administration has strengthened the counterrevolutionary organization of society in all directions," he noted.[11] And for Marcuse as well, it was a counterrevolution without a revolution: "Here, there is no recent revolution to be undone, and there is none in the offing."[12] The result is what Marcuse called "the new counterrevolutionary phase"[13]—or what I call today "the Counterrevolution."[14]

Even more, Marcuse identified, within that "new counterrevolutionary phase," a tendency toward fascism—suggesting that it would likely "prepare the soil for a subsequent fascist phase."[15] The differences with Hitler's Germany were clear, and Marcuse emphasized, "History does not repeat itself exactly."[16] However, Marcuse warned that there was evidence of a protofascist "syndrome" on the horizon. The turn to law and order, the explosion of violence, the vindictiveness, the attack on the liberal arts—all of these were signs of danger on the horizon. The counterrevolutionary forces would eventually turn to "proto-fascism," Marcuse warned, as capitalism progressed beyond its most advanced stage of monopolistic state capitalism.[17]

I am struck by how Marcuse almost foresaw, in his crystal ball, our current political predicament. Quoting William Shirer from the *New York Times*, Marcuse ominously wrote that "we may well be the first people to go Fascist by the democratic vote."[18]

The Human Condition of Endless Struggle

In the end, there is no place to hide. No refuge. No shelter. There is no intimate realm to retreat to. No personal domain that will protect us. There's no way to avoid it.

At every moment, we shape our political condition, in every little thing we do. That is our political predicament.

Invariably and at all times, each one of us is both the author and subject of our political condition—and it is a struggle. Every microscopic choice, every decision, even the most minute ones, will have consequences for the world we live in. This is the utterly excruciating reality of our existence—from the smallest gesture to the greatest, we shape our social relations and human condition. Whether we mindlessly ignore the homeless panhandler on the street or deliberately pull the execution switch, what newspaper we buy and book we read, whether we retire and cede the ground or blog or hack—entire political regimes are built on those choices. A world is shaped by each one. Each and every one, minute or profound—they all shape our human condition.

This is why—although it may sound entirely counterintuitive—work on ourselves, transformations of ourselves in the narrowest sense, must necessarily accompany political action and the quest for justice. There is no tension between ethics and politics here. There is no priority of one over the other—there is no passage from one to the other. The two are inextricably linked insofar as our every choice, our every action form the foundation of our political condition. To act or not to act, and how to act, or not, are ethical choices that are entirely political. There is no natural equilibrium in politics—and there never will be. Each moment is produced by the infinite actions and inactions of each and every one of us. There is nothing but a constant struggle over resources, wealth, reputation, force, influence, values, and ideals—nothing but constant power struggles.

Those who understand this, for the most part, try to dissimulate it in order to gain the upper hand. The art in politics is to put up a façade, a veneer of civility and normality: to make it seem as though politics is not a battle, to calm and appease at the very same time that we strategize and engage. "The presidency is bigger than any of us," we are told. "We must all work hard to ensure a successful transition" because "one presidential administration must follow the other."[19] Those are the arts, the *technē* of politics, intended to soothe and distract, and simultaneously to lead (or, rather, mislead) the subject and citizen, to make them believe that they need not always preoccupy themselves with politics, or truly get their hands dirty, or get too involved, or protest too vehemently. They should contain themselves, play by the rules, or let their elected representatives take care of matters. Politics is not warfare. Things are under control.

"Enjoy your family and your private life." "Go shopping again." "Pursue your personal projects and ambitions," we are told, and all will work out for the best. Nothing could be further from the truth. No, things will not work out for the best; instead, others will decide how to restructure laws and taxes, redistribute wealth, and benefit themselves. "The pursuit of self-interest leads to the common good"—that is perhaps the greatest illusion of all. This would be a farce if it were not so tragic. It is in fact a strategy that merely allows others to determine the "common good," or allows others to claim, reassuringly, that our political condition is under control, well regulated, or ruled by norms. But it is not. It is not *under control*, except insofar as it is entirely *controlled*. It is shaped by our every action and inaction.

We are in inherently violent confrontations because we are, inevitably, and necessarily, in opposition and in competition with other people's projects and values. Politics is a struggle in this sense. It is not a regulated game. It is not agonism, but antagonism. We are inexorably in a clash, in a realm of scarcity, against others who have different utopic values. In this struggle, critical theorists need to be strategic in their deployment of tactics—which I will turn to in part III of this work—but everything has to be aimed at achieving our shared critical values.

Critical philosophy has now wasted too much energy and time on internecine epistemological struggles between materialists and interpretivists, between foundationalists and postfoundationalists, between the Frankfurt School, Foucault, postcolonial thinkers, queer theorists and more—when all along, critical theorists have been making a similar point: that we are in the grip of illusions and myths that construct our world in these unjust ways and render it tolerable. Critical theory has spent too much time on its epistemological detour. It needs to move forward now, first to recognize its shared set of values and second to move on to praxis. Nietzsche spoke of the death of God, but of the proliferation of his shadow.[20] We seem to be constantly living in new shadows. It is time to get out from under them—including the last one, namely the specter of violence, which I will discuss next.

CHAPTER 12

The Problem of Violence

The human condition of endless political battle immediately raises the specter and problem of violence. If the critical horizon indeed includes unending struggle, how is it possible to reconcile those potentially violent practices with the critical values of compassion, respect, and solidarity? How could critical philosophy even consider embattled political praxis if a reconstructed critical theory arcs toward those critical values? Critical thinkers have struggled with this dilemma for decades and constantly face the problem of violence. In reaction to black bloc protesters who destroyed property at an antifascist demonstration in UC Berkeley in 2017, for example, Judith Butler condemned the physical violence. "The turn to violence," she wrote, "further destroys hope and augments the violence of the world, undoing the livable world."[1] Instead of violence or insurrection, Butler embraced an ethic of love. Others as well have turned to King, Gandhi, and the tradition of nonviolent resistance in order to avoid the contradictions.

The line demarcating physical violence from nonviolent protest serves as one of the most common recourses to resolving these questions. It distinguishes peaceful assemblies, nonviolent social movements, and political organizing from vanguard revolution, separatist insurrections, and certain forms of political disobedience. For many critical theorists today, especially given the demise of a Marxian philosophy of history, that bright line determines what is or is not acceptable practice.

The trouble is that, once again, we face an illusion: the very concept of violence that we traditionally employ is a construct of liberal political theory that embeds in it a particular vision of society. The ways that we typically think of violence—in terms of both the distinction between physically violent versus physically nonviolent actions, and between physical and property damage versus other harms—are the product of a liberal conception of state power and liberty. As a result, they are loaded with particular liberal values. This presents a real quagmire and is difficult to unpack. The future of critical praxis would be a lot simpler if critical theory could just ignore the problem of violence and stick with the liberal definition. But that would undermine the entire project of reconstructing critical theory.

This is an area of theoretical quicksand, so a word of caution is in order: the problems of violence can be disorienting. If they become *too* disorienting, please rejoin the conversation in part III, after I explore the quagmire in this chapter (chapter 12) and various ways of resolving it in the next (chapter 13).

The Pervasiveness of Violence

The problem of violence actually permeates reconstructed critical theory. Violence is not just in play in situations of armed resistance or insurrectional strategies. It pervades all modalities of resistance, even nonviolent forms of organizing. Seeking change in society—or, for that matter, maintaining the status quo—is inherently violent in the sense that it necessarily entails redistributions, affects ownership rights, upsets educational practices, and involves political and economic transformation: these inevitably involve impositions of values on many people who do not necessarily share a critical vision of society. It necessarily entails changes that would affect people's lives, life prospects, and well-being. Reinstituting a robust inheritance tax in the United States, for instance—which is necessary—is a violent act: it is enforced through the penal law on threat of fines or incarceration. For the wealthy, it is the functional equivalent of someone taking their property; but instead of having a gun at their head, they are threatened with tax enforcement and penal sanctions. It would be blinking reality to ignore the violent dimensions of social reform or revolution. From a critical theory perspective, the problem of violence comes up even in nonrevolutionary strategies: transforming society (or not) necessarily entails redistributions that are inherently coercive.

Liberal political theory does not need to confront this problem because it defines the contours of violence in such limited ways that it claims never to be imposing values on others. In the liberal view, violence is cabined essentially to disobeying the law, damaging private property, and physically harming others. The liberal concept of violence is what allows liberal political theorists to avoid the hard questions of violence.

The Liberal Conception of Violence

Since Hobbes and Locke, the liberal tradition has narrowly defined violence as the illegitimate interference with the legitimate pursuits of other individuals. Force or fraud, coercion or misrepresentation: these are the exceptional circumstances that justify the state's use of force against its citizens. So long as subjects are legally pursuing their ends, so long as they are staying within the hedges or fences of law, they are not to be disturbed. So long as they are not interfering with each other in pursuit of their personal interests, subjects are left alone.

As Max Weber reminded us, the liberal state has a monopoly on the legitimate use of force. A liberal government is entitled to use legitimate force, even physical violence, to prevent subjects from getting into each other's way or harming each other. Getting in each other's way, in fact, is conventionally defined as a crime—either a crime of violence or a property offense. By contrast, state enforcement of the law, or even the justified use of lethal force or capital punishment, is not viewed as violence. In the liberal view, in essence, violence is conceptualized as individuals getting in each other's way, whereas state policing and enforcement of the laws are not considered violent. These are, respectively, illegitimate and legitimate forms of coercion.

In the liberal schema, then, the problem of violence is limited to interpersonal acts of aggression and property damage—following the model of what we call street crime. The laws themselves never do violence to individuals unless they are misapplied or violated. Economic conditions do no violence to people, nor does the accumulation of capital. Violence—or, more technically, illegitimate violence—is limited to actions of subjects against each other or against the state. (Hobbes went somewhat further regarding the latter, arguing that resistance to the sovereign would amount to rebellion.)[2]

This narrow liberal definition of violence effectively masks all the potential violence that the state or economic conditions might wreak upon its subjects. So, for instance, the failure to maintain proper water utilities in Flint, Michigan, from 2014 to 2016, which resulted in the exposure of over 100,000 residents (including thousands of children) to lead contamination and potential brain damage, was not violent, strictly speaking, in the liberal view. The 2008 economic meltdown and the collapse of the mortgage-backed securities market, which caused tens of thousands of Americans to lose their jobs, health insurance, homes, and retirement savings, with potentially devastating health consequences for many, were not violent according to the liberal view. These forms of harm are masked by the liberal definition of violence. None of them fall in the neat category of one subject using force or fraud against another, or of a state actor illegitimately using force. The fact is, however, that they are systemic forms of violence that may actually cause more overall physical harm than all property crimes combined.

Arguably, liberal theorists could stretch the boundaries and argue that the Flint water crisis and the 2008 financial crisis included actionable misrepresentations. It might even be possible, if there were malicious intent or extreme negligence, to imagine possible prosecutions—and some commentators have argued for that. There is nothing absolutely preventing it. But the fact is, from the dominant or mainstream liberal perspective, those are not incidents that would typically be called "violence." And that's because violence is limited to the interpersonal, to the model of one subject interfering with another's pursuit of liberty or enjoyment of property, or to the state acting ultra vires. It is imagined essentially along the model of street crime. That's just how violence is generally understood in liberal terms.

Now, this liberal understanding of violence has significant effects on our political condition. Just as the illusion of liberal legalism naturalizes political outcomes and renders them legitimate as products of merit, the narrow liberal definition of violence also produces its own illusions that naturalize political outcomes. It gives rise, for instance, to the impression that interpersonal physical violence is somehow far more serious, in kind and degree, than the harm produced by economic conditions—even when the latter may be quantitatively far worse in scope. The first calls for state intervention; the second does not.

The liberal state focuses its police and enforcement powers on common-law crimes, but it ignores (and thereby protects from criticism and oversight) economic harm. This means that the liberal state focuses aggressively on street crime and ignores economic exchanges, even when the latter produces detrimental health and personal outcomes. This then produces what I have described as "neoliberal penality": the paradox of mass incarceration and a police state on questions of common-law crimes, but a laissez-faire attitude in the area of political economy.[3]

The Critique of Violence

Critical philosophy has challenged the liberal conception of violence for years. Under the rubric of a "critique of violence"—from Walter Benjamin's writings on the subject through Derrida's *The Force of Law* to Žižek's essays in *Violence*—critics have questioned the state's monopoly on the legitimate use of force and the narrow liberal definition of violence. These critiques often begin with a critique of the state, which then, naturally, exposes its violence.

Benjamin began, for instance, with a clear denunciation of the legitimacy of state force. The liberal theoretic conception of violence rests on a limited, state-centric notion of violence, he argued. The use of lethal force by the police is not violence in the liberal view, but rather the justified use of force; violence tends to be limited to unlawful (not falling within a legal justification, such as necessity) applications of physical force, deliberately and directly applied. In this way, the liberal definition of violence excludes violent actions of the state that are justified: the death penalty, law enforcement, police or military action, or self-defense.[4] Political violence becomes either ultra vires action by the state or a state agent, or (most of the time) the violence of individuals.

Benjamin and other critics of violence then expand the category of violence to include more ordinary power struggles in both the public and personal realm: to broaden the notion of violence to include the effects of poverty, lack of health care, discrimination, domestic relations, and other elements. This is the idea of "objective violence," which Žižek defines, in contrast to "subjective" or interpersonal physical violence, as the forms of systemic violence that have no identifiable authors but still pervade our world, hidden or masked by all the subjective violence that we so easily identify.[5] It is the idea expressed by Benjamin that extortion, or means-ends rationality, is itself a form of violence. It is the idea that violence pervades ordinary relations between state and citizen, as well as the interpersonal. It is structural. It is pervasive. It suffuses relations of power.

Foucault, notably, developed this critique using the metaphor of civil war. As opposed to the Hobbesian idea of a war of all against all, ending with the establishment of public order, Foucault sought to reinstate the notion of civil war *within* the Hobbesian commonwealth. Civil war, for him, is not the collapse of a political union that would plunge us back into a state of nature. It is not opposed to political power; rather, civil war constitutes and reconstitutes it. Civil war is, in his words, "a matrix within which elements of power come to function, are reactivated, break up." Political relations must be viewed through the prism of war: "Contrary to what political theory usually assumes, civil war is not prior to the constitution of power; no more than it is what necessarily marks its disappearance or weakening. . . . Civil war takes place on the stage of power."[6]

In a letter to Daniel Defert dated December 1972, Foucault wrote that he had begun to analyze social relations on the basis of "the most criticized of all wars: not Hobbes, nor Clausewitz, nor class struggle, but civil war."[7] This notion of civil war and the related concepts of discipline and delinquency are the keystones to his theory of knowledge-power. The idea of civil war, for Foucault, marked a break with previous analyses—notably those that deploy the concepts of repression, exclusion, and transgression—and a turn to the productive functions of civil strife.

The critical theorists of violence, then, begin to see violence everywhere. Benjamin, for instance, even perceived violence in the legal, nonviolent action of the striking worker. Žižek makes a similar move in the first of his "sideways reflections" in *Violence*: to expose the symbolic and structural forms of violence that surround us every day—not only in state relations, but also with each other. These do not have the typical physical trappings of physically violent acts. Violence here is the economic system that imposes early death on the poor and unemployed. Violence is the coercive dimensions of the free market. Violence is the gender norms that produce domination and the racial stereotypes that aggress persons of color.

In this way, violence extends even beyond state action, to our ordinary social interactions. It becomes possible to see how much violence is needed to maintain an ordered society. This is where Sartre, Benjamin, and Foucault come together. By placing existential freedom above everything else, and social relations as limits on our freedom, Sartre too imagined violence in practically all social interactions. As the tape recorder plays, at the bitter end of *The Condemned of Altona*:

> The century might have been a good one had not man been watched from time immemorial by the cruel enemy who had sworn to destroy him, that hairless, evil, flesh-eating beast—man himself. One and one make one—there's our mystery.[8]

For Sartre, in a world marked by scarcity, all actions that are antagonistically related to the projects of other men are violent. Along these lines, physical violence is no different from conceptual mystification or nonphysical acts of protest or liberation. Sartre broke down the distinctions between public and private, between state and citizen, between personal and political, to argue that we are all necessarily implicated in a violent struggle for existence and betterment in a world marked by scarcity.[9]

The violence that surrounds us: Marx saw it well and described it for us in his discussion of what he called "primitive accumulation"—all the policing that it takes to begin to accumulate capital. Weber agreed. He described the grueling discipline, military and industrial, required to mold men and women to a Protestant ethic. Foucault, especially, minutely detailed the timetables, grids, measured movements, and repetitions needed to produce the docile body of the Industrial Revolution. Recall the earlier passage about the accumulation of bodies necessary for the accumulation of capital. In the nineteenth century, Foucault reminds us, we learned not to punish *less*, but to punish *better*—without leaving traces on the body, without disfiguring beauty with brutality, without showing the violence.

There is so much violence hidden today, veiled behind a polished veneer. Wealth is concentrated in the hands of the tiniest few, who accumulate it beyond any possible imaginable use, while others roam the streets destitute and begging—literally sleeping on the pavement. The poor police their own neighborhoods and guard their brothers and sisters behind bars. But we do not see it. We do not want to see it. We do not want to see it to such a desperate extent that we tell ourselves stories about our own ingenuity and enterprise, about the virtues of hard work, about the American Dream. We lavish attention on the few lucky people who escape their lot and make it to the top. We praise the sweat and tears of those who turn their lives around. And we refine elaborate political theories of liberalism that privilege individual responsibility, self-sacrifice, and self-interest: liberal theories that claim to be entirely neutral as to the good life and to set forth only procedural rights and rules that would allow each and every one of us to pursue our ambitions freely, unhindered by others. We build an intricate politics on the foundation of individualism, independence, merit, and responsibility. We construct a line around physical violence. What an illusion! Perhaps it is the most sophisticated, politically. They go hand in hand: the illusion of liberal legalism and the liberal illusion of violence. The amount of hidden violence—violence we do not even see—that is necessary to maintain urban, suburban, or rural existence is frightening.

Once critical theory exposes the illusions, the world becomes much more complicated. There is far more violence that surrounds us, to begin with. There is harm all around—not just in the physical violence that takes place domestically and on the streets, but in economic structures and property relations. The Millian harm principle, that most intuitive of all liberal principles, is of no avail; it serves only as a limiting principle to government action where there is harm. However, today we see harm almost everywhere. There isn't a way out using the rule of law because laws necessarily impose values and redistribute resources. Even our own actions appear violent now. They inevitably impose a particular vision on others. They cannot *not* affect others. In a society shaped by relations of power, it is impossible to act without confronting others. We are inevitably violent ourselves.

In part, we have become better at identifying violence. We have learned to talk about racial microaggressions. We have begun to document police killings. We have stopped thinking—for the most part—that marital rape is just part of the marital bargain. We've started to notice campus rape. We've begun to understand that imposing our values will do violence to others. It makes little sense to quantitatively compare the amount of violence today to that of other periods in history or other centuries or places[10]—such as, for instance, mid-twentieth-century Europe, or even the Middle Ages—because the legibility of violence has changed over time. (Also, more often than not, we construct those earlier periods in order to make ourselves look more enlightened. We create museums of inquisitorial torture instruments filled with fakes from the eighteenth century.) No—if we honestly look around us today, there is no doubt that we are surrounded by violence.

As critical theorists, we now see the violence in ways that we did not see it before. It has become more legible at both the local and the global level. We see the violence and brutality of disciplinary actions. This is, in part, the effect of Foucault's work—perhaps the first genuine "Foucault effect," before governmentality. We now see how routine forms of discipline displace the overtly corporal in order to control us better—we now recognize the violence of discipline. We see the violence that we inflict on our brothers and sisters trying—as we and our parents did—to better their lives.

In the liberal view, so much of this is hidden by the harm principle and notions of force or fraud—and so many of us (even the most critical among us) default to the physical/nonphysical violence distinction. We so often end up privileging the physicality of harm, somehow. We are just wedded to it, practically unable to see past it. But critical theory has always resisted and tried to expose the forms of violence that surround us: the excessive accumulation of private property (and its police enforcement), the residential patterns that are no more than racial segregation now imposed by real estate values, the evisceration of public education, the two fists of the state—workfare and mass incarceration. It takes remarkable amounts of violence, tucked away, to maintain this peaceful existence of ours. Critical theory has taught us that there is no nonviolent way of proceeding—that all political interventions are necessarily violent, that the matrix of social relations is civil strife, or class struggle, or racial or gender conflict.

The Dark Side of Violence

Things become doubly complicated when we recognize the potential pleasure in violence—the dark side of humanity, a touchstone of critical theory—as well as the possible productivity of violence. Here, the quicksand almost suffocates.

It is to Nietzsche that we practically always turn when we raise these issues—to Nietzsche and his fellow travelers, before and after him: to the Marquis de Sade, to the film director Pier Paolo Pasolini, to writers like Georges Bataille or Jean Genet, and to that disturbing literary strand that extolls the dark side of humanity, the human underbelly. One can almost hear them laughing at all this—all this discomfort with cruelty, all this squeamishness. What a waste of time and energy, and how weak, they might say. Our discomfort simply reflects a slavish morality, the fact of our own frailty. Nietzsche, Pasolini, Bataille—they line up far better with civil war: expect torture, understand that it is part of the process, anticipate it, prepare for it, know it, and use it yourself. Don't imagine a time without torture, violence, or cruelty.

"Let us not become gloomy as soon as we hear the word 'torture,'" Friedrich Nietzsche advised in his meditations in *On the Genealogy of Morals* in 1887; "there is plenty to offset and mitigate that word [torture]—even something to laugh at." Nietzsche reminded us of the ugly truth: men often take pleasure in cruelty and torture. In fact, there has rarely been a time without them. To cause suffering, Nietzsche observed, can be "in the highest degree pleasurable," and "fundamentally," he added, "this world has never since lost a certain odor of blood and torture." Pain and suffering have always functioned well for us, in one way or another. "Man could never do without blood, torture, and sacrifices when he felt the need to create a memory for himself," Nietzsche wrote.[11]

Sade's *120 Days of Sodom* (1785) laid the groundwork for much of this—confronting us, appalling us into seeing the possibility of obscene pleasure in pain. Sade's novel is, as advertised, "the most extreme book in the history of literature."

It reads in passages, especially in later chapters, like a numbing laundry list of sexual torture scenes. One could go on endlessly—the manuscript is a parade of horrifying violent acts presented as *jouissance*. The presentation tells it all: "the escalating sex-crimes of four libertines who barricade themselves in a remote castle with both male and female victims and accomplices for a four-month, precipitous orgy of sodomy, coprophagia and rape leading inexorably towards torture and human decimation."[12] The sexual torture in Sade's book is *the* extreme—presented as the extreme form of pleasure.

Coprophagia—yes, look that word up in the dictionary. Or watch Pasolini's 1975 film *Salò, or the 120 Days of Sodom*, based on Sade's fantasies, to see what it might look like: one of the adult male tormentors at his pretend wedding force-feeding feces to his young male "bride." Pasolini piles onto Sade's already shocking narrative new layers of hell from Dante's *Inferno*, leading us after an *Ante-Inferno* down, rather than up, to the "Circles of Manias, Shit, and Blood." Pasolini's film ends with the murder of most of the male and female victims in horrifying ways, including scalping, burning, and hanging—a remnant of the auto-da-fé—under the watching gaze of the four fascist libertines. Yes, torture is mastery, and here, apparently, utterly orgasmic joy.

The sadistic pleasure in the film is conjoined with a drive to legalize the violence. It is not a coincidence that Pasolini places his *Salò* in fascist Italy. It symbolizes a call for order, for command structures and hierarchy, for uniforms and black boots, for rules, for the chain-of-command—and, yes, for the rule of law. The law soon becomes another form of terror in itself: drawing up a list of approved methods, making clear the consequences, and spelling out the inquisitorial procedures. The legal framework contributes and enhances the torturous methods.

Joseph Fischel has analyzed and dissected the TV series *To Catch a Predator* and explored, phenomenologically, the feelings that we experience when the culprit is caught, when justice is done in the case of a heinous offender. Fischel writes about the high we feel, the excitement, when a bad guy is caught. He uses an expression: "Getting just feels like getting off."[13] We are, it seems, constantly in the abyss with Nietzsche. We can hardly escape, on any side. We are caught in the sovereignty of desire, not wanting to hear it, but desiring to punish it as well. We are caught, as Didier Fassin notes in his lectures by that name, in a desperate will to punish, or, as William Connolly writes, in the desire to punish.[14] And the truth is that this sovereignty of desire that we try to escape and avoid at all times, it explodes in every direction.

Fassin and Connolly remind us that there is often a pleasure in punishment, a desire for revenge, a will to punish. It is like the will to power. It is there and it makes little sense to deny it or ignore it. It is not just a will for recognition of the other. It can also be a form of satisfaction, of pleasure. There is a sadistic will to punish. It is reflected in Donald Trump's speech, in his oratory. "In the good old days, he'd be taken out on a stretcher," Trump said, at a rally, of a heckler. "In the good old days"—that is a euphemism for days of more valor, masculinity, bare-knuckle fighting. "Let's stop being politically correct": that is a coded way of being tolerant of or even enjoying violence.[15]

Nietzsche also reveals not just our pleasure in violence, but the productivity of violence—all the work that it does. To deny or ignore or sideline all that would be dishonest—another illusion. It has to be discussed and recognized at the very least, because it functions so powerfully in real life and has functioned so often in history. History is just littered with the productivity of violence. How could one imagine escaping that history?

As I argued in *The Counterrevolution*, violence and terror have been extremely productive, historically. They serve to terrorize revolutionary insurgents, to scare them to death, and to frighten the masses as well, to prevent them from joining insurgent factions. The use of torture or so-called enhanced interrogation methods, the targeted drone assassination of high-value suspects, the indefinite detention under inhuman conditions—these are shows of strength, demonstrations of who is in control, who will protect better, who has the resolve to win or the barbarity to prevail. They not only eviscerate the enemy, they also alarm others into submission and obedience, into fidelity. Terrorizing is an essential and inescapable part of winning: fear, trembling, and terror constitute an essential strategy of the counterrevolution. Waterboarding is no *mere* torture. It is instead a *terrorizing technique* intended to crush with deadly fear those it touches, and strike with terror anyone else who might even imagine sympathizing with the revolutionary minority.

In effect, these techniques do much more. They display a mastery that appeals to and seduces the masses. They delimit and delineate what it means to be free, who is good and evil. They legitimize the guardian class, even the entire ideological system. They strike the fear of death in the hearts of the enemy—and one's own people. Torture, throughout history, has always done far more than what is expected of it. It has always done so much work. One might even go so far as to say that violence is the linchpin of the Counterrevolution. It alone, through all of its productivity, is what conquers the hearts and minds of the masses.

These violent practices exude a will to mastery. If anything, they call to mind that "life-and-death struggle," that "trial by death" that Hegel identified at the heart of his phenomenology of human existence in the nineteenth century, and that Alexandre Kojève in the next century placed as the touchstone of Hegel's thought.[16] Hegel recognized this will to mastery as an essential driving force in human development, as a foundational step, motivated by a deep need for recognition and a drive to conquer the other. The deep desire for recognition by others, on this account, is laced with violence and tied to this struggle to the death.

It is a trial to the death that achieves mastery and works by instilling the deepest fear—indeed terror—into the heart of the other: In that moment of near-death, the subject is gripped with a fear of death, with a fear "not of this or that particular thing or just at odd moments, but its whole being has been seized with dread; for it has experienced the fear of death, the absolute Lord. In that experience it has been quite unmanned, has trembled in every fibre of its being, and everything solid and stable has been shaken to its foundations."[17] Hegel was speaking here of the struggle to the death between master and slave, between lord and bondsman. He was speaking of terror, precisely—about that trembling feeling and the fright and the flight. As Adriana Cavarero reminds us in her book *Horrorism*, the word *terror* traces etymologically to "the physical experience of fear as manifested in the trembling body . . . making it tremble and compelling it to take flight."[18] We are, with Hegel's master-slave dialectic, at the very heart of terror.

Violence manifests this will to master, to prevail, to dominate. These can be important in political struggle. They are surely important in warfare. War, Georges Bataille reminds us, is nothing else than "the unleashed desire to kill."[19] They are also important to ethics. This is the "Nietzschean view that life is essentially bound up with destruction and suffering," in Judith Butler's words.[20] Writing in the wake of these traditions—from Sade to Nietzsche—Maurice Blanchot reminded us of the deep ethical dimensions here: that our lives are "founded on absolute solitude as a first given fact." As Blanchot explained in *Lautréamont et Sade*, the Marquis de Sade reminded us, "over and over again in different ways that we are born alone, there are no links between one man and another." The result would be a unique ethic—perhaps not one that we would all subscribe to, but an ethic nonetheless: "The greatest suffering of others always counts for less than my own pleasure.

What matter if I must purchase my most trivial satisfaction through a fantastic accumulation of wrongdoing? For my satisfaction gives me pleasure, it exists in myself, but the consequences of crime do not touch me, they are outside me."[21] How far is this from self-interest, so valued in liberal thought since the eighteenth century, one might ask? What Nietzsche ultimately revealed, alongside Sade and later Bataille and Pasolini, is the darker side of our psyche, the unsavory dimension of the will to power, the desire for recognition, the ambition of mastery—in sum, the *productivity of violence.*

This reminds me of a passage from Bataille's personal diaries in about April or May 1944—which he published shortly thereafter as part of his *Somme athéologique: Sur Nietzsche.* It starts with an account of torture in the news pages of the *Petit Parisien,* April 27, 1944. "From a news item on torture," he starts writing: "eyes gouged out, ears and nails torn off, the head cracked open through repeated butcher blows, the tongue cut off with pincers . . ."[22]

"As a child," he continues, "the very idea of torture turned my life into a burden. I do not, still today, know how I would endure it . . . The earth today," Bataille goes on, "is covered by flowers—lilacs, wisteria, irises—and the war at the same time is buzzing and humming: hundreds of planes fill the nights with the sound of mosquitoes." A few paragraphs later, Bataille jots down, "the carnage, the fire, the horror: this is what we can expect in the coming weeks, it seems to me. . . . Seen today, from afar, the smoke of a fire in the vicinity of A."[23]

Next paragraph: "Meanwhile, these last few days count among the best of my life. So many flowers everywhere! The light is so beautiful and incredibly high . . ." And then, the next: "The sovereignty of desire, of anguish, is the hardest idea to hear."

Should we hear it—this sovereignty of desire? Should we listen to this "hardest idea to hear"? Should we allow ourselves to listen, especially when what we're hearing is so troubling, so repulsive at times, so unacceptable? Bombs are falling. Warplanes are buzzing. The Final Solution is at its apex. And these are among "the best days of my life"? That, I take it, is utterly unbearable.

At this point, critical theory is disarmed, it would seem. The critique of violence really only unmasks *us,* and *our* violence, and *our* pleasures. It unmasks the productivity of violence, throughout history. To ignore this idea would be blinking reality. It would be falling dupe to another illusion. The fact is, violence has been an extremely productive force throughout human history, since antiquity at least.

The Productivity of Violence

Sophocles' tragedy *Oedipus the King* has captured our imagination for centuries for its questions of destiny, power, and sexuality. But it is perhaps on the question of violence that the tragedy turns. At the heart of Sophocles' *Oedipus*, at the pivotal moment where truth finally emerges for all to see and all to recognize, at the decisive passage that turns tragic, at the instant of the peripeteia, there is a torture scene:

> *Oedipus:* So, you won't talk willingly—then you'll talk with pain.
> *The guards seize the shepherd.*
> *Shepherd:* No, dear god, don't torture an old man!
> . . . I wish to god I'd died that day.
> *Oedipus:* You've got your wish if you don't tell the truth.
> *Shepherd:* The more I tell, the worse the death I'll die . . .
> *Oedipus:* You're a dead man if I have to ask again. . . .
> *Shepherd:* Oh no, I'm right at the edge, the horrible truth—I've got to say it![24]

Hidden in plain view, at the very heart of Sophocles' play, there is the threat of torturous death that alone—at the culmination of a whole series of unsuccessful inquiries—produces the truth: it is torture that elicits the shepherd's confession. It is violence that allows Oedipus to recognize and realize his fate. But more than that—it is violence that reaffirms the order in Thebes, that reestablishes harmony in ancient Greece.

The social order is restored and set aright when Oedipus finally recognizes this "horrible truth." Violence produces truth in Sophocles' tragedy, but more than that, it constitutes and reestablishes the social order of antiquity—a social order where gods rule, oracles tell truth, prophets divine, fateful kings govern, and slaves serve.[25] The structure of Sophocles' play—in parallel with the structure of the investigation that Oedipus leads—reflects the three-part hierarchy of ancient Greece: the divine realm of gods and prophets, the sovereign realm of kings and queens, and the ordinary realm of the people (here, the messenger from Corinth and the slave). That social order had been upended by Oedipus defying his fate—not only by Oedipus, but by Jocasta as well; it is only through the torture of the servant that the truth of Oedipus' crimes is uncovered and the just rule of the gods reestablished.

Torture is the productive force that reveals the truth in *Oedipus.* The prophet Tiresias had exposed Oedipus in his cryptic way, but he had not been believed, either by Oedipus or by the choir—after all, who could trust an angry soothsayer? Creon and Jocasta had said enough to render bare Oedipus' guilt, but they too had done so in a way that was not entirely convincing to the choir or the king himself. It was only in the third iteration, with those of lowest social rank—the ordinary plebeians, the servants, and the workers—that the truth would emerge. But it would emerge only by means of torture. As Page DuBois argues in her monograph on slavery and torture in Greek antiquity, *Torture and Truth*, the idea of truth that we hold so dear today in Western thought is indissolubly tied to the practices of torture and violence. In ancient times, as today, violence can function as the metaphorical touchstone of truth, and simultaneously as the means to establish social hierarchy and difference.[26]

Throughout history, violence has enabled and fueled political economic regimes and artistic progress. The medieval period was shaped by practices of confiscation. Confiscation threads through the entire history of the Inquisitions. Confiscation was a central element of the edicts of King Peter II of Aragon in 1197, Pope Innocent III's *Vergentis in senium* in 1199, and the various decrees of Holy Roman Emperor Frederick II from 1220 to 1232.[27] The construction of empires was built on these violent practices. This is also reflected in Foucault's analysis of the political economy of feudal law in *Penal Theories and Institutions.*[28] Foucault integrates confiscation as part of a much larger political economy of criminal justice that became, during the High Middle Ages, a primary space for the circulation of riches. These practices and effects, it seems, extend well into the present and shape our political condition. The parallels between the judicial invention of confiscation in the twelfth and thirteenth centuries, on the one hand, and the contemporary use of criminal fines in small municipalities like Ferguson, Missouri—where such fines represent the second-largest source of municipal revenue—should not escape us.

The point of all of this is that the experience of violence organizes much of civil life, and to ignore it is to put on blinders—or worse, to willingly embrace an illusion. Violence is, tragically, productive. That is a key lesson in critical philosophy.

CHAPTER 13

A Way Forward

A reconstructed critical theory exposes the naive way that people so often speak about violence. It also unveils the pervasiveness of violence. It exposes, at times, the pleasure in violence and the productivity of violence. But once it unveils and sees violence throughout our human condition of endless political struggle, it only accentuates the puzzle: How can the reality of struggle and violence be reconciled with core critical values of compassion, dignity, and respect? How can we move forward toward a reconstructed critical theory and renewed critical praxis in the face of inevitable violence?

The logical place to turn for answers is the critique of violence itself—in its different manifestations. The various critiques of violence help expose its pervasiveness but also, in the process, offer justifications of violence. Perhaps they provide guidance as well on how to distinguish legitimate from illegitimate violence.

Three Critiques of Violence

In the process of unveiling and redefining violence, the critiques of violence draw distinctions that justify certain forms of violence. The question, then, is whether they offer viable means to resolve this puzzle.

Nonviolent Violence

Walter Benjamin redefines violence in instrumental terms, as a practice that is used to attain an end. In the context of a workers' strike, Benjamin defines the strike as "violent" when, and only when, it is deployed as a form of extortion to achieve an end, such as better wages or conditions—when it takes place, in his words, "in the context of a conscious readiness to resume the suspended action under certain circumstances that either have nothing whatever to do with this action or only superficially modify it." In that case, the strike is "violent" insofar as it represents "the right to use force in attaining certain ends." This is the "political" strike that Benjamin discusses, as distinguished, originally by Sorel, from the "proletarian general strike" Benjamin discusses next.[1]

In the context of a "revolutionary general strike," defined as one intended to overthrow the government, the question of violence becomes more complicated for Benjamin. This proletarian general strike, Benjamin explains, "sets itself the sole task of destroying state power." It is viewed by the state as being violent insofar as it is intended to be lawmaking—and the function of violence is understood to be lawmaking (or law-preserving). From the state's perspective, the workers' strike is legal and nonviolent, but the proletarian general strike is pure violence and must be repressed by violent means. But for Benjamin, by contrast, this second type of strike, which falls under the rubric of violence and is discussed as a type of violence, is nevertheless "nonviolent" violence.[2] Benjamin explains:

> While the first form of interruption of work is violent since it causes only an external modification of labor conditions, the second, as a pure means, is nonviolent. For it takes place not in readiness to resume work following external concessions and this or that modification to working conditions, but in the determination to resume only a wholly transformed work, no longer enforced by the state, an upheaval that this kind of strike not so much causes as consummates. For this reason, the first of these undertakings is lawmaking but the second anarchistic.[3]

"*Während die erste Form der Arbeitseinstellung Gewalt ist, da sie nur eine äußerliche Modifikation der Arbeitsbedingungen veranlaßt, so ist die zweite als ein reines Mittel gewaltlos.*" In English: "the second, as pure means, is nonviolent (*gewaltlos*)."[4] Massimiliano Tomba refers to this as "nonviolent violence."[5]

Nonviolent violence: Benjamin valorized this kind of anarchistic strike, intended by its very action to break down the state and simultaneously instantiate this breakdown. It feels like pure action, or pure disobedience, not soiled by extortionate demands, pure in its intentions. It enacts a new political relation. It resembles, in many ways, the euphoria and enactments of the Occupy Wall Street movement: the idea that the general assembly was at one and the same time both a form of resistance and a prefiguration of a new political relation. The anarchistic strike, as revolutionary movement, represents, in Sorel's words, "a clear, simple revolt" that leaves no place for "the sociologists or for the elegant amateurs of social reforms or for the intellectuals who have made it their profession to think for the proletariat." For Benjamin, this is a "deep, moral, and genuinely revolutionary conception" that cannot be branded simply "violent."[6]

Benjamin characterizes the "nonviolent," following Sorel, as the pure revolutionary movement, as the purity of the act of resistance. "Sorel rejects every kind of program, of utopia—in a word, of lawmaking—for the revolutionary movement." Insofar as the anarchistic revolt seeks nothing else than the destruction of the state—and not some kind of lawmaking—it is nonviolent. It is only "allegedly" violent. Benjamin writes that "the violence of an action can be assessed no more from its effects than from its ends, but only from the law of its means." "The law of its means": that is, the rightness of its means. We must judge actions not by the justness of their ends, but from the rightness of their means.[7]

Destruction of the state—that is what Benjamin admires and valorized in his critique: "on the abolition of state power, a new historical epoch is founded." Benjamin wants to imagine an attack on law, believing that "revolutionary violence, the highest manifestation of unalloyed violence by man, is possible."[8] It is divine, destructive, revolutionary violence that Benjamin advocates. And so he ends his essay:

> All mythical, lawmaking violence, which we may call executive, is pernicious. Pernicious, too, is the law-preserving, administrative violence that serves it. Divine violence, which is the sign and seal but never the means of sacred execution, may be called sovereign violence.[9]

In this, Benjamin was close to Foucault. He was in the territory of relations of power modeled on matrices of civil war.[10]

In sum, Benjamin favored anarchist revolution that involved an instantiation of a self-transformative practice, as opposed to a logic of means and ends. He opposed, most centrally, the state monopoly of violence and power, the legalistic mindset of proceduralism and means-ends rationality (the priority of the right over the good), and natural law–oriented just ends (the priority of the good over the right). In this sense, he opposed the state, positive law, and natural law. He embraced instead forms of resistance that are law-destroying—as opposed to violence, which he defined as lawmaking or law-preserving. He had in mind—he favored—a kind of "nonviolent violence" that is a means all in itself, not in relation to an end (not even a just end).

The difficulty with Benjamin's position, especially today, is that it is frozen in time, caught in the foundational utopian moment of early critical theory. It depends on its utopian foundation, and in that sense is circular: Benjamin's attribution of nonviolent violence is only nonviolent insofar as it accords with his utopian vision. But once we have overcome those foundational horizons, his justification of violence no longer functions. His notion of divine violence—that it is destructive and not ends oriented, but rather is aimed at the end of the state—does not help us if indeed we no longer believe in the dogma of the withering state. Another problem is that Benjamin's is a cryptic endorsement of violence—few ever understood fully what he really meant by "divine violence." Even Slavoj Žižek, when he engages Benjamin's critique within the larger framework of his own work, *Violence*, acknowledges that these pages are "dense"—a sophisticated way of saying difficult to understand.[11] Benjamin's idea, in the end, that the type of violence that might finish the state is nonviolent seems more mystifying than enlightening. It too rings of illusions.

Vanguardism

For his part, Žižek makes a number of sideways reflections in *Violence*. He expands the definition of violence so that it includes not only instances of physical violence—the type of events that we habitually refer to when we think of violence, such as urban riots, violent crime, street crime in effect, and domestic abuse, all of which he refers to as "subjective violence"—but also objective and systemic violence. Second, he ties acts of violence to the loss of a neighbor relation.[12] In a final twist, he turns violence on its head to make it reveal our cultural selves. So the abuses at Abu Ghraib—in contrast to the brutal methods of the Middle Eastern interrogators—really reflect our American ethos more than anything else.[13]

This leads to three lessons, Žižek tells us. First, condemning violence explicitly is just ideological masking—"an ideological operation par excellence, a mystification which collaborates in rendering invisible the fundamental forms of social violence."[14] This accords with the argument, given earlier, that critical theory must reconceptualize violence. Herein lie the strength and relevance of Žižek's intervention. But there is little more of use. Žižek argues, second, that it is harder than one thinks to be truly violent. It exhausts and takes effort to be truly evil.[15] This is hardly convincing. Third, and perhaps most puzzlingly, he says that the most violent thing to do at times is nothing. Voter abstention in today's democracy, for instance, is really more powerful than other acts, he claims. Those are his closing words: "If one means by violence a radical upheaval of the basic social relations, then, crazy and tasteless as it may sound, the problem with historical monsters who slaughtered millions was that they were not violent enough. Sometimes doing nothing is the most violent thing to do."[16] That final point is surely provocative, but not convincing in the least. In the end, Žižek oddly seems to endorse passivity as *the* most violent form of (in)action. I read this simply as a provocation.

Elsewhere, Žižek does advocate violence, or at least "harshness." In his August 2011 article in the *London Review of Books*, "Shoplifters of the World Unite," he discusses the London riots, criticizing the rioters and other recent protesters (the Spanish *Indignados*, the Greek protest movement, and even the Arab Spring) for failing to articulate a program. "This is the fatal weakness of recent protests," Žižek writes. "They express an authentic rage which is not able to transform itself into a positive programme of sociopolitical change. They express a spirit of revolt without revolution."[17] Buried in the last line of the article, Žižek calls for vanguardism: "This is clearly not enough to impose a reorganization of social life. To do that, one needs a strong body able to reach quick decisions and to implement them with all necessary harshness."[18] Not so subtly, Žižek expresses his penchant for a Leninist vanguard party and for that dose of disciplinary terror he extols elsewhere.[19] The notion of "all necessary harshness" borders on violence, but it depends too much on a preconceived and fixed utopian foundation, namely Leninism. It presents the same problem as Benjamin, then: it too is wedded to a foundational horizon that is no longer sustainable if we reconstruct critical theory.

Self-transformation

A final area to explore is the writings of Frantz Fanon and Jean-Paul Sartre, who more openly advocated violence. For Fanon, the violence of the colonized subject is a form of catharsis and self-transformation. The violence of the oppressed transforms the self, he argues, and it cleanses the past. As he proclaimed in *The Wretched of the Earth*, "Violence is a cleansing force": "For the colonized, life can only materialize from the rotting cadaver of the colonist."[20]

There is a particularly poignant passage in *The Wretched of the Earth*, in which Fanon conveys this cathartic element by examining Aimé Césaire's play *And the Dogs Were Silent*. In that play, the rebel is confronted by his mother. He must defend himself against the charge of barbarity for having killed his master. The mother is distressed. "I had dreamed of a son who would close his mother's eyes," she says—struck by the fate that now awaits her son. "Spare me, I'm choking from your shackles, bleeding from your wounds," she says. "God in heaven, deliver him!"[21]

The son responds: "The world does not spare me . . . There is not in the world one single poor lynched bastard, one poor tortured man, in whom I am not also murdered and humiliated."[22] And then, the son goes on to describe the night:

> It was a November night . . .
>
> And suddenly clamors lit up the silence,
>
> we had leapt, we the slaves, we the manure, we beasts with patient hooves. . . .
>
> The master's bedroom was wide open. The master's bedroom was brilliantly lit, and the master was there, very calm. . . . and all of us stopped . . . he was the master. . . . I entered. It's you, he said, very calmly. . . . It was me, it was indeed me, I told him, the good slave, the faithful slave, the slave slave, and suddenly my eyes were two cockroaches frightened on a rainy day . . . *I struck, the blood spurted: it is the only baptism that today I remember.*[23]

The killing was a transformative moment of pure violence for the son—one that was not simply a means to some end, but in itself a pure means, a baptism. It was, in itself, that "cleansing force."[24]

Fanon suggests that violence is, in itself, an action that purifies past injustice and oppression, that cleanses or reboots social relations, that transforms the oppressed into a fully human person. It is not simply a means to an end, but a form of baptism. Banu Bargu explains it in these terms: "violence is not viewed simply as a means to an end, justified by the legitimacy or desirability of the end, but becomes formative and redemptive of the colonized subject, if not even therapeutic: violence is the process of the constitution of the colonized into a human being." Bargu writes that, for Fanon, violence is "a means of subject formation."[25]

Sartre, like Fanon, developed a dialectical understanding of violence as an act that gives birth to a new and better human. The fact that the anticolonial rebel takes arms and is willing to die for his brothers and sisters means that he has overcome death and is a "dead man *en puissance*." By accepting death and seizing the violent act, the rebel has broken the hold of scarcity and gives his life for his fellow's humanity. He has placed the freedom and humanity of others above his own existence, in a Hegelian sense. And this fraternity then gives rise to the first institutions of peace, grounded on a praxis of liberation and socialist fraternity.[26]

In other words, the self-transformation that attends certain violent acts can justify the use of violence, even though they do not constitute a means to that end. The problem is that this too is hardly convincing. Many things may be cathartic, but that does not mean they are valuable. It is entirely plausible that a deeply racist and supremacist person could feel the same form of cathartic baptism in enacting violence against a person of color. The difference, of course, is the relations of power that construct a situation in which the colonized subject for Fanon or the oppressor here confront the act of violence. But this highlights that violence *tout court* is not justified, and catharsis or self-transformation alone does not render violence a critical praxis. Context matters, as does the way that power circulates through different encounters. For Fanon, not all violence—even baptismal violence as a pure end—would serve the liberatory aspirations envisioned by him, or Benjamin for that matter. So the criteria would have to include not just self-transformation, but a normative evaluation of the political circumstances. But once we go down that path, the question of justification becomes inevitably instrumental. It is inextricably related to a normative assessment of the political situation. It reduces to a means-ends or strategic calculation. That may ultimately be right, as I consider in part III, but it means that violence is not justified merely because it transforms the wretched of the Earth or serves as a form of catharsis.

The classic critiques of violence, it turns out, hardly offer a convincing way forward. To be sure, they do reveal that the workers, or the colonized, or the young protesters in the *banlieue* that deploy violent means of resistance (torching cars or breaking windows) are themselves immersed in a violent world and subject to the violence of the state, the police, and social workers. They show that the whole milieu is violent, structurally and objectively. They highlight, as Fanon does, the unconscionably oppressive character of the colonial system—and unearth its pervasive violence. But by distinguishing between legitimate and illegitimate forms of violence, in a world pervaded by violence, these critiques of violence set up criteria that either are too foundational, are too instrumental, or simply break down. At times, they fail to offer comprehensible criteria at all and gesture to the divine or to inaction in a way that is simply unconvincing. And this, then, makes it difficult to critique what we might consider illegitimate violence.

Benjamin's litmus test—namely, avoiding means-end rationality or instrumental reason—and his embrace of an anarchist, antistate ethos are noble but seem unhelpful for reconstructed critical theory today. They are far too foundational or dogmatic—as if the withering of the state were an orthodoxy. Žižek, for his part, is at times merely provocative, and at other times too rigidly Leninist—as if a vanguard party were the solution to everything. And Fanon's criteria of catharsis and self-transformation are too encompassing.

There are really several problems with Fanon's and Sartre's positions. First, it has to be the case that the political context of the violence will matter. One can only imagine that, *pace* Benjamin, the ends would cast a shadow on the legitimacy of the means.[27] Second, as Arendt reminds us, the exigency of death and feelings of solidarity—the self-transformation—can be very short-lived. They are not necessarily permanent self-transformations, as Arendt responds:

> It is true that the strong fraternal sentiments collective violence engenders have misled many good people into the hope that a new community together with a "new man" will arise out of it. The hope is an illusion for the simple reason that no human relationship is more transitory than this kind of brotherhood, which can be actualized only under conditions of immediate danger to life and limb.[28]

Finally, one has to ask: how can critical theorists tell others to engage in violence when they themselves do not put their lives at stake? How can you only *theorize* violence? How can you glorify divine violence or nonviolent violence if you are not yourself engaged in armed revolutionary struggle?

The classic critiques of violence relativize the use of violence to shield certain privileged or foundational modalities of resistance. They do not provide a solution to the puzzle of violence from the perspective of an intellectual project like critical philosophy, which places compassion, respect, and solidarity at the top of its value system. Moreover, the fact that these critiques are essentially apologia of violence ultimately undercuts their effectiveness as critiques of *state* violence. In the end, they create criteria of violence that do not withstand scrutiny—when they offer criteria at all.

Three Possible Resolutions

How, then, do we resolve the critical puzzle—namely, that our political condition involves endless struggle, struggle that is necessarily violent, but that, at the same time, a reconstructed critical theory expressly embraces the values of compassion and mutual respect? How is a critical horizon even possible given this tension? Taking a purely instrumental route is a cop-out—another grand illusion. The idea that we could bracket our values and violently impose a just society, in which violence would then disappear, not only is unrealistic but defies everything that reconstructed critical theory stands for. It is pure mystification—and dangerous at that, because it is likely, actually, to push us onto the path of authoritarianism. Anyone who would be so vicious as to champion a state of exception—even a temporary use of what would have to be overpowering violence, to quickly get the job done—would likely be the kind of person who would abuse that license. We would be right back at where we started: facing an illusion. How, then, can critical philosophy move forward? This section will set aside three possible avenues that have been advocated by critical theorists, before proposing a more promising path forward in the next and final section of this chapter.

Interpreting Violence Away

You will recall that a radical critical philosophy of illusions rests on the infiniteness of interpretation. It rests on the lack of any foundation. What if we returned to this insight to simply interpret violence away? Let me explain what I mean.

If we live in a world characterized by the infinite regress of interpretations, going vertically all the way down, then might it not be the case that the entire argument itself—the proposition that the struggle for justice is necessarily violent in a human condition of endless struggle—is just another interpretation, and, in that sense, is nothing more than an imposition of a will to power?

What would that mean, you may ask? Would it, then, be possible to rethink violence entirely? Would it be possible to reconstruct a conception of violence in such a way as to wash away the problem of violence? Nietzsche, you will recall, famously spoke of the invention rather than the origin of knowledge.[29] What would it mean to take that insight seriously—particularly in the most tangible place of all, in the realm of violence?

What it might mean is that the claims that have been circulating throughout this chapter—namely, that violence functions in such and such a way, that the struggle for justice is inevitably violent, that violence may be justified if it is cathartic, etc.—that all those myriad claims are, well, invented. We invent our relation to violence. This does not, in any way, deny its facticity. A punch in the face is still a punch in the face, and it does not become any more consensual. Those facts do not change. The victims did not ask for the violence they endure, and they are not to be blamed. Again, that does not change. But it is what we *claim* to know about these facts that is invented. What they tell us about when violence is justified, when it is legitimate—all these things are, well, invented. All of that is made up. It tells us more about who we are and what we want to believe than anything reliable about reality. And, in the process of these inventions, we shape our own subjectivity—we shape who we are.[30]

The invention of knowledge, rather than its origin: this surely would destabilize our interpretation of violence. It highlights the creativity of interpretation. It also asks us to question what is motivating the invention. Our critique of violence may have multiple meanings and functions, all of which do a lot of work. But what we say about violence and the critical horizon, in the end, is our imposition, our interpretation, our reading, our will. Our stories of violence tell us more about our history than they do anything about violence per se.

This may all be correct, but ultimately what it does, once again, is to politicize the situation—which is directly in line with a reconstructed critical theory. Treating the liberal conception of violence as an invention seems right. What it underscores is that the liberal project privileges private property, wealth accumulation, and possessive individualism. Treating the critical conception of pervasive violence as an invention highlights that the critical project is a will to equality, compassion, and respect. In other words, they reveal that these interpretations are political. They are not just about an abstract notion of liberty or about ensuring that everyone can pursue their vision of the good; they also are political inventions that have material distributive consequences. They have effects of reality on our social and political conditions.

But, of course, that is the very point of a reconstructed critical theory. It is the whole point of understanding that critical philosophy is motivated by political values and is a political project. This does not help us resolve the quagmire of violence and the critical horizon. Instead, it brings us back to square one: how do we reconcile our critical values with our critical horizon of endless struggle?

Doing Violence to Violence

A second path forward might be to turn the critique back on itself: perhaps we should, as Simone de Beauvoir suggested of the Marquis de Sade, burn our own justifications of violence. Perhaps we should violently turn against our own critiques and apologias of violence—against the very idea that the struggle for justice is inevitably violent. "*Faut-il brûler Sade?*" Beauvoir asked.[31] Or, for our purposes, should we burn our own understanding of violence—burn our theories at the stake? Recall that Sade's son burned the ten volumes of his final work, *Les Journées de Florbelle.* Should we throw Sade's and Nietzsche's works onto the pyre? Should we destroy Bataille's books as well? What about Pasolini's films? Should we simply extinguish the apologias of violence—Benjamin as well, and Žižek and Fanon—and be done with violence once and for all? Could we, even if we decide we should?

Now, remarkably, Beauvoir answered her own question in the negative. She read into Sade an ethic—misguided in certain respects, but an ethic nonetheless, related centrally to freedom. Judith Butler similarly tried to find in Sade something useful for a feminist theory, for a philosophy of freedom, or possibly for a philosophy of sexual freedom. Butler writes:

> Although one may well conclude that Sade has little in common with feminism, it is important to note that he defended sexual freedom and the expressive impulses of individuals. Moreover, Sade did not believe that sexuality was meant only to satisfy the requirements of procreation.[32]

For both Beauvoir and Butler, the task was to seek "neither to romanticize nor to vilify Sade," but rather "to understand the ethical significance of Sade." And of course, there is always some redeeming ethical feature to discover in Sade or Pasolini. With Pasolini, for instance, it was his political conviction and queer sexuality; his opposition to the fascist nature of the state and the authoritarian nature of the Church. For Sade, it was his philosophical tendency—as a philosopher of the *boudoir* or *de la boue*, to be sure, but as a philosopher nonetheless, who questioned man's true nature at a time when man was becoming almost divine. As Butler remarked, "feminism and philosophy ought not to participate in anti-intellectual trends, it ought to distance itself from inquisitorial practices, . . . its intellectual task is to remain open to the difficulty and range of the human condition."[33]

In locating his torture chamber in fascist Italy, immediately post-Mussolini (July 1943), Pasolini targets fascism itself in *Salò*—the Italian bourgeoisie, the desire for fascistic power, the submission to order, the following of orders. In his film, Pasolini sides with Albert Camus, who, as Butler reminds us, saw in Sade the precursor to the fascisms and totalitarianisms of the twentieth century. As Camus noted of Sade, "Two centuries in advance and on a reduced scale, Sade exalted the totalitarian society in the name of a frenzied liberty that rebellion does not in fact demand. With him the history and tragedy of our times really begin."[34] Pasolini's Sade becomes, in this sense, the origin of modern fascism.[35] And Pasolini's deployment of the three circles of hell, with their allusion to Dante's *Inferno*, challenges more forcefully than most other works the Catholic Church—one of Pasolini's most impassioned and frequent political targets.

The Marquis de Sade, for his part, targeted the sexual repression of his own aristocratic peers in a purportedly pedagogic or perhaps didactic manner, as evidenced by his *Philosophy in the Boudoir*. This is the ethical dimension, something about a way of living one's life in one's work—at least that is what Simone de Beauvoir and Judith Butler seem to suggest. "He argues, in effect, that under conditions of bourgeois morality, where the interchangeability and indifference of individuals reign, sexual cruelty is a way to reestablish individuality and passion," Butler notes, with Beauvoir.[36] Sade is exposing the unrestrainable truth of nature, of our warped nature.

By contrast to the newfound faith and Enlightenment belief in the compassion of man, in the goodness of natural man, in Jean-Jacques Rousseau's concept of man in his natural condition—as Dominique Lecourt emphasizes in his reading[37]—Sade demonstrated in his writings the twisted timber of humanity. If you want to follow nature and natural man, as the Enlightenment thinkers did, Sade tells us, then *look at this!* "This book," Georges Bataille writes of *120 Days of Sodom*, "is the only one in which the mind of man is shown *as it really is*. The language of *120 Days of Sodom* is finally that of a universe which degrades gradually and systematically, which tortures and destroys the totality of the beings which it represents."[38] Imprisoned in the Bastille, having encouraged the revolutionaries from his prison window, liberated and liberating others, it is said that Sade embodied, despite it all, an element of liberation sexology—a revolution for the libertines. His writings also betray a unique morality that, as Maurice Blanchot and Georges Bataille remind us, rests on our own solitude as humans—"absolute solitude as a first given fact."[39] These are important ethical and political questions. There must be some value, then, along political and moral dimensions, to Sade's interventions, as well as Pasolini's.

Plus, both Sade and Pasolini were themselves the objects of the punitive arm of the state—of the will to punish, of the sovereignty of desire. Sade: eleven years in Vincennes and the Bastille on what appear to have been a familial *lettre de cachet*, three years at Bicêtre, another twelve years in the Charenton asylum, and more, for a total of about thirty-two years of his life in closed institutions. Pasolini: tried by the Italian government for offense to the Italian state and religion, in 1963, many years before *Salò*. Did they not suffer enough for their sins—or for their courage? Perhaps. And, perhaps, we as a society should not condemn Sade or Pasolini, or Nietzsche—any more than we, at least the former colonizers among us, should not condemn Frantz Fanon when he advocates violence against the children of the colonizers, that same violence of the colonizers.

No, it seems that violently sacrificing our own critiques and apologias of violence reflects an anti-intellectualism or antitheoretical sentiment that is far too simplistic. It solves nothing—and it does us all an injustice. It would be like embracing an illusion. We must not burn Nietzsche or Sade, we must not self-censor our critiques of violence, because there is always resistance embedded, something ethical there that we need to search for rather than extinguish. To collectively condemn, in other words, is too easy—and so false. It does nothing. We need to do more somehow; even at the extreme, even at the limit, even here with violence. We need to understand it—dark side and all—and then resolve the puzzles of critical praxis.

The point is that collective condemnation is, just that, too simple, too easy. And the dream of a world without violence is, again, just that: a dream, an illusion. We need to plumb the complexity of the human soul, with all its dark sides, and simultaneously reimagine the place of excess and violence. Or perhaps, we must take it upon ourselves to condemn, but only as ethical beings, not as a society.

Radical Nonviolence

A third path is to radically eschew violence, force, and compulsion, along the model of Mahatma Gandhi: to turn all the suffering onto oneself and completely avoid compelling others to change, so as to inspire others to self-transformation instead. This was the model of *Satyagraha* that Gandhi developed and lived. It rests, I argue, on the recognition of the critique of violence: recognition that everything we do outwardly is a form of aggression against others, and therefore everything we do should be oriented inwardly.[40]

The neologism *satyagraha* that Gandhi coined—the literal meaning of which is "to hold on to truth," "to cling to truth," or "a tenacity in the pursuit of truth"[41]—refers to a personal ethic and self-transformation through which an individual remains true to his or her ideals of justice, and seeks to convince or convert others by working on himself or herself and taking on the burden of the sufferings of injustice. The term is often simplified, in translation, to mean "nonviolent resistance," and at a practical level, it is narrowly associated with the imperative of nonviolence. But the concept has to be understood through the larger framework of an ethic or a faith that gives people the strength to turn the suffering of injustice onto themselves. The resulting nonviolence is not a practical maxim or a political strategy—although it is always political and strategic—so much as it is the necessary product of steadfastly staying true to one's ethical or spiritual beliefs and the ethical imperative not to hurt others.

The concept of *satyagraha* recognizes the pervasiveness of violence in social interaction, and tries to contain it. It does so by means of three core elements: truth, self-care, and suffering. The first is true belief or faith—holding onto a personal truth—that empowers and lends force to *satyagraha*. Gandhi often defines *satyagraha* as "Truth-force" (*satya* means "truth")—though in other places, he also refers to "Soul-force" or "Love-force." It is only when the believer is entirely committed to "the truth of his cause," Gandhi emphasizes, that he will have the force to succeed with nonviolence.[42] That faith in the truth of the cause ensures that the reformer will not lash out at an opponent, but instead work harder on himself or herself, and be prepared to sacrifice himself or herself. In this sense, *satyagraha* does not give rise to an instrumental form of nonviolence, but rather to an unconditional, entirely committed faith, like a spiritual belief or a moral commitment.

The second component is work on the self, rather than on others: nonviolent resistance requires self-transformation. It involves work by and on the individual himself or herself. It cannot be achieved from outside the person. It is deeply subjective. Gandhi explained this while discussing the case of protest at temples, where he opposed such actions as blocking the way of those who refused to admit the untouchable. "The movement for the removal of untouchability is one of self-purification," Gandhi wrote. "No man can be purified against his will." He explained that any and all steps, even in drastic situations, "have to be taken against ourselves."[43] These are, as Mantena explains, "practices of ascetic self-mastery."[44] As Gandhi wrote, "Satyagraha presupposes self-discipline, self-control, self-purification." Notice the omnipresence of the self. It is care of self that comes first. As Gandhi explained, "the doctrine came to mean vindication of truth not by infliction of suffering on the opponent, but on one's self."[45]

The third, and perhaps most important, element is self-suffering: the willingness to bear the suffering of injustice, to take that suffering onto oneself, is at the very heart of remaining true to oneself and converting one's opponents. It is via suffering that one truly demonstrates the sincerity of one's beliefs and the stakes of justice. It is also the most powerful way to convince others to change themselves. It shows that the *satyagrahi* is not there to hurt, but rather to impress upon others the justice of one's position. Self-suffering—or the broader concept, for Gandhi, of "the law of suffering"—is what converts others, in Gandhi's view. *Conversion* is the operative term: "I have deliberately used the word *conversion*," he wrote. "For my ambition is no less than to convert the British people through non-violence, and thus make them see the wrong they have done to India." And it operates through the emotions and affect of the opponent. The goal is to "draw out and exhibit the force of the soul within us for a period long enough to appeal to the sympathetic chord in the governors or the law-makers."[46]

For Gandhi, nonviolence had to extend to thought as well as action. It meant avoiding anger; it excluded even swearing and cursing. It implied, in the anticolonial context, scrupulously avoiding "intentional injury in thought, word or deed to the person of a single Englishman." It even involved being courteous and polite toward the police who are arresting you and the prison officials who are detaining you.[47] Gandhi wrote:

> It is a breach of Satyagraha to wish ill to an opponent or to say a harsh word to him or of him with the intention of harming him. And often the evil thought or the evil word may, in terms of Satyagraha, be more dangerous than actual violence used in the heat of the moment and perhaps repented and forgotten the next moment. Satyagraha is gentle, it never wounds. It must not be the result of anger or malice. It is never fussy, never impatient, never vociferous. It is the direct opposite of compulsion. It was conceived as a complete substitute for violence.[48]

Gandhi's practices of fasting represent the kind of work on the self and the suffering that characterizes and defines *satyagraha*.[49] His views on direct action were extremely nuanced and contextual. Civil disobedience was not always appropriate; it had to be judged based, for instance, on whether individuals were doing it because they expect some personal gain.[50] In addition, fasting could be used for good or ill, depending on the context. "Even fasts may take the form of coercion," Gandhi wrote, adding that "there is nothing in the world that in human hands does not lend itself to abuse."[51]

There is a pragmatic dimension to *satyagraha* that should not be ignored. In fact, Gandhi justified violence under certain extremely limited circumstances of domination and weakness—in cases of extreme self-defense or helplessness—not as a form of *satyagraha*, but as a form of vulnerable self-defense. "I do believe that where there is only a choice between cowardice and violence, I would advise violence," he wrote, adding, "I took part in the Boer War, the so-called Zulu rebellion and the late War." The illustration he gives is of a time when he was almost fatally assaulted and he would have wanted his son to defend him, even using violence. He adds, "I would rather have India resort to arms in order to defend her honour than that she should in a cowardly manner become or remain a helpless witness to her own dishonor."[52] In situations of helplessness, of utter weakness, violence may be appropriate.[53] But he then added, "I do not believe India to be helpless. I do not believe myself to be a helpless creature."[54]

The problem with this third path, though, is that it is, honestly, too demanding and also too absolute.[55] Gandhi's writings are of unparalleled exigency: one must take the burdens of injustice on oneself; turn suffering onto oneself; purify oneself as an exemplar to others; fast and engage in civil disobedience when appropriate, at sacrificial cost; bear no anger or resentment against one's oppressors; or even remain celibate or, if married, chaste. The full measure of Gandhian *satyagraha* is arduous. And regardless of the criticisms of Gandhi's actual practices and weaknesses—he has been criticized for hypocrisy, for misogyny, and even for racism and casteism—Gandhi's writings, taken on their face, demand a level of commitment and persistence that is practically unparalleled in other political traditions and impossible to achieve. They call for the kind of existence exemplified—as Gandhi himself suggested—by Buddha and Christ. One can hardly imagine a more demanding and exigent standard.

Nonviolence of this sort, I believe, is too demanding and does not offer a viable path forward for a critical horizon. It is, first, practically impossible to instantiate except in a watered-down and instrumental version. The idea, for instance, that one must not love one's children more than others is far too demanding. Remaining celibate or chaste, again, is too demanding, honestly. Avoiding evil thoughts toward one's oppressor: not realistic, possibly counterproductive. Assuming all the suffering, taking it all on oneself in order to convert others: at the end of the day, that does not ethically seem right.

Moreover, it is far too dangerous. In many situations, it would mean leading sheep to slaughter. Gandhi's writings about Jewish resistance in 1936 and 1938, where he espoused *satyagraha*, is a case in point. As Uday Mehta notes, "Gandhi's words provoked shock, controversy and considerable condemnation"[56]—and rightfully so, even if they were pronounced before many knew the worst of it. Nonviolence may be appropriate in some limited conditions, but not all. In part, this reflects again the problem with foundational thought—with the inappropriate generalization of one particular foundation. It would be misguided to resolve the problem of violence by adopting wholesale Gandhi's notion of *satyagraha.*

Satyagraha did function in the 1920s and 1930s in India, in a country of hundreds of millions of inhabitants that was governed, in contrast, by a handful of British civil servants and soldiers. It had political effects in the context of a military occupation and a vast disproportion of population, in a situation where the occupying force—as is so often the case—lacked legitimacy and moral authority. These factors conspired to make *satyagraha* so potent then. But *satyagraha* is not the answer to the broader problems of violence in critical theory. It does not resolve the critique of violence.

A More Promising Path Forward

There is, however, a more promising path forward: to understand violence as a necessary part of human existence, of social interaction, and of our human condition, but not to valorize or embolden it. Violence, in this view, is integral to human experience—from nightmares, to death and loss, to separation, to natural catastrophes. Violence, fear, and terror are part of becoming fully human. They are an inevitable element of human development. But they are only a few among a set of forces that shape the human experience. The task of critical theory is to curate that balance and, in the process, to reduce and devalue the role of violence.

The famous passage on the master-slave dialectic in Hegel's *Phenomenology of Spirit* might offer a path forward.[57] Alexandre Kojève's reading of Hegel before World War II—especially his lectures from 1934 to 1939 at the *École pratique des hautes études*—put the dialectic of master and slave at the center of many contemporary readings of Hegel's *Phenomenology*. It is Kojève who proposed a reading of Hegel in which the gradual achievement of the highest form of knowledge and recognition happens through a series of dialectics that are almost all modeled on that of master and slave. It would lead to some excesses;[58] and one need not embrace it in its entirety, nor Hegel's dialectic for that matter. But it does provide material for interpretation to resolve the problem of violence. Let me explain.

Three forces drive the confrontation between master and slave, in Hegel's account. The first is the desire for recognition—the desire to be viewed as a fully human person.[59] Hegel writes, early in his analysis of this encounter between master and slave, "Self-consciousness exists in and for itself when, and by the fact that, it so exists for another; that is, *it exists only in being acknowledged*." The struggle between those who will become master and slave begins, in fact, because of the quest for recognition. Each of the actors engages in this life-and-death struggle to be certain of himself—barring which, as Hegel writes, "he has not attained to the truth of this recognition as an independent self-consciousness."[60]

Kojève explains that in this struggle, "the Master is the man who went all the way in a Fight for prestige, who risked his *life* in order to be *recognized* in his absolute superiority by *another* man."[61] In doing so, the master has overcome nature, in the sense that he has shown that he is not governed by natural fear or self-preservation, but that recognition by another human is more important than death. He has also expressed the desire for an idea of recognition, overcoming mere biological function. It is in this sense that Hegel writes, "Death certainly shows that each staked his life and held it of no account."[62]

The master thus achieves recognition by making the slave work for him. The former now leads a life of pleasure, while the slave toils for another. But this has the potential—the paradoxical or dialectical potential—of undermining the master's recognition because he is now no longer recognized by a full human, but rather only by a slave: "What now really confronts him is not an independent consciousness, but a dependent one. He is, therefore, not certain of *being-for-self* as the truth of himself. On the contrary, his truth is in reality the unessential consciousness and its unessential action."[63] "The outcome," Hegel writes, "is a recognition that is one-sided and unequal."[64]

Recognition remains a motor of history for Hegel, however—which explains in part the role of recognition in the later writings of Axel Honneth, Jay Bernstein, and other contemporary descendants of the Frankfurt School.[65] It is the universality of the desire for recognition that drives this fight to the death, and (at least in the reading of Kojève) feeds the historical account. As Kojève says, "human, historical, self-conscious existence is possible only where there are, or—at least—where there have been, bloody fights, wars for prestige." This is the desire to master, to defeat the other, without which there would be no battle, no conflict. But it is self-defeating in the end. From the perspective of recognition—that first driving element of the conflict—"mastery is an existential impasse," as Kojève writes.[66]

The second motivating force of the dialectic between master and slave—and the one that interests me most here—is the encounter with nothingness, with *le néant* (and right here, incidentally, one sees well the influence of Kojève on Sartre). It is the encounter with nothingness that forces the slave to face his death, his own mortality, and to overcome his human condition. It is here that Hegel uses the language of violence and terror—terror, recall, which in its etymological origins traces to the act of trembling, of the physical experience of fear and the manifestation of a trembling body.[67] It traces to terror as fear, dread, trembling, shaking to one's foundations. It is by means of fear, terror, and trembling that the slave, according to Hegel, "rids himself of his attachment to natural existence in every single detail; and gets rid of it by working on it."[68] Hegel writes in *The Phenomenology of Spirit*, regarding the slave in his encounter with the master:

> This consciousness has been fearful, not of this or that particular thing or just at odd moments, but its whole being has been seized with dread; for it has experienced the fear of death, the absolute Lord. In that experience it has been quite unmanned, has trembled in every fibre of its being, and everything solid and stable has been shaken to its foundations. But this pure universal movement, the absolute melting-away of everything stable, is the simple, essential nature of self-consciousness . . .[69]

It is important to underscore here that it is terror—the terror of the battle to the death with the master, the struggle of life and death—that forces the slave to face up to nothingness, to his mortality. The terror is necessary. It is a necessary step in his development. Kojève explains: "Through animal fear of death (*Angst*) the Slave experienced the dread or the Terror (*Furcht*) of Nothingness, of his nothingness. He caught a glimpse of himself as nothingness, he understood that his whole existence was but a 'surpassed,' 'overcome' (*aufgehoben*) death—a Nothingness maintained in Being."[70]

The important point for us—and this is crucial—is that terror acts as a central motivating force in the struggle for recognition and human development. It would not be possible to achieve forms of self-recognition without it.

The third and final motivating force is, of course, the relation to labor. For Hegel, it is by means of his toil that the slave overcomes his own nature and realizes a conceptual end that makes possible comprehension, science, techniques, and art.[71] It is only "through his service," Hegel writes, that the slave "rids himself of his attachment to natural existence in every single detail; and gets rid of it by working on it."[72] Or, to be more blunt, he says: "Through work, however, the bondsman becomes conscious of what he truly is."[73] It is by means of his work that the slave recognizes that he too can overcome and dominate nature—just as the master had in the struggle by pursuing his own desire to be recognized above and beyond his biological existence—and thus the slave recognizes his freedom and autonomy.[74] Hegel writes, "Work, on the other hand, is desire held in check, fleetingness staved off; in other words, work forms and shapes the thing."[75] This line of reasoning is what would breathe life into Marx's fixation with labor and, later, into Horkheimer's placement of labor and economic production at the heart of his critical social theory. For all this to happen, Hegel suggests, there need be the two formative moments of fear and service. And that would be not just any fear, but absolute terror—the utmost dread. It is only then that labor can produce its effects. The slave, Hegel maintains, "realizes that it is precisely in his work wherein he seemed to have only an alienated existence that he acquires a mind of his own."[76]

To sum up, the three motivating forces are recognition, terror, and labor. Does that mean that we "need" torture and cruelty? Of course not—especially if we believe that we are part of a human community that can recognize its faults and excesses and seek a shared intellectual project. Also if we realize that when we do face our own mortality, our nothingness, as we do all the time—in our youth, in our nightmares, with the loss of our parents—we are all facing the terror of death. So there need be no valorization of terror or violence, nor any justification.

Instead, we need to understand Hegel's argument as allegory and take a few steps back.[77] As history, or even as phenomenology, Hegel's account is undoubtedly lacking.[78] As method, as a dialectic with necessity, it is not persuasive. However, as metaphor, the Hegelian narrative shows, brilliantly, the place of violence in the formation of one's identity, consciousness, and subjectivity. It would be practically impossible to imagine human self-development without it—or without the desire for recognition or the work of labor. These are all integral to our human experience. The question, then, is how to balance them properly—not eliminate any one of them but to calibrate them properly so as not to be governed too much by any one of them.

The path, then, is to acknowledge the inevitable violence of social transformation, to handle it with care and compassion, and to ensure that it is not concentrated on particular actors or groups. It must be treated, as Bentham would have done, as a disutility—even though it serves the greater ambition of emancipation. We must be careful and distribute it as evenly as possible. The classic critiques of violence end up justifying violence. That cannot be right. Instead, we need to recalibrate human experience to deemphasize terror and violence, to the benefit of the other modes of human interaction. Because it is impossible to exorcise it, we should devalue violence instead—again, within a radical theory of values—and spread its burden equitably.

Distributing it equitably, not sacrificing anyone, sharing the burden, being extremely careful: those are far more promising ways forward. They are critically important. I will end here with a passage from Herbert Marcuse's *One-Dimensional Man*, channeling François Perroux. Marcuse is critiquing the reification of universal categories—how the universals of country or class or political ideals so often lead us astray, lead us to sacrifice lives. Let me end then on a word of caution:

> They believe they are dying for the Class, they die for the Party boys. They believe they are dying for the Fatherland, they die for the Industrialists. They believe they are dying for the freedom of the Person, they die for the Freedom of the dividends. They believe they are dying for the Proletariat, they die for its Bureaucracy. They believe they are dying by orders of a State, they die for the money which holds the State. They believe they are dying for a nation, they die for the bandits that gag it. They believe—but why would one believe in such darkness? Believe—die?—when it is a matter of learning to live?[79]

From Critical Horizons to Critical Praxis

Before moving on to critical praxis in part III, it may be useful here to review and recast the argument thus far, placing the first two parts, parts I and II, in conversation.

Early critical theory was wracked by a tension between its theoretic commitments on the one hand and its emancipatory or utopian ideals on the other. The first included a commitment to reflexivity and historical constructivism that highlighted the fact that humans are shaped by their historical circumstances (in other words, by the changing relations of power and modes of production that construct the present); and that humans have the ability to shape the course of history by affecting those relations of production and power. The second, the emancipatory ambition, was oriented toward the goal of creating a just society for all women and men, which entailed consideration of the needs of the community and social justice; and it was infused by a Marxian philosophy of history that gave it direction.

These two elements pointed in potentially different directions, both internally and between them. First, the commitment to reflexivity could push in two very different directions depending on one's conception of history. With a robust philosophy of history that determined a trajectory for humanity, the element of reflexivity called for knowledge of the present moment and of what was to be done in practice; along these lines, reflexivity required a correct social theory that could guide humans in their praxis. But with a contingent conception of history, the element of reflexivity pointed in the opposite direction: toward the idea of a radical historical construction of subjectivity that was far more open normatively and agnostic about how to instantiate the emancipatory ideal.

The second, the emancipatory ambition, could also push in two very different directions depending on one's sensibility regarding epistemological and normative foundations. With a strong commitment to foundations, the emancipatory ambition pointed toward norms and ideals that could be generalized to others, almost in a universal (or at least, in a contextualized and historized but generalized) way; along these lines, it was possible to imagine people agreeing on a normative order and on the basis for moral and political judgment. But with less attachment to foundations, the emancipatory ambition pointed toward far more self-oriented ideals: toward a more ethical or aesthetic sense of emancipation and justice.

In effect, the unique ways in which these central elements of early critical philosophy could be combined and inflected led to very different critical interventions: at one extreme, theories that advanced the possibility of a correct social analysis that could determine for others what was to be done; and at the other extreme, theories that proposed ethical practices that were not intended to give normative guidance to others. In other words, at one end critical theories that believed in truth and normative foundations; at the other end theories that aspired to self-emancipation as an ethical or aesthetic form.

Max Horkheimer's original project for critical theory in 1937 blended a strong consciousness of reflexivity with a Marxian philosophy of history, pushing his theoretical framework toward the necessary construction of a correct social theory to properly interpret the present and guide human action forward. He grounded the normativity of critical theory in an updated analysis of capitalism that allowed him to speak in normatively foundational terms about what was to be done. The combination of reflexivity, his philosophy of history, and his emancipatory ideals led to strong normative foundations that animated the early program of the Frankfurt School.

By contrast, a wave of critical challenges in the 1960s and 1970s embraced the reflexive element of critical theory and the emancipatory ambition, but it rebelled against Marxian philosophy and history, pushing the critical project in another direction altogether. Emphasizing Nietzsche rather than Marx or Kant or Hegel as the source of critique, Deleuze and Foucault reoriented the critical project toward a genealogical method that rested on a far more contingent conception of history and analyzed social formations as the product and interaction of the microphysics of power and subjectivity. From that perspective, there were no normative foundations, but simply spaces of normative contestation.

To be sure, Foucault's writings in the early 1970s, perhaps his most marxisant, did propose a correct theory about punitive discipline that oriented his readers toward a model of civil war; but his later writings disturbed those theories. It became clear that he was not interested in laying normative foundations, but in tracing their history. He was not interested in truth, but in the history of truth-making. In his last writings, Foucault upped the ante on reflexivity, gradually focusing primarily on practices of the self. Rather than ground his actions on normative foundations, Foucault sought instead to lead his political life like a work of art and developed the idea of an aesthetics of existence.

Edward Said, Gayatri Chakravorty Spivak, Judith Butler, Homi Bhabha, and other postcolonial, critical race, and queer theorists pushed these critical challenges to interrogate their own hidden foundations of Eurocentrism, ethnocentrism, and heteronormativity, for instance, and resisted even further the urge for normative grounding and truth.

Confronted by these and other critics, the later generations of the Frankfurt School ultimately abandoned Marx's philosophy of history, but they nevertheless constructed equal, if not stronger, normative foundations—if anything, augmenting the tensions within critical theory. Jürgen Habermas developed a theory of communicative action that ultimately converged on a Kantian notion of universality and political liberalism. Axel Honneth and Rahel Jaeggi replaced Marx's philosophy of history with a Hegelian learning process that inflected their writings, each in their own ways, with normative foundations to argue for socialism or the ability to critique ways of life, respectively. Seyla Benhabib and Rainer Forst drew on Habermasian discourse ethics to make claims to justification and normativity, ultimately pushing critical theory toward Arendtian conceptions of the right to have rights or Kantian ideals of universality through reason, respectively. The controversies produced deep disagreement about normative foundations, objectivity, and truth that were primarily fought on the terrain of epistemology (namely, on questions of ideology, knowledge-power, or regimes of truth). The central points of conflict—epistemological and normative foundations, objectivity, and truth—overlapped in the sense that the normativity rested on contested epistemological bases.

This led critical theory into a lengthy epistemological detour. Critics fought over what we could know about the present and history. The different tendencies of critical theory diverged most deeply on the question of what we could know or say for others, as opposed to what we could know or say just for ourselves. Both extremes were reflexive in their own way—they just pushed reflexivity in different directions. Some went toward the idea that reflexivity calls for the affected subjects to decide how to reach agreement on political principles and normative orders; others, by contrast, went toward the idea that reflexivity calls for the subjects to work on themselves only.

If one could imagine the various fields of human inquiry aligned along a spectrum going from the more universal to the more individual—from what may apply for all to what may apply only to the self, from the objective to the subjective—it would be possible to align them from the extreme of ontology at one end to that of aesthetics at the other. Most thinkers are far more likely to believe that questions of being and existence in ontology can be resolved for everyone than to think that judgments of aesthetics could apply to everyone. The existence of things, people are more likely to believe, are real and universal for everyone; aesthetic taste, by contrast, is far more likely to be thought of in individualistic terms. If such a spectrum existed, we could probably align the fields of human inquiry in the following way (with the caveat that epistemic truth qualifies all these statements and therefore could also be considered the overarching discipline): ontology, epistemology, jurisprudence, politics, morality, ethics, and aesthetics.

This imaginary axis—what is likely to be the case for all versus what is likely to be the case only for the self—is central to understanding the cleavage between the strands of critical theory. The early generations of the Frankfurt School pushed the fields of law, politics, and morality toward the ontological side of the spectrum; by contrast, the poststructuralists in the 1960s pushed law and politics, as well as epistemology, toward the ethics and aesthetics side, and essentially sidelined morality. The tendency of the former was reflected in the scientific side of Marx's work. It persisted in Horkheimer's political economic analysis. It recurred in Habermas's later writings, and especially in his debate with John Rawls. It could be felt every time that critical theorists, such as Steven Lukes, return to a strong version of false consciousness or of ideology critique and real interests. It is, in essence, the impulse to truth and certainty in the face of contested politics and crises. But it always clashed with the other core aspects of critical philosophy and the original impetus to counter traditional or positivist social science. And the recurring confrontations pushed critical philosophy into a quagmire.

In trying to resolve and get us past the epistemic detour that has moved critical theory away from praxis, I have argued for a position that does not ground normativity in agreement or universality, nor in a philosophy of history or social learning, nor in a correct social theory, but rather in a contextualized and historicized choice of values. It would be a mistake to call this position antifoundational because it does embrace critical values that have value (namely, its emancipatory ambition). It could more likely be described as counterfoundational, though the rubric itself is of little importance.[80]

Making a claim of truth or justification for others is, in the end, nothing more than an imposition of the part for the whole, and in that sense, it is inevitably the product of relations of force in a milieu marked by endless power struggles. It is a milieu that is entirely shaped by history and by relations of power and production, and in that sense, all potential value choices are contextual, historical, and situated. Most important, these are values for oneself only, not to impose on others—not even critical theorists.

The idea that a political, moral, or legal judgment could be in any way true or correct for others—or for that matter, reasonable—is nothing more than a vain attempt to achieve consensus or resolution in a manner that masks the relations of power that make a part stand for the whole. In the end, we need to get beyond the idea of objective normative foundations in law, politics, and morality. This is not to embrace skepticism. It does not deny the existence of things. In the ontological domain, there is being and existence, and in that sense, one can speak of facts. But that way of thinking cannot extend to law or politics. One cannot speak of reasonable normative orders or political principles that would apply to others; that is trying to extend the ethical or aesthetic onto others. Given the need for reflexivity, we can embrace critical values only for ourselves. That is the only way to return critical theory to its ambition: to change the world. That lays the groundwork for a critical theory of praxis.

PART III

Renewing Critical Praxis

Just as a reconstructed critical theory, understood as a radical theory of illusions and critical values, frees us from unfounded epistemological foundations and too simplistic utopias, a renewed critical praxis should liberate us from ready-made modes of practice—whether it is the need for a vanguard party, class struggle, or, for that matter, leaderless assemblies and occupations. It frees us from dogma about political action and opens wide the space of revolt. A reconstructed critical theory goes hand-in-hand with a reflexive, contextual, and situated strategic approach that seeks not to realize a predetermined privileged praxis, but to interrogate and explore unique strategies in time and space in order to push really existing social and political arrangements in an egalitarian and socially just direction, recognizing the need to constantly reexamine how power circulates in our own critical theory and practices.

Critical praxis too must be situated, contextualized, and grounded in specific historical, geographical, social, and political circumstances—this is, again, the critical imperative of reflexivity. Just as a reimagined critical horizon aims at critical values and not abstract concepts, and just as those critical values are always situated and contextualized, a renewed critical praxis calls not for abstract categories like nonviolence or revolution, but instead an individually tailored, specific assessment of tactical engagement in each historical, geographical, and political space. A vanguard of intellectuals may perhaps be appropriate or useful in some discrete situations, but never as either a default or a constant. There is no one size that fits all, but at the same time, nothing is off the table. When, for instance, Slavoj Žižek declares that "a dose of this 'Jacobin-Leninist' paradigm is precisely what the left needs today,"[1] the response of critical praxis theory is: careful, not if it is just because you are a die-hard Jacobin-Leninist and think those methods are always necessary; but that does not mean that we rule out those practices.

The "today" in Žižek's statement is the most operative term, but we need to make sure that it is an authentic "today" and a here and now, in this location, not just a rhetorical ploy or trick. There may well be a specific time and place when Jacobin-Leninist tactics might be called for, but it should never be a paradigm for paradigm's sake. There is no universalism and little portability to critical praxis. Portability in the context of critical praxis, in fact, is especially dangerous.[2] Praxis must be determined in a deeply contextualized manner. It must be punctual, with a unique GPS location, date, and time stamp. It must be responsive to the exceptional time and place constraints because there is no utopian landing strip, nor is there a fixed target—rather, there is always another historical space in which power circulates in new and unprecedented ways. In this sense, a renewed critical praxis calls for *a radical critical theory of strategies and tactics.*

The crucial point is that contemporary critical theorists must constantly reexamine how power circulates in time and space. This is key: the central element of reflexivity requires that we, critical theorists, be aware of the constantly changing nature of our historical situation and of the ways in which we affect it, such that our own critical thinking, writing, speech, and actions are simultaneously the subject and object of a critical inquiry. We are, therefore, investigating not only what praxis to engage in, but also the very ways in which we investigate and relate to one another. This is why critical philosophy is so concerned with the relation between theory and practice. It is also why we need to interrogate the formula "What is to be done?" That formulation of the action imperative (and alternative ones as well) needs to be constantly interrogated because the critical task is precisely to explore how power circulates in new and changing situations—and the space of critical praxis *itself* changes as critical theorists debate, communicate, and struggle over the praxis imperative and act in response. This is the beauty of a reconstructed critical theory—not its weakness, but its strength: it poses the question of how power circulates within its *own* domain as well, within the very field of critical praxis. It is eager to reexamine whose voices are heard, whose are silenced, whose are legible or illegible, and who can speak and who cannot.

In my view, this requires that the question "What is to be done?" be reformulated. The action imperative at the heart of that formula is important (in fact essential), but the phrasing has had a way of privileging the voices of some people over others, and of undermining the critical values of equality and solidarity. It is insufficiently reflexive. It presupposes too much about the "we" who are to do something and the corresponding field of action.[3] Instead, I will propose, for myself, in part IV, to reformulate the question into one that I ask myself, not others: "What more am *I* to do?" This, I believe, turns the tables on the action imperative, reorients it toward myself, and places responsibility where it should. It also confirms that praxis and theory must constantly confront each other. "What more can I do, and how is what I am doing working?" entails not only a question about the necessity of my own praxis, but also a question about how it relates to critical philosophy. Before getting to my own reformulation, though, I will examine in this part some new ways of thinking about critical praxis in the twenty-first century.

CHAPTER 14

The Transformation of Praxis

In his essay "No Way Out? Communism in the Next Century" in volume 3 of his edited collection *The Idea of Communism*, Slavoj Žižek poses a real challenge to a radical critical theory of illusions and values: even if we all agree that there are no inherent laws of economics, that abstract regime types are not determinative, that material distributions are the product of the second-order rules and regulations, and that we have control over those distributional outcomes—in other words, even if we agree that our social condition is politically chosen and can be changed to align with our critical values—this question still remains: Can the social transformation occur through political reform, or must there be a revolution? In effect, can the transition be gradual and incremental, or must there be a radical rupture from the present? What kind of critical praxis is really required?[1]

In posing this question, Žižek draws on a passage by Joseph Stiglitz, the Columbia University economist and Nobel laureate, who argues that the social problems we face are the result not of any inexorable inequality inherent to capitalism, nor of inherent laws of capitalism or internal contradictions, but instead are the product of deliberate political decisions. The problem is not economics—in effect, it is politics. Stiglitz is responding to Thomas Piketty's book *Capital in the Twenty-First Century*, in a review titled, tellingly, "Democracy in the Twenty-First Century," which emphasizes that the problem is not the laws of capital but our liberal-democratic political system. Stiglitz writes there, and Žižek quotes at length:

> What we have been observing—wage stagnation and rising inequality, even as wealth increases—does not reflect the workings of a normal market economy, but of what I call 'ersatz capitalism.' The problem may not be with how markets should or do work, but with our political system, which has failed to ensure that markets

> are competitive, and has designed rules that sustain distorted markets in which corporations and the rich can (and unfortunately do) exploit everyone else . . . Markets, of course, do not exist in a vacuum. There have to be rules of the game, and these are established through political processes . . . Thus, Piketty's forecast of still higher levels of inequality does not reflect the inexorable laws of economics. Simple changes—including higher capital-gains and inheritance taxes, greater spending to broaden access to education, rigorous enforcement of anti-trust laws, corporate-governance reforms that circumscribe executive pay, and financial regulations that rein in banks' ability to exploit the rest of society—would reduce inequality and increase equality of opportunity markedly. If we get the rules of the game right, we might even be able to restore the rapid and shared economic growth that characterized the middleclass societies of the mid-twentieth century. The main question confronting us today is not really about capital in the twenty-first century. It is about democracy in the twenty-first century.[2]

Stiglitz's argument, you will notice, is consonant with a radical theory of illusions and values: the problem is not the abstract regime type, but the second-order rules and regulations in American capitalism today, including the lack of an inheritance tax, low corporate tax rates, and unlimited executive pay.

Žižek's response to Stiglitz is important: this may all be right and good, but for real political change to occur, there would need to be much more than just freely chosen and gradual redistribution. Real transformation would require fundamental social change. It would require a revolution, in fact—and not just a metaphorical, political revolution, as Bernie Sanders proposed. It would require real revolution. In other words, it would be impossible to implement all those necessary second-order legal and political reforms without a more fundamental social upheaval. Žižek writes: "Here the change required is not political reform but a transformation of the social relations of production—which entails precisely revolutionary class struggle rather than democratic elections or any other 'political' measure in the narrow sense of the term. . . . Radical changes in this domain need to be made outside the sphere of legal 'rights.'"[3] Rehearsing Marx's distinction between human emancipation and civil and political rights as presented in *On the Jewish Question*, Žižek emphasizes the need for revolution over reform. His challenge boils down to whether we could achieve true social transformation and critical emancipation through democratic modes of deliberation, or whether a revolution is necessary.

This was, you will recall, the debate between Eduard Bernstein and Rosa Luxemburg at the beginning of the twentieth century. Bernstein argued, based on his reading of Engels, that the transformations of capitalism and improved social conditions had abated the class war and called for the end of a war paradigm. He advocated for parliamentary reforms and party politics rather than revolution. "Engels is so thoroughly convinced that tactics geared to a catastrophe have had their day that he considers a revision to abandon them to be due even in the Latin countries where tradition is much more favourable to them than in Germany," Bernstein wrote. Citing Engels, he asked, "If the conditions of war between nations have changed, no less have those for the war between classes. Have we forgotten this already?" Bernstein argued that social democrats had to get beyond the war paradigm, beyond catastrophe and revolution, and work instead for legislative victories, juridical guarantees, and established power. Rather than revolution, war, and upheaval, Bernstein recommended a struggle for political rights and legislative reform: "the struggle for the political rights of the worker, the political activity of workers in towns and municipalities for the interests of their class, as well as the work of organising workers economically." The task for social democrats, he argued, in italics for emphasis, was to find "*the best way to extend the political and industrial rights* of the German working man." The task ahead was to organize workers politically, train them for democratic politics, and push for better working conditions and more democracy.[4]

The heart of Bernstein's debate with Rosa Luxemburg was whether to wage war—class war and proletarian revolution—or to engage in parliamentary politics. Luxemburg understood that well, which is why she portrayed the dispute as going to the very heart and soul of Marxism and social democracy. The question of reform or revolution, for her, was equivalent to, or, in her words, "equals for the Social Democracy the question: 'To be or not to be?'"[5] The question went to the very core of social democracy. And Luxemburg could not have been clearer as to her position on that question: "The question of reform and revolution, of the final goal and the movement, is basically, in another form, but the question of the petit-bourgeois or proletarian character of the Labor movement."[6] In other words, reformists betray the proletariat.

In these debates, critical theorists have disagreed for decades. They have rehearsed many of those earlier arguments. They ultimately have gone in different directions. Jürgen Habermas, for instance, veered toward communicative action and eventually reached a political reformism quite similar to political liberalism;

in contrast, Žižek remained true to the other extreme and to Lenin. Regardless of the divergence, these debates bring us to the heart of the next and final question: Having reconstructed critical theory as a radical theory of illusions and values, what is the way forward to achieving these critical values and a more just society? What form should critical action take today in specific contexts? Does it necessarily call for revolutionary action? Does it call instead for an uprising, an occupation, or political disobedience? Or, in certain cases, for civil disobedience—or is civil disobedience too wedded to liberal legalism? Might it entail social protest movements like #BlackLivesMatter or #MeToo? What about riots? Hacking? Whistleblowing? If there is such a thing as a critical praxis that *differs* from liberal political practices, what should it look like? Before responding, it is important to begin again with a short history of the present to get a sense of where critical praxis is located today.

The Historical Trajectory

From its inception in the nineteenth century through at least the mid-twentieth century, critical philosophy was mostly guided by Marxist and socialist ideas that placed the worker and class struggle at the center of political engagement. Some strands of critical theory were more individualist, anarchist, or oriented toward personal practices, such as psychoanalysis, and less oriented toward collective action. In the 1960s, some theorists tried to integrate different strands, such as Herbert Marcuse in *Eros and Civilization*. But for most of its early history, the struggle of workers defined the historical narrative, identified the central political problem, and provided one foundational response: class warfare. Marx and Engels's *Manifesto of the Communist Party* opened precisely on that note: "The history of all hitherto existing society is the history of class struggles."[7] For almost a century after the *Manifesto*, much of the critical Left placed its praxis under the banner of class struggle.

The importance of class struggle produced a more coherent vision on the critical Left of what was to be done. The struggle was to take the form of a social revolution—either with the help of a vanguard party, through forms of syndicalism or in more democratic ways—or radical reform. There were, of course, sharp disagreements along those lines, leading to continued, voluminous debate over revolution versus reform. But most agreed about one thing: class struggle. So the question of political action—what was explicitly referred to, at the time, as *praxis*—predominantly passed through a workers' movement that would bring about social transformation. It would translate, through the ages and various contexts, into internationalism, syndicalism, anti-imperialism, and anticolonialism. With Mao, it extended to agricultural workers, or what were referred to as "peasants," and later colonized subjects. Regardless, for the most part, there was a coherence to, and almost a consensus about, the question of what was to be done: class struggle against the bourgeoisie.

That consensus evaporated by the mid-twentieth century. To be sure, some theorists still held onto it. Immanuel Wallerstein wrote in 2019, the year of his death, "Class struggles are eternal."[8] But for the most part, class became one of a number of other dimensions of struggle, including race, gender, ethnicity, sexual orientation, and religion. The shift gave rise to an explosion of varied experiments of different modalities of revolt. New forms of praxis burst forth. Occupy Wall Street and the global Occupy movement, #BlackLivesMatter, Tahrir Square, Nuit Debout, temporary autonomous zones (TAZs) in Notre-Dame-des-Landes, Lyon and elsewhere, Gezi Park, the London riots, Standing Rock, and the *Indignados* movement in Spain: these historical events reimagined political action. They also led to renewed critical theorizing about political practice. The Movement for Black Lives and #MeToo movements inspired important critical reflections on questions of leadership and representation in the writings of Cathy Cohen, Barbara Ransby, Keeanga-Yamahtta Taylor, Deva Woodly, and others.[9] The Occupy movement and assemblies prompted new thinking on the performativity of assembly in Judith Butler's writings, on the political potential of the multitude in Michael Hardt and Toni Negri's work, and on old and new concepts of civil disobedience and "political disobedience" in the works of W. J. T. Mitchell and Mick Taussig, Brandon Terry, Sandra Laugier and Albert Ogien, Frédéric Gros, Robin Celikates, and others.[10]

Rather than revolution, many spoke about riots and insurrections. The practices changed. New forms and bricolage emerged, and new words did too.[11] Often, these diverse practices—of leaderless occupations and general assemblies at Tahrir Square or Zuccotti Park, of spiritually tinged gatherings or even nation-building at the Standing Rock reservation, of hunger strikes in Turkey or Pelican Bay Prison—clashed with more classical conceptions of praxis and triggered uneasy reactions among critical theorists. Some expressed frustration at these newer modalities of revolt. The leaderless aspect was particularly fraught, and substantial disagreement emerged about practices at Occupy Wall Street.

These tensions and conflicts posed the question: How should we think about critical praxis when the dialectical imagination is so fractured? What should critical action look like, especially at a time when right-wing populist movements have cannibalized segments of the working class, turning old-style class warfare into anti-immigrant and ethno-racist conflict?

Critical theorists today face many of the threats that earlier critics stared down. Like Walter Benjamin, Theodor Adorno, and others in the 1920s and 1930s, we face a troubling conjuncture of crises in world history that are challenging our understanding of both our present and possible futures. But something important has changed. The coherence of both critical theory and praxis in a world of class struggle has fractured, and with that, the clear compass of earlier times. The historical trajectory has placed us in a different situation today. It has fractured the relationship between critical theory and critical praxis.

The Fracture of Theory and Praxis

Class struggle was, in a sense, the theoretical glue that kept critical praxis together: so long as the Marxist and socialist ideas of class conflict dominated, then theory could effectively dictate practice. To put it simply, class warfare implied proletarian revolution; and if the first dissipated, so would the second. In fact, it is no coincidence that Eduard Bernstein, in his debate with Rosa Luxemburg, argued, based on his authoritative reading of Engels, that the historical conditions had changed and that class struggle should no longer be viewed through a war paradigm.[12] Bernstein's dilution of the concept of class warfare was the first weakening in the theory-praxis link to revolution. As the paradigm of class warfare weakened, so did the coherence of praxis, and so did the link between theory and praxis. The coherence of critical praxis, in effect, was tied to a certain understanding of the unity of theory and practice. That understanding may well have been present at least through the early writings of the first generation of the Frankfurt School, but it quickly vanished with World War II at midcentury and with the political turmoil and student movements during the Cold War.

Before the war, the unity of theory and practice remained tight. Still, in 1937, Horkheimer professed an abiding faith in that unity and in the paradigm of class warfare. He specifically wrote about that "unity of theory and practice," which he defined as "the idea of a theory which becomes a genuine force, consisting in the self-awareness of the subjects of a great historical revolution."[13] For Horkheimer, there was a harmonious relationship between theory and practice—one in which critical theory unified the duality and militated in favor of a vanguard role for the critical intellectual. There was in fact both a theoretical and a practical aspect to critical theory, as evidenced in his subtle formulations, in the very semantics of his writings: "The economy is the first cause of wretchedness, and critique, *theoretical and practical*, must address itself primarily to it." Seamlessly, in the fabric of his prose, Horkheimer joined the theoretical and practical dimensions. We do not need "simply the theory of emancipation," he proclaimed, but "the practice of it as well."[14] Horkheimer believed in radical transformation, revolutionary change, rather than gradual or incremental social change. He gestured toward the need for revolutionary change: "The change which [critical theory] seeks to bring about is not effected gradually," he wrote.[15]

However, the war, and later the student revolts of the late 1960s and 1970s, shook this unity, broke the link to praxis, and brought to a head the tension within the Frankfurt School. Two starkly opposed positions emerged, represented on the one hand by Herbert Marcuse and on the other by Theodor Adorno.

Marcuse and many students still advocated for the unity of theory and practice, and with it, a renewed call for revolution. Unity was, in fact, the very slogan and the heart of the emerging New Left at the time. As Marcuse wrote in his book *Counterrevolution and Revolt* in 1972, emphasizing the point in italics: "The petrification of Marxian theory violates the very principle which the New Left proclaims: the *unity of theory and practice*."[16] Theory had to guide practice. As Marcuse explained, "A theory which has not caught up with the practice of capitalism cannot possibly guide the practice aiming at the abolition of capitalism." Marcuse not only argued for the unity of theory and practice—one that admittedly "is never immediate" but necessary—he also advocated strenuously for a radical New Left movement inspired by and inspiring to the students and their revolt. Marcuse called for a revolution that involved "a radical transformation of the needs and aspirations themselves, cultural as well as material; of consciousness and sensibility; of the work process as well as leisure." He called for a "new relationship between the sexes, between the generations, between men and women and nature." He demanded "a new sexual morality, the liberation of women" to fight against the material conditions of capitalism. This was a New Left that would be built by freeing Marxian thought of its dogmatic, Marxist interpretations and updating it to address the new conditions of late capitalism. "Marxian theory remains the guide of practice, even in a non-revolutionary situation," Marcuse declared in 1972.[17] Notice the careful use of the term "Marxian" rather than "Marxist," which was a deliberate and careful signaling mechanism by means of which Marcuse was referring to a reconstructed reading of Marx, rather than to what was called "vulgar" Marxist dogma. In all this, Marcuse sought to empower the younger generations, in which he identified this unity of theory and praxis.

In *One-Dimensional Man* especially, Marcuse set forth a clear political program and ways to measure its success—all implied by Marxian theory. He called for "the pacification of existence." He identified what people would need to sacrifice (for those who live in affluent societies), and how progress could be measured. The program was explicit: the refusal of all toughness and brutality, active disobedience and refusal, protest—or, famously, in his words, the "Great Refusal."[18] For Marcuse, as he wrote nearly a decade later in *Counterrevolution and Revolt*, the "most advanced counter-force" was the radical student movement, which he added, "must become a political weapon."[19]

In contrast, confronted by those very same student protests, Theodor Adorno retreated even more from praxis to theory, debunked the call to action, and dismissed revolution. He underscored the dialectical—and thus negative or discontinuous—relationship between theory and praxis. The relationship was one of contradiction, opposition, and tension, not unity. Only the productive clash of theory and praxis could advance either one.

Throughout the history of critical theory, Adorno maintained, there never was unity. Theory did not "imply" praxis. There was, in fact, practically no attention to praxis. Whenever Adorno himself intervened with a practical result, "it happened only through theory," as he emphasized in his "Marginalia to Theory and Praxis" in 1968–1969. He attacked the idea that Marx was praxis-oriented. Marx's *Capital*, Adorno wrote, had "no program for action." To be more precise, he wrote, "The theory of surplus value does not tell how one should start a revolution." "In regard to praxis generally," he added, "the anti-philosophical Marx hardly moves beyond the philosopheme." And Adorno's own key works (not only *Dialectic of Enlightenment*, but also more politically engaged research like *Authoritarian Personality*), he contended, were not oriented toward praxis. There was no practical intention.[20]

Adorno maintained that the relationship between theory and praxis is dialectical: the two are neither unified as one nor distinct as two; instead, they are in a relation of "discontinuity."[21] In the words of Adorno, targeting Marcuse, "The dogma of the unity of theory and praxis, contrary to the doctrine on which it is based, is undialectical: it underhandedly appropriates simple identity where contradiction alone has the chance of becoming productive."[22] In other words, theory does not imply praxis. Praxis is not the application of theory. Neither is it subordinate to the other. It is only in their "polar relationship" that either of them can be productive. In this, as noted previously, Adorno agreed with what Horkheimer had argued after the war, two decades earlier in *Eclipse of Reason* (1947): "Today even outstanding scholars confuse thinking with planning."[23]

The net effect, though, was a fracturing of the coherence of praxis and a privileging of theory. The priority of theory at the expense of the coherence of praxis was stunning. In *Eclipse of Reason*, Horkheimer situates himself at a time of crisis at the end of the war: the democratic regimes that had prevailed, alongside the Soviet Union, confronted a veritable crisis, as technical progress and knowledge were accompanied by mass manipulation and what Horkheimer called a "process of dehumanization."[24] Horkheimer was deeply concerned that the ambition of liberal democracy—what he called "the idea of man"—would succumb and that the West might face a resurgence of totalitarianism and fascism. Horkheimer writes, "Whether this situation is a necessary phase in the general ascent of society as a whole, or whether it will lead to a victorious re-emergence of the neo-barbarism recently defeated in the battlefields, depends at least in part on our ability to interpret accurately the profound changes now taking place in the public mind and in human nature." The looming threat at this moment, in 1946, was the resurgence of fascism—a form of government that was always much more efficient than democracy. But notice—and this is key: the future will depend "on our ability to *interpret* accurately the profound changes," Horkheimer writes.[25]

To "interpret": we are in the realm of *theoria*. We are in the contemplative. Faced with the crisis of democratic disillusionment and of what he calls "dehumanization"—faced with what we face today, the looming rise of the New Right—Horkheimer calls for "interpretation." Indeed, he goes even further: in the next paragraph, Horkheimer essentially foreshadows Adorno's "Marginalia on Theory and Praxis" two decades later. His goal, he writes, is to "throw some light on the philosophical implications of these changes"—to enlighten, to "throw some light," to theorize, not to offer guidance on praxis.[26]

Adorno, in "Marginalia on Theory and Praxis," affords the same privilege to theory, even at the expense of theorizing a coherent praxis. To be sure, Adorno criticizes the pristine Kantian notion of theory—and refuses to "refract[] theory through the archbourgeois primacy of practical reason proclaimed by Kant and Fichte." He states that he does not intend to subsume praxis to theory. But nevertheless, Adorno evinces a distinct preference for theory. He criticizes those who focus on the "effectiveness here and now" of theory. He chides the call for action—so often associated, he writes, with bloody reality. He defends against the students' call for praxis. He writes at length of the "error of the primacy of praxis." At times, Adorno is hostile, even aggressive, toward praxis: "[Praxis] becomes in its turn ideology. There is a sure sign of this: the question 'what is to be done?' as an automatic reflex to every critical thought before it is fully expressed, let alone comprehended. Nowhere is the obscurantism of the latest hostility to theory so flagrant. It recalls the gesture of someone demanding your papers."[27]

The question "What is to be done?" interpellates the subject as a police officer would, "demanding your papers"—think here of what could only be the sharpest of contrasts with Althusser (even though Althusser also would be accused of privileging theory over praxis). Adorno writes that Marx "by no means surrendered himself to praxis."[28] The notion of "surrendering" oneself to praxis sounds the alarm. And the danger of action is precisely how Adorno concludes his piece:

> [Praxis] appears in theory merely, and indeed necessarily, as a blind spot, as an obsession with what is being criticized; no critical theory can be practiced in particular detail without overestimating the particular, but without the particularity it would be nothing. This admixture of delusion, however, warns of the excesses in which it incessantly grows.[29]

The sharp contrast between Adorno and Marcuse leaves little doubt that Adorno was targeting Marcuse in his resistance to the excesses of praxis—and, no doubt, for this reason, Marcuse became the champion thinker of the Frankfurt School among the rebellious students who rose up in 1968 and thereafter. In any event, the resistance to practice, even among some of the most critical of critical theorists, effectively fragmented the coherence of critical praxis. This was accompanied by a broader structural transformation in the revolutionary forms of revolt.

Structural Shifts in Critical Praxis

Alongside the structural transformation of critical horizons and utopias discussed in part II, critical philosophy experienced a structural transformation of critical praxis. A shift from Marx to Mao, as well as to later insurrectional practices, moved critical theory away from the modern concept of revolution to more situated uprisings, revolts, and political disobedience—to new modalities of uprising. This reflected, in part, a movement away from the Eurocentric model of revolution and toward practices of insubordination that were shaped during the colonial wars. "In the dominated colonial peripheries," Étienne Balibar explains, "there were no 'revolutions' but only 'resistances,' 'guerillas,' 'uprisings' and 'rebellions,'" and in contrast to the latter, the great revolutions of the nineteenth century "were supposed to be *political processes typical for the center* because they involved a participation of 'citizens' who exist only in the nation-states."[30] In effect, the mid-twentieth-century insurrections were, to the modern concept of revolution, what the periphery was to the center.

From revolution to uprising, from Europe to its colonies: this captures well the shift and resulting fragmentation of critical praxis during the twentieth century. It produced, by midcentury, four models on the more radical, revolutionary side of praxis.

There was, first, an *insurgency model of uprising* that could be traced directly to Mao's military strategies pre-1949. This model rested on Mao's tripartite division of society, and it inspired the growth of small, separatist cells or wider national liberation movements.[31] This was the model of the Front de libération nationale (FLN) in Algeria and of other liberation movements throughout the Global South. It was the model of insurgency that eventually gave rise to counterinsurgency warfare practices in Indochina, Algeria, Malaya, and Vietnam.

There was, second, a model of the *constant upending of revolutionary accomplishments*, based on Mao's Cultural Revolution from 1966 to 1968 (or at least to the time of the disbanding of the Red Guards). This model rested on the idea of the inevitable return of self-dealing and self-interest, of elitism and complacency. It reflected Mao's idea that the Chinese Communist Party had become the bourgeoisie. This model was one that gave rise to the call for "permanent revolution" that we heard in Latin and South America.

There was, third, a model of more *creative insubordination*, especially in some of the receptions of Maoism in the West in the 1960s and 1970s as an alternative to the Soviet archetype of communism. Militants in France, Italy, and other places drew on Mao's writings to develop alternative ways of thinking and challenging relations of power—some through new forms of popular justice, others through leaderless inquiries. A good illustration here, again, is the debate between Michel Foucault, Benny Lévy, and André Glucksmann in 1971.

And finally, there emerged a model of *Maoist-inspired insurrection* that had elements of early insurgency theory, but was isolationist or separatist from the masses. Mao here is less an explicit point of reference than a central but silent identifier. This model is what I would call *separatist insurrectional*, and it was reflected in the more extreme violent movements of the 1970s and 1980s in Western Europe and the United States, such as the Baader-Meinhof Group, the Red Brigades in Italy, or the Weather Underground Organization. The model differs sharply from the modern concept of revolution. It has a sharply different episteme: a small-bore, tactical episteme of guerilla fighting, associated with rebellion and insurrection, as opposed to the modern revolution.

These structural transformations greatly influenced practices of critical revolt at the turn of the twenty-first century. There were, naturally, a range of practices, but two major styles, or poles, emerged in the West in the first decade of the twenty-first century, alongside the parliamentary practices of socialist and social democratic parties: at one end, a set of more radical insurrectional movements in continuity with the historical transformations already discussed; and at the other end, a set of more open, prefigurative, nonviolent social movements that have evolved in part in opposition to the previous models—including, for instance, Occupy Wall Street, #BlackLivesMatter, and Standing Rock in the United States. Each of these styles and movements have been fruitfully theorized by contemporary collectives and thinkers such as the Invisible Committee for the first, and Michael Hardt and Antonio Negri, Judith Butler, and others for the second.

Insurrectional Cells

The first style of separatist insurrectional movements manifested around the world, from El Salvador and Peru in the 1980s to Nepal and Kashmir in the 1990s. These insurrectional practices took different forms and inspired separatist cells in Europe and elsewhere. The Invisible Committee, an anonymous group of anarchist activists in France, gave theoretical expression to this approach in a series of books, beginning with their first, *The Coming Insurrection*, published in 2007.

The Coming Insurrection views the world through the prism of civil war. What lies ahead is the "emergence of a brute conflict," the Committee writes. It is a civil war between different visions of society—between "irreducible and irreconcilable ideas of happiness and their worlds." It is useless, the Committee tells us, to get indignant, to get involved in citizens' groups, to react to news stories, or to wait for change or the revolution. "To no longer wait is, in one way or another, to enter into the logic of insurrection. It is to once again hear the slight but always present trembling of terror in the voices of our leaders. Because governing has never been anything other than postponing by a thousand subterfuges the moment when the crowd will string you up, and every act of government is nothing but a way of not losing control of the population."[32]

Rather than join citizens' groups or assemblies, the Committee advocates a form of separatism, secession, and isolation. France, the Invisible Committee tells us, is "the land of anxiety pills," "the Mecca of neurosis." Rather than embrace the neurotic masses, the insurrectional project is to withdraw to communes, to isolate oneself, and to remove oneself from the people. "Far more dreadful are *social milieus*, with their supple texture, their gossip, and their informal hierarchies," the Invisible Committee writes. "Flee all milieus. Each and every milieu is orientated towards the neutralization of some truth." Even anarchist milieus must be forsaken because what they do is "blunt the directness of direct action." Activists today must form communes instead of blending into the population. They must remove themselves from the toxicity of the general population. The masses are to be viewed with caution and suspicion, not the least of which because "we expect a surge in police work being done by the population itself."[33]

The Committee sets forth strategies for insurrection: demonstrations need to be wild and unexpected, not disclosed in advance to the police; they must lead the police, rather than be herded by them; they must take the initiative; harass and distract the police in order to attack elsewhere; choose the terrain; take up arms and maintain an armed presence, even if this does not mean an armed struggle; and use arms sparingly and infrequently. The central idea is of an uprising that represents "a vital impulse of youth as much as a popular wisdom."[34] This was an important model at the turn of the century, inspired clearly by Mao's trajectory of insurrectional practices over the course of the twentieth century.

Leaderless Assemblies as Prefigurative Movements

At the other extreme, another broad style embraced a very different ethic. Reacting in part against the patriarchal, "great man," and top-down character of most traditional critical praxis, these movements aspired to leaderless—or inversely, what could be called "leaderful"—and more egalitarian, ideologically open, democratic procedures. They attempted to prefigure the political processes that they aspired to, rather than viewing their militancy as a temporary, albeit necessary, means to achieve the society they wanted to live in.

Naturally, these movements took different forms. Some of the organizations within the Movement for Black Lives, for instance, were more centralized and hierarchical, such as the Black Youth Project 100 (BYP100), but most of the others aspired to be leaderless, such as Occupy Wall Street, Nuit Debout, or other organizations within #BlackLivesMatter. Many of the movements were ideologically open in the sense that there was often no policing of views, censorship of political ideologies, or establishment of a party line. There was rarely, in these new movements, a vanguard party. To the contrary, many of the militant movements had a unique ethical and political stance of equality and respect that went against the very idea of hierarchical power, the latter being mostly viewed as patriarchal. They deployed new technologies and had a strong digital presence on social media—using Facebook, Twitter, Instagram, Google+, and every other digital medium as a way to horizontalize authority.[35] They honed their political ethos and strategies around notions of equality and skillfully deployed digital disobedience toward that end.

Some of these new movements were more attentive to membership and representation. BYP100, for instance, restricted membership to persons who were between eighteen and thirty-five years old, and it was by definition Black and young. Beyond that, to become a member of BYP100, the person had to attend an orientation meeting, participate in two chapter meetings, and attend a public event. The organization was wedded to democratic principles: "Leaders are nominated, elected, and constantly rotated; the bulk of decisions must be ratified by a majority vote."[36] Other large-scale protests like Occupy Wall Street and Nuit Debout were more leaderless and equally egalitarian. What these movements all shared, though, was that they did not endorse political parties or political actors. For the most part, they maintained themselves outside mainstream politics.

In their very organization, many of these movements inserted their principles of equality into the way they functioned and operated. The aspirations and values were included in the movement structures themselves. In this sense, they were acting out what Barbara Ransby called "group-centered leadership practices." This did not mean that there were never recognized individuals, and even some celebrities, in these movements. What it meant, according to Ransby, was that everyone in the group responded to the will of its members. "The Movement for Black Lives is distinctive because it defers to the local wisdom of its members and affiliates, rather than trying to dictate from above," Ransby explained. This was, in her words, a "better model for social movements," and it represented "a choice, not a deficiency." The reason that it represented a better model, Ransby argued, was that it turned over the decision-making to those people on the ground who had the best understanding of the problems they faced and who were in the best position to carry out their own solutions. "People are better prepared to carry out solutions they themselves created, instead of ones handed down by national leaders unfamiliar with realities in local communities," she wrote.[37]

In *Notes Toward A Performative Theory of Assembly*, Judith Butler explored the performative dimensions of these assembly-based movements to expose how the physical gathering of bodies and the material element of assemblies precede, constitute, and make possible political expression. For her, the performative nature of assembly is a precondition for expression, and the materiality of assembly fashions the discursive realm. As Butler writes: "*The assembly is already speaking before it utters any words* . . . By coming together it is *already* an enactment of a popular will. . . . The 'we' voiced in language is already enacted by the gathering of bodies, their gestures and movements, their vocalizations, and their ways of acting in concert."[38]

This enactment of a "we" by means of physical assembly—both being present and being absent for those who are in prison or have been disappeared—is, for Butler, an essential precondition to expression and speech. It forms—or it performs—the medium within which claims for inclusion are expressed. It is the way to initiate claims to be "we the people" or, even further, "we are *still* the people." Butler explains that "when bodies assemble on the street, in the square, or in other forms of public space (including virtual ones) they are exercising a plural and performative right to appear, one that . . . delivers a bodily demand for a more livable set of economic, social, and political conditions no longer afflicted by induced forms of precarity."[39]

Butler argues that "acting in concert can be an embodied form of calling into question the inchoate and powerful dimensions of reigning notions of the political," and this works in two ways: first, by enacting contestation; and, second, by exposing precarity. In other words, assemblies serve as incipient forms of popular sovereignty. They give rise to forms of popular will and help shape our conception of the will of the people. The bodily nature of assemblies exposes the precarity of these lives. They reveal the lived existence in the shadows, but also the resounding claim that this condition of precarity is intolerable. As Butler notes, "the bodies assembled 'say' we are not disposable, even if they stand silently."[40]

Butler's central point is that the materiality of assembly, the corporeal presence of people assembled in the square, has a force of its own, independent of what is said, and serves as the precondition for what gets said. Assembly, in and of itself, matters. It says and does a lot. Or, as she writes: "the basic requirements of the body are at the center of political mobilizations—*those requirements are, in fact, publicly enacted prior to any set of political demands*."[41] This is, for Butler, the power and importance of these types of assemblies.

From insurrectional, separatist communes to prefigurative, egalitarian democracies, the turn of the twenty-first century served as a laboratory of critical praxis as critical theorists and practitioners rebuilt on the crumbling foundations of class struggle.

CHAPTER 15

The Landscape of Contemporary Critical Praxis

The historical context changed once again in the first decades of the twenty-first century. More openly xenophobic and racist movements emerged around the world with the growth of far-right parties in Europe and the Tea Party and then the Trump presidency in the United States, the Brexit debacle, and the rise of authoritarian leaders in Turkey, Russia, the Philippines, India, Brazil, and elsewhere. Across a spectrum of political issues, from immigration to social welfare to sexual orientation, the gloves came off, and the critical Left is facing a far more vocal and popular authoritarianism and extreme New Right—with even the more traditional conservative parties, like the Republican Party in the United States, revealing their ugliest underbellies. The lines of political demarcation are becoming more polarized, violent, and confrontational.

This presents a real challenge to critical praxis. The reason is that critique is often sharper when it confronts liberal ideology. That was surely the case with the immanent forms of criticism, discussed in chapter 5, that used the aspirations and ideals of liberalism—for instance, the promise of greater equality in the face of an unequal world or the potential of freedom in an unjust society—to motivate its assessment. Critique is often at its strongest when it can leverage the rhetoric of its interlocutor. But when the opposition is openly racist, sexist, homophobic, xenophobic, nationalistic, and supremacist, there is little to be gained from immanent critique. In a raw power struggle over values, there is hardly much need for sophisticated theory. And in the early twenty-first century, the critical Left faced precisely that: political leaders like Donald Trump, who was openly and proudly—and vociferously—Islamophobic, racist, and misogynist; Rodrigo Duterte, who campaigned on his willingness to kill citizens accused of drug dealing in the Philippines; and Recep Erdoğan, who openly imprisoned political opponents in the name of democracy in Turkey. While critique may function well in the face of liberalism, it is effectively disarmed against these forms of authoritarianism. Here, the subtleties of critique become less convincing.

It should not come as a surprise that the leading critical theorists in wartime have so often joined the ranks of the state apparatuses that they ordinarily would have critiqued or had critiqued in the past. After all, where was the Frankfurt School in wartime? At the U.S. Office of Strategic Services (OSS), which was the forerunner of the Central Intelligence Agency (CIA). Franz Neumann, who had just published a book on Nazi Germany, *Behemoth: The Structure and Practice of National Socialism*, in 1942, as well as Marcuse and Otto Kirchheimer, the coauthor of *Punishment and Social Structure* with Georg Rusche in 1939, all worked for the OSS under its head, the Republican Wall Street lawyer William Donovan. Neumann in fact took charge of the Research and Analysis Branch of the OSS for Donovan. As John Herz, who worked in Neumann's unit, quipped, "It was as though the left-Hegelian World Spirit had briefly descended on the Central European Department of the OSS."[1] Horkheimer was also reportedly part of the OSS. Meanwhile, Adorno, Herta Herzog, and Paul Lazarsfeld became involved in the Princeton Radio Project (later Columbia University's Bureau of Applied Research), which served intelligence functions.[2] And, to be honest, what else would one do, faced with a regime like the Third Reich—especially as a Jew in exile in the United States?

Similarly, today, we face a new constellation. The rise of far-right parties and movements has shifted the landscape of critical praxis. Critical theory no longer faces a type of liberalism that, in the United States for instance, hypocritically and cruelly fueled mass incarceration and replaced welfare with so-called workfare. It no longer faces a Democratic administration that, in the 1990s passed pro-prison tough-on-crime measures, and in the 2000s ratcheted up drone strikes and legally justified the first targeted assassination of American citizens abroad. Rather, it faces New Right political leaders who are openly Islamophobic, homophobic, xenophobic, misogynist, and racist.

In response, in the early twenty-first century, a lot of critical theorists retreated—perhaps justifiably—to the liberal institutions of resistance: whether they be the American Civil Liberties Union (ACLU) and human rights nongovernmental organizations (NGOs), the attorneys general of liberal states like Washington or New York, or even the Federal Bureau of Investigation (FBI), the CIA, and special counsel Robert Mueller, who led a two-year investigation into Trump and his campaign's illicit dealings with Russia during the 2016 presidential election. They fell back on the liberal bastions, as critical theorists did at midcentury. And it may well be that one effective strategy today is to do just that: to lock arms with liberals, to tone down the critique, to work together until better times manifest themselves.

But not all critical theorists take that position. Instead, many contemporary critics now advocate for an array of new or reconstructed practices, ranging from a return to revolution to more conventional democratic forms of parliamentary politics. At this point, let me start again at what we might call the two extremes, before exploring the many other praxis proposals that have emerged in the broader conversation.

The Vanguard and Revolution

Some critical theorists urge a return to vanguard revolutionary practices. There is, of course, a distinguished lineage to this approach, going back to Lenin or earlier, which is also evident in the early work of the Frankfurt School.[3] In the context of the Arab Spring uprisings of 2011, for instance, critical thinkers such as Tariq Ali and Perry Anderson advocate for a more concerted anti-imperialist strategy and vanguard revolutionary practice. The only way for the Arab uprisings "to become revolution," Anderson writes, is for the region as a whole to undo the 1979 Camp David Accords: "The litmus test of the recovery of a democratic Arab dignity lies there."[4] Ali, for his part, points us directly back to Lenin as the proper guide to rethink the Arab uprisings—and revolt more generally.

In his 2018 book *The Dilemmas of Lenin: Terrorism, War, Empire, Love, Revolution*, Ali draws our attention back to Lenin's *April Theses*. Lenin pronounced those theses at meetings of Soviets in Saint Petersburg held in early April 1917 (between the first revolution of February 1917 and the Bolshevik Revolution of October 1917). In his *April Theses*, Lenin argued for a second, truly proletarian revolution to succeed the first bourgeois revolution. Lenin's *Theses* were highly controversial among Marxists at the time because of their vanguardism, and there naturally were sharp differences in strategy and tactics. But the *April Theses* were, as Ali reminds us, a clarion call to vanguard action at a time when the revolutionary leadership was adrift—a provocative (in Ali's words, "explosive") and extremely controversial call for a second, truly socialist revolution to overcome the first, bourgeois revolution.[5]

At that time, Lenin called on his party members to unleash in effect a second revolution—in terms that would have had a special resonance in Egypt in 2011:

> The specific feature of the present situation in Russia is that the country is *passing* from the first stage of the revolution—which, owing to the insufficient class-consciousness and organisation of the proletariat, placed power in the hands of the bourgeoisie—to its *second stage*, which must place power in the hands of the proletariat and the poorest sections of the peasants.[6]

These words, Ali notes, "paved the way for the revolution in October 1917."[7] They laid the groundwork for a leaderful, vanguard revolution—precisely the type of practice that was consciously avoided by many in Tahrir Square, and later in Zuccotti Park and at the Place de la République. Ali's message is clear: what is needed at our assemblies today is a second uprising, a truly vanguard revolution. That alone will produce lasting change, according to Ali.

Ali is not alone. Žižek also advocates a Jacobin-Leninist stance. Recall how he argues for "a dose of this 'Jacobin-Leninist' " medicine. Žižek offers a passionate defense of popular and communist revolutions—from Robespierre to 1917 to Mao's Cultural Revolution. He calls for the four strict invariants of communism: "strict *egalitarian justice*, disciplinary *terror*, political *voluntarism*, and *trust in the people*."[8] The reason is that Žižek really wants to push us beyond uprising, back to revolution. He is fed up with uprisings like Occupy, which merely bring about the return of the same. He aspires to some kind of intervention that will push the riots and disobedience into a new social order. Thus, he writes:

> what if contemporary dynamic capitalism, precisely in so far as it is "worldless," a constant disruption of all fixed order, opens up the space for a revolution which will break the vicious cycle of revolt and its reinscription, i.e., which will no longer follow the pattern of an eventual explosion after which things return to normal, but will assume the task of *a new "ordering" against the global capitalist disorder*? Out of revolt we should move on shamelessly to enforcing a new order. (Is this not one of the lessons of the ongoing financial meltdown?) This is why the focus on capitalism is crucial if we want to reactualize the communist Idea: today's "worldless" dynamic capitalism radically changes the very coordinates of the communist struggle—the enemy is no longer the State to be undermined from its point of symptomal torsion, but a flux of permanent self-revolutionizing.[9]

To achieve this, Žižek advocates that we reimagine the state: not that we seize state power, nor that we seek the dissolution of the state entirely, but that we reconfigure the state into a nonstatal form. We need to radically transform the state, as Lenin suggested. And the only way that will be possible is if the three separate factions of the working class unite. As Žižek explains, the condition of postmodern capitalism has split the working class into three parts, each with a very different ideology and way of life. There are the intellectuals, who are mostly liberal, hedonist, and multicultural; the workers, who are more populist and fundamentalist now; and then the marginalized outcasts. In each of these three classes or factions, identity politics plays out in a different way: "postmodern multicultural identity politics in the intellectual class, regressive populist fundamentalism in the working class, half-illegal initiatic groups (criminal gangs, religious sects, etc.) among the outcasts." What all three classes share is the dependency on identity politics now that there is no more of a universal public sphere. Žižek's strategy, then, is to reunite the three factions. He closes the essay as follows: "The old call 'Proletarians, unite!' is thus more pertinent than ever: in the new conditions of 'post-industrial' capitalism, the unity of the three fractions of the working class *is* already their victory."[10]

Revolutionary class struggle has served, and can always serve, as a model for critical praxis. As an aside, though, it is worth recalling, at least for a moment, the dark side of vanguard communism: how Leninism led to Stalinism, to the Molotov–Ribbentrop Pact of nonaggression in 1939 and the Soviet Gulag; and how Maoism led to the Great Famine of 1959–1961 and to the concentrated violence of the Cultural Revolution. In armed warfare, naturally, there have been successful models of vanguard insurgencies based on the military strategies of Mao, Che, and others; but those were armed insurrections led by armed insurgents attempting to gain independence or violently overthrow a government. That might still be a model for critical praxis today, but it is important to emphasize that in many places today, it would likely lead to wide-scale incarceration and death. It should not be advocated lightly by theorists who are not willing to put themselves at the forefront and risk their own lives. It should also remind us of the courage of those women and men who engage in protest and uprisings. It reminds me of the words—recalled by Soha Bayoumi—of an activist, Mina Daniel, who was killed in October 2011 by the Egyptian military in Maspero, near Tahrir Square, during a peaceful Coptic protest: "You are not going out to make a revolution and live; you are going out to make a revolution and die . . . for your siblings, for your children, for anyone, so that others can enjoy this beautiful thing."[11]

Political Parties and Movements

At the other extreme of the praxis spectrum, some critical theorists advocate for political reform through parliamentary parties, trade unions, and nonviolent social movements. The approach is increasingly visible in the United States, in part because of the presidential bids by Bernie Sanders in 2016 and 2020. Those, along with Alexandria Ocasio-Cortez's election in 2018 to the House of Representatives, gave momentum to the Democratic Socialists of America. In France, Jean-Luc Mélenchon founded a new populist and social democratic party in 2016, La France insoumise, which advocates for a constitutional convention and the creation of a new republic that would transform the private ownership of capital. In Spain, Pablo Iglesias founded in 2014 a leftist populist party, Podemos, that challenged European austerity measures and became one of the country's largest political parties. Not everyone on the critical Left agrees or supports these politicians or parties, but these movements certainly comprise critical praxis. They represent precisely the kind of new parties and movements that Seyla Benhabib, for instance, commended in *Critique, Norm, and Utopia*: "those new social movements, which on the one hand fight to extend the universalist promise of objective spirit—justice and entitlements—and on the other seek to combine the logic of justice with that of friendship."[12]

Some critical theorists rally behind even more centrist leftist parties, such as the Social Democratic Party of Germany, the Democratic Party in the United States, or the French Socialist Party. In effect, the idea here, in terms of critical praxis, is that the political ambitions should conform to those of critical philosophy, but the practical implementation follows more conventional political strategies of electoral politics. The approach may feel conventional, or even conservative, to some—perhaps even noncritical—but if it is deployed in furtherance of critical values, there is no reason that it could not be considered an instrumental critical praxis.

"What is critical about it?" you may ask. The answer is the potentially emancipatory egalitarian project in many of these political movements and parties. Bernie Sanders is a good illustration. Sanders appropriates the term *political revolution* to express the radical emancipatory nature of his political project. This is not to suggest physical violence or revolutionary action, but to emphasize that gradual reform, even of the Barack Obama variety, will not fundamentally change the United States and produce equality. His point, in speaking of a revolution, is to suggest that there needs to be more radical parliamentary and executive reforms against the hegemony of corporations and corporate interests. But his praxis is entirely electoral and legislative. Like the Jacobin-Leninists, it deploys the term *revolution*, but it is really at the other extreme of the political spectrum.

The fact that Sanders usually qualifies *revolution* with the word *political* is important. It reflects a more conventional approach. The meaning of the term *revolution* has undergone change over time, as we have seen, and, in its modern meaning, connotes *social*, as opposed to merely *political* revolution: as Hannah Arendt and Reinhart Koselleck showed, the modern conception of Revolution is associated with a social transformation that goes beyond political change.[13] In this light, Sanders's use of the qualification *political* is astute and strategic. His intervention focuses us back on the political—almost as if he is shedding his earlier socialist identity to assume his current democratic socialist identity. The shift from revolution *tout court* to *political* revolution chastens his political position, putting it more in line with democratic socialist reform.

The reform agenda that Sanders sets out in his *Guide to Political Revolution* is nevertheless pretty radical—and with the exception, perhaps, of nationalized industry, it would satisfy many of the social ambitions of a utopian socialist state.[14] It is possible that Sanders's program is even more leftist and audacious than that of, say, former Socialist president François Hollande of France. Sanders's *Guide* is a remarkable text that not only argues convincingly for equitable positions, in detail, but also directs the reader to websites and organizations that address the points he raises. It is an *applied* intervention with a how-to approach. In part because he has been in Congress since 1990, Sanders knows how to pitch a policy proposal and measure its effects: a transaction tax of just 0.5 percent on stock trades would raise $300 billion a year—enough to make colleges and universities tuition-free for every American. Sanders proposes to transform American society along the following lines, all spelled out with detailed policy proposals:

- A national single-payer health care system, currently known as "Medicare for All"
- Tuition-free higher education
- A federal jobs program

- A living minimum wage, with paid parental and sick leave and vacations
- An increase in the number of union jobs
- A progressive estate tax
- Abolition of the death penalty, private prisons, and militarized police forces
- A path to citizenship for undocumented residents[15]

From the perspective of critical theory, one of the most interesting aspects of Sanders's approach is that he does not deploy notions of ideology or false consciousness. Throughout his narrative, Sanders repeats the idea that we all know "what is really going on." There are no illusions. There is no need to lift the veil. Everybody knows and understands the way that the political system favors and subsidizes large corporations. He says, "Americans *see* that there are different rules for the rich and powerful than for everyone else."[16] Throughout, Sanders underscores that we know what is going on.

There is no need for ideology critique, then—no need to lift any veil. All that we need is to mobilize in the face of these injustices. Sanders is cognizant of the paradoxes of capitalism, and he exposes them at every turn: the system actually underwrites large corporations such as Walmart, which does not pay its workers a living wage and does not seem to care that they must rely on food stamps, subsidized housing, and other public benefits funded by taxpayers. Hence, in a sense, Walmart is receiving public subsidies that, as one of the most profitable companies in America, it surely does not need. Sanders also describes the fraud and misrepresentation of large banks.[17] He is relentless in showing the lie of advanced capitalism.

We know the truth, Sanders argues. The only thing missing, then, is for the younger generation to mobilize and do what is necessary. He dedicates his book to "the younger generation," encouraging them to convert their "idealism and generosity of spirit into political activity," and acknowledging that only they will be able to "create a lot better world than the one my generation left you."[18] His message is clear: it is only the younger generation who will get us out of this mess. If anything, Sanders's *Guide* has gone beyond critique—to pure praxis. The imperative is not to enlighten or unveil. We all know this, he insists. The imperative, instead, is to encourage and incite the younger generation to mobilize, for they alone will be able to improve our world. One could summarize Sanders's approach, borrowing from the last line of Marx's and Engels's famous manifesto, as follows: Youth of this country, unite!

Sanders's agenda may fail in some critical aspects. Amna Akbar criticizes Sanders for being insufficiently attuned to relations of power and for insufficiently challenging the national security state.[19] Brandon Terry argues that the Sanders campaign was insufficiently attuned to class conflict within African American communities. The social problems associated with crime and policing, he argues, are not just problems of racism, but they lie at the intersection of race and class, wealth, and poverty. Adam Tooze faults Sanders for his nationalist and patriotic appeals.[20] But these critiques, more than anything, raise a genuine conundrum: whether it is even possible to engage American electoral politics honestly from a critical perspective. Is it possible for an *electoral* strategy—especially one that has any chance of winning—to be genuinely *critical*? And can legislative lobbying tactics, like those contained in the former congressional staffers' *Indivisible: A Practical Guide to Resisting the Trump Agenda* (2016), serve as critical praxis?

The fact is that these political practices are fundamentally electoral strategies and are, by definition, embedded within a constitutional framework, dependent on the existing political system, and are not seeking change even at the level of a constitutional amendment. They are entirely nonrevolutionary in the modern sense. They are not intended to transform the *structures* of political power—just the democratic balance and outcomes. As a result, in certain respects, they may well fall short of genuine critical values, and certainly fall short of an earlier critical consensus of class warfare. For instance, making unionization easier is not the same as creating a political economy in which the workers control the means of production; a minimum living wage is not the same as a minimum standard of living; and Medicare for All still depends on private doctors.[21] Nevertheless, it is surely the case that a society constructed along Bernie Sanders's lines—and all the other myriad proposals like banning fracking, reforming personal income tax, closing tax loopholes, banning the box, legalizing marijuana, etc.[22]—would be radically different from the current American political landscape. They might be radical, but are they radical enough to be called critical?

The problem, if there is any, is tied then to this specific modality of praxis: democratic electoral politics, at least in the United States in these times, does not allow much more than what Sanders proposed with any likelihood of winning a presidential election. So the mode of action places constraints on the political horizon. There is more, though. The problem also may relate to the reified nature of critical utopias. The formal resistance to characterizing Sanders's platform as truly critical reveals a certain rigidity in what it takes to be considered a paradigm shift:

certain forms of reorganizing our political economy, such as facilitating unions and using progressive taxation, may not qualify as sufficiently critical, whereas other forms of reorganizing our political economy, such as shifting the means of production to the workers, would. But that, of course, is far too foundational. It rests on an antiquated, dogmatic Marxist view. The real problem, then, comes back to the question of utopian foundationalism. As I argued earlier in part II, we would be far better off if we imagined critical utopias not through the lens of abstract regimes of political economy, but rather as a substantial movement toward our critical values. Our critical utopias should not aim at particular, rigid regime types, but should consist instead of material change in the direction of our critical ideals.

There are two more points to make. First, on the question of the confrontation of critical praxis and theory, it is worth noting the tension here. Electoral and parliamentary politics, as a form of critical praxis, pushes toward explicit policies and platforms. It forces political actors to position themselves and make proposals. It does not allow political actors to step back. If you are running for office, realistically, it is not enough to say that you are going to create a space for the voices of those who are not being heard to be heard. Only with great difficulty can you make the move that the founding intellectuals did in the manifesto of the *Groupe d'information sur les prisons* (GIP) and declare, as the GIP manifesto did, "It is not for us to suggest reform. We merely wish to know the reality. And to make it known almost immediately, almost overnight, because time is short."[23] The idea of simply letting others be heard does not function well in electoral politics. The closest you get is the so-called listening tour, which has become increasingly popular among politicians as a way for them to claim to be learning something from the people and to postpone policy details until they get that feedback. But electoral politics does not go well with the art of stepping back. Amna Akbar correctly speaks about the need for progressive movements today to listen and make a space for the discourse of the less advantaged; and she stresses that "we do not have the answers."[24] The trouble is, it is not clear how that works with electoral politics as a mode of praxis.

Second, as many observe today, one of the central problems facing critical philosophy is that its field has narrowed. Critical theory has become increasingly limited to the academy and to professional critics—as Didier Fassin and Linda Zerilli argue in *A Time for Critique*. If we are going to redress this problem, then, as critical theorists, we may need to be more generous with nonacademics and nonprofessional critics. The fact of simplicity alone—or of "sloppy sociology" as

Adam Tooze says—cannot be a response to a practical guide like Sanders's, which is intended to be a political platform, not a doctoral dissertation. This is especially the case because simplicity may be serving other ends.[25]

Let's take a closer look, for example, at one of the purportedly simplistic areas in Sanders's *Guide*—namely, immigration reform. Sanders was criticized for only proposing solutions related to the *existing* undocumented persons in this country and failing to address the larger question of "open borders"—a particularly tricky question for a socialist-friendly agenda, given the long-standing tension between, on the one hand, its history of internationalism, and, on the other hand, the parochialism of some national unions and domestic workers who fear that open borders would invite too much labor and thus depress domestic work and wages.

A look at Sanders's *Guide* makes clear that many of the proposals on immigration are indeed focused on the undocumented who are already on American soil. When Sanders describes immigration reform in detail, he focuses, "first and foremost," on "creating a path for the eleven million undocumented people in our country to become lawful permanent residents and eventually citizens"; his immigration reform also includes shoring up the DREAM Act for those in the military or attending college, ending family deportation sweeps, family detention and private detention facilities, and imposing measures on employers to prevent exploitation of the undocumented.[26]

These particular measures indeed focus on the undocumented who are already on American soil. But there are other recommendations that extend this action further. Sanders writes:

- Immigration reform must create viable and legal channels that match our labor market needs and promote family cohesion.
- Immigration reform must eliminate the three-year, ten-year, and permanent "bars."
- In light of a historic refugee crisis, immigration reform means reaffirming our commitment to accepting our fair share of refugees.
- And lastly, immigration reform means recognizing that inequality across the world is a major driving force behind migration. The truth is, our free-trade policies are exacerbating inequality by devastating local economies, pushing millions to migrate. We must rewrite our trade policies to end the race to the bottom and instead work to lift the living standards of Americans and people throughout the world.[27]

Those proposals are more open ended, and they also address some of the supposed root causes of migration. Sanders's discussion of immigration embeds a lengthy discussion of the impact of the North American Free Trade Agreement (NAFTA)—recognizing that migration and economic trade policies have to be addressed together. But even more, and more generously, it is not at all clear that the "path to citizenship" proposals are limited to only current undocumented residents—or that there is grandfathering going on. Sanders defines the phrase *pathway to citizenship* as openly applying to any and all "undocumented immigrants living in the shadows."[28] There is no caveat that this applies only to *present* undocumented residents; a proper system with a path to citizenship would apply prospectively to new undocumented residents as well. Some of the vocabulary is jarring on a first read—and Tooze underscored this following passage: "PATHWAY TO CITIZENSHIP: a system that allows undocumented immigrants who are in good standing to pay a fine, learn English, and *go to the back of the line* for the opportunity to become citizens."[29] The language about going "to the back of the line" is somewhat harsh; but in truth, all it means is that there is a queue: the most recently entered undocumented resident should not get their papers before another undocumented person who was here before them. Surely we can agree on that. There should be a chronological order to this process. So one way to read this platform is that, although it does not talk about "open borders" per se, it takes the approach of both addressing the root causes of migration and trying to put in place a process that would effectively create the possibility of far more open or porous borders. On its face, it is more than simply focused on the current undocumented population. And if we read it closely, with more of a Straussian touch—given especially the limitations of democratic electoral politics *as a mode of critical praxis*—then surely there is a strong indication of the direction of change, in relation to our shared critical values.

My point is *not* that we should not read critically or confront this praxis using critical theory. On the contrary, critical confrontation is necessary and especially productive when it highlights conceptual problems.[30] My point instead is twofold: first, that electoral politics as praxis puts certain constraints on political speech that may require us to read more subtly democratic electoral proposals; and second, that we need to discard antiquated reified utopias and begin to think and imagine more critically *en situation*. To move critique outside the academy and beyond professional critics, we can start by being more generous toward actors like Sanders and fellow travelers.

Left Populism

In dialogue with and in close proximity to these types of reform projects, Chantal Mouffe, in her book *For a Left Populism*, advocates more explicitly for an egalitarian, open, and embracing populist political strategy that could serve to unite all those who have been marginalized by the neoliberal global hegemony during the past forty years. As a discursive and rhetorical political device, Mouffe argues, left populism can construct an all-embracing "we the people" around the unsatisfied demands of all those left behind and opposed to the ruling powers. Mouffe identifies elements of this left populist project in the political discourse of Bernie Sanders and Jean-Luc Mélenchon, and in the approach of the Podemos and Syriza parties. Yet it represents a different form of praxis from Sanders's political revolution because it focuses more on the social movement and less on electoral politics. It is also more radical because it expressly embraces the contested term *populism*. Although it may evolve into parliamentary politics, Mouffe is primarily concerned with the broader, populist, grassroots movement.

Mouffe repeatedly underscores that her political project is constructivist and anti-essentialist: she is not trying to instantiate a "real people" and does not favor a hostile or exclusionary notion of "the people." She views politics through the perspective of agonism rather than antagonism, of adversarial relations rather than friend/enemy relations.[31] Her project is to unite those who have been left behind, by means of a more compelling discourse of equality, social justice, and popular sovereignty.

Mouffe tries to avoid the near-consensus of academic criticism of the term *populism* by stating up front that her project is about praxis, not theory. She proposes a political intervention, not a theory of populism, and she emphasizes that she has "no intention to enter the sterile academic debate about the 'true nature' of populism."[32] Nevertheless, those academic debates haunt the project, insofar as they pose real risks and challenges associated with populist movements.

Mouffe is not alone in calling for a left-leaning populist movement. Nancy Fraser also advocates for a progressive populism of a Marxian type. In a fascinating conversation with Rahel Jaeggi, in which Jaeggi ultimately asks Fraser, "What is to be done?" Fraser responds in a militant and urgent way: "My instinct is to seize the moment and go on the offensive," she states, as she then develops a Marxian left populism. Fraser refers to this as "progressive populism," and elsewhere as the "progressive-populist protection-plus-emancipation scenario." It is founded on Marxism but is intended to include within the concept of the working class—in the "*whole* working class," she writes, as does Mouffe—women, immigrants, people of color, and workers in domestic, agricultural and service sectors. It is, effectively, an updated Marxism in light of both Fraser's extensive writings on financialized capitalism and the rise of New Right populism. (In the end, though, the financialization of capital does not seem to be central to the praxis; in this sense, Jaeggi can say that what Fraser proposes "sounds a bit like the old left-wing strategy.")[33]

In advancing her progressive populism, Fraser adopts several classically Marxist-Luxemburgian positions, including first, that the contradictions of capitalism "are sharpening"; second, that the root of the crises today are "the multiple, deep-seated contradictions of capitalism"; third, that the crisis will not be resolved by "tinkering with this or that policy"—in other words, not by reform, siding with Luxemburg against Bernstein; and fourth, that resolution "can only go through the deep structural transformation of this social order," in other words, revolutionary change. Fraser embraces a leftist populism, like that of Chantal Mouffe, which includes not just the old-style working class, but women, minorities, immigrants, and other marginalized populations; which tries to attract potential allies within the right-wing populist movements; which applauds the vision of Sanders, Corbyn, Mélenchon, Podemos, and early Syriza; and which is based on the basic idea that neoliberalism as ideology has crumbled. "I repeat," Fraser emphasizes: "as a *hegemonic* project, neoliberalism is finished; it may retain its capacity to dominate, but it has lost its ability to persuade." Fraser draws a few lines in the sand, and these create a slightly separatist aura at times: she cautions against leaning into neoliberalism, like lean-in feminism, and proposes instead to separate it out, with "feminism for the 99 percent." Fraser also warns against false allies on the Right—proposing instead to carefully exclude racists and fascists.[34] To summarize this, she states that:

> We must break definitively both with neoliberal economics and with the various politics of recognition that have lately supported it—casting off not just exclusionary ethnonationalism but also liberal-meritocratic individualism. Only by joining a robustly egalitarian politics of distribution to a substantively inclusive,

class sensitive politics of recognition can we build a counterhegemonic bloc that could lead us beyond the current crisis to a better world.[35]

Almost uniformly, critical scholars criticize the turn to populism, predominantly because of the dangers presented by resurgent right-wing populism, but also in response to these calls for a left populism. Jan-Werner Müller, in his book *What Is Populism?* argues that populism is inherently an antipluralist strategy that, when it succeeds (invariably with the collaboration of more traditional conservative elites), veers toward exclusionary practices and mass clientelism.[36] Nadia Urbinati, in her article "Political Theory of Populism," maintains that populism is parasitic to democracy, insofar as it exploits democratic failures by means of an us-and-them logic; and that when it takes power, it inevitably pushes the notion of the people into an extreme or authoritarian direction, leading to the distortion of democratic institutions and practices (e.g., the rule of law, separation of powers, and checks and balances).[37] Jean Cohen, in "What's Wrong with (Theories of) Left Populism?" highlights specifically the dangers of *left* populism, arguing that it cannot avoid the authoritarian pitfalls of populism more generally.[38]

The confrontation with these academic critics of populism, though, makes clear that Chantal Mouffe is focused on *how to gain power*, whereas most of these critiques of populism are focused on the populist style of governing *when in power.*[39] But even with this distinction in mind, the core claim of the academic critics is that a populist mode of gaining power will inevitably distort democracy in practice. In other words, there is path dependence: it may not be possible to separate the way in which a movement takes power from the way that it exercises power. There is, certainly, evidence for this. (Donald Trump rose to power on a New Right exclusionary populism, and then he accentuated the exclusionary nature of his politics in office. There is also evidence for this on the left side of the populist spectrum—in Latin America, for instance.) Mouffe, however, responds by proposing a version of populism that is egalitarian and emphasizes social justice, in an effort to disrupt this path dependence. But it is, of course, difficult to evaluate her call for a left populism as a form of critical praxis when the very definition of *populism* itself is so contested. To give Mouffe a fair reading, the place to begin is to delineate more clearly her use of the term *populism*, especially as compared to other contemporary usages; and then to articulate her use of the *left* aspect of the term *left populism.*

Mouffe's Idea of Populism

Mouffe articulates a narrow definition of what she calls populism. Drawing in part on her long collaboration with Ernesto Laclau, Mouffe specifies that she understands populism

> as a discursive strategy of constructing a political frontier dividing society into two camps and calling for the mobilization of the "underdog" against "those in power." It is not an ideology and cannot be attributed a specific programmatic content. Nor is it a political regime. It is a way of doing politics that can take various ideological forms according to both time and place, and is compatible with a variety of institutional frameworks.[40]

Let me highlight, then, three aspects of Mouffe's definition of *populism*.

First, *discourse*: Populism is a way of speaking and of doing politics that constructs a subject for purposes of political action. Mouffe emphasizes repeatedly that her approach is, in her words, "anti-essentialist." She does not suggest that there is a "real" people out there, but that populism rhetorically constructs a political subjectivity that can be called "the people." Mouffe intends to appropriate the term as a rhetorical and political device to create a movement in these fractured times. The neoliberal hegemony, she argues, is falling apart. The discursive strategy of "the market" is breaking down. And there is an opening for a new way of speaking and doing politics. We are at a time, she argues, in which "the possibility arises of constructing a new subject of collective action—the people—capable of reconfiguring a social order experienced as unjust."[41]

Second, *power*: Populism separates "the underdog" from "those in power." Notice that the distinction is between those in society who lose and those who have power. Power is key, and it is to be understood as something that one has, as a possession—it is to be understood in a pre-Foucaultian way. The structure is similar to the Marxian model of class struggle, but Mouffe emphasizes that the underdogs include a far more copious range of dominations, along gender, sexual, racial, and ethnic lines. The "underdog" label is intended precisely to reject class essentialism and broaden the category to include women, trans* and other sexual minorities, and racial and ethnic minorities as well. It is a copious concept that is supposed to reflect and grasp "the multiplicity of struggles against different forms of domination."[42]

Third, *strategy*: Populism is intended to serve as a political intervention. It is not intended to get at the essence of what *populism* might mean. "I have no intention to enter the sterile academic debate about the 'true nature' of populism," Mouffe emphasizes. Her use of the term is entirely strategic and punctual. It is intended to function as a partisan political device in these specific times: "in the present conjuncture, it provides the adequate strategy to recover and deepen the ideals of equality and popular sovereignty that are constitutive of a democratic politics."[43]

Along these dimensions, Mouffe strategically uses the term *populism* as a political-rhetorical device to construct a new political subjectivity for those who are out of power at a time when the neoliberal hegemony has fractured.

Mouffe's Idea of the Left

Chantal Mouffe tries to discard the left/right distinction as the basis of her discursive strategy, and to replace it with the distinction of the underdog versus the powerful. In this sense, the term *left* is no longer a cardinal term for Mouffe. It is, instead, a descriptive term, a qualifier, an adjective—one intended to capture long-standing democratic values of equality and popular sovereignty, as opposed to long-standing liberal values of property and liberty, understood as possessive individualism. This represents an intellectual turn for Mouffe, who writes:

> When I wrote *On the Political* [in 2005,] I suggested reviving the left/right frontier, but I am now convinced that, as traditionally configured, such a frontier is no longer adequate to articulate a collective will that contains the variety of democratic demands that exist today.... Such claims—the defence of the environment, struggles against sexism, racism and other forms of domination—have become increasingly central.... [As a result,] the "populist" dimension is not sufficient to specify the type of politics required by the current conjuncture. It needs to be qualified as a "left" populism to indicate the values that this populism pursues.[44]

Here too, I will highlight three aspects of Mouffe's use of the term *left*.

First, *democratic*: The adjective *left* stands in for a centuries-long struggle between liberals and democrats, in the political theory sense of the terms. The contrast that Mouffe draws here is between, on the one hand, the tradition of political liberalism that upholds the ideals of the rule of law, checks and balances, and individual freedom, which trace back to Locke and C. B. Macpherson's concept of possessive individualism; and on the other hand, the tradition of democratic governance that traces to the Greek *demos* and produces a variety of democratic models (representative, constitutional, pluralist, etc.). For Mouffe, the qualifier *left* maps onto the latter democratic tradition. It is important to note that, for her, the competing tradition of liberalism is what led to neoliberal hegemony, the rule of the market, and the nefarious policies of privatization, austerity, and deregulation.[45] It is also worth noting that the distinction serves to disambiguate the unitary idea of "liberal democracy," which Mouffe views as confused, paradoxical, irreconcilable, and the source of many of our problems today.

Second, *equality and social justice*: At the core of that left/democratic tradition are the values of equality and popular sovereignty—which at times Mouffe refers to as "equality and social justice." The "central ideas" and the very "grammar" of the democratic tradition are those two values. By embracing the democratic tradition, she intends to promote these central values of equality and social justice: "The democratic logic of constructing a people and defending egalitarian practices is necessary to define a *demos* and to subvert the tendency of liberal discourse to abstract universalism."[46]

Third, *the people*: It is by mapping the term *left* onto this democratic tradition that Mouffe intends to construct "we the people," as opposed to the experts, the oligarchs, and those in power. When we view politics from this egalitarian democratic perspective, we see the fundamental opposition as being between, on the one hand, those who are oppressed and claiming political relief—who are making "unsatisfied demands"—from, on the other hand, those who have power and exercise it as oligarchs. The idea of "left populism" thus becomes "a discursive strategy of construction of the political frontier between 'the people' and 'the oligarchy,' [that] constitutes, in the present conjuncture, the type of politics needed to recover and deepen democracy."[47]

Along these dimensions, then, Mouffe strategically uses the term *left* to contrast her notion of "the people" from that of right-wing populists. For the latter, the "we" of "we the people" consists of citizens and patriots of the nation and excludes immigrants and racial, ethnic, and sexual minorities. By contrast, the "we" of left populism aims to embrace all persons who are making unsatisfied claims against those in power—all those who are challenging the oligarchy, all those who are voicing democratic demands. As Mouffe explains, "this requires the establishment of a chain of equivalence among the demands of the workers, the immigrants and the precarious middle class, as well as other democratic demands, such as those of the

LGBTQ community. The objective of such a chain is the creation of a new hegemony that will permit the radicalization of democracy."[48]

Mouffe's Political Strategy

Chantal Mouffe's political goal is to assemble a larger and broader constituency that includes, through an open and less judgmental rhetoric, many right-wing populists. The strategy is to unite and confederate all of those who are expressing democratic claims against those in power, not by adopting the anti-immigrant perspectives of the far right, but by offering a more compelling discourse and by "orientat[ing] those demands towards more egalitarian objectives." Mouffe emphasizes: "I believe that, if a different language is made available, many people might experience their situation in a different way and join the progressive struggle."[49] Through the use of examples, Mouffe signals precisely what type of politics she proposes. She draws on the case of Jean-Luc Mélenchon's party La France insoumise and acknowledges her intellectual debt to Mélenchon and François Ruffin; she refers to the Syriza party in Greece and the Podemos party in Spain; she also describes Bernie Sanders as clearly exhibiting a left populist strategy.[50] These are the kinds of popular political movements, parties, and actors that Mouffe has in mind.

Mouffe—and Laclau, working with her earlier—view populism as the full potential of democracy, almost as the telos of democracy. It is the populist movement that fully realizes the central values of democracy—namely, equality, social justice, and popular sovereignty. Populism is for Mouffe (and Laclau), in the words of Nadia Urbinati, "democracy at its best, because the will of the people is constructed through the people's direct mobilization and consent. It is also politics at its best, because it employs only discursive devices and the art of persuasion."[51]

The question, though, is: how does Mouffe's embrace of the term *left populism* respond to the broadsides against populism that characterize most of the literature and research on populism—which is predominantly negative and uses the term *populist* in a predominantly pejorative sense? To be sure, Mouffe is not interested in either sterile academic debates or purely definitional questions. But the question that arises is whether those other critiques of populism undermine her argument. There are at least four such critiques:

First, *the antipluralism of populism*: Populism, Jan-Werner Müller argues, should not be understood primarily as a form of antielitism. It may be (and often is) anti-establishment, but it is not the only political form that opposes the establishment.

That is not really what makes populism unique. Instead, he writes, "the hallmark of populists is that they claim that they, and they alone, represent the people (or what populists very often refer to as 'the real people')." In this respect, Müller emphasizes, populists are antipluralist: they are intolerant of other views, exclude others as illegitimate, and shut out wide swaths of the population through exclusionary identity politics. The principal strategy of populists is to claim a unique, moralized right to the people, to delegitimize anyone else's claim, and to always paint themselves as the silent majority facing off against corrupt and crooked opponents who are only promoting their self-interests (whether in or out of office). Whether they are winning or losing, they will always argue that "corrupt elites were manipulating the process behind the scenes."[52]

Second, *the democratic distortions of populism*: Nadia Urbinati worries that populism has, embedded within it, tendencies that push it toward authoritarianism or totalitarianism. The reason, she suggests, is that populism is most often tied to strong leadership or, as Laclau noted, most often takes "the name of the leader."[53] Populism rarely involves a claim to direct self-government. And when it then comes to power, it is most often under the leadership of a strong figure who enforces the division of the people against the institutions of governance. In this sense, Urbinati views populism as parasitic to democracy—as a mode of politics that exploits democratic failures by means of an us-and-them logic, but that, as such, must necessarily transform when it takes power. That transformation is inevitably problematic because it pushes the notion of the people (now the majority) into an authoritarian direction. So it risks disfiguring the institutions of democracy. Urbinati suggests that "populism in power is an extreme majoritarianism,"[54] and she adds:

> populism is structurally marked by a radical partiality in interpreting the people and the majority; this implies that, if it comes to power, it can have a disfiguring impact on the institutions, the rule of law, and the division of powers, which comprise constitutional democracy.[55]

The danger of populism, for Urbinati, is what happens when it prevails and transforms constitutional forms of democracy.

Third, *the fascistic tendencies of populism*: Jean Cohen focuses on the pitfalls of left populism: namely, that, whether as a discourse, strategy, logic, or language, it always evokes the need to create unified people embodied by a leader, and in the process, constructs a frontier between us and them, separating the true people from the rest of the population. Left populism, Cohen argues, is really defined by Mouffe only in terms of its opposition to neoliberalism and technocratic discourse; but that ignores all the other registers (xenophobic, among others) on which it operates. While not directly addressing populism, Jason Stanley's *How Fascism Works: The Politics of Us and Them* intersects this critique, and also raises alarms about populist methods.[56] Stanley writes, "The most telling symptom of fascist politics is division. It aims to separate a population into an 'us' and a 'them.'"[57] He notes that many political movements play on such distinctions, including leftist and even communist movements, so the *bases* for the distinctions are more telling. He also argues that fascist strategies appeal to national, racial, ethnic, and religious distinctions. The question for us is how far that might extend—and whether it extends to left populism.

Fourth, *the threat of nepotistic democracy*: As Urbinati notes, another group of scholars, including Kurt Weyland, Guillermo O'Donnell, and Alan Knight, associate populism in power with a particular form of unmediated and uninstitutionalized governing that depends on nepotistic favors to maintain control over a majority. Weyland describes how a "personalistic leader seeks or exercises government power based on direct, unmediated, uninstitutionalized support from large numbers of mostly unorganized followers." O'Donnell speaks of populism in power as "a form of a 'delegative democracy,' a gigantic machinery of nepotistic favors with an orchestrating propaganda that imputes the difficulty in delivering on promises to the conspiracy, international and domestic, of an all-powerful global machinery."[58] The danger here is that, once in power, populism will have no other way of maintaining itself than to engage in mass nepotistic clientelism.

These four challenges raise a number of difficult questions. The first concerns whether the potential defects of populism in power necessarily attach to populism as a social movement. Most of these challenges are aimed at populist regimes, not populism used *as a political strategy to gain power*. Assuming, for instance, that Bernie Sanders has an element of populism in his makeup, does that necessarily mean that, in power, he would gravitate toward authoritarianism? Whether he has an element of populism is disputed,[59] though there are passages from the very first pages of his *Guide to Political Revolution* that support such an interpretation:

> *The American people* understand that health care is a right for all and not a privilege, and that in a competitive global economy we must make public colleges and universities tuition-free.

> *The American people* know that in the midst of massive wealth and income inequality the very rich have got to start paying their fair share of taxes . . .
>
> That's not Bernie Sanders talking. That's what poll after poll *shows the American people want.*[60]

Here, Sanders boasts of having taken on the entire "establishment" and makes a deep emotional appeal to his audience to join a revolutionary movement. He exhorts his readers, "This is your country. Help us take it back. Join the Political Revolution."[61]

So, there are populist elements to his rhetoric. But there is no reason to believe that, hypothetically, Sanders would succumb to the defects of populism in power. The reason for this is that his style of populism seems different than the populism of regimes in power. Chantal Mouffe's does as well. Mouffe is trying to imbue left populism with an ethos of equality, social justice, and popular sovereignty. Those values inherently resist—or are intended to resist—the dangers that the critics identify. She emphasizes the democratic values that oppose authoritarianism, dictatorship, and delegation. The core of Mouffe's left populism is a form of radical democracy that is neither representational nor delegative. Moreover, the centrality of social justice is intended to embrace *all* marginalized populations—and not exclude minorities. It is an open populism, including even those who lurch right.

This raises the question of whether it is possible to craft a left populist praxis that would avoid the pitfalls of prior populist experiences. More concretely, is it possible that someone like Bernie Sanders *in power* could avoid the problems of really existing populism, such as its authoritarian tendency, mass clientelism, and democratic distortions? What about someone like Jean-Luc Mélenchon? Did this happen in Greece with Syriza? This entire debate, though, more than anything, reveals the ambiguity of the term *populism*—the nominalist difficulty of applying an abstract label to phenomena that are inextricably really existing singularities in history. To go straight to the heart of the matter: the minute we go beyond a basic, minimalist definition of *populism* as antielitism and ascribe to the term certain characteristics—such as a strong leader, an exclusionary frontier, or the Schmittian friend/enemy distinction—we fall into the nominalist trap, in other words, the trap that nominalism tries to avoid by favoring the study of historical singularities over the naming of phenomena.

What this means is that any discussion of "populism" should be preceded by an extremely careful analysis of the ways in which the word is being deployed, so that the ensuing argument is not already embedded within the definition. In effect, any use of the term should be prefaced by the equivalent of one of those Wikipedia "disambiguation" pages to distinguish among the following meanings of *populism*:

- *Populism (minimalist description)*: A political technique that appeals to "we the people," as opposed to the elite, and thus operates as a form of antielitism.
- *Populism (social movement)*: A social movement that contests the ruling political power as elitist and not representative of the people; this is intended to be opposed to "*populism (in power)*," when a movement takes power and governs.
- *Populism (authoritarianism)*: A pejorative use of the term, which rests on the argument that *populism (minimalist description)* necessarily tends toward authoritarianism (defined as nonpluralist and illiberal) if it becomes *populism (in power)*.
- *Populism (false ideology)*: Another pejorative use of the term, which captures the purely strategic, instrumental, and hypocritical deployment of "we the people" in order to advance the political empowerment of a leader or party that in fact constitutes an elite or minority of the population.
- *Populism (Latin America post-1945)*: This term refers to classical, neoliberal, and neoclassical populist regimes in Latin America, including those of Peron, Menem, and Kirchner in Argentina; Chávez and Maduro in Venezuela; and others in Brazil, Peru, and Bolivia.[62]

In the end, I am not sure that it is useful to retain the term *populism* as a label. It may cause more confusion than clarity. But if we do use the term, then I am convinced that we need to use more careful language. I would argue that it is possible to have a *populism (social movement)*, like that of Bernie Sanders, that does not necessarily tend toward *populism (authoritarianism)*; or, for that matter, a *populism (social movement)* like Occupy Wall Street, which does not favor a strong leader. The notion of the 99 percent during the Occupy movement was precisely a rhetorical appeal to the people, as opposed to the elite 1 percent. It was *populist (minimalist description)*. And there was a lot to the Yellow Vest movement in France in 2019 that had a *populist (social movement)* air to it, including the extensive use of the French flag; in addition, that movement was entirely leaderless, but it made the same claim: to represent the people in opposition against the oligarchs.

As a nominalist myself, I am uneasy retaining the label *populism*, especially because it engenders more confusion and argument-by-definition than clarity. But if we do retain the term, then it is crucial that we disambiguate as much as possible. Moreover, if we recuperate a narrow definition of *populism (minimalist description)*, I believe the questions become more empirical than abstract or theoretical. The question of authoritarianism or antipluralism is less a question of what is inherently true about populism than an empirical and historical claim, and the questions asked would be, empirically, for instance: What are the additional attributes (or variables) that tend to push *populism (minimalist description)* toward *populism (authoritarianism)*? Can the appeal to "the people" be successful on the left? How much coalition building is possible from the right populists (as Müller asks)? In too much of the discussion, there is a slippage into *populism (authoritarian)* without sufficient argumentation as to its necessity. Is it inherent in the logic of *populism (minimalist description)* that it becomes authoritarian—in a kind of synthetic, a priori manner? Or, rather, is it that history demonstrates that it is more probable than not? And have we been sufficiently careful to select our pool of historical examples? What about the American nineteenth-century agrarian movements and, much later, Occupy?

The trouble with the term *populism*, naturally, plagues many other political terms as well, especially those like *neoliberalism*, which are predominantly used in a derogatory manner. In fact, we might say that if a political label is being used in a pejorative way, it is inherently unstable. But other terms as well, such as *fascism, liberalism, totalitarianism, democracy*, and *pluralism*, call for similar care and disambiguation. This does not mean that we should get rid of all political concepts, and in this, I agree with Jean Cohen; however, it does raise the central question of what exactly to do with them—whether to construct ideal types and definitions, perform genealogies of their usage, or map them in space and time. Regarding the latter, it may well be that, rather than define these labels, it would make more sense to locate really existing social movements and political regimes in a space demarcated by certain key dimensions, such as the concentration or dispersal of political force, whether in the hands of one person, or one party, or one branch, or the entire social body (by referendum); the ease or difficulty of contestation of political power, of resistance to political or civil domination; or the privileging of a social or political hierarchy (privileging an elite) versus more horizontal and equal social relations (treating all citizens equally). We tend to use political labels by clumping together a few historical regimes as illustrations of the term, such as combining

Chávez and Morales as "left populists," which then tells us something about their level of authoritarianism; or Mussolini and Hitler as "fascists" and Hitler and Stalin as "totalitarians," which again tells us something about the inherent qualities of fascism or totalitarianism. But that really inverts the argumentative logic.

I started this discussion by saying that the debate over populism is an object lesson for nominalism—maybe I should have written "abject." It really does highlight the quagmire of applying abstract labels to really existing singularities. In the final analysis, I would clear the ground and contest the assumption—advanced by many critics today—that there is anything inherently and necessarily authoritarian about *populism (minimalist description)*. Then I would return with fresh eyes to Chantal Mouffe's call for a left populism and ask the direct question: Can it work? In the United States, for instance, would it have helped counter the power grab by Donald Trump and the New Right in 2016? Mouffe argues for a soft form of strategic discourse of populism on the left to assemble a broad coalition of all those who have been left behind—not just the working class, but also women, persons of color, sexual minorities, immigrants, marginalized populations—to unite them against the oligarchs, against those in power. The important question, in the end, is whether it can work.

#BlackLivesMatter and New Social Movements

One new type of social movement that has met with success is the Movement for Black Lives. It is "new" in the way in which it deploys social media communication and the hashtag as galvanizing forces. It is not so much populist as it is popular, unless one retains the very minimal definition of *populism (minimalist description)* as representing antielitism—or better yet, here, antiestablishment. The use of the hashtag and social media amplification has already been picked up by other social movements, such as #MeToo. A number of critical theorists, including Barbara Ransby, Keeanga-Yamahtta Taylor, and Deva Woodly, have offered compelling analyses of these new social movements and highlighted their potential for critical praxis.

The #BlackLivesMatter movement burst onto the scene in the aftermath of George Zimmerman's acquittal at his trial in Florida for the murder of Trayvon Martin.[63] An activist, Alicia Garza, wrote a post on Facebook in July 2013 that went viral. Her partner, Patrisse Cullors, took a snippet from that post, made it one word, added the hashtag, and thereby created one of the most potent political memes and social movements of the twenty-first century. Another acquaintance, Opal Tometi in Brooklyn, developed a social media platform to deploy the term and connect the emerging networks of activists. By August 2015, Twitter's ten-year anniversary, #BlackLivesMatter was the third-most-used social-issue hashtag for the platform's entire history.[64] Other hashtag social movements, like #MeToo, would emerge in its wake.

The context of #BlackLivesMatter was tragic: a rash of videos of police shootings or killings of unarmed Black men and women exposed a tragic phenomenon that otherwise would have gone unnoticed or been deemed justified, and both *The Guardian* and the *Washington Post* began keeping track of the numbers, documenting around 1,000 fatal police shootings per year. The videos and stories went viral, and the rapid succession of deaths shocked the entire country. Eric Garner died of asphyxiation from a chokehold and being smothered under the weight of several New York Police Department officers on the streets of Staten Island, New York, on July 17, 2014. A month later, on August 9, 2014, an unarmed eighteen-year-old young man, Michael Brown, was shot dead in Ferguson, Missouri, by police officer Darren Wilson. Two months later, on October 20, 2014, on the Southwest Side of Chicago, police officer Jason Van Dyke unloaded sixteen rounds of his 9-mm semiautomatic service weapon into seventeen-year-old Laquan McDonald. The wave of police killings continued on and off camera, around the country, with the police shooting deaths of twenty-eight-year-old Akai Gurley in a Brooklyn stairwell on November 20, 2014; twelve-year-old Tamir Rice in a Cleveland park on November 22, 2014; fifty-year-old Walter Scott, shot in the back five times on April 4, 2015, in North Charleston, South Carolina; thirty-two-year-old Philando Castile, pulled over in a suburb of Saint Paul, Minnesota, and shot seven times on July 6, 2016, while peacefully trying to explain his situation; thirty-year-old Charleena Lyles, shot in front of her four children in Seattle after calling the police about an attempted burglary on June 18, 2017; and the deaths in police custody of thirty-seven-year-old Tanisha Anderson in Cleveland, slammed on the pavement while being arrested, and of twenty-eight-year-old Sandra Bland, found hanging in her jail cell in Waller County, Texas, on July 13, 2015—all African American men and women.

It was during the protests in Ferguson and throughout the country in response to these events that the #BlackLivesMatter movement was born.[65] The movement consisted of a range of activism, extending from individual acts of resistance to local collectives to national organizations, all self-identifying as part of a broader movement for Black lives, antiracism, and racial justice. The key element was *self*-identification. There was no authoritative policing, no institutional judge of who could legitimately claim to be part of the movement; and perhaps as a result, the edges and boundaries of the movement were fluid.

There was, on the one hand, the hashtag #BlackLivesMatter itself, which remains a unique phenomenon today and does an enormous amount of work on its own. It might be worth stopping here for a moment—on the hashtag *itself*—to explore how this phenomenon represents a new form of uprising and how it challenges the very notion of a movement. The hashtag is a radical new form of politics, in large part because almost anyone can deploy it. The hashtag resists appropriation. It can spread on its own, and it has a certain malleability, so that it can be redeployed in different and new contexts of antiracist protest. As a result, it can be seen pervasively and has resilience. It does not allow the identification of leaders. And it resists the organizational form because the hashtag, almost in its very identity, resists appropriation. In this, the hashtag is brilliantly responsive to the problems that have plagued social movements to date.

There were, on the other hand, a number of local and national organizations that coalesced into a larger national Movement for Black Lives, with several specific policy platforms—local organizations in Chicago, for instance, such as Assata's Daughters, We Charge Genocide, Black Lives Matter–Chicago, and the People's Response Team; national organizations like the Black Lives Matter Global Network (that traces back to Garza, Cullors, and Tometi) and the Black Youth Project 100 (BYP100), an outgrowth of Cathy Cohen's Black Youth Project at the University of Chicago; as well as over thirty chapters of #BlackLivesMatter across the country. These groups varied somewhat in their organization and leadership. But one thing that united them all is a commitment to avoiding the model of the single heroic male leader that is so common to prior movements and revolutions—from Robespierre and Danton; to Marx and Lenin; to Mao, Gandhi, and Che Guevara; to Martin Luther King Jr. and Malcolm X. There is hardly a modern revolution or revolutionary project that is not associated with a great man. (Not surprisingly, all the major counterrevolutions today are headed by charismatic male figures as well.) The thread that ties together all the various facets of the Movement for Black Lives is the direct challenge to that history. And in this, as Barbara Ransby underscores, we can see the strong influence that Black feminist and LGBTQ theorists and practitioners have had on many of the leaders of the movement.[66] As the website of the Black Lives Matter Global Network recounts, in its herstory:

> Black liberation movements in this country have created room, space, and leadership mostly for Black heterosexual, cisgender men—leaving women, queer and transgender people, and others either out of the movement or in the background to move the work forward with little or no recognition. As a network, we have always recognized the need to center the leadership of women and queer and trans people. To maximize our movement muscle, and to be intentional about not replicating harmful practices that excluded so many in past movements for liberation, we made a commitment to placing those at the margins closer to the center.[67]

These movements are also developing, on these bases, new forms of "group-centered leadership practices," in Ransby's words. These authorize decision-making by those on the ground, who have a better understanding of the community's problems and how to implement solutions than do top-down institutions and associations.

The Movement for Black Lives is now "a movement of movements." This term captures perfectly the diversity of groups, projects, alliances, and organizations that make up the larger movement for Black lives and that is represented by the hashtag #BlackLivesMatter. The expression has been used, recently, in other contexts, including with regard to the movements challenging neoliberal globalization,[68] or to the New Left more generally.[69] And the term has been deployed more recently in various debates, pro and con—suggesting that it may indeed have negative potential if it is associated with a desire to control or rein in other movements, or to privilege one organization or set of actors over another.[70] But if we think of the *singular* in "a movement of movements" not as an identifiable organization, or set of actors, or even a single actor, but rather as the larger whole which is greater than the parts of all the various organizations for Black lives—from BYP100 to the Black Lives Matter Global Network, to the chapters of #BlackLivesMatter, to all the groups that militate side by side, like Assata's Daughters, We Charge Genocide, and the People's Response Team—then the term seems to capture perfectly what is going on today. If we speak of the larger phenomenon that is associated with the hashtag and made up of all the organizations and groups, then we do seem to have a "movement of movements"—one that indeed seems to resist appropriation or cooptation. That is perhaps, ultimately, the theoretical genius of the hashtag and the larger movement: it cannot be coopted because it cannot be pinned down or associated with any particular group or person. It makes the movement ultimately larger than any of its constituent parts, broader than any of the specific organizations, and longer-lasting than the present constellation.

Many activists in these social movements seek to leverage the momentum of gatherings and nonviolent protest to push assemblies into a more direct political process. As Jelani Cobb documents in *The New Yorker*, the Movement for Black Lives is pushing in new directions and getting more involved in public policy platforms, and some activists are even jumping into the electoral fray, such as DeRay McKesson, who ran an unsuccessful mayoral campaign in Baltimore in 2016.

One of the movement's strengths, theoretically, is that it rejects a politics of respectability. BYP100, for instance, specifically positions itself *against* a politics of respectability, claiming to speak on behalf of "ALL Black people," including the most marginalized LGBTQ folks. Their agenda, they say, is "not meant to advance politics of respectability—we want ALL Black people to be able to live in their dignity." With a strong national coordinator, Charlene A. Carruthers, they do not present as leaderless or starry-eyed. They set out their positions and their demands clearly, backed up with research and community sentiment, in a twenty-four-page "Agenda to Keep Us Safe," which includes lengthy "References and Additional Resources."[71] BYP100 flips the famous Occupy slogan about the bottom 99 percent and the top 1 percent: in their self-presentation, they associate themselves more closely with the bottom 1 percent, which can be understood only in relation to Occupy. As they write on their webpage: "We envision a more economically just society that values the lives and well-being of ALL Black people, including women, queer, and transgender folks, the incarcerated and formerly incarcerated as well as those who languish in the bottom 1 percent of the economic hierarchy."[72]

It has many other strengths as well. One is the fact that it contains organizations that are so well organized, using these new and innovative table structures (i.e., tables for communications, policy, law, healing justice, electoral justice, etc.) to reach policy proposals, as Shanelle Matthews demonstrates.[73] Another is the fact that there is a deep engagement with the state and with policy, but no ambition to be the state. There is also the resonance with the Foucaultian idea of critique as the desire "not to be governed thusly." Finally, consider the way in which the organizations repoliticize the public sphere, as Deva Woodly emphasizes—and the potential for democratic experimentation that these movements express.

As Woodly suggests, the Movement for Black Lives revives and repoliticizes the public sphere by countering a growing "politics of despair." The various manifestations of #BlackLivesMatter protest, then, should not be understood as prepolitical. They themselves are inherently political, and they may be what allows a democracy to correct itself—because as Woodly notes, the institutions certainly do not seem capable of correcting themselves.[74]

A rich debate has emerged between the strands of Black joy and dandyism in the movement (in effect, over the desire not be reduced to victimhood and death) versus the elements of Afro-pessimism and the dark truth that the movement itself was born from fatal encounters of young Black women and men with the police. Kendall Thomas ultimately argues for recognition of the foundational element of mourning and Black death in the movement to fight against injustice itself and as a motivating force. "I am pessimistic. I am pessimistic," Thomas declares in a powerful intervention. "We fought for and won this new legal order . . . and yet have prisons which are filled with black and brown citizens in complete compliance with the law. . . . I think there is something to the claim by the Afro-pessimist Frank Wilderson. The notion of black citizenship in the US is an oxymoron. . . . At the same time, the #BlackLivesMatter movement has given us joy and it gives me hope. But the challenge is to hold on to both ends of the chain at once: the pessimism, which provokes the passion to rage against injustice, and at the same time that joy that gives us a vision of the future that allows us to imagine that another world is possible."[75]

An Illustration from Chicago

To imagine how this other world is possible, it is useful to look, for instance, at how Black youth movements crystalized in response to the shooting death of Laquan McDonald in Chicago, and to the fact that the state's attorney, Anita Alvarez, waited almost 400 days to indict police officer Jason Van Dyke in the fatal shooting. With T-shirts bearing "Adios Anita" and a flurry of social media posts carrying the hashtag #ByeAnita, a group of young activists mobilized and rallied against Alvarez.[76]

"Two down, one to go!" The chant started quietly and then caught on, resonating across the victory ballroom at the downtown Holiday Inn in Chicago. The Democratic state's attorney candidate, Kim Foxx, had just unseated Alvarez in the March 2016 primaries. The "first down," of course, was former Chicago police superintendent Garry McCarthy, who was quickly sacrificed by Mayor Rahm Emanuel as soon as the cover-up of the McDonald shooting began to be exposed and the political heat was turned on. McCarthy was fired on December 1, 2015. Alvarez was the next to fall, with Foxx taking 58 percent of the primary vote, against Alvarez's 29 percent. Fox was elected state's attorney in the fall of 2016.

The young activists were probably responsible for taking down the prosecutor. Alvarez had been leading her challengers in the polls well into February 2016;[77] but the concerted efforts of these activists, on the streets and on the Internet, turned the tide. According to newspaper reports, the young activists who buoyed Foxx's campaign were predominantly young African American organizers in movements such as the Black Youth Project 100, Assata's Daughters, and We Charge Genocide.[78] These are a new set of popular, bottom-up, militant organizations, often interlinked, with an interesting new political character and a strong digital presence on social media. The presentation of the People's Response Team on their Facebook page is characteristic:

> The People's Response Team is a team of concerned community members committed to supporting efforts to end police violence in Chicago. We do not collaborate with law enforcement. We aim to respond to, document, and investigate fatal police shootings in Chicago and connect family members and loved ones with emotional, social, and legal support. Many of us are members of We Charge Genocide, Chicago Alliance Against Racist and Political Repression (CAARPR), Black Lives Matter—Chicago, and other grassroots organizations challenging police violence.[79]

What is interesting is that these movements did not explicitly endorse the other candidate, Foxx. They mobilized against Alvarez and succeeded in getting her out of office, but they did not actively campaign for Foxx. As Kampf-Lassin reports, "While none of these groups explicitly endorsed Foxx, they did work diligently to make sure Chicagoans did not vote for Alvarez. Brenna Champion, an organizer with BYP100, said that the group canvassed, knocked on doors throughout the city with their anti-Alvarez message, and reached out to 2,500 voters who planned to vote for Foxx, focusing on African-American voters, largely on college campuses."[80]

In fact, not only did they *not* endorse Foxx, some of the groups made it clear that they also had their eye on her. @AssataDaughters stated this explicitly in the "collective victory" statement they posted online:

> Chicago Black youth kicked Anita Alvarez out of office. Just a month ago, Anita Alvarez was winning in the polls. Communities who refuse to be killed and jailed and abused without any chance at justice refused to allow that to happen. We did this for Rekia. We did this for Laquan. We won't stop until we're free, and Kim Foxx should know that well.[81]

"Kim Foxx should know that well": an ominous statement to the candidate who had unseated Alvarez—reflecting the particular strategy of these young activists.

And, of course, both in Chicago and at the national level, they confronted and challenged—and intensified—relations to older, more well-known civil rights figures, such as Jesse Jackson, Sr., and the Democratic establishment—not just Hillary Clinton, then running for president, but Bill Clinton as well. Some of this can be chalked to generational shifts, but it also reflects more radical politics. The BYP100, for instance, advocates in the long term for the "outright abolition of the police department and the prison system," as well as "reparations, universal childcare, a higher minimum wage, the decriminalization of marijuana," and other reforms.[82] There is a different political sensibility at play, especially with regard to the political establishment. In this way, these movements revive public discourse and engagement. Deva Woodly emphasizes how the Movement for Black Lives repoliticized the public sphere and demonstrates the potential of democratic experimentation, especially by countering the growing "politics of despair."[83] The various manifestations of #BlackLivesMatter protest, she explains, are not just prepolitical or prefigurative—they are inherently political practices that allow democracy to correct itself. These movements offer new models for critical praxis.

Occupations and Assemblies

Alongside these new social movements, novel forms of occupation and general assembly proliferated in the early twenty-first century: Tahrir Square, January 2011; Zuccotti Park, November 2011; Taksim Gezi Park, May 2013; Place de la République,

March 2016; Champs-Élysées, December 2018; Hong Kong, June 2019. The images have now become iconic. The mode of uprising as well: assembly, occupation, and leaderlessness. These events galvanized a new style of resistance—a pastiche of earlier autonomist movements and assembly practices. Some critical thinkers criticized them as disorganized, episodic, and doomed to failure. Critics argued that they would inevitably either morph into ordinary party politics (like Podemos in Spain) or play into the hands of their opponents (like the Muslim Brotherhood in Egypt or the far-right Rassemblement national in France). Disavowing more radical insurrectionary approaches, some argue, may feel safer, but it will ultimately fail and undermine the critical ambition. Other critical theorists, however, see potential in these novel forms of assembly.

In *Notes Toward a Performative Theory of Assembly*, Judith Butler explores the power of assembly. Butler draws on theories of performativity—which she developed in the context of gender—to suggest that assemblies have enacted a particular form of "we the people," in which the precarious have gathered to contest their own precarity and proclaim loudly to those in power that "we are part of the people and we are still here."[84] Butler explicitly embraces these new political forms. A frequent speaker at the global Occupy movement, she sees promise in such nonviolent strategies.

Butler elaborates on the productive ways in which already existing assemblies shape our politics. Butler praises the productive performative dimensions that emanate from the materiality and physicality of people assembling either in public or virtually, on digital platforms. Assembly is the condition of possibility for forming a people that does not act merely as a group of individuals, but as a collective. "The thesis of this book," Butler writes, "is that none of us acts without the conditions to act, even though sometimes we must act to install and preserve those very conditions."[85] Assembly is, in this sense, the expression of precarity and opposition to the resulting social exclusion. It is an act of defiance in the face of domination.

Rather than subsume the bodily assembly within discourse, Butler tries to peel off the assembly of bodies from what is said, in order to give independent meaning to the bodies. The assembly, she argues, is a precondition for speech. It prefigures what is said: "*the assembly is already speaking before it utters any words*," Butler writes.[86] "The specific thesis of this book," she states, "is that acting in concert can be an embodied form of calling into question the inchoate and powerful dimensions of reigning notions of the political."[87]

Butler advocates for an ethical form of assembly that is nonviolent—nonviolence as an ethical and tactical matter, not as an absolute or imperative or in a transhistorical way, but rather as a tactical matter in these times. Silently, she objects to the Foucault of the early 1970s, who mapped social relations on civil war. As if directly addressing *The Punitive Society*, Butler writes to distinguish herself from "those who can only read the tactic as hatred and the continuation of war by other means."[88] For Butler, materiality precedes expression. She is challenging, as Hana Worthen underscores, the "privileging of a political subject constituted by speech."[89] Assembly, Butler argues, is neither discursive in itself (it is not a form of speech) nor prediscursive. It cannot be reduced to the utterances (written or oral) that it produces. It is not just a vehicle or form of speech. Forms of assembly do work and perform separately from what people say: "forms of assembly already signify prior to, and apart from, any particular demands they make."[90] Butler is drawing a distinction, in effect, between "forms of linguistic performativity" and "forms of bodily performativity": "They overlap," she writes; "they are not altogether distinct; they are not, however, identical with one another."[91] What she argues, as Lee Pierce notes, is that "the freedom of assembly is not simply different from the freedom of speech but 'may well be a precondition of politics itself.' "[92] And in this sense, again as Pierce writes, "the 'the' of *the* assembly is misleading. The assembly is not so much a noun—a stable identity that 'is'—but a verb, a disruptive 'doing' that produces, however fleetingly, 'a new form of sociality on the spot.' The assembly is a form, albeit a form that takes many forms, of 'exposure' through which vulnerability is mobilized, returning to the political scene what is too often excluded in the name *of* politics."[93]

Assembly, then, is bodies congregating. It is the materiality and physicality of people coming together and laying claim to a public space. It includes mass demonstration and social movements. These forms of assembly are performative in the sense that, according to Butler, they "reconfigure the materiality of public space and produce, or reproduce, the public character of that material environment." They dispute "the very public character of the space."[94] In a passage that resonates with the typical forms of protest in a city like Paris—where the space and path of protest are so rigidly drawn by the prefecture, where any deviations from the official path result in arrests, and where protesters constantly try to take the demonstrations out of the proscribed route—Butler writes:

> As much as we must insist on there being material conditions for public assembly and public speech, we have also to ask how it is that assembly and speech

> reconfigure the materiality of public space and produce, or reproduce, the public character of that material environment. And when crowds move outside the square, to the side street or the back alley, to the neighborhoods where streets are not yet paved, then something more happens.[95]

When protesters move into the side streets and try to create nonsanctioned spaces of protest, "something more happens"—indeed, they contest the authority to limit and contain protest (and they usually get arrested). Butler argues that these forms of defining space challenge boundaries between public and private—showing or otherwise revealing that politics is already in the private, in the home, in the personal.

Now, to suggest that assembly can affect our conceptions of politics is perhaps somewhat tautological because that is often the very purpose of assembly. So it may be important to distinguish further between performance and productivity. To say that assembly can unveil the politics in the home, on the street, or in the neighborhood seems certainly right. In fact, it is because many have come to understand that the personal is political, and that the public/private distinction is problematic, that they are in the street protesting. But beyond that, we could say that assembly does other things. Assemblies can be prefigurative. They can create democratic forms that do not exist elsewhere. They can instantiate relations between citizens that are uncommon, equal, even glorious. They can do all these things. These are productive effects for sure. And one could use the discourse of performativity to say that assemblies "perform" these things. But the difference between productive and performative is that the political is more hidden in performativity—and it is not hidden in assembly. Before, when we performed gender unknowingly, we did not think that it was a political act. But when we perform assembly, we do that precisely *because* it is a political act. There may be hidden dimensions that we ignore because of our biases; however, we are in the street or on the square to perform politics. The performative theory of assembly, in sum, does not render something political that wasn't before. It just becomes another vocabulary to talk about its productivity: we assemble to challenge the political status quo, to instantiate new forms of interpersonal relations, to prefigure new modes of democracy, to trouble in all these ways established political relations. But we do that intentionally and by design, regardless of the language we use. We can call it "performative," we can call it "organizing," we can call it "subversive," but all along, we knew what we were doing—which was not the case with gender previously. Butler writes: "Many of the massive demonstrations and modes of resistance we have seen in the last months not only produce a space of appearance; they seize upon an already established space permeated by existing power, seeking to sever the relations between the public space, the public square, and the existing regime." In this way, they contest state legitimacy and in themselves "threaten the state with delegitimation."[96] This is certainly right. But, I would argue, that is what is intended in the act of assembly.

In contrast to Butler's more theoretical approach to assembly, Michael Hardt and Antonio Negri provide a handbook intended not just to analyze, but to stimulate, encourage, and foster assembly-style social movements. Hardt and Negri offer guidance on how to organize, how to assemble, how to revolt, how to seize power, and how to transform society. At the most concrete level, faced with leaderless social movements like Occupy Wall Street or the Arab Spring uprisings, they offer a list of tangible organizational principles—almost commands—for leftist revolt.

First, do not give up on leadership. Do not go leaderless. Instead, "transform the role of leadership by inverting strategy and tactics":[97] reverse the traditional relationship between leaders, followers, leadership, and their tasks. Whereas conventionally leaders (or the vanguard) were tasked with setting strategies and the followers (or the masses) were in charge of implementing the tactics, Hardt and Negri want to flip that on its head: the assembled masses should be in charge of broad strategies, and the appointed leaders should be responsible for deciding on tactics. Strategy, they suggest, is the long-term vision for society. Here, we look far into the future, we "*see far*, across the entire social field." The idea is to plan for the long term and to create overarching, cohesive activities. Tactics, on the other hand, are shorter term and concern immediate arrangements of forces. They are specific, contextual, local interventions that require knowledge of the circumstances on the ground. These are circumstances that often involve threats of violence and quick decision-making. They can be regrouped, Hardt and Negri suggest, under the rubric of "counterpower": "confronting the existing power structures, especially regarding questions of force and under the threat of violence, often requires prompt decision-making."[98] With that division, Hardt and Negri propose to rethink leadership: "*strategy to the movements and tactics to leadership*." This simultaneously will eliminate any recognizable form of sovereignty, or at least modify it such that it will produce nonsovereign leadership and make possible nonsovereign institutions. "Our hypothesis," they write in the opening, "is that decision-making and assembly do not require centralized rule but instead can be accomplished together by the multitude, democratically."[99] In this sense, as Joshua Smeltzer emphasizes, their model represents "the inversion of this revolutionary division of labour: leaders will take on a tactical role while the multitude forms strategy 'from below.' "[100]

Second, do not avoid organization: "the critique of traditional forms of leadership should not be confused with a refusal of organization." Leftist movements today seem to attribute a lot to chance and fortuity. However, Hardt and Negri argue, none of the successful leftist revolts left anything to happenstance. They were all minutely planned and organized. There is no "spontaneity" to effective protest, they suggest, adding, "Distrust anyone who calls a social movement or a revolt spontaneous."[101] Contemporary leftist revolts need to be equally organized and prepared: everything has to be charted out ahead of time. Organization is key.

Third, do not avoid institutions: "the critique of modern administration must be accompanied by the creation of alternative administrative forms. The point is not to be done with Weber but to run Weber in reverse." Institution building is often viewed with suspicion by leftists, Hardt and Negri tell us. But that too is a mistake. Today, leftist movements must build new institutions—specifically nonsovereign institutions. More than ever, in fact, we need "institutions to foster continuity and organization, institutions to help organize our practices, manage our relationships, and together make decisions." Inventing these new institutions is precisely what they mean by taking power.[102]

Fourth, and most important, seize power: the overall objective should be to seize power.[103] Many social movements focus too much attention on the movement itself and its general assemblies. Often times, there is even deliberate resistance to power and politics. Hardt and Negri argue strenuously against this. "We have little sympathy with those who want to maintain their purity and keep their hands clean by refusing power," they write. "In order to change the world, we need to take power."[104]

Now, all these concrete directives are grounded on a particular diagnosis of our social condition and political economy. In other words, the tactical proposals—and I emphasize the word *tactical* because, within their own framework of leadership, Hardt and Negri could be leading only on tactics, not on strategies—are superstructural (in a Marxist sense) to more profound analyses of our current social and economic condition. The two foundational pieces to their diagnosis of our present condition—two central elements of their worldview that shape their activist directives—involve, first, the new forms of social production (how we produce today as workers) and, second, the new forms of neoliberal political economy.

First, in their view, there is a new and increasingly social nature of production that we have to understand properly because it grounds both new ways of revolt, as well as new models for social relations for the future. The key point here is that resistance precedes power and shapes power, so to understand how to combat and seize power, we first need to understand our forms of revolt—the social production of the multitude. They explain:

> a political realism that begins with power gives us an upside-down image of the world and masks the real movements of social development. If you begin with power, you will inevitably end up seeing only power.
>
> Today's forms of neoliberalism and financial command should really be understood as *reactions* to projects of freedom and liberation. In a kind of intellectual shorthand, in other words, resistance is prior to power. This methodological principle highlights not so much that struggles for freedom come before new structures of power chronologically (although this is often also true), but rather that the struggles are the principal authors of social innovation and creativity, prior, so to speak, in an ontological sense.
>
> First methodological principle of political realism: *begin with the multitude*.... We need to begin with a materialist analysis of the passions of the multitude.
>
> The key is to grasp the increasingly *social* nature of production in a double sense: both how and what the multitude produces. The multitude, first, both within and outside capitalist relations, produces socially, in expansive cooperative networks. And, second, its products are not just material and immaterial commodities: it produces and reproduces society itself. The social production of the multitude in this double sense is the foundation for not only rebellion but also the construction of alternative social relations.[105]

There are, then, new forms of social production—new "processes of cooperative social production and reproduction," with "technologies, modes of production, and forms of life," with "new subjectivities of production and reproduction." The starting point, for them, is the new digital milieu of youth. They talk about machinic subjectivities and a machinic assemblage. This is intended to capture an existence, materially, in the digital age, and theoretically, in post-Nietzschean humanism. They draw extensively on Deleuze and Guattari. According to Hardt and Negri, youth today in the digital age, who are absorbed in this machinic milieu, are in fact entirely submerged in forms of resistance: "their very existence is resistance." Based on these machinic subjectivities, youths themselves must invent new forms of resistance. This can be achieved, for Hardt and Negri, by these subjectivities *embracing* rather than resisting the entrepreneurial ethic so closely associated with our neoliberal condition. "The important thing," they write, "is to incarnate the energy, responsibility, and virtue of the entrepreneurial spirit. You can go into business, launch your own start-up, or organize a project for the homeless."[106]

Second, Hardt and Negri argue that neoliberalism is a *reaction* to new modes of social reproduction. All of the transformations of capitalism, in their view, react to social change. Fascism, they argue, was a reaction to revolutionary movements; state socialisms were a reaction to communist internationalism; and neoliberalism, they contend, was a reaction to new forms of social reproduction. Because it is *reactive*, neoliberalism must be understood as reacting to and producing new forms of subjectivity. Subjectivity, for Hardt and Negri, is key to understanding all this: the struggle of reaction and production, the struggle of neoliberalism, is precisely a struggle over subjectivity. In their words, italicized by them, "*Subjectivity, in other words, is not a given but a terrain of struggle.*" And this is particularly the case in the context of the political economic field—where the capitalist modes of production face off against "the immeasurable, over-flowing forces of enlarged social production and reproduction, which reside in and produce the common."[107]

The battle over subjectivities, then, requires in their view both a destituent and a constituent element: a destituent element to undo the neoliberal processes of subjectivation; and a constituent element to construct these machinic assemblages described earlier. It is in this way that, to understand fully the current social situation described here of social domination, Hardt and Negri turn to and investigate "the ways that neoliberal governance and the power of finance today both extend and transform the modes of capitalist exploitation and control."[108]

In prophetic terms, Hardt and Negri announce the coming of a "new Prince"—"A Prince of the multitude." By this, they are referring to the multitude taking power through radical innovation, new democratic institutions, and the pursuit of a commons under those conditions of social reproduction. It is here that they call for the creation of new social relations through the passage from private property to the commons. They argue for the creation of new machinic subjectivities. And they urge new democratic institutions based on the entrepreneurial instincts of the multitude, new forms of self-organization, and self-administration.[109]

Hardt and Negri propose concrete "fixes" because they buy into the notion that these leaderless movements have not had long-lasting effects. Their book, in an important way, is motivated by failure: the failure of movements like Occupy or the *Indignados* to have tangible, positive effects and outcomes—"to achieve lasting change and create a new, more democratic and just society."[110] Their manual is born of failure and fueled by the threat of counterrevolutionary forces. The question, they say in opening their book, is urgent and pressing precisely because of the New Right and fascist reactions, because of the counterinsurgency strategies of surveillance and states of exception.

In this respect, it is important to emphasize the difference compared to Butler—a major difference: Butler never says that these leaderless uprisings have little effect. On the contrary, her task is to unearth their performative effect, to examine how these assemblies actually affect politics, the public space, the public/private divide. The contrast with Hardt and Negri couldn't be sharper. Butler looks at these assemblies and sets out, in a constructive way, to figure out everything that they do—all the ways in which they have deeply transformative effects that we fail to appreciate fully. Hardt and Negri look at these assemblies and set out to fix them, change them, guide them so that they become more effective and succeed at bringing about true revolution. Butler cajoles protest by confessing her youthful thrill for protest. She says, "I experience a certain thrill, dating back to my adolescent years, when bodies get together in the street."[111] She inspires, and in many ways seduces, resistance—though she remains apprehensive of those very desires. Hardt and Negri, by contrast, openly, unabashedly, persistently call for revolt and try hard to inspire and foster revolt. They end their manifesto, of sorts, in the voice of an "exhortation":

> Assembly is becoming a *constitutive* right, that is, a mechanism for composing a social alternative, for taking power differently, through cooperation in social production. The call to assembly is what Machiavelli would call an exhortation to virtue. More than a normative imperative, this virtue is an active ethics, a constitutive process that on the basis of our social wealth creates lasting institutions and organizes new social relations, accompanied by the force necessary to maintain them. We have not yet seen what is possible when the multitude assembles.[112]

The opening epigraph of the preface is from Césaire: "Here poetry equals insurrection." The book itself is dedicated to freedom fighters.[113]

Butler evinces very different sensibilities than Hardt and Negri do. In fact, I would even gainsay that Butler is aware of the tension herself because, in that very sentence where she discusses the thrill of assembly, I think she indexes Hardt and Negri as a foil: "At the outset, I confessed that I experience a certain thrill, dating back to my adolescent years, when bodies get together in the street, *and yet I am quite suspicious of those political views that hold, for instance that democracy has to be understood as the event of the surging multitude.*"[114] Butler is deploying philosophy of language to phenomenologically reveal the power of the assembly. For their part, Hardt and Negri are stoking the flames to produce effective revolt. And they maintain a Marxian register of class warfare at times. Our world, they tell us in the opening, "is a world constructed in social cooperation but divided by the domination of the ruling classes, by their blind passion for appropriation and their insatiable thirst for hoarding wealth."[115] Both of these approaches, however, see in assembly a promising new critical praxis.

Political and Civil Disobedience

I have written extensively about the Occupy Wall Street movement as a form of what I call "political disobedience," as opposed to civil disobedience, especially with W. J. T. Mitchell and Michael Taussig in *Occupy: Three Inquiries in Disobedience.*[116] Political as opposed to civil disobedience does not accept the legitimacy of the existing legal regime. By contrast to Martin Luther King Jr. or Mahatma Gandhi, the politically disobedient do not break the law to be punished and to expose the injustice of the law. They do not accept the constitutional structure or the very notion of the rule of law. Instead, they challenge the existing political system. Their disobedience is political in nature, not civil.

Civil disobedience has a long, storied history and deep philosophical and activist roots in Henry David Thoreau's *On the Duty of Civil Disobedience*, Mahatma Gandhi's writings on *Satyagraha* (nonviolent resistance), Martin Luther King Jr.'s *Letter from Birmingham City Jail*, and Hannah Arendt's writings on civil disobedience as a form of lobbying in *Crises of the Republic.* It is conventionally defined as the act of disobeying a positive law to suffer legal punishment and thereby convince others of the injustice of that law or of a legal regime as a whole—of slavery and war for Thoreau, colonialism and imperialism for Gandhi, white supremacy for King, and encroaching authoritarianism for Arendt. Today, a number of contemporary critical theorists advocate a renewed attention to civil disobedience in democracies as a powerful tool to achieve social reform. In their work *Pourquoi désobéir en démocratie?* Sandra Laugier and Albert Ogien address head on the countermajoritarian difficulties typically associated with civil disobedience and resolve them in its favor. Frédéric Gros, in a book titled *Désobéir,* explores and maps out the various forms of disobedience that mirror the various types of expected obedience to authority in political theory. Others have enriched the conversation as well, especially Robin Celikates, Candice Delmas, Alexander Livingston, Todd May, and Brandon Terry.[117]

In contrast to civil disobedience, political disobedience can be defined as a form of insubordination that contests not only unjust positive laws, but also the very political system that gives rise to those laws. It thus challenges the docility of civil disobedience, refusing to respect the punishment associated with breaking unfair laws. It involves flouting rules, not to challenge their legality but because they are simply intolerable. This type of practice has become increasingly common along sovereign borders, where local farmers are giving aid and assistance to undocumented immigrants in defiance of the law, as well as in so-called sanctuary cities, which openly resist the legal enforcement of immigration laws. The ambition here is not to suffer punishment as a way to reveal the immorality of the law, but to defy laws that are considered immoral. It takes a different ethical position toward praxis. It is much closer to what Foucault described in his 1978 lecture, "What Is Critique?" where he suggested that critique is about not being governed "*like this,*" not, as he had originally formulated, in being governed less or not at all, but in not being governed *in this way.*[118]

Here too, praxis and theory confront each other in interesting ways. Political disobedience can prefigure egalitarian forms of democracy, insofar as it aspires to be leaderless, nonhierarchical, and not means-ends driven, or merely instrumental, and avoids being coopted by conventional party politics. It can implement and immediately realize a critical vision of equality, serving as an exemplar of what is possible. Leaderlessness, as an aspiration, helps create a community and mutual respect for all the participants. The resistance to formulating policy demands reflects healthy skepticism regarding easy answers and technocratic solutions. In addition, political disobedience, particularly practices of illegal occupations or squatting, can contain important elements of creativity, spontaneity, and pleasure. As Taussig observed at Zuccotti Park, the humor, creativity, and artwork of the slogans and posters were memorable.[119] Stefan Jonsson highlights the aesthetic aspects of political disobedience.[120] These forms of protest are sensual and pleasurable events, Jonsson underscores, and one cannot fully grasp them absent that dimension. That was certainly the case with Occupy Wall Street, as it had been, decades earlier, with May 1968.

To understand political disobedience, it is crucial to highlight the way that it opens up possibilities for individuals that many no longer believe exist. That was, at least, the palpable feeling that one got reading the texts emerging from the Occupy movement—the numerous, short, moving interventions. It is what you heard, for instance, in the voice of Manissa Maharawal in *Occupy!*—a moving collection of essays by Occupiers—as she rides her bike home after an intense debate at Occupy over issues of racism, classism, and patriarchy: "Later that night I biked home over the Brooklyn Bridge and I somehow felt like, just maybe, at least in that moment, the world belonged to me as well as to everyone dear to me and everyone who needed and wanted more from the world. I somehow felt like maybe the world could be all of ours."[121] This feeling pervades the personal accounts from the protests. A deep current of emancipation, liberation, renewed hope, and political and spiritual reawakening runs through those stories. There was an intense feeling of exuberance in the collective assemblies, in the communal sharing, in the lived experiences of the Occupiers. "What unified this disparate throng was a tangible sense of solidarity, a commitment to the cause of the occupation, but also an evident commitment to each other," the Writers for the 99 Percent recount in their "inside story" of Occupy Wall Street. "It was not unusual for food, packets of cookies or pretzels, or bottles of water to be passed hand-to-hand around the rows, shared by strangers who had just become comrades."[122] There was an overwhelming sense of community. The Occupiers found pleasure in protest. The dancing ballerina, the drumming circles, the mimes, the human microphone, the imaginative, hilarious, and haunting posters—these were key features of the occupation at Zuccotti Park, and of political disobedience more generally. You will recall here Deleuze and Guattari's *Anti-Oedipus*, where they write: "Revolutionaries often forget, or do not like to recognize, that one wants and makes revolution out of desire, not duty."[123] Desire is key to political disobedience—as it is to many of these other forms of critical praxis.[124]

Hacking and Whistleblowing

Political disobedience tends to be a collective enterprise, as we saw with Occupy, Nuit Debout, or Hong Kong—but it need not be. Just as Thoreau developed a highly individualistic, almost libertarian conception of civil disobedience, there are myriad instances of individual acts of political disobedience: hacking, whistleblowing, and ordinary acts of resistance, for example.[125] In the civil disobedience context, there has been active debate on the question. Hannah Arendt, for instance, turned the collective and public aspects of civil disobedience into a requirement, referring to Thoreau as engaged not in civil disobedience, but instead in conscientious objection. There has been less of a debate on this question in the context of political disobedience; but there's no good reason to believe that the individual/collective distinction matters as much. The critical theorist James C. Scott has analyzed ordinary (and often individual) forms of political disobedience under the umbrella of infrapolitics and ordinary acts of resistance. These are precisely the kinds of individual acts that disrupt, cause chaos, and jam the system—often in a less open, explicit, and cooperative way than with assemblies or social movements. This praxis is traditionally associated with marginalized and disempowered populations—though it need not be. It can take many forms, and it is captured well today, for instance, by denial of service attacks and other forms of hacking, whistleblowing, and individual acts of resistance.

Infrapolitics, according to Scott, is the space of struggle of the nonelites and involves "surreptitious resistance." It is, for instance, "poaching and squatting" on such a large scale that it restructures the control of property, "peasant tax evasion," or "massive desertion by serfs or peasant conscripts" that brings down entire regimes. These are down-to-earth, low-profile stratagems designed to minimize appropriation. In the case of slaves, these stratagems have typically included "theft, pilfering, feigned ignorance, shirking or careless labor, footdragging, secret trade and production for sale, sabotage of crops, livestock, and machinery, arson, flight, and so on." Scott argues that these stratagems of infrapolitics are a foundational form of politics. They are "the building block for the more elaborate institutionalized political action that could not exist without it."[126] They reflect the situation of being cornered, dominated, and powerless in the face of an all-powerful state with all the tools—and lashing back in whatever way you can. At times, they are purely individual. At others, they can constitute a mob or a riot—or what E. P. Thompson described so brilliantly under the rubric of the moral economy of the crowd. They can take many different forms.

Hacking is one modern type of infrapolitics. In a table analyzing ordinary acts of resistance, Scott observes that a recurring style of infrapolitics is masked resistance. He refers to it as anonymous resistance, in fact. He speaks of "disguised resisters," "masked appropriations," and "anonymous threats."[127] It is almost as if Scott prefigured the hacker collaborative Anonymous. Hacking and hacktivism grew up, in part, as a form of infrapolitics enacted by marginalized communities that felt that their anonymity was important to protecting their members and keeping them safe. It is a form of resistance that is intimately tied to the digital age, but it actually developed earlier, in an analog age, with the hacking of public phones using false tones.

Emmanuel Goldstein, a hacker and the publisher and editor of the magazine *2600: The Hacker Quarterly* (his real name is Eric Gordon Corley, but he uses a pen name derived from the fictional opposition leader in George Orwell's *1984*), defines *hacktivism* as trying to use the system against the system: to figure out how the system works, to get inside it, to master it, and then to turn it against itself. Hacking, as a form of resistance, plays centrally on the notions of visibility and invisibility. That is what WikiLeaks founder Julian Assange tried to do: to expose corporate secrets or governmental secrets; to render transparent our government. At the same time, it depends on anonymity and invisibility. It often depends on forms of encryption, the use of Tor, creating or breaking through firewalls, and getting back at people through anonymous attacks or denial of service.

One of the major hacking incidents was when, early in the history of WikiLeaks, Mastercard and other credit card companies refused to allow people to use their credit cards to give money to the organization. As a result, one of Anonymous's first acts was to launch a denial of service attack on all the banks and credit card companies that were impeding the fundraising efforts of WikiLeaks. But what really put WikiLeaks on the map was the leak by Chelsea Manning, a U.S. army soldier, of a video of an Apache helicopter attack in Iraq: trying to share, trying to render visible, trying to render transparent what the war in Iraq was about, who were the casualties, and what was being carried out.

It is challenging to critically explore and theorize hacktivism as a leftist political practice when, at the same time, Cambridge Analytica, a British political consulting firm, is engaging in forms of unauthorized digital analyses on behalf of right-wing politicians and given the Russian hacking of American institutions and voters in support of Trump.[128] A few years ago, perhaps, hacking and hacktivism were much more solidly associated with anarchist-leaning attacks on the establishment. They were almost exclusively linked to radical Leftist forms of truth-telling and whistleblowing—to Anonymous, to WikiLeaks and Assange, and to Chelsea Manning and Edward Snowden. In effect, they were associated with forms of political contestation that had an anarchist, sometimes libertarian, but certainly radical nature to them, predominantly on the Leftist, anticapitalist, anti-imperialist side of the spectrum.

As Gabriella Coleman emphasizes in her article "Weapons of the Geek," we need to be more nuanced about the politics of hackers—as she correctly argues, "the ideological sensibilities that animate hacker politics are diverse: just as we can locate liberal hackers and projects, so too can we identify radical hackers and projects and see how both engender social change."[129] But it is fair to say that these sensibilities were (and still are) predominantly on the more radical Left. Emmanuel Goldstein provides a brilliant history in his essay "Hacktivism and the Hacker Promise,"[130] as does Coleman in her article. The political valence was linked, theoretically and historically, to what Coleman refers to as "the cultural cultivation of antiauthoritarianism" within hacker circles.[131]

Today, things may be changing, at least in the public imagination. Hacking has undergone an ideological drift—no longer so tightly associated with resistance to power and often, now, connected to more authoritarian political tendencies. If I had to identify a moment, a tipping point, I think it would be when Assange effectively threw his support behind Donald Trump and against Hillary Clinton in the 2016 presidential election. It was at that moment that hacktivism began to feel as much authoritarian as anarchist. Today, I fear, it almost seems as if hacking has become superpowered and militarized. It is as if the power of hacking were recognized as being so great, in our digitized age and geopolitics, that it was captured by the military superpowers. For instance, with news stories about Russia's ability to turn off the American power grid now dominating the public imagination of hacking, at least more so than denial of service attacks, hacking has a new militarized valence.[132]

Closely tied to hacking today is whistleblowing—in fact, many of the highest-profile hacks have been acts of whistleblowing. Some theorists, such as Candice Delmas, argue that subjects may have a duty to engage in government whistleblowing as an illegal act of uncivil but principled disobedience. Delmas proposes that whistleblowing effectively exceeds civil disobedience. The purpose is not to contest or repeal laws about secrecy so much as to expose wrongdoing. Plus, many whistleblowers attempt to evade the law and keep from getting caught. As Delmas emphasizes, "Many whistleblowers seek to evade punishment." In this sense, it is not civil disobedience, but rather, according to her, justified illegal resistance—or what she calls "principled disobedience."[133] By contrast, William Scheuerman offers a defense of whistleblowing as an act of civil disobedience in furtherance of a conception of the rule of law.[134]

The cases of Chelsea Manning and Edward Snowden, whose actions involved the United States, are at the center of the debate over whistleblowing.[135] Most on the critical Left view their actions as both justified and a form of political praxis. The debate, when there is any, is about how to understand their actions and their way of life. Snowden is theorized at times as the truth-teller, or the Foucaultian *parrhesiast*, in the writings of such scholars as Lida Maxwell, Charleyne Biondi, and John Rajchman. At other times, Snowden is portrayed as a civil disobedient in the best tradition of the rule of law, in the writings for instance of William Scheuerman and others. And at other times, he is the paradigm of uncivil disobedience, as in the writings of Candice Delmas.[136] In any event, the overarching consensus is that whistleblowing is a key modality of critical praxis today.

Killjoy Politics

Closely tied to acts of individual political disobedience is the killjoy ethic that the critical theorist Sara Ahmed develops under the rubric of "killjoy feminism." In *Living a Feminist Life* and earlier works, including *The Promise of Happiness* and *Willful Subjects*, Ahmed outlines the practice of the feminist killjoy and willful feminist subject as a way of being and living a feminist life.[137] The killjoy ethic is a type of unrelenting frank speech and uncompromised confrontation of sexism and racism. It represents a form of praxis that contests, in everyday life, domination and oppression.

The feminist killjoy is a woman who challenges sexism or racism in spaces where people would rather not hear it—where they would prefer to ignore it and enjoy the moment. Ahmed uses the illustration of a family dinner around the dining room table—the protected setting for the performance of the family—that is disrupted by the feminist woman or girl (in this case, Ahmed herself, as a child) raising issues of sex discrimination.[138] She recalls getting slowly wound up in the face of disturbing sexist (or racist) statements, holding it in for a while as she gets more and more upset, and then finally speaking out, but realizing that no one wants to hear her. "The feminist killjoy appears here: when she speaks, she seems wound up. I appear here. This is my history: wound up."[139] These moments are accompanied with what Ahmed refers to as "the eye-roll": eyes begin to roll at this moment, in an expression of frustration with feminism and feminists, attributing to the feminist the responsibility for creating the uncomfortable moment.

The killjoy feminist becomes a nuisance the moment she describes the problem—as if the problem had not been there before her, but that she created it. Discussing another time that she called out racism, Ahmed points out how the killjoy becomes responsible for the problem, as if she introduced it into the room, when it was there all the while, but unacknowledged. "Racism was on my mind because racism was in the room," Ahmed writes. Racism was present before, but unacknowledged, and it is as if calling it out is the problem. It is as if the feminist or antiracist person is the one who is looking for a problem. She adds, "It is as if these problems are not there until you point them out; it is as if pointing them out is what makes them there."[140]

The willful feminist is the woman who embraces the notion of willfulness—itself a term, when used about women, that connotes a will that is wanting in some way. As Ahmed writes, "feminists are judged as willful women as a way of dismissing feminism as a screen behind which a will lurks: a will that is wanting." The willfulness of girls, as opposed to the "strong will" of boys, is perceived as a fault and tied to disobedience. It is something that society must tame, in order to ensure obedience to the broader social order. In a similar way to the killjoy, the "willful child" is portrayed as responsible for the problems. "To be called willful is an exclamation of why we ruin things," Ahmed writes. "We are assumed to cause our own ruin, as well as to ruin things for others."[141] Here too, Ahmed advocates embracing and reclaiming willfulness. Following Alice Walker, she wants to claim willfulness as an act of self-description.

Embracing willfulness, Ahmed proposes a form of militantism. In a conclusion headed "A Feminist Army," she uses the metaphor of arms, from an important passage from a Grimm fairy tale, to trigger a discussion of the revolutionary sign of the clenched fist, which becomes for her the paradigm image of feminist life and liberation. It is the revolutionary sign of the clenched fist, placed within the symbol for women, that captures these notions of killjoy, of willfulness, and of disobedience. "A feminist does not lend her hand; she too curls her fist," Ahmed writes. "When a hand curls up as a feminist fist, it has a hand in a movement." And into a telling reference to the famous dictum of Audre Lorde, Ahmed concludes the part of her book called "Becoming Feminist" with the following formulation: "the arms that built the house are the arms that will bring it down." Ahmed comes back to Lorde's famous statement—"the master's tools will never dismantle the master's house"—later in the book. With a slightly different take this time, Ahmed writes: "In that unflinching 'will never' is a call to arms: do not become the master's tool!"[142]

Sara Ahmed's book is a remarkable critical theoretic intervention that does not operate in the usual manner of critical theory. In fact, she specifically positions her intervention in confrontation with traditional critical theory, as well as with the entire tradition that cites predominately male theorists and, both openly and subliminally, privileges male work (subliminal, as when you use the word *seminal* to identify the most important contributions to thought. "Seminal," she writes: "how ideas are assumed to originate from male bodies.")[143] The substance of Ahmed's feminism overlaps and infuses her methodology, with the result that hers is not an explicit, direct, or open engagement with male-dominated critical theory, but instead an orthogonal intervention aimed at displacing the critical theory discourse with her own feminist embodiment.

Ahmed proceeds in a personal voice that highlights the affective dimensions that lead her, and maintain her, passionately and militantly, in feminism. She traces the sensational nature of feminism—both in the sense of the affects and sensations that brought her to feminism, and in the sense of the reactions against feminism as being a "killjoy." Those sensational experiences are what nourish her feminism. It is the sensations of injustice, exploitation, assault, and marginalization, humiliation, and frustration—the combination of all these shattering experiences and life-transforming events that motivates her feminist praxis.

Ahmed's practice of killjoy feminism is a militant, engaged, constant, and unbending will to create a new world for women and persons of color to inhabit, to live, to find themselves. She recurrently draws the parallel between feminism and antiracism and between sexism and racism, and embraces an intersectional approach. Although she speaks predominantly about feminism and sexism, she writes as a woman of color, and her discourse is equally applicable—although raising naturally different issues and different dimensions—to the question of racism and discrimination against persons of color.

Ahmed's distinct relationship to the world of critical theory—her conflictual relationship, that is—is what produces the unique discursive texture and the urgency of her text. She writes in the tradition of Black feminists, feminists of color, poets, and writers, referring predominantly to authors such as Audre Lorde, bell hooks, Gloria Anzaldúa, and Judith Butler, but also Virginia Woolf, Toni Morrison, and George Eliot. She has a citation policy and theory of not citing any white male authors. She writes: "In this book, I adopt a strict citation policy: I do not cite any white men." She specifies that by the term "white men," she is targeting an institution, in part the institution of critical theory, that privileges certain authors; and she notes that she "might need to add cis, straight, and able-bodied to the general body I am evoking."[144] Her citation policy has expository and theoretical effects and pushes her toward, or perhaps reflects, a more personal, experiential, and almost phenomenological approach to theorizing and toward her deep engagement with feminist theory and authors.

The thrust of the killjoy practice is to make feminism a life question. She is discussing "living a feminist life," which entails how to live in such a way. She recognizes that for doing this, she will be judged as being judgmental.[145] But she refuses to desist for that reason. She willingly embraces the judgmental dimension of asking and answering the question of how to live a feminist life.

Sexual assault, sexual exploitation, and sexual oppression are central motivating forces in Ahmed's work. It is, in fact, the experience of sexual assault and harassment that forms her central experiences and memories of the sensation of injustice and wrongness, and that contributes to Ahmed's take on feminism. She describes, courageously, her own experiences of sexual assault, sexual touching, and sexual harassment. These experiences and sensations are deeply associated with becoming a girl or a woman, Ahmed argues, and they give rise to a feminist consciousness. They are central to the definition of sexism that Ahmed uses in the book *Living a Feminist Life*. Drawing on bell hooks's definition of feminism as "the movement to end sexism, sexual exploitation, and sexual oppression," Ahmed emphasizes that these definitional elements are important precisely because they have *not* ended. One key element for the feminist movement is precisely to emphasize that these have not ended, and that we do not live in some kind of "post-feminist fantasy." She is attentive to intersectionality and argues that feminism cannot be separated from the questions of race, colonialism, slavery, and capitalism. "Intersectionality is a starting point, the point from which we must proceed if we are to offer an account of how power works."[146]

Ahmed's writings are especially inspiring to those who think that they are always raising issues that no one wants to hear or see, or are told that they are the ones with the problem. It is especially powerful for those who have experienced the feeling of someone telling them that the problem is not in reality, but in their head. "Even to describe something as sexist and racist here and now can get you into trouble," Ahmed writes. "You point to structures; they say it is in your head. What you describe as material is dismissed as mental."[147] These are the experiences that push her to a very personal form of theoretical work, written in a very personal voice, drawing on personal experiences, and making a personal intervention.

Ahmed is entirely correct that theory, and especially critical theory, create a loaded space that has extraordinarily hierarchical relations and lots of, in her term, "capital." However, her rejection, or displacement, of theory rests in part on experiences with what I would call idiotic political theorists. It may be too much of a reaction against the type of effete theorist that protects herself or himself from politics. Ahmed discusses an experience from which she came out thinking, "if theory is not politics, I am glad I am not doing theory!" She mentions that, "it was a relief to leave that space in which theory and politics were organized as different trajectories."[148] If, however, we view critical theory and the critical method as an expression of a *political project*, then surely there shouldn't be this kind of rejection of theory.

In a part of *Living a Feminist Life* titled "Living the Consequences," Ahmed addresses the difficult consequences of being a feminist and the resilience that is required to do so. She coins another term: "feminist snap," which she defines as "how we collectively acquire tendencies that can allow us to break ties that are damaging as well as to invest in new possibilities." It is about the difficulties of diversity work: about being shattered, about being exhausted, about feeling depleted. These have effects. They slow the feminist killjoy. There may be times when she no longer reacts as quickly, or even reacts at all. They lead to transformations. This is especially true for the feminist of color, whose very presence may alter and disrupt even a grouping of white feminists.[149] "Feminist snap" builds on the multiple connotations of the infinitive *to snap*: from the biting, to the brisk, cracking sound after a break. Ahmed uses the term *snap* to symbolize that moment when the feminist simply cannot take it anymore.[150] Ahmed also explores and reimagines the Middle English word *hap* (chance), which is at the root of both words like *happiness* and words like *happenstance*. This is a topic developed earlier, in her 2010 book, *The Promise of Happiness*, where she devoted much attention to the question of how the notion of happenstance was hollowed out of happiness—the question of how happiness lost its way. Ahmed associates a certain queerness with the term. "To affirm hap is to follow a queer route: you are not sure which way you are going; maybe you let your feet decide for you," she writes.[151]

Ahmed argues for a revival of lesbian feminism. This is, she tells us, her conviction: doing so is necessary "in order to survive what we come up against, in order to build worlds from the shattered pieces." She constructs a structural or institutional argument for a lesbian feminism. It is based on the fact that the feminist struggle is a struggle against structures, and that it involves the constant chipping away of those structures, structures that are the least visible. Parts of the structures are heteronormativity and male dominance. To understand those structures and institutions, to interpret them, Ahmed argues for lesbian feminism as the lived experience that gives the proper tools for interpretation.[152] "Lesbian feminism can bring feminism back to life," she writes.[153]

As virtual appendices to her book, Ahmed offers both a killjoy survival kit and a killjoy manifesto. The survival kit is intended to offer tips on everything from books to read and keep handy to humor, feelings, and bodily movements. The manifesto—itself an item in the survival kit—offers principles to live by. These two are squarely in the domain of praxis.

Survival means having close at hand the books of Audre Lorde, bell hooks, Judith Butler, Virginia Woolf, and others—but especially books by Lorde and Butler. It also means having feminist objects around you, feminist tools such as a pen, a keyboard, and a table, and even perhaps a blog; it also means taking some time off as a killjoy, possibly having pets or another killjoy nearby, and retaining a sense of humor, though never laughing when jokes are not funny, when jokes are sexist. Ahmed's survival kit includes things like wiggling and dancing—and finally, of course, writing a manifesto.[154]

Ahmed expresses her manifesto as a series of principles. There is a set of negative principles, of things that she is not willing to do, not willing to compromise. These include making others happy; laughing at jokes that are offensive; getting over histories, even though those histories aren't over; and being included in a system that is unjust. There is, inversely, a set of positive things that she is willing to do: to cause unhappiness; to support other feminists who caused unhappiness; to reject the life that others think she should lead; to snap, to break bonds, to be a killjoy; and to put back the *hap* in *happiness*.[155]

Ahmed militates for a killjoy moment, which is where she ends her manifesto in the book. "I am willing to participate in a killjoy moment," she proclaims: that is the last and tenth principle. It is what she calls a rebellious command. On the penultimate page, she writes, in bold, one line at a time:

> **Killjoy?**
> **Just watch me.**
> **Bring it on.**[156]

Autonomous Zones

Closely connected to the practice of lesbian feminism is the idea of creating autonomous zones. These consist, most often, of noninsurrectional separatist movements that seek to create communities, often through a squatting model that does not involve violence, but rather community, new forms of property, and various forms of collaboration. The ambition of these temporary spaces is generally to avoid formal state structures of control. They are often referred to as *temporary autonomous zones* (TAZs), in part in homage to the poetic anarchist writings of Hakim Bey by that name. They can also aspire to be permanent, or as Bey suggested, "Permanent TAZs," in a 1994 article by that title.

A well-known example of a TAZ, which has attempted to become a permanent autonomous zone, is the autonomous zone of Notre-Dame-des-Landes, outside Nantes, France. This zone and others—in Rouen, Lyon, and elsewhere in France—are referred to as *Zones à défendre* (ZADs) and have generally involved peaceful occupations of land, often with a significant environmental aspect. In the case of Notre-Dame-des-Landes, the zone began as a protest movement against the building of a new, large airport outside Nantes to service all of western France. The physical presence of the protesters, through a form of squatting on agricultural land where the airport was going to be built, started a long-term alliance between leftist activists, anarchists, environmentalists, and local farmers. The ZAD brought down the airport construction project eventually, after ten years of occupation and protest. In the process, the activists invented new forms of nonproperty, which the French state has tried to violently repress and demolish.

Hakim Bey's *The Temporary Autonomous Zone* (1985) offers a seductive, poetic vision of anarchist separatism. His is a romantic vision drawing on the imagination of the pirate alcove, the explorers going native, the artists living a limit experience. Bey embraces the fugitive, the deviant in all ways. The vision that he offers is a creature of our postrevolutionary moment—of the lapse in that modern conception of Revolution elaborated in the writings of Reinhart Koselleck. The revolutionary ideal, Bey warns, is behind us—a thing of the past. What lies ahead are uprisings and insurrections. His poetics are strident: "realism demands not only that we give up *waiting* for 'the Revolution' but also that we give up *wanting* it. 'Uprising,' yes—as often as possible and even at the risk of violence."[157] He explains the appeal of the uprising: "The concept of the TAZ arises first out of a critique of Revolution, and an appreciation of the Insurrection. The former labels the latter a failure; but for us *uprising* represents a far more interesting possibility, from the standard of a psychology of liberation, than all the 'successful' revolutions of bourgeoisie, communists, fascists, etc."[158]

For Hakim Bey, the TAZ already exists—it has been with us for centuries and is with us today. We are in it now, at least for the lucky ones among us: "a certain kind of 'free enclave' is not only possible in our time but also existent." It is the experience of Tortuga, the pirate enclave, but also of the explorers who preferred to stay, of early Madagascar, or just of the space where we have escaped. For Bey, it is the party "where for one brief night a republic of gratified desires was attained." For one brief night, or for two or three years, he notes.[159]

The zone allows us to get outside or beyond the state—without conceding to the state. The relationship is that of having overcome the state, escaped it, and ignored it; and being a step ahead. "The TAZ is like an uprising which does not engage directly with the State, a guerilla operation which liberates an area (of land, of time, of imagination) and then dissolves itself to re-form elsewhere/elsewhen, *before* the State can crush it."[160] In the zone, we discover other ways to be fully ourselves, and we withhold judgment.

"In the end the TAZ is almost self-explanatory," Bey writes. "If the phrase became current it would be understood without difficulty . . . understood in action."[161] Understood in praxis, that is. Increasingly, autonomous zones are becoming a form of critical praxis.

The Common

Bearing a family resemblance to the autonomous zone, a number of critical theorists envisage the idea of creating what they call "the common."[162] For thinkers such as Hardt and Negri, Žižek, Alain Badiou, and Pierre Dardot and Christian Laval, in conversation with others, Étienne Balibar, Aristides Baltas, Eduardo Cadava, Rosalind Morris, and Mikhaïl Xifaras, the common represents another type of practice. The idea here is to focus praxis on the creation of a framework of shared property extending from the creative commons and copyleft regimes to open access to goods and services to shared property ownership (including of the Earth itself). The idea is not to place common property in the hands of the state, but to instantiate a genuine common. The term tends to be used in the singular, as opposed to *commons*, to contrast it with the metaphor of the common green and the literature on the tragedy of the commons.

The project of "the common" takes us back to the *material* roots of praxis—to Marx, to capital, to private property, to the idea of the commons. It does so, though, by once more flipping things on their head. The return to political economy here places the *law* of private property at the very heart of the analysis. Law, rather than being merely superstructural and epiphenomenal, moves center stage—and this is not any kind of law, not the usual public or constitutional law, but rather private law, the law of private property and of commercial transactions. This represents a double move: first, theoretically, one might say, from Giorgio Agamben back to Marx; but second and more important, from Marx to Critical Legal Studies and beyond.

Perhaps the best way to understand the idea of the common is to draw on the term's secondary connotation. Rather than focus on the typical objectives of seizing power or sovereignty, or resisting states of exception or counterrevolutions, this practice focuses instead on the more common and pervasive forms of domination today: relations of property ownership that determine our daily existence. It focuses on what is more commonly oppressive and omnipresent—namely, the ubiquitous milieu of property law within which we live and breathe daily.

This represents then, as I have mentioned, a two-step movement or corrective. The first corrective is the return to Marx and political economy: the return to the core considerations of capital, private property, modes of production, and material interests. Here, we place property relations at the heart and center of the debate—and we try to transform those relations. This first corrective resonates elegantly with the central idea of praxis. It was, after all, the failure of German idealism to confront the *material* conditions of existence that fueled Marx's dialectical materialism. The shift from contemplation to action—from interpreting the world to changing it—was grounded, for Marx, on the first imperative, to privilege political economy.

One hears this loudly in Michael Hardt and Antonio Negri's *Commonwealth*, published in 2009. Hardt and Negri argue that we need to displace our obsession with sovereignty, fascism, and states of exception—with Agamben, essentially—and return to Marx: "Just as Kant sweeps away the preoccupations of medieval philosophy with transcendent essences and divine causes, so too must we get beyond theories of sovereignty based on rule over the exception, which is really a holdover from old notions of the royal prerogatives of the monarch. We must focus instead on the transcendental plane of power, where law and capital are the primary forces." Their constant refrain is that all the talk of "states of exception" and "fascism" hides the more fundamental way in which power operates in society: the focus on violence and sovereign power "eclipses and mystifies the really dominant forms of power that continue to rule over us today—power embodied in property and capital, power embedded in and fully supported by the law." Also, the obsession with sovereignty and violence means that we become politically disengaged and disarmed by the weight of the state. We lose the very ability to resist, reform, and transform when the domination becomes too oppressive. "There can be no political engagement with a sovereign fascist power," Hardt and Negri write; "all it knows is violence." We need to focus instead on the common forms of power, they say: "The primary form of power that really confronts us today, however, is not so dramatic or demonic but rather earthly and mundane."[163]

The second corrective is to Marx, or perhaps later Marxism: the praxis intervention here, centrally related to property relations and modes of production, does not relegate law to a superstructural place in society. Law is not the outside, nor are we habitually situated outside law. Everything happens within a space that is constituted by law. In this debate, law and capital are integrally intertwined, such that the core of praxis may well become *legal* praxis. For Hardt and Negri, the phrase "the republic of property" at the heart of their book *Commonwealth* inextricably intertwines law *and* capital. Their critique, they write, "must show how capital and law intertwined together—what we call the republic of property—determine and dictate the conditions of possibility of social life in all its facets and phases."[164]

If Marxists indeed relegated law to the margins—if, for instance, Pashukanis is properly interpreted as hostile to the emancipatory potential of legal reform, as he often is—then we are now in a very different place, as evidenced especially by the deployment by Hardt and Negri of Critical Legal Studies. In fact, in *Assembly*, Hardt and Negri urge us to take the final leap beyond Critical Legal Studies: "Legal projects to reform property and limit its power have certainly had beneficial effects but now we need finally to take the leap beyond." To those, like the law scholar Thomas Grey, who believe that the law of property evolved, especially through American Legal Realism, toward a conception of "bundles of rights" that might eventually "dissolve" on their own, Hardt and Negri say no, it will not happen on its own—we need to take the final and decisive step to create the commons as "*nonproperty*."[165]

Instead of legal regulation, Hardt and Negri propose, in essence, democratic regulation of this common. It is not held by the state, nor is it subject to legal regulation. It must be determined and regulated by democratic decision-making—by "more expansive democratic experiences that are open to others" and the "new, fuller form of democracy." They add: "We wholeheartedly endorse [Elinor] Ostrom's claim that the common must be managed through systems of democratic participation."[166]

In *Assembly*, Hardt and Negri respond to the critiques that Critical Legal Studies scholars leveled at their earlier work, *Commonwealth*, and they reformulate somewhat their proposal for a common—integrating the history of American Legal Realism and Critical Legal Studies and the related understanding of private property as "bundles of rights," as well as Harold Demsetz and the Chicago School economists.[167] Their revised theory of the common does not differ that much from the original version, except to address specifically the question of the internal and the external of the law. As Hardt and Negri make clear in *Assembly*, any notion of the common must propose eventual ways of *managing* the common goods: there must be a democratic mechanism for determining its use—which would be a form of regulation. So the common will remain fully regulated, but regulated through democratic forms—democratic management, rather than in a monopolistic manner. There must be open and equal access, and democratic decision-making—as we saw, Hardt and Negri argue, at Zuccotti Park. This entails, of course, a regulatory framework—whether we call it legal or not. It functions as a legal language—as Balibar suggests: "This is the idea that, *more than ever*, an institution of the common (or a communist society) will need a juridical system of categories and rules, because it will need to *regulate* the distribution of moments (part of life), activities, and use values *between the collective and the proper* (or the individual). This amounts to anticipating a *meta-level* in the definition of 'property,' which has essentially an ethical (or anthropological) function, but which must be formulated in the language of law, or in a legal grammar."[168] And it entails as well the design of institutions, as Camille Robcis emphasizes in her work.[169]

The debate among these thinkers often centers on using a term like *management* or *regulation* versus *law, juridical,* or *legal regulation.* But that is of minor consequence. As I argue in *The Illusion of Free Markets,* all economic spaces are regulated, fully regulated, and whether we call those forms of regulation *laws* or *norms* or simply *regulations,* they are the mechanisms that distribute wealth and resources in society. That will not go away with the common. There will have to be democratic governance (assuming a democracy) or simple governance of the use of property. No critical thinker, I would like to believe, could possibly believe that there can be an unregulated economic space. Hardt and Negri speak of institutions and organizations, and decision-making, and mechanisms to determine use. That's what others, lawyers, call law. And the fact there can be no unregulated space is precisely why the notion of the free market is a myth, why the idea of overregulation is also an illusory trope, why the term deregulation is a euphemism for reregulation, and why Ronald Reagan was simply redistributing, not deregulating in the 1980s. It is why neoliberalism is a regulatory mechanism, and not a form of deregulation. If you agree with all this, as any critical thinker must, I believe, then there is no major disagreement between Hardt and Negri and their critics, such as Mikhaïl Xifaras. It is rather a question of terminology. Hardt and Negri engage Critical Legal Studies and discuss concrete forms of the common, including code, immaterial property, and intellectual property, but ultimately remain on the political terrain of democratic decision-making. Others, such as Xifaras, place lawyers and law reform more centrally in the process of social transformation—not to say the revolutionary process. As Xifaras writes, "The wish, or the project, I make here would be to reconcile political radicality with concrete practice, by getting politically radical critical theories to better speak the language of the law, or, to put it another way, to better articulate internal and external critique of the Law."[170]

The project of the common is also what motivates the encounters and publications spearheaded by Slavoj Žižek under the rubric of "The Idea of Communism." It is in fact the very question that motivated and set the agenda for the series of volumes: "to discuss the perpetual, persistent notion that, in a truly emancipated society, all things should be owned in common."[171] Žižek too proposes a notion of the common—but a new one that would have revolutionary implications. This is at the heart of his demonstration in his essay "How to Begin from the Beginning" in the first volume of the collection. Žižek argues there that we need to begin by rethinking communism from scratch, following Lenin's recognition, in 1922, that the only way forward is to start again and again from the beginning: "we definitely have to 'begin from the beginning,' that is, not to 'build further upon the foundations' of the revolutionary epoch of the twentieth century (which lasted from 1917 to 1989), but to 'descend' to the starting point and follow a *different* path."[172] In this, Žižek accompanies Alain Badiou, who also urged us to hold on to the "communist hypothesis," but to rethink entirely its modality and expression. In fact, Badiou urges us to rethink even its core elements, including property and the state. By turning to the idea of communism, and liberating ourselves from its experience, we can begin anew to reimagine its modalities and propose entirely new "political experimentation," in Badiou's words, taken up again by Žižek.[173] It invites, as Peter Hallward suggests, "a certain amount of free or 'reckless' speculation, a reflection on communism as a project or possibility independent of the legacy of formerly existing communism."[174]

In his essay, Žižek identifies four contradictions—what he calls "antagonisms"—within contemporary capitalism that will ultimately bring its downfall: first, climate change; second, intellectual property and its tension with the idea of private property; third, biotechnologies and their socioethical implications; and fourth, new walls and slums as new forms of apartheid. For Žižek, the first three of these contradictions articulate three different aspects of the notion of the common—what he calls external, cultural, and internal dimensions.[175] Žižek argues that in all three of these dimensions, the global grab for the common and unremitting privatization risk total apocalypse—what he calls "the self-annihilation of humanity itself." It also goes hand in hand with a fragmentation of the working class into three sectors: the intellectual creators, the manual laborers, and the marginalized unemployed, as discussed earlier. The chasms between these three segments then further empower the state. (This allows Žižek to radicalize the notion of the proletariat, arguing that we all have become the proletariat in the condition of potential annihilation—of potentially losing everything. "This triple threat to our entire being makes us all in a way proletarians, reduced to 'substanceless subjectivity,' as Marx put it in the *Grundrisse*.")[176]

Beyond this, Žižek also warns against what some of us call neoliberal penality. Over and above the four aforementioned antagonisms, Žižek tells us, there is a broader and more deeply embedded contradiction in postmodern capitalism, which drives our current inequalities and eventually must lead to political change. This is the contradiction between the increasingly "deregulated" state of postmodern capitalism and its increasing policing functions, which are necessary to extract rent. "Perhaps therein resides the fundamental 'contradiction' of today's 'postmodern' capitalism: while its logic is deregulatory, 'anti-statal', nomadic/deterritorializing, etc., its key tendency towards the 'becoming-rent-of-profit' signals the strengthening role of the State whose (not only) regulatory function is ever more omnipresent."[177] In effect, because capitalism is gradually becoming an economy of rent-seeking—of rent profits off intellectual labor in the digital age—the state is actually *increasing* its power and policing rather than disappearing.

Only the idea of the common—the idea of communism—pays attention to the fourth contradiction: apartheid inequality, or what Žižek calls "the gap that separates the Excluded from the Included."[178] This is what makes it unique. All other practices can address the first three antagonisms in reformist ways. Only a politics that takes the fourth into consideration will be emancipatory: it alone will focus on the problem of inequality.

This is the core of the idea of communism—and it sheds light on the path forward, for Žižek: to unite the three separate factions of the working class. As Žižek explains, the condition of postmodern capitalism has split the working class into three parts, with very different ideologies—"each part with its own 'way of life' and ideology."[179] The strategy, then, must be to reunite the three. Žižek closes the essay by proclaiming: "The old call 'Proletarians, unite!' is thus more pertinent than ever: in the new conditions of 'post-industrial' capitalism, the unity of the three fractions of the working class *is* already their victory."[180]

This is, then, a fully emancipatory philosophy. Žižek speaks of his political position and aspiration as representing "the new emancipatory politics." "It is thus crucial to insist on the communist-egalitarian emancipatory Idea," Žižek writes, "and insist in a very precise Marxian sense." He distinguishes between communism and socialism, associating the latter with authoritarian-imposed community: "communism is to be opposed to socialism, which, in place of the egalitarian collective, offers a solidary organic community—Nazism was national socialism, not national communism." According to Žižek, socialism is compatible with anti-Semitism, populism, and even modified forms of capitalism.[181]

For Balibar too, the idea of communism allows him to synthesize and define communism. On the one hand, to define who "we communists" are—that is, for Balibar, those of us who "desire to *change the world in order to become transformed ourselves*."[182] That would be, in Rosalind Morris's words, those with a "relentless commitment to our shared goal of radical equality."[183] On the other hand, for Balibar, the idea of communism also allows him to identify its praxis. Only by reaching toward the abstraction of the idea of communism is it possible to isolate what precisely characterizes communist action or praxis. And what Balibar proposes here is that "they/we [communists] are participating in various 'struggles' of emancipation, transformation, reform, revolution, civilization; but in doing that we are not so much 'organizing' as 'de-organizing' these struggles."[184]

What is clear from this is that the path to the common can take different routes—a legal reformist one, say, for Xifaras, and a revolutionary one for Žižek. For Xifaras, existing law is indeterminate and malleable and can be pushed into radical directions, both right and left, from within. Law, he writes, is "malleable and open enough to allow the thinking and practicing of radical alternatives from within the legal system." As a result, he adds, "alternatives spoken in the language of the Law can be no less radical, but for sure more concrete than others."[185] In this, I agree, and articulate this position explicitly in *The Counterrevolution*, where I demonstrate how the rule of law has been twisted from within since 9/11 to achieve radical counterrevolutionary ends. As I argue in chapter 12 there, titled "A State of Legality," we do not live today in a state of exception, but in a state of legality, because the rule of law, in the end, is so malleable.[186] This is true in matters of private law as well. I agree with Xifaras that there is just as much pliability there. He is undoubtedly correct, for instance, that the free software movement "illustrates how greatly malleable legal technicalities are and . . . how alternatives can be built from within."[187] But Étienne Balibar is also undoubtedly right to supplement Xifaras's *juridical* intervention—regarding the constitutive nature of law—with a similar *economic* intervention. That is what Hardt and Negri do, when they refer explicitly to the conjuncture of "capital *and* law," when they argue that the two are "intertwined together," or when they use the expression "the republic of property."[188]

The complementarity of economics and law is essential to the idea of the common. The conclusion that Balibar draws—namely, that "law and economy are coextensive and mutually constitutive"[189]—is important, and it highlights the dual nature of this form of praxis.

Socialism

In a slightly different register, Axel Honneth fleshes out a new vision for socialism in his book *The Idea of Socialism.* Although Honneth does not give practical guidance and shies away from praxis, there is ample material for critical practitioners to confront this theoretical work with their praxis and vice versa.

As you will recall from chapter 4, Honneth's starting point is his observation of a significant discontent among ordinary citizens in Western democracies about their socioeconomic condition, combined with what he calls a "widespread outrage" that has no clear direction or expression. He originally published his book in 2015, before the rise of the New Right around the globe. As a result, he does not identify the rise of the Alternative for Germany (AfD) party in Germany or the election of Donald Trump in the United States, or the fact of Brexit, as expressions of this discontent. Instead, he remarks on the rudderless aspect of the outrage and on a certain quietude. Honneth searches for explanations for this "sudden decline in utopian energy"[190] and goes through a few—the collapse of communism in general in 1989, the rise of postmodernism, a fundamental shift in our sense of history—before reaching what he believes is the closest, though still yet lacking, explanation: a contemporary form of reification of the concept of social relations, such that we no longer even believe in the possibility of change. We have come to believe that things are inevitable.

So the question that Honneth poses is the following: "why do visions of socialism no longer have the power to convince the outraged that collective efforts can in fact improve what appears 'inevitable'?" To respond, he first reconstructs the original idea of socialism in order to demonstrate how and why that original idea has become antiquated. He then attempts to reconfigure the idea of socialism for our contemporary times. The historical account bears the method of a learning process, and in that sense has a strong Hegelian flavor. Honneth describes the history of the original idea of socialism and locates it as a direct product of capitalist industrialization.[191] He highlights how the term *socialist* was first used to refer to the works of Grotius and Puffendorf; but it only comes into fruition, to its proper usage, in the 1820s and 1830s in relation to Robert Owen in England and Charles Fourier in France, who refer to themselves as "socialist."

The original idea of socialism was to try to make the world more "social," expressed in the efforts to develop a cooperative society, to establish collectivities that Charles Fourier called *phalanstères*, or to facilitate solidarity among workers and people. Honneth draws heavily on Émile Durkheim, who studied and formulated the idea of socialism as having at its core a shared ambition to master economic processes under the authority of society, as represented by the state. The history that Honneth illustrates is one in which the originators of the idea of socialism were grappling primarily with the relationship between the value of liberty and of fraternity in the wake of the French Revolution—and its famous trinity. Regarding the early thinkers, Owen, Fourier, and Saint-Simon, Honneth suggests that their main struggle was to expand on the *liberal* notion of freedom to align it better with the value of fraternity: to shed the self-interested and egotistical dimensions of liberal freedom associated with the postrevolutionary bourgeoisie. He sees the same in the second wave of socialists—Louis Blanc and Pierre-Joseph Proudhon. Here too, the notion of freedom had to be expanded from the pursuit of private interests to a much more solidaristic appeal aligned with fraternity.[192]

Honneth identifies a number of what he calls "birth defects" in the original idea of socialism, each tied to a core assumption—and each of which, I would argue, can be tested against critical praxis. The first is an excessive and exclusive focus on economics as the only organizing principle for freedom, which ignores the questions of politics and democracy and deliberation. He writes, in a distinctly Habermasian tone, that "early socialists simply ignored the entire sphere of political deliberation." The second is an assumption that the spirit of socialism already exists and is incarnated in the workers and proletariat. This produces a certain kind of fatalism and quietude. Third, Marx imposed on the project a philosophy of history that made it impossible to think about changing capitalist society gradually. This made it impossible to think about ways of reforming economic organization. As Honneth writes, "Because they were convinced that the revolution was inevitable in the near future, they saw no cognitive or political benefit in attempts at gradual change in the present."[193] Remedying each of these defects would orient critical praxis in a distinct direction.

The first birth defect, then, is the failure to see democratic popular rule and democratic politics as possible spheres of emancipation—as spaces that could provide for forms of social freedom alongside economics. Honneth locates the heart of this problem in Marx's essay *On the Jewish Question*, published in 1844, where he identifies a clear transference from political rights to economic emancipation. This placed a heavy burden on socialists throughout the ages because it meant that they could produce real transformation only based on a wide-scale "communitarian reorganization of the economic sphere." As a result, the project turned into an insurmountable hurdle of economic communitarian reorganization. This completely ignored the realm of the political as a space of freedom and reorganization, at least until after World War II, when the Social Democratic Party of Germany began to talk in earnest about "democratic socialism." This leads Honneth to articulate and develop his alternative Hegelian position—namely, "to abandon the views of socialism's founding fathers and further develop the idea of socialism by drawing on Hegel's theory of freedom."[194]

The second birth defect is the assumption that there is already an oppositional movement in existence in society that reflects socialist ideals. Marx was particularly responsible for assuming class interests, but the Frankfurt School would raise empirical doubts about this sociological fiction. The history of postindustrialization, the disappearance of the revolutionary proletariat, and the reduction of the blue-collar working class in the overall labor market would contribute to making it impossible to believe anymore in the preexistence of such revolutionary subjects. Of course, this produces a true crisis for socialism today because the fact that there is no embodiment of its ideals in a proletariat class or other actually existing movement, or in society more generally, means that socialism now is nothing more than a competing political theory. And in this, as Honneth shows, "socialism was struck to the core, for it could no longer claim to be the theoretical expression of a living movement."[195] It has effectively become nothing more than one type of normative theory, as opposed to another.

The third birth defect is the idea of the inevitability of revolution, of the coming catastrophe, of the necessary dissolution of capitalism. The major problem with this assumption is that it undermines the possibility of any experiments or reforms other than radical revolution. It devalues the role of human agency and human actions, turning them into secondary players, given that the forces of history will necessarily prevail. There's a sense in which actually, as in Joshua Clover's approach, there need not even be explicit knowledge by the actors because these events are going to happen in any case. The Frankfurt School may have mitigated some of this by offering a more limited version of historical inevitability, but it did not do away with it entirely. This may cause, in the first place, political complacency, and, in the second place, limitations on imagination and experimentation.[196]

It is lack of experimentation that, according to Honneth, produced the exclusive economic solution of replacing the market economy with a planned economy. This became a real handicap because it deprived everyone of the opportunity to experiment with other forms of economic relations to achieve social freedom. Honneth maintains that each of these three defects was essentially tied to the historical context of *industrialization*, and that it's precisely for this reason that the post–World War II period of deindustrialization coincided directly with the rapid decline of the socialist ideals.[197]

To reconstruct the idea of socialism for today's needs, Honneth proposes that we shed these three birth defects, get beyond the Marxist dogmatic assumptions and push socialism in the direction of democratic politics. In the process, he offers a much thinner vision of socialism, shorn of its Marxian philosophy of history and assumptions about the proletariat, and far more connected to the Habermasian public sphere. Socialism, for Honneth, should not be rigid, but experimental. Honneth challenges the conventional socialist utopia of a centralized planned economy. He challenges the equation of capitalism with market economy as a way to open up the possibility of alternative approaches to markets. What he is trying to do is "open[] up space for alternative uses of the market." Drawing on the ideal of more horizontal and solidaristic relations, Honneth argues that there are really three market models: first, the market model of Adam Smith; second, the idea of an "association of free producers" who govern themselves (early socialists); and third, a more democratic, deliberative process of governing the economic sphere. This last alternative is a Habermasian-inspired approach, which he describes as "citizens engag[ing] in democratic will-formation and assign[ing] to the government the task of steering and supervising the process of economic reproduction in the interest of the well-being of society." Honneth argues that we need experimentation about which of these approaches is the best, suggesting that we should not predetermine, but instead simply experiment with the market, with civil society, or with the democratic constitutional state as different ways to organize and achieve social freedom in the economic sphere. Despite all this, while Honneth wants to drop the idea of a necessary revolution and of the revolutionary proletariat, he does want to hold on to some form of historical agreement, so that socialism is not just another political theory. In this sense, Honneth writes about "historical anchoring." This is the Hegelian normative foundation of his project.[198]

Honneth advocates for various kinds of experimentation and economic initiatives. Throughout the discussion, there is a recurring return to communication as an essential part of socialism. This is captured in his idea that socialism must understand itself "as part of a historical process of liberation from dependencies and barriers to communication." Honneth argues that socialism should be thought of as a struggle for recognition—one that is associated with the French Revolution and the sentiment at that time of the need to break down barriers to communication in the economic sphere. So the notion of "communication" gains importance as the text proceeds—harking back to Habermas's theory of communicative action. Honneth also argues that socialism should avoid feeling the need to find representatives of its consciousness, as Marxists had with the proletariat. He suggests that we search instead for "the real expression of the future" in the traces of existing institutions and shifting mentalities, rather than in "the most frequent appearances of social movements."[199]

A problem with Honneth's proposal, naturally, is that he engages no practical questions. As a result, the proposal remains too contemplative. There is one passage where Honneth discusses theory versus practice. There, he derives the original relationship between theory and practice from the idea of social freedom. He argues that the original socialists believed that the engine of revolution "could already be found in the prevailing social relations," and thus the engine of revolution was already part of and present in society. As a result, he writes, "the relationship between theory and practice would consist in educating, informing or enlightening a clearly defined social group."[200] That is, in succinct form, the vanguard role of the intellectual, and it was well rehearsed in Horkheimer's 1937 article. Honneth argues that we should set that mode of the intellectual aside—based on many of the arguments discussed already. But while he is willing to set aside that model, he does not really propose one of his own. So we are left with little guidance on the new role for critical theorists.

Nevertheless, there are ways to see forward. Honneth's substantive proposal is fully consonant with a radical theory of illusions—especially his emphasis on experimentation and his willingness to reexamine economic interventions. I am troubled about his focus, in this day and age, in the West at least, on the question of social freedom, given that wealth and income inequality are such major problems in Western democracies today. I do not want to privilege material over social and cultural matters, but am not sure whether social freedom is the crux of the problem today in the spaces that Honneth privileges. It is equality, and with inequality comes the marginalization of different groups and a lack of autonomy. The two go hand in hand, naturally, but it makes little sense to privilege freedom, as Honneth does.

The result, I think, is that Honneth proposes relatively little, concretely, about how to achieve economic equality and social justice.[201] I also have concerns that opening the concept of social freedom to the democratic public sphere does not provide enough guidance. It assumes a Habermasian relationship to the public sphere that remains, in my opinion, tied to notions of reasonableness and rational argument that are out of place, especially today, with the rise of the New Right and phenomena like Brexit. To be sure, we can feel more socially included when we participate politically. That is surely a form of social freedom. But without further guidance as to how to participate politically, it tells us little. Any discussion would need to go to the next step and take on issues from the most concrete (voter suppression and disenfranchisement and how to combat those) to the most praxis-oriented (whether to occupy and how, or to form temporary autonomous zones). To gesture to the political is simply not enough.

Honneth's idea of experimentation, nevertheless, is important and confirms the argument, discussed earlier in chapters 6 and 7, that critical theory calls for constant reexamination of what it has unveiled, as well as relentless confrontation with praxis. Insofar as Honneth abandons a Marxian philosophy of history and the myths surrounding the working class and the proletariat, he pushes critical theory in the direction of a far less foundational enterprise. The need for experimentation reflects precisely the idea that there can be no fixed utopian vision. It parallels the idea of the illusion of free markets and of state-controlled economies. The idea of experimentation is very consonant with the argument in part I of this work.

At the same time, the notion of experimentation offers one way out of the perpetual dilemma between reform and revolution. One recurring argument against reform is that it might ease tension, let off steam, prevent social reality from becoming so unbearable as to trigger a real revolution. But that argument actually assumes a philosophy of history. It rests on the belief that there will be a revolution in the future. It almost buys into the Marxian and early socialist idea of the inevitability of revolution. After all, it wouldn't matter to let off steam unless it prevented the inevitable revolution. But if we no longer cling to a philosophy of history and do not believe that there will necessarily be a revolution at all, then not engaging in reformist activity means actually doing nothing, pure and simple. It means neither reforming nor contributing to a future revolution. It means no longer trying to change the world. It would be like waiting for Godot.

As a coda, in his Marc Bloch lecture at the École des hautes études en sciences sociales in Paris in June 2019, Honneth wedded the idea of socialism to more concrete practical proposals intended to realize fully the project of a more unified European Union (EU). He argued for the need for unified European socialist parties, for coordinated European radio and television, and for the requirement of a common second language for all European citizens. He also argued for the need for equality of opportunity and equality in outcomes within and among EU countries, including wealth and income outcomes; otherwise, he suggested, the citizens of the various countries will not be able to deliberate on equal footing. Finally, he made a bold proposal for a European New Deal, on the model of Franklin Delano Roosevelt's New Deal in the United States in the 1930s. He argued for a massive collective investment in infrastructure and institutions in order to guarantee equality within the context of Europe. Here, Honneth was far more policy-oriented.

Honneth reached these proposals on the basis of a historical-theoretical analysis with a distinct Hegelian dimension. Actual historical events—for the most part failures, atrocities, and crimes—bring about political resolutions to problems that allow the people, who are affected by those failures, to get past the conflicts. Honneth used four historical situations in particular. The first was the wars of religion, which he argued produced the theoretical opposition between Hobbes on the one hand and Rousseau and Kant on the other. It produced an opposition between an authoritarian sovereign, as a way to guarantee social order, and a republican or deliberative democratic solution that privileges autonomy in self-government. The second historical illustration was the exploitation of the proletariat in the eighteenth and nineteenth centuries during the Industrial Revolution. An equal failure of Europe, this crisis produced three theoretical solutions: first, the notion of class struggle and revolution, as reflected in the work of Marx and Engels; second, a more reform-oriented approach reflected in the legal regulatory structures of the administrative state, that gave rise to the welfare state in the twentieth century; and third, the theory of trickle-down economics. Here too, Honneth argued that these three competing resolutions continue to have effects in the present. The third historical catastrophe was European colonialism, which, he argued, remains unresolved today. European countries and the European public sphere still have not resolved that historical catastrophe, though it has given rise to competing approaches, as reflected in the responses of European countries faced with the influx of immigrants from Syria, the Middle East, and North Africa. The fourth catastrophe was the Holocaust, one of the worst crimes of all, Honneth maintained, which he portrayed as bringing about a continental transformation to a form of self-discipline in Europe. It is the atrocities of Nazi Germany that brought about the first attempts, in the 1950s, to create a joint market, from which there emerged European solidarity.

Honneth argued that the European Union now serves as a minimal moral standard. It represents a way to institutionalize public debate and to prevent crimes and atrocities on the Continent. European solidarity serves to prevent worse outcomes in the future. It is not civilization or success, but rather crimes, that push history, in his view. The European Union is necessary as a way to ensure that Europeans will not destroy each other. What World War II and the Holocaust brought about, he argued, is the creation of the European public sphere, a deliberative, democratic European space. He proposed that the contradictions arising out of European failure are the very source of the Continent's solidarity. Solidarity is created not because of consensus, harmony, or success, but rather conflict and social contradiction.

At a practical level, I am troubled by the way that Honneth evacuates relations of power from the formation of these historical resolutions. There is little discussion, for instance, of how France and Germany are jockeying for power within a more unified Europe, in a geopolitical confrontation with China and the United States. The analysis revolves more around ideas and public discourse than power. The issues of power and relations of power are also somewhat elided in the call for a New Deal and the analysis of the U.S. experience. Ira Katznelson has written at length about the way in which the New Deal in America was the product of the Southern states strategizing to maintain white supremacy.[202] Race and racial politics were at the heart of the New Deal, as well as, for a while, the fear of and the attraction to fascism, at least for Roosevelt. Those power struggles were elided in Honneth's discussion, with the New Deal presented as a rational and successful solution to the Depression—an odd echo of the earlier debates between Habermas and Foucault. Despite that, Honneth's proposals did not shy away from possibilities for action. On the contrary, they visualize how the idea of socialism could be tied to a political and juridical program, at least in the European context.

Judicial Lawmaking

All this raises the role of law in critical praxis. Legal transformation is certainly central to the earlier idea of the common, as well as to the idea of socialism. There, it reflects a deliberate strategy—whether, for instance, to privilege law over economics in the pursuit of the common. By contrast, there are times when there is no choice but to litigate as a form of critical praxis. A woman or man on death row or in extreme forms of solitary confinement has few other weapons at their disposal. They have their lives, which they can and sometimes do weaponize—I will discuss that shortly—but, at least in the United States, they can also litigate, file state post-conviction and federal habeas corpus challenges, and legally resist their confinement and sentence. These are critical acts aimed at emancipation and equality—at the very least, the right to equal treatment under law. The same is true for refugees seeking asylum or women exercising choice and control over their bodies.

For the lawyer as activist, litigation in court can become a form of praxis. Here, legal practice needs to be understood more broadly than just the liberal exercise of individual rights. Jack Greenberg describes the broader vision of social justice litigation under the rubric of "litigation campaigns" that produce what he calls "judicial law making."[203] He argues that lawyers can achieve through litigation what Congress can achieve through passing bills or presidents signing them into law. Litigation in the courts, he suggests, can be lawmaking when it aims at collective change.

Greenberg, a civil rights lawyer at the NAACP Legal Defense Fund who argued *Brown v. Board of Education* and other landmark cases, as well as a law professor and dean at Columbia University, had firsthand knowledge of the costs and protracted nature of litigation campaigns and their risks and failures. As he knew all too well, "a series of cases is likely to be protracted, costly, require extensive effort and be of uncertain outcome."[204] These often involve complicated questions of timing, selecting the right plaintiffs and venues for litigation, patience, and flexibility—and a sense of when and how to shift strategies.

The campaign for desegregated schools is a case in point—a decades-long campaign that started in the 1920s, involved different strategies over time, and extended into unforeseen directions, like litigation over busing. The first goal of that litigation campaign was to create physically equal—segregated but equal—facilities for whites and blacks, in part because of the *Plessy v. Ferguson* (1896) precedent, which seemed like it could not be circumvented. So the first goal of the campaign was to create physical equality, so that the schools for black children would be as good (in terms of the facility) as the schools for white children. Gradually, the strategy evolved toward making segregation too expensive for the states and counties to maintain dual, separate systems rather than having a unified school system. It then shifted to challenging segregation in higher education first, to create useful precedent there. Charles Houston, William Hastings, and Thurgood Marshall at the

NAACP Legal Defense Fund began litigating for equality in the law school setting. There were far fewer students of color applying to law schools (only three African American persons in the state of Mississippi for instance). It was thought that this would likely meet less resistance in the judiciary, having such a limited impact, but it potentially would create favorable law. This was a targeted approach that, as hoped, ended up creating favorable precedent on the question of stigma and equality, which was then used during the *Brown* litigation. That incremental approach also had value, in that it demonstrated that institutions could be desegregated without anything catastrophic happening. It contributed, ultimately, to the remarkable reversal and victory. As Justice William Brennan noted in his opinion in *NAACP v. Button* (on the question of access to the membership rolls of the NAACP): "In the context of NAACP objectives, litigation is not a technique of resolving private differences; it is a means for achieving the lawful objectives of equality of treatment by all government, federal, state, and local for the members of the [African American] community, in this country."[205]

Litigation is a form of political expression and praxis. It is not just a technique for resolving private differences. But of course, its successes can be mitigated by reactionary social change. The successes of school desegregation, for instance, were mitigated through voluntary housing segregation so that, today, in the United States, private housing choices and segregation predominantly by wealth create and maintain even more insidious forms of school segregation. They are almost more insidious because it is not the state that is enforcing segregation as a matter of law or de jure, but rather, it is the result of purportedly private choice, so it has become de facto segregation that appears far more natural. It appears as though the residential patterns are arising naturally from the free market, when in fact they are the product of a political economy that creates new forms of segregation, residential and educational, which in some cases and in some cities are even worse than what existed before. Regardless of the healthy debate over the failures, unintended consequences, and backlash against judicial decisions like *Brown*, litigation resulting in decisions like *Loving v. Virginia* in 1967 (which rendered unconstitutional miscegenation laws that prohibited interracial marriage) or *Obergefell v. Hodges* in 2015 (which constitutionalized same-sex marriage) represents stunning forms of critical praxis.[206]

Judicial lawmaking has, without doubt, an antidemocratic nature. It is a countermajoritarian act, almost by definition. This may undermine its effectiveness as a form of critical praxis. Gerald Rosenberg makes this point in his book

The Hollow Hope.[207] Rosenberg argues that the Supreme Court has far less power to change society than we tend to think it has. Rosenberg develops what is called a "constrained view of the courts," and his argument, essentially, is that the historical record reveals that it was not the Court's decision in *Brown v. Board of Education*, but rather the political will starting about ten years later, in about 1964–1965, and the civil rights legislation that Congress passed at that time, that really had the effect of undoing segregation. Rosenberg argues that judicial lawmaking is a lot less powerful and effective than we tend to think it is. There are several reasons for this, he suggests. The first is the nature of constitutional rights: these do not touch on many substantive areas of justice. While the courts have interpreted the equality principle to attach to race and gender, they have not extended it to poverty, which has limited their constitutional reach on matters of social justice. Second, the courts do not have the power to enforce their decisions, and they therefore need the cooperation of the executive branch to enforce recalcitrant parties and Congress to pass legislation. This necessarily entails negotiation and compromise. In retrospect, Rosenberg is undoubtedly correct in suggesting that the courts, when they declare rights, do not have a mechanism to change public opinion or enforce their decisions; and it is clear that, as a countermajoritarian force, judicial lawmaking will encounter significant resistance, as *Brown* did.

But those judicial decisions nevertheless affect subsequent political debate. It is not clear whether President Lyndon Johnson would have turned to the enforcement of civil rights without the declarations from the Supreme Court in the *Brown* and other decisions, nor is it clear how long it would have taken to get civil rights statutes passed into law. There are important ways in which a decision like *Brown* can serve as justification for people to argue, militate, get votes, and promote social transformation. Barring *Brown*, it is hard to imagine that would have happened in the 1960s. It is hard to imagine that, without the Supreme Court's imprimatur, without the idea that racial equality is part of the Constitution, the course of history would have been the same. I do not know how much longer it would have taken to desegregate—but I am certain it would have taken longer. Just how constrained the courts are, critics will disagree; however, there is no doubt that these Court decisions had effects and shaped political opinion even if they also can have backlashes and cause unintended consequences.

With regard to the backlash question, there is no doubt there can be unintended consequences. Paul Butler makes this argument in the context of *Gideon v. Wainwright*, which established the right to counsel in 1963. *Gideon* was the impetus for public defender systems and the appointment of counsel in felony cases. Many believe that these systems are inadequate today—and they surely are—but they have been transformative nevertheless. Butler argues, though, counterintuitively, that the process of guaranteeing the accused representation served to make us more complacent and comfortable with racialized mass incarceration. He contends that Americans would not tolerate the present levels of incarceration today if they knew that the men and women who were incarcerated did not have attorneys. In other words, the right to counsel may have facilitated racialized mass incarceration.[208] This argument has been made in the context of the death penalty as well, especially by Carol Steiker and Jordan Steiker.[209] There, the argument is that the Supreme Court's due process protections have in fact legitimated the system of capital punishment without having any real protective effect; it may even have legitimated the broader criminal justice system—I will come back to this point in chapter 18 of this book. As counterfactuals, these legitimation theories are hard to prove or to falsify. And the very same arguments can be leveled against practically all other forms of critical praxis: nonrevolutionary social movements may blunt revolutions, and revolutions may cause counterrevolutions. Once again, the only way to address these arguments properly will be in the highly situated and contextualized circumstances of unique struggles for social justice—with GPS-, date- and time-stamped analyses.

Peaceful Secession

Rather than reform or revolt, and somewhat in line with the idea of autonomous zones, some critical theorists urge peaceful secession. We have seen this strategy deployed in the Catalans recently, and also in the United States, with "Calexit" and other movements of individual states to secede from the country. The thrust here is not to create an isolated cell or commune along more insurrectional lines, but rather to redefine borders in such a way as to create a community that is more compatible with one's own critical values.

Often, the secessionist approach is insular: one region, or one state, or one people calls for secession. However, it need not be that way. One could imagine, for instance, an effort in the United States to break up the country into more politically homogenous and coherent units—in the same way in which the former Czech

Republic was broken into different countries. The idea would be for different regions of the country to all agree to govern themselves separately—in effect, to agree to disagree about the major political issues and policies of the day.

The fact is, some Americans believe deeply and earnestly in private health care, gun ownership rights, pro-life values, the death penalty, and closed borders. Other Americans believe sincerely and profoundly in universal health care, public education, gun control, unions, the right to asylum, and family choice. The cleavages between these different values and views of society may simply become too deep at some point, and citizens may decide to effectively sort themselves into two or more sovereign states based on popular referenda. One could imagine, for example, separate sovereign states in America—such as New England, the Republic of Texas, the Republic of California, the Southern States, the American Heartland, and Native Lands, among other sovereignties—and this could be a matter of popular decision-making. The underlying practice would involve creating more homogenous units, in terms of values and ideals, to approximate more rapidly a new critical horizon.

Outright Insurrection

Other critical thinkers advocate instead for a return to outright insurrection. Critical theorists, such as Giorgio Agamben and Jacques Rancière, are often associated with the anonymous collective the Invisible Committee, discussed earlier in chapters 8 and 14, which explicitly militates for insurrection in its series of books, *The Coming Insurrection* (2007), *To Our Friends* (2014), and *Now* (2017). Some commentators have suggested that the writings of the Invisible Committee, in certain passages, bear striking resemblance to those of Agamben and Rancière.

In *The Coming Insurrection*, the Committee explicitly calls for a cellular, separatist insurgency. It offers very precise prescriptions for action, including the following:

> Expect nothing from organizations. Beware of all existing social milieus, and above all, don't become one.
>
> Form communes.
>
> Get organized in order to no longer have to work.

Plunder, cultivate, fabricate.
Flee visibility. Turn anonymity into an offensive position.
Organize self-defense.
Abolish general assemblies.
Liberate territory from police occupation. If possible, avoid direct confrontation.
Take up arms. Do everything possible to make their use unnecessary. Against the army, the only victory is political.
Depose authorities at a local level.[210]

"Abolish general assemblies." The Committee signals, in no uncertain terms, that it is arguing against the recent tradition of occupations and general assemblies and advocating a far more radical posture. It goes so far as to propose a weaponized insurgency, although it is careful to emphasize that it does not fetishize armed resistance. It embraces weapons in order not to use them. The idea is that an a priori refusal to arm oneself or to handle weapons is equivalent to powerlessness. Power is achieved by having weapons, but not using them. The idea is to get to the point where it is no longer necessary to use arms because all the other strategies of unseating local authorities work. "When power is in the gutter," the Committee writes, "it's enough to walk over it."[211]

Many of the tactics that have been deployed recently in antifascist and antigovernment protests draw on these insurrectional writings. In protests in 2018 in Berkeley, Oakland, and Paris, for instance, so-called black bloc tactics were inscribed within an insurrectional frame. These tactics generally involved breaking windows, burning garbage, tires, or cars, and throwing projectiles at the police, and generally are carried out by black-clad protesters equipped with helmets, goggles, and face coverings. The tactics trace back to the squatter and other autonomist movements in Europe in the 1980s and to the World Trade Organization (WTO) protests in Seattle in 1999. In certain locations, such as Western Europe, they have become routine at protest marches. In France, protests were traditionally headed, in what was called the *cortège*, by union representatives, and they were strictly policed by union security forces. In more recent times, though, the protest marches have been preceded in what is called the *cortège de tête*, by individual protesters, including black bloc protesters, who defy the requirement to get march permits and take on law enforcement agents (national police, military gendarmes, etc.) that are policing the march. Individual protesters now also regroup in smaller clusters outside the perimeter of the permitted protest route in order to expand the space of contestation and inject the protest more into the public space. These tactics violate the protest permit and are often severely repressed by police, resulting in large-scale confrontations and arrests.

These insurrectional practices are often physically dangerous. At the 2018 May Day protests in Paris, for instance, a *cortège de tête* with hundreds of black bloc protesters encountered a police force, and the ensuing violence resulted in over 200 arrests and a handful of injuries. In some cases, the practices have led to accusations of sabotage, conspiracy, and terrorism. This was the case of the Tarnac Nine—a group of nine or ten alleged anarchists living collectively in the French rural commune of Tarnac in the Corrèze department of France and purportedly associated with the Invisible Committee—who were accused in 2008 of obstructing power cables of the high-speed railroad system in France. Those charges were ultimately dismissed; but the accusations weighed on the activists and continue to circulate. Like vanguard revolutionary practices, these insurrectional strategies may involve potentially treasonous practices that may expose individuals to incarceration, physical injury, and possibly death. In this sense, they should not be advocated lightly, especially not by armchair critical theorists. Nothing is off the table, but it is important to emphasize the risks of any strategy—as well as the trade-offs.

The Invisible Committee's latest book, *Now*, is remarkably rich in ideas and theoretical imagination. Whether one agrees or not with the overall intervention—which promotes a vision of destituent insurrection and communalist living—the work itself is chock-full of provocative, critical theoretic insights. The Committee positions itself against critique and criticism, arguing that we now live in times that explicitly value domination, and therefore the subtlety of critique is no longer required. Nevertheless, its book is filled with critique and critical theory. The Committee seeks to unmask illusions and expose how power circulates in society and how to challenge and contest that. It unveils the "illusion of unity" that has done "*its work of fooling people*," and shows that we live instead in an increasingly politically fragmented reality.[212] It sets forth a vision of critical praxis that places, at its heart, the value of action itself, for its own sake. It offers a reversal of the ends and means relation: action is not undertaken as a means toward an end, but as an end in itself. There are, to be sure, internal tensions in the book that may lead some readers to question the coherence of the intervention.[213] But it would be wrong to focus on those minor tensions; instead, it would be better to focus on the significant contributions to contemporary critical thought and praxis—four in particular.

Destituent Power: Avoiding the Counterrevolution

The central argument in *Now*, in a chapter titled "Let's Destitute the World," calls for destituent rather than constituent power: to knock down rather than reconstitute political institutions. For the Committee, the recurring problem with political action is that it always reproduces old forms of domination. Young student leaders become state ministers. Revolution turns into counterrevolution. This is what the Committee calls "the iron cage of counter-revolution": the fact that revolutionary movements always reconstitute the power relations that they first attacked.[214]

To escape the cycle, the Committee argues for a new type of power—destituent insurrections—that it presents in opposition to constituent insurrections.[215] The idea is to constantly avoid the reproduction of domination by always escaping it, exiting, disengaging. The Committee writes:

> where the "constituents" place themselves in a dialectical relation of struggle with the ruling authority in order to take possession of it, destituent logic obeys the vital need to *disengage from it*. It doesn't abandon the struggle; it *fastens on to the struggle's positivity*. It doesn't adjust itself to the movements of the adversary but to what is required for the increase of its own potential. So it has little use for criticizing.[216]

How can we understand this destituent power? Perhaps by means of a comment that the Committee makes about communism: "It's not a question of fighting *for* communism. What matters is the communism that is lived *in the fight itself*. The true richness of an action lies within itself." In other words, there has to be a reversal of the ends and means relation: as stated before, action is not undertaken as a means toward an end, but as a means in itself. This should remind us of Walter Benjamin, who, in *Critique of Violence*, imagines the possibility of violence as only a means. For their part, the Committee claims to draw inspiration from Deleuze, Guattari, and Lyotard.[217] The Committee then gives very concrete examples of what it has in mind with regard to destituent power:

- "To destitute the university is to establish, at a distance, the places of research, of education and thought, that are more vibrant and more demanding than it is—which would not be hard—and to greet the arrival of the last vigorous minds who are tired of frequenting the academic zombies, and only then to administer its death blow.

- "To destitute the judicial system is to learn to settle our disputes ourselves, applying some method to this, paralyzing its faculty of judgment and driving its henchmen from our lives.
- "To destitute medicine is to know what is good for us and what makes us sick, to rescue from the institution the passionate knowledges that survive there out of view, and never again to find oneself alone at the hospital, with one's body handed over to the artistic sovereignty of a disdainful surgeon.
- "To destitute the government is to make ourselves ungovernable. Who said anything about winning? Overcoming is everything."[218]

According to the Committee, the idea is not to attack these institutions, but to let them wither and die: "The destituent gesture does not oppose the institution. It doesn't even mount a frontal fight, it neutralizes it, empties it of its substance, then steps to the side and watches it expire. It reduces it down to the incoherent ensemble of its practices and makes decisions about them."[219]

To Build and Destroy

The destituent power combines two necessary elements, according to the Committee: a moment of separation, associated with the Latin etymology of *destituere*: "to place standing separate, raise up in isolation; to abandon; put aside, let drop, knock down; to let down, deceive"; and a moment of destruction, represented by the breaking of windows and property. The first represents the secessionist and separatist removal to the collectivity, apart from capitalism and liberal society; the second is an attack on capitalism, on private property, on consumption, on "the world of capital."[220] The first is a communalist ideal, which I will come to next; the second is a violent anarchist action.

With the first point—on separation—the Committee proposes a form of insurrectionary secession: "We mean the decision to desert, to desert the ranks, to organize, to undertake a secession, be it imperceptibly, but in any case, *now*." This secessionist element is tied to the concept of fragmentation that is so important in chapter 2, "50 Nuances of Breakage." The idea that "the world *is fragmenting*" and that "the illusion of unity can no longer *do its work of fooling people*" bolsters the impetus for secession. "The states are coming apart at the seams," we are told; and this can only reinforce the logic of secession. The Committee attributes to the *cortège de tête* a prefigurative role of secession: of the creation of an autonomous vitality separating itself from the corpse of conventional protest marches, or what they call "funeral processions."[221]

With the second point—on destruction—the Committee argues that riots afford "the paradoxical virtue of freeing us from" the anxiety that the government tries to instill in its citizens through a culture of fear. The riot, in its view, is productive and achieves value: "The organized riot is capable of producing what this society cannot create: lively and irreversible bonds." The Committee rehearses the Fanonian theme of self-transformation: "One never comes out of one's first riot unchanged... In the riot there is a production and affirmation of *friendships*, a focused configuration of the world, clear possibilities of action, means close at hand." The riot, the Committee suggests, makes the true conflict appear. It gives a face to the enemy. It has an enlightening or "incandescent" effect. "The riot is formative by virtue of what it makes visible."[222]

But the important theoretical point is that the second can be understood only as a positive thing through the lens of destitution. As the Committee says, "It's only from the destituent standpoint that one can grasp all that is incredibly constructive in the breakage." The ideal of destitution, then, brings together creation and destruction: it is "desertion and attack, creation and wrecking, and all at once, *in the same gesture*." The combination of the two is what the Committee calls "communism": "Communism is the real movement that destitutes the existing state of things."[223]

Communism

The Committee makes passing references to communism throughout the book, but then, in the final chapter, it ends on that theme. It defines "what we call 'communism'" in terms of the need for reassembling the fragmented singularities: "it's the return to earth, the end of any bringing into equivalence, the restitution of all singularities to themselves, the defeat of subsumption, of abstraction, the fact that moments, places, things, beings and animals all acquire a proper name—*their* proper name. Every creation is born of a splitting off from the whole." It is this splitting off that then brings about the potential promise of communism, which is precisely the act of relinking the fragments.[224]

It is through communalism, friendship, and love that the Committee sees a path forward. In response to the isolation of our digital existence, it urges us to leave our phones behind and come together in community: "In the face of all that, the thing to do, it would seem, is to leave home, take to the road, go meet up with others, work towards forming connections, whether conflictual, prudent, or joyful, between the different parts of the world. Organizing ourselves has never been anything else than loving each other." The Committee recognized in Nuit Debout an element of this coming together, and praised Nuit Debout for this aspect: it was, the Committee wrote, "the site of wonderful encounters, of informal conversations, of reunions after the demonstrations." But the discussion devolved into endless talk and a bureaucratic view of politics that leads nowhere. The model of peaceful general assemblies and the open discussion forum, the Committee argues, ends up becoming nothing more than a "bureaucracy of the microphone." Nuit Debout, the Committee writes, "made the misery of assemblyism not just a theoretical certainty but a shared experience."[225]

The communism that the Committee espouses in the final chapter of *Now* is one of community, love, and friendship. It involves a form of community that "nullifies all the axioms of economy and all the fine constructions of civilization." It involves a form of love of the world and of one's kindred. It involves friendship tied to fraternity in combat and equality among friends. The Committee ends *Now* precisely at the point of communism, leaving the reader there. But it is not a vision of communism as an end point or as a utopia. It is instead communism as a process of community, love, and friendship. It is a process, not a state. "For us, therefore, communism is not a finality. There is no 'transition' towards it. It *is* transition entirely: it is *en chemin*, in transit."[226] This reflects the idea of politics, expressed earlier in chapter 11, as a constant struggle, not in an instrumental way, but as an end in itself. It is in the struggle, in the destitution and destruction, in the ZAD, that we form bonds and that singularities achieve community. In the end, the vision of politics that the Committee offers is one of return and isolation in solidarity with friends and physical combat against the state and police. It is the life of the anarchist communitarian.

The Role of Critique

In the Committee's work, there is little explicit role for critical theory. There is a sense throughout that what we need is action, not critique—praxis, not *theoria*. "This world no longer needs explaining, critiquing, denouncing. We live enveloped in a fog of... critiques and critiques of critiques of critiques." The reason is that our political condition today has rendered explicit forms of domination that had previously been hidden. There are no longer any liberal veils. The gloves are off. According to the Committee, "We live in a world that has established itself *beyond any justification*. Here, criticism doesn't work, any more than satire does. Neither one has any impact."[227]

The Committee does not affirm truth as Steven Lukes or Hannah Arendt does in "Truth and Politics." Instead it takes a humble approach, suggesting that there is room to debate truth. "In what follows we don't claim in any instance to convey 'the truth' but rather the perception we have of the world, what we care about, what keeps us awake and alive," the Committee writes. "The common opinion must be rejected: truths are multiple, but untruth is one, because it is universally arrayed against the slightest truth that surfaces."[228]

The Committee remarks on the fragmentation and dissipation of traditional concepts of law's universality, and its replacement with new legal norms, centered on the law of the enemy and exceptional terrorist legislation. It focuses on a relatively obscure German legal scholar, Günther Jakobs, who, influenced by Carl Schmitt, developed a jurisprudence around the criminal law of the enemy as a different, separate sphere of legality.[229] This notion of an internal enemy that feeds the "penal law of the enemy" bears great resemblance to the notion of the internal enemy at the heart of counterinsurgency theory and of the American Counterrevolution today.

The Committee stresses throughout *Now* the urgency of the call to action and its determination: "there isn't, there's never been, and there never will be anything but now," it emphasizes. "It is the present, and hence the locus of presence. It is the moment, endlessly renewed, of the taking of sides. . . . The current disaster is like a monstrous accumulation of all the deferrals of the past, to which are added those of each day and each moment, in a continuous time slide. But life is always decided now, and now, and now." This urgency of the present and the need for action is compelling, especially as it is conjoined with such determination on their part. "The epoch belongs to the determined."[230]

There are strong Foucaultian themes throughout the text: on the courage of truth, on discipline, on civil war, on relations of power, and on the history of police in the seventeenth century. When the Committee reflects on the genealogy of the police and on the *police des grains*, they are essentially picking up on Foucault's work in *Security, Territory, Population* (which is also at the heart of *The Illusion of Free Markets*). The theme of civil war is also particularly important—and ties back to the 1973 lectures *The Punitive Society*. There is, in so many countries, the Committee writes, "a form of civil war that will no longer end." The resonance with Foucault's discussion of the matrix of civil war is hard to escape. And when the Committee writes, "All *social* relations in France are power relations," one hears a clear echo of Foucault. They even place this discussion under his sign, referring specifically to Foucault's theory of power.[231]

The Committee's enthusiasm for riots is also proximate to Joshua Clover's theory of riot prime in *Riot. Strike. Riot.* As noted earlier in the introduction to this book, Clover proposes an understanding of riots as a contemporary form of political resistance. He suggests that the history of uprisings has gone through three periods, correlating to the stages of capitalism, and that we have now entered a new period of uprisings that can be called "riot prime"—a new age of riots marked by the French riots of 2005 and 2009 in the Paris *banlieues*, the Greek riots of 2008, the London riots of 2011, the Ferguson protests and riots of 2014, and the Baltimore riots of 2015.

"Riots are coming," Clover writes. "They are already here, more are on the way, no one doubts it. They deserve an adequate theory."[232] Well, he offers one, and it resonates with the Committee. Other theorists address the form of the riot too. Candice Delmas argues, in fact, that these acts of rioting may be justified as one archetype of uncivil principled disobedience. Discussing the riots that followed the brutal police abuse of a young man named Théo L. in Aulnay-sous-Bois, outside Paris, in February 2017, and the resulting nights of violent rioting in Bobigny, Argenteuil, and Saint-Denis—including the burning of cars and tires, looting, and physical attacks on the police—she argues that those actions were morally justified, and therefore should not be punished. She says, "When uncivil disobedience is morally justified, in my view, agents ought not to be punished by the state."[233]

In the end, in light of the contemporary fragmentation of politics, the Committee advocates for the destitution of power, institutions, and the economy, to give way to a form of living in common. It calls for destituent insurrections, drawing on the historical illustrations of May 1968 and other insurrectionary communes, rather than for the recurring "constituent itch" of collectivities like Occupy Wall Street or Nuit Debout. And it does so urgently because "there will never be anything but now": "life is always decided now, and now, and now."[234]

The Committee's writings are themselves a form of communal and commune praxis in an autonomous zone. The author of the final chapter of *Now* writes poetically about sitting underneath an "old sequoia sempervirens," and then mentions their friends at work: "In this print shop dominated by an antique Heidelberg

4 Color which a friend ministers to while I prepare the pages, another friend glues, and a third one trims, to put together this little samizdat that we've all conceived, in this fervor and enthusiasm, I experience that continuity."[235] Reflecting on the sense of community and purpose that their praxis engenders, the author concludes—as I will too:

> There is no myself and the world, myself and the others, there is me and my kindred, directly in touch with this little piece of the world that I love, irreducibly. There is ample beauty in the fact of being here and nowhere else. . . . For what is friendship if not equality between friends?[236]

The Undercommons

The call for insurrection echoes in the undercommons. Stefano Harney and Fred Moten, in their masterful work *The Undercommons: Fugitive Planning & Black Study*, invite critical theorists to overcome their complacency—or what they call their "negligence"—and become truly subversive. Critique, criticism, and the critical stance within the academic setting, Harney and Moten argue, merely reproduce the forms of hierarchy and the illusions of meritocracy that lie at the root of injustice and inequality in our society. Far from undermining the problems, critical scholars create them. Harney and Moten write that, hand in hand with their more conventional colleagues (liberals and conservatives), critical scholars reinforce the structures of domination that oppress "the undercommons"—those "Maroon communities of composition teachers, mentorless graduate students, adjunct Marxist historians, out or queer management professors, state college ethnic studies departments, closed-down film programs, visa-expired Yemeni student newspaper editors, historically black college sociologists, and feminist engineers." Critical scholars reproduce a hierarchical space that is the very condition of possibility of our tiered universities, overlooking—or blindly ignoring—the living and working conditions in the undercommons. Critical scholars believe themselves to be fighting for justice and combatting the "school-to-prison pipeline," but quite the opposite is likely true: "perhaps more universities promote more jails," Harney and Moten write. "Perhaps it is necessary finally to see that the university produces incarceration as the product of its negligence."[237]

So instead of doing critique, Harney and Moten propose tearing things down. Rather than critical theory, they call for subversion, for the "subversive intellectual," in Jack Halberstam's words—the subversive intellectual who is "unprofessional, uncollegial, passionate, and disloyal."[238] Subversion is key. Deviance is central. Harney talks about "hacking concepts and squatting terms."[239] The goal is to break down and break up, to shatter the institutions that reproduce privilege; and not just to abolish those institutions, but to dismantle the very society that makes those institutions possible. "Not so much the abolition of prisons," Harney and Moten write, "but the abolition of a society that could have prisons, that could have slavery, that could have the wage, and therefore not abolition as the elimination of anything but abolition as the founding of a new society."[240]

To dismantle, to destitute, to abolish: these are the verbs of the undercommons. As Halberstam writes:

> we refuse to ask for recognition and instead we want to take apart, dismantle, tear down the structure that, right now, limits our ability to find each other, to see beyond it and to access the places that we know lie outside its walls. We cannot say what new structures will replace the ones we live with yet, because once we have torn shit down, we will inevitably see more and see differently and feel a new sense of wanting and being and becoming.[241]

Here, we are close to the destitution of institutions that the Invisible Committee calls for in *Now*—as Halberstam underscores as well. The Committee speaks of destituting the university, the judicial system, medicine, and the government—and making ourselves "ungovernable" in the process. The Committee writes, in similar terms as Harney and Moten, about not just abolishing institutions, but abolishing the society that needs them: "To destitute is not primarily to attack the institution, but to attack the need we have of it," it declares in *Now*. "It's not to criticize it . . . [but] to administer its death blow." The Committee also does not spare critics or militants, stating that "the more they criticize power, the more they desire it and the more they refuse to acknowledge their desire."[242]

The undercommons is a space of disorder, of wildness, of improvisation. It is a space of radical resistance and contestation—and tearing down. A space of refusal. It bears a resemblance, Moten and Harney suggest, to the idea of communism.[243] It deviates. It is deviant. It is close to what I called, in an earlier piece, the politics of spleen.[244]

Moten and Harney's *The Undercommons* cuts to the quick. It places a mirror up to critical thinkers and forces us to examine our own role, as professors, as graduate students, as undergraduates—especially at elite institutions—in perpetuating and reproducing the structures of domination that make possible a society that enslaves or incarcerates en masse. There is no point in sugarcoating their intervention. The professionalized critical scholar is nothing less than a counterrevolutionary in their view. Moten and Harney write:

> A professional education has become a critical education. But one should not applaud this fact. It should be taken for what it is, not progress in the professional schools, not cohabitation with the Universitas, but counterinsurgency, the refounding terrorism of law, coming for the discredited, for those who refuse to write off or write up the undercommons.[245]

We are back at the counterrevolution—but this time, the counterrevolutionary is the critical scholar. And in response, Harney and Moten propose stealing and dismissing: "if the critical academic is merely a professional, why spend so much time on him? Why not just steal his books one morning and give them to deregistered students in a closed-down and beery student bar, where the seminar on burrowing and borrowing takes place. Yet we must speak of these critical academics because negligence, it turns out, is a major crime of state."[246]

The element of pure deconstruction, of radical dismantling, is both appealing and troubling. How else could we possibly—ethically, honestly—deal with the gross injustices that surround us but to tear it all down? How can those in the undercommons recover psychologically, but by tearing it all down? Fanon surely had it right: violent dismantling is necessary. It is cathartic. It brings about a new beginning, a new human. And we cannot know what will come after this, or what ideals and institutions we shall have. The act of destruction itself is liberating. Plus, there is value in the opposition itself, in the struggle against domination, in the constant effort to resist the hegemonic or dominant class. That is the energy of the politics of spleen. It is the limit experience, living in the garret or the undercommons—living on the edge, creating a subculture, and not being constrained by the convention.

Incrementalism, reformism, working within the system, using the master's tools—those are mind-numbing. And they coopt. Power corrupts. When one works from the inside, one starts to see what that inside power can get—what it tastes like, how it feels—and one slowly becomes less radical. Injustices seem less stark or compelling. A little power tastes good, one becomes soft. Plus, how can we talk about a just society when we are embedded in this one and have so fully internalized its values and assumptions?

There have been acts of dismantling: tearing down the Berlin Wall without having a clear plan of where that would lead East Germans; tearing down the Bastille before knowing what that would entail, or what would follow monarchy. These are leaps into the void. They may be necessary. They may be dangerous. It is that danger that attracts some but worries others—even those who are inclined to agree with the underlying praxis. As Steve Sawyer asks in conversation, "If we tear institutions down, do we just give way to the bully with the biggest stick?" You might respond, "Can it get any worse? For someone sitting in the undercommons today, what is there to wait for?" And how can we even ask anyone to wait? We cannot be patient about the undercommons—we might not live to see the proper moment to contest. But can it get worse? Perhaps. It surely did at various times in the twentieth century. Can we be sure that there are no better models readily available that we could try to transpose? Are there other university systems in other countries that try to avoid such severe hierarchies and rankings, that try to place all institutions at the same level (so that the degree from one might be equivalent to that of any other university in the country), that try to maintain free higher education, and try to reduce disparities between professorial ranks or try to treat instructors in equitable ways? Could we imagine a reconstructed university that treats all its instructors fairly as civil servants and strives to have a unified system, without hierarchies or rankings? Are there existing models of medical or judicial systems, or of forms of governing that avoid the undercommons? If the answer is no, then perhaps, with Harney and Moten, we may need to tear down before knowing what comes next: times of extreme crisis may call for extreme action.

Weaponizing Life

In her book *Starve and Immolate: The Politics of Human Weapons*, Banu Bargu details another form of extreme action: forms of resistance undertaken by political prisoners in Turkey and Ireland, as well as by others in desperate situations around the globe, including such self-destructive acts as the hunger strike, the fast to death, self-mutilation, self-immolation. Bargu refers to these practices as *the weaponization of life*, and she draws on Foucault's notion of biopolitics, and more broadly, on his analyses of various forms of power (sovereignty, discipline, security), in order to describe and diagnose the power relations within which these practices are embedded. These often include solitary confinement in supermax prisons and other forms of hypercoercive or marginalizing conditions. Bargu characterizes these political situations as *biosovereignty*, a contradictory amalgam of early modern conceptions of sovereignty and of Foucaultian biopolitics, but empowered and augmented by the very interaction between the two. And in reaction to this biosovereignty, Bargu identifies the weaponization of life as a new form of resistance—what she calls *necroresistance*. Her book navigates between the two. It is located in the space where "the *biopoliticization of sovereignty* meets the *necropoliticization of resistance*."[247]

The weaponization of life entails the militant turning his or her life into a political weapon of struggle. The practices range from death fasts and self-immolation (which were practiced in Turkish prisons from 2000 to 2007—the focus of Bargu's case study—and continue today)[248] to other forms of self-mutilation and suicide attacks. These practices have a long history, going back to the Russian anarchists who engaged in hunger strikes in the late nineteenth and early twentieth centuries; the suffragette hunger strikes in Great Britain in 1909 and thereafter, and in the United States in 1917; the Buddhist monks in South Vietnam who practiced self-immolation during the 1960s; the 1981 hunger strikes of Irish republican prisoners, including Bobby Sands; the 2013 prisoner hunger strikes at Pelican Bay State Prison in California—and, of course, the several hunger strikes of Mahatma Gandhi.

Bargu brings together these various types of practices and provides a full articulation and description of them:

> As a tactic, the weaponization of life encompasses a series of practices that range from varieties of nonlethal self-mutilation (which include forms of amputation, maiming, infection with disease, sewing of eyes and mouth, temporary starvation, all inflicted by and upon oneself) to the more fatal actions of self-immolation (understood as setting oneself on fire), temporally indefinite hunger strikes, fasts unto death, self-killing (through a variety of methods including hanging, drinking pesticide, slitting wrists, overdosing on medication, and swallowing cyanide capsules), and forms of suicide attack (involving, again, different forms of actions such as the detonation of bombs strapped upon the body, driving a loaded vehicle into a target to induce explosion, participation in military assaults with no chance of survival, and so on).[249]

These forms of praxis, Bargu suggests, are at first blush almost inexplicable—too extreme, too demanding, too severe—given the political stakes, even the extraordinary political stakes of solitary confinement and punitive excess. As she writes, "The ends simply did not seem to measure up to the means." But ultimately, Bargu makes sense of these practices by rethinking and reformulating our categories of power. Her objective—and ours as well, I should think—is not to judge these acts of courage and sacrifice, but to understand them and what they reveal about our present. As Bargu says, "Not to excuse or justify human weapons, nor to condemn or vilify them, but to reckon with them; to engage, earnestly and critically, with their intervention into politics."[250]

In bringing together these weaponized forms of resistance, Banu Bargu lays out for us another type of critical praxis: one that is extreme. They are often associated with deeply asymmetric relations of power. They involve profound forms of self-sacrifice. They often rest on very different logics and rationales—with Gandhi, for instance, opposed to fasting when it entails a form of moral coercion or blackmail against the state. And they are often associated with an ethical, or even theological, dimension in their proximity to penance and sacrifice of self. The dangers are, naturally, self-evident. But these are situations, one has to believe, in which this form of praxis may feel like the only possible way to resist power.

Sacrifice and Penitence

The sacrificial dimension of some of these practices of the self sometimes bears a resemblance to forms of penitence. There is a sense in which Bruno Latour also ends here, in his book *Down to Earth: Politics in the New Climatic Regime*, in a practice of penance—though far less self-destructive. Latour calls for recognition and confession of one's own faults (here, Europe's exploitation of nature and colonies), and leading by example. Telling and retelling the truth of climate change are not the solution, Latour suggests. Imposing the facts of global warming will not help. The reason is that facts alone are ineffective. They require trust first. And trust, he contends, has vanished today. As a result, praxis does not call for better or more reporting, more facts, or more studies. Rather, it calls for practices of the self that address the deficit in trust today—for acts that rebuild our shared practices and common world.

The answer is not to simply reimpose the norms and institutions from the past, Latour argues. Those political and disciplinary norms—of liberal tolerance, for instance—went hand in hand with Western exploitation of others. He does not seek a return to a past of normalized politics, but rather a dramatic confessional push forward. And this begins, for him, through confession, penance, and example. In this, there is a strongly monastic dimension to the final chapters of *Down to Earth.* The orientation of praxis has a distinct spiritual valence. It is penitence that Latour is after. His points are as follows:

- Europe must confess its guilt: "Continental Europe is said to have committed the sin of ethnocentrism and to have claimed to dominate the world, and therefore it has to be 'provincialized' to bring it down to size."
- Europe must be humble and honest: "Europe, because of its history, has to plunge in first because it was the first to be responsible."
- Europe must lead by example: "[Europe] can no longer claim to dictate the world order, but it can offer an example of what it means to rediscover inhabitable ground."[251]

"Europe, that Old Continent, has changed its geopolitics" since Brexit and Donald Trump's election in the United States, Latour writes. Now "Europe is alone, it is true, but only Europe can pick up the thread of its own history." Europe's past is its strength—bureaucratic, managerial, and ready to be provincialized. It must seize those strengths and seek penance. It must seek that "*second chance that it in no way deserved.*"[252] Confession. Penance. Mercy. Those are the spaces where Bruno Latour ultimately lands.

Polyvalent Approaches

And then, other critical theorists embrace polyvalent forms of resistance—finding allies and embracing various strategies, but not privileging one approach over others. In the face of newly empowered far-right movements and their constant attacks on minorities—from Muslims, to #BlackLivesMatter activists, to refugees and immigrants, to trans* persons—multiple forms of resistance may be necessary and none, perhaps, should be off the table. Form assemblies and jam the system. Be insurrectional and secessionist. Litigate to enjoin the Muslim ban, occupy and assemble, canvass areas, and protest. These may all be important strategies, depending on the specific time and location, and there may be no reason to exclude any of them or take any off the table. As Robin D. G. Kelley argues, there is virtue to employing a diversity of strategies and tactics. "Sometimes we confront power directly," he notes, but "other times, we struggle to build power where we are—through collectives, mutual aid, community economic development, and the like."[253]

Talal Asad argues for more polyvalent forms of political engagement that contest authority at different levels, or, in his words, that "address numerous overlapping bodies and territories."[254] Asad is discussing slightly different questions, but his analysis is perfectly pertinent. Taking polyvalent approaches means not always seeing conflict and aiming resistance at the same target. Asad reminds us of the remark that Foucault made in the context of the Iranian Revolution: "Concerning the expression 'Islamic government,' why cast immediate suspicion on the adjective 'Islamic'? The word 'government' suffices, in itself, to awaken vigilance."[255] It is vigilance across the board that would be called for—without any specific privilege. It must involve multiple strategies of resistance at different levels. Here, then, are Asad's words:

> The idea of numerous nonhierarchical domains of normativity opens up the possibility of a very different kind of politics—and policies—that would always have to address numerous overlapping bodies and territories. Procedures to deal with differences and disagreements would include civil pressure directed against authorities, such as civil disobedience, to make officeholders accountable. . . . The tradition of *amr bi-l-ma'ruf* could form an orientation of mutual care of the self, based on the principle of friendship (and therefore of responsibility to and between friends) not on the legal principle of citizenship. . . . The same tradition might find its way to collective acts of protest against excessive power (and so there have to be notions of power's temporalities and bounds). . . . The risk of a military force being formed to create an exclusive territorial body would have to be met not merely by constitutional barriers but also by the work of tradition in the formation, maintenance, and repair of selves who are bonded to one another.[256]

A range of critical praxis may well be called for—from political disobedience and care of the self, to collective acts of protest and constitutional litigation. In the situated context of struggle, the answer may be to deploy various combinations of these critical practices.

As critical theorists today, then, we face a wide array of possible practices. We are no longer bound only by class struggle and revolution—although those too should not be off the table. The questions become: How do we, critical theorists, move forward? And how do we overcome the philosophical resistance to the action imperative? The answer must be to confront forms of critical praxis with critical theory—and vice versa—as I have tried to do in this chapter. Amy Allen argues, in *The End of Progress*, that the "truly critical," in her words, is "to engage in the ongoing self-clarification of the struggles and wishes of our postcolonial—by which I mean formally decolonized but still neocolonial—age."[257] Seyla Benhabib reminds us that we also need a proper understanding of present crisis tendencies. "Critical theory must also be a theory of crises," she emphasizes—in addition, that is, to a theory of emancipation.[258] Judith Butler emphasizes the need to reflect and not rush into action.[259] And to be sure, we need self-understanding, better analyses of the crisis moment, and reflection on praxis. But all of these must be combined with a more sustained confrontation of praxis and theory. We need to return to the heart and ambition of critical philosophy: namely, not just interpret the world, but change it. And that will call for sustained attention to the action imperative.

When one goes back to the debates of the 1960s and the multiplicity of factions, cells, and groupuscules, one is inundated with terms that today most people cannot even recognize. When Castoriadis was describing how his party, Socialism or Barbarism, was constituted in 1946, and at whom it was targeted—especially its journal by that name, started in March 1949—he explained that "the main audience of the group and of the journal was formed by groups of the old, radical left: Bordigists, council communists, some anarchists and some offspring of the German 'left' of the 1920s."[260] Many of us critical theorists would not even recognize those terms today—the variety of situated, engaged, praxis-oriented interventions, groups, communities. There was, at the time, such a battle over critical praxis, and such deep commitments. We need to renew that energy and refocus critical philosophy on its core: critical praxis.

Today, there are a wide range of modalities of contemporary critical praxis, from the left populism of Mouffe to theories of assembly with Butler, Hardt, and Negri; to the idea of a common; to the radical anarchist separatism of the Invisible Committee and the explosive undercommons of Harney and Moten; to electoral and parliamentary politics; to vanguard revolution; and to the weaponization of life. There is a remarkable and varied space of praxis. The question is: how should critical theorists and practitioners then engage this new space of critical praxis?

CHAPTER 16

The New Space of Critical Praxis

At this point, it is time to put all this together. As I argued in part II, our political condition is one of endless struggle: a constant and unending battle to distribute resources equally and fairly, with no illusion of stability or equilibrium. The struggle is unavoidably violent. There is no way around that. Seeking change in society—just like maintaining the status quo—is necessarily violent in the sense that it imposes values on others who may not share the same ideals. It inevitably entails redistribution. It will affect ownership, rights, and possession. It implicates educational, societal, and personal transformations. These are all violent effects if we properly understand violence and are honest with ourselves.

Revolutions are inevitably violent. The same is true with uprisings. But social transformation more generally is violent as well. Even Gandhian *satyagraha* is violent when we realize what it would entail emotionally for our children, families, and loved ones. Some practices are not *physically* violent—like Occupy Wall Street—but they are equally violent in trying to transform distributions of wealth and well-being. There is, however, no reason or need to valorize the violence of critical praxis. There is no reason to create justifications that embolden the violence—no reason to seek out or accentuate the violence. On the contrary, there is every reason to try to minimize and devalue violence and to do our best to distribute it equitably, so no one group or individual suffers the brunt of societal change.

In the end, it is far too simplistic to draw the line of critical praxis at *physical* violence, first, because the enforcement of any kind of distributional rules will require the threat or application of force (as it does in capitalist regimes through, for instance, the criminal enforcement of trespass laws), and second, because the line of physical violence is a liberal illusion that masks the structural violence that pervades social relations. Naturally, physical violence *is* a powerful signifier. There is no doubt about that. The sight of German shepherds attacking peaceful civil rights protesters in the South in the 1960s galvanized public opinion. The sight of police officers pepper-spraying peaceful Occupiers, or of militarized SWAT teams confronting peaceful protesters—those images galvanize political opinion. Inversely, peaceful civil disobedience, as opposed to black bloc tactics, will have effects of reality, and vice versa.

Instead of drawing overly simplistic lines, the path forward should seek to devalorize violence and distribute it equitably. No one individual or group should bear the concentrated weight of social transformation. No single individual should feel the brunt of critical praxis. The weight of social change should fall on everyone equitably. It should not be concentrated. Ultimately, this is an ethical question—perhaps the most important ethical question: critical praxis should be conducted carefully and hesitantly, with respect, care, humility, and thoughtfulness; not with glee or delight, but instead always conscious of the harm it distributes, vigilant and watchful of not exceeding what is strictly necessary. Praxis should not be targeted at particular individuals or groups, but rather equitably distributed across society and classes. As an ethical matter, we should avoid strategies that concentrate, rather than distribute, the burdens of political transformation.

It would be nice to imagine that violence would ultimately recede—or that, in a more equitable society, there would be less need for social transformation and redistribution, and thus less need for violence. It would be lovely to imagine a society where there is greater equality and opportunity for all, and therefore less interpersonal struggle. To imagine a society where equality itself limits the extent of violence, a world where the wealth disparities are not so sharp, where there is good public education and health care—and as a result less need for social change. If we achieved such a world, wouldn't there be less violent struggle between individuals? Yes, that would be nice to imagine. But this too is another illusion—and a dangerous one. It might justify more violence today to achieve a less violent society in the future. That is usually how illusions work. We must let that one go, too.

Rethinking Critical Praxis

What this entails for critical praxis is a careful, respectful, contextual, case-by-case analysis of our political struggles that responds to the exact situation and the actually existing political economic regimes in which we, critical theorists, find ourselves. There can be no generalized theory of nonviolence or self-sacrifice, or for that matter of leaderlessness, or of a vanguard party, or of Revolution. Every critical practice has to be precisely designed for the specific time and space, with humility and care. Here too, we need to resist foundations and universalizations that may be entirely inapplicable in different geopolitical or temporal contexts.

In effect, in the same way in which critical values should be understood through a contextual lens, with humility, as Amy Allen reminds us, critical praxis must also be deeply situated in time and space, and careful. The idea of portability in critical praxis makes no sense. A hunger strike or self-sacrifice would likely not have worked in 1936 Germany—and Gandhi's writings advocating that approach were simply off the mark in that regard. The idea of generalizing from one situated political context to another is dangerous. An armed vanguard revolutionary movement in the United States today, for example, would get crushed. The disproportionality in weaponry and technology, in the face of American military might, is estopping. This may not have been the case in Russia in 1917, nor in China in 1948, but in the United States today, the asymmetries and imbalances are far too overwhelming to expect any type of armed uprising to succeed. That is why the American New Right, for instance, has engaged in a protracted cultural and populist revolution, rather than an armed revolt (for the most part, at least, so far).

It is important to recognize that all social movements and tactics are inevitably situated. Political disobedience of the type manifested in Occupy Wall Street—which many of us, myself included, had perhaps erroneously interpreted as apolitical or outside politics—was in fact deeply ensconced within the political-historical moment of a centrist Democratic administration. Occupy was effectively pushing, or trying to push, President Barack Obama to the left—a model that may be totally inappropriate under another presidential regime. The Occupy movement made sense and was tactically sophisticated during the Obama administration, but it would make no sense under a Trump presidency. The model of the *Groupe d'information sur les prisons* (GIP) may have been effective, insofar as it was, under a repressive Gaullist regime. But again, one can hardly imagine it being effective in times of open and blatant punitiveness such as today.

Critical praxis is inevitably situated and calls for specific, contextual assessment and discussion. It should not come as a surprise that Lenin's "What Is To Be Done?" is precisely such a detailed tract. It is not ageless. It is not portable. It is a historical artifact. That is what our critical praxis should aspire to: winning a struggle and then becoming a historical artifact that may not be replicable.

In *Assembly*, Michael Hardt and Antonio Negri draw a distinction between strategies and tactics: strategies, or the broader goals of the movement, they argue, should be decided by the assembled multitude, by the people. In contrast, shorter-term and more localized tactics should be designed by the movement leaders. In this way, Hardt and Negri try to accommodate the newfound desire for leaderlessness with the reality (or at least their idea of the reality) of social movements. They propose an illuminating distinction, even if it may need to be reformulated. Critical philosophy does set the overarching critical values, so the critical horizon is indeed determined by the collectivity through debate and exchange; but the medium-term strategies and short-term tactics are ultimately decided by critical actors on the ground, and in that sense, they are inevitably left to the critical practitioners who know better the field of action and who situate their praxis accordingly.

There is a deep contextual element to critical praxis, as there is to critical values: our political interventions are situated in time and place. In fact, I am not sure I would be writing or publishing this book in a different political situation. My own interventions—including my work on the illusion of order and the myth of free markets—are situated. I could well imagine a political context where I would advance different arguments. That is the essence of critical thought. It is not universalizing or generalizable. It is not absolute in this sense. It does not allow the universalization of our maxims.

It is imperative to avoid collapsing things or being too reductionist or simplistic. Despite the pervasiveness of violence and the continuity between physical and systemic violence, it is important to remain careful about the exercise of power and the distributional effects of critical praxis. Just because political action is inherently violent does not mean that anyone should turn a blind eye to the harm of physical violence, rush to cause needless harm, or enjoy it. On the contrary, it means that people should be careful, respectful, humble, and deliberate, and minimize and devalue the violence, not value it—and certainly not inflate it.

I ended *The Counterrevolution* hand in hand with William of Ockham during the Inquisition, drawing inspiration from his struggles against despotic power. That was not an accident. Ockham well understood the imperative to limit things to what was absolutely necessary. That was the essence of Ockham's razor: not to engage in the unnecessary, not to compound beyond necessity. But at the same time,

Ockham recognized acutely the need to resist, to struggle, and to contradict. That is our human condition—a constant, consuming, and unending struggle. There is no equilibrium, remember. There is no end of history. There is just a constant battle over distributions in society. I ended with Ockham to emphasize that our task will not end, that we are part of a relentless struggle—but that we should be careful not to exceed what is strictly necessary. Neither we, nor others, nor the state should act more than is necessary, and this especially applies to the use of force. As Ockham reminded us: "Subjects should be warned not to be subjugated more than is strictly necessary."[1]

The paradigm for critical praxis, then, is not to embrace an abstract form or style of action generically—occupation, insurgency, hunger strike, Jacobin-Leninism, and so on—but rather to discover, in each unique context and *en situation*, the best method to counter the forces that push us toward servitude and inequality. The key is to *counter*, once again, but the goal must be to get past its reactivity so as to produce a constant, autonomous forward movement of critical practice.

In terms of method, then, critical theory and critical praxis should constantly confront each other—as the Movement for Black Lives has done in rejecting a politics of respectability, and as Occupy Wall Street did in challenging ordinary politics and prefiguring new forms of democracy. That is, after all, the point of infinitely testing and revaluing our beliefs and material conditions: to ensure that we are not deluding ourselves again, to test our critical praxis against our *theoria* with the blows of a hammer. In the end, critical praxis calls for constant reminders:

First, there are no universals. Actions have to be judged in context, *en situation*, and nothing should be off the table. Desperate times may call for desperate acts, but different times will call for different praxes. Physical violence might well be called for in a colonial setting, as Fanon did. It may be appropriate in the form of riots at other historical and geopolitical points, as Clover suggests. But in other discrete contexts, in the current social media age, it may not be advised—naturally, this would need to be evaluated closely and contextualized. Physical violence may backfire if the traditional media pounces on it out of commercial self-interest, and the footage goes viral. That happened early on in Hong Kong in 2019, during protests against proposed legislation allowing for the extradition of accused persons to China. It happened in France, in 2018 and 2019, during the Yellow Vest movement, and during the Antifa protests in California in 2017. In certain contexts, violence may deprive critical actors of the moral high ground. But all these questions would need to be evaluated, in each context, on the ground.

In this respect, although I may not subscribe to the justificatory analysis that Candice Delmas proposes in her book *A Duty to Resist*, I nevertheless come out in a similar place on the use of violence. In the context of Antifa violence, Delmas emphasizes that Antifa activism has probably saved lives, as an empirical matter. Delmas recounts the experience of Cornel West, who was scheduled to give a sermon in Charlottesville, Virginia, on the day of the infamous "Unite the Right" rally in August 2017, and, the next day, found himself and twenty others (many clergy) surrounded by white nationalists, without police protection. Had it not been for about 300–350 anarchists and antifascists, West recalls, "we would have been crushed like cockroaches . . . We would have been completely crushed."[2] Delmas analyzes the justifications for the use of violence, especially as a form of collective self-defense, and ends up arguing that, although it may be better to avoid violence and use nonviolent means, physical violence should not be taken off the table. "The bottom line," Delmas writes, "is that, amid a surge of hate groups, we shouldn't wholesale reject antifa tactics. Instead we need to think carefully about their justifications and whether the combination of justification and action passes the test of political obligation."[3] That may not be my discourse exactly. I prefer to speak in the language of strategy rather than justification. But I end up essentially in a similar place as Delmas.

Second, when considering various tactics—hunger strike, occupation, electoral mobilization, litigation, insurrection, and others—there are, again, no universals. Different forms will function in different contexts. As stated previously, Occupy Wall Street may have functioned in the setting of the Obama administration, but it would not under a Trump presidency. There is a need for *situated* intervention. That being said, there is a need for constant insubordination: the struggle is unending and has to be considered as a permanent pushback against the forces of tyranny and inequity. The paradigm should be a constant countering, where the countermove ends up achieving autonomy so that it is no longer merely reacting to the opponent, but instead becomes a powerful moving force. It must become an autonomous political form: a constant countering that overcomes its own reactivity to become a force of its own.

Third, we need to resist foundational thinking and adamantly overcome the hegemonic ideas we oppose. The deceit of hegemonic ideas is that we begin to believe and internalize them. That's true of the neoliberal ideas of market efficiency. It is equally true of counterinsurgency governmentality. We begin to think that the masses are passive and can be swayed one way or the other; or that there is only a small minority that is prepared to actively resist—or a small guardian class that is maintaining an oppressive system. Part of what makes these ideas so powerful is that we begin to absorb them, to internalize them in our own thinking about how to resist. We begin to believe them or stop asking questions. But they are just illusions: the myth of natural orderliness in economics that has come down to us from the divine order of the first economists; the delusion of an economic sphere that is somehow self-regulated; the illusion of an insurrection, of a small, active minority ready to sway the passive masses. These are all illusions. The "passive masses": nothing could be further from the truth. That counterrevolutionary vision of society—of a tripartite division of society, with the passive masses in the middle—is pure fiction. It is far too simplistic and misleading. The masses have never been passive. And they are not passive today. They know what they want, and they know what they are doing. When they are quiet, they tolerate. They might tolerate because they are scared, because they think the alternative would be worse, or because they have been taught to tolerate. But they do not tolerate because they are inherently passive. Whether in an authoritarian or democratic regime, the political system always depends on the authorization and legitimacy of the people. What Gandhi made clear through his inspiring acts of nonviolent resistance is that a regime—even an oppressive regime that wields all the military force—cannot survive if it does not have the backing or support of the citizens.

In the end, critical theory cannot dictate a critical praxis—no more than critical praxis can dictate critical theory. The relationship between theory and praxis is not one of implications or applications, but of confrontation, in order for each one to test the other with a sounding hammer.

Reformulating the Praxis Imperative

Critical theory itself, therefore, cannot answer the question "What is to be done?" There is no unidirectionality from critical theory to praxis. There has to be a confrontation of praxis and theory. This confrontation must occur *en situation*—located precisely in space and time. Theory cannot dictate to others what to do. It can only confront one's own praxis.

As a result, the traditional question of critical praxis—namely, "What is to be done?"—needs to be reformulated so that it does not police others, so that it does not ask for your papers, as Adorno said, so that it does not dominate others. The praxis imperative should not reenact forms of social hierarchy. It should not silence some or re-create other traditional forms of privilege. It should not contribute to the suppression of voices. Instead of declaring to others what is to be done or what they should do, the action imperative has to be reformulated.

But that task itself—the task of reformulating the very question "What is to be done?"—must remain open to all critical theorists. Each and every critical theorist should have the opportunity to reformulate it themselves (or not). The task of reformulating, no more than the action imperative itself, must not silence any voice or privilege any voice. Everyone should address it so that no single person seizes the ground or takes up too much space.

For myself, rather than ask, "What is to be done?" I will turn the question on myself and ask: What am I doing, what more am I to do, and how are my actions working? This idea is not new—even if it is always overdue.

Colliding Theory and Praxis: A Model

In the early 1970s, Michel Foucault took part in a prison resistance movement and worked with others to organize the GIP. Rather than tell others what was to be done, Foucault began by asking himself about his own critical praxis. This would lead to an entirely different practice, in which the GIP tried to create a space where those who were most affected by prisons could speak and be heard. The experiment served to reframe the praxis question. It also demonstrates the way in which critical theory and praxis could productively confront each other. In effect, the GIP offers a window into the fifth model of the relation between theory and praxis discussed in the introduction to this book: the model of contradiction and confrontation, of the CERN Large Hadron Collider.

The form that Foucault's political action took was the direct product of his confronting critical praxis with critical theory. At the same time, his critical praxis would fundamentally confront and reshape his philosophical work. The confrontation of theory and practice was utterly remarkable—and extremely instructive as a critical model. Specifically, the form, structure, and practices of the GIP were a deliberate result of critical confrontations with the praxis of popular tribunals and political prisoner status, which Maoist activists were advocating at the time. Some historical background will help.

Following the student and worker uprisings of May 1968, the French government cracked down on nonparliamentary political organizations. What followed was the massive arrest of several hundred Maoist militants and their detention in French prisons. The Maoist political organization *La Gauche prolétarienne* demanded at first that the prisoners receive political prisoner status. Danielle Rancière and Daniel Defert asked Foucault to conduct a popular tribunal to air these grievances—on the model of the popular tribunal that Jean-Paul Sartre had just conducted in northern France against mining magnates. Foucault agreed to participate, but in a different way, confronting these forms of praxis with discourse theory. After much discussion among a number of intellectuals, the GIP emerged on the model of a discursive intervention: it would be a vehicle to allow discourses to be heard, a way to allow prisoners, whose voices were still inaudible, to become audible. The GIP was imagined in direct opposition to popular tribunals, in part (at least for Foucault) as a result of his theoretical work in *The Archaeology of Knowledge*. To see this, one need only examine the following three dimensions of the GIP.

First, by contrast to alternative forms of engagement, such as a formal commission of inquiry or a popular tribunal (originally proposed and extensively debated with other Maoists)[4], the GIP was organized so as to allow incarcerated persons to be heard—rather than be spoken for. This involved a number of subelements, including:

- *The (relative) anonymity of the organizers*: Rather than have a named and appointed spokesperson, along the model of Sartre as prosecutor and judge of a popular tribunal, the effort went toward diffusing authority and avoiding designated speakers. Still today, few of the central figures are known—Danielle Rancière, Christine Martineau, Jacques Donzelot, and Jean-Claude Passeron would all be participants, working on the original survey, but they remain somewhat anonymous.[5] Domenach, Foucault, and Vidal-Naquet signed the original manifesto, but practically all the other communiqués were unnamed, signed generically by the GIP.
- *The leaderlessness of the organization*: Insofar as the objective was to make it possible to hear the incarcerated persons and their families, rather than to speak

on their behalf, there was a concerted effort not to identify or allow leadership positions within the GIP.

• *The choice not to say what to do, but to allow the voices of the prisoners to be heard*: As the GIP manifesto declared, "It is not for us to suggest reform. We merely wish to know the reality. And to make it known almost immediately, almost overnight, because time is short."[6] The effort throughout was "about letting speak those who have an experience of prison."[7]

Second, by contrast to the original impetus of the *Gauche prolétarienne*, the GIP challenged the distinction between political and common-law prisoners. Whereas at first the Maoist militants attempted to obtain political prisoner status for their colleagues,[8] the GIP took the position that *all* prisoners were political prisoners: that the prison and the penal system were political institutions. This confrontation also was in continuity with Foucault's critical theory of penal law. It intersected with his 1972 lectures, *Penal Theories and Institutions*, where Foucault had developed a political theory of penal law. One can see how this affected the praxis of the GIP from the initial manifesto onward, where the object of the political intervention became the prison *tout court*, not the detention of militants only, or of political prisoners.[9]

Finally, the GIP intervention ended at the moment of the creation of an autonomous—actually the first—organization of and for prisoners, the *Comité d'action des prisonniers* (CAP). The central mission of the GIP (namely, creating the conditions of possibility so that the voices of the incarcerated could be heard) was achieved when the prisoners formed their own association—thereby triggering, with elegance, the dissolution of the GIP.

In this sense, the unique praxis of the GIP emerged from the conflict of earlier practices with discourse analysis, more specifically with Foucault's writings ranging from the *History of Madness* to *The Archaeology of Knowledge* to *The Order of Discourse*. As Foucault himself confided to Daniel Defert, his involvement in the GIP was, in his words, "*dans le droit fil de l'Histoire de la folie*" ("in a straight line emanating from *The History of Madness*").[10] Foucault's interventions on the prison consisted of direct dialogue and constructive tension with his lectures at the Collège de France. Foucault explored at the Collège the ways in which societies used legal forms to produce truth. Reading Homer's *Iliad*, he explored how the ancient Greeks used agonistic competition between heroes to reestablish the social order; how early Germanic law used compensation to resolve the blood feud; how medieval jurists employed various ordeals or social status to render justice; and how we had graduated, in the West, to processes of examination and expertise to find and justify the truth in contested legal disputes—to tell justice, to engage in what he called "*jurisdiction*." On December 9, 1970, at the moment of his very first lesson at the Collège, Foucault indicated that his research seminar (distinct from his main lectures) would focus on the production of truth in the context of nineteenth-century penality.[11] Only a few weeks later, Foucault combined those intellectual interests with the declaration, on February 8, 1971, of the GIP manifesto. There was, then, an intimate connection between Foucault's archaeology of knowledge and mode of discourse analysis circa 1970 and his political engagement with the GIP.

The feedback loop was also remarkable. Foucault's political praxis pushed his theoretical reflections toward both the idea of a "political economy of the body" and the need to supplement the archaeological approach with a more genealogical analysis of power. In effect, Foucault's theoretical work in the early 1970s informed his political engagement, but reciprocally, his political praxis reshaped his theoretical writings.[12] This is well documented in Daniel Defert's oral history of the period, *Une Vie politique*,[13] as well as in a range of recent research on the GIP[14] and documentary film work.[15] Foucault's practical engagements reshaped his thinking and significantly influenced the writing of his book on prisons, *Discipline and Punish* (1975)—which Foucault himself explicitly recognized in the work itself. You will recall the telling passage in *Discipline and Punish*, cited earlier, where Foucault writes: "That punishment in general and the prison in particular belong to a political technology of the body is a lesson that I have learnt not so much from history as from the present. In recent years, prison revolts have occurred throughout the world."[16]

The creative tension and effect of praxis on theory operated on a number of levels. First, Foucault's practical engagements helped refocus his theoretical analysis on the materiality and the bodies of the prisoners—the bodies that form both the locus of punishment and the source of resistance. What *Discipline and Punish* succeeds in doing is to augment the traditional Marxian political economy with what Foucault referred to expressly as "a political economy of the body." Second, the GIP engagement helped refocus his analysis of the relationship between juridical forms and truth—which was the very project he set for himself at the Collège—on the juridical form of *imprisonment* that is tied inextricably to the form of *examination*. Third, it revealed to Foucault that his archeological approach was not entirely sufficient for the task he had set for himself, and a genealogical method was necessary. The firsthand experience of the prison and witnessing of the routinized, homogenous uniformity of isolated confinement, intolerable prison conditions, and the day-in-and-day-out repetitiveness and recurrence of prison life manifested to Foucault the difference from the ideals of the prison reformers of the eighteenth century, thereby revealing to him that an archaeological approach alone was insufficient, and a genealogical method was necessary. Archaeology would have entailed the derivation of the prison from the theories of the eighteenth- and nineteenth-century reformers. Foucault discovered that that was impossible, and instead he had to seek its development in a genealogy of morals. You can hear this first in 1973, in his lectures on *The Punitive Society*, where you get a clear turn to the penitential; and of course, we received the full articulation in 1975.

Fourth, and perhaps most important, the GIP engagements turned Foucault's attention to the productive aspects of penality. Right after he visited Attica Prison in New York State in April 1972—his first direct access to a prison, an experience which he describes as "overwhelming"[17]—Foucault shifted the focus of his analysis. Upset and "undermined" by this visit, Foucault began an analytical transition towards the "positive functions" of the penal system: "the question that I ask myself now is the reverse," he explained at the time. "The problem is, then, to find out what role capitalist society has its penal system play, what is the aim that is sought, and what effects are produced by all these procedures for punishment and exclusion? What is their place in the economic process, what is their importance in the exercise and the maintenance of power? What is their role in the class struggle?"[18]

Fifth, Foucault's involvement in the GIP produced a new awareness of the seriousness of these struggles—something that would behoove us. Foucault's turn to the notion of civil war as the basic matrix to understand social order was a direct outgrowth of this period. It loomed largest in 1972 and 1973, right during and after the peak of the prison riots in France—the revolt in the Ney prison of Toul in December 1971, the Charles-III jail of Nancy on January 15, 1972, and the prisons of Nîmes, Amiens, Loos, Fleury-Mérogis, among others.[19] After the revolt at Toul, on January 5, 1972, in a joint press conference of the GIP and the *Comité Vérité Toul*, Foucault declared that "what took place at Toul is the start of a new process: the first phase of a political struggle directed against the entire penitentiary system by the social strata that is its primary victim."[20] Civil war came to the fore just at this time, in his lectures at the Collège de France.

Foucault's praxis sharpened his awareness of the stakes of the battle. His lectures at the time were peppered with indignation, almost anger, against those who misjudge the seriousness of the political struggle:

> We are forever in the habit of speaking of the "stupidity" of the bourgeoisie. I wonder whether the theme of the stupid bourgeois is not a theme for intellectuals: those who imagine that merchants are narrow-minded, people with money are mulish, and those with power are blind. Safe from this belief, moreover, the bourgeoisie is remarkably intelligent. The lucidity and intelligence of this class, which has conquered and kept power under conditions we know, produce many effects of stupidity and blindness, but where, if not precisely in the stratum of intellectuals? We may define intellectuals as those on whom the intelligence of the bourgeoisie produces an effect of blindness and stupidity.[21]

And Foucault added, in the margin of his manuscript: "*Those who deny this are public entertainers. They fail to recognize the seriousness of the struggle.*"[22]

It may be possible to summarize all this by saying that the 1973 lectures *The Punitive Society*, the book *Discipline and Punish*, and the militancy of the GIP, working all together, formed a philosophical act, what Gilles Deleuze referred to as "a theoretical revolution,"[23] which was aimed to deconstruct the distinction between political and common-law prisoners, actualize a civil war matrix, and build alliances in society among critical theorists, political militants, and criminal justice practitioners. As Foucault famously said of the book he was writing, *Discipline and Punish*: "The little volume I would like to write about the disciplinary systems, I would want it to be useful for an educator, a guard, a magistrate, a conscientious objector. I don't write for a public, I write for users, not for readers."[24]

There were other important elements of the GIP engagement that involved dimensions of frank speech, of a mode of life, and of an aesthetics of existence. These are themes and concepts that flourish in Foucault's later lectures, and yet they are reflected in the way in which the members of the GIP were proceeding. They relate closely to Foucault's discussion of the Cynics, as well as of the Cynics' mode of life and their critique of their surroundings, all of which are developed in great depth in his last set of lectures in 1984, *The Courage of Truth.*

Critical theory as a way of living, as a mode of life: this is, as Foucault explored in *The Courage of Truth*, the characteristic life of the Cynics—of those philosophers in the tradition of Antisthenes and Diogenes of Sinope who, from the fifth century

BCE to the fifth century CE, espoused a simple mode of life that challenged most of the conventions of society. There are certain key concepts associated with the Cynics, at least in Foucault's reading: an aesthetics of existence, frank talk, and life as a work of art.[25] Cynic practice is all about a particular mode of life. And on Foucault's reading, this mode of life is inextricably linked to a certain form of truth-telling, a particular ethical form of *parrhesia*. As we know, truth-telling is by no means limited to the Cynics, but the Cynics are in part defined by their truth-telling. "The Cynic is constantly characterized as the man of *parrhesia*, the man of truth-telling," Foucault tells us.[26] If anything, it is the kind of *parrhesiastic* truth-telling that is characterized by "insolence": this is a term that he began to deploy in relation to the frank speech of the Cynics.

In helping the prisoners to be heard, and in paving the way for them to create their own prisoners' action organization, the CAP, Foucault's praxis had at its center a mode of life geared toward independence, simplicity, and autarky. This resonates distinctly with the Cynics, who Foucault would study and approximate in his final years. Throughout all these periods, it was the confrontation between critical theory and praxis that pushed both Foucault's critical theory and the critical praxis. This is precisely the model of contradiction—of the Large Hadron Collider.

My goal, too, is to collide critical theory and critical praxis as if by the Large Hadron Collider. For me, the only way to do that is to stop asking the question "What is to be done?" and to ask instead, of myself, "What more am I to do?" and "How does what I am doing work?" I must confront my own critical practice using critical theory, and my own critical theory with critical praxis. Let me now turn to that final task.

PART IV

Reformulating Critique

"What more am I to do?" In reformulating the question of praxis in this way, I would like to underscore both the action imperative and personal responsibility. I hope to put pressure on my own praxis, to push myself further, to be demanding of myself, to responsibilize myself. I do not ask anything of you, nor am I suggesting what you or other critical theorists should do. This is, in the end, a reflexive act intended to place the onus on myself alone.

For the longest time, I was troubled by the fact that so much of my early political practice fed into a narrow civil and political rights framework rather than a broader critical emancipatory framework. In my litigation and organizing on behalf of women and men on death row, I spoke mostly, early on, in a language of civil and human rights advocacy. I channeled most of my interventions through the judiciary and targeted primarily the institutions and organs of criminal law. My efforts at tackling broader issues of racism, poverty, and the punitive state were most often funneled through capital litigation, and in the process were cabined in a certain way. However, over time, by constantly challenging my praxis with critical theory—and vice versa—I evolved to a broader framework of abolitionism, now aimed not only at ending capital punishment, but at abolishing the broader punitive paradigm of American governing and society. This has pushed my praxis into new areas, such as challenging Donald Trump's Muslim ban, participating and counseling protesters at Occupy Wall Street or in Garland Hall at Johns Hopkins, or taking on repressive law enforcement practices at Standing Rock. Alongside my continuing death penalty litigation and ongoing challenges to racist law-and-order practices, like broken-windows policing and racial profiling, these other interventions have nourished a broader, abolitionist ethic—the product of a constant clash of critical theory and critical praxis.

"What more am I to do?" That is the challenge that a reconstructed critical praxis theory has led me to pose to myself. It dares me to confront my critical praxis with critical philosophy, and my critical theory with praxis. In that clash, in that contradiction, in that brutal and relentless confrontation, I hope to push my critical theorizing further, to overcome illusions that stand in its way, to drive myself toward proper forms of political action—and ultimately to not only interpret the world, but to change it or contribute, in whatever small way that I can, to our human emancipation.

CHAPTER 17

Reframing the Praxis Imperative

To always push myself, and not others, to constantly confront my political actions with critical theory, and critical theory with my praxis: that is the challenge of a reconstructed critical praxis theory, as I understand it. Perhaps you or others will reformulate the question "What is to be done?" differently. Some ultimately may decide to stick with Lenin's original formulation. Others, perhaps, will prefer to ignore the invitation entirely. But for me, staying true to the reflexivity at the core of critical philosophy, the action imperative at the very heart of the relationship between *theoria* and praxis must be turned back on myself, relentlessly.

In January 2019, I was in Paris to teach my annual seminar at the École des hautes études en sciences sociales. On Saturday, January 12, protesters demonstrated in Paris and in cities across France—from Bourges to Bordeaux to Toulouse—in what they called "Act IX" of the Yellow Vest movement. According to the official count by the Ministry of the Interior of the French government, there were 84,000 protesters across the country, and they faced an equal number of law enforcement officers from the national police, *Compagnies républicaines de sécurité* (CRS), and *gendarmerie*.[1] A total of 80,000 police officers were mobilized and deployed around the country to manage any possible unrest—along with military-grade armored tanks, flash-balls, water cannons, and other weapons—resulting in an astounding one-to-one ratio: one police officer for every Yellow Vest protester. The number of Yellow Vests at Act IX was up slightly from the week before, which seemed to signal that the movement, which began on November 17, 2018, was not dissipating. The conjuncture on January 12 was especially important: President Emmanuel Macron was slated to deliver a "*Lettre aux français*" the next day, and the "National Debate" over the political questions raised by the movement was scheduled to begin in three days.

I had researched the movement extensively before arriving in Paris, and I spent that Saturday afternoon at the protest at the Place de l'Étoile and along the Champs-Élysées. From what I could tell, Act IX was relatively peaceful compared to other Saturdays, with the weight of power on the side of the overwhelming militarized police force. To be sure, there were tear gas canisters fired and the police used water cannons; but compared to other previous Yellow Vest "acts"—and to typical manifestations in Paris—the space of protest was relatively subdued. Along the Champs-Élysées, steps from the CRS, national police, and gendarmes, Yellow Vest protesters tagged the fortified and boarded-up banks and stores, while other Parisians and tourists continued to shop in the nearby luxury boutiques.

The Yellow Vest movement had been aptly described, by Étienne Balibar and Antonio Negri, as a "*contre-pouvoir*," perhaps one of the only counterpowers to President Macron.[2] All the potential institutions that could serve as a check to executive power were, at the time, missing in action. The National Assembly was filled with Macron's hastily assembled delegates. The Sénat was hardly to be heard from. The judiciary did not serve that function in France. The major oppositional parties—the Socialist Party on the left and the Republicans on the right—had imploded and disappeared. The print media was docile and predominantly opposed to the Yellow Vest movement. The few voices that could be heard, and only dimly, were Jean-Luc Mélenchon's *insoumis* on the farther left and the new *Rassemblement national* of Marine Le Pen on the far-right (formerly the *Front national*). As a result, the Yellow Vest movement effectively stood as perhaps the only counterweight to Macron. At the time, they apparently had the support of the majority of the French people. About 72 percent of the public supported the movement as of December 1, 2018;[3] it was widely believed that a majority of the French people still supported them at the time of Act IX, despite a series of unfavorable videotaped incidents that had gone viral.

In an essay published a month earlier, in December 2018, Étienne Balibar offered a nuanced analysis of the movement.[4] He situated the movement as a reaction against neoliberalism. The historian Ludivine Bantigny, in another essay, situated the uprising in the context of unprecedented inequality in France, calling it, with admiration, "*un événement*."[5] Antonio Negri, in a series of essays, saw the multitude in the Yellow Vests, but he warned of what he imagined would come in response: "a long period of repression."[6] In his piece, Balibar ended up offering advice on how the Yellow Vest movement might gain momentum, suggesting that local political institutions, the city halls in municipalities around the country, should welcome the movement and its reform agenda. Balibar suggested the following:

> I therefore suggest that all this could be given concrete form, opening up a dialectic of self-representation and governmentality, if municipalities (starting with some of them that set an example: those most sensitive to the urgency of the situation or most open to democratic invention) now decided to open their doors to the local organization of the movement, and declared themselves ready to pass on its demands or proposals to the government.[7]

The municipalities, in fact, had contributed to the momentum of the Yellow Vest movement by opening their doors and hosting what they called, remarkably, "*cahiers de doléances*"—notebooks in which ordinary citizens and residents could write down their grievances about their social and political situations. I say that this is remarkable because that was the exact name given to the notebooks during the buildup to the French Revolution in 1789, and those earlier *cahiers de doléances* have a mythic existence in the French imagination as part of what caused the uprising against Louis XVI. The mere fact that there were, again, such grievance notebooks was radical.

Balibar's proposal that the municipalities open their doors to the protesters and, more important, that the Yellow Vest protesters work and cooperate with local officials—an idea that for the most part, they resisted at that time—seemed to me reasonable and strategic for the movement. But it was precisely here that I realized that I had to turn the tables on myself, and rather than ask, "What is to be done?" I had to ask myself, "What am I to do?" It is precisely here that I felt the urge to resist the typical role that critical intellectuals assigned themselves in the late twentieth century and still today—whether it is the "*intellectuel universel*" supposedly modeled on Sartre, the "*intellectuel spécifique*" that Foucault embraced, or even the "*intellectuel singulier*" that Balibar had uncovered in his book *Libre parole*.[8]

It is not my role to tell the movement what to do. I can only ask: what am I doing? And so, in this situation too, the questions I began to ask myself were: On that Saturday at the Étoile, why did I not pull on a yellow vest? Why did I decide to remain merely an observer?

A few days later, I participated in a scholarly panel to reflect on the Yellow Vest movement with Balibar, Bantigny, and Negri. And it was precisely in that context that everything came together for me on these questions. From the perspective of a reconstructed critical theory, I realized, my task is not to engage in sage advice to others or to assume the function of a counselor to insurrections. It is instead to reflect, confront, and motivate my own political action, so as to act more critically tomorrow and the day after.

Turning the Question on Oneself

The fact is that, at the time, the Yellow Vest movement challenged many of the political formations and public policies that I too oppose. First, it was aimed, in large part, at the ills of neoliberalism and our new forms of entrepreneurial surveillance capitalism, which are so detrimental to ordinary people. It aimed at our new, Uberized economy, where destitute women and men are incentivized to exploit their own meager possessions, like their cars, bikes, or apartments, to earn a paltry, self-employed rate of pay with no social benefits. As Negri suggests, the movement represents the "expression of a rejection of the logics of neoliberalism—a rejection probably brought against those logics in a moment of acute crisis."[9] On this point, there is substantial overlap with my own views on neoliberalism.[10]

Second, the movement targeted the excesses of our militarized police state. These too are problems that I have addressed for decades in my own work in the United States. Many of the grievances of the Yellow Vest protesters mirror those of the Occupy Wall Street movement, with which I was involved in solidarity, and which I admired from a critical theory perspective.

When I looked closely at the spoken words of, for instance, Christophe Dettinger, a retired boxer (French light-heavyweight champion in 2007 and 2008) and self-identified Yellow Vest protester, I felt a deep resonance with his grievances. There was a lot of controversy surrounding Dettinger because he physically assaulted a policeman at the protests in Paris on January 5, 2019. The video went viral, as did his apology—both of which you can see at *The Guardian* at a link sponsored by the newspaper.[11] Supporters of Dettinger quickly raised more than 100,000 euros on a crowdfunding site named Leetchi, which was shut down by political opposition in outrage. Dettinger then posted this apologia *qua* political manifesto on YouTube, to explain himself to his fellow Yellow Vest protesters:

> Dear Yellow Vest friends,
>
> Here we go, let me present myself. My name is Christophe. . . . I'd like to present things to you the way I feel them.
>
> I've participated in the eight Acts . . . I've been at every protest every Saturday in Paris.
>
> I've seen the repression. I've seen the police gas us. I've seen the police hurt people with flashballs. I've seen injured people. I've seen retired people get gazed.
>
> Me, I'm just a normal citizen. I work. I'm able to pay my bills at the end of the month, though it's complicated.
>
> But I am protesting for those who are retired, for the future of my children, for single women . . .
>
> I am a Yellow Vest. I have the people's anger in my breast.
>
> I see all these presidents, I see all these cabinet members, I see the whole state binging on us, sucking us dry. They're not even capable of leading by example. They show no example. They gouge themselves off our backs. And it's always us, the little ones, who pay.
>
> I feel concerned because I'm French. I'm proud to be French. I'm not far-left, I'm not far-right. I'm just an ordinary citizen. Citizen lambda. I'm a Frenchman. I like my country. I like my motherland. I like everything.[12]

Notice that this is not so much Marxist class struggle as French revolutionary talk. The enemy is not the bourgeoisie or the managing class, but the state—the presidents and their ministers. It is pitched in a decidedly *ancien régime* revolutionary register. Dettinger's discourse is tinged with citizenship and patriotism. He emphasizes repeatedly that he is a citizen, that he loves his country and his homeland. I would hesitate to jump to the conclusion that he has a xenophobic or anti-immigrant position. He may have such sentiments, but he also may, possibly, simply be trying to emphasize that he's not a habitual protester and bears no animus to France. (I'll come back to this.) His claim that he is neither an extreme leftist or rightist is important. He's trying to deny having any ideology. "This is not about political ideology," he is essentially saying, and "it is not about party politics either." All presidents and ministers, regardless of their party, are corrupt and exploit the little person.

Much of this discourse resonates with leftist ideals of equality, solidarity, social justice, and anti-neoliberalism. Many of the positions of the Yellow Vest movement strike me as important, strategically astute, and sympathetic. *So, why did I not don a yellow vest?* That, I take it, is the critical praxis question. It is not what should I do, but what am I doing? Why am I or am I not participating, acting, engaging in protest, and how?

Ultimately, in this personal confrontation, it became clear to me why I had not joined the protest. But again, the point is not whether to join or not—it is to confront praxis and critical theory. There were, it turns out, a few reasons why I hesitated to wear a yellow vest. First was the concern that there was a latent, identitarian dimension to the protest that did not equally valorize the suffering of persons of color or of others who are marginalized in the *banlieues* or have been struggling to decolonize France for decades, along the lines of race, postcolonialism, ethnicity, gender, and sexual difference, to name a few. Second was the concern about the patriotic, nationalistic language and symbols. I have argued elsewhere that we had not paid sufficient attention to the words that Donald Trump used and, as a result, have not recognized the neofascist, white supremacist, ultranationalist counter-revolutionary turn that has been taken in the United States. I felt that I needed to assure myself, through further research and investigation, that the Yellow Vest movement's appeal to citizenship, nationality, and *patrie* in their declarations and manifestos were not in fact the New Right in another guise.

So, rather than put on the yellow vest, I decided at the time to assume the mantle of *compagnon de route*—the fellow traveler, a deeply contested term from the 1960s, but one that I felt was perfectly suited to the times. Fellow travelers in the twentieth century, famously, did not join the Communist Party, but they sympathized with the aims and goals of the communists and were willing to work with the communist movement. The term became controversial because many fellow travelers did not distance themselves from Stalinism in time. Thus, their fellow traveling became a form of collaboration with the worst of Stalin's Soviet Union and the Western European communist parties that remained faithful to Stalin. The same problem, of course, could arise in the context of the Yellow Vest movement—although there, the cost of not disavowing the movement would be far smaller given that it could peter out on its own.

The role of fellow traveler, I believe, was perfectly suited to my position vis-à-vis the Yellow Vest protesters, so resurrecting that contested term felt appropriate. It allowed me to highlight my degrees of separation from the movement, and spell out, clearly, the lines that I would draw for myself—again, not for others, but for myself in my critical praxis:

- I reject any affirmative or prescriptive nationalism: it may be okay to be proud to be French (or Algerian, or Haitian, or American for that matter) in a cultural sense (even if there are so many dark sides to all these histories, from collaboration with the Nazis, to Papa Doc in Haiti, to American slavery); but it is never okay to denigrate others for having a different national identity. National pride in itself is not necessarily out of bounds; but there is *no* room for discrimination on the basis of national origin and *no* place for patriotism as a normative grounding of the movement. Citizenship cannot serve as a source of distinction or discrimination.
- I reject any xenophobic, racist, ethnic, sexist, or sexual phobias: here too, there is absolutely *no* place in a popular movement like this for discrimination against those who are, in many ways, even more marginalized than the working class.
- I reject the call to a "people" defined in ethnocentric ways: insofar as there is reference to a "people," and therefore a "populist" dimension to the movement, it must have a porous boundary that does not serve to exclude or police identity. The term "people" has to be understood merely as the "collective assembled," not the *Volk*.

As I confronted my praxis with critical theory, those were lines that I drew and that I would not cross in my own praxis. At the time, they pushed me to guard against wearing a yellow vest, while standing beside the protesters, being willing to carefully defend the movement, and calling myself a fellow traveler. The term *compagnon de route*, in fact, seemed more appropriate than ever—not only because of the historical conjuncture, but also because the movement was taking over the *ronds-points* (roundabouts) on the roads and highways across France, because of the symbolism of their yellow road safety vests, and, of course, because President Macron had named his party "La République En Marche!"

Being a "*compagnon de route*" thus allowed me to express some areas of doubt, other areas of admiration, and some astonishment.

First, admiration: it was remarkable that the Yellow Vest movement had raised such critical issues of inequality and social injustice so quickly, and in such an apparently spontaneous and autonomous way—in the sense that it was not the product of an established political party calling its constituents to action, nor of a clear political ideology. It was stunning that, in such a short span of time, it had mobilized a counterpower in France, made up of what might be called, by analogy, the 99 percent. The fact, for instance, that the country, only two months later, was going through a process of people writing their grievances by hand in *cahiers de doléances* in *mairies* around France, and that they had triggered the most serious and prolonged national debate in the country since perhaps the Revolution, was amazing and historically haunting.

Negri described the movement as a "multitude," using the term that he and Hardt had coined in their book of that title. Negri wrote, "There is undoubtedly in France a multitude that is rising up with violence against the new misery wrought by neoliberal reforms."[13] What I saw at Act IX, and what I was surprised by, was that the crowd was large in number, but it did not feel so much like a collective or a multitude as like a congregation of individuals, couples, families, and friends. The numbers were astounding, but I was struck by the *individualized* nature of the uprising: it had the appearance of individual actors; or small family units, rising up as single individuals; or couples, just themselves, as "person *lambda*," finding others who are also exasperated, rather than a multitudinal uprising. It felt as if these particular persons wanted to make themselves heard in their own right, as citizens *lambda*.

From what I could tell from my participant observations on that Saturday, January 12, but also from what I had read in my research, many of the Yellow Vest protesters in Paris had come with their spouses or partners and a few friends—women and men, some partnered, others not. They were wandering around, somewhat unsure of the process, unsure of the rules of protest, trying to stick together. I heard many of them watching out for each other—asking each other where their friend who came with them was, for instance. They were not, for the most part, habitual protesters. There were, of course, interspersed, both far-right and far-left, black-clad militants. But for the most part, the protesters were not professionals and looked somewhat unaccustomed to what they were doing.

The leaderless aspect of the movement was brilliant strategically—and picked up perfectly on notions of political disobedience from the Occupy movement.[14] It protected the movement from appropriation, as well as from being sullied by any one individual. It reflected the idea that the individual protesters did not want to be represented or spoken for, but rather wanted to present themselves—or so it seemed. They wanted to engage the political field on their own terms and in their own words. One older protester was sitting on a bench on the Champs-Élysées, with a megaphone, orating. A woman, perhaps his wife, sat next to him, looking on approvingly. Other protesters would walk by, listen, engage, chat, applaud at times, and then move on. But he was really just expressing himself—and his indignation.

If there was one unifying theme, it was one constant refrain: "*Macron, démission!*" ("Macron, resign!"). I even heard a few times, "*Macron, en prison*"—which oddly reminded me of Donald Trump's call to "Lock her up." But, yes, the one theme that seemed to unite most of the protesters was a certain hatred, a visceral hatred, of Macron *Rex*. His personality, his discourse, and his attitude seemed to drive the Yellow Vests over the edge. The sentiment was omnipresent. It practically defined the protests that day. And this, of course, complicated things for many on the Left because the protest was perceived, as a result, to be a referendum on Macron's policies, including his support of Europe and of climate reform. It was precisely because of this that many on the Left opposed the movement, seeing it as a threat to the European Union and more cosmopolitan politics. (During the election, naturally, many on the Left opposed Macron and would have preferred another candidate, but now that he was president, many preferred to work within the political system rather than try to expel him from the Élysée and deal with the unknown, especially the possibility of an extreme right replacement.)

It was also politically meaningful to be on the Champs-Élysées for a mass demonstration. Protest marches usually are in the more popular, less wealthy neighborhoods in Paris, mostly around the Bastille and the Place de la République. This was another striking (and, I felt, admirable) feature of the Yellow Vest movement: the protesters were directly confronting the extreme wealth inequalities and excess consumption right in the space of excess luxury. The battle cry for that Saturday's protest, somewhat amusingly, was "*On va faire les soldes à Paris!*" ("We are going to shop the sales in Paris!"), and the intention was to march on the Grands Boulevards, precisely where all the large department stores are located.[15] Of course, the *cortège* went through the Place de la Bastille, as it began further east at Bercy, where the Ministry of Finance is located; but the rallying point was, and had always been, the Étoile. The fact that the protests were taking place at the most chic neighborhood of Paris is telling. It was a protest aimed at wealth inequality and the excesses of the elite.

Most banks were boarded up in Paris, even outside the area of the Saturday marches. For instance, even in the Latin Quarter, on the Left Bank, far from any of the marches, the BNP and Société Générale branches had their windows permanently boarded up—not just on the weekends, but permanently. Banks in Paris had become the symbol, and now incarnation, of fortress capitalism. Equally surprisingly, the boarded-up and secured luxury stores near the Champs-Élysées remained open, and a few wealthy-looking customers were still shopping, only meters away from the protest. I was amazed to see luxury stores like Fendi, Gucci, and others, heavily guarded by private security, boarded up, gated (in the sense that the doors and any windows had iron security bars on them), but nevertheless open to a handful of swanky buyers. It felt surreal. In the background, you could hear flash-balls.

Second, then, outrage: at the Étoile, it felt that there were more police officers than protesters. *Le Monde* reported that there were 80,000 police officers deployed around the country, which is about as many as the official count of protesters: a one-to-one ratio, as previously mentioned. (If only education were like that. Could you imagine one teacher for each student? What a beautiful world that would be.) At the perimeter on the West boulevards of the Étoile, I heard a gendarme order protesters within the perimeter to take off their yellow vests if they wanted to go outside the perimeter. The protesters were blocked in by a row of shielded, militarized police officers, and this particular officer told the protesters, loudly, "If you want to leave, you first need to take off your yellow vest, line up, and then go through there," pointing. I am not sure if he said something about being checked, or searched. (However, the police were searching the bags of anyone crossing into the perimeter.) It felt odd to hear this officer order people to take off their yellow vests as a condition of exiting the protest—an odd limitation on expression and protest. The military-police hardware was impressive—the tanks, the armed trucks with shovels and water cannons, the massive number of paramilitary officers in SWAT gear. I understand, of course, that there was vandalism and broken windows, and also that there had been injuries at past protests. But still, the amount of military hardware and police was overwhelming. It is so plain, today, that liberal democratic regimes rely on the police state.[16]

Third, doubts: the act of putting on the vest, of wearing it, is the only thing that identifies anyone as a member of the protest group. It is a small act. Now, one definitely has to be committed to enter the perimeter of the protest wearing a yellow vest because the area is heavily policed by armed paramilitary officers. Not everyone is willing to walk up to a member of the CRS in full gear and ask him for permission to pass through the perimeter and into the fray. Most people who have not been at a protest before or are not accustomed to doing so would feel hesitant.

But on the other hand, of course, most who are used to protesting would feel little fear and easily don the vest.

It is worth spending a moment thinking about this aspect: one becomes a protester simply by physically putting on a yellow vest. It slips over your clothes easily. You can put it on and take it off easily. In that sense, it is a bit like the pink hats from the Women's March against Trump that took place the day after his inauguration. Everyone has a yellow vest in their car. Many are accustomed to wearing them—sanitation and transportation workers, little kids going to the park from school, crossing guards, and others, all wear a yellow vest regularly. (Actually, the grade-school children had started wearing orange safety vests at the time to avoid confusion!) So the only real cost of donning the yellow vest was the fear of being accosted or confronted by someone else or by the police. This, of course, means that it may be difficult at times to distinguish so-called authentic protesters from those who are there to rumble with the police, entertain themselves, or simply out of curiosity. Of course, the official count that Saturday was 84,000 people across France—and official counts tend to underestimate—so it seems clear that there were lots of protesters, and it is hard to imagine that the question of authenticity would involve anything more than a fraction of those present.

Perhaps the very question of authenticity is inappropriate with a popular, grass-roots movement like this. Perhaps I should no more distinguish between authentic protesters and rabble-rousers, than between political and common-law prisoners. The fact is, there was no party to belong to, nor any ideology to subscribe to. These women and men just seemed to share a rageful sense of indignation that compelled them to don the yellow vest and show their political anger. A *casseur/casseuse* (defined as someone who joins the protest and breaks windows, loots, or vandalizes) may also be full of anger and indignation at his or her political and economic condition, so this person may well be the perfect illustration of a Yellow Vest protester. These are political acts of uprising. Just as all crime is political, all uprising is too. As Foucault so brilliantly demonstrated in *Penal Theories and Institutions* in 1972, penal law is political practice; this should extend to protest as well. So it is not clear, in the end, whether I should engage in the exercise of policing the boundaries of the protest movement, although it continues to trouble me. Antonio Negri discusses this as well in an essay.[17] The fact that the question even comes up, and needs to be repressed, suggests something different about these particular protests.

Fourth, finally, surprise: honestly, I am somewhat surprised at the discourse on (and particularly the condemnation of) the vandalism and acts of violence by protesters. Many of my leftist colleagues complained bitterly that these Yellow Vests were "*des voyous*" (thugs, hoodlums). And no doubt there were incidents of violence—for instance, the arson at Fouquets on the Champs-Élysées. But it is hard to characterize a predominantly peaceful day of protest in this way. Return to the retired boxer, Christophe Dettinger, for a minute: many people, including people on the Left, appropriately decried the assault that he committed—it made the cover of a major weekly. And many pointed to him as evidence of the hooliganism of the Yellow Vest movement. But I have to say that I find it hard to impugn a movement of 84,000 plus protesters on the basis of a few people who turn violent. To dismiss the movement as "*une bande de voyous*" because a minute fraction of them turned to violence—in a movement built on anger—seems politically irresponsible to me.

In the end, these admirations and doubts, and questions, left me (at least at the time) tentatively willing to declare myself a *compagnon de route* to the Yellow Vest protesters, but not prepared to don the vest myself. In this way, I hoped at least to emphasize the places where I would not skid off the road—under any circumstance.

How Does My Critical Praxis Work?

At the panel a few days after Act IX, when I spoke about being a "fellow traveler," a young philosopher standing in the back of the auditorium challenged the idea, confronting my own praxis with critical theory. He cut me to the quick. He was, not surprisingly, the only person in the auditorium of about 250 people who openly professed that he had worn a yellow vest at the protests. His questions stopped me in my tracks—the perfect confrontation of theory and praxis: "If you don't wear a yellow vest, if you're just a fellow traveler," he asked, "then aren't you ceding ground to the New Right? Aren't you enabling the very thing you fear most—namely, that the protest movement will get captured by the right-wing *Rassemblement national*?"

I slowly started to formulate a response while others asked more questions. I would have ventured an answer to the young philosopher, but ultimately I felt that I needed to leave the last words to my guests, especially to Ludivine Bantigny, who had given the audience so much hope—symbolized by a photograph she projected of a Yellow Vest protester with the word "*Espoir*" imprinted haphazardly on the back of her or his vest. Later, as the young philosopher and I walked out of the auditorium together, and he began rolling his cigarette, I learned his name: Vincent Jarry.[18]

Jarry's question highlighted the fact that we—or rather I—still have not fully grasped what is at stake with leaderless social movements today, despite all the writing on political disobedience. I continue to cling to antiquated or static notions of identity, ideology, party—or even static ideas of left and right. But in our conversation—in his confrontation of my praxis—it became clearer to me that I have to, once and for all, get beyond those outdated concepts of identity and ideology when I confront the challenges of, or participate in, a leaderless movement. Jarry was right: the leaderless and open nature of new social movements today means that we either participate, and thereby help give meaning to the movement, or we leave the field open for others to define the movement. The very notion of an "identity" of the movement—especially a passive identity—is obsolete in today's universe of leaderless protest. It is every individual who is willing to march, to make a poster, to carry a banner, or to write our *revendications* on a yellow vest, that effectively gives voice to the movement.

You will recall Judith Butler's writings on the performative nature of assemblies, where she argues that the physical gathering of bodies and the material element of assemblies precede, constitute, and make possible political expression.[19] I would push this one step further, perhaps in a more concrete direction. The issue is not just assembled bodies and the general notion of a popular will, but more exactly all the minutiae of who exactly assembles, in the most microscopic detail. When people don the yellow vest, *who* they are, *what* they look like, and *what* they say and write on the back of their vest—all those expressive functions, including expression itself, the ink on the vests, the signs protesters carry, the words they say—have effects on reality. What they look like, their class appearance, their skin tone, their gender, their clothes, their hair, their shoes, their weight, the way they walk, talk, look—all aspects of their appearance shape the movement itself. The French flags and white faces on the Champs-Élysées at Act IX, the very look on people's faces in the *défilé* at another Yellow Vest protest, Act X, the presence or absence of minorities, the words on the back of the vests and on the front of the banners—those constitute and transform, moment by moment, week by week, the trajectory of the movement. They define the movement at any moment. And that turns on whether *we* are there—*we*, as in, you and me.

Presence itself turns into a form of truth-telling, or what Foucault referred to as "veridiction." It has real effects. It can be contested, and in the context of the Yellow Vests, it functions differently from the judicial words that J. L. Austin famously discussed—those illocutionary acts such as marrying or sentencing someone. Nothing needs to be said by anyone authorized to enact laws. Everything is accomplished simply by our presence, in all its richness of symbolic interaction.

Contestation works differently here as well. At a recent Yellow Vest protest, some Antifa protesters attacked and excluded right-wing, *Action française* Yellow Vest protesters. Internal policing and exclusion was taking place. There were attempts to shape and define the movement. And when some Yellow Vest protesters claimed to speak for others, routinely they were threatened and forced to step back.[20] There is also a powerful dimension of authenticity associated with the social status of the person wearing the yellow vest. A protester who really has a hard time making ends meet at the end of the month has more legitimacy and authenticity than one who is well off.

But within these constraints, the leaderlessness of the movement allows a certain truth-telling and truth-making. It makes possible a concrete, constitutive performativity. Wearing the yellow vest gives—or is the only way to *try* to give—meaning to the movement.[21] Being a fellow traveler is almost impotent in that sense. This contrasts sharply with more traditional political practice. For instance, someone wearing a *France insoumise* T-shirt or carrying its flag is not able to refashion or shape the meaning and significance of that party as easily as by talking or by writing things on their vest. Jean-Luc Mélenchon is the one who will effectively define the party's identity. Members can try to push and nudge and cajole. They can at times go ahead of their party or syndicates—as some workers did in France, in 1968, when they went on strike against the dictates of the General Confederation of Labour (*Confédération Générale du Travail*, or CGT) and other unions. But that will eventually catch up with them—as it did, precisely, in 1968, when the CGT ordered the termination of the strikes (essentially at the behest of the Soviet Union). In a leaderless protest, by contrast, each individual constitutes and gives direction to the movement.

Balibar, Bantigny, Negri, and members of the audience warned about and feared a rightward drift of the Yellow Vest movement. That was the looming threat and risk of the *événement*—that it might empower Le Pen's *Rassemblement national*. And there were serious geopolitical concerns, given the rise to power of the Five Star movement in Italy and of the ÖVP and FPÖ in Austria, Brexit, and the rightward drifts in Eastern Europe, Brazil, Turkey, India, the United States, and other countries. But one of the only ways to avoid that is precisely, as Vincent Jarry suggested, to participate.

Chantal Mouffe argues, in her latest book, that left populism may offer far-right militants a new language and political register to express their grievances. It may be the only way, in fact, to swing those voters to the left. Mouffe notes that Mélenchon's party was able to draw some supporters from Marine Le Pen, and in Britain, Jeremy Corbyn attracted a share of the right-wing UK Independence Party (UKIP) votes—we might think here of the Donald Trump–Bernie Sanders swing voters.[22] Mouffe wagers that a conciliatory left populism, one that does not accuse but invites, might be able to win far-right votes. The truth, Mouffe contends, is that many on the far right are attracted to right-wing parties because they think that they are the only parties taking their concerns seriously: "I believe that, if a different language is made available, many people [on the populist right] might experience their situation in a different way and join the progressive struggle."[23] Isn't this yet another reason, then, to participate rather than to sit on the sidelines and judge the movement as a *compagnon de route* inevitably must?

As I left Paris to return to teach at Columbia University, another Yellow Vest protest was getting underway, called "Act X," on Saturday, January 19, 2019. The Ministry of the Interior reported that Act X mobilized the exact same number of protesters as the week before—84,000 Yellow Vests.[24] The protests were scattered across the country—in Paris and Toulouse, of course, but also in Bordeaux, Nancy, Rennes, Rouen, Caen, Lyon, Dijon, and elsewhere; this was on the same day, incidentally, as the Women's March in the United States. In Paris, the number of protesters reached 7,000 according to the French state, down from 8,000 the week before, but other cities (and a greater number of them) saw increases. The count was a particularly sensitive matter for both the state and the movement. The "National Debate" was launched on the previous Tuesday, January 15, 2019, and President Emmanuel Macron had spent a combined total of thirteen hours responding to 1,200 mayors on Tuesday and Friday, January 15 and 18—in two question-and-answer marathons lasting six-and-a-half hours each, with 600 mayors in two regions of France, Normandie and Occitanie. The big question on everyone's mind was whether the launch of the National Debate and President Macron's thirteen hours of face time would dampen, assuage, or abate the Yellow Vest movement. To the surprise of many, it did not—at least not for Act X.

Once again, the police were there—and everywhere—in an overwhelming display of force. The French government, again, mobilized and deployed 80,000 law enforcement officers, meaning that, if we take their numbers at face value, there was one police officer for every yellow vest. The media reports about the police force said that it was, once again, overwhelming. Whereas previously the Paris protests had been less organized and clustered around the Étoile at the Champs-Élysées, Act X resembled a more traditional protest march, a more classic *défilé* on the Left Bank. It started at the Invalides and proceeded along the left bank of the Seine, down the Boulevard St. Michel to the Place d'Italie, toward more popular neighborhoods, and it felt like it contained more union members and Mélenchon supporters.

Act X was dedicated to all the yellow vests who have died in the movement, and it resembled a more traditional *cortège* procession. There were more militants with CGT logos or *France insoumise* logos on their yellow vests. But according to news reports, this was not the case in Toulouse, where the protests were far more chaotic and violent—and which had become, according to the media, the epicenter of the movement.[25]

Many questions were swirling around the Yellow Vest movement and the National Debate. There was growing controversy over the use of flash-ball weaponry, which had seriously injured protesters. There was also a serious question surrounding the use of violence by the protesters, especially the burning of Fouquets on the Champs-Élysées. There was great uncertainty about the future and potential trajectory of the Yellow Vest protest movement, as well as daunting questions about the future of French politics. It was a truly exceptional moment in French history, somewhat *inédit*, marked by the spontaneous drafting of *cahiers de doléances* around the country, the triggering and hurried organization of a dizzying and vast national debate, and calls of all kinds for different and more radical political procedures. Antonio Negri and others spoke of turning the French Assembly into an "*assemblée constituante*," which would have pushed the situation into even more uncharted territory. These were weighty matters that called for deep reflection and care.

In the immediate moment, though—at least for me—the most punctual dilemma remained Vincent Jarry's original question—one that raises critical questions of meaning, veridiction, performativity, and praxis.

Donna Haraway writes: "The only scientific thing to do is revolt! Movements, not just individuals, are critical. . . . Revolt! Think we must; we must think. Actually think, not like Eichmann the Thoughtless. Of course, the devil is in the details—how to revolt? How to matter and not just want to matter?"[26]

"How to matter and not just want to matter?" Haraway asks. What more am I to do? How, then, must I revolt? That was the question I posed myself—and posed again, thanks to Jarry. Was it right to remain a *compagnon de route*? Should I have participated in a way that lent meaning to the movement? What could I have written on the back of a yellow vest? Under which banner would I have walked, and what poster would I have carried? Did being a fellow traveler, or even editorializing about it, accomplish anything? How did it confront the punitive paradigm of governing?

As my plane took off the runway at Roissy Charles de Gaulle, and I looked out the porthole for a last glance at Paris, all I could see was a question: "What more should I have done?" It is that question that I pose to myself now, in lieu of "What is to be done?" Let me now address the question more directly in relation to the longer trajectory of my own political praxis. In a very real sense, this is, for me, the heart of the enterprise and the struggle that gave shape to this book.

CHAPTER 18

What More Am I To Do?

This book was born of my own struggles—born from years, or rather decades, of torment, conflict, and contradiction between my political engagements and my critical theorizing. It is the outgrowth of a seemingly irreconcilable, intolerably frustrating rift that always separates the two and gnaws at them both—and constantly haunts me.

It grows, on the one hand, out of decades of political interventions, of litigation and community organizing, of marches and canvassing, of commissions of inquiry and giving testimony, counseling, and writing editorials. Alone, and with friends and colleagues, I have deployed the range of activist methods over a lifetime, applying for protest permits and organizing anti-nuke marches; representing prisoners at disciplinary hearings, indigent tenants being evicted, and disabled individuals who were denied benefits; litigating on behalf of those condemned to death, deprived of humane prison conditions, or wrongfully convicted; serving on human rights commissions in Latin America and Africa; testifying before Congress; canvassing for presidential candidates; and counseling protesters and litigating on their behalf. For three decades, alongside Bryan Stevenson, Steve Bright, George Kendall, Randy Susskind, and now Alexis Hoag, I have represented men condemned to death in Alabama or later sentenced to life imprisonment without parole. With Tom Durkin, I sued President Donald Trump the moment he signed the Muslim ban on behalf of a Syrian medical resident at a hospital in Chicago named Amer Al-Homssi, whose J-1 visa was immediately cancelled at the airport in Abu Dhabi. I took on the case of Musab Zeiton, a dual Libyan-British national admitted to a master's program at Columbia University who got caught in the Muslim ban as well. Noah Smith-Drelich and I sued law enforcement in North Dakota for outright abuses of the rights to protest, assemble, and pray at the Standing Rock reservation.

I have lobbied and organized to defeat intolerable federal judicial nominations, to pass racial justice legislation, to abolish the death penalty. I counseled protesters during the Occupy Wall Street movement and at Garland Hall at Johns Hopkins University. I have published countless editorials and signed petitions and amicus briefs. I have marched against wars and oppression. Throughout my life, I have fought for social justice as a lawyer and litigator, as a political activist and organizer, in Montgomery, Alabama, and at the Southern Prisoners' Defense Committee in Atlanta, as far back as the Legal Aid Bureau and Prison Legal Assistance Project in law school and the Alliance to Reverse the Arms Race in college. Those endless struggles have shaped how I think about critical praxis.

At the same time, this project grows directly out of years of engaging in critical theory—poring over poststructuralism and Critical Legal Studies, critical race and queer theory, feminism, postcolonialism, and deconstruction, as well as existentialism and German idealism. It grows out of years of confronting radical thinkers like Nietzsche, Marx, and Freud, and years of writing on the illusions of order and free markets, on racial bias in algorithms and prediction, on the devastating impact of neoliberalism, on our expository society and new forms of counterinsurgency governmentality, on political disobedience. It builds on years of editing the lectures that Michel Foucault gave on the punitive society at the Collège de France, or on the role of avowal at Louvain (with Fabienne Brion), or on Nietzsche at Vincennes, and of editing Foucault's book *Surveiller et punir*; of organizing seminars, workshops, and reading groups on critical theory, uprisings, and critical praxis. Alone and with friends and critical thinkers, I have toiled in these fields for decades—starting with a thesis in college on Sartre, Fanon, and political violence, followed later by a dissertation on subjectivation and social meaning. I have had the privilege of working with remarkable critical theorists, from Sheldon Wolin, Raymond Geuss, and Rüdiger Bittner in college, Duncan Kennedy, Janet Halley, and Martha Minow, in law school, to Seyla Benhabib and Richard Tuck in graduate school. I have conducted research on everything from asylums and prisons to Nazi gun laws and our culture wars. I have spent years debating with students on everything from social theory to penal law and procedure.

But throughout those decades and years of militancy, the activism and the critical philosophy clashed violently. They relentlessly collided, confronted and contradicted each other—each one jamming against the other, neither leaving the other alone. Was I merely legitimating injustice by representing capital defendants in what often felt like show trials, or was I really dismantling these unjust institutions and practices? Was I participating in constructing the fiction of due process, or was I demolishing it? Were these human rights interventions sapping more radical movements of more solidaristic possibilities and undermining more radical leftist projects? Was the Foucaultian turn to subjectivation helpful to political protest, or was it deflating earlier work on power? How was it even possible to answer the question "How to revolt?" when so many voices are not heard, especially my friends and clients sentenced to death and their families?

For decades, my critical theorizing challenged, and most often undermined, my political activism—and vice versa, my interventions confronted and deconstructed my critical theory. The dream of any unity of theory and praxis turned out to be just that: a point on the horizon, always vanishing. This all came to a head with the growing crises at the turn of the twenty-first century—with the climate change crisis, the rise of the New Right, Brexit, the pandemic, and the elections of Erdoğan, Trump, and Bolsonaro, among others. The crises came one after another, heightened, in quick succession. And it seemed that critical theory, at least in the United States, had little to say. If anything, it was beating a hasty retreat and confessing that it had "run out of steam," as Bruno Latour suggested.[1] Critical intellectual giants were raising the white flag of surrender. Critical theory itself was in crisis.

When I was fully immersed in representing a man sentenced to death, the turmoil and questions calmed. I suddenly felt that I knew what I was doing and why. You may think that critical theory nourished my struggles on behalf of my friends and clients on Alabama's death row—Doyle Hamm, Phillip Tomlin, Kenneth Magwood, Arthur Giles, Walter McMillian, Pernell Ford, Jason Williams, Timothy Davis, Robin Myers, among others, and now David Wilson. You may think that it is because I am a critical theorist that I went down to Montgomery to represent these condemned men. But it's exactly the opposite—I practically had to turn off the critical theory to get the job done. What motivated me and nourished my struggle was the injustice in their capital cases, to be sure, but more than that, it was their lives. It was the fact that their lives were at risk and that they had no one to fall back on. It was the fact that the state of Alabama was doing everything in its awesome power to sacrifice their lives in order, supposedly, to restore others' well-being and strengthen the moral fabric of society. These were human sacrifices, presumably for the benefit of the rest of us. But even that was too theoretical. It was just their lives. It was the fact that their fragile lives hung in the balance. It was the fragility of life.

Confronting Critical Theory

I immersed myself in these death penalty cases and represented these condemned men, not so much as a result of critical theory but because I felt I had no choice. I first learned about the scale and extent of injustice in these death penalty cases as a third-year law student. A lawyer from Atlanta named Joseph Nursey, from a public-interest law center named Team Defense, came to speak to class at the invitation of my professor, Max Stern, for whom I was working as a teaching assistant. Nursey told us about the death penalty cases he was working on. He told us about one where the defense attorney was so drunk that he was escorted to jail with his client, locked up, and came to court directly from the drunk tank the next morning. He told us about one where the defense attorney referred to his client using racial epithets in open court. He told us about one where a third-year law student represented a capital defendant, thanks to the permissive licensing rules of the state courts. He told us about a case—or rather many cases—where all the African American potential jurors were struck off the venire in predominantly African American counties. He told us about cases where defense counsel presented no mitigating evidence at sentencing. The injustices and lack of minimal legal representation, due to the race, poverty, and mental illness of the accused, were too astounding to even imagine, and too shocking to ignore. By the end of that class, I had decided that I would go to the South and see if all this was really true, and if so, that I too would represent women and men on death row.

I quickly organized an independent clinical externship for myself for the month of January in 1989, thanks to Professor Betsy Bartholet, and headed to the Southern Prisoners' Defense Committee (SPDC) in Atlanta (now the Southern Center for Human Rights). The moment I began to work on my first case—that of George Daniel, in Russell County, Alabama, with Bryan Stevenson—I saw firsthand the unconscionable, simply shocking quality of representation by appointed counsel. At the time, and still today, there was no statewide public defender service in Alabama, so in most small counties, local judges appointed inexperienced attorneys whose compensation was capped at $1,000 per case. In George Daniel's case, his trial attorney had clocked in eight hours of pretrial investigation—eight hours total. The state psychiatrist who testified that Daniel had antisocial personality disorder was a quack who had falsified his credentials and never had *any* higher education, let alone a medical degree. I could go on for pages about his case. It rattled my soul.

The minute I encountered firsthand the blatant racism in the second case I worked on—that of Albert Jefferson, in Chambers County, Alabama, with Ruth Friedman—I knew. The prosecutor in Jefferson's case had his secretary type up the names of all the potential jury venire members into four lists, headed "Strong," "Medium," "Weak," and "Black," and then started striking jurors from the bottom of the "Black" list, so that Jefferson, a young African American man, faced an all-white jury.[2] The moment I watched, in admiration, Steve Bright put on evidence at a hearing in William Anthony Brooks's case in Chattahoochee County, Georgia, to recuse the trial judge because he was racist—and heard all the evidence—I knew.

As I drove back to Atlanta from death row at Holman Prison in Atmore, Alabama, with Bryan Stevenson on Wednesday, January 18, 1989—a day I will never forget, having met four men who had been sentenced to death (Albert Jefferson, Willie Tabbs, Vernon Madison, and Walter McMillian, who kept insisting he was innocent and was later proved to be so) and having listened to their stories and what they told us about their trials and their lawyers, I knew. In fact, the minute I began to work with the extraordinary lawyers at SPDC, Steve Bright, Ruth Friedman, Bryan Stevenson, Clive Stafford-Smith, I knew what I had to do. I had no choice but to move to the South and represent men and women on death row. There were a few things in my background that undoubtedly contributed to this. I came from a family of French Jewish refugees on my father's side, some of whom, but not all, were fortunate enough to escape the Holocaust; and several close family members had put their lives at risk to combat Nazi oppression. Some of the critical philosophy that I had read and studied also undoubtedly contributed. But it was mainly the injustice and the lives that compelled me. Yes, it was the fragility of life.

When I moved to Montgomery, Alabama, the next year to work with Bryan Stevenson, it was not a critically theorized intervention. If anything, it was impulsive. I did not consider myself a death penalty abolitionist. I did not philosophically interrogate capital punishment. I did not strategically analyze what I was doing. I felt compelled, that's all. I had to go to the South because of the blatant racism and discrimination on the basis of poverty, class, and mental illness that I had witnessed. I was not strategizing how to end the death penalty or achieve a just society. I just had to represent these women and men on death row because their lives were at stake. If anything, I avoided or resisted critical theory.

My litigation, legal representation, and organizing—no less than critical theory itself—forged a double-edged sword. It could easily serve to legitimize, rather than undermine, the capital punishment system. Law can easily play that role, particularly in a country like the United States, with its long history of slavery and lynchings, and the ugly racism behind the death penalty. Indeed, it was one of my mentors, Carol Steiker, and her brother, Jordan Steiker, in an early article, "Sober Second Thoughts," published in 1995, who laid out the counterintuitive but compelling argument that the purported failures of the death penalty were actually what has made it endure. All our procedural struggles—all my ongoing litigation, all the Supreme Court jurisprudence—were actually what legitimated the death penalty in this country.

Taking a leaf out of Foucault's *Discipline and Punish,* but drawing more explicitly from Max Weber and Antonio Gramsci, Carol Steiker and Jordan Steiker argued that the failures of Eighth Amendment jurisprudence could not just be thought of as failures—they had to be analyzed in terms of their productive effects. Just as Foucault had refused to stop at the failures of the prison, and instead forced us to see the productive effects of those failures—in that case, the production of docile bodies, of the category of the delinquent as a means to distribute punishment, of the accumulation of men necessary for the accumulation of capital—Steiker and Steiker turned our attention to the *productive* effects of Eighth Amendment dysfunctionality.

The death penalty, they argued at the time, was both overregulated and underregulated: overregulated because there was so much intricate jurisprudence and so many technicalities that had no effect; but underregulated because the courts never really looked at the merits of cases. The result was layers upon layers of proceduralism, with no substantive review. In their view, Eighth Amendment jurisprudence was both too messy and too meaningless. But these failures, they suggested, served another function: to legitimize the death penalty and the larger criminal justice system.

Steiker and Steiker forced me to rethink the functionality of law. As they wrote, "You can't know that a thing is not being done well until you know what it is that is being done." And it turned out, in their view, that Eighth Amendment jurisprudence was actually doing *something* well—namely, legitimating capital punishment and, more broadly, the American criminal justice system. It induced, in their words, "a *false or exaggerated* belief in the normative justifiability of something in the social world—that is, [a] belief in the absence of or in contradiction to evidence of what the phenomenon is 'really' like."[3]

Their analysis, and similarly that of the historian Douglas Hay on the legitimating functions of clemency, of Foucault on the productive functions of the prison, and of

Gramsci on the hegemonic functions of ideology—these struck at the core of my critical praxis. In more colloquial terms, I had become a cog in the system, rather than a wrench. I had become *part* of the death penalty system. Rather than stopping it in its tracks, I was helping it function better.[4]

From a critical perspective, I also often asked myself how much more could be done to change the world and what I was foregoing. I wondered what better ways there were to ensure that others avoid Doyle Hamm's poverty and upbringing or the racial discrimination that plagued Kenneth Magwood's and Arthur Giles's lives. I questioned whether broader legal challenges might help improve the world or render society more just. I worried about the amount of time, of years, of resources, that it takes to try to save one life, when so many others are going through similar experiences without anyone paying attention or lending a hand. Would I not be better off investing at the front end than at the back end, in education rather than in eleventh-hour capital defense? Instead, I was dedicating a lifetime to keeping a few women and men from the butcher, or delaying one or two executions—in the process, often producing sentences of life imprisonment without parole that are hardly worth living, lives that so many of my friends and clients did not want to live.

For the longest time, the contradictions were so unbearable that I mostly tried to avoid them. I never lectured about the death penalty, never made it a focus of my critical scholarship, or even taught it much. I only wrote two short, unplanned pieces on capital punishment: one about the remarkable decision of the Supreme Court of South Africa abolishing the death penalty back in 1995; and another, in a moment of weakness, predicting the abolition of the death penalty in the United States by 2050. Somehow, instinctively, I always felt that it would only make my legal representation more difficult if I critically theorized what I was doing. I litigated the death penalty passionately, yes, as I've done for three decades now, but for many years, I did not critically examine or talk about it.

Faced with lives at risk, I mostly did not allow myself to stop and think. I immersed myself in my cases and did everything I could to keep my friends alive. It's as simple as that. I appealed to every possible court, multiple times if possible. I found legal ways to delay their executions, calculating days and postal delivery times and summer recesses to stave off the butcher. And I did it all because these men and women needed a lawyer. It was not that I was qualified—I certainly was not when I first took these cases, one year out of law school. With no legal experience to speak of, I had no place taking their lives in my hands. But no one else more qualified was willing to represent them. Bryan Stevenson and I had tried to obtain pro bono counsel for the men I would later represent, but there was nothing attractive or interesting about their cases—no innocence claims, no blatant evidence of prejudice, few mitigating circumstances—and so no one stepped up. Thus, when the time came, we would, and I did. It was like emergency medical triage: we, death row lawyers, privileged the most threatened life—the woman or man closest to the execution chamber, or facing a statute of limitations. That most precarious life would receive immediate attention. Whoever was going to suffer the most, we jumped in there. It was in part why we represented the men and women on death row before tackling sentences of life imprisonment without parole. To do otherwise, from a moral or ethical perspective, seemed to be squandering precious time and resources.

Not all revolutionaries or radical theorists think this way. In fact, true revolutionaries often believe that they know how to sacrifice some individuals for the greater good of everyone. Maximilien Robespierre and Mao certainly did. Most, if not all, accomplished military generals do. Napoleon and Patton certainly did. And many critical theorists do as well. When Žižek, for instance, writes about the four invariants of communism, including "disciplinary *terror*," and calls for a dose of that Jacobin-Leninism, he is alluding precisely to the sacrifice of some for the greater good of the cause.[5] And, it's important to note, this is not a radical position. Most welfare economists think this way as well, as do major corporations and legislatures: life has a statistical value, and most social and corporate policies weigh the costs of lost life (precisely using the statistical value of life) against the welfare benefits to society. This is true across the board in the United States, whether it has to do with the recall of a defective automobile part or emissions standards for clean air.

Walter Benjamin, too, resisted the idea that protecting life at all cost is the first imperative. That was his central starting point and critique of liberalism in *Critique of Violence*: there is something more important than just being alive at all costs, and it has to do with the quality of the life we lead. Liberalism leads us down the wrong path, Benjamin argued, in placing life, bare life, as its first priority. Life per se is not worth preserving. In fact, when you start down that road, you end up justifying anything, any violence, Benjamin warned.[6] This is consonant with the view, commonly expressed, that a life on death row, or a life in prison without the possibility of parole, may not be worth living at all. Some men and women on death row volunteer for this reason; many are opposed to negotiating a plea for this reason. It is not a stretch to suggest that, for many critical theorists, these calculations might militate *against* death penalty representation—especially if it serves only to legitimize the punitive state.

But what of the values of compassion, and respect, and equality that also are central to critical philosophy? Yes, I could now look back and draw on those values of compassion and respect, and especially on the obligation—as I discussed in chapters 12 and 13 on the inevitable violence of critical theory—to spread the burden of violence with care and equity. Those facing execution are suffering the most concentrated form of state violence—of the inequalities in society that sacrifice persons of color, the poor, the mentally ill. These are the men and women, those on death row or behind bars, who bear the concentrated brunt of our unjust society. They are carrying the greatest burden of a wayward society that pays little to no attention to public education, public health, poverty, and discrimination. For all the reasons discussed earlier about the need to distribute the burden equitably and carefully, and not to concentrate the violence, these incarcerated men and women, especially those facing death, deserved my primary focus.

But, to be honest, there was—and still often is—a gap between my critical theory and my praxis. I went to Montgomery and continue to represent the condemned not for these critical theoretic reasons, but in spite of them; not because I was an abolitionist—I wasn't one when I went South in 1989—but in spite of that; not because I was religious, no, not out of faith—rather, perhaps, out of my lack of faith. I represented the condemned simply and purely because of their lives—because of the uniqueness of Doyle Hamm's life, the fragility of Kenny Magwood's life, the inimitability of Phillip Tomlin's life. Because of the tangible, physicality of life itself.

The incommensurability and uniqueness of life prevented me from critically unwinding my representation or doing anything differently. I would not cost out their lives. I would not sacrifice them or let them go, even if I could have deployed my time more effectively in other struggles. There was something incommensurate about a life in front of me. There was something too valuable—paradoxically, perhaps, for the very reasons that Kant spoke of: namely, the inviolability of life, the ethical obligation to never treat life instrumentally, precisely because life is incommensurable. "Paradoxically," I say, because, for Kant, life was so inviolate that he advocated for the death penalty. It was so inviolate, that is, that he lost his reason. There was also something about friendship, loyalty, and fidelity that drew me to these men whom I had represented for so long. Many years ago, I told them (and others since) that I would be there for them until one of us was no longer alive.

I have, so far, kept my word. I cannot imagine not doing so. These men depend on me, in a way that only they and I understand. We have spent years talking to each other, as I am sure you realize.

This may sound presumptuous. The idea that these condemned men depend on me surely sounds a bit inconsiderate. It is also not exactly correct. When you get down to it, it is probably the other way around. Yes, it's probably the exact opposite. It turns out that it is I who needed them. And I still do. I need these men because in the end, I do not know how any of us—especially any of us who are trained attorneys, but any of us, just as human beings—how any of us would *not* give part of ourselves to help another. How could anyone live their life without giving to someone else?

In conversation, François Ewald diagnosed the conflict, ultimately, and without prompting, as the product of a Sartrian decision *en situation* that carried with it certain consequences, but nothing more. It was an ethical choice I made, Ewald told me, and one that I am simply sticking with. He suggested that the dilemma would never even have presented itself to Foucault because Foucault did not cost out life. Foucault always took the viewpoint of the oppressed, the subjugated, the "*soumis*." Foucault always took the side of the *infâmes—les hommes et femmes infâmes*, like Herculine Barbin, Pierre Rivière, or those incarcerated in the Bastille. He would have put himself in the shoes of the person on death row. So he never would have had to interrogate himself about the ethical trade-offs. There is something to this point. It may explain Foucault's lack of normative grounding and his turn instead to an aesthetics of existence. For me, though, it all happened fortuitously: an event, a speaker at law school, a visit to death row that January in 1989 to meet four men, a decision to move to Montgomery. The inability of Doyle Hamm, Kenny Magwood, and Phil Tomlin to find a lawyer led to me becoming their lawyer. That's all. It was a decision, perhaps an ethical choice *en situation*, one that carried with it certain consequences, but nothing more. It is an ethical choice I made—one I stuck with, one I am sticking with to this day.

Rethinking Critical Praxis

After three decades of litigation and struggling to confront critical theory, having expanded the scope of my political interventions, I have a different relationship today to my praxis and critical theory. I have come to see that the death penalty forms part of a larger punitive paradigm of governing in the United States that extends far and wide to militarized policing and total information surveillance, and how the racism and classism in criminal justice must be challenged as part of a larger style of punitive governing that creates and depends on fabricated internal enemies and a counterinsurgency paradigm of warfare. In the process, my praxis has expanded to contest the creation of these internal enemies at home through challenges to such actions as the Muslim ban, order-maintenance policing, racial profiling, and repressive policing of speech and protest. The constant conflict between theory and praxis has pushed both—never toward unity, but instead toward an endless friction that has transformed, energized, and shocked both. It is only as a result of that friction that I have, on the one hand, broadened the scope of my political interventions and, on the other hand, formulated a more encompassing critique of what I now call the American Counterrevolution.

I have seen enough. I have witnessed, in my death penalty litigation, the grossest forms of injustice and barbarity—even in cases where I did not immediately think that I would have sympathy. I have seen, firsthand, how the thirst for vengeance and order can distort and disfigure humans. How the perverse quest for human sacrifice can deface not only august institutions, like the federal judiciary, but individual justices on the U.S. Supreme Court. I have learned that we, humans, are not sufficiently trustworthy to be entrusted with life. I have also witnessed enough of the punitive state, as it fabricates and demonizes internal enemies—whether it is the disorderly or panhandlers, or Muslims, or peaceful protesters, or immigrants, or persons of color. I have also heard enough of the justifications, even by liberals and progressives, of the supposed efficiency of racial profiling or Muslim surveillance, of the purported success of order-maintenance policing, or of the need to target and assassinate even American citizens abroad, without trial or due process.

Today, I approach my praxis as an abolitionist, not just of capital punishment, but of the prison system as well, and more broadly of our punitive society. I engage in my praxis in dialogue with the compelling abolitionist writings of brilliant critical theorists such as Amna Akbar, Angela Davis, Ruth Wilson Gilmore, Allegra McLeod, and Dorothy Roberts. In conversation with these writings, and of course with those of Foucault on the prison and governmentality, I have changed how I understand and engage in praxis. In the death penalty context, I have gravitated away from the more limited focus on the inadequacy of counsel and toward a broader ethics of abolition; but beyond that, I have come to embrace the abolition of the punitive paradigm of governing—this is now my horizon. We should not be caging humans; rather, we should do everything we can to invest and research and find ways to avoid needing to punish them. We should not be creating internal enemies, but instead reject the very framework of counterinsurgency warfare. That is, for me, my hope, my goal, my ambition—and my struggle. It is not simply ensuring that the accused receive adequate counsel, nor just holistic representation, even though that is a must. We ultimately must get beyond the punishment paradigm and achieve instead a society that operates more on an educational or well-being paradigm—one that aspires to support, encourage, and nourish everyone equally, rather than ignore and wait to punish people. And to those who immediately respond by asking what I would do with the murderers among us—my friends and clients, that is—I would respond, with McLeod, that these women and men are but a tiny fraction of the 2.2 million persons behind bars today in the United States, and their situation should not hold us back from achieving our broader aspirations. We can place their situation on hold for the time being, figure it out later; but in the meantime, there is so much to do to go toward the ethical goal of abolition, of not locking our brothers and sisters in cages, of getting beyond the punitive paradigm, that we should not let a tiny fraction get in the way.

As Harney and Moten write in their provocative critical work on the undercommons, the ambition of abolition should not just be to abolish the death penalty or racism, but also to abolish the societies that make those possible. What they advocate for, you will recall, is "not so much the abolition of prisons, but the abolition of a society that could have prisons, that could have slavery, that could have the wage, and therefore not abolition as the elimination of anything but abolition as the founding of a new society."[7]

That is what I aspire to now. My ambition is not simply to impose new meaning on my critical praxis, but to reorient it, expand it, and challenge it. I realize, though, that however much I would like to place my praxis under an abolitionist ethic, however much I would like to resist the possibility of legitimating the institutions and practices of capital punishment, I ultimately do not control the meaning of my praxis.

Early on, I read and was taken by Sartre's play *Dirty Hands*, and I have been haunted ever since by the question of giving meaning to one's actions. In large part, *Dirty Hands* raised the question of whether one can ever, in fact, give meaning to one's acts. Sartre thought so, I would argue, and he tried to impose meaning on his own work—for instance, by prohibiting the performance of the play in any country in which the local Communist Party did not agree to its performance.[8]

But I read *Dirty Hands* differently, and still do today. Hugo, the protagonist, a young, idealistic intellectual, ultimately shoots down and kills the Leftist leader, Hoederer, in a fit of jealousy—thereby accidentally completing the mission that he had been assigned by the more stringent Leftist faction, but until then failed to complete. Hugo insisted on staying pure and true to his ideals, but he had become fond of Hoederer, the man, that life. Fond of the way he smoked and spoke and thought. Hoederer, in contrast to Hugo, was the practical leader who compromised, negotiated, and made deals and arrangements to pursue what he believed would ultimately lead most successfully to a communist state. Hoederer dirtied his hands. Hugo would not, and, sent to kill Hoederer, could not. It was only when Hugo accidentally stumbled onto Hoederer embracing Hugo's wife, Jessica, misinterpreting the act as infidelity, that Hugo finally pulled the trigger. Released from prison two years later, he was effectively given the option of repudiating any potential political dimensions of his murder of Hoederer. His own more extreme Leftist faction, it turns out, had shifted strategies, entering into the very alliances that Hoederer had pursued. If Hugo claimed that he had killed Hoederer due to a fit of jealousy, he could be recuperated and put back to use by his political faction. If he claimed to have killed Hoederer for his politics, he himself would be gunned down. In the final scene, agonizing over whether to remain true to his ideals, Hugo kicks the door open and screams, "Unrecuperable!" At that point, the curtain falls, but the audience knows that he will be gunned down.

Hugo seized the moment of his suicide to give meaning to his actions. And Sartre, I believe, would have preferred that Hugo could do so. Sartre thought that one could give meaning to one's own acts. "I consider me, myself, as the signifier," Sartre said.[9] But I have no doubt that, in the end, Hugo would not have the last word. The living would. They could place Hugo's dead body in the red-light district and feign a tryst gone bad. Or they could frame his ex-wife, or Hoederer's successors. There is no reason to assume that his faction wanted to be legally responsible for Hugo's death. He was hardly worth that much.

Spivak reminds us of how difficult it was for her grandmother's sister, Bhubaneswari Bhaduri, to give meaning to her suicide. Bhaduri, you will recall from chapter 2, left a suicide note, and even waited until she was menstruating to kill herself. She too had failed to fulfill her mission to assassinate a political leader that the radical faction—in her case, angling for Indian independence—had assigned her. "I asked her nieces. It appears that it was a case of illicit love."[10] Indeed, how difficult it is for anyone to speak—impossible, I would say, if what we mean by that is the ability to impose meaning on one's actions. Bhaduri could not accomplish this—or perhaps she could only through the voice of Spivak. Hugo certainly could not. He is not only dead, but also a fictitious character. As for myself, I know I too cannot. But that will not stop me either from embracing an abolitionist ethic and representing the condemned or repudiating the argument that my actions merely serve to legitimate the death penalty in this country. Only time will tell, but I do believe that we are moving toward an abolitionist horizon.

In confrontation with Weber, Gramsci, Marx, and legitimation theory, I see better how legal weapons, even litigation over civil and political rights, can challenge the punitive state. These may be the state's weapons, but they can be turned against the state, to prevent it from executing the condemned—from exercising its full power in a situation where it is at its most powerful: where the state faces down, most often, an impoverished and despised person who has confessed to murder, lacks any resources whatsoever, and has no one to turn to. It is the ultimate confrontation of a Goliath at its most mighty—in the realm of crime and punishment, in the unquestioned space of security and policing—with an entirely subjugated David, isolated in solitary confinement, on a desperate path since the moment he was born. This should be quick work for the state—a swift display of power. And yet the litigation takes place as a power struggle, as an ordeal, with condemned prisoners using every weapon they can get their hands on—including at times the weaponization of life, and at other times, due process and liberal legalism.

These tactics form a critical praxis. There is no reason to be dogmatic or categorical about what weapons we use. In battle, in struggle, I am prepared to use any weapon, especially when I am as desperate as my condemned friends are. I do not take literally Audre Lorde's famous proviso that "the master's tools will never dismantle the master's house."[11] That must be read metaphorically, or perhaps better, in the way that Sara Ahmed interprets it, as you will recall from chapter 15: "In that unflinching 'will never' is a call to arms: do not become the master's tool!"[12] This comes back, once again, to the problem of nominalism and the naming of categories. *Pace* Marx, there is no reason to exclude civil and political rights, or scorched-earth litigation, from an emancipatory and abolitionist agenda.

The Problem of Truth

In his seminar on the death penalty, held during 1999–2000, Jacques Derrida explored, among many other things, four historically important or world-historic executions—Socrates, Jesus Christ, Joan of Arc, and Mansur al-Hallâj, a Persian mystic, writer, and teacher of Sufism who was executed in 922. Derrida proposed that all four of them were killed for claiming to speak the truth—for presenting themselves as the voice of God, or for hearing God, and for that reason, for speaking truth. "I am truth," Christ and al-Hallâj literally said, as Derrida emphasizes. "I am the witness, I can witness a truth bigger than me and you."[13]

Derrida felt like an outsider, an interloper to capital punishment—and expressed concern about not simply doing feel-good work in the seminar. He asks, "How can you talk about the death penalty in a seminar like this in a way that it is not just a feel-good discussion, especially when we know or believe we will never be the executioner, or the condemned, or the lawyers, or the governors with the power to pardon?" Derrida mentions the federal resource centers that opened in the early 1990s, which was where I worked in Montgomery. Mine was called, at the time, the Alabama Capital Representation Resource Center—today people know it as the Equal Justice Initiative (EJI). Derrida mentions how President Bill Clinton reduced the federal budget for the centers, and then, in 1996, signed the Antiterrorism and Effective Death Penalty Act of 1996, which limited the appeals of death row prisoners.[14] I lived through that. It was an odd sensation to feel so interpellated by Derrida in this way. But it does not relieve me, in any way, of Derrida's concern—of the need to take precautions against engaging in no more than a feel-good discussion. I pray, again in my agnostic way, that I have avoided that.

In any event, Derrida may be right that, for the exceptional women and men who have been executed in history, those historical figures, there was an element of truth-telling. They did speak a truth that others did not want to hear. They confronted their peers—the complacency, the established wisdom of their peers—and in so doing, they were frightening. They were destabilizing. They threatened the social hierarchy. They challenged the power structure. At the very least, they were an utter nuisance and a bad influence on the young—or so their contemporaries thought.

But it is less likely that we are killing *parrhesiastic* speech today—that we are killing truth-telling speech when we sentence to death a person convicted of a capital offense in the United States or elsewhere (in China, for instance). There may, on occasion, be truth-tellers, but I do not sense that that is what we are doing with my friend Doyle Hamm. It may well be that we sentence them to death in order to kill the truth about our own weak human nature. Perhaps we kill because the condemned tells us the truth about ourselves. In killing a woman or man convicted of homicide, perhaps we think that we are being cleansed of a truth about ourselves. But it is unlikely that we are executing many of these men and women on death row in America because they are telling truths in the way that Socrates, Christ, Joan of Arc, and al-Hallâj were.

Perhaps, instead, we need to explore how truth comes in at the other end: it is only the certainty of truthful belief that allows us to execute someone. It is only our self-righteousness, our utter faith in ourselves as knowers of right and wrong, as knowers of facts, that allow us to kill another. It is only when we are so sure about the need to eliminate a criminal or cleanse society of the abnormal or mentally ill that we act in such a cruel fashion.

I recall, when visiting the Goethe Universität in Frankfurt am Main, Germany, to deliver a lecture, suddenly realizing that the university was built in and around the massive corporate headquarters of I. G. Farben, which were constructed before the war. Farben was the largest chemical company in Europe, and it patented and manufactured Zyklon B, which became the preferred chemical agent to exterminate over one million Jews. Farben collaborated with the Schutzstaffel (SS) in running Auschwitz, and it actually had a plant in the concentration camp itself, as well as more massive chemical plants near Auschwitz III-Monowitz, a factory facility that used over 80,000 slave laborers—one subsidiary was called IG Farbenindustrie AG Auschwitz.

The history of those concentration camp killings is harrowing and well documented in the Auschwitz album.[15] It reveals how the killings evolved, starting with the desire to eliminate the mentally ill and abnormal. It began with the elimination of mental patients, and then it extended to the handicapped, the chronically ill, the aged. It was part of a euthanasia program, in the lineage of eugenics—that is, in the lineage of science and truth. The documentation is telling. Let me reproduce it at length here. We need to be reminded. We need to remember. We need to recall the rationality of it all, the systematicity, the protocols:

> The Nazis first began using poison gas as a means for mass murder in December 1939, when an SS *Sonderkommando* unit used carbon monoxide to suffocate Polish

mental patients. One month later, the head of the Euthanasia Program decided to use carbon monoxide to kill the handicapped, chronically ill, aged, and others who had been put in his charge. By August 1941 approximately 70 000 Germans had been murdered in five euthanasia centers, which were equipped either with stationary gas chambers or with mobile gas vans.

In the summer of 1941, the Germans commenced murdering Jews en masse in a systematic fashion. After several months, it became clear to them that the mass murder method they had previously employed, of shooting, was neither quick nor efficient enough to serve their needs. Thus, based on the experience gained in the Euthanasia Program, they began using gas chambers to annihilate European Jewry.

In December 1941, the SS inaugurated the large-scale use of gas vans at the Chelmno extermination camp. These worked by piping exhaust fumes into the enclosed vehicle through a special tube. 40–60 victims were jammed into the van at a time, and after several minutes, they were suffocated. However, this method was insufficient for the millions of Jews that the Nazis intended to kill. Therefore in 1942, as part of Aktion Reinhard, (the program to exterminate Jews in the *Generalgouvernement*)—they built three extermination camps equipped with large, stationary gas chambers. Belzec, which commenced operation in March, had three gas chambers located in a wooden barrack; Sobibor, where the killings began in May, housed its gas chambers in a brick building and Treblinka, which was established in July, had three gas chambers that could be hermetically sealed. At each of the three camps, hundreds of thousands of Jews were murdered by exhaust gas from diesel engines. During the summer and fall of 1942 the Nazis enlarged the existing gas chambers and added new ones.

When transports arrived at Sobibor, Treblinka, and Belzec, a few of the victims were chosen to join *Sonderkommando* units, while a few others with various skills were selected to work in repair shops which served the camp staff. The rest of the victims were sent on an assembly line, where they were stripped of their possessions and clothing and their hair was cut. They were then pushed into the gas chambers with their arms raised so the maximum number of people could be jammed in. Babies and young children were thrown in on top of the crowd. After the victims had been gassed and killed, the *Sonderkommando* men would remove the bodies from the chamber and bury them.

The Nazis continued to search for a more efficient method of mass murder. After some experimentation on Soviet prisoners of war, the Nazis found a commercial insecticide called Zyklon B to be an appropriate gas for their needs.

> Zyklon B, a form of hydrogen cyanide, was put to use in the extermination center at Auschwitz. Over its four years of existence, more than one million people were gassed to death there. However, the Nazis were not satisfied with the rate of extermination. During the summer of 1942 plans were made to build newer, more efficient gas chambers and crematoria ovens to dispose of the corpses. The project was completed under the direction of the company JA Topf und Soehne, by the spring of 1943, allowing Auschwitz to become the Nazis' main killing center.
>
> Some of the Nazis' other camps also contained gas chambers, but they were not used on a regular basis for mass extermination. Gas chambers functioned at Mauthausen, Neuengamme, Sachsenhausen, Stutthof, and Ravensbrueck. All of these gas chambers utilized Zyklon B to kill their victims.[16]

Notice how the atrocities advanced: it started with the mentally ill; then the physically disabled; then the chronically ill and aged. It began and developed scientifically. It rested on science and medicine. It extended to Jews, Roma, homosexuals, and opponents. I do not mean to draw a comparison between the American death penalty and the legacy of slavery and the Holocaust. They are incommensurable. But surely there are similarities in the way that truth functions in each. It is only when we are so sure of ourselves that we are willing to rid the world of the others, of criminals, of the abnormal. It is when we are so sure of our truth that we build execution chambers. We do have a way, we humans, of feeling righteous about getting rid of the defective, of cleansing ourselves of the abnormal. As a result of difficulties with lethal injection, the state of Alabama, as well as the states of Oklahoma and Mississippi, are now developing execution protocols using nitrogen gas.[17] They have not yet decided whether to use gas chambers or simply gas masks. We will know more about how they plan to gas the condemned soon. They are writing the protocols. Truth can, indeed, be murderous.

The Politics of Death

The broader ambition of abolishing the punitive society, which now animates my critical praxis, relates and confronts in critical ways the writings of Michel Foucault from the early 1970s. At that time, Foucault exposed the thoroughly political nature of penal law and procedure. Especially in his lectures *Penal Theories and Institutions* in 1972 and *The Punitive Society* in 1973, Foucault demonstrated how penal practices are, through and through, political. He also exposed, in his militancy with the *Groupe d'information sur les prisons* (GIP), how all common-law prisoners are in fact political prisoners.

These insights are, for the most part, elided in death penalty cases in the United States. Capital crimes have a way of naturalizing the process entirely, sanitizing it of its political nature. To be sure, many Americans recognize the racial discrimination that plagues capital punishment in this country, not to mention its disparate impact on the poor and disadvantaged. But far too few connect these dots to the larger punitive society and fully grasp the extent to which the death penalty, as a practice, enforces a social order and white supremacy in this country. A social order in which, literally, the lives of white people are worth more than the lives of persons of color.[18] A social order in which the lives of indigent and poor persons are sacrificed so that the social fabric can be reknit.

Interestingly, the European experience with the death penalty was perceived as being far more political than the American experience. In France, for instance, the death penalty was viewed as being politically tainted by the judicial and governmental killings during the Commune and World War II. Victor Hugo spoke of a "political death penalty" after the Commune in 1870—of the resumption of the "political death penalty" that had been abolished in 1848.[19] In his seminar on the death penalty, Derrida notes that European countries abolished the death penalty at a time when Europe was weary from the political travesties of human killing, in the wake of the two world wars, and disgusted at the barbarity of humanity. Capital punishment had become too political, not to mention tainted. By contrast, in the United States, there is a general perception that the death penalty is purely a matter of criminal law—not of politics. There is an awareness of disparities based on race, but even that is not generally perceived as "political." Bryan Stevenson is trying to change that understanding and make us realize that capital punishment and racialized mass incarceration in this country are the historical legacy of racism—of slavery and lynchings and Jim Crow. EJI's Legacy Museum: From Enslavement to Mass Incarceration and its memorial to the victims of racial terror lynchings in the American South, the National Memorial for Peace and Justice, in Montgomery, powerfully demonstrate the historical continuity and expose the racial and political nature of punishment in the United States today.[20]

In his book on the American death penalty, *Peculiar Institution*, David Garland argues that the radically local nature of democracy in the United States explains the continued existence of the death penalty. The explanation lies, Garland writes, "above all, in the distinctive character of the American state and the radically local, popular majoritarian control of the power to punish."[21] Garland tries to escape the discourse of American exceptionalism, suggesting that the history of America's relationship to the death penalty is not that different from that of other countries, especially Western nations. It may feel exceptional today because of the European ban on capital punishment, but the trajectory of decreased use and selective abolition, early abolition in some states, and the overall trends are not out of line with other Western countries.

Garland rejects arguments of culture or punitiveness, focusing instead on the idiosyncratic nature of local American democracy—what Tocqueville observed and wrote about in the nineteenth century. The day-to-day administration of the death penalty is determined, Garland writes, by the "micro-physics of local politics—of group relations and status competition, professional rivalry and ambition, and the venal give-and-take of political exchange." It has become, in his words, "a resource for political exchange and cultural consumption," a symbolic measure that serves primarily communication purposes.[22]

This helps explain it, but it does not go all the way. Garland usefully draws on part of the Foucaultian framework—the microphysics—but one could go further to show how those microphysics cohere, overall, to breathe life into a social order that privileges white life. Here, rather than pointing simply to microphysics, I would reach further to Foucault's work on the function of avowal in criminal justice in *Wrong-Doing, Truth-Telling*, where he demonstrates how our ordinary practices can help establish and reestablish social order. In the same way in which Antilochus' quasi-avowal reconstituted the hierarchy of ancient Greece and its social order of male heroes, these death penalty practices reconstitute white supremacy and racialized social hierarchy in America. It is that broader social order, that larger political reality of the punitive state, that I target with my praxis—not just the local politics and microphysics, but the overarching social order of punitiveness and racial hierarchy.

Rethinking Strategies and Tactics

As a result of the settlement of one of my decades-long death penalty cases, I have the ability to represent another person on death row, should there be a need and desire on her or his part. I now have the time and resources to file an appearance on behalf of a new client. Doing that is never easy. It requires a lot of coordination with attorneys who are monitoring capital cases, identifying the right stage to file an appearance, and ensuring that one is not harming rather than helping. There are certain stages of capital cases where it makes sense to enter—whether on the first appeal, at the beginning of the state postconviction review, or at the stage of the federal habeas corpus petition—but that is also changing right at the present moment. As a result of the adoption of fast-track legislation in some states, for instance, the timing of the direct appeal or state postconviction review has changed, which requires additional coordination. This is a highly contextualized and situated area. To make a long story short, there are significant strategic questions that need to be addressed before identifying or responding affirmatively to a condemned person's request for assistance, and this takes time, reflection, and attention.

Perhaps at this juncture, though, it is time to step back and rethink, for myself at least, strategies and tactics—as well as broader challenges to the punitive state. Freed from the immediate threat of the previous execution, I can revisit some of the critical contradictions between praxis and critical theory. There have been a number of campaigns that have had a broad impact and made significant inroads against capital punishment. Across the country, innocence projects and capital litigators have uncovered and proved a client's innocence in over 150 death penalty cases, achieving their exoneration. Although each of these cases—such as Walter McMillian's in Alabama—involves intense labor, creating the institutional framework of innocence projects has had an enormous impact, almost greater than the sum of its parts. Lawyers and nonprofit organizations have also mounted broad class action challenges to the methods of execution, especially lethal injection, that have stalled the death penalty in many states, at the federal level, and across the nation while the U.S. Supreme Court considered the constitutional issues surrounding the use of those poisonous cocktails. There also have been broad-scale challenges to executing juveniles and persons suffering from mental disability that have also significantly narrowed capital punishment in this country. These campaigns have had a significant influence.

Having now more time and resources, and brilliant new colleagues and student collaborators, I can perhaps imagine a broader strategic challenge to the death penalty and the punitive state for these times. It may be possible, for instance, to identify the handful of counties that are producing the few remaining capital sentences, and to target resources there at the trial level. In 2019, only thirty-four death sentences were meted out across the country, with concentration in just a few counties. Perhaps one could envisage a project to target those counties—or perhaps develop another broad strategy. I need not distract you with the details; surely I can and will work those out. But the confrontation of critical theory and praxis has led me to rethink what I am to do next and to set for myself a series of difficult challenges.

In these abolitionist efforts, I too seek to render unmanageable the punitive paradigm of governing. In this, I critically test—with a hammer, that is—the concept of "ungovernability" that the Invisible Committee proposes in its writings. The Invisible Committee notes, at the end of a long series of examples of what it means to "destitute" institutions—for instance, the university, the judicial system, or medicine—that "to destitute the government is to make ourselves ungovernable."[23] Yes, I need to collide this with my praxis.

Some critical theorists object to the notion of ungovernability, suggesting that it is too naive and unworkable. "Only the dead are ungovernable," says Stathis Gourgouris, who writes extensively about the need for a "left governmentality" that avoids the pitfalls of left populism. To speak of ungovernability, he argues, evades the hard question of *how* we should govern ourselves. The goal instead, Stathis suggests, should be "to erase the difference between those who govern and those who are governed."[24] By contrast, I now feel that the ambition to "make ourselves ungovernable" may both be productive and enlightening—enlightening, especially, because it finally allows me to articulate and formulate something that has always bothered me about Foucault's discussion of governmentality and critique in his famous lecture, "What Is Critique?"

In that 1978 lecture, Foucault notoriously defined critique as the "art of not being governed in this manner." There is a lot of back-and-forth in the early part of his lecture about that precise definition. Foucault rephrases it several times, referring to critique as "how not to be governed *like this*, by these people, in the name of these principles, in view of these objectives, by the means of these procedures," as how to not be "governed like this, for this, and by them," as "the art of not being governed," as "the art of not being governed like this and at this price," as "not wanting to be governed," as "not wanting to be governed like this," and as "*l'art de n'être pas tellement gouverné*."[25] This last formulation is especially confusing in translation. It has been misleadingly translated as "the art of not being governed so much," when in fact the French term *tellement* can also be properly translated as "thusly": so it should read, in my view, "the art of not being governed thusly." Especially in light of the misguided effort by some scholars to impose a neoliberal film on Foucault, it is important to avoid improperly overlaying a laissez-faire connotation on Foucault's definition of critique.[26]

It is clear from his 1978 lecture that Foucault does not interpret critique as the desire to not be governed *at all*—since, as he acknowledges, the idea of not being governed *at all*, as if there is somewhere outside of governmentality, makes no sense. This is undoubtedly correct, and it aligns perfectly with the earlier argument in chapter 7 that there is no unregulated space. It is clear that Foucault does not intend for critique to mean being governed *less*—here too, the idea of *more or less governmentality* makes no sense. Again, this is undoubtedly right, as I argue in *The Illusion of Free Markets.* Critique is a question, for Foucault, of resisting a particular way of being governed. It is, in his words:

> How to not be governed *like this*, by them, in the name of these principles, in view of those objectives and by means of such procedures, not like that, not for that, not by them?[27]

In other words, critique is resisting to be governed *thusly*.

Something bothered me about this formulation for years, but I could never put my finger on it—until I began earnestly reflecting on the notion of "making ourselves ungovernable," in the words of the Invisible Committee, especially in the context of abolishing the punitive society. What I realize now is that Foucault's definition of critique, however correct, remains too docile because it somehow accepts that we will inevitably be governed. It forces us to ask what ways of being governed might be better. But that is not the question I want to ask, in the end. I do not want to be spending my time justifying a form of governmentality; rather, I want to be challenging it and the next form as well—I want to be dedicating myself to finding the best argument against the next best form of governing.

The problem with the concept of "ungovernability," we are told, is that no one but the dead is ungovernable. This makes it a useless or childish ambition. Foucault certainly shared this intuition that critique is *not* about not being governed *at all*—that any notion of being ungovernable is unrealistic, that we cannot not be governed in one way or the other. But what I find attractive or provocative in the Invisible Committee's formulation—and this is something I have only now been able to put my finger on in my confrontation of my praxis with critical theory, even though it has always haunted my reading of Foucault's lecture—is that my ambition, ultimately, *is* to be ungovernable, even if I know that I cannot be ungoverned. My ambition is not to spend my time justifying a form of governmentality; others can do that (they do it all the time). They do it very well—all too well. I want to be spending my time critiquing and finding the problems because few do that properly, relentlessly. I want to be justifying the *ungovernability*, not the governability.

In other words, the realist reaction to all this—the mature, reasonable position that no one can be ungoverned, so we have to find the mode of governability that is most tolerable—*draws us into the project of governing* and distorts our vision. It forces us to spend our time conducting the wrong exercise: justifying a form of governing, rather than challenging it. I now appreciate—thanks to this confrontation between my praxis and the Invisible Committee's theory—the many parallels that confirm my discomfort and my hesitations.

Take, for instance, my friend and colleague Harold Koh, the former dean of Yale Law School. After a long and brilliant career as a human rights advocate, he was nominated by President Barack Obama and confirmed by the U.S. Senate to serve as the legal adviser to the U.S. Department of State under Secretary of State Hillary Clinton. In that capacity, Koh effectively wrote the rules of engagement to justify the use of lethal force in drone strikes. That is, precisely, an activity that amounts to justifying a form of governing—perhaps in a manner that we might all agree was better than the rules of engagement under the prior administration of President George W. Bush. But how on Earth does someone who has dedicated his life to human rights then allow himself to become, in effect, an executioner? He did so precisely by buying into the notion that we are necessarily governed—and that we therefore have to justify a less nefarious form of governing rather than stubbornly insisting on our ungovernability.

That, to me, is intolerable. I want to be the one who finds the best argument *against* execution protocols, not *for* them, who spends his time *challenging* our mode of governing and punitive society, rather than *justifying* it. And it is not simply a question of wanting to maintain clean hands, or not being willing to dirty them. My hands are just as dirty. I am not absolved. But I am just unwilling to expend—or, rather, viscerally opposed to expending—my intellectual resources on justifying punishment or executions. That is why I am an attorney for the condemned and why I could never be a prosecutor—even a progressive prosecutor. This is a question of how I spend my time—my short time on this Earth. It is about what I dedicate my life to.

Another parallel: the idea of being "leaderless" in relation to the Occupy Wall Street movement. No one believes, really, that it is possible for a protest movement to be entirely leaderless. No one is that naive. But it is the *aspiration* that matters. The goal, in certain movements, should be leaderlessness; and to best achieve that goal, it may be necessary to hold out the ambition of being leaderless rather than putting aside the ideal. Rather than arguing about a limited need for leaders, however limited, I will spend my time formulating arguments against leadership, relentlessly.

To return then to abolition: to those who reject the idea of prison abolition because there may always be, at the extreme, a justification for detaining someone, I respond that I will spend my time trying to construct the best argument *against* incarceration, not *for* it. I have spent too much time close to prison, and even more, my friends and clients have lived too much time in prison, for me to be the one to figure out the best justification for incarceration (even limited incarceration). I refuse to be the person formulating the best argument in favor of the prison. I will be the one trying my best to construct the most compelling argument for abolition.

In the same vein, then, I do not want to spend my time or energy or intellectual capacity figuring out how better to be governed, or how to be governed differently. I want to dedicate myself to always pursuing the best argument for how to make us ungovernable. And it was only in reading and debating the Invisible Committee—in struggling over that phrase "to make ourselves ungovernable" and my own praxis of abolition—that this all came together for me, and that I finally understood what bothered me about the idea of "not wanting to be governed *like this*."

Another critical concept that the Invisible Committee deploys is "destitution." In its work, the Committee privileges destituent over constituent power. Its use of the concept of destitution is one of the more novel aspects of its intervention. It has become its trademark. But it is important to recognize and underscore that the Committee links the concept of destitution to the moment of creativity. In other words, it holds that destitution is inherently tied to creativity. It is a two-step dance: creation *and* destitution. The Committee describes this twofold relation thusly: "the revolutionary gesture no longer consists in a simple violent appropriation of this world; it divides into two." Those are the two moments—and there are *two* moments: "On the one hand, there are worlds to be made, forms of life made to grow apart from what reigns, including by salvaging what can be salvaged from the present state of things, and on the other, there is the imperative to attack, to simply destroy the world of capital." This is, it emphasizes, a "two-pronged gesture." Those two moments, of making and breaking, of production and destitution, are integrally related for the Committee. "It's only from the destituent standpoint that one can grasp all that is incredibly constructive in the breakage," it says.[28]

This resonates, in my mind, with the radical critical theory of illusions that I developed in part I of this work. The idea of a radical critical philosophy of illusions is that the act of unmasking an illusion—the central theoretical intervention in critical theory—will necessarily activate the production of a new illusion that will need to be unmasked later. In other words, there is a two-step movement that involves both destitution and production. In my view, critique is necessarily an endless cycle: destitution creates something that will need to be unmasked, which in the process of unmasking will create something else that will need to be unveiled, ad infinitum. In this way, the radical theory of illusions is a relentless succession of destitution and creation, in which we are endlessly implicated. This duality is what the Invisible Committee calls "desertion and attack, creation and wrecking."[29] This captures the productivity of negativity. It reflects the endlessness of critique—and of political struggle as well.

Abolition as ungovernability is the moment of destitution, but it needs to be paired with the moment of creation—all the while recognizing that someday, even abolition itself may be a hindrance. (But there will be plenty of time to deal with that later.) For the moment, it is important to emphasize that destituting the punitive paradigm must go hand in hand with finding a new paradigm to replace it. Education could surely serve as a placeholder while I continue to explore.

On Law and Politics

As I do continue to explore, I must also confront the question of how to incorporate legal praxis into the political. We saw this question arise earlier in chapter 15, in the context of the common. It was there, most specifically, that we encountered reflection and debate over the relation between critical legal practice and political praxis. That debate can shed light on a similar question in the abolition context: How does the specific critical legal praxis relate to the broader political engagement? Can or should I privilege the legal practice—or rather subsume it, or even efface it—within the political intervention? The question is particularly relevant given the possibility that legal practice has the potential to legitimate, rather than undermine, the institutions of criminal law. The analogy to the earlier debate over the common is instructive here.

Michael Hardt and Antonio Negri, you will recall, argued that the common can overcome the juridical sphere. It can surpass and render defunct the law of property. They imagine the common as a space beyond law, regulated instead by democratic mechanisms and decision-making. By implication, they view the struggle for the common as a predominantly political fight, not a legal fight. By contrast, Mikhaïl Xifaras argued that private lawyers and critical legal innovators are already creating the common through copyleft and creative commons innovation. Xifaras contends that, rather than pretend to leave law behind, it would be far more effective to get private lawyers to critically reconfigure law. Drawing on the Critical Legal Studies tradition, especially in its private-law manifestations in the work of Duncan Kennedy and David Kennedy, but also Morton Horowitz and Roberto Unger, Xifaras proposes a big picture of private law—what could be called, provocatively, a vision of "Big Law." This vision empowers lawyers, especially private lawyers, to become the vanguard of social change because they are at the source of the internal critique of law, have the greatest technical expertise to understand and transform law, and are in the best position to oversee the eventual regulatory mechanisms.

There is both a more imperialist and a nonimperialist way to interpret Xifaras's position. On the first reading, critical legal scholars view themselves as the intellectual vanguard at the frontline of the struggle, leading the charge for the common: critical lawyers have the greatest skill and are positioned at the most pivotal location to achieve change. In this view, in practical terms, the common will be created by legal reformers or revolutionaries only within the space of law, legal institutions, and legal practice. In the second, nonimperialist reading, critical legal scholars simply enlist and train law students to participate in the broader political mission of overcoming private property and creating a common. This is a more pedagogical project—to reshape legal education so that law students are taught the internal critique of law and become empowered to instantiate the project of the common.

In my reading, Xifaras proposes an expansive view of critical legal intervention, along the lines of the first interpretation: law is constitutive of our social reality and will remain constitutive in the future. The common—in other words, the possibility of a shared communal regime that is neither state-owned nor private property, but where use is determined and managed by democratic decision-making—can, does most effectively, and perhaps must emerge from an internal critique of private law. The common is a product of legal transformation and necessarily entails legal regulation. Law comes before, during, and after, and it forms the very substratum on which new property regimes can emerge but must remain rooted.

I say "provocatively," though, when I call this the vision of "Big Law" because the term, naturally, has another, more common, street definition. Big Law also refers to the set of large corporate law firms, such as Skadden Arps, or Cravath, Kirkland & Ellis, or Baker McKenzie, that dominate and shape the flow of young attorneys and of the legal profession. Big Law is understood, in common parlance, to mean the "collection of huge law firms in major cities (particularly NYC) where thousands of Ivy Leaguers and honor students make six-figure salaries straight out of law school." The Urban Dictionary goes on to say, "They usually quit after a couple of years of virtual slavery, but if they stay in the game, they end up running the country."[30] That's not that far from the truth.

But this raises a real question of whether it is possible to maintain a big *critical theoretical* vision of law without also considering the *political reality* of Big Law. The two are necessarily interconnected. It is precisely the relationship between the two meanings of Big Law that may doom the imperialist critical legal project—even though, at a purely theoretical level, critical legal theory may be correct, and on a more limited nonimperialist ambition, the pedagogical political project is also necessary. Nevertheless, the fact remains that the political economy of Big Law undermines the potential that radical political change will come from private lawyers engaging in the internal critique of the law. What this entails is that, in all likelihood, we may need to turn to other equally constitutive dimensions of social reality to create radical social change, while recognizing that any future political regime will necessarily be governed through mechanisms and processes that can be qualified as "juridical." They will certainly be governed by second-order rules and regulations, whether we call those "juridical," which makes sense, or "political," which also makes sense.

This, again, raises important questions about how critical legal praxis differs from, on the one hand, the democratic processes that Hardt and Negri describe for the purposes of regulating the common, and, on the other hand, the regular litigation strategies that a hard-hitting lawyer working with the American Civil Liberties Union (ACLU) would engage in, whether on the common or on abolition. With regard to the common, the question is whether the common can emerge from within law, whether it would eventually be regulated by law, and what role lawyers might play in the emancipatory project and its future elaboration. With regard to abolition, the question is whether the political transformation can be led from within law, by critical lawyers, or whether a lawyer litigating from within is compromised. Naturally, it is not a question of mutual exclusion—but rather of priority, privilege, and importance. These are classic questions that go to the rightful place of radical jurists in social change.

In continuation with the thrust of this book, I would displace the conversation one notch—from the purely theoretical register to a more praxis-oriented and reflexive dimension. The high theoretical discourse over the common masks what I think is really at stake—namely, where the real space of militant action lies. The theoretical agreements and slight disagreements between Xifaras and Étienne Balibar, and their broader theoretical engagement with Hardt and Negri, distract from what in my opinion is the more fundamental and crucial question at issue: the question of political praxis, of strategy, and of the likely spaces of effective political struggle.

The stakes of the dispute, ultimately, are not about the theoretical niceties regarding the liminal spaces of law, its boundaries, or even its shadows. Rather, the stakes boil down to where it makes most sense to put our energies (or rather my energy) to seek social change: whether in the political or the legal domain, or, to put it in another way, given the reality of legal practice today and of Big Law, in the multitude, in the people, or in the elite (of which lawyers, especially private lawyers, form a part). Of course, the obvious answer to this question is "both"—this is not an either/or, it should be a both/and. Both the common and abolition will depend on both the multitude and the lawyers, and we should be attuned to this in our pedagogy, regardless of whom we are teaching or other considerations.

With regard at least to the project of creating a common, law students who (predominantly) are headed to Big Law and corporate lawyers making six or more figures are not the most promising wellspring of radical social change. As a matter of simple algebra, there are far more nonlawyers in this world, in the multitude, than there are lawyers. For the elite lawyers to seize the terrain of politics and jockey for a vanguard position, relying on their claim to technicity and expertise, can have only regressive or reactionary effects. To push out the multitude or militants through a claim to greater knowledge of the field of private law strikes me as counterproductive. There is, as Xifaras suggests, a conflict of the faculties. And it is truly disciplinary—in both senses of the term. My position is that when private lawyers try to gain the upper hand in the knowledge-power struggles within critical theory—vis-à-vis Hardt and Negri, for instance—they are doing a disservice to an emancipatory political future.

Another way to say this is that the imperialist political ambition of the internal critique of private law suffers from a heuristic fallacy—think here of the availability heuristic: we fail to consider the fact, first, that there is a minuscule number of trained private lawyers in society as a proportion of the overall population; and second, that the proportion of critical legal thinkers within that group is infinitesimal. So focusing on the *legal* transformation and the knowledge claims of private lawyers over the essentially similar ambitions of political actors and the multitude is probably a nonstarter. In effect, the *political economy* of Big Law—I am referring to the two meanings of the term, both the idea of law playing a privileged role in social transformation and the collection of large NYC law firms—is not promising for social change toward a common. So, while I mostly agree with the theoretical claims of Xifaras and, more broadly, with Critical Legal Studies, and while I admire and support the pedagogical project of the internal critique of the law, I do not believe that we, critical legal theorists, should be teaching lessons to political activists or trying to seize the space of social change. That, I think, dooms the transformative project to failure. Let me explain this point in more detail.

On the question of the common: I agree with the three theoretical premises of the internal critique of law as reflected in the writings of Critical Legal Studies. First, the law is undoubtedly indeterminate and malleable, and it can be shaped in radical directions from within, from both right and left. Second, it is undoubtedly the case that the common, should it emerge, will be a fully regulated space—whether we decide to call the regulatory mechanisms "law," or "norms," or "management," or whatever. It will be regulated in a *juridical* manner: the evolution from private property, understood as bundles of rights, to some other conception of the common does not involve a passage beyond the law. Third, law and political economy are constitutively intertwined. As noted earlier, this is the sense in which Hardt and Negri refer to the conjuncture of "capital *and* law," when they argue that the two are "intertwined together," or when they use the expression "the republic of property."[31]

It is precisely because I substantially agree on the three foundational premises of the argument for the common, especially on the coconstitutive nature of social reality, that I reach a different conclusion: namely, that the real question is which domain to privilege in our praxis. Given that law and political economy are mutually constitutive, the crucial question then becomes one of *prioritizing* and *privileging certain spaces of action over others*. What is at stake is not whether the internal critique of law is right, but rather whether to focus on particular (juridical) forms of intervention and to favor certain (legal) types of actors, or others. Marx's privileging of political economy, to be sure, should not relegate law to the superstructure or belittle the place of law, or suggest that law is not constitutive. But that does not mean that, with regard to mutually constitutive elements, we might not want to privilege one over the other in our praxis. In other words, while law and political economy are inextricably part of the analysis and of revolutionary praxis (to which we may need to add other constitutive elements), the real question is whether we privilege one field or space over the other in terms of our militancy, or one set of actors or knowledges.

Another way to put this is to ask: what do we gain by privileging the legal dimensions of the constitutive law-and-political-economy nexus? First, we rope the lawyers back in. That is important and can be useful. Second, we see new spaces to intervene and new ways to change society: many spaces of legal contestation open up to us. But what do we lose? First, there is a legal technicity that privileges law-trained experts—an elite. Second, and more important, we are focusing on a corps of actors who may be more resilient to political influence because they often are subservient to corporate interests.

We need to keep our eyes on the prize: changing the world to create a more just society. And the question, then, is whether critical legal scholars jockeying for the privileged knowledge-power position will help us get there. If the critical legal thesis is limited to the idea that we should render legal education critical and encourage law students and private lawyers to engage in critical praxis, then there is no problem. But if the ambition is more imperial—in other words, if the ambition is for the legal field to become, in some loose sense, the vanguard of the revolution—then I have to think that the political economy of Big Law will doom the project. The fact is that the field of private law and legal practice is dominated by Wall Street law firms, corporate interests, and capital, and the law school pipeline for private law goes straight to Big Law.

So the question is: among mutually constitutive elements, what will offer the greatest leverage? This is the perspective, I think, that Balibar may be getting at when he asks, and answers: "which are the *forces*, or the combination of forces, which, in a given situation, make it possible (inevitable) to cross the threshold, rise from the interpretation of the rules to their change? Is that the Supreme Court? Or the political movements? Or the social classes? . . . I am tempted to say (having in mind civil rights, abortion, social legislation): the 'force' is *a non-legal combination of legal agents and actions*. But this is just a formula."[32]

I would tweak that formula so that it reads, instead of just "legal agents," rather "militants." And I would not say "nonlegal," because the regulatory mechanisms have to be a central component of all this, but rather "strategic." So in effect, I would propose: *The force is a strategic combination of militants and actions that swell up from the multitude and that necessarily have political, economic, and legal components.* If we look around, especially abroad, at the spontaneous eruption of the Yellow Vest movement in 2018 or the Hong Kong protests in 2019, or the rise both in the United States and abroad of a popular, neofascist New Right, it is not at all clear that private law or, more broadly, Big Law is the space of political agitation.

This is surely the case in the abolition context as well. Although lawyers and legal scholars are fighting for abolition—and I count myself among them—there are far more nonlawyers challenging the punitive state today. The #BlackLivesMatter movement and Critical Resistance, among others, have mobilized legions of women and men. This does not mean that critical jurists should not continue their constitutive work of transformation. This does not diminish the need for critical legal praxis in any way. But it does means that anyone who is strategically observing from up high—as a field commander or general would view large-scale battlefield warfare—will probably be training their binoculars on what is going on in the streets and boulevards right now, rather than in the law offices. And it explains why some people may maintain their sights on other (equally mutually) constitutive fields of revolutionary action. If the ambition is to abolish the punitive society, there must indeed be multifaceted strategies, including important juridical critique and invention. Further, any movement toward abolition will necessarily implicate *legal* transformation. New forms of legal regulation will necessarily be involved. Law will be constitutive, and mutually so, with society and economy. But the forces that bring about the change, the paths of transformation, the fields of struggle may not be, most importantly, in the legal field. I doubt it will be private lawyers leading the charge. [As a public-law jurist, I would maintain that far more positive social change has been the product of public-law reform, through equal protection, due process, and other constitutional and statutory (habeas corpus) channels, than through private law reform—but I will leave that dispute aside.]

In conclusion, then, I would put the emphasis elsewhere: not on abstract theoretical questions, but on *praxis*—and on my own praxis in particular. The question is *what to focus on* in terms of our practical engagements. And in this respect,

Hardt and Negri have something important to contribute: they are not necessarily saying that law is irrelevant, or that we can get "beyond" law. Rather, they are arguing that democratic forces (the multitude) are more likely to push us—through assembly and other forms of organizing—beyond the punitive state. It is not an either/or for the law. It is a realization that the momentum will come from the multitudes rather than from the elite.

I do not take these questions lightly. I have struggled over them for decades. I rarely discuss this, but I was formed and cut my teeth on Critical Legal Studies in the late 1980s, as a law student under the guidance of mentors and close friends, Duncan Kennedy, David Kennedy, Martha Minow, and other critical thinkers, including Clare Dalton (my contracts professor my first year—the very year that she was denied tenure for being a critical legal scholar), Mort Horowitz, and Roberto Unger. I returned in the mid-1990s in part to work closely with these and other critical legal thinkers, Terry Fisher, Janet Halley, Christine Desan, and others. I worked closely with Carol Steiker, who pioneered Gramscian legitimation theory in death penalty jurisprudence. But my subsequent decades in critical theory, in constant virtual conversation with Foucault and Deleuze, Nietzsche, and contemporary critical thinkers, have churned those earlier years of critical legal study and added multiple dimensions to the "constitutive" nature of the social world. This is just my way of confessing how much I have struggled with this debate over the internal critique of the law—and agonize and pore over its complexities and implications.

In the end, I do not believe that it is strategically wise to build a praxis-for-all from a praxis for lawyers. Mikhaïl Xifaras ends his impassioned plea in the following terms: "*Let us hurry to render the (internal) critique of law popular.*"[33] I will certainly continue to try to do this when teaching law. But on the broader political scale, I am skeptical that we would be able to render such an elite project truly popular. That particular conflict of the faculties and struggle over knowledge-power is unlikely to bring about radical social change. I would and will continue to place my energy and hopes in a broader critical political praxis and space.

The Challenge of Power and Popular Will

This raises two other challenges, both to praxis and critical theory, regarding first, the question of power, and second, the question of the general will. Regarding the first, as you will recall, Michael Hardt and Antonio Negri advocate seizing power. They argue vociferously that critical social movements must "smash the state" and "take power."[34] In the context of the abolitionist horizon, this is somewhat fraught, although there is no doubt a lot of traction to the idea.

Gavin Newsom, governor of California, single-handedly imposed a moratorium on the death penalty when he took office in 2019, thereby postponing, perhaps indefinitely, the executions of 737 men and women on California's death row. With the stroke of a pen, he changed the lives of hundreds of condemned persons. In France, President François Mitterrand did the same. At the time of his election as president in 1981, popular opinion in France strongly favored capital punishment. But despite that fact, Mitterrand declared during his campaign that he opposed the death penalty and that, if elected, he would abolish it. When asked about his position, he responded honestly: "In my conscience, in the deepest recesses of my faith, I am opposed to the death penalty. . . . I don't need to read the opinion polls to know that a majority of the people favors the death penalty: I'm a candidate for President of the Republic. . . . I say what I think, what I sincerely believe, my deepest spiritual attachments, my faith, my concern for our civilization. I am not in favor of the death penalty."[35] Once elected, Mitterrand and Robert Badinter, his justice minister, introduced legislation that ultimately abolished the death penalty.

So what about seizing power, through whatever mechanism, and using it to abolish the punitive state? If it were possible, surely it would be better than just taking a single death penalty case. But this action also raises a number of conundrums, starting with the familiar problem that wracked the student revolutions of 1968—the question of whether meaningful social change can be achieved by taking state power or whether instead there must be a more fundamental transformation of the mechanism and institutions that reproduce power. Power or the reproduction of power: that issue permeated the late 1960s. That was precisely the debate that Foucault and Louis Althusser had in the early 1970s.[36] The case of Patrice Lumumba and the Congolese revolution was on everyone's mind at that time. Shortly after the Congo gained independence from Belgium in 1960, the country's first prime minister, Lumumba, was assassinated and replaced by his former military general, Mobutu Sese Seko, who later became president and military dictator, and the country devolved into a corrupt dictatorship beholden to the same powers that had governed it before. The most common explanation was that the structures of power had not changed. The economy of the country had not changed. The political institutions were still beholden to the former colonial powers and multinationals that extracted resources from the Congo. Hardt and Negri are keenly aware of this problem: it is not enough, they say, to simply put new people in power, even well-intentioned people. No, we have to think more ambitiously about taking power and transforming power. They explain the idea as follows: "to take power, not simply by occupying the existing offices of domination with better leaders, but instead by altering fundamentally the relationships that power designates and thus transforming power itself."[37]

When I confront my own praxis with these critical ideas, I realize that I have little option but to struggle to transform the reproduction of power. Running for office or seizing power may be an option for others, but I am far too honest and open with my abolitionist ambitions to ever hope to be elected or nominated to power (this raises the problem of the general will, which I will come to next). Others may have the *technē* to seize power. Others had battlefield experience—like Che Guevara or Mao or, perhaps, General David Petraeus. Still others have a skill for electoral politics. But for critical praxis to succeed, it must come from each of us confidently, firmly, deeply, and conscientiously.

Along those lines, and having spent a lifetime in higher education, I must orient my praxis toward the reproduction of power. Victor Hugo wrote, "The writers of the eighteenth century *destroyed* torture; the writers of the nineteenth century, I have no doubt, *will destroy* the death penalty."[38] Hugo was certainly right, speaking of himself and the way in which he wrote so eloquently to inspire others, like François Mitterrand would a century later. For a charismatic leader like Mitterrand, it took the eloquence of Hugo. It would take someone of Mitterrand's stature and respect in the United States—someone with his authority—to end the death penalty. Cases of innocence are important, as are botched executions, tragically, and the executions of the vulnerable—these all have important effects on public opinion. But it may take someone with a lot more political capital to affect public perception.

The question of popular will presents a number of challenges in the context of an abolitionist praxis. The fact is, a majority of the American population favors the death penalty. Although support for the death penalty has varied over time, since the early 1970s and the era of the modern death penalty in this country, public opinion polls have always favored capital punishment, from highs of 78 percent in 1996 to lows of 55 percent in 2017.[39] The numbers are far higher in support of prison; only a tiny fraction of Americans favor prison abolition. And support for the police is even higher in this country. As the #BlackLivesMatter movement demonstrates, and as Larry Sherman proves statistically, the United States is a divided nation when it comes to confidence in the police and the punitive state, with one section of the country far more comfortable than the other. But these two segments are very unequal in size and wealth. The vast majority of Americans, especially white Americans, have far more trust in the police than they do for almost any other institution.[40] Thus, to suggest that the abolitionist ethic I hold is popular, reflects the will of the people, or bears any relation to a general will would be blinking reality.

Many critical theorists hold on to the idea of the popular will. Some, as we saw earlier with Chantal Mouffe, aspire to populism. Judith Butler makes a claim to "We the People." She contends that "the collective assembling of bodies is an exercise of the popular will, a taking up or taking over of a street that seems to belong to another public, a gathering up of the pavement for the purposes of action and speech that press up against the limits of social recognizability."[41] Those assembled, in other words, made a claim to the general will. At the same time, however, the popular will is a deep problem for critical and democratic theory, and for thinking about uprisings today. Butler recognizes the dilemma: "the efforts to associate a particular uprising or mobilization with democracy itself is a temptation as thrilling as it is erroneous—it cuts short the conflictual process through which the idea of the people is articulated and negotiated." So a central question is whether the assembled people are ever "we the people"; or, in Butler's words, "whether any given assembly really represents the people as such."[42]

The problem is acute in the abolition context. Those at Occupy Wall Street may have felt that they were speaking for the people—especially for those who were too affected to be able to speak out, who had lost their homes or jobs or health care. But it is far harder for abolitionists to feel, self-righteously, that they are speaking for the people. Butler is insistent—and in this I deeply admire her—that we include, in any analysis of popular will, the silence of those in prison who cannot be heard, as well as all others who have been silenced.[43] She insists that we include all the people who are missing. These are the "constitutive exclusions" that Chantal Mouffe and Ernesto Laclau discuss in their book *Hegemony and Socialist Strategy*.[44] But even so, adding the 7 million women and men who are under correctional supervision is unlikely to really constitute a general will.

It is a genuine question whether we can interpret assemblies like Occupy or other antiprecarity demonstrations as being "true or promising examples of the popular will, the will of the people," when in fact they may be transient and fluid—or worse, small in number. How does an assembly claim to speak for the people or to express a general will? The thesis of Butler's book, you will recall, is that assemblies serve as incipient forms of popular sovereignty. They give rise to forms of popular will and help shape our conception of the will of the people. And the bodily nature of assemblies exposes the precarity of these lives. It reveals not only the lived existence in the shadows, but also the resounding claim that this condition of precarity is intolerable. "The bodies assembled 'say' we are not disposable, even if they stand silently," as Butler says.[45]

The assembly does performative work in communicating strength, especially when it is a robust assembly. The "*Marée populaire*" (popular wave) on May 26, 2018, in Paris and all around France, was a perfect illustration. The count of bodies was high: 31,700 in Paris according to some reports, 80,000 according to the General Confederation of Labour (*Confédération Générale du Travail*, or CGT). But even more important, the diversity of the "*Marée populaire*" did work: the fact that assembled together were political parties, and syndicates, and associations from the *banlieue*, that fact alone, the fact of assembly and sharing the street, was extremely meaningful. Butler wants to reject the idea of defining "the people" based on metrics, or what she calls demographic forensics.[46] But that is often precisely how we fight over the significance of protest. It is a key weapon in the democratic arsenal. Building a broad, numerous, and diverse movement around abolition must be the priority.

The Women and Men

And, most important, what of the women and men who are condemned or incarcerated, and whose voices can hardly be heard, muffled by the iron bars, the cinderblock walls, and the barbed wire? How can I place them and their critical praxis at the forefront of my own political struggles?

Here again, the formulation of the action imperative "What is to be done?" may mislead. These women and men themselves are engaged in critical praxis, as Allegra McLeod shows brilliantly in her discussion, in *A Time for Critique*, of the hunger strike led by members of the Short Corridor Collective, a reading group initiated by men imprisoned in solitary confinement, for decades, at the California Pelican Bay State Prison Security Housing Unit.[47] These men, including Todd Ashker, Sitawa Jamaa, Arturo Castellanos, and Antonio Guillen, all classified by the state as belonging to racially identified prison gangs, surreptitiously began to read together and pass underground notes on a variety of critical texts on subjects ranging from the Irish prison hunger strikes to the Black Panthers, as well as on the writings of Michel Foucault and Cesar Chavez. Through their praxis, these men developed their own critique of their conditions of confinement and of the punitive state. Their critical exercise inspired a hunger strike, which ultimately resulted in the release of hundreds of prisoners from decades-long solitary confinement, as well as contributing to the abolitionist movement across the country.

Banu Bargu documents the use of hunger strikes by prisoners in Turkey, as well as in Ireland. In the United States, we have seen the widespread weaponization of life in prisons—of hunger strikes and labor strikes. We have also been allowed into and seen the harrowing conditions in prison through photos and videos surreptitiously sent by prisoners from contraband cell phones to family, the media, and advocates.[48] Prison conditions severely limit the range of praxis, but not the will to resist or the ambition for abolition. My role on the outside is to support these efforts in every way I can—and to support prisoners' families and friends on the outside as well. Accompanying the children of the condemned always hurt the most.

In the end, on my part, critical praxis remains today an ethical matter: an ethical decision *en situation* about the irreducibility and fragility of life—about human frailty. Instinctively, I too have always placed myself in the shoes of the subjugated, of the young refugee fleeing, of the accused, of the infamous, of the powerless: the disorderly, the profiled, the targeted, the internal enemy. How could I not? How else could I live life than by helping others? How else? Especially, as I have the privilege and the ability, the honor, to stand before justice for those in need. How else could I lead life? And more important, what more must I now do?

CHAPTER 19

Crisis, Critique, Praxis

"What more am I to do?"

I came to this question reluctantly. For quite a few years, I preferred the old formulation. I had few qualms about saying what had to be done. Perhaps it was because of my gendered upbringing, or the entitlement of being white or European, or the privilege of being the son of a refugee who fled Nazi Europe, or my growing up during the post-1968 era—or just my sense of urgency. I felt more comfortable saying what we had to do—if only more courageous people had spoken up in the 1930s or 1960s, perhaps we would not be where we are now. I felt comfortable using that floating signifier *we* too often and too easily. I still do, you might argue. But as I confronted my praxis with critical theory, I slowly advanced, first, to a middle ground, at least for a while: I began to believe that each and every one of us, critical thinkers, should provide our own GPS-, date-, time-stamped answer to the question "What is to be done?"[1] But then, ultimately, I came to realize that the question itself needed to be reformulated. In confrontation with my brilliant students—in their constant resistance to answering the question for others, in their critique of the question itself, in their puzzlement at the audacity of the formulation—I began to grasp fully the need for fuller reflexivity.

"What more, then, am I to do?" Yes, that is the only question that I can ask now, and I can pose it only to myself. It is the only question that I can try to answer—and I can answer it only for myself, in constant confrontation with critical theory and my critical praxis. And even though, as reformulated, the praxis imperative has become a personal quest, I decided to respond to it in public in order to carve out a space to guard against the many other critical voices that still want to tell me and others what to do. I have been tempted many times to erase this last part of the book, part IV—even at times, the entire manuscript—as I gradually came to reformulate the question of praxis. If, in the end, the question can be addressed solely to oneself, if one must ultimately confront only one's own praxis and theory, does it even need to be answered out loud, in public? Perhaps not—and perhaps I will regret doing so. But I nevertheless remain concerned that others will continue to tell me or us, on the critical Left, what is to be done, and at this point, I want to resist that with all my force.

That is precisely the problem: the claim to truth, the dangerous appropriation of truth, the will to truth. The problem is claiming to know what others should do. And I desperately want to counter that, to expose it, to push it back. I decided not to erase part IV or to abandon this project (even though by the end of it, I realized I could do so comfortably), precisely to create room for me and anyone else to resist the claims to truth by others. The earlier intuition of specificity—of time-, date-, and location-stamps—remains poignant and pressing. The question that I pose to myself, and my answers and confrontations, must be situated in these specific times of crisis. Whether called a new climatic regime (by Bruno Latour), the Chthulucene or Capitalocene (by Donna Haraway and Jason Moore, respectively), financialized capitalism (by Nancy Fraser), "Neoliberalism's Frankenstein" (by Wendy Brown), or as I do, the Counterrevolution—no matter what its name, we have entered a new historical epoch.[2]

We are suffering today from decades of neoliberal government policies and a global grab for the commons that has triggered a cataclysmic climate crisis in the shadow of an endless global war on terror since 9/11. In the United States, we are experiencing a new style of governing, both at home and abroad, modeled on the counterinsurgency paradigm of warfare. It is accompanied at the domestic level by growing inequalities, and at the international level by a global grab for the commons. These crises have been precipitated by a series of illusions, including, first, the belief in the efficiency of free markets; second, the fictitious creation of internal enemies; and third, faith in the neutrality of the rule of law. Together, these have enabled our leaders to legalize intolerable practices in the global war on terror and distract their (and our) attention from the climate crisis, while lining the pockets of the wealthiest in society.

It is precisely in the context of these crises and the critique of these illusions that I confront my critical praxis and theory today. In a few decades, if the Earth still exists to shelter us, readers may look back at this part of the book as hopelessly outdated. But the analyses of crises, illusions, and critical praxis are inevitably momentary and temporal. They are a snapshot. They can stand, inevitably, for only a moment, and then, they become artifacts, a mere archive. They become entirely out of date. That is, for instance, the fate of Lenin's tract *What Is To Be Done?* Today, that text is virtually incomprehensible because it addressed so minutely its own moment and crises. Rabocheye Dyelo, Iskra and Zarya, Martynov, the League of Russian Social-Democrats Abroad, the Cadets, the Bezzaglavsti, Krichevsky—Lenin's entire tract is practically unintelligible to the modern reader; and justifiably so. It is situated, contextualized, engaged in its time and space. May we all hope to write and prevail, and then become incomprehensible, an archive, a figment of history—and ultimately find ourselves to be outsized masses of marble, floating down rivers on barges. One can only hope that our theory and praxis will be worth transporting down the river and not simply tossed into the river. But even that would be okay.

Yes, we unveil and then, one day in the future, we will be unveiled ourselves. My ambition is that someday, this discussion of crises and praxis in part IV will be incomprehensible, discarded, nothing more than a forgotten folio in the archive in a more equal and solidary world. But let me take things, here, in order: crises, illusions, and praxis. Let me be as timely, punctual, and specific as possible. And may this all someday be incomprehensible and anachronistic. I will start with the crises.

Times of Crisis

To contextualize my analysis properly, I need to specify how and where I am located in these times of crisis. Most of my early praxis centered around the death penalty and the issues of race, poverty, and mental illness in the United States. It gradually expanded, first, to the broader issues of racism, classism, and animus across the American punitive society as I took on the broken-windows and order-maintenance theories of policing, racial and Muslim profiling, biased algorithms, digital surveillance, and the larger topic of neoliberal penality—the way in which neoliberalism has fueled racialized mass incarceration. Gradually, I expanded my praxis and critical theory to include global surveillance and the war on terror, and then the broader punitive paradigm of counterinsurgency governmentality, leading to my most recent work on the American Counterrevolution and my representation of individuals caught in Donald Trump's Muslim ban, as well as domestic protesters repressed by the punitive state. Today, I place all these actions and critical theory under the larger rubric of the abolition of our punitive society and counterinsurgency paradigm of governing, and relate it to the broader problem of the global grab for the commons, which has produced our global climate crisis. In other words, the more specific crises that I tackled in any one political intervention—whether it was capital punishment, or racialized mass incarceration and neoliberal penality, or the counterinsurgency paradigm of governing—are now imbricated and must be understood in a more interconnected way.

Also, importantly, I have always taken the position that my praxis needs to focus on my own backyard. I have practically always engaged in political action in the United States, where I live. I have never felt comfortable criticizing or intervening in other countries or addressing the problems of others. From early on, I resisted American human rights paradigms that did not make room for a conception of human rights violations happening right here, on American soil. I have always thought that it is far too arrogant to speak about injustice elsewhere, when we Americans have so much injustice to work through in our own country.

For that reason, practically all of my interventions and legal practice have been focused on the United States. In this, I have always thought, silently, with Voltaire's Candide, that I must tend to my own garden. I read *Candide* when I was young, and the concluding line has always stuck with me: "*Il faut cultiver notre jardin.*"[3] One negative consequence of this, of course, is the U.S.-centric nature of my praxis and of my analysis of crises. The U.S.-centricity of my work—and, so often, of this book—is born of this humility. It is not intended to be a form of imperialism. I have not found it possible to counter the imperialist-sounding aspects of this U.S.-centricity, precisely because of my attachment to candid humility. It is not my place to speak for others or about others' countries and problems. With these caveats, let me turn then to an analysis of the crisis moment that has shaped my confrontation of praxis and theory.

When *The Counterrevolution* went to press, the true character of Donald Trump's variation of the American Counterrevolution had not yet fully revealed itself. During the presidential campaign and the first months of his presidency, Trump experimented with every possible counterinsurgency strategy. He vowed a return to waterboarding and even worse torture. He warned that he would refill the camp at Guantánamo Bay, this time with U.S. citizens. He endorsed warrantless—and even suspicionless—infiltration of mosques, and spoke of establishing a national registry for Muslim Americans. And once in office, President Trump immediately signed the Muslim ban, excluding nationals from predominantly Muslim countries, and filled his administration with U.S. military counterinsurgency experts.

Trump played every note of the counterinsurgency score, accenting two leitmotifs: first, the creation, out of whole cloth, of an internal enemy composed of Muslims and Hispanics, #BlackLivesMatter protesters, and sexual minorities; and second, winning the hearts and minds of ordinary Americans through distraction techniques like Twitter and palace intrigue. The buildup to the 2018 midterms was particularly revealing, as Donald Trump whipped up fear, in a crescendo-like manner, over the threat of an enemy "caravan" coming up from Latin America, and then deployed military troops to the U.S.-Mexican border to keep out, in his words, the "animals."

Many Americans believed that Trump was just playing the reality-TV performer, similar to when he starred in *The Apprentice*—firing top-level aides on a whim, tweeting to get on the news, stoking conspiratorial plots. Many thought that Trump was just trying to be entertaining, or craved attention. Some thought that he was simply a buffoon. After all, he had told his closest aides that he wanted his presidency to be like a TV series, each day being another episode where he conquered an opponent. But gradually, as the fog of the distractions lifted, the true face of Trump's regime became apparent. Far from entertaining or merely distracting, he put in place a new and even more ominous variant of the American Counterrevolution: a neofascist, white supremacist, ultranationalist form of governing through counterinsurgency. Whereas George W. Bush's variation was marked by the raw brutality of waterboarding, indefinite detention, and illegal eavesdropping, and Barack Obama's version was characterized by the technocratic and legalistic use of targeted drone strikes (including the killing of a U.S. citizen and his sixteen-year-old son abroad) and globalized total surveillance, Donald Trump infused the American Counterrevolution with a fascistic, white supremacist ultranationalism that pushed counterinsurgency governing in an entirely new and portentous direction: an American New Right Counterrevolution. Trump tied the ultranationalism to an "America First" doctrine that unleashed domestic exploitation of the Earth and a grab for the global commons, cut relations with long-standing allies, and withdrew from international treaties like the Paris Climate Accords, pushing the country into a downward spiral on global climate change.

President Trump's constant use of New Right language and logic—a toxic blend of antebellum white supremacy, twentieth-century fascism, European far-right movements of the 1970s, and today's self-identified American "alt-right"—pushed the Counterrevolution into new terrain and the country toward violent social conflict. Trump's words and deeds empowered and enabled an upsurge of white nationalists and extremist organizations—from AtomWaffen to the Proud Boys to the Rise Above Movement.[4] Amplified by social media, Trump's actions incited unstable men to commit violence via pipe-bomb mailings, synagogue attacks, and mass shootings.[5]

The words Trump used, the things he was willing to say, when he said them, where, how, how many times—everything about Trump's discourse was deliberate and intended for consumption by the New Right. When Trump repeatedly accused a reporter of "racism" for questioning him about his embrace of the term "nationalist," he was deliberately drawing from the toxic well of white supremacist discourse and directly addressing that base.[6] Trump's increased use of the term "globalist" in interviews and press conferences[7]—including to describe Jewish advisers and Republican opponents, such as Gary Cohen or the Koch brothers[8]—was a knowing use of an anti-Semitic slur, in the words of the Anti-Defamation League, "a code word for Jews."[9] Trump's self-identification as a "nationalist,"[10] especially in contrast to "globalists" like George Soros, extended a hand to white nationalists across the country. His pointed use of the term "politically correct," especially in the context of the Muslim ban,[11] spoke directly to followers of far-right figures such as William Lind.

Practically every day, Trump created new internal enemies for the American people. One day it was the Reverend Al Sharpton, an African American leader from New York City, who he called a "con-man" who "Hates Whites & Cops!"[12] The day before, it was Representative Elijah Cummings, an African American politician from Maryland, who he accused of being a "racist,"[13] and the entire Black community of Baltimore, which he described as a "rodent infested mess."[14] Not long before that, it was four newly elected congresswomen—Alexandria Ocasio-Cortez, Ilhan Omar, Ayanna Pressley, and Rashida Tlaib—all young women of color, whom he treated as anti-American and racist against whites, and whom he told to "go back and help fix the totally broken and crime infested places from which they came."[15] Just before that, he called immigrants trying to cross the U.S.-Mexico border an "invasion of drugs and criminals coming into our country," declaring the situation a national emergency.[16] And before that, right at the start of his presidential campaign, he demonized all Muslims and Muslim Americans, demanding the "total and complete shutdown of Muslims entering the United States,"[17] associating

Muslim Americans with jihad and Sharia law, and calling for a Muslim ban and renewed warrantless surveillance of Islamic mosques.

Trump methodically engaged in verbal assaults that threw fuel on his political program of closed borders, nativism, social exclusion, and punitive excess. Even his cultivated silences and failures to condemn right-wing violence, such as in the fatal aftermath of the "Unite the Right" rally in Charlottesville,[18] or regarding pipe-bombing suspect Cesar Sayoc, communicated directly to extremists. In real time, we watched a New Right discourse come to define the American presidency. The term *alt-right* is too innocuous when this new political formation is, in truth, neofascist, white-supremacist, ultranationalist, and counterrevolutionary.

Building on the ugly history of white supremacy in this country, as well as on European far-right movements of the late 1960s and 1970s, a New Right emerged in the United States. It lies at the core of our crises in this country today. The central tenets of this American New Right are that Christian heterosexual whites are endangered, that the traditional nuclear family is in peril, that so-called Western civilization is in decline, and that whites need to reassert themselves. George Shaw, an editor at a leading New Right publishing house and the editor of *A Fair Hearing: The Alt-Right in the Words of Its Members and Leaders* (2018)—a collected volume intended to give voice to the self-identified "alt-right," including well-known figures such as Richard Spencer, the cofounder of AltRight.com, the evolutionary psychologist Kevin MacDonald, Jared Taylor, the founder of *American Renaissance*, and Augustus Invictus, a 2018 candidate for the Republican nomination for the U.S. Senate seat in Florida—opens his introduction on the race question as follows: "If alt-right ideology can be distilled to one statement, it is that white people, like all other distinct human populations, have legitimate group interests."[19]

The main goal of the American New Right, Shaw explains, is to discuss "the one topic that white conservatives are not allowed to discuss"—namely, "Race." All the recent conservative losses, in his words, represent "a transfer of power from white males to one or another nonwhite and/or non-male fringe group."[20] Spencer, in his contribution to *A Fair Hearing*, describes the superiority of certain athletes who are "white, and not just white, but Anglo and Germanic," with clear reference to Aryan supremacy.[21] A main guidepost of the New Right, Shaw highlights, is that "Jews not only wield obscene levels of power in Western societies, they use that power to damage native white populations."[22]

"White genocide is underway," Shaw warns, and those responsible are Jews, Muslims, leftists, and nonwhites.[23] Note how these claims of white genocide and

Jewish power resonate with President Trump's discourse. His last campaign ad in 2016 vilified three opponents, all Jewish: George Soros, Federal Reserve chair Janet Yellen, and Lloyd Blankfein, the chief executive officer (CEO) of Goldman Sachs.[24] In August 2018, on Twitter, Trump parroted white nationalist propaganda that the South African government was engaged in a genocidal campaign against white farmers.[25]

In all this, the American New Right draws heavily on European thinkers. Thanks to efforts like Steve Bannon's 2018–2019 European tour and the increasing exchange of ideas and publications, this movement is beginning to form part of what could be called a "Nationalist International"[26]—though the U.S. arm of this movement remains somewhat distinct because of American exceptionalism on race and its history of slavery. Shaw's collected volume includes, for instance, a chapter by the intellectual leader of the Swedish New Right, Daniel Friberg. The European influence is evident.

The French New Right thinker, Guillaume Faye, author of a leading manifesto of the European New Right called *Why We Fight: Manifesto of the European Resistance*, published in 2001 and translated into English in 2011, identifies the greatest threats to European civilization as "demographic decline," "homophilia," and "xenophilia"—the latter of which, he writes, is "improperly called 'anti-racism.'" With a doctorate from Sciences Po and a reputation as a founder of the French New Right in the late 1960s, Faye now puts forward an extreme geneticism. "A people's long-term vigour lies in its *germen*," Faye writes, "in the maintenance of its biological identity and its demographic renewal, as well as in the health of its mores and in its cultural creativity and personality. On these two foundations a civilization rests." A civilization or people who ignores this, he warns, "inevitably perishes."[27]

Similarly, Friberg, of the Swedish New Right, in his manifesto *The Real Right Returns: A Handbook for the True Opposition*, published in English in 2015, argues against "uncontrolled immigration," "sexual liberalism," the "right to birth control," and radical feminism, as well as "'humanism,' 'liberal democracy,' 'tolerance,' and 'human rights,'" or to sum up: "equality, feminism, mass immigration, postcolonialism, anti-racism, and LGBT interests." He also says that "Jews, homosexuals, Muslims, or other minorities" constitute groups who are indifferent to the interests of "Europe's native populations" and "traditional European values." When, on a visit to Europe in 2018, Donald Trump spoke of Europe "losing its culture," he was speaking directly to the new political constituency built on this concept of white genocide.[28]

The central strategy of the European New Right is to convert antiracism to racism—to make us believe that concern about white supremacists or promotion of multiculturalism is actually "racist." Antiracism, it turns out, is a ruse. "In the guise of combating racism and xenophobia," Faye argues, antiracism "encourages discrimination in favor of aliens, the dissolution of European identity, the multi-racialisation of European society, and, at root, paradoxically, racism itself." Or, as Faye says, emphasizing the words in boldface, "**anti-racists use their fake struggle against racism to destroy the European's identity, as they advance cosmopolitan and alien interests.**" For this reason, Faye emphasizes that antiracism "in fact is an inverted racial obsession. What's called 'anti-racism' is but a pathological expression of xenophilia." He adds that "to be 'anti-racist' is . . . to be part of a movement which is directly linked to a reckless hatred for Europe and her history."[29]

This core strategy has been incorporated into American New Right discourse. This and other New Right ideas, like the trope of "cultural Marxism,"[30] circulate back and forth across the Atlantic. Multiculturalism is now racist: "'diversity' and 'multiculturalism' do not ultimately enrich white lives," Shaw contends, "but rather tend to make white societies poorer, more dangerous, and finally unlivable for whites." Richard Spencer builds on this line of reasoning. Race becomes, in his words, "a weapon used against [whites] in all aspects of life: affirmative action, the 'diversity' racket, white Guilt, white privilege, etc." To combat this "double standard," Jared Taylor concludes that it is vital to recognize that white racial pride and preference are not "hate" or "racism"; on the contrary, they constitute "healthy racial/national pride." Whites must be allowed, in Taylor's words, "the right to pursue their unique destiny free from the embrace of large numbers of people unlike themselves."[31]

A policy paper titled "POTUS and Political Warfare," written in May 2017 by Rich Higgins when he was at the White House as a member of the strategic planning office of the National Security Council, advances the same charge against antiracism and multiculturalism. "Group rights based on sex or ethnicity," Higgins wrote, "are a direct assault on the very idea of individual human rights and natural law around which the Constitution was framed. 'Transgender acceptance' memes attack at the most basic level by denying a person the right to declare the *biological fact* of one's sex."[32] (Note that the Trump administration has urged the U.S. Supreme Court to affirm its ban on transgender personnel in the military.)

The rise of this American New Right discourse afforded Donald Trump cover to radicalize his long-standing tribalism. Back in the New York City of the 1980s and 1990s, Trump's interventions as a local race warrior were widely regarded as the quixotic folly of a real-estate magnate. For instance, he took out full-page ads in not one, but four New York City newspapers,[33] at a cost of $85,000, following the rape of a jogger in Central Park and the arrest of five African American and Hispanic teenagers, to declare in all caps "BRING BACK THE DEATH PENALTY. BRING BACK OUR POLICE." (Despite the DNA exoneration of the five youths in 2002, Trump never apologized, but instead doubled down on his charge.)[34] But by 2019, Trump was no longer a local player. He had become a New Right president, buoyed by a domestic base and increasingly global far-right movement built on white supremacist propaganda.

President Trump was no mere entertainer or buffoon, as many wanted to believe. Instead, he was carefully, skillfully, and consistently speaking directly to hardline nationalist supporters in their (and now his) exact language, using their tropes and memes. This is patently clear if you closely study his press conferences, campaign speeches, and tweets. In 2018, for instance, at a White House news conference, Trump rehearsed perfectly the New Right's core argument regarding the racism of antiracism.[35] The exchange occurred during questioning by Yamiche Alcindor, of *PBS Newshour*, when she asked Trump whether this self-identification as a "nationalist" might embolden white nationalists. Read the exchange closely, or even better, view it yourself here on YouTube (https://youtu.be/7bSMiSTdthE):[36]

Yamiche Alcindor (PBS Newshour): On the campaign trail, you called yourself a "nationalist." Some people saw that as emboldening white nationalists. Now people are also saying. . . .

President Donald Trump: I don't know why you say that, *that is such a racist question.*

Alcindor: There are some people who are saying that the Republican Party is now supporting white nationalists because of your rhetoric.

Trump: Oh, I don't believe that, I don't believe that, I don't believe that. Why do I have my highest poll numbers ever with African Americans? Why do I have among the highest poll numbers with African Americans? *That's such a racist question.*

[Alcindor tries to intervene]

Trump: Honestly, I know you have it written down and everything. Let me tell you, *that is a racist question.*

[Alcindor tries to intervene]

Trump: You know what the word is? I love our country. I do. You have nationalists, you have globalists . . . But to say that, what you said, is so insulting to me. It's a very terrible thing what you said!

Not once, not twice, but three times Trump accused Alcindor of asking a "racist question." It is hard to imagine a more immaculate illustration of how to turn antiracism into racism. Trump knew exactly what he was doing—as he did when he disparaged "globalists" and Soros, mocked "political correctness," or used demeaning and dehumanizing expressions such as "infest," "animals,"[37] "rapists,"[38] "rodent infested," and "shithole countries"[39] to describe immigrants, Black neighborhoods, and Haiti and a number of African nations. These are deliberate fodder for his white nationalist base.

Trump and the New Right were deeply conscious of the importance of language. In fact, many of the New Right texts consist, at their core, of what they call "metapolitical" dictionaries that redefine, recast, and infuse with political meaning ordinary terms. Faye's *Why We Fight* is essentially an alphabetized glossary—practically 200 pages of the 271-page book list definitions. Friberg too includes a lengthy metapolitical dictionary in his *The Real Right Returns*.[40]

Language is political. Interpretations are political, as I discussed in chapter 7. And for the New Right, it is the main site of struggle—the main battle, in Friberg's words, is over "shaping people's thoughts, worldviews, and the very concepts which they use to make sense of and define the world around them." The core concept of "metapolitics," central to New Right thought, is intended to redeploy the Frankfurt School's notion of ideology: to undo what the New Right sees as all the deconstructive cultural work that has been accomplished by the Left since the mid-twentieth century. American extreme Right thinkers also embrace "the metapolitical dimension" and its key influence on politics, emphasizing that today, as Collin Liddell writes, "the left entirely dominates the metapolitical realm in America, through its control of Hollywood, the media, and academia."[41]

As Jason Stanley demonstrates in *How Fascism Works* (2018), these extreme-right writings function along proto-fascist lines. The parallels are unmistakable. "Demography is destiny," Shaw writes. Diversity is making "white societies poorer, more dangerous, and finally unlivable for whites," he adds. Friberg talks of "natural selection," women's "natural role in society," and the right of "Europe's native populations" to self-determination and self-defense. Faye writes, "The base of everything is biocultural identity and demographic renewal." This contemporary discourse works in the same linguistic way as in classical fascism.[42]

Empowered by President Trump, the New Right radicalized itself in the United States. An entire part of Shaw's volume *A Fair Hearing* is explicitly titled "Counterrevolution," and it spells out extreme methods to "rout" the Left. This includes a chapter on how to "physically remove" leftists. The language is violent and explicit. "Physically removing leftists has gained so much traction because the idea is instinctively both logical and appealing," Invictus writes, continuing:

> The *means* of physically removing leftists, however, is not as simple. While throwing commies from helicopters *à la* Pinochet has become the alt-right's favorite policy proposal, this is clearly an inefficient solution. The Pinochet regime only executed 120 communists in this manner, and we are faced with many thousands of times this number.[43]

It should not come as a surprise that a "Free Helicopter Rides"[44] meme grew among far-right extremists, or that there have been sightings of right-wing protesters wearing T-shirts celebrating Pinochet and others, bearing the legend "Antifa Removal Unit"; or that the expression *Right Wing Death Squad* (*RWDS* for short) has entered chat-room discourse.[45]

The New Right explicitly adopted a warfare paradigm of political conflict. "Civil war is already upon us," Invictus writes. Europe "**is at war**," Faye writes, in boldface. And the relation to Maoist insurgency theory is explicitly made, for instance by Rich Higgins, who argues that Trump was the target of what he calls "political warfare" that traces directly to Mao's strategies. "Political warfare is one of the five components of a Maoist insurgency," he writes. "Maoist methodologies employ synchronized violent and non-violent actions that focus on mobilization of individuals and groups to action."[46]

The explicit foundation of the ongoing struggle that Trump purportedly faced was modeled on Maoist insurgency theory—and, of course, we know what the proper response to a Maoist insurrection is: counterinsurgency practices. The writings made clear that an "internal enemy" must be defeated. The insurgents include Muslims and Hispanics, the Movement for Black Lives, civil rights advocates, and trans* persons (what Higgins refers to as "ACLU and BLM" and "transgender acceptance"), and now, as well, the "Cultural Marxists." The result was a radicalization of the counterrevolutionary politics that we have seen since 9/11.[47]

Herbert Marcuse was remarkably prescient in forecasting this kind of counterrevolutionary development in the 1970s. At the time, he already was warning, ominously, that "we may well be the first people to go Fascist by the democratic vote."[48] We were, I believe, insufficiently attentive to how carefully crafted Trump's New Right discourse and politics were and how they deliberately encouraged and mobilized extremists and normalized them as a core political constituency. Trump enabled extremists through what sociologists refer to as "scripted violence."[49] We tended to say that Trump was "dog-whistling" to white nationalist supremacists; but it was far more blatant—and serious—than that. Speaking openly to the New Right, Trump was rallying and emboldening a counterrevolutionary politics that is at the very heart of the central crises that we face today.

Hand-in-hand with this new counterrevolutionary politics, Trump promoted an "America First" doctrine that unleashed a U.S. grab for the global commons and undermined all efforts at stemming global climate change. This formed part of a broader desire to seize the global commons—or whatever is left of it—with the dismantling of the Soviet Union and the precipitous privatization of industry, utilities, and finance in the former Eastern bloc, the capitalization of the Chinese economy, the deregulation of Western European economies, and the devastating impact of the fiscal policies of the International Monetary Fund (IMF) across Africa and Latin America. Mainstream economists document the plummeting percentage of property held in public trust in the United States, but also in China, Japan, and across Europe—with several of these countries having effectively placed their commons in hock. In other words, the amount of commons has shrunk. Thomas Piketty, Emmanuel Saez, and their colleagues have documented this well for China, Japan, Europe, and the United States.[50]

Combined with decades of economic neoliberalism in the United States, the grab for the commons has had long-term economic effects of wealth concentration and elite consolidation. As Piketty, Saez, Anthony Atkinson, and their colleagues have demonstrated, the United States has experienced a steady concentration of wealth by the wealthiest, beginning in the 1970s and continuing to the present day. The results are disparities and inequalities that are unimaginable. Today, the three richest Americans, Bill Gates, Jeff Bezos, and Warren Buffett, hold more than the combined wealth of 50 percent of Americans.[51] The 100 richest Americans hold about as much wealth as all of the country's 42 million African American residents. The 186 richest boast as much wealth as all of the country's 55 million Latinos.[52] America's 400 wealthiest individuals have more wealth than about two-thirds (or 64 percent) of Americans.[53] Whereas most Americans believe that the compensation ratio for a CEO compared to a low-skilled factory worker *should* approximate about 6.7:1, and while most Americans estimate that the ratio is probably more like 30:1, the actual ratio of CEO compensation to unskilled workers today hovers around 354:1. Back in 1965, it stood at 20:1.[54] Since then, the disparity has increased almost 18-fold.

Inequalities in the United States have also been fueled and aggravated by the deliberate creation of a carceral state that builds on and parallels the slavery of the country's past. The United States imprisons people at rates that would be considered inhuman almost anywhere else, and that circumstance distributes life consequences along racial and ethnic lines. The life chances of a Black man between the ages of adolescence and young adulthood being incarcerated are one in three. Prisons and jails are filled with young men and women of color. Jackie Wang documents the connection between the carceral state and racism in her explosive book, *Carceral Capitalism*, which ties together the techniques of racial capitalism and the carceral state in America.[55] Wang examines specifically the history of predatory lending and parasitic governance, which she argues includes five key elements: financial states of exception, automated processing, extraction and looting, confinement, and gratuitous violence. These key elements are summarized in the subtitle to her book: *Essays on the Contemporary Continuum of Incarceration: The Biopolitics of Juvenile Delinquency, Predatory Policing, the Political Economy of Fees and Fines, and Algorithmic Policing*. Wang shows not only that race is central to even seemingly benign and automated procedures, and how these techniques represent new forms of racial discrimination, but also how these techniques are meant to stave off crises of capitalism. She convincingly shows that practices of racial discrimination and subordination are not incidental to capitalism, but rather are inherent and indispensable to it.

At the global level, the inequalities are even more obscene. Sam Moyn reminds us that "a mere eight men controlled more wealth than half the inhabitants of the planet—several billion people."[56] We have witnessed, in effect, the decomposition of a period of social reconstruction after World War II and the wars of colonial independence featuring markedly increasing inequality throughout the globe:[57] a hegemonic form of economic neoliberalism no longer contained by the threat (or even the existence) of communism, an oppressive globalized and financialized political economy run from the corporate headquarters of finance, oil, data, and commercial multinational giants and G7 through G20 government leaders, and a run on the global commons, extending even to our shared planet, the Earth. Since the last third of the twentieth century, in effect, we have witnessed a structural transformation of the human condition—one that is about to accelerate with the explosive growth of artificial intelligence and the expected diminution by half of global employment.

These inequalities are not independent of, but tie directly to, the global climate crisis we face today. As Bruno Latour argues in his book *Down to Earth: Politics in the New Climatic Regime*, the climate change crisis lies at the center of these transformations:

> The hypothesis [of this book] is that we can understand nothing about the politics of the last 50 years if we do not put the question of climate change and its denial front and center. Without the idea that we have entered into a New Climatic Regime, we cannot understand the explosion of inequalities, the scope of deregulation, the critique of globalization, or, most importantly, the panicky desire to return to the old protections of the nation-state—a desire that is identified, quite inaccurately, with the "rise of populism."[58]

In this book, Latour paints a haunting portrait of our current crisis: global climate change, the product of Western exploitation of nature and colonized peoples, has created a vicious circle of growing inequality, ultranationalist isolationism, and strategic climate denial that is now being deployed tactically by the rich to protect themselves (somewhat in vain) from impending doom. We are, Latour tells us, on a *Titanic*—that is an exaggeration, but just barely. The rich are pretending to deny the impending disaster so as not to alarm the popular classes and to gain advantage during the wreck. "The ruling classes understand that the shipwreck is certain," Latour writes. "They reserve the lifeboats for themselves and ask the orchestra to go on playing lullabies so they can take advantage of the darkness to beat their retreat before the ship's increased listing alerts the other classes!"[59] The trouble is, of course, that this very strategy will ensure that no one survives the catastrophe.

Latour traces the history of our crisis back to the fall of the Berlin Wall and the collapse of the Soviet Union. At that time, three forces got underway: the global rise of deregulation, or what I would call "neoliberalism"; an explosion in inequality; and a systematic effort at climate denial. These three forces reflected what Latour calls "a single historical situation: it is as though a significant segment of the ruling classes (known today rather too loosely as 'the elites') had concluded that the earth no longer had room enough for them and for everyone else."[60]

This was the culmination of centuries of exploitation and domination of continental Europe over its neighbors, colonies, and the Global South. It has produced a breakdown of trust and shared social life. The result is that we are now at the brink of the precipice—if, that is, we have not already gone over it. In the United States, the election and policies of Donald Trump were the culmination, or final realization, of the end point of this history. And unless the West—and here Latour speaks only of continental Europe, or what he calls "Old Europe"—takes responsibility, recognizes its guilt for its previous centuries of exploitation, achieves humility, and leads the way forward toward climate reason, there is no hope. "We are the ones who started it—we of the old West, and more specifically Europe," Latour emphasizes.[61]

Meanwhile, in the United States, President Trump did everything possible to deny the climate crisis, empower carceral capitalism, and increase inequality—the latter, for instance, through a so-called tax reform bill signed into law in December 2017. We know that these were all the product of deliberate political choices. What Piketty and his colleagues convincingly show is that the economic transformations causing increased inequality are not the product of inherent laws of capital, autonomous forces of economics, or natural historical developments—instead, they are the product of deliberate human choice: the product of our actions and politics.[62] In this sense, Marx was wrong to think that there were inherent contradictions and laws of capital accumulation; and twentieth-century economists, such as Simon Kuznets, were wrong to suggest that primitive or mature capitalism has specific tendencies toward accumulation.[63] The differing trends are the product, instead, of political and legal choices. The sharp increases in inheritance taxes in the United States in the early twentieth century, and the elimination of such inheritance taxes later that century, are political choices with significant economic impact.

These are choices that we made and continue to make. So, for instance, the famous Beveridge Plan in England in 1942 promised social welfare benefits to soldiers in exchange for their willingness to put their lives at risk: this pact founded the welfare state in England during the war, and it had significant redistributive effects. Similarly, the elimination of inheritance taxes in the United States under

President George W. Bush at the turn of the twenty-first century had significant redistributive effects. All these political choices shape the equality curves—and all of them are the product of our individual actions and inactions, not of economic laws or political determinism. They are the outcome of political actions and choices of ordinary women and men. And they have frightening consequences, insofar as these wealth accumulations explain in part the rise of extreme right-wing populist movements and the New Right in the United States and around the globe in the early twenty-first century, and the election of strongmen leaders—not just Donald Trump and Russia's Vladimir Putin, but also Recep Tayyip Erdoğan in Turkey, Rodrigo Duterte in the Philippines, Narendra Modi in India, Viktor Orbán in Hungary, and Jair Bolsonaro in Brazil.

The mounting inequalities in the United States have already triggered an increasing number of uprisings. The dawn of the twenty-first century witnessed a number of revolts in the United States, from the Tea Party challenge to a perceived consolidation of Democratic Party power in Washington, to the Occupy Wall Street movement on behalf of the 99 percent, to the #BlackLivesMatter and broader movement against the lived—and fatal—inequalities of African Americans and persons of color, to the rise of a New Right that believes that it itself is the victim of the increasing inequality in American society. "The political revolution is just beginning," Bernie Sanders writes in his *Guide to Political Revolution*, published in 2017 after the election of Donald Trump. "The economy, health care, education, the environment, social justice, immigration: What role will YOU play?" Sanders asks.[64] With graphics showing the real average income of the top 0.01 percent, 1 percent, and bottom 90 percent, CEO pay disparities, starvation wages, and mass incarceration; with chapters on health care, higher education, climate change, and policing—Sanders calls for radical political mobilization. "This is your country. Help us take it back," Sanders writes. "Join the Political Revolution."[65]

Sanders's use of the term "Revolution," the Occupy movement's appropriation of the notion of an "Occupation," the New Right's adoption of the language of "Counter-Revolution" and of fascist and white supremacist imagery—these are fighting words and images. They represent a call to arms. They reflect the high stakes and the seriousness of the crises today. And they signal, possibly, the coming of stormier political times—under the cloud and ticking noise of global climate change.

Critique and Illusions

In the previous parts of this book, and in a set of earlier writings, I have attempted to expose both the ideational forces and the strategic factors that have shaped our perilous political condition in the United States today and the crises we face—or at least, as I understand them in the confrontation of my praxis and critical theory. I have tried to expose not only the illusion of liberalism and of the liberal definition of violence—but also, the illusion of Marxian utopias and philosophies of history. This work builds on earlier writings, which I will just reference here.

In *The Illusion of Free Markets*, I documented the rise of neoliberal penality and its effects on our punitive society in the United States. I traced a genealogy of the myth of the free market, from divine notions of orderliness tied to natural law in the work of the first economists in the eighteenth century, through the more secular ideas of self-interest, expertise, and informational advantage reflected in more conventional nineteenth-century laissez-faire theories, to cybernetic notions of spontaneous order elaborated by Friedrich Hayek in the mid-twentieth century, and ultimately to the more scientific and technical economic theories of the Chicago School concerning the efficiency of competitive markets. I demonstrated that the myth of the free market went hand-in-hand with a punitive society—that the illusion of natural order was from its inception joined at the hip, and remains tied, to the purported need for the strict policing and punishment of those who are viewed as "disorderly." I exposed the fundamental paradox of neoliberal politics—what I and others refer to as "neoliberal penality": in the country that has done the most to promote the idea of a hands-off government, we run the largest prison complex in the entire world.[66] I revealed how these illusory beliefs in free markets have had devastating effects on our contemporary politics by hiding wealth distributions, making them seem natural, and thereby reducing our willingness to critically examine our political condition.

By obscuring the rules and making the outcomes seem natural and deserved, neoliberal politics make it easier for certain market players to reorganize economic exchange in such a way as to maximize their take, which ultimately augments social inequality. Increased social inequality, in turn, has its own dynamics that tend to demand heightened punitive repression to maintain that social order. It facilitates the police state and mass incarceration by making it easier to resist government intervention in the economic sphere, but to embrace aggressive forms of policing and punishing that result in even greater inequality and mass incarceration.

In *Exposed: Desire and Disobedience in the Digital Age*, I then analyzed how the digital age has transformed the circulation of power in society and facilitated total surveillance. In particular, I showed how our own desires render us transparent to social media, corporations, and the intelligence services of the government—and the new ways in which the government and commerce know everything about us and shape us. The important point here is that we live in a new digital era that has profound effects on how politics function and how power circulates in society. I call it an "expository society" because it is our own expositions and exhibitions that are disarming us. But the central implication is that relations of power are changing dramatically as a result of technological innovation and centralizing knowledge in the hands of a digital elite. It has created a space of total information awareness.

Next, in *The Counterrevolution: How Our Government Went to War Against Its Own Citizens*, I exposed our new, dominant, but hidden paradigm of governing: the counterinsurgency method, which we have embraced in the United States and now are turning against our own citizens. I showed how we govern today, at home as well as abroad, by a mode of political engagement infused with counterinsurgency theory. It is a strategy of governance that creates, out of whole cloth, a fictitious internal enemy—Muslims, Mexicans, police protesters, "radical black extremists," and other minorities—and then puts in place tactics of total information awareness, elimination of those minorities, and pacification of the "ordinary" American in an effort to win the hearts and minds of the ordinary, passive masses and control our political condition. When, as today, there really is no domestic insurgency or insurrection in the United States, the counterinsurgency mode of governing becomes what I call "The Counterrevolution": a counterrevolution without a revolution, a counterinsurgency without an insurgency. This Counterrevolution has, today, successfully concentrated political power in the hands of a small minority of citizens, composed of cabinet members and national security advisors, congressional leaders, high-tech chairpeople, and captains of industry. These elites control the flow of digital data and the direction of drones and special operations, repress internal protest, and make possible an unprecedented concentration of wealth.

Those prior writings, along with the earlier chapters of this book on the illusions of legal-liberalism and of the liberal conception of violence, serve to clear the ground of various myths that operate to render tolerable today's inequalities, attacks on minorities and immigrants, punitive state, and climate denial. They set the stage for the most pressing question: What more am I to do?

In beginning to frame a response, I have taken for granted, naturally, that my orientation needs to be guided by the critical values and practices of critical philosophy. But let me just explain why, quickly. I start from the inexorable fact that, today, the New Right, including the Republican Party in the United States, has embraced a conservative vision that rests on ideals of natural hierarchy and white supremacy—a vision that not only eschews equality, but even abandons basic notions of sufficiency: one that does not even aspire to universal health care, subsistence benefits for the unemployed, or other basic welfare safeguards. As a result, it is patently clear that right and conservative ideologies will not advance the cause of social justice. Not only will they not promote equality, they will not even provide for the basic needs of people. By the same token, most centrists and liberal Democrats have embraced a style of neoliberalism that has also essentially given up on the promise of equality. That was true of President Obama, who explicitly and openly endorsed Chicago School notions of the free market. The illusions of liberalism that I have tried to expose, of course, point in the same direction.

As a result, one must look to the critical Left and critical philosophy, alone, to find answers for a more equitable and just society. To be sure, at a theoretical level, there may be fruitful conversations with centrists who espouse, for instance, a capabilities approach, like Amartya Sen and Martha Nussbaum; or those who argue for a "maxi-min" principle, by which fairness is determined by whether it will maximize those who have the least; or philosophical egalitarians; or even those, like Derek Parfit, who are prioritarian on sufficiency but believe that the priority of a sufficient life for all will lead to greater equality. It is even conceivable that some of these philosophical approaches may be as productive as more leftist philosophical stances. And there may even be times when there may be useful strategic coalitions on particular issues—such as criminal justice reform and the Right on Crime movement—that reach across the political spectrum. But my concern here is not with philosophical arguments, contemplation, or temporary coalitions. My goal is not simply to make the argument for a more equal society, nor is it to rehash the merits of the sufficiency versus equality debates, or to bridge differences. These are all theoretical or academic questions—and we are past those. The type of inequality that we face today, in the United States and around the globe, is simply intolerable, and there is no point arguing about the merits of redistribution. On the question of political engagement, then, the only place to look today, I believe, is on the critical Left, with critical philosophy.

Critical Praxis

The crises are prodigious, to be sure. But they can be overcome. There is no need to descend into dark despair that may only serve to render us passive and resigned—as Horkheimer and Adorno did during the war, warning us, "The downfall of Fascism will not necessarily lead to a movement of the avalanche."[67] No, there is no need for such gloom. What we need instead is to see clearly what is happening—and to act now. Critical theory cannot content itself with diagnosing crises, unveiling illusions, and revealing our present political situation—and stop there. It cannot settle for crisis and critique. It cannot retreat there as its sole form of praxis. It must move forward to critique and praxis. I must act, continue to act, and confront my critical practices with critical theory.

To begin with, by way of background and as should be clear from part II, it is essential to reject economic and historical determinism, and to work with, against, and within the really existing structures and institutions in the United States. Marx predicted that the long-term reduction in the profitability of capitalist production would ultimately lead to its downfall. But he based his theory on a nineteenth-century preoccupation with labor. He believed that only labor created surplus value, and as capitalist managers tried to beat their competition by using more machine labor, the rate of return on capital would ultimately decrease to the point of unprofitability. This would lead to the collapse of capitalism. He had a fixed formula for the rate of return that was a factor, in the denominator, of the ratio of labor to machinery; so the laws of capitalist competition would lead ultimately to its demise—alongside cyclical crises of capital accumulation that would produce unemployment and ravage society.

But notice that this was a fixed law of capital. Although Marx was surely right about the importance of surplus value tied to human labor, he was wrong to imagine a law of capital that led to the reduction of the rate of return; and his theoretical structure does not address a postindustrial economy. The point is not to search for economic laws, but to identify the practices and rules and regulations that redistribute wealth. In this sense, I am much closer to post-Keynesian and heterodox economists like Esteban Pérez and others.[68] Keynesians were too sanguine in believing that the problems of capitalism were questions of market failure that could be remedied. Post-Keynesians and heterodox economists seem more on track when they argue that the problems are much deeper and there has to be a constant corrective mechanism: there needs to be constant and continuous oversight of the regulatory mechanisms that continually adjust and regulate markets to ensure fair distribution. Just as we face a political realm of constant struggle, the regulation of economic exchange calls for constant interventions.[69]

On this basis, I then orient my praxis along three temporal axes—immediate political priorities, medium-term objectives, and (at least for me) one long-term project. The immediate priority for me today is to stop in its tracks the punitive society in this country, to end the downward spiral to authoritarianism and racial hierarchy, and to push the country not just back to where it was on climate change before the Trump administration, but even further. My work and litigation on abolition alone are inadequate to stem all these crises; so on this front, I need to join the efforts of others to deal with climate change and push back the American Counterrevolution in its proto-fascist, white supremacist, New Right iteration. Given present circumstances, this calls for an effort combining several actions: first, litigating, challenging, blocking, and delaying counterrevolutionary policies as much as possible, as lawyers did in the context of the Muslim ban or the citizenship question on the 2020 census; second, fostering a groundswell critical leftist movement; third, investigating and exposing the corruption of the New Right; and, fourth, challenging New Right federal court packing.

In terms of litigation and militancy, I will continue relentlessly to advocate and litigate against our punitive society, alongside the Equal Justice Initiative, Southern Center for Human Rights, NAACP Legal Defense Fund, Center for Constitutional Rights, American Civil Liberties Union (ACLU), and other public-minded groups that are in the best position to support and coordinate the efforts of militants and attorneys. The history of effective litigation campaigns—from desegregation to near-abolition of the death penalty to same-sex marriage—makes clear the central role of coordination. Plaintiffs have to be picked carefully, jurisdictions have to be selected, and timing has to be coordinated. Nothing can be left to chance. There needs to be direct communication, and it needs to be coordinated through the leading public-interest centers. In every legal challenge I have brought—whether against Trump and the Muslim ban with Tom Durkin in Amer Al-Homssi's case in January 2017, against discriminatory delays in Musab Zeiton's case in August 2017, against the lethal injection of Doyle Hamm throughout 2017 and 2018, or assisting Noah Smith-Drelich in our litigation against North Dakota law enforcement for their repressive practices at the Standing Rock reservation—I have always worked closely with these organizations, and I cannot underscore more emphatically the importance and value of doing so.

The next priority is to support, nourish, and empower a leftist groundswell movement in order not only to take the levers of power, but also to transform the reproduction of power. It is crucial in this context, I believe, to encourage greater political participation by the disengaged and first-time voters; to build coalitions on the ground with them and with those providing support and services to those who are disengaged and disenfranchised; and most important, to follow their lead, to find ways to allow their discourse to be heard so that they can orient our agenda—in the same way in which the *Groupe d'information sur les prisons* (GIP) served to allow the voices of prisoners to be heard. I need to create space for the next generations to speak and give us direction. I need to help create the space for a groundswell to emerge. I need to nourish it and support it. I have some ideas—which I will get to shortly. In the meantime, though, I think it would be best to avoid using labels from the past that carry unnecessary luggage—whether it is *democratic* or *socialist*—and instead focus on the values of equality, compassion, and respect that critical theory embraces. In electoral politics now, I believe that the "hundred flowers" approach is the right way to proceed. There is far too wide an ideological spectrum right now on the Left for anyone to impose a party line. What is needed is a voting bloc that can stop the American Counterrevolution. The best way forward is precisely to let local militants fully represent their constituencies. As Mao famously said in 1956, "The policy of letting a hundred flowers bloom and a hundred schools of thought contend is designed to promote the flourishing of the arts and the progress of science." The same can be said now about the flourishing of an opposition coalition. In terms of exposing the New Right's corruption, I believe that that is the task for special counsels and prosecutors. Not everyone is well qualified for doing this (and I certainly am not), so those who have the positions of authority, skills, and ambition will need to take the lead. Finally, in terms of the federal bench, the Left needs to challenge as vigorously as possible New Right nominations.

In all of this, it is key to interpret better and unceasingly. I argued in chapter 7 that a radical hermeneutics of interpretation should guide our political battles and these struggles that are brewing, this political storm. Thanks precisely to our interpretive training, critical thinkers have always known the vital importance of interpretation and how to lend meaning to things. The critical Left should be able to seize the upper hand because we have been doing this and have known this for so long. We should never give up, even in the face of brilliant interpreters and meaning-makers like Donald Trump or Steve Bannon, but instead do what we do best: offer a better interpretation, change the meaning, propose a reading. We knew that first. Donald Trump became a master at it. Notice how Trump and his meaning-makers were so rapidly able to take up the idea of "fake news" that the Democrats had first seized on. Especially after Pizzagate, Trump appropriated that meaning and turned it around, so that today, the *New York Times* and the liberal media are more closely associated with this concept of "fake news" in the public imagination than Trump himself. Trump was a brilliant interpreter. That is how he got elected. "Lock her up." "Clinton for Prison." Those were brilliant—and yes, despicable, but also brilliant—interpretations. Trump was a meaning-maker like few others. But remember, interpretation is our skill, our *technē*, what we grew up on. And now, more than ever, is the time to refine it and redeploy it. The Left began to do that. "Nasty woman." "You can grab them by the pussy," Trump said. Well, the opposition made a lot of pink pussyhats and marched. That was reclaiming the meaning, giving another interpretation, another spin on it. And I believe it had the potential to start a pink revolution.

The critical Left needs to challenge New Right interpretations and impose our own, better interpretations. And by "better," I mean interpretations that orient the world toward a critical horizon. Clifford Geertz had proposed that an interpretation is "better" than another when it serves to shed light on other situations. What recommends an interpretation, he wrote, "is the further figures that issue from them: their capacity to lead on to extended accounts which, intersecting other accounts of other matters, widen their implications and deepen their hold."[70] This remains too contemplative, I would argue. What recommends an interpretation is not just what it enlightens, but whether and how it pushes really existing political conditions in the direction of critical values. Critical praxis can achieve this in myriad ways—always boldly, with a hammer. Recall, with Nietzsche, the promise of tomorrow's *Daybreak*:

> There are no scientific methods which alone lead to knowledge! We have to tackle things experimentally, now angry with them and now kind, and be successively just, passionate and cold with them. One person addresses things as a policeman, a second as a father confessor, a third as an inquisitive wanderer. Something can be wrung from them now with sympathy, now with force; reverence for their secrets will take one person forwards, indiscretion and roguishness in revealing their secrets will do the same for another. *We investigators are, like all conquerors, discoverers, seafarers, adventurers, of an audacious morality and must reconcile ourselves to being considered on the whole evil.*[71]

Now, regarding the longer-term project: for myself, I believe that it is essential to open the space of critique and praxis to all the voices of contemporary critical thinkers in equal time and with equal space. This is a strategy of empowering those who are not heard and creating a groundswell among those who are most affected by the crises. For me, that means teaching about just societies, promoting justice, and supporting the brilliant and motivated students and activists dedicated to justice, critique, and praxis. It means, for me, creating social networks among critical theorists that reinforce leftist values, building alliances, and trying to create a space for critical praxis theory.

The future lies in taking a long view of history—not a Marxist, determinist vision of history, but rather a long, laborious view of history. In this, I draw as well, paradoxically, on conservative thinkers and bend their theories toward a critical Left future. I have in mind, in particular, the moralist tradition of Edward Banfield and James Q. Wilson and the historical tradition of the Annales School. Edward Banfield and his disciple, James Q. Wilson, were offensive thinkers, to be honest. Political scientists, urbanists in particular—recall their central thesis, that moral backwardness is characterized by present-orientedness, whereas moral superiority is marked by future-orientedness. You may recall that Banfield infamously published a book about southern Italian society titled "The Moral Basis of a Backward Society." He had spent the summer in southern Italy with his wife, who spoke a little Italian—he did not—and interviewed some of the residents of the small town of Chiaromonte, in the region of Basilicata, in 1955. What he argued, in the book he published three years later in 1958, was that the short-sightedness of the southern Italian people, who purportedly acted only on the short-term immediate interests of their families, was the source of their "moral backwardness" and plight. In later work, including some in collaboration with his disciple, James Q. Wilson, he argued that the problem with inner-city residents in the United States, and minorities more generally, was similarly their present-orientedness—in contrast to the future-orientedness of the upper class. Together, Banfield and Wilson oriented forward conservative thought, which had traditionally looked backward. For its part, the Annales School of historiography developed the concept of "*la longue durée*," the long view of history—coined by Marc Bloch and Lucien Febvre, the two historians who founded the journal *Annales d'histoire économique et sociale* in 1929. They focused on the deeper structures that influence, but do not determine, history. These historians, in their own words, preferred to "neglect[] surface disturbances" and instead "to observe the long and medium-term evolution of economy, society, and civilization."[72] In effect, they were choosing to unearth the deeper, long-term forces that shape, but do not dictate, our future.

Rather than reject these schools of thought as reactionary, I have come to see in them a key to critical praxis. Much of the attention among critical practitioners is focused on the here and now—rightfully so, given the immediacy of the crises. The assemblies are prefigurative models of democracy that we instantiate here and now. Tariq Ali's call for a second revolution at Tahrir Square, similarly, was temporally immediate. The Invisible Committee's latest intervention, its 2017 book *Now*, captures well this temporal dimension. But we should not let the urgency of the immediate crises blind us to the future: to the deeper structures and forces that shape us, our desires, our ambitions. It is equally important to be future-oriented. Not on moral grounds, but on political grounds. It is vital to till the fields, laboriously, for rewards that we might reap in the future; to create institutions of a different vein to shape future politics (like the Federalist Society, but for the Left). This is slow social network labor that reinforces certain values, shapes possibilities, and builds reputations. The time-consuming labor of shaping ideas and desires is important. It is precisely how conservative organizations were built over decades and have now come to dominate. Popular dissatisfaction and the desire "not to be governed in this way" are what bring about social uprisings, perhaps; but those are shaped by decades-long struggles.

There is, I believe, a pressing need for this long-term investment in networks, ideas, institutions, and organizations that promote the human values of equality, compassion, and solidarity. I believe that we need more concerted groundwork to promote critical thought that pierces illusions, and at the same time nurtures the critical values and strategizes about tactics. This is hard, ungrateful work, unsatisfying in the short term, thankless. It involves a time horizon that is hard to bear.

In the midst of the last major crises—after the events of May 1968, the repressions, and the rethinking of power that have taken place—Foucault reminded us of the stakes of the political struggle.[73] He emphasized how serious the political struggle is. I cannot stress enough how right he was—even if we need to replace his notion of civil war, which is too binary and time-bound, with the concept of endless battles. The political situation today is critical. Not only that, but the neoliberal consumerist horizon is so terribly seductive. Consumption is so frighteningly powerful, and the digital age so awfully distracting. In the face of that, now more than ever, critical theorists need to reorient critical praxis for the twenty-first century. We now need to do the long, hard work of reinforcing existing institutions, alliances, and networks, and creating new ones that will instill the values of equity and compassion, especially among the generations to come.

We are, in the United States, far down a dangerous path today. Few realize the magnitude of the historical shift, even though so many of us have heard the alarm bells. But unless and until we begin to recognize the truly epochal transformation that crystalized counterinsurgency warfare strategies into a new mode of governing post 9/11 and, especially under President Trump and this new Supreme Court that he has helped mold, into a new constitutionally counterrevolutionary form of government—unless we realize that we are now living the American Counterrevolution—it will be impossible to resist it properly. The priority now—as the priority would have been in 1932 Germany—is to defeat the American Counterrevolution.

Most important, I believe that this requires creating equal space for critical theorists, for the young, for those who are disengaged, for first-time voters and militants, to be heard and to lead. For myself, then, I will place my greatest energies toward building critical community with a long view of history that promotes the values of the critical Left. I will help build critical spaces that are oriented toward praxis, not just contemplation. I will foster social networks among critical theorists that reinforce critical values and build lasting alliances. In the end, politics is a constant, endless battle. We must never forget our political condition; instead, we must struggle as intelligently and critically as possible. That is the only way to win this coming battle, to continue fighting what is, in effect, an endless struggle.

To constantly refocus critical philosophy onto its main objective, to change the world, and its most important dimension, critical praxis: that is my mission. It is what orients all my praxis and political interventions. My great fear, in this effort, is that it will appear too reductionist. That is always what keeps us away from praxis. It seems naive. It is not as elegant or fancy as theory or contemplative philosophy. It sounds crude at times; and we intellectuals fear that most. What makes praxis so uncomfortable for theorists is that it concretizes the theoretical analysis. Without fail, it seems, the praxis analysis feels flat-footed. Those final chapters in our books—the ones that address the inevitable question from the audience, "Well, what should we do about it?"—they always feel like the shallowest part of the theoretical enterprise. Those are the parts we always regret.

Well, maybe the problem is that we should regret them—and we should constantly rewrite them. That is where we produce our own illusions. Those are the sections that may need the most rethinking. Or maybe the problem is precisely that we do not yet have a rich enough discourse on critical praxis. Perhaps we do not have as much of a critical theoretical tradition on praxis precisely because we shirk it. Maybe that is the whole point of this book.

I was reminded recently of a comment by Walter Benjamin about Bertolt Brecht.[74] You may recall from chapter 2 that their relationship was important, and in the eyes of Adorno and Horkheimer, troubling and controversial. Their plan to start a journal, *Krise und Kritik*, was viewed with suspicion. Yet Benjamin saw value in Brecht's direct approach and political honesty:

> There are many people to whom a dialectician means a lover of subtleties. In this connection it is particularly useful when Brecht puts his finger on 'crude thinking' which produces dialectics as its opposite, contains it within itself, and has need of it. . . . Action can, of course, be as subtle as thought. But a thought must be crude in order to come into its own in action.[75]

Yes, that frankness, that directness, that frank speech, they have value. I believe that they clear a path forward. There is indeed value to doing philosophy with a hammer.

The space of critique and praxis must be open on equal terms to all contemporary critical thinkers. That is the very point of not reformulating the action imperative for others, but creating room for everyone to reformulate for themselves. To further this ambition, I will continue to foster critical spaces that are open to all critical thinkers to propose, intervene, object, but remain steadfast in the enterprise of renewing critical praxis theory. The space of critical praxis must not silence or privilege, but instead allow all critical thinkers to be heard in their own voices, with equal respect and equal time.

Conclusion

In her book, *Staying with the Trouble: Making Kin in the Chthulucene*, Donna Haraway urges us to rethink our present crises and abandon the notion of the Anthropocene, as well as the more properly named Capitalocene, in favor of what she calls the "Chthulucene." She defines the Chthulucene, with an extra *h*, as a way to rethink our period through the figure of the spider *Pimoa cthulhu*, an eight-legged tentacular arachnid that makes its home in Sonoma and Mendocino counties in California.[1] It is, she observes, obscene to place humans at the heart of the Anthropocene—as Haraway writes, "Surely such a transformative time on earth must not be named the Anthropocene!"[2] This is not just for theoretical reasons, but for practical ones as well. We must, Haraway argues, rethink (or better think) these categories in order to practice, and practice better. "We must think!" Haraway urges us.[3] And with that—with real thinking, thinking that can lead to action, to revolt, to the right *way* to revolt—Haraway urges us to act: "The unfinished Chthulucene must collect up the trash of the Anthropocene, the exterminism of the Capitalocene, and chipping and shredding and layering like a mad gardener, make a much hotter compost pile for still possible pasts, presents, and futures."[4]

To create this space for thinking and action—for theory and praxis—confronting the two, relentlessly: that is the lesson here, for me. And it calls for a new concept of the critical space of theory and practice. It calls for radically rethinking the space of *theoria* and *praxis*. It is precisely this space that Carolin Emcke, an author, war correspondent, and critical theorist from Berlin, explores when she travels back and forth from the university and critical philosophy to regions in crisis, to elaborate and inhabit what she calls the "spaces of praxis." At times, these are "hidden spaces, restricted spaces, gendered spaces." At other times, they are "contested territory." And still at other times, they entail "space in a broader sense as visibility: different strategies to make invisible people visible."[5]

The way I see it, this space of critique and praxis must be a new *Zone à défendre* (ZAD)—a creative and productive autonomous zone. Looking over my own trajectory to this point, I discern a new way to think about the project of critical philosophy. It is a space, itself, of relentless confrontation and conflict, where we not only strive toward realizing critical ambitions, but constantly clash and collide our practices with our critical theory. It is, in this sense, a temporary autonomous zone, a TAZ: a space of open experimentation at the outer limits, willing to reconsider all our critical ideas and practices, each in our own way. From this perspective, one can imagine the space of critical praxis theory, just like the Earth today, as a space at risk. The two, perhaps, are symbiotically related: They may depend on each other. They are both in need of defense—and of constant radical rethinking and action.

This new space of critical praxis theory makes room for critical thinkers to engage in action and critique: to reformulate their practices, subject them to searing criticism, unmask the resulting illusions, and act again and think again. It protects a critical space for each of us to reformulate anew the action imperative "What is to be done?" in our own way. It affords space for everyone to be heard, on equal terms and with equal voice.

For me, critical theorizing must turn inward. I must confront my own political engagements *en situation*. This, I believe, is in line with the reflexivity at the origin of critical philosophy, of critical theory in the 1920s, and of the new waves of critique since the 1960s; but it is also a radical departure from certain strands of critical philosophy that throughout, and, paradoxically, veered toward foundationalism and truth. "The history of all hitherto existing society is the history of class struggles": That was brilliant and captured something essential at the time, but it turns out to be too universalizing.[6] Our struggles today are racial as well, and gendered, and sexualized, and ethnic. In many specific contexts today, in the United States, the struggle is not between the working class and capitalist managers only or primarily, but between working poor whites and working poor blacks, between female athletes and male athletes, between transgender and heteronormative ways of being. Class struggle, it turns out, is not a universal, even if it infuses and shapes in part those other struggles. We are, today, well past the redistribution versus recognition debate, in an intersectional space that challenges race, gender, sexuality, class, faith, and other vital aspects of the self.[7] Most of the older critical mantras are outdated as well. The state is not always the enemy, and its withering may not always be beneficial. A vanguard party is not always the best praxis. Charismatic leadership—or for that matter, its opposite, leaderless movements—are not always in order. Nonviolence is not always called for.

There has always been tension at the heart of critique and criticism between the subjective dimension of discerning and judging, and the objective dimension of diagnosing crisis moments and shaping the course of history—both embedded in the etymology of the terms critique and crisis, as discussed earlier. There has also often been tension, within the first subjective dimension, between exercising that faculty only within one's private space, or instead in the public sphere. This latter tension was captured well by Kant's recommendation to use reason in a private realm but to obey at the professional or public level. "*Argue as much as you like and about whatever you like, but obey!*" Kant wrote, on behalf of the enlightened ruler.[8]

Seyla Benhabib and Reinhart Koselleck trace the historical evolution of these tensions to the various ways in which the term *critique* or *criticism* was used in antiquity, medieval times, and pre-Revolutionary and post-Revolutionary Enlightenment. They discern a dialectic. In ancient and medieval usage, they suggest, there was a direct link between subjective judgment and decision-making on the one hand, and the determination of objective moments of crisis on the other. They were operating, as it were, in a two-dimensional plane. The idea, prevalent in areas such as medicine, was that judgments should be formed at those moments of truthful diagnoses of illness or health crises. In pre-Revolutionary Enlightenment, Benhabib and Koselleck argue, criticism had reverted to the subjective only. Criticism became the art of judging the beauty or truth of objects. It would only be after the Revolution that people began, once again, to relate the concepts, so that reason would be applied to public acts and to the state. This reflected, Benhabib writes, "the dialectic of early bourgeois Enlightenment": the ancient meaning of critique was renewed and, once again, "the art of the critic does not remain confined to the evaluation of private, non-public matters, but extends itself to judging reasons of state as well." And so, "on the eve of the French Revolution, 'criticism' means the exercise of rational evaluation which reveals the 'crisis' of the absolutist state to be an objective, historical process."[9]

For too much of its history, from the mid-nineteenth to the mid-twentieth centuries, critical philosophy was wedded to an overly deterministic position regarding the objectivity of historical processes. But today, the problem with critical theory is that it has reverted too much to the form of criticism that Benhabib and Koselleck identified with the pre-Revolutionary period—to the academy, to the professoriate—and thus retreated too much from the public sphere.

The task of a reconstructed critical praxis theory is to revive, in a new way, the relationship among these various dimensions to enable firm, subjective judgments about critical praxis to be made in conjunction with a solid evaluation of our political crises, cognizant of the historical dimensions. The turn to self-criticism—the reformulation of the question of critical praxis as "What more am I to do?"—is by no means intended to be a return to the purely subjective aesthetic judgment, but instead to promote political praxis and more critical engagement in the public sphere, chastened by the elements of domination and social hierarchy.

In the final part of this work, part IV, I proposed how I would reformulate the action imperative for myself. I did so in order not to shirk my own responsibility—not to abuse my author's prerogative, but also not to punt on the most important question of all: "What more am I to do?" Having done so, I will close this work by borrowing a page from Bruno Latour. Latour concludes his book, you will recall, with an invitation: "There, I've finished. Now, if you wish, it's your turn to present yourself..."[10] I have done so now. If you like, perhaps you will reformulate the praxis question as well. This book is an invitation. I hope you will be willing to continue the conversation, confrontation, and endless struggle.

Postscript

> A.1. Human activities are estimated to have caused approximately 1.0°C of global warming above pre-industrial levels, with a *likely* range of 0.8°C to 1.2°C. Global warming is *likely* to reach 1.5°C between 2030 and 2052 if it continues to increase at the current rate. (*high confidence*)
>
> —United Nations, Intergovernmental Panel on Climate Change, *Special Report on Global Warming of 1.5°C* (2018).[1]

We live in revolutionary times. Revolutions are occurring all around us. The collapse of the Soviet Union and the privatization of Russia and the former Eastern Bloc are revolutionary. The capitalization and neoliberal turn in China are revolutionary—as are their effects throughout Africa and Asia. The rise of the New Right in Germany, Italy, Austria, Hungary, Poland, France, and elsewhere in Europe, and the consolidation of authoritarian power in Brazil, India, Turkey, and the Philippines are revolutionary. And the looming cataclysm of climate change is revolutionary.

Many people deny this. Most people believe that we live in a post-revolutionary age—that the time of grand revolution and national liberation is behind us. But the idea that we are past revolutions is myopic. The notion that the modern concept of Revolution is behind us, or that the revolutionary ideal is too exigent, is deeply misleading. The problem is that we hardly see the revolutions coming. We barely feel them when they are taking shape. We scarcely recognize them in the present. We tend to identify them only in the rearview mirror. But revolutions are everywhere around us.

A revolution—or, rather, a Counterrevolution—is happening right now, before our eyes, in the United States. It is tearing down an embattled social welfare state and replacing it with a greedy, heartless one that massively redistributes wealth to the national security, military, domestic law-and-order, and punitive constituencies. It is repudiating all our efforts to reverse global climate change. It is eviscerating public education and replacing it with charter and private schools. It is Christianizing our way of life—constraining women's reproductive choices, punishing sexual minorities, reestablishing patriarchy, and reinforcing extreme and capital punishment. It is silencing and punishing dissenting voices, multiculturalism, and racial, ethnic, sexual, and political differences.

Entangled in the snare of the present, blinded by the apparent necessity of our existing institutions and political arrangements, it is hard to even imagine the extraordinary political transformations that lie ahead. But they undoubtedly will be great—some even unimaginable—just as democratic elections must have appeared unimaginable in feudal times or during the *ancien régime*. It is, today, practically impossible to imagine, in North America, something different from a liberal democracy, but surely that time will come.

The political future in North America is wide open, and practically unimaginable, as it is around the world, especially in all the hot spots today—on the Korean peninsula; in the Persian Gulf and Middle East; around the Mediterranean; throughout Latin America; in Brussels, Moscow, and Beijing; in sub-Saharan Africa. Fearing the unknown, many of us cling to the modicum of political stability we have, trying not to challenge or rock the boat too much—even when the status quo is so intolerable and appalling. Many of us hardly believe in the possibility of a radically different future. This is not new. Few foresaw the French Revolution. Practically no one predicted the fall of the Berlin Wall or the collapse of the Soviet Union—not even the experts. No one forecast the Arab revolutions. Most were surprised by Brexit and stunned by the election of Donald Trump as U.S. president. But there are more to come, and it will, in rapid succession.

These upheavals—upheavals so unexpected they cannot even be predicted by the experts—are precisely the product of the endless and relentless political struggles that mark our political condition. They have dramatic effects on the prospect, for each and every one of us, of realizing our ideals and values. They severely affect the human condition, equality, solidarity, autonomy, well-being, welfare—life itself. And everything we do as individuals—every choice we make, every action we take—affects these struggles and upheavals.

This is the unbearable and daunting reality: every one of our most minute actions will affect these upheavals. Unbearable, indeed. Agonizing and excruciating. The burden is almost too much to bear—which is why so much of the history of political thought has been consumed by futile efforts to derive schemes or structures or principles that would lighten the load. That would prevent sliding into, or away from, authoritarianism. That would allow us to go on with our personal lives, in private, without interfering with anyone else. That would allow us to believe that the private pursuit of self-interest will work out for the greater good of humanity. Imagine that! Private greed serves the public good . . . What dupes we are, humans. How prone to illusions. And how futile, how counterproductive are all these myths! As if institutional fixes or legal regimes could solve our problems, when instead it all comes back to *who we are, each and every one of us, and what we do.* The challenge is daunting—almost overwhelming. But there is no choice.

Critique and praxis: a radical critical philosophy of illusions entails a radical theory of values and demands a radical theory of action. This book proposes a critical praxis theory for the twenty-first century that confronts these revolutionary times and challenges the intolerable that is all around us. Faced with the utter singularity and endlessness of the struggle, it offers contextualized critical theory and praxis, *en situation*, relentlessly confronting each other, and it lays the groundwork for equality, compassion, respect, social justice, and autonomy. It is urgent. Time is running out.

Bernard E. Harcourt
New York City
January 1, 2020

Notes

The Primacy of Critique and Praxis

1. To be more precise I could use the term *radical critical philosophy.* The term *critical philosophy,* without the qualifier *radical,* is usually associated with Kant in the late eighteenth century and his three critiques—of pure reason, of practical reason, and of judgment. It is usually defined by means of Kant's critical project to rid us of our illusions about our ability to know things really and to search instead for the conditions of possibility of knowledge. Despite this association, many contemporary critical thinkers trace critical philosophy elsewhere—to Nietzsche for Gilles Deleuze, to Hegel or Marx for others. The aim of this book is to reclaim the term *critical philosophy,* without needing to add the word *radical,* to refer to a way of being that privileges critical praxis. For this reason, I will mostly drop the qualifier *radical.* The terminological confusion and, ultimately, the central tension over the meaning of critical philosophy traces back to Kant. I will return to this point later.
2. Karl Marx, "Eleventh Thesis," *Theses on Feuerbach,* in *The German Ideology* (London: Lawrence and Wishart, 1938).
3. Richard Bernstein analyzed the concept of *praxis* in a monograph in 1971 that was, for me, formative when I first read it in about 1983. His book *Praxis and Action: Contemporary Philosophies of Human Activity* (Philadelphia: University of Pennsylvania Press, 1971) should serve as a backdrop to mine. In addition, Nicholas Lobkowicz's *Theory and Practice: History of a Concept from Aristotle to Marx* (Notre Dame, IN: University of Notre Dame Press, 1967) is formative in tracing the history of the concept of *praxis.* Seyla Benhabib, in her book *Critique, Norm, and Utopia: A Study of the Foundations of Critical Theory* (New York: Columbia University Press, 1986), 1–3, traces this history as well. I am indebted to these books and would like to think of this work as a continuation of the historical arc presented there.
4. See Lobkowicz, *Theory and Practice,* for an exhaustive treatment of this history.
5. Bernstein, *Praxis and Action,* 11–83.
6. Max Horkheimer, "Postscript," 244–252, in Max Horkheimer, *Critical Theory: Selected Essays* (New York: Continuum, 1992), 246; see also Max Horkheimer, "Traditional and Critical Theory," 188–243, in Max Horkheimer, *Critical Theory: Selected Essays,* trans. Matthew J. O'Connell et al. (New York: Continuum, 1992), 197, 215, 229.
7. Sartre wrote that "in the first phase of the revolt killing is a necessity: killing a European is killing two birds with one stone, eliminating in one go oppressor and oppressed." Jean-Paul Sartre, preface to Frantz Fanon, xliii–lxii, *The Wretched of the Earth* (New York: Grove Press, 2004), lv.
8. Michel Foucault, "Prisons et asiles dans le mécanisme du pouvoir," in *Dits et Écrits,* vol. 2: *1970–1975,* ed. Daniel Defert, François Ewald, and Jacques Lagrange (Paris: Gallimard, 1994), 523–524 (my translation).

9. Angela Y. Davis, *Are Prisons Obsolete?* (New York: Seven Stories, 2003).
10. Judith Butler, *Notes Toward a Performative Theory of Assembly* (Cambridge, MA: Harvard University Press, 2015), 32.
11. Chantal Mouffe, *For a Left Populism* (New York: Verso, 2018), 9 ("This book is meant to be a political intervention and it openly acknowledges its partisan nature.")
12. Sara Ahmed, *Living a Feminist Life* (Durham, NC: Duke University Press, 2017).
13. Horkheimer, "Traditional and Critical Theory," 233.
14. See Jean-Paul Sartre, *Les Mains sales* (Paris: Gallimard, 1948); Horkheimer, "Traditional and Critical Theory," 231; Nancy Fraser and Axel Honneth, *Redistribution or Recognition? A Political-Philosophical Exchange* (New York: Verso, 2003); Herbert Marcuse, *Counterrevolution and Revolt* (Boston: Beacon Press, 1972).
15. Horkheimer, "Traditional and Critical Theory," 231; 231; 231; 231; 232; 214; 215.
16. Max Horkheimer, *Eclipse of Reason* (London: Bloomsbury, 1974), viii. As we will see, that represented a shift from his writings in 1937. For example, see Horkheimer, "Traditional and Critical Theory," 231.
17. Horkheimer, *Eclipse of Reason*, viii (emphasis added).
18. Horkheimer, *Eclipse of Reason*, 130.
19. Horkheimer, *Eclipse of Reason*, 130.
20. Horkheimer, *Eclipse of Reason*, 130; 131; 132.
21. Theodor W. Adorno, "Marginalia on Theory and Praxis," 259-278, in *Critical Models: Interventions and Catchwords*, trans. Henry W. Pickford (New York: Columbia University Press, 1998), 277, 278.
22. Adorno, "Marginalia on Theory and Praxis," 277; 268; 276; 276.
23. This is most evident in *La Société punitive. Cours au Collège de France (1972–1973)*, ed. Bernard E. Harcourt (Paris: Gallimard/Seuil, 2013); and *Théories et institutions pénales. Cours au Collège de France. 1971–1972*, ed. Bernard E. Harcourt (Paris: Gallimard/Le Seuil, 2015). As I mentioned in the course context to *The Punitive Society*, these were the times of his most marxisant years (putting aside the early 1950s, when he was a member of the French Communist Party). See *The Punitive Society: Lectures at the Collège de France 1972–73*, ed. Bernard E. Harcourt, trans. Graham Burchell (New York: Palgrave Macmillan, 2015), 278-279.
24. That period left distinct traces of Marxism in the final two chapters of Foucault's first book. See Michel Foucault, *Maladie mentale et personalité* (Paris: Presses universitaires de France, 1954).
25. Michel Foucault, "Confinement, Psychiatry, Prison," interview by David Cooper et al., 178–210, in *Politics, Philosophy, Culture: Interviews and Other Writings 1977–1984*, ed. Lawrence D. Kritzman, trans. Alan Sheridan (New York: Routledge, 1988), 197.
26. Foucault, "Confinement, Psychiatry, Prison," 197.
27. I will discuss his abolitionist politics and praxis from the early 1970s later in chapter 16.
28. Michel Foucault, *The Use of Pleasure*, Vol. 2 of *The History of Sexuality* (New York: Vintage, 1990), 6; 5.
29. In recent work, I try to correct this misperception and argue that the publication in 2018 of the fourth and final volume of *The History of Sexuality, Confessions of the Flesh*, provides the key to link Foucault's later work on subjectivity to his earlier, more directly political writings on knowledge-power. See Bernard E. Harcourt, "Foucault's Keystone: *Confessions of the Flesh*. How the Fourth and Final Volume of *The History of Sexuality* Completes Foucault's Critique of Modern Western Societies" (November 30, 2019). Columbia Public Law Research Paper. Available at SSRN: https://ssrn.com/abstract=3497030 or http://dx.doi.org/10.2139/ssrn.3497030. It is also important to emphasize that Foucault's exploration of the history of the desiring subject focused attention on truth-telling, *parrhesia*, and the courage of truth, which are archetypal political practices. Breaking silence *is* praxis, as the Reverend Martin Luther King Jr. so brilliantly demonstrated in his sermon against the Vietnam War from the pulpit at Riverside Church in New York in April 1967, just a year before his assassination. Martin Luther King, Jr., "It Is Time to Break Silence," in *A Testament of Hope: The Essential Writings of Martin Luther King, Jr.* (San Francisco: Harper & Row, 1986); on the radicality of King's

philosophy, see Brandon Terry, "MLK Now," *Boston Review*, September 10, 2018, http://bostonreview.net/forum/brandon-m-terry-mlk-now. Émile Zola also famously illustrated this point in *J'accuse*, his tract in defense of Alfred Dreyfus published in January 1898—for which Zola was convicted of libel and had to flee France. Foucault himself staked out contentious political positions in manifestos and editorials throughout his life.

30. Here too, Marx prefigured the epistemological turn with his analysis of commodity fetishism—his exploration of how capitalist subjects perceive objects in terms of market exchange value rather than the social relations and modes of production embedded in them. As Peter Baehr demonstrates well, Marx's social theory of unmasking has been the most influential of all. Peter Baehr, *The Unmasking Style in Social Theory* (London: Routledge, 2019), 3. But other thinkers such as Antoine Destutt de Tracy and Étienne de La Boétie had foreshadowed the ideological turn even earlier. And, of course, Marx was not alone in lighting this path. Other hermeneutists of suspicion, such as Nietzsche and Sigmund Freud, contributed importantly as well and paved significant competing avenues.
31. Horkheimer, "Traditional and Critical Theory," 213; 214 (emphasis added).
32. Regarding the intellectual, Horkheimer wrote, "His own thinking should in fact be a critical, promotive factor in the development of the masses." Horkheimer, "Traditional and Critical Theory," 214.
33. See, e.g., Luc Boltanski, *De la Critique. Précis de Sociologie de l'émancipation* (Paris: Gallimard, 2009); Luc Boltanski and Laurent Thévenot, *On Justification: Economies of Worth* (Princeton, NJ: Princeton University Press, 2006); Stephen Best and Sharon Marcus, "Surface Reading: An Introduction," *Representations* 108, no. 1 (2009): 1–21; Bruno Latour, "Why Has Critique Run out of Steam? From Matters of Fact to Matters of Concern," *Critical Inquiry* 30, no. 2 (2004): 225–248. See also Yannick Barthe and Cyril Lemieux, "Quelle critique après Bourdieu?" *Mouvements* 5, no. 24 (2002): 33–38.
34. Didier Fassin, "How Is Critique?" in *A Time for Critique*, ed. Didier Fassin and Bernard E. Harcourt, 13–35 (New York: Columbia University Press, 2019).
35. Erdmut Wizisla, *Walter Benjamin and Bertolt Brecht—The Story of a Friendship* (New Haven, CT: Yale University Press, 2009); Reinhart Koselleck, *Critique and Crisis: Enlightenment and the Pathogenesis of Modern Society* (Cambridge, MA: MIT Press, 1988).
36. Axel Honneth, *The Idea of Socialism: Towards a Renewal* (Cambridge, UK: Polity Press, 2017), 5.
37. Bruno Latour, *Down to Earth: Politics in the New Climatic Regime* (Cambridge, UK: Polity Press, 2018), 1.
38. Seyla Benhabib traces the intertwined lives and thoughts of many of these exiled critical theorists and other intellectuals, including Adorno, Hannah Arendt, Benjamin, Isaiah Berlin, Albert Hirschman, Gershom Scholem, and Judith Shklar. See Seyla Benhabib, *Exile, Statelessness, and Migration: Playing Chess with History from Hannah Arendt to Isaiah Berlin* (Princeton, NJ: Princeton University Press, 2018).
39. See Eduard Bernstein, *The Preconditions of Socialism*, ed. and trans. Henry Tudor (Cambridge: Cambridge University Press, 1993); and Rosa Luxemburg, *Reform or Revolution and Other Writings* (Mineola, NY: Dover Publications, 2006); and Luxemburg, *Organizational Questions of Russian Social Democracy* (Creative Commons: 2017), https://archive.org/details/Leninism_Or_Marxism_New; and Vladimir Ilyich Lenin, *What Is To Be Done? Burning Questions of Our Movement* (New York: International Publishers, 1929).
40. *Groupe d'information sur les prisons* (GIP), "Le GIP vient de lancer sa première enquête" (1971), in Philippe Artières, Laurent Quéro, and Michelle Zancarini-Fournel, eds., *Le Groupe d'information sur les prisons: Archives d'une lutte 1970–1972* (Paris: IMEC, 2003), 52:

> Il s'agit de laisser la parole à ceux qui ont une expérience de la prison. Non pas qu'ils aient besoin qu'on les aide à "prendre conscience": la conscience de l'oppression est là parfaitement claire, sachant bien qui est l'ennemi. Mais le système actuel lui refuse les moyens de se formuler, de s'organiser.

41. Gayatri Chakravorty Spivak, "Can the Subaltern Speak?" 21–78, in *Can the Subaltern Speak? Reflections on the History of an Idea*, ed. Rosalind C. Morris (New York: Columbia University Press, 2010).
42. Michel Foucault and Gilles Deleuze, "Intellectuals and Power: A Conversation Between Michel Foucault and Gilles Deleuze," in *Language, Counter-memory, Practice: Selected Essays and Interviews*, ed. Donald F. Bouchard, trans. Donald F. Bouchard and Sherry Simon (Ithaca, NY: Cornell University Press, 1977), 214–215.
43. Spivak, "Can the Subaltern Speak?" 27.
44. Michael Hardt and Antonio Negri, *Assembly* (New York: Oxford University Press, 2017), 133; 63; xx, 39, 69, 70.
45. Mouffe, *For a Left Populism*, 22.
46. Jack Halberstam, "The Wild Beyond: With and for the Undercommons," introduction to Stefano Harney and Fred Moten, *The Undercommons: Fugitive Planning & Black Study* (Wivenhoe, UK: Minor Compositions, 2013), 6.
47. Sara Ahmed, *Living a Feminist Life* (Durham, NC: Duke University Press, 2017).
48. Ruth Wilson Gilmore, *Golden Gulag: Prisons, Surplus, Crisis, and Opposition in Globalizing California* (Berkeley: University of California Press, 2007).
49. Some philosophers will prefer to conceive of these three parts as epistemology, normativity, and practical philosophy. Part I will propose a resolution of the epistemological controversies in order to motivate a reconstructed critical theory. Part II will propose a situated and contextual normative theory of values to guide the political interventions. Part III will propose different ways of political action. In part IV, I will return to each of these in dialogue with my own critique and praxis.

Toward a Critical Praxis Theory

1. Richard Bernstein, *Praxis and Action: Contemporary Philosophies of Human Activity* (Philadelphia: University of Pennsylvania Press, 1971), x; Nicholas Lobkowicz, *Theory and Practice: History of a Concept from Aristotle to Marx* (Notre Dame, IN: University of Notre Dame Press, 1967), 9. For more recent work on the concepts of work and creation, see Giorgio Agamben, *Creation and Anarchy: The Work of Art and the Religion of Capitalism* (Stanford, CA: Stanford University Press, 2019).
2. Bernstein, *Praxis and Action*, x.
3. In this regard, I feel a tension between Bernstein's and Lobkowicz's readings of the ancients. For Lobkowicz, the different modes of life are competing ways of living, and we have to choose between them.
4. Michel Foucault, "What Is Enlightenment?," in *The Essential Works of Foucault, Vol. 1: Ethics: Subjectivity, and Truth*, ed. Paul Rabinow (New York: The New Press, 1997), 303–319. Kant is an important figure in the historical trajectory of theory and praxis. In his distinction between the first and second critique—between *The Critique of Pure Reason* and *The Critique of Practical Reason*—and, perhaps in a more accessible way, in his short essay "On the Common Saying: 'This May Be True in Theory, But It Does Not Apply in Practice,'" Kant formulated a highly rationalist position—one that I will come back to at the end of chapter 4. See generally Lobkowicz, *Theory and Practice*, 120 et seq.
5. Foucault, "What Is Enlightenment?," 309.
6. Bernstein, *Praxis and Action*, 51; 53; 53; 55; 56.
7. Bernstein traces some of these praxis moments in the preface to *Praxis and Action*, xi–xii.
8. Bernstein, *Praxis and Action*, 34–35.
9. This is relevant to my call for a radical theory of illusions. Marx's and Feuerbach's critiques of Hegel were to expose the myths and illusions in his theory of *Geist*: the mystification of a spirit that has agency when it is the agency of humans; the mystification of the self-alienation of spirit when it is human alienation in fact. Bernstein, *Praxis and Action*, 39. It is through a series of unveilings of illusions

in Hegel that Marx would march forward—but of course, my point is that this would produce another set of illusions in Marx that we need to unmask. The transformative method that Feuerbach develops and Marx appropriates—the method of transforming the putative subject acting (*Geist*) into the result instead of real active humans, and vice versa, is all a practice of demystification. Bernstein, *Praxis and Action*, 39. The illusion, the myth that Marx would enact, was the idea of species-being that he would take from Feuerbach.

10. See, e.g., Chantal Mouffe, *For a Left Populism* (New York: Verso, 2018), 70.
11. Étienne Balibar, "Dire, contredire: sur les formes de la *parrêsia* selon Foucault," 81–120, in Étienne Balibar, *Libre parole* (Paris: Galilée, 2018).
12. Balibar, "Dire, contredire," 100 (all translations in text are mine).
13. Balibar, "Dire, contredire," 119.
14. Balibar, "Dire, contredire," 112 (italics in original).
15. Balibar, "Dire, contredire," 118.
16. Étienne Balibar, "Gilets jaunes: le sens du face à face," *Praxis 13/13* (blog), January 12, 2019, http://blogs.law.columbia.edu/praxis1313/etienne-balibar-gilets-jaunes-le-sens-du-face-a-face/; Toni Negri, "Gilets jaunes: un contropotere," *Praxis, 13/13* (blog), January 11, 2019, http://blogs.law.columbia.edu/praxis1313/antonio-negri-gilets-jaunes-un-contropotere/.
17. Étienne Balibar, "'Gilets jaunes': The Meaning of the Confrontation," *openDemocracy*, December 20, 2018, https://www.opendemocracy.net/can-europe-make-it/etienne-balibar/gilets-jaunes-meaning-of-confrontation.
18. Balibar, "Dire, contredire," 111.
19. As Martin Saar suggests, referring both to Nietzsche and Foucault, "Genealogy always deals with relation to self and with (however abstract) reflexivity." Martin Saar, "Genealogy and Subjectivity," *European Journal of Philosophy* 10, no. 2 (2002): 232.
20. Michel Foucault, "Interview with Christian Panier and Pierre Watté (May 14, 1981)," 247–252, in Michel Foucault, *Wrong-Doing, Truth-Telling: The Function of Avowal in Justice*, ed. Fabienne Brion and Bernard E. Harcourt, trans. Stephen W. Sawyer (Chicago: University of Chicago Press, 2014), 247.
21. Foucault, "Interview with Christian Panier and Pierre Watté," 247.
22. Foucault, "Interview with Christian Panier and Pierre Watté," 248. In further prompting on the relation to his books, Foucault responds:

    In the same way, the book on prisons stops in 1840 and I have often been told: "This book constitutes such an indictment of the penitentiary system that we don't know what to do once we have read it." To tell the truth, it is not an indictment. My question simply consists in saying to psychiatrists and to the personnel of the penitentiary: Are you capable of enduring your own history? Given that history and what it reveals for the system of rationality, the type of proof, the postulates, et cetera, the ball is now in your court." And what I would like would be for them to tell me, "Come work with us," instead of hearing people say, as they sometimes do, "You are keeping us from our work." No, I am not keeping you from your work. I am asking you a certain number of questions. So let's try now to work together to elaborate new modes of critique, new modes of questioning, to attempt something else. *This is my relationship to theory and practice.*

    Foucault, "Interview with Christian Panier and Pierre Watté," 249 (emphasis added).
23. I am referring here to Foucault working in psychiatric hospitals, not to the *Groupe d'information sur les prisons* (GIP), of course. I discuss the GIP in chapter 16.
24. Bruno Latour, *Down to Earth: Politics in the New Climatic Regime* (Cambridge, UK: Polity Press, 2018), 106.
25. Jack Halberstam, "Strategy of Wildness," *Praxis 13/13* (blog), February 25, 2019, http://blogs.law.columbia.edu/praxis1313/jack-halberstam-strategy-of-wildness/.

26. I should emphasize that I could not and would not claim the privilege of being part of the undercommons. It would be obscene for me to speak on behalf of or place myself in the undercommons, or even as a fellow traveler. As a tenured professor at an elite, Ivy League school, it would be unseemly and the worst form of arrogance for me to claim the undercommons. Second, and more important, the undercommons is a challenge to knowledge and knowledge formation. It is a direct challenge to *who* has knowledge. It says that those who have conventionally held knowledge—like tenured professors, like critical theorists—have fraudulently maintained their hold on power by taking advantage of their positions of authority and structures of hierarchy. They no longer have legitimacy. They should step back. The only legitimate intervention is the action from the undercommons. And in this sense, I am not in a position to claim to endorse this; I am the legitimate target.
27. Axel Honneth, *The Idea of Socialism: Towards a Renewal* (Cambridge, UK: Polity Press, 2017), 5.
28. Joshua Smeltzer, "Review of *Assembly*, by Michael Hardt and Toni Negri," *LSE Review of Books*, January 31, 2018.
29. Michael Hardt and Antonio Negri, *Assembly* (New York: Oxford University Press, 2017), xviii.
30. Hardt and Negri, *Assembly*, 290; 289; 134.
31. Hardt and Negri, *Assembly*, 69.
32. Slavoj Žižek, "No Way Out? Communism in the Next Century," in *The Idea of Communism*, vol. 3: *The Seoul Conference*, ed. Slavoj Žižek and Alex Taek-Gwang Lee (New York: Verso, 2016), 256; 257.
33. Banu Bargu, *Starve and Immolate: The Politics of Human Weapons* (New York: Columbia University Press, 2014); Massimiliano Tomba, *Insurgent Universality: An Alternative Legacy of Modernity* (New York: Oxford University Press, 2019).
34. Bargu, *Starve and Immolate*, 9 (emphasis added); 9.
35. Bargu, *Starve and Immolate*, 20; 20; 27; 9.
36. Tomba, *Insurgent Universality*, 226–228.
37. Joshua Clover, *Riot. Strike. Riot* (New York: Verso, 2016), 3.
38. Clover, *Riot. Strike. Riot*, 129 (italics in original).
39. Clover, *Riot. Strike. Riot*, 175.
40. Theodor W. Adorno, *Negative Dialectics* (New York: Continuum, 1973); see generally Critique 7/13 Seminar, Columbia Center for Contemporary Critical Thought, December 18, 2019, available at http://blogs.law.columbia.edu/critique1313/7-13/.
41. Amy Allen, *The End of Progress: Decolonizing the Normative Foundations of Critical Theory* (New York: Columbia University Press, 2016), xiv.
42. Allen, *The End of Progress*, xii, xiv.
43. Seyla Benhabib, "Critique and Emancipation: Comments Prepared for the *Emanzipation Conference*" (Lecture, Humboldt-Universität zu Berlin, May 25, 2018), 6.
44. Benhabib, "Critique and Emancipation," 6 (emphasis added).
45. Let me just make the point here that eliminating the dimension of necessity does not render the concept of illusion—or ideology, for that matter—noncritical or neutral in Karl Mannheim's sociological usage or Raymond Geuss's "non-pejorative" sense. Karl Mannheim, *Ideology and Utopia: An Introduction to the Sociology of Knowledge* (New York: Harcourt, Brace and Company, 1940); Raymond Geuss, *The Idea of a Critical Theory: Habermas and the Frankfurt School* (Cambridge: Cambridge University Press, 1981), 5. It remains a belief that naturalizes relations of power and masks social distributions, as I demonstrate in chapters 5–7. This loaded meaning of illusion, or ideology, bears a family resemblance to some analytic philosophical definitions of the term, such as that of Tommie Shelby, who defines it as "a widely held set of associated beliefs and implicit judgments that misrepresent significant social realities and that function, through this distortion, to bring about or perpetuate unjust social relations." Tommie Shelby, *Dark Ghettos: Injustice, Dissent, and Reform* (Cambridge, MA: Harvard University Press, 2016), 22.

46. Page DuBois, *Torture and Truth* (New York: Routledge, 1991). Foucault, in his first lectures at the Collège de France, *Lectures on the Will to Know* (1970–1971), explores money as a measure of truth. Michel Foucault, *Lectures on the Will to Know: Lectures at the Collège de France, 1970–1971*, ed. Arnold Davidson, trans. Graham Burchell (Basingstoke, UK: Palgrave Macmillan, 2013). See also Michel Foucault, *An Introduction, Volume 1, The History of Sexuality*, trans. Robert Hurley (New York: Vintage, 1990), where Foucault links the questions of torture, truth, and confession, as well as slavery (see especially Michel Foucault, *La Volonté de savoir* (Paris: Gallimard, 1976), 79).
47. Stephen Best and Sharon Marcus, "Surface Reading: An Introduction," *Representations* 108, no. 1 (2009), 2.
48. Best and Marcus, "Surface Reading," 2.

Part I: Reconstructing Critical Theory

1. Amy Allen, *The End of Progress: Decolonizing the Normative Foundations of Critical Theory* (New York: Columbia University Press, 2016), 5, vii.
2. The notion of a ruthless, unending critique was captured so powerfully in that famous passage from Marx's letter to Arnold Ruge: "If the designing of the future and the proclamation of ready-made solutions for all time is not our affair, then we realize all the more clearly what we have to accomplish in the present—I am speaking of *a ruthless criticism of everything existing*, ruthless in two senses: The criticism must not be afraid of its own conclusions, nor of conflict with the powers that be." Karl Marx, "For a Ruthless Criticism of Everything Existing," originally in the *Deutsch-Franzosische Jahrbucher* (1844), reproduced in *The Marx-Engels Reader*, 2nd ed., ed. Robert C. Tucker, trans. Ronald Rogowski (New York: W. W. Norton, 1978), 12–15.
3. Axel Honneth, *The Critique of Power: Reflective Stages in a Critical Social Theory*, trans. Kenneth Baynes (Cambridge, MA: MIT Press, 1991), xv (Honneth proposes to "provide a reconstruction of the history of critical theory in the form of a learning process" and to "make[] use of the Hegelian method for the history of philosophy"); Rahel Jaeggi, *Critique of Forms of Life*, trans. Ciaran Cronin (Cambridge, MA: Harvard University Press, 2018).

1. The Original Foundations

1. Max Horkheimer, "Traditional and Critical Theory," in *Critical Theory: Selected Essays*, trans. Matthew J. O'Connell et al. (New York: Continuum, 1992), 208; 208, 210, 227; 213; 216–217; 217; 218; 219; 221; 233; 241; Max Horkheimer, "Postscript," in *Critical Theory: Selected Essays*, trans. Matthew J. O'Connell et al. (New York: Continuum, 1992), 246; 248; Horkheimer, "Traditional and Critical Theory," 215.
2. Horkheimer, "Traditional and Critical Theory," 197.
3. Horkheimer, "Traditional and Critical Theory," 200; also see 210.
4. Horkheimer, "Traditional and Critical Theory," 208, 207; 208.
5. Horkheimer, "Traditional and Critical Theory," 229; 231.
6. Horkheimer, "Traditional and Critical Theory," 188.
7. Horkheimer, "Traditional and Critical Theory," 227.
8. Horkheimer, "Traditional and Critical Theory," 209; 218.
9. Horkheimer, "Traditional and Critical Theory," 227.
10. Horkheimer, "Traditional and Critical Theory," 213; 218, 225; 234; 215; 215; 226.
11. Horkheimer, "Traditional and Critical Theory," 202; see also the bottom of 204 in particular; and 207, where he suggests that critical theory can plan class distinctions.

12. Horkheimer, "Traditional and Critical Theory," 204; 213; Horkheimer, "Postscript," 244; Horkheimer, "Traditional and Critical Theory," 232.
13. Also see Seyla Benhabib, "Comments Prepared for the *Emanzipation Conference*," lecture, Humboldt-Universität zu Berlin, May 25, 2018. As Benhabib explains, "Horkheimer's remarkable achievement in 'Traditional and Critical Theory' is to develop this philosophy of praxis into a critique of the epistemology of his contemporaries, i.e. positivist social sciences as well as the phenomenology of Edmund Husserl. Via this move, Horkheimer returns to Kant: critical inquiry is once more in the service of autonomy and emancipation. By disclosing that the world of social facts *are the work* of humans themselves, it is possible to end the alienation from and enslavement to a social reality that dominates them. Emancipatory knowledge is knowledge in the service of demystifying (*Entlarvung*) the supposed objectivity of the social world, and above all, of the so-called 'laws' of capitalism."
14. Horkheimer, "Traditional and Critical Theory," 214; 213, 214; 214.
15. Horkheimer, "Traditional and Critical Theory," 221; 221.
16. Raymond Geuss, *The Idea of a Critical Theory: Habermas and the Frankfurt School* (Cambridge: Cambridge University Press, 1981), 2–3.
17. Horkheimer, "Traditional and Critical Theory," 237; 214; 214.
18. Horkheimer, "Traditional and Critical Theory," 242; 242; 242.
19. Horkheimer, "Traditional and Critical Theory," 195; 194.
20. Horkheimer, "Traditional and Critical Theory," 194; 197 ("The latter believe they are acting according to personal determinations, whereas in fact even in their most complicated calculations they but exemplify the working of an incalculable social mechanism.")
21. Horkheimer, "Traditional and Critical Theory," 198.
22. Walter Benjamin, "Theses on the Philosophy of History," in *Illuminations*, ed. Hannah Arendt (New York: Schocken, 1968), 253–265.
23. This discussion is drawn from my essay "Counter-Critical Theory: An Intervention in Contemporary Critical Thought and Practice," *Critical Times* 1, no. 1 (2018): 5–22, https://ctjournal.org/index.php/criticaltimes/article/view/9.
24. "*Krise und Kritik* Memorandum," c. 1930, in Erdmut Wizisla, *Walter Benjamin and Bertolt Brecht—The Story of a Friendship* (New Haven, CT: Yale University Press, 2009), 188.
25. Benjamin made this comment in conversation with Ernst Bloch in 1931, as reported by Max Rychner and quoted in Wizisla, *Walter Benjamin and Bertolt Brecht*, 76 (emphasis added).
26. See the stenographic memorandum of conversations among Benjamin, Brecht, and Ihering, from 1930, reproduced in Wizisla, *Walter Benjamin and Bertolt Brecht*, 203–206. See also Horkheimer, "Traditional and Critical Theory," 242.
27. *Krise und Kritik* minutes from November 1930, quoted in Wizisla, *Walter Benjamin and Bertolt Brecht*, 190 (emphasis added).
28. Wizisla, *Walter Benjamin and Bertolt Brecht*, 42; 66.
29. Wizisla, *Walter Benjamin and Bertolt Brecht*, 76 (emphasis in original).
30. Wizisla, *Walter Benjamin and Bertolt Brecht*, 75; 80.
31. Walter Benjamin, *The Correspondence of Walter Benjamin, 1910–1940*, ed. Gershom Scholem and Theodor W. Adorno, trans. Manfred R. Jacobson and Evelyn M. Jacobson (Chicago: University of Chicago Press, 1994), 368; see also Wizisla, *Walter Benjamin and Bertolt Brecht*, 68. Note that in the *Correspondence*, the journal is referred to as "*Krisis und Kritik*," and the letter is addressed to "Gerhard Scholem," see *Correspondence*, 368, 367. I retain the usage from Wizisla's book because *Krise und Kritik* is more consistent with every other mention of the title, and Gerhard Scholem changed his name to Gershom Scholem when he moved from Germany to Israel. Special thanks to Fonda Shen.
32. On Theodor Adorno's, Max Horkheimer's, and Friedrich Pollock's views of Brecht, see Wizisla, *Walter Benjamin and Bertolt Brecht*, 62–63; Martin Jay, *The Dialectical Imagination: A History of the Frankfurt*

School and the Institute for Social Research, 1923–1950 (Berkeley: University of California Press, 1973), 201–203. See generally Michael W. Jennings, *Dialectical Images: Walter Benjamin's Theory of Literary Criticism* (Ithaca, NY: Cornell University Press, 1987), 3; Uwe Steiner, *Walter Benjamin: An Introduction to His Work and Thought*, trans. Michael Winkler (Chicago: University of Chicago Press, 2010), 18–20, 145; Susan Buck-Morss, *Dialectics of Seeing: Walter Benjamin and the Arcades Project* (Cambridge, MA: MIT Press, 1989); and Susan Buck-Morss, *The Origin of Negative Dialectics: Theodor W. Adorno, Walter Benjamin, and the Frankfurt School* (New York: Free Press, 1979).

33. Wizisla, *Walter Benjamin and Bertolt Brecht*, 71; 91; 71; Jennings, *Dialectical Images*, 3.
34. Reinhart Koselleck, *Critique and Crisis: Enlightenment and the Pathogenesis of Modern Society* (Cambridge, MA: MIT Press, 1988), 5.
35. Theodor W. Adorno, "The Actuality of Philosophy" (1931), *Telos*, no. 31 (1977): 120–133, 127; 120; 126; 128, 131; 129; 130.
36. Adorno, "The Actuality of Philosophy," 129.
37. Max Horkheimer and Theodor W. Adorno, *Dialectic of Enlightenment*, trans. John Cumming (New York: Continuum, 1969), 221; 221.
38. Max Horkheimer and Theodor W. Adorno, preface to *Dialectic of Enlightenment*, trans. John Cumming (New York: Continuum, 1969), ix; ix.
39. Horkheimer and Adorno, *Dialectic of Enlightenment*, 34–36.
40. Horkheimer, "Traditional and Critical Theory," 235; 236.
41. Horkheimer and Adorno, *Dialectic of Enlightenment*, 34–36.
42. Horkheimer and Adorno, *Dialectic of Enlightenment*, 35.
43. Horkheimer and Adorno, *Dialectic of Enlightenment*, 34; 34.
44. Horkheimer and Adorno, *Dialectic of Enlightenment*, 35–36.
45. Horkheimer and Adorno, *Dialectic of Enlightenment*, xi.
46. Horkheimer and Adorno, *Dialectic of Enlightenment*, xi; 42.
47. See Martin Saar, "X—What Is Social Philosophy? Or: Order, Practice, Subject," *Proceedings of the Aristotelian Society* 118, no. 2 (2018): 207–223, 215, 217 (proposing a theory of "social philosophy" that is a critique of power and that draws on Axel Honneth and Horkheimer at the same time as Foucault and Étienne Balibar); see also Martin Saar, "Genealogy and Subjectivity," *European Journal of Philosophy* 10, no. 2 (2002): 231–245; and Martin Saar, *Genealogie als Kritik: Geschichte und Theorie des Subjekts nach Nietzsche und Foucault* (Frankfurt: Campus, 2007).
48. Rahel Jaeggi, *Critique of Forms of Life* (Cambridge, MA: Harvard University Press, 2018); Steven Lukes, "In Defense of False Consciousness," *University of Chicago Legal Forum* (2011): 29–52, http://chicagounbound.uchicago.edu/uclf/vol2011/iss1/3/.

2. Challenging the Frankfurt Foundations

1. Gilles Deleuze, *Nietzsche et la philosophie* (Paris: Presses Universitaires de France, 1962), 2.
2. Gilles Deleuze, *Différence et répétition* (Paris: Presses Universitaires de France, 1968), 4 (when the French reference is cited in these notes and the passage is in English in text, these are my translations unless otherwise indicated).
3. Deleuze, *Différence et répétition*, 1.
4. Deleuze, *Nietzsche et la philosophie*, 223.
5. Personal conversation with Daniel Defert, June 9, 2019, discussing forthcoming edition of Foucault's lectures and writings on Nietzsche.
6. Michel Foucault, "Truth and Juridical Forms," in *Power*, vol. 3 of *The Essential Works of Foucault (1954–1984)*, ed. James D. Faubion, trans. Robert Hurley (New York: New Press, 2000), 32.

7. Max Horkheimer, "Traditional and Critical Theory," 188–252, in *Critical Theory: Selected Essays*, trans. Matthew J. O'Connell et al. (New York: Continuum, 1992), 214.
8. Michel Foucault, *Qu'est-ce que la critique?*, ed. Henri-Paul Fruchaud and Daniele Lorenzini (Paris: Vrin, 2015), 43–44; Michel Foucault, *"Il faut défendre la société." Cours au Collège de France, 1976*, ed. Mauro Bertani and Alessandro Fontana (Paris: Gallimard/Le Seuil, 1997), 30; Michel Foucault, *Naissance de la biopolitique. Cours au Collège de France (1978–1979)*, ed. Michel Senellart (Paris: Gallimard, 2004), 21–22; Michel Foucault, "Adorno, Horkheimer, and Marcuse: Who Is a 'Negator of History'?," in *Remarks on Marx: Conversations with Duccio Trombadori* (New York: Semiotexte, 1991), 115–130; and Michel Foucault, "Structuralisme et poststructuralisme," in *Dits et Écrits*, vol. 4: *1980–1988*, ed. Daniel Defert, François Ewald, and Jacques Lagrange (Paris: Gallimard, 1994), 431–457.
9. See, e.g., Pierre Klossowski, *Nietzsche et le cercle vicieux* (Paris: Mercure de France, 1969); Jacques Derrida, *De la grammatologie* (Paris: Minuit, 1967); Sarah Kofman, *Nietzsche et la métaphore* (Paris: Galilée, 1972); Sarah Kofman, *Nietzsche et la scène philosophique* (Paris: Galilée, 1979); and also the essays by Klossowski, Jean Wahl, and others in *Cahiers de Royaumont. Nietzsche* (Paris: Minuit, 1967) and later, Jacques Derrida, *Éperons. Les styles de Nietzsche* (Paris: Flammarion, 1978); Jacques Derrida, *Limited Inc* (Evanston, IL: Northwestern University Press, 1988). It would also, of course, be essential to trace the Freudian critical branch through Jacques Lacan, but that will have to wait for the next book. See Jacques Lacan, *Écrits* (Paris: Seuil, 1966); Jacques Lacan, *Le Séminaire de Jacques Lacan, Livre XI, "Les quatre concepts fondamentaux de la psychanalyse"* (Paris: Seuil, 1973).
10. Friedrich Nietzsche, "On Truth and Lie in a Nonmoral Sense (1873)," 17–49, in *On Truth and Untruth: Selected Writings*, ed. and trans. Taylor Carman (New York: HarperCollins, 2010), 29–30.
11. For a discussion of the term *history of truth*, its Pascalian origins, and Foucaultian uptake, see Étienne Balibar, "Dire, contredire," in *Libre parole* (Paris: Galilée, 2018), 99 and articles cited at 99 n.1.
12. My translation; the original title is Georges Dumézil, *Servius et la fortune: Essai sur la fonction sociale de louange et de blâme et sur les éléments indo-européens du cens romain* (Paris: Gallimard, 1943).
13. Michel Foucault, *Lectures on the Will to Know: Lectures at the Collège de France, 1970–1971, and Oedipal Knowledge*, ed. Daniel Defert, trans. Graham Burchell (Basingstoke, UK: Palgrave Macmillan, 2014), 84.
14. Georges Dumézil, *Servius et la fortune*, cited in Michel Foucault, *Wrong-Doing, Truth-Telling: The Function of Avowal in Justice*, ed. Fabienne Brion and Bernard E. Harcourt, trans. Stephen W. Sawyer (Chicago: University of Chicago Press, 2014), 28.
15. This is discussed in the English edition of the course context of the Louvain lectures, in Foucault, *Wrong-Doing, Truth-Telling*, at 271–272 and following pages.
16. In large part, the antifoundationalism of these writings, and of poststructuralism more generally, was also motivated by the critique of structuralism, which was viewed as overly scientistic. In this sense, poststructuralism was a form of postfoundationalism. See Bernard E. Harcourt, *Language of the Gun: Youth, Crime, and Public Policy* (Chicago: University of Chicago Press, 2006); Oliver Marchart, *Post-Foundational Political Thought: Political Difference in Nancy, Lefort, Badiou, and Laclau* (Edinburgh: Edinburgh University Press, 2007), 2.
17. Foucault, "Truth and Juridical Forms," 86.
18. The quintessential "animal functions" consist of "eating, drinking, procreating," and Marx contrasts these with "human functions," which consist of laboring freely and productively. Labor is "*life-activity, productive life* itself . . . the life of the species . . . life-engendering life"; or, as Marx emphasizes, "free conscious activity is man's species character." Karl Marx, "Economic and Philosophical Manuscripts of 1844," in *The Marx-Engels Reader*, ed. Robert C. Tucker, trans. Ronald Rogowski, 2nd ed. (New York: Norton, 1978), 75–76. The alienation of labor is problematic on these grounds because it turns life as labor into a mere means for existence: "What is animal becomes human and what is human becomes animal." Marx, "Economic and Philosophical Manuscripts," 74.

19. Foucault, "Truth and Juridical Forms," 86; 86–87.
20. Michel Foucault, *Discipline and Punish: The Birth of the Prison*, trans. Alan Sheridan (New York: Vintage, 1979), 220–221 (emphasis added); 221; 221. As he proposed elsewhere: "Necessary for the accumulation of capital, there was an accumulation of men, or, if you like, a distribution of the labor force with all its somatic singularities." Michel Foucault, *Psychiatric Power: Lectures at the Collège de France, 1973–1974*, ed. Jacques Lagrange, trans. Graham Burchell (Basingstoke, UK: Palgrave Macmillan, 2006), 71.
21. Foucault, *Discipline and Punish*, 25–26.
22. Foucault, *Psychiatric Power*, 55; see also 71-72.
23. Foucault, *Psychiatric Power*, 71, 72.
24. Foucault, "Truth and Juridical Forms," 87.
25. Foucault, "Truth and Juridical Forms," 87.
26. Max Horkheimer, "The Latest Attack on Metaphysics," 132–187, in *Critical Theory: Selected Essays*, trans. Matthew J. O'Connell et al. (New York: Continuum, 1992), 159.
27. Rahel Jaeggi, *Critique of Forms of Life*, trans. Ciaran Cronin (Cambridge, MA: Harvard University Press, 2018), 213.
28. In this, there is a clear parallel with Amy Allen, who writes that "even our local and contextual judgments about progress in history, whenever we feel compelled to make them, must be ongoingly and relentlessly problematized." Amy Allen, *The End of Progress: Decolonizing the Normative Foundations of Critical Theory* (New York: Columbia University Press, 2016), 229.
29. Deleuze, *Nietzsche et la philosophie*, 1; 97; 1; 97, 2; 1; 119.
30. Deleuze, *Nietzsche et la philosophie*, 100; 1.
31. Deleuze, *Nietzsche et la philosophie*, 107.
32. Deleuze, *Nietzsche et la philosophie*, 108; 59.
33. Gilles Deleuze, *Nietzsche, sa vie, son œuvre: avec un exposé de sa philosophie* (Paris: Presses universitaires de France, 1965); Gilles Deleuze, *Présentation de Sacher-Masoch: Le froid et le cruel* (Paris: Minuit, 1967), 102; Gilles Deleuze, *Foucault*, trans. Séan Hand (Minneapolis: University of Minnesota Press, 1988), 129–130; Gilles Deleuze, "Mystère d'Ariane Selon Nietzsche," in *Critique et Clinique* (Paris: Minuit, 1993), 126–134.
34. Georges Bataille et al., eds., "Nietzsche et les Fascistes: Une Réparation," *Acéphale: Religion, sociologie, philosophie* 2 (1937): 17–21.
35. *Acéphale*, as you know, means "headless." This headless man, according to Bataille, would point us both to the "surhumain" [the superhuman] and to the death of God. Bataille would write in his essay "Propositions," that *l'acéphale*, the headless man, is the mythic representation of "the superhuman that IS fully 'death of God.' " Georges Bataille, "Propositions," in "Nietzsche et les Fascistes: Une Réparation," ed. Georges Bataille et al., *Acéphale: religion, sociologie, philosophie*.
36. See, e.g., Deleuze, *Différence et répétition*, 384.
37. Deleuze, "Mystère d'Ariane Selon Nietzsche," 126–134.
38. Gilles Deleuze, "Nietzsche," in *Gilles Deleuze: Pure Immanence: Essays on a Life*, ed. John Rajchman, trans. Anne Boyman (New York: Zone, 2001), 92.
39. Deleuze, *Nietzsche et la philosophie*, 77.
40. Gilles Deleuze, *Nietzsche and Philosophy*, trans. Hugh Tomlinson (New York: Columbia University Press, 2006), 68.
41. Deleuze, *Nietzsche and Philosophy*, 68.
42. Deleuze, *Nietzsche et la philosophie*, 81. At the conference at Royaumont in July 1964, he further develops this interpretation of the eternal return. See Gilles Deleuze, "Conclusions sur la volonté de puissance et l'éternel retour," in *Cahiers de Royaumont. Nietzsche*, ed. Gilles Deleuze (Paris: Minuit, 1967), 285. He does so again four years later, in *Différence et répétition*, 15.

43. Deleuze, "Conclusions," 285. For a different interpretation of the concept of eternal return, not as practical doctrine but as dramatic representation, see Robert Gooding-Williams, *Zarathustra's Dionysian Modernism* (Palo Alto, CA: Stanford University Press, 2002).
44. Deleuze, "Conclusions," 285 ("En toutes choses, l'éternel retour a pour fonction de séparer les formes supérieures des formes moyennes, les zones torrides ou glaciales des zones tempérées, les puissances extrêmes des états modérés. 'Séparer,' ou 'extraire,' ne sont même pas des mots suffisants, car l'éternel retour *crée* les formes supérieures. C'est en ce sens que l'éternel retour est l'instrument et l'expression de la volonté de puissance: il élève chaque chose à sa forme supérieure, c'est-à-dire à la *nième* puissance.")
45. Deleuze, *Différence et répétition*, 15–16.
46. Gilles Deleuze, in Michel Foucault and Gilles Deleuze, "Intellectuals and Power: A Conversation Between Michel Foucault and Gilles Deleuze," in *Language, Counter-memory, Practice: Selected Essays and Interviews*, ed. Donald F. Bouchard, trans. Donald F. Bouchard and Sherry Simon (Ithaca, NY: Cornell University Press, 1977), 214–215.
47. Gilles Deleuze and Félix Guattari, *Anti-Oedipus: Capitalism and Schizophrenia*, trans. Robert Hurley, Mark Seem, and Helen R. Lane (Minneapolis: University of Minnesota Press, 1983), 104, 118; see also Gilles Deleuze and Félix Guattari, *A Thousand Plateaus: Capitalism and Schizophrenia*, trans. Brian Massumi (Minneapolis: University of Minnesota Press, 1987), 215; John Protevi, "Fractures of the State: Deleuze and Guattari on Ideology," in *Edges of the State* (Minneapolis: University of Minnesota Press, 2019).
48. Foucault's early writings on Nietzsche will be published as part of the series *Cours et travaux avant le Collège de France* (Paris: Gallimard/Le Seuil, forthcoming [expected 2024]).
49. Michel Foucault, "Nietzsche, Freud, Marx," in *Dits et Écrits, vol. 1: 1954–1969*, 564–579 (Paris: Gallimard, 1994), 570; Michel Foucault, "Nietzsche, Freud, Marx," in *The Essential Works of Michel Foucault, vol. 2: Aesthetics, Methods, and Epistemology*, ed. James D. Faubion, trans. Robert Hurley et al., 269–278 (New York: New Press, 1998), 275; Michel Foucault, "Nietzsche, la généalogie, l'histoire," in *Dits et Écrits, vol. 2: 1970–1975*, 136–156 (Paris: Gallimard, 1994), 156. Foucault would return to this theme not only in the 1964 text, but also in *The Order of Things*, which underscores that "thought . . . is a perilous act. Sade, Nietzsche, Artaud and Bataille have understood this on behalf of all those who tried to ignore it." See Michel Foucault, *Les Mots et les choses: Une archéologie des sciences humaines* (Paris: Gallimard, 1966), 339; Michel Foucault, *The Order of Things: An Archaeology of the Human Sciences*, trans. Alan Sheridan (New York: Vintage, 1994), 328.
50. Foucault published his translation of Kant's *Anthropology* in 1964 with the publisher Vrin, but did not include his introduction for reasons discussed by Daniel Defert, François Ewald, and Frédéric Gros in their presentation; see Michel Foucault, *Introduction à l'*Anthropologie, in *Anthropologie du point de vue pragmatique*, by Immanuel Kant (Paris: Vrin, 2008), 8–9.
51. The text first turns to Nietzsche at the end of the ninth section of the introduction, immediately after Foucault has critiqued phenomenology. Foucault deploys the notion of the eternal return to describe the way in which post-Kantian philosophers always return to reflections on the a priori, the originary, and finitude—in other words, to the illusions from which philosophers have tried for centuries now to emancipate themselves. Foucault's introduction plays with Nietzsche's language of the eternal return, of philosophizing with a hammer, of the dawn, as a way to emphasize the recurring problem of existential and psychological phenomenologies. Foucault writes there, pointing to Nietzsche's words and most identifying expressions, "*c'est là, dans cette pensée qui pensait la fin de la philosophie, que résident la possibilité de philosopher encore, et l'injonction d'une austérité neuve.*" Foucault, *Introduction à l'*Anthropologie, 68. That *austérité neuve* (new austerity) represents the quest for an end to illusions.
52. Foucault, *Introduction à l'*Anthropologie, 76–78; 78.
53. Foucault, *Introduction à l'*Anthropologie, 78 (my translation); 79.

54. Defert, Ewald, and Gros, "Présentation" to Foucault, *Introduction à l'*Anthropologie, 8–9.
55. Foucault's essay is published, alongside the contributions of Deleuze, Pierre Klossowski, Karl Löwith, Jean Wahl, and others, in *Cahiers de Royaumont. Nietzsche* (Paris: Minuit, 1967). All references in this chapter, though, are to Michel Foucault, "Nietzsche, Freud, Marx," in *Dits et Écrits, vol. 1: 1954–1969* (Paris: Gallimard, 1994), 564–579. English-translation references are drawn from Michel Foucault, "Nietzsche, Freud, Marx," in *The Essential Works of Michel Foucault, vol. 2: Aesthetics, Methods, and Epistemology*, ed. James D. Faubion, trans. Robert Hurley et al. (New York: New Press, 1998), 269–278.
56. For example, Foucault writes in *Les Mots et les choses* on page 572 (*The Order of Things*, page 269) that the techniques of the Renaissance were also techniques to eradicate suspicion: "one can say that allegoria and hyponoïa are at the bottom of language and before it, not just what slipped after the fact from beneath words in order to displace them and make them vibrate, but what gave birth to words, what makes them glitter with a luster that is never fixed." Here, we see clearly that the various epistemological layers were always in a relationship with this question of the suspicion of truth.
57. Foucault, *Les Mots et les choses*, 33–36 (*The Order of Things*, 18–22).
58. Foucault, "Nietzsche, Freud, Marx," 569 (English, 271-272). He discusses this on page 311 of *Les Mots et les choses* (*The Order of Things*, 298), where he writes: "The first book of *Das Kapital* is an exegesis of 'value'; all Nietzsche is an exegesis of a few Greek words; Freud, the exegesis of all those unspoken phrases that support and at the same time undermine our apparent discourse."
59. Foucault, "Nietzsche, Freud, Marx," 569 (English, 275).
60. Foucault, "Nietzsche, Freud, Marx," 571 (English, 275).
61. Foucault observes that, in order to understand this, one need only look at the etymology of *agathos* in Nietzsche's *On the Genealogy of Morals*. When Nietzsche tells us that words have always been invented by superior classes, he is not pointing to a signified, he is imposing an interpretation. The model for understanding these hermeneutics, then, can be found in paragraphs four and five of the first essay of the *Genealogy of Morals*, in which Nietzsche develops an analysis of the word *good* and shows that its meaning is linked to the group that is speaking in different historical, cultural, and geographical periods. What is important here is not so much the fact of doing philology, of using a classical philological technique that seeks to find the meaning of words through filiation so as to return to a form of original signified. Rather, it is to show at every little stage, in all these various contexts, how those who are speaking use the word and thereby impose meanings on it, how they create signs in temporal and political contexts and in the context of their own group. It is there that Nietzsche finds, for example, the notion of nobility, of superiority. He finds that the contingent political attachments inherent to the way in which we use a word in one culture or another evoke something like nobility: "With regard to a moral genealogy, this seems to me a fundamental insight; that it has been arrived at so late is the fault of the retarding influence exercised by the democratic prejudice of the modern world toward all questions of origin." Friedrich Nietzsche, First Essay, paragraph four, *On the Genealogy of Morals*, trans. Walter Kaufmann and R. J. Hollingdale (New York: Vintage, 1989), 28. So it is necessary to travel through history to find the way in which these signifieds have been steeped in certain conceptions of race, and we see the importance of race in the fifth paragraph of this text: " 'the rich,' 'the possessors' (this is the meaning of arya; and of corresponding words in Iranian and Slavic)"; Nietzsche, *Genealogy of Morals*, 29. We find the notion of race, notion of nobility, notion of force, of the blonde person in opposition to the dark native with black hair. "The Celts, by the way, were definitely a blonde race; it is wrong to associate traces of an essentially dark-haired people which appear on the more careful ethnographical maps of Germany with any sort of Celtic origin or blood-mixture"; Nietzsche, First Essay, paragraph five, *Genealogy of Morals*, 30. The aryan notion itself is imposed on the notion of "good" and "evil." For Foucault, this is an example of the imposition of interpretation that one finds in Nietzsche, and that thus would give us the infinite task of trying to understand how different meanings have been imposed through time.

62. Foucault, "Nietzsche, Freud, Marx," 571 (English, 275).
63. Foucault, "Nietzsche, Freud, Marx," 571 (English, 275).
64. Deleuze, *Nietzsche et la philosophie*, 1; this refers, naturally, to Nietzsche, "Götzen-Dämmerung oder wie man mit dem Hammer philosophiert" (Twilight of the idols or how to philosophize with a hammer). Friedrich Nietzsche, *Twilight of the Idols and the Anti-Christ*, trans. R. J. Hollingdale (New York: Penguin, 2003).
65. Foucault, "Nietzsche, Freud, Marx," 574 (English, 278).
66. Foucault, *Les Mots et les choses*, 275 (*The Order of Things*, 263); Foucault, *Les Mots et les choses*, 353 (*The Order of Things*, 342).
67. Foucault, "Nietzsche, Freud, Marx," 571 (English, 275).
68. Foucault, "Nietzsche, Freud, Marx," 570 (English 275); Michel Foucault, "Nietzsche, la généalogie, l'histoire," in *Dits et Écrits, vol. 2: 1970–1975* (Paris: Gallimard, 1994), 136–156, at 156; see also Foucault, *Les Mots et les choses*, 339 (*The Order of Things*, 328).
69. The essay "Nietzsche, Genealogy, History" was published in a *festschrift* to Jean Hyppolite, a volume entitled *Hommage à Jean Hyppolite* published by the Presses Universitaires de France in 1971 and reprinted in *Dits et Écrits* in 1994. As Defert recounts, the rereading and intellectual labor that produced the essay began in 1967 at the cusp of the student revolts.
70. In the files containing the draft manuscript, Defert notes: "Nietzsche 1967–1970: rereading of Nietzsche, Summer 1967." Fonds Michel Foucault, NAF 28730, Boîte 65, Bibliothèque nationale de France.
71. Daniel Defert, "Chronologie," in *Michel Foucault: Oeuvres*, ed. Frédéric Gros, 2 vols. (Paris: Gallimard /Pléiade, 2015) 1: liii. ("Je lizarde Nietzsche; je crois commencer à m'apercevoir pourquoi ça m'a toujours fasciné. Une morphologie de la volonté de savoir dans la civilisation européenne qu'on a laissée de côté en faveur d'une analyse de la volonté de puissance.")
72. Not surprisingly, the same was true of Foucault's texts at the time, especially, for instance, "Truth and Juridical Forms" in 1973, which opens with Foucault alternately deploying the terms *appearance, invention, birth, origin, formation, emergence*, and *stabilization*.
73. Nietzsche, "On Truth and Lie in a Nonmoral Sense," 17.
74. Foucault, "Leçon sur Nietzsche," in *Leçons sur la volonté de savoir. Cours au Collège de France (1970–1971)*, ed. Daniel Defert (Paris: Gallimard/Seuil, 2011), 195.
75. Foucault, "Nietzsche, la généalogie, l'histoire," 144; Michel Foucault, "Nietzsche, Genealogy, History," in *The Foucault Reader*, ed. Paul Rabinow, 76–100 (New York: Pantheon, 1984), 84. This notion of irruption will be important for Sarah Kofman as the inspiration for certain titles that she uses to speak about *Ecce homo* and about Nietzsche's work. The notion of irruption lends itself to the task of detecting different relations of force, relations of power, domination. We see this on page 145 (English, page 85) of "Nietzsche, la généalogie, l'histoire," where Foucault speaks precisely of dominators and dominated.
76. Foucault, "Nietzsche, la généalogie, l'histoire," 155 (English, 95): "The historical analysis of this rancorous will to knowledge."
77. A year earlier, in the winter of 1969–1970, Foucault had delivered lectures on Nietzsche at the experimental university at Vincennes. He subsequently reworked those manuscripts for other lectures, notably his three conferences at McGill (including this "Lesson on Nietzsche"), his later lectures in Rio in 1973, and portions of his Collège de France lectures on "Penal Theories and Institutions" in 1972.
78. Foucault, "Leçon sur Nietzsche," 199.
79. Foucault, "Leçon sur Nietzsche," 208.
80. Colin Koopman, *How We Became Our Data: A Genealogy of the Informational Person* (Chicago: University of Chicago Press, 2019), 23.

81. In a draft article titled "On Possibilising Genealogy," Daniele Lorenzini argues for a unique notion of genealogy that he calls the possibilising dimension of genealogical inquiry, and he locates it in Foucault's writings, especially on the notion of counterconduct and of the critical attitude. This possibilising form of genealogy, which is different from the two classic ways of thinking about genealogy (as vindication of core concepts or as a way to unmask or debunk), clearly distinguishes Foucault's conception from Nietzsche's. See Daniele Lorenzini, "On Possibilising Genealogy," draft presented at the "Critical Work" workshop of the Columbia Center for Contemporary Critical Thought (CCCCT) on April 19, 2019 (on file with author). Meanwhile, Amy Allen and Colin Koopman have identified a form of genealogy that they call "problematizing genealogies," which they associate with Foucault, by contrast to the debunking genealogical approach of Nietzsche and the vindicatory approach of Bernard Williams. See Colin Koopman, *Genealogy as Critique: Foucault and the Problems of Modernity* (Bloomington: Indiana University Press, 2013), 60; Amy Allen, "Beyond Kant Versus Hegel: An Alternative Strategy for Grounding the Normativity of Critique," 243–261, in *Feminism, Capitalism, and Critique: Essays in Honor of Nancy Fraser*, ed. Banu Bargu and Chiara Bottici (Cham, Switzerland: Palgrave Macmillan, 2017), 256. For a careful analysis of the differences between Nietzsche's and Foucault's genealogical methods, see also Martin Saar, *Genealogie als Kritik: Geschichte und Theorie des Subjekts nach Nietzsche und Foucault* (Frankfurt: Campus, 2007); and Martin Saar, "Genealogy and Subjectivity," *European Journal of Philosophy* 10, no. 2 (2002): 231–245.
82. Foucault, *La Société punitive*, 231–232; Foucault, *Discipline and Punish*, 26–27.
83. Foucault, *La Société punitive*, 233.
84. Arlette Farge and Michel Foucault, eds., *Le Désordre des familles: Lettres de cachet des Archives de la Bastille au XVIIIe siècle* (Paris: Gallimard, 1982).
85. Jacques Donzelot, *La Police des familles* (Paris: Minuit, 1977); Jacques Donzelot, *L'invention du social: Essai sur le déclin des passions politiques* (Paris: Fayard, 1984).
86. Foucault, *La Societé punitive*, 234.
87. Foucault, "Truth and Juridical Forms," 86; Foucault, *Discipline and Punish*, 25–26.
88. Louis Althusser, "Ideology and Ideological State Apparatuses," in *Lenin and Philosophy and Other Essays*, Ben Brewster, trans. (New York: Monthly Review Press, 1970), 121–176.
89. Foucault, *La Societé punitive*, 237; 239 (my translation).
90. Foucault, "Truth and Juridical Forms," 5–6; 6.
91. Bernard E. Harcourt, situation du cours to *La Société punitive. Cours au Collège de France (1972–1973)*, ed. Bernard E. Harcourt (Paris: Gallimard/Seuil, 2013), 271–314; Bernard E. Harcourt, course context to *The Punitive Society: Lectures at the Collège de France 1972–1973*, ed. Bernard E. Harcourt, trans. Graham Burchell (New York: Picador, 2015), 265–300; Bernard E. Harcourt, notice to *Surveiller et Punir. Naissance de la prison*, ed. Bernard E. Harcourt, in *Michel Foucault: Oeuvres*, vol. 2, (Paris: Gallimard/La Pléiade, 2015), 1462–1475.
92. Foucault, "Truth and Juridical Forms," 9.
93. Foucault, "Truth and Juridical Forms," 12.
94. Foucault, "Truth and Juridical Forms," 12 (my translation).
95. Foucault, "Truth and Juridical Forms," 5.
96. Evidently, I have not developed some of these other strands of critical philosophy; instead I will refer the reader to relevant secondary readings, including Vincent Descombes, *Le Même et l'autre* (Paris: Minuit, 1979); François Dosse, *Histoire du structuralisme*, 2 vols. (Paris: Découverte, 1992); Jane Gallop, *Reading Lacan* (Ithaca, NY: Cornell University Press, 1985); and Elisabeth Roudinesco, *Jacques Lacan and Co.: A History of Psychoanalysis in France, 1925–1985*, trans. Jeffrey Mehlman (Chicago: University of Chicago Press, 1990).
97. Louis Althusser, Étienne Balibar, Roger Establet, Pierre Macherey, and Jacques Rancière, *Reading Capital: The Complete Edition*, trans. Ben Brewster and David Fernbach (New York: Verso, 2016);

Louis Althusser, "Ideology and Ideological State Apparatus" (Notes Towards an Investigation), in *Lenin and Philosophy and Other Essays*, trans. Ben Brewster (New York: Monthly Review Press, 2001), 85–126. On Althusser's earlier scientific reading of Marx, see generally *Critique 13/13* (blog), November 13, 2019, http://blogs.law.columbia.edu/critique1313/5-13/.

98. Jürgen Habermas, *Legitimation Crisis*, trans. Thomas McCarthy (Boston: Beacon Press, 1975).
99. Paulo Freire, *Pedagogy of the Oppressed* (New York: Continuum, 1968); see generally *Critique 13/13* (blog), October 23, 2019, http://blogs.law.columbia.edu/critique1313/4-13/. Jacques Rancière also wrote in a similar vein in Jacques Rancière, *The Ignorant Schoolmaster: Five Lessons in Intellectual Emancipation* (Stanford: Stanford University Press, 1991).
100. Walter Benjamin, "Some Remarks on Theoretical Foundations, 1930," in *Walter Benjamin and Bertolt Brecht—The Story of a Friendship*, ed. Erdmut Wizisla (New Haven, CT: Yale University Press, 2009), 206–207.
101. Edward Said, *Orientalism* (New York: Vintage, 2003), 10.
102. Said, *Orientalism*, 326.
103. Said, *Orientalism*, 203; 204.
104. Said, *Orientalism*, 187, quoting a letter from Flaubert to the poet Louise Colet.
105. Said, *Orientalism*, 187-190.
106. Said, *Orientalism*, 2; 3; 3.
107. Said, *Orientalism*, 82.
108. Said, *Orientalism*, 328.
109. Said, *Orientalism*, 325.
110. Said, *Orientalism*, 325–326.
111. Homi K. Bhabha, *The Location of Culture* (New York: Routledge, 1994); Dipesh Chakrabarty, *Provincializing Europe: Postcolonial Thought and Historical Difference* (Princeton, NJ: Princeton University Press, 2000); Partha Chatterjee, *The Nation and its Fragments: Colonial and Postcolonial Histories* (Princeton, NJ: Princeton University Press, 1993); Gayatri Chakravorty Spivak, *A Critique of Postcolonial Reason: Toward a History of the Vanishing Present* (Cambridge, MA: Harvard University Press, 1999); for more recent work building on postcolonial and subaltern studies, see Anupama Rao, *The Caste Question: Dalits and the Politics of Modern India* (Berkeley: University of California Press, 2009).
112. Gayatri Chakravorty Spivak, "Can the Subaltern Speak?," in *Can the Subaltern Speak? Reflections on the History of an Idea*, ed. Rosalind C. Morris (New York: Columbia University Press, 2010), 21–78. Spivak's original essay was published in 1985 as "Can the Subaltern Speak? Speculations on Widow Sacrifice," *Wedge* 7/8 (Winter/Spring 1985): 120–130. A longer version was published in 1988 in *Marxism and the Interpretation of Culture*, ed. Cary Nelson and Lawrence Grossberg (Urbana: University of Illinois Press, 1988). Another long version was published in Spivak, *A Critique of Postcolonial Reason*, 244–311. It is this latter version that was reproduced in Rosalind Morris's 2010 collected volume, and which I will refer to in all subsequent citations.
113. Spivak, "Can the Subaltern Speak?," 43; 43.
114. Spivak, "Can the Subaltern Speak?," 45. Other critical theorists, such as Ann Laura Stoler, would further elaborate these limitations of Foucault's work, emphasizing his tunnel vision of the West. See Ann Laura Stoler, *Race and the Education of Desire: Foucault's History of Sexuality and the Colonial Order of Things* (Durham, NC: Duke University Press, 1995).
115. Spivak spared Derrida in all this, claiming that "the early Derrida seemed aware of ethnocentrism in the production of knowledge." Spivak, "Can the Subaltern Speak?," 45. But, to be honest, that seemed a bit self-interested, it turns a blind eye to Derrida's similar faults, and does little more than contribute to the petty, internecine battles of influence between Derridians and Foucaultians, as well as others.
116. Spivak, "Can the Subaltern Speak?," 62–63. For a personal rendition of this story, explaining the filiation as well, see Gayatri Chakravorty Spivak, "In Response: Looking Back, Looking Forward,"

in *Can the Subaltern Speak? Reflections on the History of an Idea*, ed. Rosalind C. Morris (New York: Columbia University Press, 2010), 228–229.

117. Spivak, "Can the Subaltern Speak?," 63.
118. For the different iterations of this reaction, see Spivak, "Can the Subaltern Speak?," 63.
119. Said, *Orientalism*, 335.
120. Spivak, "Can the Subaltern Speak?," 63.
121. Partha Chatterjee, "Reflections on 'Can the Subaltern Speak?': Subaltern Studies After Spivak," in *Can the Subaltern Speak? Reflections on the History of an Idea*, ed. Rosalind C. Morris (New York: Columbia University Press, 2010), 82.
122. For critical work in those other areas, see, e.g., Janet Halley, "Sexuality Harassment," in *Directions in Sexual Harassment Law*, ed. Catherine MacKinnon and Reva Siegel (New Haven, CT: Yale University Press, 2002), 80–104; Cheryl Harris, "Whiteness as Property," in *Critical Race Theory*, ed. Kimberlé Crenshaw, Neil T. Gotanda, Gary Peller, and Kendall Thomas (New York: New Press, 1996), 276–291; David Kennedy, "The International Human Rights Movement: Part of the Problem?," *European Human Rights Law Review* 15, no. 3 (2001): 101–125; Duncan Kennedy, "The Stakes of Law, or Hale and Foucault!" *Legal Studies Forum* XV, no. 4 (1991): 327–366; Duncan Kennedy, "Critique of Rights in Critical Legal Studies," in *Left Legalism/Left Critique*, ed. Wendy Brown and Janet Halley (Durham, NC: Duke University Press, 2002), 178–228; Duncan Kennedy, *A Critique of Adjudication: Fin de Siècle* (Cambridge, MA: Harvard University Press, 1997); Justin Desautels-Stein, *The Jurisprudence of Style: A Structuralist History of American Pragmatism and Liberal Legal Thought* (Cambridge: Cambridge University Press, 2018); Richard T. Ford, "Beyond 'Difference'": A Reluctant Critique of Left Identity Politics," in *Left Legalism/Left Critique*, 38–79; Patricia J. Williams, *The Alchemy of Race and Rights* (Cambridge, MA: Harvard University Press, 1991); Iris Marion Young, *Justice and the Politics of Difference* (Princeton, NJ: Princeton University Press, 1990); Todd May, *The Political Philosophy of Poststructuralist Anarchism* (University Park: Pennsylvania State University Press, 1994); Murray Bookchin, *Social Anarchism or Lifestyle Anarchism: An Unbridgeable Chasm* (Chico, CA: AKPress, 1995); Lewis Call, *Postmodern Anarchism* (Lanham, MD: Lexington, 2000); Vivien Garcia, *L'anarchisme aujourd'hui* (Paris: L'Harmattan, 2009).
123. Judith Butler, *Gender Trouble: Feminism and the Subversion of Identity* (New York: Routledge, 1990); Judith Butler, *Notes Toward A Performative Theory of Assembly* (Cambridge, MA: Harvard University Press, 2015), 28. Butler draws specifically on Jacques Derrida, *Limited Inc* (Evanston, IL: Northwestern University Press, 1988); Pierre Bourdieu, *Language and Symbolic Power* (Cambridge, MA: Harvard University Press, 1991); and Eve Kosofsky Sedgwick, *Epistemology of the Closet* (Berkeley: University of California Press, 1990).
124. Butler, *Notes Toward A Performative Theory of Assembly*, 28.
125. Butler, *Notes Toward A Performative Theory of Assembly*, 28–29.
126. Butler, *Notes Toward A Performative Theory of Assembly*, 33.
127. Judith Butler, "Contingent Foundations: Feminism and the Question of 'Postmodernism,'" in Seyla Benhabib, Judith Butler, Drucilla Cornell, Nancy Fraser, and Linda Nicholson, eds., *Feminist Contentions: A Philosophical Exchange*, 35-57 (New York: Routledge, 1995), 39.

3. Michel Foucault and the History of Truth-Making

1. Michel Foucault, *Wrong-Doing, Truth-Telling: The Function of Avowal in Justice*, ed. Fabienne Brion and Bernard E. Harcourt, trans. Stephen W. Sawyer (Chicago: University of Chicago Press, 2014), 20. See also Michel Foucault, *Discourse and Truth, and Parrēsia*, ed. Henri-Paul Fruchaud, Daniele Lorenzini, and Nancy Luxon (Chicago: University of Chicago Press, 2019), 222–224 ("my intention was not to deal with the problem of truth, but with the problem of the truth-teller or of truth-telling,

or of the activity of truth-telling. I mean that it was not for me a question of analyzing the criteria, the internal or external criteria through which anyone, or through which the Greeks and the Romans, could recognize if a statement was true or not. It was a question for me of considering truth-telling as a specific activity, it was a question of considering truth-telling as a role. . . . What is the importance of telling the truth, who is able to tell the truth, and why should we tell the truth, know the truth, and recognize who is able to tell the truth? I think that is at the root, at the foundation of what we could call the critical tradition of philosophy in our society.")

2. Michel Foucault, *Qu'est-ce-que la critique?*, ed. Henri-Paul Fruchaud and Daniele Lorenzini (Paris: Vrin, 2015), 33, 58.
3. Colin Koopman, *How We Became Our Data: A Genealogy of the Informational Person* (Chicago: University of Chicago Press, 2019), 23.
4. Foucault, *Qu'est-ce-que la critique?*, 35, 37, 38.
5. Foucault, *Qu'est-ce-que la critique?*, 42–44, 45, 47; 47; 51, 53, 55.
6. See Foucault, *Wrong-Doing, Truth-Telling*, 39.
7. Michel Foucault, *L'Ordre du discours*, 225–259, in Michel Foucault, *Oeuvres*, Volume 2, ed. Frédéric Gros (Paris: Gallimard/Pléiade, 2015), 254–255. Foucault's interest in studying sexuality dates much further back. See Michel Foucault, *La Sexualité, Cours donné à l'université de Clermont-Ferrand. 1964, suivi de Le Discours de la sexualité, Cours donné à l'université de Vincennes. 1969*, ed. Claude-Olivier Doron (Paris: Gallimard/Le Seuil, 2018).
8. The reception of the Collège lectures has always been somewhat disjointed, in no small part due to the publication process and the idiosyncrasies of the decisions about what to publish first. The root of that problem was a dispute that stemmed from the fact that Alessandro Fontana had intended to publish an Italian edition of the 1976 lecture series, "Society Must Be Defended." As a result, and despite Foucault's stated desire that there be no posthumous publication of his work, the heirs ultimately agreed to allow the lectures to appear, on the principle that these had been public lectures—public performances, if you will. The 1976 lectures thus first appeared in an official French edition, but following that, the editors decided to begin with the courses that had the best audio documentation. This circuitous publication process was thus marked with a kind of odd and disjointed feeling: a text like his 1982 lectures on the *Hermeneutics of the Subject* would then be followed by something much earlier and seemingly unrelated. Ultimately, the last lectures published would be the first ones given, and the transcriptions were based solely on handwritten manuscripts and notes, as recordings were unavailable. In the unique case of *The Punitive Society* (1973), the current text is based on the written transcript of an audio recording that has since disappeared. As a result, the earliest lectures, *Lectures on the Will to Know* (1971), *Penal Theories and Institutions* (1972), and *The Punitive Society* (1973), were the last to be published. Now that the lectures are all published and can be read in chronological order, what emerges is a history of truth.
9. Foucault's surviving notes and manuscripts, preserved by Daniel Defert, have been turned over to the BnF, and they include 37,000 pages of handwritten notes, including an archive of his extensive readings and lecture notes in law.
10. Foucault returns to this scene and this analysis in the 1981 Louvain lectures, *Wrong-Doing, Truth-Telling*, in which he devotes an entire lecture to the production of truth in Greek antiquity. See Foucault, *Wrong-Doing, Truth-Telling*, First Lecture, April 22, 1981, 27–55.
11. Michel Foucault, "Truth and Juridical Forms," in *Power*, vol. 3 of *The Essential Works of Foucault (1954–1984)*, ed. James D. Faubion, trans. Robert Hurley (New York: New Press, 2000), 37; 35.
12. It is, ultimately, only through torture that the slave confesses to having saved Oedipus' life.
13. Foucault, "Truth and Juridical Forms," 33; 35; 45; 49.
14. Michel Foucault, *Mal faire, dire vrai. Fonction de l'aveu en justice*, ed. Fabienne Brion and Bernard E. Harcourt (Louvain-la-Neuve, Belgium: Presses universitaires de Louvain, 2012).

15. Michel Foucault, *"Society Must Be Defended": Lectures at the Collège de France, 1975–76*, ed. Mauro Bertani and Alessandro Fontana, trans. Arnold I. Davidson (New York: Picador, 2003), 57–62, 70; 52.
16. The discussion in Foucault, *"Society Must Be Defended,"* 52–54, particularly evokes such realist theories.
17. Foucault, *"Society Must Be Defended,"* 54; 57.
18. This new historical-political discourse intersects with Marx directly, as Foucault makes the connection between race war and class war, a connection that Marx had mentioned in his letter to Joseph Weydemeyer of March 5, 1852.
19. Michel Foucault, *The Birth of Biopolitics: Lectures at the Collège de France, 1978–1979*, ed. Michel Senellart, trans. Graham Burchell (Basingstoke, UK: Palgrave Macmillan, 2008), 32.
20. Foucault, *Birth of Biopolitics*, 34–36; 84.
21. During the period 1979–1981, the titles of Foucault's lectures do not always correspond well to their content. This is because Foucault had to provide the title for the following year's lecture series the previous spring, when he had just finished his last lecture; at times, he had an idea for the next series based on where he was at that moment, but that would change by the time he actually began the following set of lectures.
22. Michel Foucault, *Naissance de la biopolitique. Cours au Collège de France (1978–1979)*, ed. Michel Senellart (Paris: Gallimard, 2004), 24.
23. Michel Foucault, *Security, Territory, Population: Lectures at the Collège de France, 1977–1978*, ed. Michel Senellart, trans. Graham Burchell (Basingstoke, UK: Palgrave Macmillan, 2007), 123.
24. Michel Foucault, *On the Government of the Living: Lectures at the Collège de France, 1979–1980*, ed. Michel Senellart, trans. Graham Burchell (Basingstoke, UK: Palgrave Macmillan, 2014), 11; 6.
25. Michel Foucault, *Subjectivité et vérité. Cours au Collège de France (1980–1981)*, ed. Frédéric Gros (Paris: EHESS/Gallimard/Seuil, 2014), 299 (my translations); Foucault, *Subjectivity and Truth: Lectures at the Collège de France, 1980–1981*, ed. Frédéric Gros, trans. Graham Burchell (London: Palgrave Macmillan, 2017), 293–294.
26. Foucault, *Subjectivité et vérité*, 16–17.
27. Michel Foucault, *The Courage of Truth: The Government of Self and Others II: Lectures at the Collège de France 1983–1984*, ed. Frédéric Gros, trans. Graham Burchell (Basingstoke, UK: Palgrave Macmillan, 2011), 8–9.
28. Michel Foucault, *Les Aveux de la chair. Histoire de la sexualité*, vol. 4, ed. Frédéric Gros (Paris: Gallimard, 2018), 351–352, 355–356.
29. Foucault, *Birth of Biopolitics*, 282–83; *Naissance de la biopolitique*, 285–286. This critique can also be discerned in two other places. First on page 271 of the English, page 275 of the French edition, when Foucault begins the discussion, rhetorically: "Is *homo œconomicus* . . . not already a certain type of subject who precisely enabled an art of government to be determined according to the principle of economy, both in the sense of political economy and in the sense of the restriction, self-limitation, and frugality of government?" Second, on page 292 on April 4, 1979, in the last lecture, where Foucault is discussing the fact that "*Homo œconomicus* strips the sovereign of power inasmuch as he reveals an essential, fundamental, and major incapacity of the sovereign, that is to say, an inability to master the totality of the economic field. The sovereign cannot fail to be blind vis-a-vis the economic domain or field as a whole." *Birth of Biopolitics*, 292; *Naissance de la biopolitique*, 296.
30. Foucault, *Birth of Biopolitics*, 276.
31. See Frédéric Gros, "Avertissement," in Foucault, *Les Aveux de la chair*, vii.
32. Ella Myers, *Worldly Ethics: Democratic Politics and Care for the World* (Durham, NC: Duke University Press, 2013).

4. The Return to Foundations

1. See, e.g., Alain Badiou, *Communist Hypothesis*, trans. David Macey and Steve Corcoran (New York: Verso, 2010); Joshua Clover, *Riot. Strike. Riot.* (New York: Verso, 2016); Jodi Dean, *The Communist Horizon* (New York: Verso, 2012); Slavoj Žižek, Costas Douzinas, and Alex Taek-Gwong Lee, eds., *The Idea of Communism*, 3 vols. (New York: Verso, 2010–2016); and the discussion *infra*.
2. Hannah Arendt, "Truth and Politics," *The New Yorker*, February 5, 1967, 50; 52.
3. Arendt, "Truth and Politics," 50; 50; 50–51.
4. Arendt, "Truth and Politics," 51; 56; 59.
5. Arendt, "Truth and Politics," 60–62.
6. Arendt, "Truth and Politics," 83; 84; 84.
7. This is precisely what sparks Steven Lukes's argument in his essay "Power, Truth, and Epistemic Closure"—namely, the argument that we need to reconstitute a political space where the norms of political debate are respected, so that truth can prevail. Steven Lukes, "Power, Truth, and Epistemic Closure," *Praxis 13/13* (blog), September 9, 2018, http://blogs.law.columbia.edu/praxis1313/steven-lukes-power-truth-and-epistemic-closure/.
8. Arendt, "Truth and Politics," 88.
9. Arendt, "Truth and Politics," 88.
10. For a synopsis of Habermas's lectures at the Collège de France from March 7–22, 1983, see Didier Éribon, "Habermas le 'moderne,'" *Libération*, March 9, 1983, 33. For Habermas's recollection of the planned encounter with Foucault, see Habermas's essay "Taking Aim at the Heart of the Present," in *Critique and Power: Recasting the Foucault/Habermas Debate*, ed. Michael Kelly (Cambridge, MA: MIT Press, 1994), 150, where Habermas reports that Foucault had suggested to him that they "meet with some American colleagues in November 1984 for a private conference to discuss Kant's essay *What Is Enlightenment?*, which had appeared two hundred years earlier." Habermas recalled that those present included Hubert Dreyfus, Richard Rorty, and Charles Taylor, and he believed that the topic would be "various interpretations of modernity, using as a basis for discussion a text that in a certain sense initiated the philosophical discourse of modernity" (Habermas, "Taking Aim," 150). For Foucault's recollection, see Michel Foucault, "Critical Theory/Intellectual History," in *Critique and Power: Recasting the Foucault/Habermas Debate*, ed. Michael Kelly (Cambridge, MA: MIT Press, 1994), 125, an interview during which he states, "The Americans were planning a kind of seminar with Habermas and myself. Habermas had suggested the theme of modernity for the seminar." The debate never took place; instead, what we have is a virtual debate, constructed by Michael Kelly and others, who collected several texts by each, to try to recreate what the debate might have sounded like. The Habermas contributions include two chapters that he wrote under the larger project of *The Philosophical Discourse of Modernity: Twelve Lectures.* This book was originally published in German in 1985 (Suhrkamp Verlag), which was after Foucault's death. The first, Chapter 9, was titled "The Critique of Reason as an Unmasking of the Human Sciences: Michel Foucault." The second, Chapter 10, was "Some Questions Concerning the Theory of Power: Foucault Again." In addition, the editors included the essay "Taking Aim at the Heart of the Present," which appeared in Jürgen Habermas, *The New Conservatism: Cultural Criticism and the Historians' Debate*, trans. Shierry Weber Nicholsen (Cambridge, MA: MIT Press, 1991), and also appeared in David Hoy, ed., *Foucault: A Critical Reader* (Oxford: Basil Blackwell, 1986). The Foucault contributions included "Two Lectures," his courses of January 7 and January 14, 1976, from *"Il faut défendre la société"*; and an interview titled "Structuralisme et poststructuralisme," retitled "Critical Theory/Intellectual History" and contained in *Dits et Écrits*, ed. Daniel Defert, François Ewald, and Jacques Lagrange, vol. 4: *1980–1988* (Paris: Gallimard, 1994), 431–457. For an excellent reconsideration of the virtual Foucault/Habermas debate, see Amy Allen, "Discourse, Power, and Subjectivation: The Foucault/Habermas Debate

Reconsidered," *The Philosophical Forum: A Quarterly* 40, no. 1 (2009): 1–28; see also Étienne Balibar, "Dire, contredire," in *Libre parole* (Paris: Éditions Galilée, 2018), 110–119, which unearths a missed conversation between discourse ethics and an agonistic counterconduct of frank speech.

11. It is, first, the political context of Foucault's "disappointment with the failure of the 1968 revolt" that renders the turn to power, in Habermas's words, "biographically intelligible." Michael Kelly, ed., *Critique and Power: Recasting the Foucault/Habermas Debate* (Cambridge, MA: MIT Press, 1994), 57. It is, second, an intellectual impasse or, in Habermas's words, "embarrassment" associated with the impossibility of explaining any transformation from one to another layer of epistemic totality. Kelly, ed., *Critique and Power*, 80.
12. Kelly, *Critique and Power*, 57; 57.
13. Michel Foucault, "What Is Enlightenment?," in *The Foucault Reader*, ed. Paul Rabinow (New York: Pantheon, 1984), 32–50.
14. Kelly, *Critique and Power*, 152; 152–153; 154.
15. Jürgen Habermas, *The Structural Transformation of the Public Sphere: An Inquiry into a Category of Bourgeois Society*, trans. Thomas Burger (Cambridge, MA: MIT Press, 1991), 36, 37, 41.
16. Habermas, *The Structural Transformation of the Public Sphere*, 160.
17. Habermas, *The Structural Transformation of the Public Sphere*, 145; 142; 177.
18. Habermas, *The Structural Transformation of the Public Sphere*, 175; 164, 175; 193; 195.
19. Habermas, *The Structural Transformation of the Public Sphere*, 4; xviii; xviii–xix.
20. Habermas, *The Structural Transformation of the Public Sphere*, 235.
21. Habermas, *The Structural Transformation of the Public Sphere*, 250.
22. See James Gordon Finlayson, *The Habermas-Rawls Debate* (New York: Columbia University Press, 2019); and James Gordon Finlayson, Fabian Freyenhagen, and James Gledhill, eds., *Habermas and Rawls: Disputing the Political* (New York: Routledge, 2011). Also see Jürgen Habermas, *Between Facts and Norms: Contributions to a Discourse Theory of Law and Democracy* (Cambridge, MA: MIT Press, 1996).
23. Jürgen Habermas, "Reconciliation Through the Public Use of Reason: Remarks on John Rawls's Political Liberalism," *Journal of Philosophy* 92, no. 3 (1995): 110; 110.
24. Jürgen Habermas, "A Reply to Critics," in *Habermas and Rawls: Disputing the Political*, ed. James Gordon Finlayson et al. (New York: Routledge, 2011), 289.
25. Jürgen Habermas, " 'Reasonable' Versus 'True,' or the Morality of Worldviews," in *Habermas and Rawls: Disputing the Political*, ed. James Gordon Finlayson et al. (New York: Routledge, 2011), 93.
26. Habermas, "A Reply to Critics," 290.
27. Habermas, "Reconciliation Through the Public Use of Reason," 128; 110.
28. See, generally, Habermas, "'Reasonable' Versus 'True,' or the Morality of Worldviews," 94, 113.
29. Habermas, "Reconciliation Through the Public Use of Reason," 117–118.
30. Habermas, "Reconciliation Through the Public Use of Reason," 131.
31. Habermas, "Reconciliation Through the Public Use of Reason," 122.
32. Habermas, "Reconciliation Through the Public Use of Reason," 126.
33. John Rawls, "Political Liberalism: Reply to Habermas," *Journal of Philosophy*, 92, no. 3 (1995): 149; 135.
34. Jürgen Habermas, "'Reasonable' Versus 'True,' or the Morality of Worldviews," 93; 96; 98.
35. Habermas, "A Reply to Critics," 284; 284; 286.
36. Habermas, "Reconciliation Through the Public Use of Reason," 110.
37. Habermas, "Reconciliation Through the Public Use of Reason," 116:

    This additional determination, however, tacitly presupposes a deontological distinction between rights and goods which contradicts the prima facie classification of rights as goods. Since the fair value of equal liberties requires the actual availability of equal opportunities to exercise these rights, only rights, not goods, can be qualified in this manner;

and 129:

> But such an a priori boundary between private and public autonomy not only contradicts the republican intuition that popular sovereignty and human rights are nourished by the same root. It also conflicts with historical experience, above all with the fact that the historically shifting boundary between the private and public spheres has always been problematic from a normative point of view.

38. Seyla Benhabib, *Critique, Norm, and Utopia: A Study of the Foundations of Critical Theory* (New York: Columbia University Press, 1986), ix; 14.
39. Benhabib, *Critique, Norm, and Utopia*, 10.
40. Benhabib, *Critique, Norm, and Utopia*, 12.
41. Benhabib, *Critique, Norm, and Utopia*, 55; 254; 267.
42. Benhabib, *Critique, Norm, and Utopia*, 13, 352; 346; 15; 346; 15.
43. Seyla Benhabib, Judith Butler, Drucilla Cornell, Nancy Fraser, and Linda Nicholson, eds., *Feminist Contentions: A Philosophical Exchange* (New York: Routledge, 1995). Benhabib had staked out some of these positions in an earlier article. Seyla Benhabib, "Epistemologies of Post-Modernism," *New German Critique* Fall 1984, no. 33 (1984): 103–127. Incidentally, in the *Feminist Contentions* debate and Benhabib's article, the contributors use the term *postmodernism*, which I find too vague in this context. Benhabib draws on the work of Jane Flax to define the term; but given the disagreements over the term, and the fact that the exchange is really about French theory in the late 1980s (mostly by Foucault, Derrida, and Lacan), I will use the term *poststructuralism* instead.
44. Seyla Benhabib, *Situating the Self: Gender, Community, and Post-modernism* (London: Polity Press, 1992). See, generally, Tony Couture, "Feminist Criticisms of Habermas's Ethics and Politics," *Dialogue: Canadian Philosophical Review/Revue canadienne de philosophie* 34, no. 2 (1995): 259–280.
45. Seyla Benhabib, "Feminism and Postmodernism: An Uneasy Alliance," in *Feminist Contentions: A Philosophical Exchange*, ed. Seyla Benhabib, Judith Butler, Drucilla Cornell, Nancy Fraser, and Linda Nicholson (New York: Routledge, 1995), 20.
46. Benhabib, "Feminism and Postmodernism," 21; 21.
47. Benhabib, "Feminism and Postmodernism," 25; 25.
48. Benhabib, "Feminism and Postmodernism," 25; 27.
49. Benhabib, "Feminism and Postmodernism," 30 (internal quotations omitted).
50. Benhabib, "Feminism and Postmodernism," 30; 30.
51. Seyla Benhabib, "Subjectivity, Historiography, and Politics: Reflections on the 'Feminism/Postmodernism Exchange,'" in *Feminist Contentions: A Philosophical Exchange*, ed. Seyla Benhabib, Judith Butler, Drucilla Cornell, Nancy Fraser, and Linda Nicholson (New York: Routledge, 1995), 115.
52. Benhabib goes on to say, "I have argued elsewhere for a 'nonfoundationalist'" justification of critical social theory and have expanded this strategy of justification in *Situating the Self*." Benhabib, "Subjectivity, Historiography, and Politics," 118.
53. Seyla Benhabib, "Claiming Rights Across Borders: International Human Rights and Democratic Sovereignty," *American Political Science Review* 103, no. 4 (2009): 691–704, reproduced in Seyla Benhabib, *Dignity in Adversity: Human Rights in Turbulent Times* (New York: Polity, 2011), 117–137; Seyla Benhabib, "The Return of Political Theology: The Scarf Affair in Comparative Constitutional Perspective in France, Germany, and Turkey," in *Dignity in Adversity: Human Rights in Turbulent Times*, ed. Seyla Benhabib (New York: Polity, 2011), 166–183; Seyla Benhabib, "Carl Schmitt's Critique of Kant: Sovereignty and International Law," *Political Theory* 40, no. 6 (2012), 688–713.
54. Benhabib, "Claiming Rights Across Borders," 118; 119. One may ask whether this position ultimately rests on what Carl Schmitt identified as a fallacy of liberalism—namely, that more discourse within a liberal democratic regime will lead to forward motion. This is the critique of Schmitt that Benhabib

herself summarizes as "the principle of government by discussion, and the assumption that opinions will eventually converge through deliberation." Benhabib, "The Return of Political Theology," 169. In this regard, Schmitt does present a real challenge. There is, after all, nothing in the discussion of the scarf affair that tells us that the jurisgenerative discourse is a move forward or normatively better. Benhabib maintains that it is empowering for women. But, then, couldn't another language or another discourse substitute for human rights talk? Why, in the end—as a normative matter—are we in a better place? Naturally, this calls for a more sustained conversation.

55. Seyla Benhabib, "Critique and Emancipation: Comments Prepared for the Emanzipation Conference" (lecture, Humboldt-Universität zu Berlin, May 25, 2018; draft on file with author), 11.
56. Benhabib, "Claiming Rights Across Borders," 137.
57. Axel Honneth, *The Critique of Power: Reflective Stages in a Critical Social Theory*, trans. Kenneth Baynes (Cambridge, MA: MIT Press, 1991).
58. Honneth, *The Critique of Power*, 99–101; xviii; 303.
59. See especially chapter 7 of Honneth, *The Critique of Power*, 203–239, on "Habermas' Anthropology of Knowledge: The Theory of Knowledge-Constitutive Interests."
60. See, e.g., Honneth, *The Critique of Power*, 100 ("Both ignore the cognitive and moral synthetic accomplishments of which social groups are capable through the cooperative interpretive efforts of their members").
61. Amy Allen, "Discourse, Power, and Subjectivation: The Foucault/Habermas Debate Reconsidered," *Philosophical Forum* 40, no. 1 (2009): 3.
62. Honneth, *The Critique of Power*, 17–18; 99, 17; 18–19, 31, 99–100; 31–35; 55, 99; 100.
63. Honneth, *The Critique of Power*, 67; 100.
64. Honneth, *The Critique of Power*, xix; xix; xv; 101; xv.
65. Honneth, *The Critique of Power*, xvii.
66. Honneth, *The Critique of Power*, 195.
67. Honneth, *The Critique of Power*, 204–210, 211, 213–222, 224–239.
68. Axel Honneth, *The Idea of Socialism: Towards a Renewal* (Cambridge: Polity, 2017), viii.
69. Honneth, *The Idea of Socialism*, 13.
70. Honneth, *The Idea of Socialism*, 15; 18; 20.
71. Honneth, *The Idea of Socialism*, 24.
72. Honneth, *The Idea of Socialism*, 52; 53.
73. Honneth, *The Idea of Socialism*, 81.
74. Honneth, *The Idea of Socialism*, 96; 97.
75. Honneth, *The Idea of Socialism*, 105.
76. Honneth, *The Idea of Socialism*, 106.
77. Honneth, *The Idea of Socialism*, 5.
78. Rahel Jaeggi, *Critique of Forms of Life*, trans. Ciaran Cronin (Cambridge, MA: The Belknap Press of Harvard University Press, 2018).
79. Jaeggi, *Critique of Forms of Life*, xi–xii; 30; xiii.
80. Jaeggi, *Critique of Forms of Life*, ix.
81. Jaeggi, *Critique of Forms of Life*, 85; 8; 2, 5; 30.
82. Jaeggi, *Critique of Forms of Life*, 8; 9.
83. Jaeggi, *Critique of Forms of Life*, 85–86; 86; see also 87; 31.
84. Jaeggi, *Critique of Forms of Life*, 212–213; 213; 31; 216.
85. Jaeggi, *Critique of Forms of Life*, 217; 315.
86. Jaeggi, *Critique of Forms of Life*, 316.
87. Jaeggi, *Critique of Forms of Life*, 15; 21, 25.
88. Jaeggi, *Critique of Forms of Life*, 29.

89. Jaeggi, *Critique of Forms of Life*, xii.
90. Rainer Forst, *Justification and Critique*, trans. Ciaran Cronin (Cambridge: Polity, 2014), viii, 1; 1.
91. Forst, *Justification and Critique*, 2.
92. Forst, *Justification and Critique*, 2.
93. Forst, *Justification and Critique*, 3.
94. Forst, *Justification and Critique*, 9–11; Rainer Forst, "Noumenal Power," *Journal of Political Philosophy* 23, no. 2 (2015): 111–127; Rainer Forst, "Noumenal Power Revisited: Reply to Critics," *Journal of Political Power* 11, no. 3 (2018): 294–321.
95. Forst, *Justification and Critique*, 11.
96. Reinhart Koselleck, *Critique and Crisis: Enlightenment and the Pathogenesis of Modern Society* (Cambridge, MA: MIT Press, 1988 [1959]), 103–104 n.15 and 103–123 (tracing in detail the etymology and usage of the terms *crisis* and *critique*); Jürgen Habermas, *Legitimation Crisis*, trans. Thomas McCarthy (Boston: Beacon, 1975 [1973]), 1–3 (discussing esp. the medical, aesthetic, and social scientific usage); Michel Foucault, *Mal faire, dire vrai. Fonction de l'aveu en justice*, ed. Fabienne Brion and Bernard E. Harcourt (Louvain, Belgium: Presses Universitaires de Louvain, 2012 [1981]), 35–40, 271–276, 287–292 (tracing the relationship between the concepts of *dikazein*, *krinein*, and truth); Michel Foucault, *Wrong-Doing, Truth-Telling: The Function of Avowal in Justice*, ed. Fabienne Brion and Bernard E. Harcourt, trans. Stephen W. Sawyer (Chicago: University of Chicago Press, 2014 [1981]), 45–50, 279–303; Seyla Benhabib, *Critique, Norm, and Utopia: Study of the Foundations of Critical Theory* (New York: Columbia University Press, 1986), 19–20 (discussing the philological and philosophical transformations of critique).
97. Foucault, *Wrong-Doing, Truth-Telling*, 50.
98. Colin Koopman, "Critical Problematization in Foucault and Deleuze: The Force of Critique Without Judgment," in *Between Deleuze and Foucault*, ed. Nicolae Morar, Thomas Nail, and Daniel Smith (Edinburgh: Edinburgh University Press, 2016), 90; see generally Colin Koopman, *Genealogy as Critique: Foucault and the Problems of Modernity* (Bloomington: Indiana University Press, 2013).
99. Colin Koopman, *How We Became Our Data: A Genealogy of the Informational Person* (Chicago: University of Chicago Press, 2019), 23.
100. Philippe Lacoue-Labarthe and Jean-Luc Nancy, *Retreating the Political* (New York: Routledge, 1997), 144. See, generally, Oliver Marchart, *Post-Foundational Political Thought: Political Difference in Nancy, Lefort, Badiou and Laclau* (Edinburgh: Edinburgh University Press, 2007) (developing a postfoundational philosophy based on the writings of Nancy, Lefort, Badiou, and Laclau); also see Jacques Rancière, *Disagreement: Politics and Philosophy*, trans. Julie Rose (Minneapolis: University of Minnesota Press, 1999).
101. Dipesh Chakrabarty, "The Climate of History: Four Theses," *Critical Inquiry* 35, no. 20 (2009): 17–40; Bruno Latour, "Anthropology at the Time of the Anthropocene: A Personal View of What Is to Be Studied," lecture to the American Association of Anthropologists, Washington, D.C., 2014; Paul J. Crutzen, John R. McNeill, and Will Steffen, "The Anthropocene: Are Humans Now Overwhelming the Great Forces of Nature?," *Ambio* 36, no. 8 (2007): 614–621.
102. Rik Peeters and Marc Schuilenburg, "Gift Politics: Exposure and Surveillance in the Anthropocene," *Crime, Law, and Social Change* 68, no. 5 (2017): 563–578.
103. Wendy Brown, *Undoing the Demos* (New York: Zone, 2015); Wendy Brown, "Neoliberalism's Frankenstein: Authoritarian Freedom in Twenty-First-Century 'Democracies,'" *Critical Times* 1 (2018): 60–79; Loïc Wacquant, *Punishing the Poor* (Durham, NC: Duke University Press, 2009); Nancy Fraser, "Legitimation Crisis? On the Political Contradictions of Financialized Capitalism," *Critical Historical Studies* 2, no. 2 (2015): 157–189; Bernard E. Harcourt, *The Illusion of Free Markets: Punishment and the Myth of Natural Order* (Cambridge, MA: Harvard University Press, 2011); Juan Obarrio, *The Spirit of the Laws in Mozambique* (Chicago: University of Chicago Press, 2014); Giorgio

Agamben, *Homo Sacer: Sovereign Power and Bare Life*, trans. Daniel Heller-Roazen (Stanford, CA: Stanford University Press, 1998).

104. Judith Butler, *Notes Toward a Performative Theory of Assembly* (Cambridge, MA: Harvard University Press, 2015), 33–38; Achille Mbembe, "Necropolitics," *Public Culture* 15, no. 1 (2003): 11–40; Achille Mbembe, *Critique of Black Reason* (Durham, NC: Duke University Press, 2017); Alexander G. Weheliye, *Habeas Viscus: Racializing Assemblages, Biopolitics, and Black Feminist Theories of the Human* (Durham, NC: Duke University Press, 2014); Saidiya Hartman, "Venus in Two Acts," *Small Axe*, 12 (2), 2008: 1–14; Kimberlé Crenshaw, "Mapping the Margins: Intersectionality, Identity Politics, and Violence Against Women of Color," *Stanford Law Review* 43, no. 6 (1991): 1241–1299; Didier Fassin, "The Endurance of Critique," *Anthropological Theory* 17, no. 1 (2017): 4–29; Amy Allen, *The End of Progress: Decolonizing the Normative Foundations of Critical Theory* (New York: Columbia University Press, 2016); Patricia Hill-Collins, *Black Feminist Thought: Knowledge, Consciousness, and the Politics of Empowerment* (New York: Routledge, 2009); José Esteban Muñoz, *Disidentifications: Queers of Color and the Performance of Politics* (Minneapolis: University of Minnesota Press, 1999).
105. Martin Saar, "X—What Is Social Philosophy? Or: Order, Practice, Subject," *Proceedings of the Aristotelian Society* 118, no. 2 (2018): 220.
106. Recall that Habermas had held Horkheimer's dual chair in sociology and philosophy from 1964 to 1971, so the lineage goes back even further to the first generation of the Frankfurt School. See "History of the Chair," Goethe Universität Frankfurt am Main, accessed August 30, 2019, http://www.fb03.uni-frankfurt.de/46159784/History_of_the_Chair?
107. Martin Saar, *Genealogie als Kritik: Geschichte und Theorie des Subjekts nach Nietzsche und Foucault* (Frankfurt: Campus, 2007).
108. Saar, "What Is Social Philosophy?," 215; 215; 218–220.

5. The Crux of the Problem

1. See, e.g., Rahel Jaeggi, *Critique of Forms of Life*, trans. Ciaran Cronin (Cambridge, MA: The Belknap Press of Harvard University Press, 2018), 205–206; 213; 214.
2. Rahel Jaeggi, "Rethinking Ideology," in *New Waves in Political Philosophy*, ed. Boudewijn de Bruin and Christopher F. Zurn (New York: Palgrave Macmillan, 2009), 63. Elsewhere, however, Jaeggi notes that her "concept of a 'strong' version of immanent criticism" is "inspired by the critique of ideology." Jaeggi, *Critique of Forms of Life*, xiii.
3. Jaeggi, "Rethinking Ideology," 75; 75–76; 77.
4. Peter Baehr, *The Unmasking Style in Social Theory* (London: Routledge, 2019), 50–69.
5. Amy Allen, *The End of Progress: Decolonizing the Normative Foundations of Critical Theory* (New York: Columbia University Press, 2016); Seyla Benhabib, *Critique, Norm, and Utopia: A Study of the Foundations of Critical Theory* (New York: Columbia University Press, 1986); Jaeggi, *Critique of Forms of Life;* Raymond Geuss, *The Idea of a Critical Theory: Habermas and the Frankfurt School* (Cambridge: Cambridge University Press, 1981).
6. See, generally, chapter 1 *supra;* Martin Saar, "Genealogy and Subjectivity," *European Journal of Philosophy* 10, no. 2 (2002): 231–245, 232, 236; Martin Saar, *Genealogie als Kritik: Geschichte und Theorie des Subjekts nach Nietzsche und Foucault* (Frankfurt: Campus, 2007).
7. Seyla Benhabib, *Situating the Self: Gender, Community and Post-modernism* (London: Polity Press, 1992); Rainer Forst, *Justification and Critique*, trans. Ciaran Cronin (Cambridge: Polity, 2014), viii. ("The guiding idea throughout is that the concept of justification is reflexive in nature and that political philosophy must build on this insight in order to link theory and practice in the right way and to avoid the blind alleys into which it all too often stumbles.")
8. Jaeggi, *Critique of Forms of Life*, 173.

9. Edward Said, *Orientalism* (New York: Vintage, 2003), 4–5.
10. Jaeggi, "Rethinking Ideology," 65.
11. Benhabib, *Critique, Norm, Utopia*; Seyla Benhabib, "Critique and Emancipation: Comments Prepared for the Emanzipation Conference" (lecture, Humboldt-Universität zu Berlin, May 25, 2018).
12. See, e.g., Forst, *Justification and Critique*, 7 ("I share Honneth's view that a critical theory should understand itself as a 'form of reflection belonging to a historically effective reason' which represents an emancipatory force."); Martin Saar, "X—What Is Social Philosophy? Or: Order, Practice, Subject," *Proceedings of the Aristotelian Society* 118, no. 2 (2018): 207–223, 208; Jaeggi, *Critique of Forms of Life*, xi ("an exploration of the conditions of what can be conceived in the tradition of critical theory as a ferment of individual and collective *emancipation processes*").
13. Luc Boltanski, *De la critique. Précis de sociologie de l'émancipation* (Paris: Gallimard, 2009), 228. See also Luc Boltanski, "Sociologie critique et sociologie de la critique," *Politix* 3, no. 10 (1990): 124–134.
14. Geuss, *The Idea of a Critical Theory*, 2; 2.
15. Immanent critique derives from Kant as well as from Hegel, to be sure. The practice indexes Kant and his notion of a transcendental critique. Kant's idea is that it is not possible to transcend our way of knowing to achieve knowledge of the object in itself, independent of the nature of our mind and the categories of space and time. Because we cannot escape or go beyond the human experience, we are locked within it in the same way that an immanent critique remains within the nature of its object. As Kant explained, "By *transcendental idealism* I mean the doctrine that appearances are to be regarded as being, one and all, representations only, not things in themselves, and that time and space are therefore only sensible forms of our intuition . . ." Immanuel Kant, *Critique of Pure Reason*, trans. Norman Kemp Smith (New York: St. Martin's, 1965), 345 (A369). In a similar way, in immanent critique, we remain within the object and do not transcend it. For a counternarrative of the birth of immanence that includes not only Kant and Hegel but Hume, and explores immanence in Foucault and Deleuze, see Colin Koopman, "Critical Problematization in Foucault and Deleuze: The Force of Critique Without Judgment," 87–119, in *Between Deleuze and Foucault*, ed. Nicolae Morar, Thomas Nail, and Daniel Smith (Edinburgh: Edinburgh University Press, 2016), 92–94.
16. Robert J. Antonio, "Immanent Critique as the Core of Critical Theory: Its Origins and Developments in Hegel, Marx and Contemporary Thought," *British Journal of Sociology* 32, no. 3 (1981): 330–345, 332.
17. Jaeggi, "Rethinking Ideology," 63.
18. As Benhabib explains, the method "refuses to stand outside its object and instead juxtaposes the immanent, normative self-understanding of its object to the material actuality of this object"; it is different from mere criticism, which by contrast "stands outside the object it criticizes" and "privileges an Archimedean standpoint." Benhabib, *Critique, Norm, and Utopia*, 33.
19. David L. Harvey, "Introduction," *Sociological Perspectives* 33, no. 1 (1990): 5.
20. Thomas Piketty, *Le Capital au XXIème siècle* (Paris: Le Seuil, 2013).
21. Max Horkheimer, *Eclipse of Reason* (London: Bloomsbury, 1974), 126; 126.
22. Max Horkheimer, "Traditional and Critical Theory," 188–252, in *Critical Theory: Selected Essays*, trans. Matthew J. O'Connell et al. (New York: Continuum, 1992), 203; 204; 204; 207, 208; 208; 212; 213.
23. Horkheimer, "Traditional and Critical Theory," 215.
24. Colin Koopman, "Problematization in Foucault's Genealogy and Deleuze's Symptomatology," *Angelaki: Journal of the Theoretical Humanities* 12, no. 2 (April 2018): 187–203, 190 (emphasis added).
25. John Rajchman, introduction to Gilles Deleuze: *Pure Immanence: Essays on a Life*, ed. John Rajchman, trans. Anne Boyman (New York: Zone, 2001), 12–16.
26. Benhabib, *Critique, Norm, and Utopia*, 47; see also 21.
27. François Ewald, *The Birth of Solidarity: The History of the French Welfare State*, ed. Melinda Cooper, trans. Timothy Scott Johnson (Durham: Duke University Press, forthcoming), [*51]; [*367].

28. Judith Butler, *Gender Trouble: Feminism and the Subversion of Identity* (New York: Routledge, 1990); Saar, "Genealogy and Subjectivity," 236. For another illustration of thin defetishizing critique, see Ian Hacking, *The Taming of Chance* (New York: Cambridge University Press, 1990).
29. Jaeggi, "Rethinking Ideology," 63; see also Rahel Jaeggi, "Ideology as Social Practice" (paper, Columbia University Political Theory Workshop, February 6, 2019).
30. Jaeggi, "Rethinking Ideology," 64.
31. Jaeggi is using the term *ideology* in its pejorative sense rather than in the neutral or affirmative senses of the term discussed by Raymond Geuss in his book *The Idea of a Critical Theory*. See Rahel Jaeggi, "Rethinking Ideology," 81 n.6; Karl Mannheim, *Ideology and Utopia: An Introduction to the Sociology of Knowledge* (New York: Harcourt, Brace and Company, 1940).
32. Rahel Jaeggi, "Rethinking Ideology," 65.
33. Rahel Jaeggi, "Rethinking Ideology," 72; 73; 73.
34. Rahel Jaeggi, "Rethinking Ideology," 76.
35. Steven Lukes, "In Defense of False Consciousness," *University of Chicago Legal Forum* 2011 (2011): 28, http://chicagounbound.uchicago.edu/uclf/vol2011/iss1/3/.
36. Steven Lukes, *Power: A Radical View* (New York: Palgrave Macmillan, 2005), 91–92 (citing Michel Foucault, *Power/Knowledge: Selected Interviews and Other Writings, 1972–1977*, ed. Colin Gordon, trans. John Mepham (New York: Pantheon, 1980), 38); Lukes, "In Defense of 'False Consciousness," 28.
37. Bernard E. Harcourt, "Radical Thought from Marx, Nietzsche, and Freud, Through Foucault, to the Present: Comments on Steven Lukes's 'In Defense of False Consciousness,' " *University of Chicago Legal Forum* 2011, no. 1 (2011): 29–51, http://chicagounbound.uchicago.edu/uclf/vol2011/iss1/4. Others as well tried to breach the divide. Seyla Benhabib, for instance, developed a version of critical social theory based on communicative action that tried to resolve the breach through an "insistence that criteria of validity, ascertained via non-foundationalist arguments, can be formulated." Benhabib, *Critique, Norm, and Utopia*, 15.
38. Jaeggi, "Rethinking Ideology," 67.
39. Jaeggi, "Rethinking Ideology," 70; 76.
40. Jaeggi, "Rethinking Ideology," 77.
41. Forst, *Justification and Critique*, 2.
42. Jürgen Habermas and John Rawls, for instance, recognize in their exchanges that there is, at the very least, an essential analogy between statements of truth and those of normative rightness, even if Rawls may prefer to avoid the term *truth* and use instead *reasonableness*, and if Habermas slips into moral truth talk. See, e.g., Jürgen Habermas, " 'Reasonable' Versus 'True,' or the Morality of Worldviews," 92–113, in *Habermas and Rawls: Disputing the Political*, ed. James Gordon Finlayson, Fabian Freyenhagen, and James Gledhill (New York: Routledge, 2011), 98; John Rawls, "Political Liberalism: Reply to Habermas," *Journal of Philosophy* 92, no. 3 (March 1995): 132–180, 149.
43. On the Habermas-Rawls debate, see James Gordon Finlayson, *The Habermas-Rawls Debate* (New York: Columbia University Press, 2019); and Finlayson et al., *Habermas and Rawls: Disputing the Political*.
44. Jürgen Habermas, "Reconciliation Through the Public Use of Reason: Remarks on John Rawls's Political Liberalism," *Journal of Philosophy* 92, no. 3 (March, 1995): 109–131, 127–128.
45. James Gordon Finlayson, introduction to *The Habermas-Rawls Debate* (New York: Columbia University Press, 2019), 2.
46. John Rawls, "Justice as Fairness: Political Not Metaphysical," *Philosophy and Public Affairs* 14, no. 3 (Summer 1985): 223–251, 230; Habermas, "Reconciliation Through the Public Use of Reason," 122.
47. Habermas, "Reconciliation Through the Public Use of Reason," 122; 126; 123–124; 125.
48. Rawls, "Political Liberalism: Reply to Habermas," 133; 141–142. (Note my emphasis, that Rawls writes, "in Habermas's view the test of *moral truth or validity* is fully rational acceptance in the ideal discourse situation, with all requisite conditions satisfied.")

49. Rawls, "Political Liberalism: Reply to Habermas," 149.
50. Habermas, "'Reasonable' Versus 'True,' or the Morality of Worldviews," 92–113.
51. Jürgen Habermas, "A Reply to My Critics," 283–304, in *Habermas and Rawls: Disputing the Political*, 290.
52. Habermas, "Reconciliation Through the Public Use of Reason," 125.
53. Habermas, "A Reply to My Critics," 290.
54. For that matter, I would argue that Rawls, who assiduously avoids the concept of truth, adopts a notion of reasonableness that inscribes within it the need for what I would call truthful judgments—this is, of course, Habermas's critique. Habermas helpfully summarizes Rawls's definition of *reasonable* as follows: "'reasonable' refers in the first instance to the attitude of people who are (a) willing to propose, agree upon, and abide by fair terms of social cooperation between free and equal citizens, and (b) capable of recognizing the burdens of argument and willing to accept their consequences." Habermas, "'Reasonable' Versus 'True,' or the Morality of Worldviews," 102. What is plain from this definition is that it likely would lead a critic to claim truth—namely, on whether people are in fact truly capable or willing. Those judgments determine whether people are being unreasonable or whether there are other grounds for deliberative breakdown. In liberal political and legal debate, that often leads to claims of truth. I will set that aside here, but in the end, it does functionally bring us back to truth again.
55. Lukes, "In Defense of False Consciousness," 19.
56. Bernard E. Harcourt, "Radical Thought from Marx, Nietzsche, and Freud, Through Foucault, to the Present: Comments on Steven Lukes's In Defense of False Consciousness," *University of Chicago Legal Forum* 2011, no. 1 (2011): 29–51, 32, https://chicagounbound.uchicago.edu/cgi/viewcontent.cgi?article=1474&context=uclf.
57. Michel Foucault, "Structuralisme et poststructuralisme," in *1980–1988*, vol. 4 of *Dits et Écrits*, ed. Daniel Defert, François Ewald, and Jacques Lagrange (Paris: Gallimard, 1994), text no. 330, 439; Michel Foucault, "Structuralisme et poststructuralisme," in *1976–1988*, vol. 2 of *Dits et Écrits*, ed. Daniel Defert, François Ewald, and Jacques Lagrange (Paris: Gallimard/Quarto, 2001), text no. 330, 1258. ("Rien ne cache plus une communauté de problème que deux façons assez voisines de l'aborder.")
58. Michel Foucault, *Sécurité, Territoire, Population. Cours au Collège de France, 1977–1978*, ed. Michel Senellart (Paris: Gallimard, 2004), 5; Michel Foucault, *Security, Territory, Population: Lectures at the Collège de France, 1977–1978*, ed. Michel Senellart, trans. Graham Burchell (Basingstoke, UK: Palgrave Macmillan, 2007), 3.
59. Michel Foucault, "Une esthétique de l'existence," in *Dits et Écrits*, vol. 4: *1980–1988*, 730–735.
60. Bernard E. Harcourt, "Reflections on Ideology and Regimes of Truth" (paper presentation, Princeton University, April 15, 2012; draft on file with author).
61. Rahel Jaeggi, "Rethinking Ideology," 77; 78.
62. Rahel Jaeggi, "Rethinking Ideology," 78–79.
63. This was the thrust of earlier analyses of ideology critique. Geuss, *The Idea of a Critical Theory*, 26. See also Martin Jay, *The Dialectical Imagination: A History of the Frankfurt School and the Institute for Social Research, 1923–1950* (Berkeley: University of California Press, 1973), 63–64.
64. See, e.g., Jürgen Habermas, " 'Reasonable' Versus 'True,' or the Morality of Worldviews," 98; John Rawls, "Political Liberalism: Reply to Habermas," 149.
65. Steven Pinker, *Enlightenment Now: The Case for Reason, Science, Humanism, and Progress* (New York: Penguin, 2018).
66. Homi Bhabha and Steven Pinker, "Does the Enlightenment Need Defending?," Institute of Art and Ideas, September 10, 2018, https://iai.tv/articles/does-the-enlightenment-need-defending-auid-1149.

67. Richard Rorty and Pascal Engel, *What's the Use of Truth?* trans. William McCuaig (New York: Columbia University Press, 2016), 43.
68. "Word of the Year 2016 Is . . .," *Oxford Dictionaries*, accessed August 30, 2019, https://en.oxforddictionaries.com/word-of-the-year/word-of-the-year-2016.
69. "2017 Word of the Year Shortlist," *Collins Dictionary*, accessed August 30, 2019, https://www.collinsdictionary.com/word-lovers-blog/new/collins-2017-word-of-the-year-shortlist,396,HCB.html.
70. See, e.g., Michiko Kakutani, *The Death of Truth: Notes on Falsehood in the Age of Trump* (New York: Tim Duggan, 2018); Daniel J. Levitin, *Weaponized Lies: How to Think Critically in the Post-Truth Era* (New York: Penguin Random House, 2016); Lee McIntyre, *Post-Truth* (Cambridge, MA: MIT Press, 2018); Cailin O'Connor and James Owen Weatherall, *The Misinformation Age: How False Beliefs Spread* (New Haven, CT: Yale University Press, 2018); Shanto Iyengar and Douglas S. Massey, "Scientific Communication in a Post-truth Society," *PNAS* 116, no. 16 (2019): 7656–7661; Stephan Lewandowsky, Ullrich K. H. Ecker, and John Cook, "Beyond Misinformation: Understanding and Coping with the 'Post-Truth' Era," *Journal of Applied Research in Memory and Cognition* 6, no. 4 (2017): 353–369; Jennifer Kavanagh and Michael D. Rich, *Truth Decay: An Initial Exploration of the Diminishing Role of Facts and Analysis in American Public Life* (Santa Monica, CA: RAND Corporation, 2018), https://www.rand.org/pubs/research_reports/RR2314.html.
71. Bernard E. Harcourt, "The Last Refuge of Scoundrels: The Problem of Truth in a Time of Lying" (July 31, 2019). Paper prepared for NOMOS and presented at the 2019 conference of the American Society for Political and Legal Philosophy on "Truth and Evidence" at Princeton University on Friday, September 27, 2019; Columbia Public Law Research Paper No. 14–628, 2019. Available at SSRN: https://ssrn.com/abstract=3433975.
72. Many, in fact, accuse the poststructuralists and "post-" theories of having caused the post-truth age. The philosopher Daniel Dennett exclaims: "I think what the postmodernists did was truly evil. They are responsible for the intellectual fad that made it respectable to be cynical about truth and facts." Carole Cadwalladr, "Daniel Dennett: 'I Begrudge Every Hour I Have to Spend Worrying about Politics,'" *The Guardian*, February 12, 2017, https://www.theguardian.com/science/2017/feb/12/daniel-dennett-politics-bacteria-bach-back-dawkins-trump-interview (quoted in Joshua Forstenzer, "Something Has Cracked: Post-Truth Politics and Richard Rorty's Postmodernist Bourgeois Liberalism" (paper, Ash Center Occasional Papers Series, Ash Center for Democratic Governance and Innovation Harvard Kennedy School, July 2018).). Some contend that it is not just postmodernists, but pragmatists like Richard Rorty who are responsible for our post-truth condition. The Harvard fellow, Joshua Forstenzer, maintains, for instance, that "Rorty's philosophical project bears some intellectual responsibility for the onset of post-truth politics, insofar as it took a complacent attitude towards the dangers associated with over-affirming the contingency of our epistemic claims." Forstenzer, "Something Has Cracked," 4.
73. Simone de Beauvoir. *The Second Sex*, trans. Constance Borde and Sheila Malovany-Chevallier (New York: Vintage, 2011).
74. Judith Butler, "Sex and Gender in Simone de Beauvoir's Second Sex," *Yale French Studies* no. 72 (1986): 35-49, 35; 45; 47. In an essay titled "Cutting the Seams, Unraveling the Thread," I propose the Big Bang as a metaphor to describe how Beauvoir's original critique serves to continually expand the space of theory and praxis. Once the initial seam that held together gender and sex is cut, the possibilities expand and expand over time, such that today, for instance, individuals who were not the same sex as they were assigned at birth and who may be in relations with others of the same or different self-identified sex can parent without child-bearing through adoption and surrogacy in ways that would confuse someone writing in 1948. See *Critique 13/13* (blog), November 16, 2019, http://blogs.law.columbia.edu/critique1313/bernard-e-harcourt-cutting-the-seams-unraveling-the-thread-comments-on-judith-revel/.

6. Reconstructing Critical Theory

1. Michel Foucault, *Mal faire, dire vrai. Fonction de l'aveu en justice*, ed. Fabienne Brion and Bernard E. Harcourt (Louvain, Belgium: Presses universitaires de Louvain, 2012), 10; Michel Foucault, *Wrong-Doing, Truth-Telling: The Function of Avowal in Justice*, ed. Fabienne Brion and Bernard E. Harcourt, trans. Stephen W. Sawyer (Chicago: University of Chicago Press, 2014), 21.
2. Foucault, *Mal faire, dire vrai*, 10; Foucault, *Wrong-Doing, Truth-Telling*, 21 (emphasis added).
3. Étienne Balibar, "Resistance, Insurrection, Insubordination," in *Equaliberty: Political Essays*, trans. James Ingram (Durham, NC: Duke University Press, 2013), 284.
4. Joseph Conrad, *The Secret Agent*, ed. John Lyon (Oxford: Oxford University Press, 2008), 52.
5. Conrad, *The Secret Agent*, 71; 51.
6. Conrad, *The Secret Agent*, 49.
7. Conrad, *The Secret Agent*, 233.
8. Conrad, *The Secret Agent*, 227.
9. Friedrich Nietzsche, *Will to Power*, ed. Walter Kaufman, trans. Walter Kaufman and R. J. Hollingdale (New York: Vintage, 1968), 419; Friedrich Nietzsche, *Twilight of the Idols and the Anti-Christ*, trans. R. J. Hollingdale (New York: Penguin, 2003), 83.
10. Michel Foucault, "Sur la justice populaire," in *1954–1975*, vol. 1 of *Dits et Écrits*, ed. Daniel Defert, François Ewald, and Jacques Lagrange (Paris: Quarto/Gallimard, 2001), 1234.
11. Michel Foucault, "*Society Must Be Defended*": *Lectures at the Collège de France, 1975–1976*, ed. Mauro Bertani and Alessandro Fontana, trans. Arnold I. Davidson (New York: Picador, 2003), 79.
12. Foucault, "*Society Must Be Defended*," 29; Michel Foucault, *Security, Territory, Population: Lectures at the Collège de France, 1977–1978*, ed. Michel Senellart, trans. Graham Burchell (Basingstoke, UK: Palgrave Macmillan, 2007), 211–212.
13. Foucault, "Sur la justice populaire, 1235.
14. Michel Foucault, *The Birth of Biopolitics: Lectures at the Collège de France, 1978–1979*, ed. Michel Senellart, trans. Graham Burchell (New York: Palgrave Macmillan, 2008), 137.
15. Michel Foucault, *The Order of Things: An Archaeology of the Human Sciences*, trans. Alan Sheridan (New York: Vintage, 1994), 379.
16. "Counter-, prefix," *Oxford English Dictionary Online*, accessed August 6, 2019.
17. Étienne Balibar, *Equaliberty: Political Essays*, trans. James Ingram (Durham, NC: Duke University Press, 2013), 205; 284.
18. Balibar, *Equaliberty*, 159.
19. Balibar, *Equaliberty*, 159.
20. These interventions have been published in Étienne Balibar, *Libre parole* (Paris: Galilée, 2018).
21. Arnold Davidson, "In Praise of Counter-conduct," *History of the Human Sciences* 24, no. 4 (2011): 30 (internal citations omitted).
22. Jacques Lezra, "Solidarity," in *Political Concepts—A Lexicon in Formation: Thinking with Balibar*, ed. Stathis Gourgouris, Jacques Lezra, and Ann Stoler (New York: Fordham University Press, 2020).
23. Ann Stoler, "Internal Frontiers," in *Political Concepts—A Lexicon in Formation: Thinking with Balibar*.
24. Balibar, *Equaliberty*, 316, n.7.
25. In this regard, I would question Étienne Balibar's suggestion that Foucault's relation to Marx could be properly described as "anti-Marx," insofar as Balibar titles his essay "*L'anti-Marx de Michel Foucault*." Especially in relation to the Foucault of the early 1970s, as I have argued, we are facing much more of a *contre*-Marx than an anti-Marx. The 1972 and 1973 lectures are determinative in this regard. Insofar as Foucault supplements, but does not displace, the accumulation of capital by the accumulation of docile bodies, what we face is a *contre*-move, at least in this most marxisant period of Foucault. See François Ewald and Bernard E. Harcourt, "Situation du cours," in Michel Foucault, *Théories et*

institutions pénales: Cours au Collège de France, ed. Bernard E. Harcourt (Paris: Gallimard/Le Seuil, 2015), 262. ("Le contre-marxisme de Foucault n'est pas un anti-marxisme.")

26. Karl Marx, "Afterword (Second German Ed.)," in *Capital: A Critique of Political Economy*, ed. Frederick Engels, trans. Samuel Moore and Edward Aveling (Moscow: Progress Publishers, 1965), 1.14.
27. Michel Foucault, "Sex, Power and the Politics of Identity," in *Ethics: Subjectivity and Truth*, vol. 1 of *The Essential Works of Foucault* (1954–1984), ed. Paul Rabinow, trans. Robert Hurley (New York: New Press, 1997): 167.
28. Foucault, *Security, Territory, Population*, 208; see also 204.
29. "Counter-, prefix."
30. Davidson, "In praise of counter-conduct," 27.
31. Davidson, "In praise of counter-conduct," 27; 126, quoting Michel Foucault, *Volonté de savoir* (Paris: Gallimard, 1976); 126; 28; 29, citing Foucault, *Security, Territory, Population*, 213.
32. Davidson, "In praise of counter-conduct," 33.
33. Jigoro Kano and T. Lindsay, "Jujutsu and the Origins of Judo," in *Transactions of the Asiatic Society of Japan*, vol. 15 (Yokohama, Japan: R. Meiklejohn and Co., 1887).
34. Kanō and Lindsay, "Jujutsu and the Origins of Judo."
35. For a detailed elaboration of this argument, see Bernard E. Harcourt, *The Counterrevolution: How Our Government Went to War Against Its Own Citizens* (New York: Basic Books, 2018).

7. A Radical Critical Philosophy of Illusions

1. This is especially apparent in Slavoj Žižek's reading of Lacan. See Slavoj Žižek, *The Plague of Fantasies* (New York: Verso, 1997); see also Slavoj Žižek, "From *Che Vuoi?* to Fantasy: Lacan with Eyes Wide Shut," in *How to Read Lacan*, ed. Slavoj Žižek (New York: Norton, 2007), 40–60.
2. Sigmund Freud, *The Future of an Illusion*, ed. and trans. James Strachey (New York: Norton, 1961), 30.
3. Sigmund Freud, *Die Zukunft einer Illusion* (Leipzig, Germany: Internationaler Psychoanalytischer Verlag, 1928).
4. Freud, *The Future of an Illusion*, 30; 25; 31; 31; 31.
5. Raymond Geuss, *The Idea of a Critical Theory: Habermas and the Frankfurt School* (Cambridge: Cambridge University Press, 1981), 39; 39; 39. Notice that, elsewhere, Geuss uses the terms *delusion* and *false consciousness* interchangeably. See, e.g., Geuss, *The Idea of a Critical Theory*, 19–20, 60.
6. Freud, *The Future of an Illusion*, 31; 31.
7. Karl Marx, *Capital: A Critique of Political Economy*, vol. 1, trans. Ben Fowkes (New York: Vintage, 1976), 176; see also Jacques Derrida, "Apparition of the Inapparent: The Phenomenological 'Conjuring Trick,'" in Jacques Derrida, *Specters of Marx*, trans. Peggy Kamuf, 156-221 (New York: Routledge, 1994).
8. Marx, *Capital*, 165.
9. Translated as "fantastic" in this and most English translations, but it should read "phantasmagoric" as in the original German, which is "*die phantasmagorische Form.*" See generally Caroline Evans, *Fashion at the Edge: Spectacle, Modernity, and Deathliness* (New Haven, CT: Yale University Press, 2007), 89 n.4; David Kazanjian, *The Colonizing Trick: National Culture and Imperial Citizenship in Early America* (Minneapolis: University of Minnesota Press, 2003), 228n.52.
10. Marx, *Capital*, 165.
11. Marx, *Capital*, 165.
12. Peter Baehr, *The Unmasking Style in Social Theory* (London: Routledge, 2019), 51.
13. Max Horkheimer, "Traditional and Critical Theory," in *Critical Theory: Selected Essays*, trans. Matthew J. O'Connell et al. (New York: Continuum, 1992), 232; Rahel Jaeggi, "Rethinking Ideology," in *New Waves in Political Philosophy*, ed. Boudewijn de Bruin and Christopher F. Zurn (New York: Palgrave Macmillan, 2009), 63–86; Geuss, *The Idea of a Critical Theory*, 26–44, especially 39–41

(contrasting ideology, illusion, and delusion); Louis Althusser, "Ideology and Ideological State Apparatus (Notes Towards an Investigation)," in *Lenin and Philosophy and Other Essays*, trans. Ben Brewster (New York: Monthly Review Press, 2001), 85–126; see also my discussion of Althusser-Foucault on ideology in Michel Foucault, *The Punitive Society: Lectures at the Collège de France 1972–1973*, ed. Bernard E. Harcourt, trans. Graham Burchell (New York: Picador, 2015), 283–289; and the discussion by Claude-Olivier Doron on the concept of ideology in Althusser and Foucault in Michel Foucault, *La sexualité, Cours donné à l'université de Clermont-Ferrand. 1964, suivi de Le Discours de la sexualité, Cours donné à l'université de Vincennes. 1969*, ed. Claude-Olivier Doron (Paris: Gallimard/Le Seuil, 2018), 245–252.

14. See Michel Foucault, "*Introduction* à l'Anthropologie," in Immanuel Kant, *Anthropologie du point de vue pragmatique* (Paris: Vrin, 2008), 76–78.
15. Michel Foucault, *Psychiatric Power: Lectures at the College de France, 1973–1974*, ed. Jacques Lagrange, trans. Graham Burchell (Basingstoke, UK: Palgrave Macmillan, 2006), 58 (emphasis added).
16. See, e.g., Foucault, *Psychiatric Power*, 77; Michel Foucault, *Discipline and Punish: The Birth of the Prison*, trans. Alan Sheridan (New York: Vintage, 1979), 200–202.
17. Michel Foucault, *The Birth of the Clinic: An Archaeology of Medical Perception*, trans. A. M. Sheridan Smith (New York: Vintage, 1994), x.
18. Michel Foucault, *Naissance de la clinique. Une Archéologie du regard médical* (Paris: Presses Universitaires de France, 1963), vi.
19. "Phantasme," *Centre National de Ressources Textuelles et Lexicales*, http://www.cnrtl.fr/definition/phantasme, accessed July 20, 2019. Foucault eventually would come to regret the emphasis on the visual or perceptive element, on the "gaze," on the idea of "medical perception," especially six years later, in *The Archaeology of Knowledge*. See Michel Foucault, *The Archaeology of Knowledge and the Discourse on Language* (London: Tavistock, 1972), 54 n.1. ("In this respect, the term '*regard* médical' used in my *Naissance de la clinique* was not a very happy one.")
20. Foucault was far more consistent in resisting the term *ideology*. For a general discussion, see Bernard E. Harcourt, "Radical Thought from Marx, Nietzsche, and Freud, Through Foucault, to the Present: Comments on Steven Lukes's 'In Defense of False Consciousness,'" *University of Chicago Legal Forum* 2011, no. 1 (2011): 29–51; and Foucault's discussion of ideology in Foucault, *The Archaeology of Knowledge*, 184; also see Michel Foucault, *Naissance de la biopolitique. Cours au Collège de France (1978–1979)*, ed. Michel Senellart (Paris: Gallimard, 2004), 107.
21. See Foucault, *Naissance de la biopolitique*, 21–22; 21; 22 ; 22. Foucault would develop these themes as well on May 27, 1978, in his lecture, "Qu'est-ce que la critique? [Critique et *Aufklärung*]," *Bulletin de la Société française de philosophie* 84, no. 2 (1990): 35–63, translated in Michel Foucault, *The Politics of Truth*, ed. Sylvère Lotringer (Los Angeles: Semiotext(e), 2007), 41–82.
22. Foucault, *Naissance de la biopolitique*, 21–22.
23. Edward Said, *Orientalism* (New York: Vintage, 2003), 6.
24. Said, *Orientalism*, 6.
25. Freud, *The Future of an Illusion*, 31.
26. See, e.g., Baehr, *The Unmasking Style in Social Theory*, Chapter 4, 70–80.
27. Bernard E. Harcourt, *The Illusion of Free Markets: Punishment and the Myth of Natural Order* (Cambridge, MA: Harvard University Press, 2011), 86–87.
28. Dotan Leshem, *The Origins of Neoliberalism: Modeling the Economy from Jesus to Foucault* (New York: Columbia University Press, 2016).
29. See generally Harcourt, *The Illusion of Free Markets*, 176–190.
30. See Douglas S. Massey, *Categorically Unequal: The American Stratification System* (New York: Russel Sage Foundation, 2008); Thomas Piketty, *Capital in the Twenty-First Century* (Cambridge, MA: Harvard University Press, 2014).

31. F. A. Hayek, *The Road to Serfdom*, ed. Bruce Caldwell (Chicago: University of Chicago Press, 2007), 124–133.
32. See, generally, Harcourt, *The Illusion of Free Markets*, 131, 142, 271 n.56.
33. Renata Salecl, *Choice* (London: Profile, 2010), 67.
34. Cathy Lynn Grossman, "Religion Colors Money Views; Survey Reveals Many See God Steering Economy, Government as Meddlers," *USA Today*, September 20, 2011; Ryan Avent, "Deus ex Machina: Faith in the Free Market," *The Economist*, September 20, 2011, http://www.economist.com/blogs/freeexchange/2011/09/deus-ex-machina.
35. Grossman, "Religion Colors Money Views."
36. Friedrich Nietzsche, "On Truth and Lie in a Nonmoral Sense (1873)," in *On Truth and Untruth: Selected Writings*, ed. and trans. Taylor Carman (New York: HarperCollins, 2010), 30 (slightly modified).
37. Michel Foucault, "Nietzsche, Freud, Marx," 269–278, in *The Essential Works of Michel Foucault*, vol. 2: *Aesthetics, Methods and Epistemology*, ed. James D. Faubion, trans. Robert Hurley et al. (New York: New Press, 2000), 277–278.
38. Friedrich Nietzsche, *On the Genealogy of Morals*, trans. Walter Kaufmann and R. J. Hollingdale (New York: Vintage, 1989), 80. See also, generally, Alexander Nehamas, "The Genealogy of Genealogy: Interpretation in Nietzsche's Second 'Untimely Meditation' and in 'On the Genealogy of Morals,'" 269–283, in *Nietzsche, Genealogy, History: Essays on Nietzsche's Genealogy of Morals*, ed. Richard Schacht (Berkeley: University of California Press, 1994).
39. Foucault, "Nietzsche, Freud, Marx," 275.
40. Nietzsche, *On the Genealogy of Morals*, 77; Foucault, "Nietzsche, Freud, Marx," 275; Theodor W. Adorno, "The Actuality of Philosophy," *Telos* 1997, no. 31, 120–133 (1997), 126; Theodor W. Adorno, *Negative Dialectics* (New York: Continuum, 1973), 5; 5.
41. See, e.g., Leslie Paul Thiele, "The Agony of Politics: The Nietzschean Roots of Foucault's Thought," *American Political Science Review* 84, no. 3 (1990): 907–925; Thibault Bardon and Emmanuel Josserand, "A Nietzschean Reading of Foucauldian Thinking: Constructing a Project of the Self Within an Ontology of Becoming," *Organization* 18, no. 4 (2011): 497–515. Some emphasize that "Foucault often referred to himself as a Nietzschean." John S. Ransom, *Foucault's Discipline: The Politics of Subjectivity* (Durham, NC: Duke University Press, 1997). (Ransom cites Foucault's essay "Nietzsche, Genealogy, History," and an interview of Michel Foucault, "Prison Talk," in *Power/Knowledge: Selected Interviews and Other Writings, 1972–1977*, ed. Colin Gordon, trans. Colin Gordon et al. (New York: Pantheon, 1980), 53; but neither of these really support the claim.) As Tuomo Tiisala reminds us, Foucault also referred to himself, at least once, as "very much 'anti-Nietzschean.'" Tuomo Tiisala, "Review of *Foucault and Nietzsche: A Critical Encounter*," ed. Alan Rosenburg and Joseph Westfall, *Notre Dame Philosophical Reviews* (2018), https://ndpr.nd.edu/news/foucault-and-nietzsche-a-critical-encounter/.

    In line with the argument in text, recent work has begun to complexify the relationship between Foucault and Nietzsche, see *especially* Daniele Lorenzini, *La Force du vrai. De Foucault à Austin* (Lormont, France: Le Bord de l'eau, 2017); Colin Koopman, *Genealogy as Critique: Foucault and the Problems of Modernity* (Bloomington: Indiana University Press, 2013); Colin Koopman, "Critical Problematization in Foucault and Deleuze: The Force of Critique Without Judgment," 87–119, in *Between Deleuze and Foucault*, ed. Nicolae Morar, Thomas Nail, and Daniel Smith (Edinburgh: Edinburgh University Press, 2016); Stuart Elden, *Foucault: The Birth of Power* (Cambridge: Polity, 2017); Amy Allen, "Beyond Kant Versus Hegel: An Alternative Strategy for Grounding the Normativity of Critique," 243–261, in *Feminism, Capitalism, and Critique: Essays in Honor of Nancy Fraser*, ed. Banu Bargu and Chiara Bottici (Cham, Switzerland: Palgrave Macmillan, 2017); the contributors to Alan Rosenberg and Joseph Westfall's edited volume, *Foucault and Nietzsche: A Critical Encounter* (2018); Tiisala, "Review of *Foucault and Nietzsche: A Critical Encounter*"; and, of course, Daniel Defert's "Situation du cours" for Foucault, *Leçons sur la volonté de savoir. Cours au Collège de France, 1970–1971* (Paris: Gallimard/Le Seuil, 2011).

42. In a draft article titled "On Possibilising Genealogy," Daniele Lorenzini argues for a unique notion of genealogy, which he calls the "possibilising" dimension of genealogical inquiry and locates in Foucault's writings, especially on the notion of counter-conduct and of the critical attitude. This possibilising form of genealogy, which is different from the two classic ways of thinking about genealogy—as vindication of core concepts or as a way to unmask or debunk—clearly distinguishes Foucault's conception from Nietzsche's. See Daniele Lorenzini, "On Possibilising Genealogy," (paper, CCCCT's "Critical Work" workshop, Columbia University, New York, April 19, 2019; draft on file with author). Amy Allen and Colin Koopman have identified a form of genealogy that they call "problematizing genealogies" and associate with Foucault, in contrast to the debunking genealogical approach of Nietzsche and the vindicatory approach of Bernard Williams. See Colin Koopman, *Genealogy as Critique: Foucault and the Problems of Modernity* (Bloomington: Indiana University Press, 2013), 60; Amy Allen, "Beyond Kant Versus Hegel: An Alternative Strategy for Grounding the Normativity of Critique," 256. For a careful analysis of the differences between Nietzsche's and Foucault's genealogical methods, see Martin Saar, *Genealogie als Kritik: Geschichte und Theorie des Subjekts nach Nietzsche und Foucault* (Frankfurt: Campus, 2007); and Martin Saar, "Genealogy and Subjectivity," *European Journal of Philosophy* 10, no. 2 (2002): 231–245.
43. Foucault, "La vérité et les formes juridiques," 550.
44. Foucault, "La vérité et les formes juridiques," 550 (my translation).
45. Foucault, "Prison Talk," 53.
46. This is not to suggest that there are no biographical connections that we can draw between written texts and their authors. Objects of study do not spring out of nowhere—and neither do political projects. It is always possible to find biographical moments to contextualize philosophical discourse or to give it meaning. So, for instance, Foucault's fascination with the discourse of madness did not spring out of nowhere. Foucault began working at a psychiatric hospital, Sainte-Anne in Paris, when he was 25 years old, in October 1951—after having attempted to take his own life in June 1950 and considered committing himself to that very hospital in July of that year. See Daniel Defert, "Chronologie," in *Oeuvres*, vol. 1, by Michel Foucault, ed. Frédéric Gros (Paris: Gallimard/Pléiade, 2015), xxxviii–xl. Foucault tutored psychology at the École normale supérieure beginning in October 1951, having received a bachelor's degree in psychology two years earlier in 1949; and his first academic appointment was as assistant professor of psychology at Clermont-Ferrand in 1960. Defert, "Chronologie," xxxix, xxxviii. The discourse on madness, as an object of study for Foucault, did not spring out of nowhere. He returned to it throughout his intellectual life—from the very first book he published in 1954 on "Mental Illness and Personality," to his course and writings on Ludwig Binswanger and his visit to the patient festival at the Swiss asylum in Münsterlingen in 1953, to his dissertation on "Madness and Unreason," to his lectures on psychiatric power at the Collège de France in 1973–1974, to his analysis of the ancient method of the interpretation of dreams in the third volume of *The History of Sexuality* published shortly before his death in 1984.

    In the same way, the discourse of sexuality did not spring out of nowhere as an object of study for Foucault. For his master class during his *aggrégation* examination in philosophy in 1951, Foucault was assigned, by lot, the topic of "sexuality," which had been proposed for the first time by Georges Canguilhem. Defert, "Chronologie," xxxix. The multiple biographical connections, too, would initiate a lifelong interest in the concept of sexuality—from his course on sexuality at the University of Clermont-Ferrand in 1964, to his course on the discourse of sexuality at the experimental university of Vincennes in 1969, to his inaugural lecture "The Order of Discourse" at the Collège de France in 1971, to his four published volumes (the last posthumously) of *The History of Sexuality*.

    This is true as well for Foucault's other lifelong object of study: Nietzsche's discourse. Foucault often recounted that he was introduced to Nietzsche through the writings of Georges Bataille, and to Bataille by Blanchot. At other times, Foucault said that he came to Nietzsche through Heidegger.

The archives suggest that Foucault first encountered Nietzsche's writings in about 1951, while a student at the École normale supérieure; a few years later, in August 1953, Foucault delved into Nietzsche's writings on history, especially the untimely meditations. Defert, "Chronologie," xxxix, xli. Foucault dedicated a course to Nietzsche in 1953-1954. It was at about that time that he started writing manuscripts on Nietzsche that remain unpublished today (those are now being edited). The earliest unpublished manuscripts seem to date from about 1953, and, according to Gérard Lebrun, Foucault began writing a text on Nietzsche in November 1954. Defert, "Chronologie," xlii. His interest in Nietzsche's texts would extend to his very last lecture in *The Courage of Truth* on March 28, 1984, a few months before his death. See Michel Foucault, *Le Courage de la vérité*, ed. Frédéric Gros (Paris: Gallimard/Le Seuil 2009), 294; see also pages 164 and 178 for a more extensive discussion of Nietzsche's cynicism, as well as pages 89–94.

It is always possible to draw biographical connections and find meanings; but those are secondary, and often misleading, to the critical method of working critical texts for our political projects.

47. Without wanting to revive old and worn rivalries, thinkers who genuinely believed in scientific Marxism would typically have conceived of themselves as laboring within a Marxian tradition. This explains how a thinker like Eduard Bernstein could write that he was "well aware" that his argument for reform and parliamentary social democracy "deviates in several important particulars from the views to be found in the theory of Karl Marx and Friedrich Engels—whose writings have exercised the greatest influence on my views as a socialist." Eduard Bernstein, *The Preconditions of Socialism*, ed. and trans. Henry Tudor (Cambridge: Cambridge University Press, 1993), 7. It also could explain how a thinker like Rosa Luxemburg could write that "Marxian doctrine" is "the most stupendous product of the human mind in the century." Rosa Luxemburg, *Reform or Revolution and Other Writings* (Mineola, NY: Dover Publications, 2006), 5. The self-conception as a "Marxian" thinker requires a positivist conception of scientific Marxism, entirely alien to what a critical theorist does when she takes philosophical discourse as object study (which would represent a very different approach to Marx's texts as well).
48. Friedrich Nietzsche, *The Gay Science*, ed. Bernard Williams, trans. Josefine Nauckhoff (Cambridge: Cambridge University Press, 2001), III, § 108, p. 109.
49. Hannah Arendt, "Truth and Politics," *New Yorker*, February 25, 1967, 88.
50. Seyla Benhabib, "Subjectivity, Historiography, and Politics: Reflections on the 'Feminism/Postmodernism Exchange,'" in *Feminist Contentions: A Philosophical Exchange*, ed. Seyla Benhabib, Judith Butler, Drucilla Cornell, Nancy Fraser, and Linda Nicholson (New York: Routledge, 1995), 118.
51. Steven Lukes, "In Defense of False Consciousness," *University of Chicago Legal Forum* 2011 (2011): 28.
52. Judith Butler, "For a Careful Reading," in *Feminist Contentions: A Philosophical Exchange*, ed. Seyla Benhabib, Judith Butler, Drucilla Cornell, Nancy Fraser, and Linda Nicholson (New York: Routledge, 1995), 129.
53. Michel Foucault, *Discourse and Truth, and Parrēsia*, ed. Henri-Paul Fruchaud, Daniele Lorenzini, and Nancy Luxon (Chicago: University of Chicago Press, 2019), 224.
54. Foucault, *Discourse and Truth, and Parrēsia*, 224. Colin Koopman offers a brilliant analysis of what he calls the method of "problematization" in both Foucault's and Deleuze's work. See, generally, Koopman, "Critical Problematization in Foucault and Deleuze," 100–108; Colin Koopman, "Problematization in Foucault's Genealogy and Deleuze's Symptomatology," *Angelaki: Journal of the Theoretical Humanities* 12, no. 2 (April 2018): 187–203, 188–191.
55. Koopman, "Critical Problematization in Foucault and Deleuze," 99.
56. Foucault, *Discourse and Truth, and Parrēsia*, 226.
57. Foucault, *Discourse and Truth, and Parrēsia*, 226.
58. Foucault, *Discourse and Truth, and Parrēsia*, 226–227n3[***] (internal brackets and quotation marks omitted).
59. Foucault, *Discipline and Punish*, 308; 308.

60. Oliver Marchart writes, "The ontological weakening of ground does not lead to the assumption of the total absence of all grounds, but rather to the assumption of the impossibility of a *final* ground, which is something completely different as it implies an increased awareness of, on the one hand, contingency and, on the other, the political as the moment of partial and always, in the last instance, unsuccessful grounding." Olivier Marchart, *Post-Foundational Political Thought: Political Difference in Nancy, Lefort, Badiou and Laclau* (Edinburgh: Edinburgh University Press, 2007), 2. Marchart's philosophy of postfoundationalism, drawing on the writings of Jean-Luc Nancy, Claude Lefort, Alain Badiou, and Ernesto Laclau, bears a family resemblance to the theory I propose here. I place emphasis, though, on the way in which new interpretations become illusions again and require constant critique. I also do not propose to go down the path of the storied distinction between politics and the political at the heart of Marchart's research, because I believe that that distinction is unnecessary and another distracting epistemological detour.

Part II: Reimagining the Critical Horizon

1. Max Horkheimer, "Postscript," in *Critical Theory: Selected Essays*, trans. Matthew J. O'Connell et al. (New York: Continuum, 1992), 250.
2. Horkheimer, "Postscript," 250.
3. Horkheimer, "Postscript," 250–251.
4. Max Horkheimer, "Traditional and Critical Theory," in *Critical Theory: Selected Essays*, trans. Matthew J. O'Connell et al. (New York: Continuum, 1992), 227.
5. Amy Allen, *The End of Progress: Decolonizing the Normative Foundations of Critical Theory* (New York: Columbia University Press, 2016), 201–202.

8. The Transformation of Critical Utopias

1. See *supra*, chapter 7; see also Bernard E. Harcourt, *The Illusion of Free Markets: Punishment and the Myth of Natural Order* (Cambridge, MA: Harvard University Press, 2011).
2. See, generally, Axel Honneth, *The Idea of Socialism: Towards a Renewal* (Cambridge: Polity, 2017), 1; Eli Zaretsky, *Why America Needs a Left: A Historical Argument* (Cambridge: Polity, 2012), 4–6. On Marx's rejection of utopianism, see Seyla Benhabib, *Critique, Norm, Utopia: A Study of the Foundations of Critical Theory* (New York: Columbia University Press, 1986), 34–35, 41–42; Amy Allen, *The End of Progress: Decolonizing the Normative Foundations of Critical Theory* (New York: Columbia University Press, 2016), 40–41. On the question of hope, see, generally, Ayse Parla, "Critique Without a Politics of Hope?" in *A Time for Critique*, ed. Didier Fassin and Bernard E. Harcourt (New York: Columbia University Press, 2019), 52–70.
3. See, for example, Alain Badiou, *Communist Hypothesis*, trans. David Macey and Steve Corcoran (New York: Verso, 2010); Jodi Dean, *The Communist Horizon* (New York: Verso, 2012); Slavoj Žižek, Costas Douzinas, and Alex Taek-Gwang Lee, eds., *The Idea of Communism*, 3 vols. (New York: Verso, 2010–2016); The Invisible Committee, *The Coming Insurrection* (Cambridge, MA: MIT Press (Semiotext(e)/Intervention series), 2009); "L'Hypothèse cybernétique," *Tiqqun* 2 (2001): 40–83.
4. Étienne Balibar, "Idea of Revolution: Yesterday, Today and Tomorrow," *Uprising 13/13* (blog), August 27, 2017, http://blogs.law.columbia.edu/uprising1313/etienne-balibar-the-idea-of-revolution-yesterday-today-and-tomorrow/.
5. Balibar, "Idea of Revolution," 24.
6. Reinhart Koselleck, "Historical Criteria of the Modern Concept of Revolution" (1968), in *Futures Past: On the Semantics of Historical Time* (New York: Columbia University Press, 2004), 52; see also Hannah Arendt, *On Revolution* (New York: Penguin, 2006 [orig. 1963]).

7. Balibar, "The Idea of Revolution," 6.
8. Simona Forti, "The Modern Concept of Revolution," September 11, 2017 (draft on file with author).
9. The seminar series "Uprising 13/13," held at Columbia University in 2017–2018 analyzed thirteen different modalities of revolt; the texts and recordings of the series are available at http://blogs.law.columbia.edu/uprising1313/1-13/.
10. Jesús Velasco emphasizes this important qualification in "The Revolution Has Been Printed," *Uprising 13/13* (blog), September 22, 2017, http://blogs.law.columbia.edu/uprising1313/jesus-r-velasco-the-revolution-has-been-printed/.
11. Mao Zedong, "Report," in *The Selected Works of Mao Tse-tung*, vol. 1 (Peking: Foreign Languages Press, 1967), 23–24.
12. Mao Zedong, "On Contradiction," in *The Selected Works of Mao Tse-tung*, vol. 1 (Peking: Foreign Languages Press, 1967), 316.
13. Mao Zedong, "On the Correct Handling of Contradictions Among the People," in *The Selected Works of Mao Tse-tung*, vol. 5 (Peking: Foreign Languages Press, 1967), 405.
14. Mao Zedong, "Talk on Questions of Philosophy," in *The Selected Works of Mao Tse-tung*, vol. 9 (Peking: Foreign Languages Press, 1967), text at notes 11–12.
15. Claire Fontaine, "1977: The Year That Is Never Commemorated," *Uprising 13/13* (blog), September 23, 2017, http://blogs.law.columbia.edu/uprising1313/claire-fontaine-1977-the-year-that-is-never-commemorated/; "*A/Traverso, Notebook #1* (October 1975), Part ¼," *Uprising 13/13* (blog), trans. Francesco Guercio, September 27, 2017, http://blogs.law.columbia.edu/uprising1313/francesco-guercio-annotated-translation-of-atraverso-notebook-1-october-1975-part-14/; see also Claire Fontaine, "Insurrection Mao," *Uprising 13/13* (blog), September 28, 2017, http://blogs.law.columbia.edu/uprising1313/claire-fontaine-insurrection-mao/.
16. Michel Foucault, "On Popular Justice: A Debate with Maoists," in *Power/Knowledge: Selected Interviews and Other Writings, 1972–1977*, ed. Colin Gordon, trans. John Mepham (New York: Pantheon, 1980), 1–36.
17. The Invisible Committee, *The Coming Insurrection* (Cambridge, MA: MIT Press (Semiotext(e)/Intervention), 2009), online version, 10; 16; 9; 18.
18. See, generally, Richard Wolin, *The Wind from the East: French Intellectuals, the Cultural Revolution, and the Legacy of the 1960s* (Princeton, NJ: Princeton University Press, 2010).
19. See Claire Fontaine, "Insurrection Mao"; Claire Fontaine, "1977: The Year That Is Never Commemorated."
20. Defert belonged to the *Gauche prolétarienne*, and Ewald was a Maoist militant in Lens during the crises there, as well as at Bruay-en-Artois. The subsequent political evolution of these intellectuals is telling; it relates to the variegated trajectories of critical theory and praxis over the late twentieth century. Defert would go on to found and run Aides, the first organization in France dedicated to fighting the HIV virus. See Daniel Defert, *Une vie politique. Entretiens avec Philippe Artières et Eric Favereau, avec la collaboration de Joséphine Gross* (Paris: Le Seuil, 2014). In addition to serving as general editor of Foucault's writings, Ewald became a professor of insurance at the Conservatoire National des Arts et Métiers, and founded and directed the École nationale d'assurances in Paris.
21. Simone de Beauvoir, *All Said and Done* (New York: Putnam, 1974), quoted in Wolin, *The Wind from the East*, 140–141.
22. See also Benhabib, *Critique, Norm, and Utopia*, 352. ("The philosophy of the subject always searches for a particular group—be it the proletariat, women, the avant-garde, Third World revolutionaries, or the Party—whose particularity represents universality as such. The politics of empowerment, by contrast, proceeds from the assumption that there is no single spot in the social structure that privileges those who occupy it with a vision of the social totality.")
23. See, e.g., Ann Laura Stoler, *Race and the Education of Desire: Foucault's History of Sexuality and the Colonial Order of Things* (Durham, NC: Duke University Press, 1995).

24. Fadi Bardawil, "Critical Blind Spots: Rethinking Left Criticism in the Wake of the Syrian Revolution," in *A Time for Critique*, ed. Didier Fassin and Bernard E. Harcourt (New York: Columbia University Press, 2019), 174–192.
25. To a certain extent, Marxist Leninism got closer to this tripartite mapping, but it was still far more binary than Maoist insurgency theory.
26. Mao, "On the Correct Handling," 384; see also Mao Zedong, "Talk on the Questions of Philosophy," in *The Selected Works of Mao Tse-tung*, vol. 9 (Peking: Foreign Languages Press, 1967), 27.

9. The Problem of Liberalism

1. Michel Foucault, *Les Mots et les choses: Une archéologie des sciences humaines* (Paris: Gallimard, 1966), 9; Michel Foucault, "Des espaces autres," in *Dits et Écrits*, ed. Daniel Defert, François Ewald, and Jacques Lagrange, vol. 2: *1976–1988* (Paris: Gallimard/Quarto, 2001), 1571–1581.
2. Michel Foucault, "Interview with Jean François and John De Wit (May 22, 1981)," 253–269, in *Wrong-Doing, Truth-Telling: The Function of Avowal in Justice*, ed. Fabienne Brion and Bernard E. Harcourt (Chicago: University of Chicago Press, 2014), 266.
3. See, e.g., Edward Said, *Orientalism* (New York: Vintage, 2003); Edward Said, *Culture and Imperialism* (New York: Vintage, 1993), 278; Gayatri Chakravorty Spivak, *A Critique of Postcolonial Reason: Toward a History of the Vanishing Present* (Cambridge, MA: Harvard University Press, 1999); Ann Stoler, *Race and the Education of Desire: Foucault's History of Sexuality and the Colonial Order of Things.* (Durham, NC: Duke University Press, 1995).
4. Dipesh Chakrabarty, *Provincializing Europe: Postcolonial Thought and Historical Difference* (Princeton, NJ: Princeton University Press, 2000).
5. Partha Chatterjee, *The Nation and Its Fragments: Colonial and Postcolonial Histories* (Princeton, NJ: Princeton University Press, 1993); Homi Bhabha, *The Location of Culture* (New York: Routledge, 1994).
6. Ann Stoler, "Ann Stoler on Reading Foucault Today," *Foucault 13/13* (blog), November 19, 2015, http://blogs.law.columbia.edu/foucault1313/2015/11/19/ann-stoler-on-society-must-be-defended-reading-foucault-today/.
7. Gayatri Chakravorty Spivak, "Can the Subaltern Speak?," in *Can the Subaltern Speak? Reflections on the History of an Idea*, ed. Rosalind C. Morris (New York: Columbia University Press, 2010), 62–63.
8. Naturally, I am using the term *liberal* here in its political theoretic meaning—not in its journalistic usage of liberal versus conservative. Liberalism here should be understood as the belief that the political collectivity should not impose its own vision of the ideals or values that individuals should seek and pursue in life, but rather establish and enforce rules that allow individuals to freely pursue their own ideals and interests without getting in the way of each other. The political collectivity, then, merely sets up the rules of society—the rules of the game—to allow political subjects to pursue their own interests unimpeded by others. This is the traditional Millian view that privileges the rules, or rights and obligations, of citizens over any particular vision of the good life; it involves what Michael Sandel and others call "the priority of the right over the good." This translates, in the legal liberal register, into the idea that a liberal regime is governed by the rule of law, and not the rule of men: that neutral rules, not self-interested arbiters, decide and adjudicate between conflicting claims of justice.
9. Jürgen Habermas, "Concluding Remarks," in *Habermas and the Public Sphere*, ed. Craig Calhoun (Cambridge, MA: MIT Press, 1992), 469. Amy Allen does a masterful job of contextualizing and interpreting Habermas's statement in *The End of Progress: Decolonizing the Normative Foundations of Critical Theory* (New York: Columbia University Press, 2016), 40–41.

10. Thomas Hobbes, *Leviathan*, ed. Richard Tuck (Cambridge: Cambridge University Press, 1996), Chap. 30, 239.
11. Hobbes, *Leviathan*, Chap. 30, 239–40.
12. Hobbes, *Leviathan*, Chap. 30, 239.
13. Hobbes, *Leviathan*, 231; 235; 235.
14. Hobbes, *Leviathan*, 235–236.
15. C. B. Macpherson, *The Political Theory of Possessive Individualism: From Hobbes to Locke* (Oxford: Oxford University Press, 1962).
16. John Locke, *Second Treatise on Government*, in *Two Treatises of Government*, ed. Peter Laslett (Cambridge: Cambridge University Press, 1988), §57, 305; 306, note to line 16 of §57.
17. Locke, *Second Treatise*, §57, 305–306.
18. Locke, *Second Treatise*, §57, 306.
19. Andrew Dilts, "To Kill a Thief: Punishment, Proportionality, and Criminal Subjectivity in Locke's 'Second Treatise,'" *Political Theory* 40, no. 1 (2012): 58–83.
20. Locke, *Second Treatise*, §17, 279 ("that *Freedom*, which is the Fence to it [Preservation]").
21. Michael Walzer, "Liberalism and the Arts of Separation," *Political Theory* 12, no. 3 (August 1984): 315–330.
22. Karl Marx, "On the Jewish Question," in *The Marx-Engels Reader*, ed. Robert C. Tucker, trans. Ronald Rogowski, 2nd ed. (New York: Norton, 1978), 26–52.
23. Marx, "On the Jewish Question," 43; 43; 42; 42.
24. Marx, "On the Jewish Question," 43; 42.
25. Marx, "On the Jewish Question," 46, quoting Jean-Jacques Rousseau, *On the Social Contract*, ed. Roger D. Masters, trans. Judith R. Masters (New York: St. Martin's, 1978), Book II, Chap. VII, 68 (emphasis in Marx, but not in Rousseau).
26. Marx, "On the Jewish Question," 35.
27. Marx, "On the Jewish Question," 46.
28. See Bernard E. Harcourt, "Foucault's Keystone: *Confessions of the Flesh*. How the Fourth and Final Volume of *The History of Sexuality* Completes Foucault's Critique of Modern Western Societies (November 30, 2019)," Columbia Public Law Research Paper, available at SSRN: https://ssrn.com/abstract=3497030, at page 14; Gary S. Becker, François Ewald, and Bernard E. Harcourt, "Becker on Ewald on Foucault on Becker: American Neoliberalism and Michel Foucault's 1979 *Birth of Biopolitics* Lectures," in vol. 7, *Neoliberalism and Risk, Carceral Notebooks*, ed. Bernard E. Harcourt (New York: U.S. Lithograph, 2011), 1–35; Gary S. Becker, François Ewald, and Bernard E. Harcourt, "Becker and Foucault on Crime and Punishment," in vol. 9, *Neoliberalism (cont'd), Carceral Notebooks*, ed. Bernard E. Harcourt (New York: U.S. Lithograph, 2013), 5–45.
29. Facundo Alvaredo, Lucas Chancel, Thomas Piketty, Emmanuel Saez, and Gabriel Zucman, "Global Inequality Dynamics: New Findings from WID.WORLD," NBER Working Paper 23119 (February 2017).
30. Slavoj Žižek, "No Way Out? Communism in the Next Century," in *The Idea of Communism*, vol. 3, ed. Slavoj Žižek and Alex Taek-Gwang Lee (New York: Verso, 2016), 243. I would note that Žižek's work is chock full of the discourse of ideology and illusions. See, e.g., Žižek, "No Way Out?," 247 ("Does this mean that there is no way out of the global capitalist universe? The bleak picture of the total triumph of a global capitalism that immediately appropriates all attempts to subvert it is itself the product of ideological imagination. It makes us blind to the signs of the New which abound in the very heart of global capitalism.")
31. See, especially, Frank Michelman, "Law's Republic," *Yale Law Journal* 97, no. 8 (1988): 1493–1537.
32. Jeff Manza and Christopher Uggen, *Locked Out: Felon Disenfranchisement and American Democracy* (New York: Oxford University Press, 2006).

10. A Radical Critical Theory of Values

1. Bernard E. Harcourt, "The Collapse of the Harm Principle," *Journal of Criminal Law and Criminology* 90, no. 1 (1999): 109–194.
2. Richard Tuck, "The Left Case for Brexit," *Dissent Magazine*, June 6, 2016. Note that Bruce Ackerman suggests in his new book, *Revolutionary Constitutions: Charismatic Leadership and the Rule of Law* (Cambridge, MA: Harvard University Press, 2019), that we should consider the United Kingdom as effectively having a constitution.
3. Richard Rorty, *Achieving Our Country: Leftist Thought in Twentieth-Century America* (Cambridge, MA: Harvard University Press, 1998), 37.
4. Rorty, *Achieving Our Country*, 30–31; 91.
5. Eli Zaretsky, *Why America Needs A Left: An Historical Argument* (Cambridge: Polity, 2012). Zaretsky develops this theme of equality as central to the project and work of Nancy Fraser in Eli Zaretsky, "Nancy Fraser and the Left: A Searching Idea of Equality," in *Feminism, Capitalism, and Critique: Essays in Honor of Nancy Fraser*, ed. Banu Bargu and Chiara Bottici (New York: Palgrave Macmillan, 2017), 263–279.
6. Zaretsky, *Why America Needs a Left*, 2 (emphasis added).
7. Zaretsky, *Why America Needs a Left*, 2.
8. Zaretsky, *Why America Needs a Left*, 4; 159–170; 15.
9. Norberto Bobbio, *Left and Right: The Significance of a Political Distinction* (Chicago: University of Chicago Press, 1996); Steven Lukes, "The Grand Dichotomy of the Twentieth Century," in *Cambridge History of Twentieth-Century Political Thought*, ed. Terence Ball and Richard Bellamy (Cambridge: Cambridge University Press, 2003).
10. Lukes, "Grand Dichotomy," 611, also quoted in Zaretsky, *Why America Needs a Left*, 4.
11. See, generally, Giorgio Agamben, *The Highest Poverty: Monastic Rules and Form-of-Life* (Stanford, CA: Stanford University Press, 2013).
12. "13/13: Ali Shari'ati and the Global Nietzsche," *Nietzsche 13/13* (blog), April 27, 2017, http://blogs.law.columbia.edu/nietzsche1313/13-13/.
13. Friedrich Nietzsche, *Thus Spoke Zarathustra*, ed. Adrian del Caro and Robert B. Pippin (Cambridge: Cambridge University Press, 2006), 78.
14. Friedrich Nietzsche, *On the Genealogy of Morals*, trans. Walter Kaufmann and R. J. Hollingdale (New York: Vintage, 1989), 72.
15. In developing a metanormative contextualist framework, Allen also draws on the work of Michael Williams, *Unnatural Doubts: Epistemological Realism and the Basis of Skepticism* (Cambridge: Basil Blackwell, 1991); and Linda Martín Alcoff, *Real Knowing: New Versions of the Coherence Theory* (Ithaca, NY: Cornell University Press, 1996); as well as Thomas McCarthy, *Race, Empire, and the Idea of Human Development* (Cambridge: Cambridge University Press, 2009).
16. Allen, *The End of Progress*, 202.
17. Allen, *The End of Progress*, 201; see also, generally, Saba Mahmood, *Politics of Piety: The Islamic Revival and the Feminist Subject* (Princeton, NJ: Princeton University Press, 2005).
18. Allen, *The End of Progress*, 195–205, drawing on Colin Koopman, *Genealogy as Critique: Foucault and the Problems of Modernity* (Bloomington: Indiana University Press, 2013).
19. Allen, *The End of Progress*, 207.
20. Allen, *The End of Progress*, 211.
21. Allen, *The End of Progress*, 215.
22. Max Horkheimer, "Traditional and Critical Theory," in *Critical Theory: Selected Essays*, trans. Matthew J. O'Connell et al. (New York: Continuum, 1992), 213.
23. Max Horkheimer and Theodor Adorno, *Dialectic of Enlightenment*, trans. John Cumming (New York: Continuum, 1996), x.

24. Horkheimer and Adorno, *Dialectic of Enlightenment*, 13; see also another quote from this book at 13 ("the freedom themselves finally came to form that 'herd' which Hegel has declared to be the result of the Enlightenment").
25. Herbert Marcuse, *One-Dimensional Man* (Boston: Beacon, 1991), 223.
26. Herbert Marcuse, *Counterrevolution and Revolt* (Boston: Beacon, 1972), 33.
27. Allen, *The End of Progress*, 27.
28. See, e.g., Allen, *The End of Progress*, 204; 195, 196, 202, 205, 229.
29. Allen, *The End of Progress*, 212.
30. Benhabib, *Critique, Norm, and Utopia*, 9.
31. Benhabib, *Critique, Norm, and Utopia*, 9.
32. Zarathustra, for instance, was a creator of values. See Robert Gooding-Williams, *Zarathustra's Dionysian Modernism* (Palo Alto, CA: Stanford University Press, 2002).
33. Martin Saar, "Genealogy and Subjectivity," *European Journal of Philosophy* 10, no. 2 (2002): 235.
34. Samuel Moyn, *Not Enough: Human Rights in an Unequal World* (Cambridge, MA: Harvard University Press, 2018), 2.

11. A Critical Horizon of Endless Struggle

1. I develop this in detail in my articles on our contemporary culture wars and how polyvalent the alliances can be. As those cases demonstrate, there is no fixed "us versus them," but rather shifting alliances that are often puzzling and counterintuitive. See Bernard E. Harcourt, "Foreword to the Supreme Court Review: 'You Are Entering a Gay- and Lesbian-Free Zone': On the Radical Dissents of Justice Scalia and Other (Post-) Queers [Raising Questions about *Lawrence*, Sex Wars, and the Criminal Law]," *Journal of Criminal Law and Criminology* 94, no. 3 (2004): 503–549; and Bernard E. Harcourt, "On Gun Registration, the NRA, Adolf Hitler, and Nazi Gun Laws: Exploding the Gun Culture Wars [A Call to Historians]," *Fordham Law Review* 73, no. 2 (2004): 653–680.
2. See Chantal Mouffe, *For a Left Populism* (New York: Verso, 2018), 93.
3. See, e.g., Michael Hardt and Toni Negri, *Assembly* (New York: Oxford University Press, 2017), 270 ("The use of arms always points in two directions: outward and inward, against the enemy and for the transformation of ourselves").
4. Joshua Smeltzer, "Review of *Assembly*, by Michael Hardt and Toni Negri," *LSE Review of Books*, January 31, 2018, https://blogs.lse.ac.uk/lsereviewofbooks/2018/01/31/book-review-assembly-by-michael-hardt-and-antonio-negri/, quoting from Hardt and Negri, *Assembly*, 254.
5. In *Assembly*, Hardt and Negri specifically discuss the use of weapons and suggest that, today, the use of arms would only harm militants (Hardt and Negri, *Assembly*, 269). However, they emphasize, "We don't mean to advocate renouncing the use of arms—on the contrary" (Hardt and Negri, *Assembly*, 270). What they mean is different kinds of arms—the arms of social programs and social entrepreneurialism, such as the democratic governance of the commune or the free breakfast program and free health clinics of the Black Panthers.
6. Richard Wolf, "Travel ban lexicon: From candidate Donald Trump's campaign promises to President Trump's tweets," *USA Today*, April 24, 2018, https://www.usatoday.com/story/news/politics/2018/04/24/travel-ban-donald-trump-campaign-promises-president-tweets/542504002/.
7. Bernard E. Harcourt, "How Trump Fuels the Fascist Right," *New York Review of Books*, November 29, 2018, https://www.nybooks.com/daily/2018/11/29/how-trump-fuels-the-fascist-right/.
8. Herbert Marcuse, *Counterrevolution and Revolt* (Boston: Beacon, 1972), 1.
9. Marcuse, *Counterrevolution and Revolt*, 1.
10. Marcuse, *Counterrevolution and Revolt*, 1.
11. Marcuse, *Counterrevolution and Revolt*, 24.

12. Marcuse, *Counterrevolution and Revolt*, 2.
13. Marcuse, *Counterrevolution and Revolt*, 24.
14. For my further discussion of this with Jeremy Scahill at *The Intercept*, see Jeremy Scahill, "The Counterinsurgency Paradigm: How U.S. Politics Have Become Paramilitarized," *The Intercept*, November 25, 2018, https://theintercept.com/2018/11/25/counterinsurgency-us-drone-strikes/.
15. Marcuse, *Counterrevolution and Revolt*, 24.
16. Marcuse, *Counterrevolution and Revolt*, 25.
17. Marcuse, *Counterrevolution and Revolt*, 24, 25.
18. Marcuse, *Counterrevolution and Revolt*, 25.
19. Loosely taken from "Transcript: President Obama's Remarks on Donald Trump's Election," *Washington Post*, November 9, 2016, https://www.washingtonpost.com/news/the-fix/wp/2016/11/09/transcript-president-obamas-remarks-on-donald-trumps-election/?utm_term=.018edb16dd49.
20. Friedrich Nietzsche, *The Gay Science*, ed. Bernard Williams, trans. Josefine Nauckhoff (Cambridge: Cambridge University Press, 2001), III, § 108.

12. The Problem of Violence

1. Judith Butler, "Protest, Violent and Nonviolent," *The Big Picture, Public Books*, October 13, 2017, http://www.publicbooks.org/the-big-picture-protest-violent-and-nonviolent/. In her book *Notes Toward a Performative Theory of Assembly*, Butler also embraces nonviolence and rejects violence. Judith Butler, *Notes Toward a Performative Theory of Assembly* (Cambridge, MA: Harvard University Press, 2015), 187 et seq. There, Butler draws explicitly on Gandhi and Thoreau, although there is a passage on page 192 where she views nonviolence as a tactic, which is, of course, extremely different from Gandhi's philosophy. In the end, she argues that "nonviolent movements, such as boycotts and strikes, cannot simply be war by other means. They have to show themselves to be substantial ethical alternatives to war . . . [by contrast to] those who can only read the tactic as hatred and the continuation of war by other means" (Butler, *Notes Toward a Performative Theory of Assembly*, 192.) Butler, then, offers the performative model of assembly as a precondition and precursor to expressive demands in a nonviolent register, as opposed, as it were, to a model of civil war.
2. Thomas Hobbes, *Leviathan*, ed. Richard Tuck (Cambridge: Cambridge University Press, 1996), Chap. 30, 232.
3. See, generally, Bernard E. Harcourt, *The Illusion of Free Markets: Punishment and the Myth of Natural Order* (Cambridge, MA: Harvard University Press, 2011).
4. Walter Benjamin, "Critique of Violence," in *Reflections: Essays, Aphorisms, Autobiographical Writings*, ed. Peter Demetz, trans. Edmund Jephcott, 277–300 (New York: Schocken, 1978), 285-287.
5. Slavoj Žižek, *Violence: Six Sideways Reflections* (New York: Picador, 2008), 11.
6. Michel Foucault, *The Punitive Society: Lectures at the Collège de France 1972–1973*, ed. Bernard E. Harcourt, trans. Graham Burchell (New York: Picador, 2015), 31; 29.
7. Foucault, *The Punitive Society*, 266.
8. Jean-Paul Sartre, *Les séquestrés d'Altona* (Paris: Gallimard, 1960), 374; see also Robert Denoon Cumming, ed., *The Philosophy of Jean-Paul Sartre* (New York: Vintage, 1965), 484.
9. Bernard E. Harcourt, "Political Violence" (senior thesis, under the supervision of Sheldon S. Wolin, Princeton University, 1984), 69–70 ("In our world united by scarcity, in our civilizations which have produced their humanity beneath the fear of death, we all are implicated in a long, violent struggle: the minute we turn into the world arena (by means of our career or the realization of our situation), we do violence to others. Sartre believed that this cycle of violence, fueled by scarcity, would lead history beyond violence, by means of violence. For only revolutionary, violent praxis can fracture the grip of scarcity (with the exception of a technological breakthrough) by inducing

rebels to forge their humanity beyond death, beyond scarcity, in complete respect of each other's situation.")

10. See Steven Pinker, *Enlightenment Now: The Case for Reason, Science, Humanism, and Progress* (New York: Penguin, 2018). Using hundreds of pages of graphs and questionable data, Pinker makes exactly the *quantitative* argument I reject. He does not fully recognize that violence has changed in legibility over time.
11. Friedrich Nietzsche, *On the Genealogy of Morals*, trans. Walter Kaufmann and R. J. Hollingdale (New York: Vintage, 1989), III, § 7, 106; II, § 6, 65; II, § 3, 61.
12. Marquis de Sade, *120 Days of Sodom* (New York: Sun Vision, 2012), back cover.
13. Joseph J. Fischel, *Sex and Harm in the Age of Consent* (Minneapolis: University of Minnesota Press, 2016), 32.
14. Didier Fassin, *The Will to Punish* (Oxford: Oxford University Press, 2017); William E. Connolly, "The Desire to Punish," 41–74, in *The Ethos of Pluralization* (Minneapolis, University of Minnesota Press, 1995).
15. Chris Deaton, "Protester Would Be 'Carried out on a Stretcher' in the Old Days, Trump Reminisces," *Washington Examiner*, February 23, 2016, https://www.washingtonexaminer.com/weekly-standard/protester-would-be-carried-out-on-a-stretcher-in-the-old-days-trump-reminisces.
16. G. W. F. Hegel, *Phenomenology of Spirit*, trans. A. V. Miller (Oxford: Oxford University Press, 1981), ¶187, 114; Alexandre Kojève, *Introduction to the Reading of Hegel: Lectures on the* Phenomenology of Spirit, ed. Allan Bloom (Ithaca, NY: Cornell University Press, 1980).
17. Hegel, *Phenomenology of Spirit*, ¶194, 117.
18. Adriana Cavarero, *Horrorism: Naming Contemporary Violence* (New York: Columbia University Press, 2008), 4.
19. Georges Bataille, *Erotism: Death and Sensuality*, trans. Mary Dalwood (San Francisco: City Lights Publishers, 1986), 81.
20. Judith Butler, *Giving an Account of Oneself* (New York: Fordham University Press, 2003), 31.
21. Maurice Blanchot, *Lautréamont et Sade* (Paris: Éditions de Minuit, 1949), 220–221; see also Bataille, *Eroticism*, 167–168, quoting Blanchot.
22. Georges Bataille, "Sur Nietzsche," in *Oeuvres complètes*, vol. 6: *La Somme athéologique* (Paris: Gallimard, 1973), 117.
23. Bataille, "Sur Nietzsche," 117; 118.
24. Sophocles, *Oedipus the King*, in *The Three Theban Plays: Antigone, Oedipus the King, Oedipus at Colonus*, trans. Robert Fagles (New York: Penguin Books, 1982), 228–230.
25. This is the reading that Foucault proposes in his second lecture in *Wrong-Doing, Truth-Telling: The Function of Avowal in Justice*, ed. Fabienne Brion and Bernard E. Harcourt, trans. Stephen W. Sawyer (Chicago: University of Chicago Press, 2014), 57-81.
26. Page DuBois, *Torture and Truth* (New York: Routledge, 1991), 152; see also Isadora Ruyter-Harcourt, "Insanity and Social Status in Classical Rome," Ancient Studies thesis (with distinction), Barnard College, Columbia University, May 2015 (on file with author).
27. Lu Ann Homza, *The Spanish Inquisition, 1478–1614: An Anthology of Sources* (Indianapolis: Hackett Publishing Company, 2006), xii. There are both asset forfeiture and confiscation in the Spanish Inquisition: the heretic suspect's property was seized and sequestered at the time of arrest, used to pay any debts or taxes owed the royal treasury, used to pay the costs of detention of the prisoner; and then, of course, when the accused was convicted of grave heresy, "the sequestrator turned the movable and immovable goods over to the Inquisition, and they were sold at public auction." Homza, *The Spanish Inquisition*, xxvii and xxviii. Throughout the archives, we read about confiscation, for instance in the inquisition trial of Isabel, wife of Bachiller Lope de la Higuera, in Castile in 1484, or in that of Marina González in Toledo in 1494. See Homza, *The Spanish Inquisition*, 16 and 49.

Gaspar Isidro de Argüello's *Instructions of the Holy Office of the Inquisition* (1484–1561), published in 1627, remarks that the goods of the dead prosecuted after their death as heretics shall also "be confiscated and applied to the Treasury and Exchequer of the King and Queen, our Lords." Homza, *The Spanish Inquisition*, 68 and 69. Argüello reproduced extensive instructions pertaining to "the receiver of confiscated goods, and to the scribe [of sequestration]." Homza, *The Spanish Inquisition*, 76–79.

28. Michel Foucault, *Théories et institutions pénales: Cours au Collège de France* (Paris: Gallimard, 2015), 138–139.

13. A Way Forward

1. Walter Benjamin, "Critique of Violence," in *Reflections: Essays, Aphorisms, Autobiographical Writings*, ed. Peter Demetz, trans. Edmund Jephcott (New York: Schocken, 1978), 282; 282. See also Georges Sorel, *Réflexions sur la violence* (Paris: Rivière, 1910).
2. Benjamin, "Critique of Violence," 291; 282–283; 291.
3. Benjamin, "Critique of Violence," 291–292.
4. Benjamin, "Critique of Violence," 291.
5. Massimiliano Tomba, "Justice and Divine Violence: Walter Benjamin and the Time of Anticipation," *Theory & Event* 20, no. 3 (2017): 579–598.
6. Benjamin, "Critique of Violence," 292, citing Sorel, *Réflexions sur la violence*; 292.
7. Benjamin, "Critique of Violence," 292; 292.
8. Benjamin, "Critique of Violence," 300; 300.
9. Benjamin, "Critique of Violence," 300.
10. Benjamin concedes that there may be nonviolent ways to resolve conflict—referring here mostly to the interpersonal ("relationships of private persons") and things like "courtesy, sympathy, peaceableness, trust." Benjamin, "Critique of Violence," 289. He also suggested that language is nonviolent—though that is hard to agree with.
11. Slavoj Žižek, *Violence: Six Sideways Reflections* (New York: Picador, 2008), 199–200.
12. Žižek, *Violence*, 46.
13. These reflect, Žižek suggests, the kind of humiliation that we inflict all the time on each other, as Americans. The practices at Abu Ghraib become nothing more than our induction or initiation of foreigners into the American symbolic world of "performance-art shows in Lower Manhattan," of "a kind of *tableau vivant* [representing] the whole spectrum of American performance art and 'theatre of cruelty,'" including "the photos of Mapplethorpe, the weird scenes in David Lynch's films, to name but two." Žižek, *Violence*, 172. (I think the reference to Mapplethorpe is off and reveals some kind of phobia.)
14. Žižek, *Violence*, 206.
15. Žižek, *Violence*, 207.
16. Žižek, *Violence*, 217.
17. Slavoj Žižek, "Shoplifters of the World Unite," *London Review of Books*, August 19, 2011.
18. Žižek, "Shoplifters of the World Unite."
19. Slavoj Žižek, "How to Begin from the Beginning," in *The Idea of Communism*, vol. 1, ed. Slavoj Žižek and Costas Douzinas (New York: Verso, 2010), 1: 217.
20. Frantz Fanon, *The Wretched of the Earth*, trans. Richard Philcox (New York: Grove, 2004), 51; 50.
21. Fanon, *The Wretched of the Earth*, 45; 45; 46 (all quoting Césaire).
22. Fanon, *The Wretched of the Earth*, 45 (quoting Césaire).
23. Fanon, *The Wretched of the Earth*, 46 (quoting Césaire; my emphasis).
24. Fanon, *The Wretched of the Earth*, 51.

25. Banu Bargu, *Starve and Immolate: The Politics of Human Weapons* (New York: Columbia University Press, 2014), 16; 17.
26. Jean-Paul Sartre, Préface to Frantz Fanon, *Les Damnés de la terre* (Paris: Maspéro, 1961), 21; 19–21; 21.
27. After all, Fanon did not even tolerate the moderate or reformist politics of his own mentor and teacher, Césaire, and was especially brutal with Senghor. Over time, Fanon distanced himself from what he called the "bards of Négritude" and the entire "cultural" approach, as he described it, of Césaire and Senghor. See Fanon, *The Wretched of the Earth*, 151, 154. He attacked Senghor in the opening chapter of *The Wretched of the Earth*, calling him a "colonized intellectual" who had no authentic connection to the struggle of colonial subjects and was still beholden to "Western values." Fanon, *The Wretched of the Earth*, 154; see also Gary Wilder, *Freedom Time: Negritude, Decolonization, and the Future of the World* (Durham, NC: Duke University Press, 2014), 134. Just a few years earlier, in 1959, Fanon had accused the "bards of Négritude" of failing to understand the national dimensions of the culture and politics of independence of the times. See, generally, Wilder, *Freedom Time*, 134.

    We know the reasons well: Fanon's nationalism was opposed to a cross-national or pan-African cultural identity, and even more so to the kind of departmentalization that Césaire advocated for the Antilles, not only from a political, but also from a pragmatic point of view. Fanon adopted, as Wilder suggests, the "paradoxical proposition: In a colonized country, nationalism in its basic, most rudimentary, and undifferentiated form is the most forceful and effective way of defending national culture." Fanon embraced a revolutionary, militantly engaged vision of the intellectual who must be part of and mobilized with the people in a violent struggle against colonialism—and he had little truck for reformists. I have little doubt that this would bleed into Fanon's assessment of violent means—and, of course, it would negate Benjamin's critique.
28. Hannah Arendt, "On Violence," in *Crises of the Republic* (New York: Harcourt Brace, 1972), 166.
29. Foucault read Nietzsche precisely in this way in "Truth and Juridical Forms," the set of lectures that he delivered in Rio in 1973. The model for knowledge, Foucault reads Nietzsche to say, is not origin, but creation, invention. On page 6 of the English translation: "When he says 'invention'"—when Nietzsche says that knowledge was invented, Foucault states—"it's in order not to say 'origin.'" Michel Foucault, "Truth and Juridical Forms," in *Power*, vol. 3 of *The Essential Works of Foucault*, ed. James D. Faubion, trans. Robert Hurley (New York: New Press, 2000), 31–456. To be invented is not to be born. It is, rather, to find, in Foucault's words, "a small beginning, one that is low, mean, unavowable"; to discover the "obscure power relations" and "small beginnings" that are "*mesquin*" and "*vilenies*"—petty, base, vile... Foucault, "Truth and Juridical Forms," 7. "Good historical method," Foucault tells us, "requires us to counterpose the meticulous and unavowable meanness of these fabrications and inventions, to the solemnity of origins." Foucault, "Truth and Juridical Forms," 7.
30. That is one of the most important consequences, at least for Foucault reading Nietzsche: "It's not God that disappears but the subject in its unity and its sovereignty." Foucault, "Truth and Juridical Forms," 10.
31. Simon de Beauvoir, *Faut-il brûler Sade?* (Paris: Gallimard, 1955) (originally published under the title *Privilèges*).
32. Judith Butler, "Beauvoir on Sade: Making Sexuality into an Ethic," in *The Cambridge Companion to Simone de Beauvoir*, ed. Claudia Card (Cambridge: Cambridge University Press, 2003), 172.
33. Butler, "Beauvoir on Sade," 187; 169.
34. Albert Camus, "L'Homme révolté," in *Essais d'Albert Camus*, ed. R. Quilliot and L. Faucon (Paris: Gallimard, 1965), 457; see also Butler, "Beauvoir on Sade," 169, quoting Camus.
35. Butler, "Beauvoir on Sade," 169.
36. Butler, "Beauvoir on Sade," 174.
37. Dominique Lecourt, "The Sadism of Foucault" (paper presentation, Foucault Colloquium at Créteil, Paris, 2014).

38. Georges Bataille, foreword to Marquis de Sade, *120 Days of Sodom* (New York: Sun Vision, 2012), 8.
39. Blanchot, *Lautréamont et Sade*, 220–221; see also Bataille, *Eroticism*, 167, quoting Blanchot.
40. For analyses of nonviolent resistance, see, generally, Akeel Bilgrami, "Gandhi, the Philosopher," in *Secularism, Identity, and Enchantment* (Cambridge, MA: Harvard University Press, 2014); Karuna Mantena, "The Power of Nonviolence," *Aeon*, March 11, 2016, https://aeon.co/essays/nonviolence-has-returned-from-obscurity-to-become-a-new-force; Todd May, *Nonviolent Resistance: A Philosophical Introduction* (Cambridge: Polity, 2015); Uday Singh Mehta, "Gandhi on Democracy, Politics, and the Ethics of Everyday Life," *Modern Intellectual History* 7, no. 2 (2010): 355–371; Brandon Terry, "MLK Now," *Boston Review*, January 9, 2018; and Brandon Terry, "Requiem for a Dream: The Problem-Space of Black Power," in *To Shape a New World*, ed. Tommie Shelby and Brandon M. Terry (Cambridge, MA: Harvard University Press, 2018), 290–324.
41. M. K. Gandhi, *Non-Violent Resistance (Satyagraha)* (Mineola, NY: Dover, 2001), text no. 3, 6; Gandhi, Editor's Notice, in *Non-Violent Resistance*, iii; Mantena, "The Power of Nonviolence"; Bilgrami, "Gandhi, the Philosopher," 105.
42. Gandhi, *Non-Violent Resistance*, text no. 3, 6; text no. 88, 202.
43. Gandhi, *Non-Violent Resistance*, text no. 88, 201; 88, 202.
44. Mantena, "The Power of Nonviolence."
45. Gandhi, *Non-Violent Resistance*, text no. 25, 77; 3, 6.
46. Gandhi, *Non-Violent Resistance*, text no. 100, 227; no. 7, 35.
47. Gandhi, *Non-Violent Resistance*, text no. 26, 79; no. 26, 78; no. 26, 79.
48. Gandhi, *Non-Violent Resistance*, text no. 88, 201–202.
49. As Bargu suggests, these practices "were formative for the constitution of modern India." See Bargu, *Starve and Immolate*, 14.
50. Gandhi, *Non-Violent Resistance*, text no. 72, 171.
51. Gandhi, *Non-Violent Resistance*, text no. 88, 202.
52. Gandhi, *Non-Violent Resistance*, text no. 55, 132.
53. Gandhi's writings about the Jews in 1938 espoused *satyagraha*, but perhaps he would have done better drawing on this justification of violence (see Gandhi, *Non-Violent Resistance*, no. 165, 348–349). Mehta discusses this productively, noting that "Gandhi's words provoked shock, controversy and considerable condemnation." Mehta, "Gandhi on Democracy, Politics, and the Ethics of Everyday Life," 366.
54. Gandhi, *Non-Violent Resistance*, text no. 55, 133. Note that, in this context, there is often a masculine dimension to nonviolence. Gandhi writes that "forgiveness is more manly than punishment" and that "forgiveness adorns a soldier." Gandhi, *Non-Violent Resistance*, text no. 55, 133. Elsewhere, he writes that mistakes at times are "preferable to national emasculation." Gandhi, *Non-Violent Resistance*, text no. 47, 115.
55. See Candice Delmas, *A Duty to Resist: When Disobedience Should Be Uncivil* (New York: Oxford University Press, 2018), 4 (arguing that the nonviolence of the Freedom Riders was "supererogatory, the work of heroes rather than ordinary people and therefore beyond moral requirement.")
56. Mehta, "Gandhi on Democracy, Politics, and the Ethics of Everyday Life," 366.
57. I am not here endorsing the Hegelian dialectic or his philosophy of history; rather, I am suggesting that, in his master-slave dialectic, Hegel put his finger on an insight worth exploring and interpreting.
58. One such excess is the idea, for instance, in his first lessons from the year 1937–1938, that all of "history is a dialectic or an inter*action* of Mastery and Slavery." Alexandre Kojève, *Introduction to the Reading of Hegel: Lectures on the* Phenomenology of Spirit," ed. Allan Bloom, trans. James H. Nichols, Jr. (Ithaca, NY: Cornell University Press, 1980), 44. Another is the idea that "the possibility of a *historical* process, of a *History*, which is, in its totality, the history of the Fights and the Work that finally ended in the wars of Napoleon and the table on which Hegel wrote the *Phenomenology* in order to *understand* both those wars and that table." Kojève, *Introduction to the Reading of Hegel*, 43.

59. Kojève, *Introduction to the Reading of Hegel*, 40.
60. Hegel, *Phenomenology of Spirit*, ¶178, 111 (emphasis added); ¶187, 114.
61. Kojève, *Introduction to the Reading of Hegel*, 45.
62. Hegel, *Phenomenology of Spirit*, ¶188, 114.
63. Hegel, *Phenomenology of Spirit*, ¶192, 117.
64. Hegel, *Phenomenology of Spirit*, ¶191, 116.
65. Jay Bernstein in particular, in his book *Torture and Dignity*, focuses on the relations between torture, recognition, trust, and dignity. See Jay Bernstein, *Torture and Dignity: An Essay on Moral Injury* (Chicago: University of Chicago Press, 2015), 311.
66. Kojève, *Introduction to the Reading of Hegel*, 41; 46.
67. Adriana Cavarero, *Horrorism: Naming Contemporary Violence* (New York: Columbia University Press, 2008), 4.
68. Hegel, *Phenomenology of Spirit*, ¶194, 117.
69. Hegel, *Phenomenology of Spirit*, ¶194, 117.
70. Kojève, *Introduction to the Reading of Hegel*, 47–48. Now, again, Kojève would push this in a direction that is somewhat absurd. In his reading, terror will become important historically through its role in the French Revolution, which will come to represent the last historical turning point of the Christian bourgeoisie (itself a slave class that has become its own slave of capital) toward the state, the empire, Napoleon, and the end of history. Kojève, *Introduction to the Reading of Hegel*, 69. "And it is only thanks to the Terror that the idea of the final Synthesis, which definitively 'satisfies' Man, is realized," Kojève lectures. "It is in the Terror that the State is born in which this 'satisfaction' is attained. This State, for the author of the *Phenomenology*, is Napoleon's Empire" (though he is not self-conscious—that requires Hegel). Kojève, *Introduction to the Reading of Hegel*, 69. In other words, Kojève interprets Hegel as self-consciously arguing that he (Hegel) is "Napoleon's Self-Consciousness. . . . This dyad, formed by Napoleon and Hegel, is the perfect Man, fully and definitively 'satisfied' by what he *is* and by what he *knows* himself to be." Kojève, *Introduction to the Reading of Hegel*, 70. This goes a bit far, though.
71. Kojève, *Introduction to the Reading of Hegel*, 49.
72. Hegel, *Phenomenology of Spirit*, ¶194, 117.
73. Hegel, *Phenomenology of Spirit*, ¶195, 118.
74. Kojève, *Introduction to the Reading of Hegel*, 49.
75. Hegel, *Phenomenology of Spirit*, ¶195, 118.
76. Hegel, *Phenomenology of Spirit*, ¶196, 119.
77. Kojève, of course, had a personal stake in all this, especially historico-politically. In a note to the second edition, written shortly after several trips to the United States, the Soviet Union, and Japan in 1959, he makes fascinating remarks about the Hegelian-Marxist end of history, locating it in the United States: "One can even say that, from a certain point of view, the United States has already attained the final stage of Marxist 'communism,' seeing that, practically, all the members of a 'classless society' can from now on appropriate for themselves everything that seems good to them, without thereby working any more than their heart dictates." Kojève, *Introduction to the Reading of Hegel*, 161, note to the second edition.
78. As history, it has far too grand a view of itself and of the teleology of history and progress. The idea of an end of history is exaggerated. The idea of rationality actualizing itself is misguided. Kojève's reading of all of history through the lens of the master-slave dialectic is entertaining and possibly brilliant—with its three-part division into an early period of mastery (a Pagan world of mastery that ends with self-defeating masters who "become Slaves of the Roman Emperor"; see Kojève, *Introduction to the Reading of Hegel*, 57, 63), followed by a period of slavish existence (the Christian world of slavery, in which the masters adopt the ideology of their slaves, "first Stoicism, then Skepticism,

and—finally—Christianity"; see Kojève, *Introduction to the Reading of Hegel*, 57, 63); and finally the advent of the end of history, which the French Revolution inaugurates, German philosophy complements, and finally, Hegel accomplishes. Kojève, *Introduction to the Reading of Hegel*, 57. The historical dialectic, which culminated in Napoleon and Hegel, is a tour de force—but it is not really convincing or worth debating. The Hegelian story is lacking from a phenomenological perspective as well. We could psychologize the account in a Freudian direction, or even more in the direction of Jean Piaget (1932), or Lawrence Kohlberg's (1958) theory of moral development. All of this could be interesting. But it would say much more about us than about reality.

79. Herbert Marcuse, *One-Dimensional Man* (Boston: Beacon, 1964), 206–207, quoting François Perroux, *La Co-existence pacifique* (Paris: Presses Universitaires de France, 1958), vol. III, 631. The passage is translated in Marcuse, *One-Dimensional Man*, 207n.2, from this original, which he includes in the text:

    On croit mourir pour la Classe, on meurt pour les gens du Parti. On croit mourir pour la Patrie, on meurt pour les Industriels. On croit mourir pour la Liberté des Personnes, on meurt pour la Liberté des dividendes. On croit mourir pour le Prolétariat, on meurt pour sa Bureaucratie. On croit mourir sur l'ordre d'un État, on meurt pour l'argent qui le tient. On croit mourir pour une nation, on meurt pour les bandits qui la baillonnent. On croit—mais pourquoi croirait-on dans une ombre si épaisse ? Croire, mourir ?... quand il s'agit d'apprendre à vivre ?

80. As noted earlier, it is possible to draw parallels between the position that I have set forth and the post-foundational philosophy that Oliver Marchart constructs in the final chapter of his book *Post-Foundational Political Thought*. See Oliver Marchart, "Founding Post-Foundationalism: A Political Ontology," in *Post-Foundational Political Thought: Political Difference in Nancy, Lefort, Badiou and Laclau* (Edinburgh: Edinburgh University Press, 2007), 154–177.

Part III: Renewing Critical Praxis

1. Slavoj Žižek, "How to Begin from the Beginning," in *The Idea of Communism*, vol. 1, ed. Costas Douzinas and Slavoj Žižek (New York: Verso, 2010), 217.
2. Gilles Gressani made this point masterfully in his analysis of Che Guevara's tactical mistakes in Bolivia in his presentation at "Histoire du present: Maoïsme, néolibéralisme et les cortèges de tête" (symposium, Amphithéâtre François Furet, Paris, June 6, 2018), http://blogs.law.columbia.edu/uprising1313/la-contrerevolution-journee-detude-du-6-juin-2018/. It is also demonstrated by Gandhi's misfire on Nazi Germany that I discuss earlier in chapter 13.
3. Daniele Lorenzini and Martina Tazzioli, "Critique's Others, Desubjugation, History: The Re-appropriation of Problems Beyond the Quest for Evidence" (working paper, August 1, 2019; on file with author).

14. The Transformation of Praxis

1. Slavoj Žižek, "No Way Out? Communism in the Next Century," in *The Idea of Communism*, vol. 3, ed. Alex Taek-Gwang Lee and Slavoj Žižek (New York: Verso, 2016), 241–242.
2. Žižek, "No Way Out?" 241–242 (quoting Joseph Stiglitz, "Democracy in the Twenty-first Century," *Social Europe*, September 01, 2014, https://www.socialeurope.eu/democracy).
3. Žižek, "No Way Out?" 242.
4. Eduard Bernstein, *The Preconditions of Socialism*, ed. and trans. Henry Tudor (Cambridge: Cambridge University Press, 1993), 4 (internal quotations omitted); 5; 5; 4.

5. Rosa Luxemburg, *Reform or Revolution and Other Writing* (Mineola, NY: Dover, 2006), 4.
6. Luxemburg, *Reform or Revolution*, 5.
7. Karl Marx and Frederick Engels, *Manifesto of the Communist Party*, ed. Frederick Engels (New York: International Publishers, 1948), 9.
8. Immanuel Wallerstein, "How to Fight a Class Struggle, Commentary No. 491," last modified February 15, 2019, https://www.iwallerstein.com/how-to-fight-a-class-struggle/.
9. Cathy J. Cohen and Sarah J. Jackson, "Ask a Feminist: A Conversation with Cathy J. Cohen on Black Lives Matter, Feminism, and Contemporary Activism," *Signs: Journal of Women in Culture and Society* 41, no. 4 (Summer 2016): 1–18; Cathy Cohen, "The Radical Potential of Queer? Twenty Years Later," *GLQ: A Journal of Lesbian and Gay Studies* 25, no. 1 (2019): 140–144, https://muse.jhu.edu/; Barbara Ransby, "Black Lives Matter Is Democracy in Action," *New York Times*, October 21, 2017, https://www.nytimes.com/2017/10/21/opinion/sunday/black-lives-matter-leadership.html; Keeanga-Yamahtta Taylor, *From #BlackLivesMatter to Black Liberation* (Chicago: Haymarket, 2016); Deva Woodly, "#BlackLivesMatter and the Democratic Necessity of Social Movements," *Uprising 13/13* (blog), November 1, 2017, http://blogs.law.columbia.edu/uprising1313/deva-woodly-blacklivesmatter-and-the-democratic-necessity-of-social-movements/.
10. Judith Butler, *Notes Toward a Performative Theory of Assembly* (Cambridge, MA: Harvard University Press, 2015); Michael Hardt and Toni Negri, *Assembly* (New York: Oxford University Press, 2017); Jodi Dean, "Claiming Division, Naming a Wrong," *Theory & Event* 14, no. 4. (2011), https://muse.jhu.edu/; W. J. T. Mitchell, ed., *Occupy: Three Inquiries in Disobedience* (Chicago: University of Chicago Press, 2013); Sandra Laugier and Albert Ogien, *Pourquoi désobéir en démocratie?* (Paris: La Découverte, 2011); Frédéric Gros, *Désobéir* (Paris: Albin Michel, 2017); Robin Celikates, "Civil Disobedience as a Practice of Civic Freedom," in *On Global Citizenship: James Tully in Dialogue*, ed. David Owen (New York: Bloomsbury, 2014), 207–228; Robin Celikates, "Democratizing Civil Disobedience," *Philosophy and Social Criticism* 42, no. 10 (2016): 982–994; Candice Delmas, *A Duty to Resist: When Disobedience Should Be Uncivil* (New York: Oxford University Press, 2018); William Scheuerman, *Civil Disobedience* (Cambridge: Polity, 2018). Alexander Livingston is also working fruitfully in this area and has a book project on civil disobedience, tentatively titled *Freedom Now: Inventing Civil Disobedience in Twentieth-Century America*.
11. See Reinhart Koselleck, "Historical Criteria of the Modern Concept of Revolution," in Reinhart Koselleck, *Futures Past: On the Semantics of Historical Time* (New York: Columbia University Press, 2004), 57 ("In politics, words and their usage are more important than any other weapon").
12. Bernstein portrayed himself as authoritative, insofar as he was Engels's literary executor, and he made that fact known in his debates with Luxemburg.
13. Max Horkheimer, "Traditional and Critical Theory," in *Critical Theory: Selected Essays*, trans. Matthew J. O'Connell et al. (New York: Continuum, 1992), 231.
14. Horkheimer, "Traditional and Critical Theory," 249 (emphasis added); 233.
15. Horkheimer, "Traditional and Critical Theory," 219; see also 220 ("there can be no corresponding concrete perception of [change] until it actually comes about.").
16. Herbert Marcuse, *Counterrevolution and Revolt* (Boston: Beacon, 1972), 34.
17. Marcuse, *Counterrevolution and Revolt*, 34; 34; 17; 17; 17; 33.
18. Herbert Marcuse, *One-Dimensional Man* (Boston: Beacon, 1991), 242, 257.
19. Marcuse, *Counterrevolution and Revolt*, 129, 130.
20. All quotations in this paragraph come from Theodor W. Adorno, "Marginalia on Theory and Praxis," in *Critical Models: Interventions and Catchwords*, trans. Henry W. Pickford (New York: Columbia University Press, 1998), 277.
21. Adorno, "Marginalia on Theory and Praxis," 276.
22. Adorno, "Marginalia on Theory and Praxis," 277.

23. Max Horkheimer, *Eclipse of Reason* (London: Bloomsbury, 1974), 130.
24. Horkheimer, *Eclipse of Reason*, vii.
25. Horkheimer, *Eclipse of Reason*, vii–viii; viii (emphasis added).
26. Horkheimer, *Eclipse of Reason*, viii.
27. Adorno, "Marginalia on Theory and Praxis," 261; 260; 260–261; 263; 268; 276.
28. Adorno, "Marginalia on Theory and Praxis," 278.
29. Adorno, "Marginalia on Theory and Praxis," 278.
30. Étienne Balibar, "The Idea of Revolution: Yesterday, Today and Tomorrow," *Uprising 1/13* (blog), August 27, 2017, http://blogs.law.columbia.edu/uprising1313/etienne-balibar-the-idea-of-revolution-yesterday-today-and-tomorrow/; see also Koselleck, "Historical Criteria of the Modern Concept of Revolution," 47, for the confessional or inquisitorial dimensions to the shift; and Ann Laura Stoler, *Duress: Imperial Durabilities in Our Times* (Durham, NC: Duke University Press, 2016).
31. I detail Mao's tripartite view of society in Bernard E. Harcourt, *The Counterrevolution* (New York: Basic Books, 2018), 29–32.
32. The Invisible Committee, *The Coming Insurrection* (Cambridge, MA: MIT Press (Semiotext(e)/Intervention), 2009) (I am using the online edition, the Invisible Committee, *The Coming Insurrection* (The Anarchist Library, 2009), https://theanarchistlibrary.org/library/comite-invisible-the-coming-insurrection, with its pagination), 8, 97.
33. The Invisible Committee, *The Coming Insurrection*, 27; 101; 118.
34. The Invisible Committee, *The Coming Insurrection*, 131–136; 14.
35. For an analysis of the use of social media in contemporary protest, see Zeynep Tufekci, *Twitter and Tear Gas: The Power and Fragility of Networked Protest* (New Haven, CT: Yale University Press, 2017).
36. Darryl Holliday, "The New Black Power: They're Young. They're Radical. They're Organized. And They're a Thorn in Rahm's Side," *Chicago Magazine*, February 22, 2016, http://www.chicagomag.com/Chicago-Magazine/March-2016/black-leaders/.
37. Barbara Ransby, "Black Lives Matter Is Democracy in Action," *New York Times*, October 21, 2017.
38. Butler, *Notes Toward a Performative Theory of Assembly*, 156–157.
39. Butler, *Notes Toward a Performative Theory of Assembly*, 181; 11.
40. Butler, *Notes Toward a Performative Theory of Assembly*, 9; 16; 18.
41. Butler, *Notes Toward a Performative Theory of Assembly*, 182.

15. The Landscape of Contemporary Critical Praxis

1. See, generally, Franz Neumann, Herbert Marcuse, and Otto Kirchheimer, *Secret Reports on Nazi Germany: The Frankfurt School Contribution to the War Effort*, ed. Raffaele Laudani (Princeton, NJ: Princeton University Press, 2013); William Scheuerman, "The Frankfurt School at War," review of *Secret Reports on Nazi Germany*, by Franz Neumann, Herbert Marcuse, and Otto Kirchheimer, *Foreign Affairs*, July/August 2013; and Thomas Wheatland, *The Frankfurt School in Exile* (Minneapolis: University of Minnesota Press, 2009).
2. Susan Cavin, "OSS & the Frankfurt School: Recycling the 'Damaged Lives of Cultural Outsiders'" (paper presentation at the 2004 meeting of the American Sociological Association, San Francisco, August 15, 2004), http://citation.allacademic.com/meta/p_mla_apa_research_citation/1/1/0/1/8/pages110188/p110188-1.php.
3. Max Horkheimer, "Traditional and Critical Theory," in *Critical Theory: Selected Essays*, trans. Matthew J. O'Connell et al. (New York: Continuum, 1992), 219; see also 220 ("there can be no corresponding concrete perception of [change] until it actually comes about").

4. Perry Anderson, "On the Concatenation in the Arab World," *New Left Review* 68 (2011): 5-15, https://newleftreview.org/issues/II68/articles/perry-anderson-on-the-concatenation-in-the-arab-world, 14, 15; see also Perry Anderson, "Two Revolutions," *New Left Review* 61 (2010): 59-96, https://newleftreview.org/issues/II61/articles/perry-anderson-two-revolutions.
5. Tariq Ali, *The Dilemmas of Lenin: Terrorism, War, Empire, Love, Revolution* (New York: Verso, 2017), 151, 164.
6. Vladimir Lenin, "The Tasks of the Proletariat in the Present Revolution," *Pravda* April 17, 1917, no. 26 (1917): *2.
7. Ali, *The Dilemmas of Lenin*, 10.
8. Slavoj Žižek, "How to Begin from the Beginning," in *The Idea of Communism*. Vol. 1, ed. Slavoj Žižek and Costas Douzinas (New York: Verso, 2010), 217; 216–217; 217.
9. Žižek, "How to Begin from the Beginning," 219.
10. Žižek, "How to Begin from the Beginning," 220; 226; 226; 226.
11. Soha Bayoumi, "Revolution, Hope, and Actors' Categories. Or What's an Engaged Scholar to Do?," October 22, 2017 (on file with author).
12. Seyla Benhabib, *Critique, Norm, and Utopia: A Study of the Foundations of Critical Theory* (New York: Columbia University Press, 1986), 352.
13. Reinhart Koselleck, "Historical Criteria of the Modern Concept of Revolution," in Reinhart Koselleck, *Futures Past: On the Semantics of Historical Time* (New York: Columbia University Press, 2004), 52; see also Hannah Arendt, *On Revolution* (New York: Penguin, 2006 [1963]).
14. Bernie Sanders, *Guide to Political Revolution* (New York: Henry Holt, 2017).
15. Sanders, *Guide to Political Revolution*, 81; 105; 25; 2 and 17–19; 16–17; 42; 166, 165, and 170; 189.
16. Sanders, *Guide to Political Revolution*, 185; 60 (emphasis added).
17. Sanders, *Guide to Political Revolution*, 8–9; 57–58.
18. Sanders, *Guide to Political Revolution*, Dedication.
19. Amna Akbar, "Gross Collective Action," *Praxis 13/13* (blog), October 21, 2018, http://blogs.law.columbia.edu/praxis1313/amna-a-akbar-gross-collective-action/. Ghislaine Pagès shares these concerns in her essay "Revolutionary in Rhetoric Only," *Praxis 13/13* (blog), October 24, 2018, http://blogs.law.columbia.edu/praxis1313/ghislaine-pages-revolutionary-in-rhetoric-only/.
20. See Bernard E. Harcourt et al., "Praxis 3/13: Indivisible: Political Revolution," public seminar, Columbia University, October 24, 2018, New York, http://blogs.law.columbia.edu/praxis1313/3-13/, video at 26:40 mark for Brandon Terry; video at 51:30 mark for Adam Tooze.
21. For a primer on the concept of democratic socialism, see Maggie Astor, "Are You a Democratic Socialist?," *New York Times*, September 22, 2018, https://www.nytimes.com/interactive/2018/09/22/us/politics/what-is-democratic-socialism.html.
22. Sanders, *Guide to Political Revolution*, 140; 41; 172; 171.
23. GIP, "Manifeste du GIP," February 8, 1971, in *1954–1975*, vol. 1 of *Dits et Écrits*, ed. Daniel Defert, François Ewald, and Jacques Lagrange (Paris: Gallimard/Quarto, 2001), text no. 86, 1042–1043; I am using Stuart Elden's translation.
24. Akbar, "Gross Collective Action."
25. Didier Fassin and Bernard E. Harcourt, eds., *A Time for Critique* (New York: Columbia University Press, 2019), 15, 47-48; Harcourt et al., "Praxis 3/13: Indivisible: Political Revolution," video at 56:10 mark for Adam Tooze.
26. Sanders, *Guide to Political Revolution*, 189, 189, 190, 191, 191, and 192.
27. Sanders, *Guide to Political Revolution*, 192; 190; 193; 193–194.
28. Sanders, *Guide to Political Revolution*, 177.
29. Sanders, *Guide to Political Revolution*, 177–178 (emphasis added).

30. So, for instance, Tooze critiqued the anachronisms in Sanders's *Guide*: it makes more reference to twentieth-century giants like IBM than to our current monopolist GAFAs (i.e., Google, Apple, Facebook, and Amazon). That reflects either an outdated analysis or sleight of hand (if in fact the hesitation to address the GAFAs is out of fear of alienating the younger generation). This is an important critique, and worth pursuing. Harcourt et al., "Praxis 3/13: Indivisible: Political Revolution," video at 58:00 mark for Adam Tooze.
31. Chantal Mouffe, *For a Left Populism* (New York: Verso, 2018), 93.
32. Mouffe, *For a Left Populism*, 9.
33. Nancy Fraser and Rahel Jaeggi, *Capitalism: A Conversation in Critical Theory* (New York: Polity, 2018), 145; 146, 149; 146 and Mouffe, *For a Left Populism*, 24; 149. In contrast to Fraser, Jaeggi places greater importance on affect. Central to her diagnosis of the present crisis is the concept of *ressentiment*. As she writes, *ressentiment* is more than just a fashionable way of speaking, "it's another tool for understanding the inner structure of those dynamics that misdirect social suffering and indignation toward reactionary, authoritarian, and proto-fascist impulses instead of emancipatory movements." Fraser and Jaeggi, *Capitalism*, 146.

    Incidentally, we see here Jaeggi's willingness to address, and judge, sentiments, affects, and in relation to those, ways of life. Regarding affect, Jaeggi is far less optimistic than Fraser and does not think we are "breaking away from neoliberalism"; she seems somewhat resigned before the rise of the alt-right. Fraser and Jaeggi, *Capitalism*, 148. Jaeggi concludes:

    > this sounds a bit like the old left-wing strategy that hopes for a "sharpening of the contradictions." This strategy didn't always work out. Rosa Luxemburg's alternative, between 'socialism or barbarism,' might not exhaust the realm of options. What we agree about, nevertheless, is that we live in an open situation. And without an emancipatory project that goes beyond the alternatives [that] people seem to be stuck with today, things might get ugly. (Fraser and Jaeggi, *Capitalism*, 149)

    The reference to "socialism or barbarism," incidentally, comes from Rosa Luxemburg's 1916 antiwar tract, *The Crisis in the German Social Democracy*, also referred to as the Junius Pamphlet, where she quotes Friedrich Engels: "Capitalist society faces a dilemma, either an advance to Socialism or a reversion to barbarism." Rosa Luxemburg, *The Crisis in the German Social Democracy: The Junius Pamphlet (1919)* (Whitefish, MO: Kessinger Publishing, 2010), 18.
34. Fraser and Jaeggi, *Capitalism*, 149; 146–147; 149; 148.
35. Fraser and Jaeggi, *Capitalism*, 149.
36. Jan-Werner Müller, *What Is Populism?* (Philadelphia: University of Pennsylvania Press, 2016); see also Jan-Werner Müller, "The Rise and Rise of Populism?," *OpenMind*, https://www.bbvaopenmind.com/wp-content/uploads/2018/03/BBVA-OpenMind-Jan-Werner-Muller-The-Rise-and-Rise-of-Populism-1.pdf.
37. Nadia Urbinati, "Political Theory of Populism," *Annual Review of Political Science* 22, no. 1 (2019): 111–127.
38. Jean Cohen, "What's Wrong with (Theories of) Left Populism?," paper presented at the *Constellations Conference* at Columbia University, New York, November 30, 2018 (on file with author).
39. This reflects, to a certain extent, the distinction that Urbinati draws between populism as "a movement of opinion" as opposed to populism as "a ruling power within the state." Urbinati, "Political Theory of Populism," 12.
40. Mouffe, *For a Left Populism*, 11.
41. Mouffe, *For a Left Populism*, 10; 11.
42. Mouffe, *For a Left Populism*, 2.
43. Mouffe, *For a Left Populism*, 9; 9.
44. Mouffe, *For a Left Populism*, 5-6.
45. Mouffe, *For a Left Populism*, 14; 11–13.
46. Mouffe, *For a Left Populism*, 6; 15.

47. Mouffe, *For a Left Populism*, 23; 5.
48. Mouffe, *For a Left Populism*, 24.
49. Mouffe, *For a Left Populism*, 22.
50. Mouffe, *For a Left Populism*, 23, 95, 20, and 81.
51. Urbinati, "Political Theory of Populism," 11.
52. Jan-Werner Müller, contribution to *Praxis 13/13* (on file with author); Jan-Werner Müller, "The Rise and Rise of Populism?," *OpenMind*, https://www.bbvaopenmind.com/wp-content/uploads/2018/03/BBVA-OpenMind-Jan-Werner-Muller-The-Rise-and-Rise-of-Populism-1.pdf. Note that Urbinati challenges Müller's emphasis on the opposition between the silent majority and the corrupt elite, suggesting that it is not unique to populism. The mantra of "we good/they bad," Urbinati suggests, is part of most partisan politics and traces back to ancient Rome: referring to John McCormick's writings, she notes that "it comes from the republican tradition that dated back to ancient Rome, whose polity was structurally based on a dualism between the people and the elite, and on popular mistrust in that elite." Urbinati, "Political Theory of Populism," 9.
53. Ernesto Laclau, quoted in Urbinati, "Political Theory of Populism," 4.
54. Urbinati, "Political Theory of Populism," 4.
55. Urbinati, "Political Theory of Populism," 3.
56. This makes sense, given that, as Urbinati shows, populism was predominantly studied in the mid-twentieth century (in the work of Edward Shils, for instance) as a subspecies of fascism. Urbinati, "Political Theory of Populism," 2.
57. Jason Stanley, *How Fascism Works: The Politics of Us and Them* (New York: Random House, 2018), xvi.
58. See Urbinati, "Political Theory of Populism," 10.
59. Jan-Werner Müller, for instance, states that Sanders is "obviously not" a populist. See "Indivisible: Political Revolution," *Praxis 3/13* (blog), October 24, 2018, http://blogs.law.columbia.edu/praxis1313/3-13/, video and blog posts.
60. Sanders, *Guide to Political Revolution*, x–xii (emphasis added).
61. Sanders, *Guide to Political Revolution*, ix; xii.
62. Regarding populism in Latin America, see Federico Finchelstein, *From Fascism to Populism in History* (Berkeley: University of California Press, 2017).
63. See Jelani Cobb, "The Matter of Black Lives," *The New Yorker*, March 14, 2016.
64. Monica Anderson and Paul Hitlin, "Social Media Conversations About Race: How Social Media Users See, Share, and Discuss Race and the Rise of Hashtags Like #BlackLivesMatter," PEW Research Center, August 15, 2016, https://www.pewinternet.org/2016/08/15/social-media-conversations-about-race/.
65. See Jordan Camp and Christina Heatherton, eds., *Policing the Planet: Why the Policing Crisis Led to Black Lives Matter* (New York: Verso, 2016).
66. Barbara Ransby, "Black Lives Matter Is Democracy in Action," *New York Times*, October 21, 2017, https://www.nytimes.com/2017/10/21/opinion/sunday/black-lives-matter-leadership.html.
67. "Herstory," Black Lives Matter, accessed August 8, 2019, https://blacklivesmatter.com/about/herstory/.
68. See, e.g., Tom Mertes, ed., *A Movement of Movements: Is Another World Really Possible?* (New York: Verso, 2004).
69. See, e.g., Van Gosse, "A Movement of Movements: The Definition and Periodization of the New Left," in *A Companion to Post-1945 America*, ed. Jean-Christophe Agnew and Roy Rosenzweig (Hoboken, NJ: Blackwell Publishing, 2006), 277–302.
70. For differing views, see Erin Mazursky, "The Rules Have Changed: How to Build a 'Movement of Movements' in the U.S.," *Medium*, November 22, 2016, accessed August 8, 2019, https://medium.com/@emazursky/the-rules-have-changed-building-a-movement-of-movements-in-the-u-s-9237ebcd930c; and "We Are a Movement of Movements," *Rivera Sun* (blog), February 13, 2014, http://www.riverasun.com/the-movement-of-movements/.

71. Janae Bonsu and Terrance Laney, "Agenda to Keep Us Safe," BYP100, 2016, http://agendatobuildblackfutures.org/wp-content/uploads/2016/01/BYP100-Agenda-to-Keep-Us-Safe-AKTUS.pdf.
72. "Home," AgendatoBuildBlackFutures.org, accessed August 9, 2019, http://agendatobuildblackfutures.org/.
73. For a discussion of this, see "#BlackLivesMatter," *Uprising 13/13* (blog), November 9, 2017, http://blogs.law.columbia.edu/uprising1313/4-13/.
74. Deva Woodly, "#BlackLivesMatter and the Democratic Necessity of Social Movements," *Uprising 13/13* (blog), November 1, 2017, http://blogs.law.columbia.edu/uprising1313/deva-woodly-blacklivesmatter-and-the-democratic-necessity-of-social-movements/.
75. Kendall Thomas, quoted in Bernard E. Harcourt, Shanelle Matthews, Kendall Thomas, Deva Woodly, and Elias Alcantara, "Uprising 4/13: #BlackLivesMatter," public seminar, Columbia University, November 9, 2017, New York, http://blogs.law.columbia.edu/uprising1313/4-13/.
76. Bill Ruthhart and John Chase, "Emanuel: Alvarez Loss Sends Clear Message on Police Reform," *Chicago Tribune*, March 16, 2016, http://my.chicagotribune.com/#section/-1/article/p2p-86244551/; Miles Kampf-Lassin, "How Black Youth Helped Unseat Anita Alvarez and Transform the Face of Criminal Justice in Chicago," *In These Times*, March 16, 2016, http://inthesetimes.com/article/18982/chicago-black-youth-anita-alvarez-kim-foxx-cook-county; see Chicago Rising, Facebook, https://www.facebook.com/OccupyChicago.
77. Sarah Schulte, "New Poll Shows Anita Alvarez Leading in Race for Re-election," ABC Chicago, http://abc7chicago.com/politics/new-poll-shows-anita-alvarez-leading-in-race-for-re-election/1184004/.
78. Kampf-Lassin, "How Black Youth Helped Unseat Anita Alvarez."
79. People's Response Team, Facebook, https://www.facebook.com/events/927190527374264/.
80. Kampf-Lassin, "How Black Youth Helped Unseat Anita Alvarez."
81. @AssataDaughters, "#ByeAnita: Our Statement on Our Collective Victory," pastebin, http://pastebin.com/7W4TkpmE.
82. Darryl Holliday, "The New Black Power: They're Young. They're Radical. They're Organized. And They're a Thorn in Rahm's Side," *Chicago Magazine*, March 2016, https://www.chicagomag.com/Chicago-Magazine/March-2016/black-leaders/.
83. Woodly, "#BlackLivesMatter and the Democratic Necessity of Social Movements."
84. Judith Butler, *Notes Toward a Performative Theory of Assembly* (Cambridge, MA: Harvard University Press, 2015), 25.
85. Butler, *Notes Toward a Performative Theory of Assembly*, 16.
86. Butler, *Notes Toward a Performative Theory of Assembly*, 156.
87. Butler, *Notes Toward a Performative Theory of Assembly*, 9.
88. Butler, *Notes Toward a Performative Theory of Assembly*, 192.
89. Hana Worthen, "Review of *Notes on a Performative Theory of Assembly*, by Judith Butler," *Critical Inquiry*, February 8, 2016. This reflects, as Mary Walsh suggests, "what may be referred to as Butler's ongoing phenomenological turn": "when bodies assemble in public spaces (including virtual ones), they assert a plural and performative right to appear, one that situates the body in the center of the political field." Mary Walsh, "Review of *Notes Toward a Performative Theory of Assembly*, by Judith Butler," *The Review of Politics* 79, no. 1, 180–183 (Winter 2017), 181.
90. Butler, *Notes Toward a Performative Theory of Assembly*, 8.
91. Butler, *Notes Toward a Performative Theory of Assembly*, 9.
92. Lee M. Pierce, "Review of *Notes Toward a Performative Theory of Assembly*, by Judith Butler," *Philosophy & Rhetoric* 50, no. 3, 356–362 (2017), 361 (quoting Butler, *Notes Toward a Performative Theory of Assembly*, 160).
93. Pierce, "Review of *Notes on a Performative Theory of Assembly*," 361.
94. Butler, *Notes Toward a Performative Theory of Assembly*, 71; 71.

95. Butler, *Notes Toward a Performative Theory of Assembly*, 71.
96. Butler, *Notes Toward a Performative Theory of Assembly*, 85; 83.
97. Hardt and Negri, *Assembly*, 290.
98. Hardt and Negri, *Assembly*, 15; 19.
99. Hardt and Negri, *Assembly*, 18; 25, 37; xiv.
100. Joshua Smeltzer, "Review of *Assembly*, by Michael Hardt and Toni Negri," *LSE Review of Books*, January 31, 2018, https://blogs.lse.ac.uk/lsereviewofbooks/2018/01/31/book-review-assembly-by-michael-hardt-and-antonio-negri/.
101. Hardt and Negri, *Assembly*, 134; 21.
102. Hardt and Negri, *Assembly*, 134; 289; 38; 39.
103. Hardt and Negri, *Assembly*, 69–72, 288.
104. Hardt and Negri, *Assembly*, 69.
105. Hardt and Negri, *Assembly*, 78.
106. Hardt and Negri, *Assembly*, 107; 123; 291; 139.
107. Hardt and Negri, *Assembly*, 222; 223.
108. Hardt and Negri, *Assembly*, 77.
109. Hardt and Negri, *Assembly*, 228; 231.
110. Hardt and Negri, *Assembly*, xiii.
111. Butler, *Notes Toward a Performative Theory of Assembly*, 134; see also 124 ["the idea of bodies on the street together gives leftists a bit of a thrill, as if power were being taken back, taken away, assumed, and incorporated in some way that portends democracy. *I understand that thrill, have even written from it*, but here I will review some of my doubts, some of which I suspect are shared." (emphasis added)].
112. Hardt and Negri, *Assembly*, 295.
113. Hardt and Negri, *Assembly*, xiii; frontpiece ("We dedicate this book . . . to those who, against all odds, continue to fight for freedom, those who suffer defeat only to stand up again, indefatigable, to combat the forces of domination. Yours is true Majesty").
114. Butler, *Notes Toward a Performative Theory of Assembly*, 134–135 (emphasis added).
115. Hardt and Negri, *Assembly*, xviii.
116. Bernard E. Harcourt, "Political Disobedience," in *Occupy: Three Inquiries in Disobedience*, ed. W. J. T. Mitchell, Bernard E. Harcourt, and Michael Taussig (Chicago: University of Chicago Press, 2013), 45–92.
117. See Sandra Laugier and Albert Ogien, *Pourquoi désobéir en démocratie?* (Paris: La Découverte, 2011); Brandon Terry, "MLK Now," *Boston Review*, January 9, 2018; Frédéric Gros, *Désobéir* (Paris: Albin Michel, 2017); Robin Celikates, "Civil Disobedience as a Practice of Civic Freedom," in *On Global Citizenship: James Tully in Dialogue*, ed. David Owen (New York: Bloomsbury, 2014) , 207–228; Robin Celikates, "Democratizing Civil Disobedience," *Philosophy and Social Criticism* 42, no. 10 (2016): 982–994; Candice Delmas, *A Duty to Resist: When Disobedience Should Be Uncivil* (New York: Oxford University Press, 2018); William E. Scheuerman, *Civil Disobedience* (Cambridge: Polity, 2018); Alexander Livingston, *Freedom Now: Inventing Civil Disobedience in Twentieth-Century America* (book project). See also Stéphane Hessel, *Indignez-vous* (Montpellier, France: Indigène editions, 2010).
118. Michel Foucault, *Qu'est-ce que la critique?* ed. Henri-Paul Fruchaud and Daniele Lorenzini (Paris: Vrin, 2015), 37–38 (emphasis added).
119. Michael Taussig, "I'm So Angry I Made a Sign," in *Occupy: Three Theories in Disobedience*, ed. W. J. T. Mitchell, Bernard E. Harcourt, and Michael Taussig (Chicago, University of Chicago Press, 2013), 3–44.
120. Stefan Jonsson, "Aesthetic Dimensions of Contemporary Protest: Methodological Considerations on Monstrous Events" (presentation, Yale University, New Haven, CT, May 11, 2018; on file with author).

121. Manissa Maharawal, "Standing Up," in *Occupy!* ed. Carla Blumenkranz et al. (New York: Verso, 2011), 40.
122. A. J., Bauer, Christine Baumgarthuber, Jed Bickman, Jeremy Breecher, and the Writers for the 99 Percent, *Occupying Wall Street: The Inside Story of an Action That Changed America* (Chicago: Haymarket, 2011), 26.
123. Gilles Deleuze and Félix Guattari, *Anti-Oedipus: Capitalism and Schizophrenia*, trans. Robert Hurley, Mark Seem, and Helen R. Lane (Minneapolis: University of Minnesota Press, 1983), 344.
124. Desire, though, can also be tamed or diverted. This is one of the central lessons—a brilliant insight—of Luc Boltanski and Eve Chiapello's *The New Spirit of Capitalism*: pleasurable revolutionary impulses can be turned against us. Luc Boltanski and Eve Chiapello, *Le Nouvel esprit de capitalisme* (Paris: Gallimard, 1999). As they show in their book, the revolutionary spirit of 1968 was tamed, mastered, disciplined, and turned back to making corporate profits by tapping the creative energy and artistic potential of the young militants—not by restricting them. Today, engineers at Google and Apple can wear jeans, tie-dyed T-shirts, and flip flops to work, live entirely creative and artistic lives, have a gym to work out in, drink cappuccinos and frappés and lattes on demand, telecommute, play video games at their computers, and re-create *Star Wars* in their own cubicles—but the fact is that all that creativity, all that energy, and all that passion are redirected and reinvested in capitalist enterprises to make a profit for their employers, and to mold desire into corporate returns. This is perhaps the dark side of desire and pleasure in revolt—and indeed, if we do not see it, we really might be led straight to the slaughterhouse, as we often have been in history. I am thinking here, of course, of fascism, of Nazism, of those dark episodes in the twentieth and now the twenty-first centuries. Here, I will again point to Deleuze and Guattari, who also reminded us of this flip side: "Even the most repressive and the most deadly forms of social reproduction are produced by desire within the organization" (Deleuze and Guattari, *Anti-Oedipus*, 344).
125. See, generally, Gabriella Coleman, *Hacker, Hoaxer, Whistleblower, Spy: The Many Faces of Anonymous* (London: Verso, 2015); Gabriella Coleman, "From Internet Farming to Weapons of the Greek," *Current Anthropology* 58, no. 15 (February 2017): S92; Bernard E. Harcourt, *Exposed: Desire and Disobedience in the Digital Age* (Cambridge, MA: Harvard University Press, 2015), 262-283; Delmas, *A Duty to Resist*; Edward Snowden, *Permanent Record* (New York: Metropolitan, 2019).
126. James C. Scott, "The Infrapolitics of Subordinate Groups," in *Domination and the Arts of Resistance* (New Haven, CT, and London: Yale University Press, 1990), 200; 192; 188; 201.
127. Scott, "The Infrapolitics of Subordinate Groups," 198.
128. Matthew Rosenberg, Nicholas Confessore, and Carole Cadwalladr, "How Trump Consultants Exploited the Facebook Data of Millions," *New York Times*, March 17, 2018, https://www.nytimes.com/2018/03/17/us/politics/cambridge-analytica-trump-campaign.html.
129. Coleman, "From Internet Farming to Weapons of the Geek," S98.
130. Emmanuel Goldstein, "Hacktivism and the Hacker Promise," *Uprising 13/13* (blog), March 16, 2018, http://blogs.law.columbia.edu/uprising1313/emmanuel-goldstein-hacktivism-and-the-hacker-promise/.
131. Coleman, "From Internet Farming to Weapons of the Geek," S95. This remains true today, and one can hear a powerful expression of it in Simona Levi's marvelous essay; see Simona Levi, "Working Notes for a R-evolution," *Uprising 13/13* (blog), March 12, 2018, http://blogs.law.columbia.edu/uprising1313/simona-levi-working-notes-for-a-r-evolution/. It rings loudly in her call to "study the law, understand it, explain it in other words, make fun of it, hack it to render it useless, destroy its authority by replacing it with a positive one that will ultimately be coopted with the bad taste and time-lag that characterises the system, clearing away whatever had been there previously and leaving a blank slate."
132. Nicole Perlroth and David E. Sanger, "Cyberattacks Put Russian Fingers on the Switch at Power Plants, U.S. Says," *New York Times*, March 15, 2018, https://www.nytimes.com/2018/03/15/us/politics/russia-cyberattacks.html.

133. Delmas, *A Duty to Resist*, 100; 21; see also Candice Delmas, "The Ethics of Government Whistleblowing," *Social Theory and Practice* 41, no. 1 (January 2015): 101; David Lyons, *Confronting Injustice: Moral History and Political Theory* (Oxford: Oxford University Press, 2013).
134. William E. Scheuerman, "Whistleblowing as Civil Disobedience: The Case of Edward Snowden," *Philosophy and Social Criticism*, 40, 7 (2014): 609–628; see also Scheuerman, *Civil Disobedience*.
135. For background on Edward Snowden, see Glenn Greenwald, *No Place to Hide: Edward Snowden, the NSA, and the U.S. Surveillance State* (New York: Metropolitan, 2014); and Luke Harding, *The Snowden Files: The Inside Story of the World's Most Wanted Man* (New York: Vintage, 2014). Regarding Manning, see Chase Madar, *The Passion of Bradley Manning: The Story Behind the Wikileaks Whistleblower* (New York: Verso, 2013); Lida Maxwell, *Insurgent Truth: Chelsea Manning and the Politics of Outsider Truth-Telling* (New York: Oxford University Press, 2019).
136. Maxwell, *Insurgent Truth*; Charleyne Biondi, "La dissidence civique dans l'impasse démocratique: Le cas Edward Snowden," Masters thesis, Institut d'études politiques, Paris, 2015; John Rajchman, "Workshop with John Rajchman: 'Citizen Four: Edward Snowden and the Question of Truth and Power,'" Columbia Center for Contemporary Critical Thought, April 10, 2015, https://www.youtube.com/watch?v=ZIvHzwXtz5Y; Scheuerman, "Whistleblowing as Civil Disobedience"; Scheuerman, *Civil Disobedience*; Delmas, *A Duty to Resist*, 21, 99–100; Delmas, "The Ethics of Government Whistleblowing," 77–105.
137. Sara Ahmed, *Living a Feminist Life* (Durham, NC: Duke University Press, 2017); Sara Ahmed, *The Promise of Happiness* (Durham, NC: Duke University Press, 2010); Sara Ahmed, *Willful Subjects* (Durham, NC: Duke University Press, 2014).
138. Ahmed subtly shows the way in which the experience of the feminist killjoy at the same time "constitutes" the family as an otherwise civil place. She writes that "to make her the cause of a tension is another way of preserving the illusion that without her, the family would be civil. I think those of us who have been killjoys around family tables probably know this; how useful we are as containers of incivility and discord." Ahmed, *Living a Feminist Life*, 37–38.
139. Ahmed, *Living a Feminist Life*, 37.
140. Ahmed, *Living a Feminist Life*, 39; 39.
141. Ahmed, *Living a Feminist Life*, 71; 73.
142. Ahmed, *Living a Feminist Life*, 85; 85; 88; 160.
143. Ahmed, *Living a Feminist Life*, 16.
144. Ahmed, *Living a Feminist Life*, 15; 270n8. (Her note 8 on page 270 is worth reading closely; Ahmed is cognizant of the bluntness of her policy, but in the end, she suggests that she may need to be blunt "in order to break a long-standing habit." Ahmed, *Living a Feminist Life*, 270n8.)
145. Ahmed, *Living a Feminist Life*, 2.
146. Ahmed, *Living a Feminist Life*, 23; 5; 5.
147. Ahmed, *Living a Feminist Life*, 6.
148. Ahmed, *Living a Feminist Life*, 8; 8.
149. Ahmed, *Living a Feminist Life*, 162; 173; 177.
150. Ahmed, *Living a Feminist Life*, 190.
151. Ahmed, *Living a Feminist Life*, 196; 197.
152. Ahmed, *Living a Feminist Life*, 213; 214–215.
153. Ahmed, *Living a Feminist Life*, 214.
154. Ahmed, *Living a Feminist Life*, 240-241; 247; 249.
155. Ahmed, *Living a Feminist Life*, 257; 261; 262; 263–264; 258; 250; 265.
156. Ahmed, *Living a Feminist Life*, 267.
157. Hakim Bey, *The Temporary Autonomous Zone* (New York: Autonomedia, 1985), 99–100. See also Mauvaise Troupe Collective, *The Zad and NoTAV: Territorial Struggles and the Making of a New Political Intelligence*, trans. Kristin Ross (New York: Verso, 2018).

158. Bey, *The Temporary Autonomous Zone*, 100.
159. Bey, *The Temporary Autonomous Zone*, 97; 132; 132.
160. Bey, *The Temporary Autonomous Zone*, 99.
161. Bey, *The Temporary Autonomous Zone*, 97.
162. For essays and exchanges among some of these critical theorists on the idea of the common, see Bernard E. Harcourt et al., "Praxis 5/13: The Common," public seminar, Columbia University, December 5, 2018, New York, http://blogs.law.columbia.edu/praxis1313/5-13/; and Bernard E. Harcourt et al., "Praxis 8/13: The Idea of Communism," public seminar, Columbia University, January 23, 2019, New York, http://blogs.law.columbia.edu/praxis1313/8-13/.
163. Michael Hardt and Antonio Negri, *Commonwealth* (Cambridge, MA: The Belknap Press of Harvard University Press, 2011), 6; 4; 5; 5.
164. Hardt and Negri, *Commonwealth*, 8.
165. Hardt and Negri, *Assembly*, 97; 91; 91, 97.
166. Hardt and Negri, *Assembly*, 99.
167. Hardt and Negri, *Assembly*, 87–89.
168. Étienne Balibar, "Law, Property, Politics: A Rejoinder to Mikhaïl Xifaras' 'The Role of Critical Theory,'" *Praxis 13/13* (blog), December 3, 2018, http://blogs.law.columbia.edu/praxis1313/etienne-balibar-law-property-politics/.
169. Camille Robcis, "Radical Psychiatry, Institutional Analysis, and the Commons," *Praxis 13/13* (blog), December 4, 2018, http://blogs.law.columbia.edu/praxis1313/camille-robcis-radical-psychiatry-institutional-analysis-and-the-commons/.
170. Mikhaïl Xifaras, "The Role of the Law in Critical Theory," *Praxis 13/13* (blog), December 2, 2018, http://blogs.law.columbia.edu/praxis1313/mikhail-xifaras-the-role-of-the-law-in-critical-theory-the-role-of-property-in-the-commons/.
171. Costas Douzinas and Slavoj Žižek, eds., *The Idea of Communism*, vol. 1 (New York: Verso, 2010), back cover catalogue copy.
172. Slavoj Žižek, "How to Begin from the Beginning," in *The Idea of Communism*, vol. 1, ed. Slavoj Žižek and Costas Douzinas (New York: Verso, 2010), 210.
173. Alain Badiou, *The Meaning of Sarkozy*, trans. David Fernbach (London: Verso, 2008), quoted in Žižek, "How to Begin from the Beginning," 211.
174. Peter Hallward, "Communism of the Intellect, Communism of the Will," in *The Idea of Communism*, vol. 1, ed. Costas Douzinas and Slavoj Žižek (New York: Verso, 2010): 111.
175. Note that Žižek uses the plural term, "the commons," in this work, whereas Hardt and Negri use the singular to differentiate their idea from the more traditional idea of the town commons.
176. Žižek, "How to Begin from the Beginning," 213; 213. In this regard, we have become *homo sacer*, Žižek tells us, borrowing here from Agamben. Also see Žižek, "How to Begin from the Beginning," 214.
177. Žižek, "How to Begin from the Beginning," 224.
178. Žižek, "How to Begin from the Beginning," 214.
179. And he adds: "Identity politics acquires a specific form in each of the three fractions: postmodern multicultural identity politics in the intellectual class, regressive populist fundamentalism in the working class, half-illegal initiatic groups (criminal gangs, religious sects, etc.) among the outcasts. What they all share is recourse to a particular identity as a substitute for the missing universal public space." Žižek, "How to Begin from the Beginning," 226.
180. Žižek, "How to Begin from the Beginning," 226. In this regard, for both Žižek and Badiou—and I might add myself, though I use the term *liberal legalism* rather than democracy—the real hindrance to revolutionary transformation is the illusion of democratic reform: "It is the 'democratic illusion,' the acceptance of democratic mechanisms as providing the only framework for all possible change,

which prevents any radical transformation of society. In this precise sense, Badiou was right in his apparently weird claim: 'Today, the enemy is not called Empire or Capital. It's called Democracy.' It is the 'democratic illusion,' the acceptance of democratic mechanisms as the ultimate frame of every change, that prevents the radical transformation of capitalist relations." Slavoj Žižek, "No Way Out? Communism in the New Century," in *The Idea of Communism*, vol. 3: *The Seoul Conference*, ed. Alex Taek-Gwang Lee and Slavoj Žižek (New York: Verso, 2016), 243.

181. Žižek, "How to Begin from the Beginning," 213; 215; 214; 214.
182. Étienne Balibar, "Communism as Commitment, Imagination, and Politics," in *The New York Conference*, vol. 2 of *The Idea of Communism*, ed. Slavoj Žižek (New York: Verso, 2013), 14.
183. Rosalind Morris, "Unpopular Politics: The Collective, the Communist, and the Popular in Recent Thai History," in *The Seoul Conference*, vol. 3 of *The Idea of Communism*, ed. Alex Taek-Gwang Lee and Slavoj Žižek (New York: Verso, 2016), 239.
184. Balibar, "Communism as Commitment, Imagination, and Politics," 14. He comes back to this notion of "de-organizing" rather than "organizing," emphasizing in a lengthy passage at the end of his essay: "But they are not building any organization of their own, not even an 'invisible' one—they are, rather, *de-organizing the existing organizations*, the very organizations in which they participate: not in the sense of undermining them from the inside, or betraying their friends and comrades in the middle of the battles, but in the sense of questioning the validity of the distances and incompatibilities (very real, most of the time) between different types of struggles and movements. In that sense they essentially perform a 'negative' function in the form of a very positive commitment." Balibar, "Communism as Commitment, Imagination, and Politics," 34. The negative dialectics of Adorno seem to loom over this passage.
185. Xifaras, "The Role of the Law in Critical Theory."
186. Bernard E. Harcourt, *The Counterrevolution: How Our Government Went to War Against Its Own Citizens* (New York: Basic Books, 2018), 213-232.
187. Xifaras, "The Role of the Law in Critical Theory."
188. Hardt and Negri, *Commonwealth*, 8.
189. Balibar, "Law, Property, Politics," 4.
190. Axel Honneth, *The Idea of Socialism: Towards a Renewal* (Cambridge: Polity, 2017), 2.
191. Honneth, *The Idea of Socialism*, 5; 6.
192. Honneth, *The Idea of Socialism*, 9; 12.
193. Honneth, *The Idea of Socialism*, 26; 26.
194. Honneth, *The Idea of Socialism*, 33; 34; 36; 37.
195. Honneth, *The Idea of Socialism*, 41–42.
196. Honneth, *The Idea of Socialism*, 42; 45; 46.
197. Honneth, *The Idea of Socialism*, 49.
198. See, e.g., Honneth, *The Idea of Socialism*, 57; 58; 59; 63.
199. Honneth, *The Idea of Socialism*, 72; 73; 73.
200. Honneth, *The Idea of Socialism*, 5; 30.
201. His discussion on that topic can be found mostly in Honneth, *The Idea of Socialism*, 69–71.
202. Ira Katznelson, *Fear Itself: The New Deal and the Origins of Our Time* (New York: Norton, 2013).
203. Jack Greenberg, *Litigation for Social Change: Methods, Limits, and Role in Democracy* (New York: Association of the Bar of the City of New York, 1974).
204. Greenberg, *Litigation for Social Change*, 10.
205. Quoted in Greenberg, *Litigation for Social Change*, 40.
206. *Loving v. Virginia*, 87 S.Ct. 1817 (1967); *Obergefell v. Hodges*, 135 S. Ct. 2584 (2015).
207. Gerald N. Rosenberg, *The Hollow Hope: Can Courts Bring About Social Change?* (Chicago: University of Chicago Press, 1991).

208. Paul Butler, "Gideon's Muted Trumpet," *New York Times*, March 17, 2013, https://www.nytimes.com/2013/03/18/opinion/gideons-muted-trumpet.html.
209. Carol S. Steiker and Jordan M. Steiker, "Sober Second Thoughts," *Harvard Law Review* 109, no. 2 (December 1995): 357–438; Carol S. Steiker and Jordan M. Steiker, *Courting Death* (Cambridge, MA: Harvard University Press, 2016).
210. The Invisible Committee, *The Coming Insurrection* (Cambridge, MA: MIT Press (Semiotext(e)/Intervention), 2009), (I am using the online edition, the Invisible Committee, *The Coming Insurrection* (The Anarchist Library, 2009), https://theanarchistlibrary.org/library/comite-invisible-the-coming-insurrection, with its pagination), 100; 100; 104; 106; 115; 117; 125; 130; 133; 136.
211. The Invisible Committee, *The Coming Insurrection*, 134.
212. The Invisible Committee, *Now* (Cambridge, MA: MIT Press, 2009), 8; 22.
213. So, for instance, the chapters address the notion of "the state of exception" in different ways. In the first chapter, "Tomorrow Is Cancelled," the Committee takes the view that the state of exception is portrayed by the state as being the rule of law—a kind of Orwellian doublespeak. "The state of emergency is the rule of law," the Committee writes (The Invisible Committee, *Now*, 10), corroborating the notion of a "state of legality" that I develop in chapter 12 of *The Counterrevolution*. Chapter 2, "50 Nuances of Breakage," picks up on this theme—suggesting that "the state of exception already reigned *in the form of the Law*" (The Invisible Committee, *Now*, 37)—but the Committee then goes on to argue that the state of exception is what we expected and is not worth protesting; instead, it must fuel a state of exception on the other side, on the side of protest. (This was Walter Benjamin's point in response to Carl Schmitt: rather than contest the state of exception, deploy it against fascism. See Walter Benjamin, "Theses on the Philosophy of History," in *Illuminations*, ed. Hannah Arendt, 253–265 (New York: Schocken, 1968), 257) But in chapter 6, "Everyone Hates the Police," the Committee suggests that the police *is* the expression of the state of exception—focusing in on the police in their daily operation (The Invisible Committee, *Now*, 117). These represent different angles on the state of exception that reflect not incoherence, but different registers and theoretical styles.
214. The Invisible Committee, *Now*, 76.
215. The Committee associates the opposite conception, constituent power, fairly or unfairly, most often with the work of Antonio Negri. The Invisible Committee, *Now*, 77, 83, 85.
216. The Invisible Committee, *Now*, 79.
217. The Invisible Committee, *Now*, 80; 79.
218. The Invisible Committee, *Now*, 81.
219. The Invisible Committee, *Now*, 81.
220. The Invisible Committee, *Now*, 78; 86.
221. The Invisible Committee, *Now*, 18; 25; 32; 13.
222. The Invisible Committee, *Now*, 13; 14; 14; 14; 15.
223. The Invisible Committee, *Now*, 87; 88; 89.
224. The Invisible Committee, *Now*, 45; 45.
225. The Invisible Committee, *Now*, 49; 54; 55; 56; 57.
226. The Invisible Committee, *Now*, 131; 132; 133; 154.
227. The Invisible Committee, *Now*, 8; 9.
228. The Invisible Committee, *Now*, 13.
229. The Invisible Committee, *Now*, 34–36. A PhD student in France, Ahlem Hannachi, wrote her dissertation on Jakobs at the Université Paris I Panthéon in 2014—but Jakobs is not that well known outside of specialized penal law circles. "*Soutenance de thèse de doctorat le 17 décembre 2014 à l'Université Panthéon-Sorbonne Paris 1*," Ahlem Hannachi-Docteur en droit (blog), June 8, 2015, http://hannachiahlemlaw.canalblog.com/archives/2015/06/08/32182838.html.

230. The Invisible Committee, *Now*, 17; 18.
231. The Invisible Committee, *Now*, 11; 22; 25, 121; 51; 115–116; 116; 25; 51; 52.
232. Joshua Clover, *Riot. Strike. Riot.* (New York: Verso, 2016), 1.
233. Delmas, *A Duty to Resist*, 70.
234. The Invisible Committee, *Now*, 17.
235. The Invisible Committee, *Now*, 131; 132.
236. The Invisible Committee, *Now*, 132–133.
237. Stefano Harney and Fred Moten, *The Undercommons: Fugitive Planning & Black Study* (Wivenhoe, UK: Minor Compositions, 2013), 31; 30; 41.
238. Jack Halberstam, "The Wild Beyond: With and for the Undercommons," introduction to Harney and Moten, *The Undercommons*, 10.
239. Harney and Moten, *The Undercommons*, 105.
240. Harney and Moten, *The Undercommons*, 42.
241. Halberstam, "The Wild Beyond," 6.
242. The Invisible Committee, *Now*, 81; 80–81; 81.
243. Harney and Moten, *The Undercommons*, 42.
244. Bernard E. Harcourt, "Foreword to the Supreme Court Review: 'You Are Entering a Gay and Lesbian-Free Zone': On the Radical Dissents of Justice Scalia and Other (Post-) Queers [Raising Questions about *Lawrence*, Sex Wars, and the Criminal Law]," *Journal of Criminal Law and Criminology* 94, no. 3 (2004): 503–549.
245. Harney and Moten, *The Undercommons*, 32.
246. Harney and Moten, *The Undercommons*, 39.
247. Banu Bargu, *Starve and Immolate: The Politics of Human Weapons* (New York: Columbia University Press, 2014), 337.
248. Eliza Egret, "Turkey Takes a Prisoner's Body and Buries It in the Middle of the Night," *theCanary*, March 18, 2019, https://www.thecanary.co/global/world-analysis/2019/03/18/turkey-takes-a-prisoners-body-and-buries-it-in-the-middle-of-the-night/.
249. Bargu, *Starve and Immolate*, 14–15.
250. Bargu, *Starve and Immolate*, 7; 350.
251. Bruno Latour, *Down to Earth: Politics in the New Climatic Regime* (Cambridge: Polity, 2018), 101; 104; 101.
252. Latour, *Down to Earth*, 100; 100–101; 106.
253. Robin D. G. Kelley, "Coates and West in Jackson," *Boston Review*, December 22, 2017, http://bostonreview.net/race/robin-d-g-kelley-coates-and-west-jackson.
254. Talal Asad, "Thinking About Tradition, Religion, and Politics in Egypt Today," *Critical Inquiry* 42 no. 1, 166–214 (Autumn 2015), 212; see also Talal Asad, "The Limits of Religious Criticism in the Middle East," in Talal Asad, *Genealogies of Religion: Discipline and Reasons of Power in Christianity and Islam* (Baltimore and London: John Hopkins University, 1993).
255. Asad, "Thinking About Tradition, Religion, and Politics in Egypt Today," 206.
256. Asad, "Thinking About Tradition, Religion, and Politics in Egypt Today," 212.
257. Amy Allen, *The End of Progress: Decolonizing the Normative Foundations of Critical Theory* (New York: Columbia University Press, 2016), xii.
258. Seyla Benhabib, "Critique and Emancipation: Comments Prepared for the *Emanzipation Conference*" (lecture, Humboldt-Universität zu Berlin, May 25, 2018; draft on file with author), 6.
259. Butler, *Notes Toward a Performative Theory of Assembly*, 123–124.
260. Dick Howard, "An Interview with C. Castoriadis," *Telos* 23 (1975): 134.

16. The New Space of Critical Praxis

1. William of Ockham, *Breviloquium de principatu tyrannico*, in *Opera Politica*, vol. 4, ed. Hilary Seton Offler (Oxford: Oxford University Press, 1997), bk. 1, chap. 4, 102 ("*Admonendi sunt subditi, ne plus quam expedit sint subiecti*"). For a discussion of my translation of this passage, see Bernard E. Harcourt, *The Counterrevolution: How Our Government Went to War Against Its Own Citizens* (New York: Basic Books, 2018), 298 n.2.
2. Cornel West, quoted in Candice Delmas, *A Duty to Resist: When Disobedience Should Be Uncivil* (New York: Oxford University Press, 2018), 244; West adds that "they saved our lives, actually."
3. Delmas, *A Duty to Resist*, 245–246.
4. Michel Foucault, "Sur la justice populaire. Débat avec les Maos," in *Dits et Écrits*, ed. Daniel Defert, François Ewald, and Jacques Lagrange, vol. 2: *1970–1975* (Paris: Gallimard, 1994), 340–369.
5. Philippe Artières, Laurent Quéro, and Michelle Zancarini-Fournel, eds., *Le Groupe d'information sur les prisons: Archives d'une lutte 1970–1972* (Paris: Éditions de l'IMEC, 2003), 30, 47 ; Kalinka Courtois, in a brilliant PhD dissertation titled "The 'Groupe d'information sur les prisons': French Intellectuals and Activism Post May '68" (defended at Columbia University on December 9, 2019), excavates the voices and names of the many GIP members who have been forgotten over time, including Edith Rose, Danielle Rancière, Hélène Cixous, Ariane Mnouchkine, Jean Genet, and others.
6. GIP, "Manifeste du GIP."
7. GIP, "Le GIP vient de lancer sa première enquête" (1971), in *Groupe d'information sur les prisons: Archives d'une lutte 1970–1972*, 52: "*Il s'agit de laisser la parole à ceux qui ont une expérience de la prison. Non pas qu'ils aient besoin qu'on les aide à 'prendre conscience': la conscience de l'oppression est là parfaitement claire, sachant bien qui est l'ennemi. Mais le système actuel lui refuse les moyens de se formuler, de s'organiser.*"
8. See, e.g., GIP, "Déclaration des emprisonnés politiques en grève de la faim" (1970), in *Groupe d'information sur les prisons: Archives d'une lutte 1970–1972*, 31.
9. Philippe Artières, Laurent Quéro, and Michelle Zancarini-Fournel, "Genèse du GIP," in *Groupe d'information sur les prisons: Archives d'une lutte 1970–1972*, 28.
10. Daniel Defert, *Une vie politique. Entretiens avec Philippe Artières et Eric Favereau, avec la collaboration de Joséphine Gross* (Paris: Le Seuil, 2014), 56.
11. Michel Foucault, *Leçons sur la volonté de savoir. Cours au Collège de France (1970–1971)*, ed. Daniel Defert (Paris: Gallimard/Seuil, 2011), 4.
12. Colin Koopman elegantly traces this influence on Foucault's methodology in his chapter, "Conduct and Power: Foucault's Methodological Expansions in 1971," in *Active Intolerance: Michel Foucault, the Prisons Information Group, and the Future of Abolition*, ed. Perry Zurn and Andrew Dilts (New York: Palgrave Macmillan, 2016), 59–74; see also the excellent pieces by Ladelle McWhorter, Lynn Huffer, Perry Zurn, and the other contributors to that volume.
13. Defert, *Une Vie politique*, 36–76.
14. See, e.g., Audrey Kiéfer, *Michel Foucault: Le GIP, l'histoire et l'action* (philosophy thesis, Université de Picardie Jules Verne d'Amiens, France, 2006), 169–172; Artières, Quéro, and Zancarini-Fournel, eds., *Le Groupe d'information sur les prisons: Archives d'une lutte 1970–1972*; *La Révolte de la prison de Nancy. 15 January 1972. Documents et propos de Michel Foucault, Jean-Paul Sartre et de militants du Groupe d'information sur les prisons* (Paris: Le Point du jour, 2013); *Active Intolerance: Michel Foucault, the Prisons Information Group, and the Future of Abolition*, ed. Perry Zurn and Andrew Dilts; *Carceral Notebooks, Volume 12 (2016): Challenging the Punitive Society*, Perry Zurn and Andrew Dilts, special eds. (New York: U.S. Lithograph, 2016); Courtois, "The 'Groupe d'information sur les prisons: French Intellectuals and Activism Post May '68' ".
15. *Sur les toits*, directed by Nicolas Drolc (Nancy, France: Les Films Furax, 2014).

16. Michel Foucault, *Discipline and Punish: The Birth of the Prison*, trans. Alan Sheridan (New York: Vintage Books, 1979), 30; Michel Foucault, *Surveiller et Punir*, ed. Bernard E. Harcourt, in *Michel Foucault Oeuvres*, vol. 2, ed. Frédéric Gros (Paris: Gallimard/La Pléiade, 2015), 291 ("*Que les punitions en général et que la prison relèvent d'une technologie politique du corps, c'est peut-être moins l'histoire qui me l'a enseigné que le présent. Au cours de ces dernières années, des révoltes de prison se sont produites un peu partout dans le monde.*")
17. J. K. Simon, "Michel Foucault on Attica: An Interview" (translated and edited from a taped conversation), *Social Justice* 18, no. 3 (1991): 26 (reprinted from *Telos*, no. 19, Spring 1974); translated into French by F. Durand-Bogaert as Michel Foucault, "À propos de la prison d'Attica" (interview with J. K. Simon), in vol. 2: *1970–1975* of *Dits et Écrits*, ed. Daniel Defert, François Ewald, and Jacques Lagrange (Paris: Gallimard, 1994), no. 137, 526; or in vol. 1: *1954–1975* of *Dits et Écrits*, ed. Daniel Defert, François Ewald, and Jacques Lagrange (Paris: Gallimard/Quarto, 2001), 1394.
18. Simon, "Michel Foucault on Attica," 28; in "À propos de la prison d'Attica," 528/1396.
19. See *La Révolte de la prison de Nancy*. Foucault gave his unreserved support for political prisoners and common-law prisoners, without making any distinction between them. As he elaborated the notion of "civil war," the very distinction—political prisoner and common-law prisoner—no longer had any sense. This is an important aspect, both theoretical and practical, of Foucault's intervention at this time. See Foucault, "Sur la justice populaire." Also see Michel Foucault, "On Popular Justice," in *Power/Knowledge: Selected Interviews and Other Writings*, trans. John Mepham (New York: Pantheon, 1980).
20. *La Révolte de la prison de Nancy*, 19 (reproduction of written manuscript).
21. Michel Foucault, "Lecture of 28 February 1973," in *The Punitive Society: Lectures at the Collège de France 1972–1973*, ed. Bernard E. Harcourt, trans. Graham Burchell (New York: Picador, 2015), 164–165.
22. Foucault, *The Punitive Society*, 165, note * (appendix to lecture 9, first folio).
23. Gilles Deleuze, "Écrivain non: Un nouveau cartographe," *Critique* 343 (December 1975): 1212.
24. Michel Foucault, "Prisons et asiles dans le mécanisme du pouvoir," in vol. 1: *1954–1975* of *Dits et Écrits*, ed. Daniel Defert, François Ewald, and Jacques Lagrange (Paris: Gallimard/Quarto, 2001), 1389–1393: *"Le petit volume que je voudrais écrire sur les systèmes disciplinaires, j'aimerais qu'il puisse servir à un éducateur, à un gardien, à un magistrat, à un objecteur de conscience. Je n'écris pas pour un public, j'écris pour des utilisateurs, non pas pour des lecteurs."*
25. Michel Foucault, *The Courage of Truth: The Government of Self and Others II: Lectures at the Collège de France, 1983–1984*, ed. Frederic Gros, trans. Graham Burchell (Basingstoke, UK: Palgrave Macmillan, 2011), 162–163.
26. Foucault, *The Courage of Truth*, 166.

17. Reframing the Praxis Imperative

1. "Acte IX: 84000 'gilets jaunes' dans toute la France, mobilisation en hausse," *Le Monde*, January 12, 2019, https://www.lemonde.fr/societe/article/2019/01/12/acte-ix-des-gilets-jaunes-attendus-a-bourges-paris-et-dans-toute-la-france_5408170_3224.html.
2. Étienne Balibar, "Gilets jaunes: Le sens du face à face," *Praxis 13/13* (blog), January 12, 2019, http://blogs.law.columbia.edu/praxis1313/etienne-balibar-gilets-jaunes-le-sens-du-face-a-face/; Antonio Negri, "Gilets jaunes: Un contropotere?" *Praxis 13/13* (blog), January 11, 2019, http://blogs.law.columbia.edu/praxis1313/antonio-negri-gilets-jaunes-un-contropotere/.
3. Clémence Bauduin, "'Gilets Jaunes': 72 percent des Français soutiennent le mouvement après le 1er décembre," December 3, 2018, https://www.rtl.fr/actu/debats-societe/gilets-jaunes-pres-de-3-francais-sur-4-soutiennent-le-mouvement-apres-le-1er-decembre-7795787626.

4. Étienne Balibar, "'Gilets jaunes': The meaning of the confrontation," *OpenDemocracy*, December 20, 2018, https://www.opendemocracy.net/can-europe-make-it/etienne-balibar/gilets-jaunes-meaning-of-confrontation.
5. Ludivine Bantigny, "*Un Événement*," *Praxis 13/13* (blog), http://blogs.law.columbia.edu/praxis1313/ludivine-bantigny-un-evenement/.
6. Antonio Negri, "Reflections on the Seventh Round of the *Gilets Jaunes*," *EuroNomade*, January 5, 2019, http://www.euronomade.info/?p=11480.
7. Balibar, " 'Gilets jaunes': The meaning of the confrontation."
8. Étienne Balibar, *Libre parole* (Paris: Galilée, 2018), 112.
9. Negri, "Reflections on the Seventh Round of the *Gilets Jaunes*."
10. Bernard E. Harcourt, "On the American Paradox of *Laissez Faire* and Mass Incarceration," *Harvard Law Review Forum* 125, no. 54 (2012): 54–68, https://harvardlawreview.org/2012/03/on-the-american-paradox-of-laissez-faire-and-mass-incarceration/.
11. Angelique Chrisafis, "€114,000 Raised for Boxer Who Punched Police at Gilets Jaunes Protest," *The Guardian*, January 8, 2019, https://www.theguardian.com/world/2019/jan/08/114000-euros-raised-french-boxer-clash-police-gilets-jaunes-protest.
12. ZAD Média News, "Christophe Dettinger," January 8, 2019, video, https://youtu.be/en57Ks6_bFU (my translation). The original French words are:

    Chers amis gilets jaunes,

    Voilà, je me présente. Je m'appelle Christophe. . . . Je voulais vous présenter les choses comme je les sens.

    J'ai participé aux huit actes. . . . J'ai fait tous les manifestations du samedi sur Paris.

    J'ai vu la répression. J'ai vu la police nous gazer. J'ai vu la police faire mal à des gens avec des flashballs. J'ai vu des gens blessés. J'ai vu des retraités se faire gazer.

    Moi, je suis un citoyen normal. Je travaille. J'arrive à finir mes fins de mois, mais c'est compliqué.

    Mais je manifeste pour les retraités, le futur de mes enfants, les femmes célibataires . . .

    Je suis un gilet jaune. J'ai la colère du people qui est en moi.

    Je vois tous ces présidents, je vois tous ces ministres, je vois tout l'État se gaver, se pomper. Ils ne sont même pas capables de montrer l'exemple. Ils ne montrent pas l'exemple. Ils se gavent sur notre dos. C'est toujours nous les petits qui payons.

    Je me sens concerné parce que je suis français. Je suis fier d'être français. Je ne suis pas d'extrême gauche, je ne suis pas d'extrême droite. Je suis un citoyen lambda. Je suis un français. J'aime mon pays. J'aime ma patrie. J'aime tout.

    See also Antoine Peillon, *Coeur de boxeur. Le vrai combat de Christophe Dettinger* (Paris: Les liens qui libèrent, 2019).
13. Antonio Negri, "French Insurrection," *Verso* (blog), December 8, 2018, https://www.versobooks.com/blogs/4158-french-insurrection.
14. Bernard E. Harcourt, "Political Disobedience," in *Occupy: Three Inquiries in Disobedience*, ed. W. J. T. Mitchell, Bernard E. Harcourt, and Michael Taussig, 45–91 (Chicago: University of Chicago Press, 2013).
15. AFP, "*À Paris, dans les pas des milliers de 'gilets jaunes' entre Bercy et l'Étoile*," LaCroix, January 12, 2019, https://www.la-croix.com/France/A-Paris-pas-milliers-gilets-jaunes-entre-Bercy-Etoile-2019-01-12-1300994935.
16. Bernard E. Harcourt, "Welcome, Nato, to Chicago's Police State," *The Guardian*, May 20, 2012, https://www.theguardian.com/commentisfree/cifamerica/2012/may/20/welcome-nato-chicago-police-state.

17. Negri, "Reflections on the Seventh Round of the *Gilets Jaunes*."
18. As we walked out together, I learned that Vincent Jarry was about to publish a book. See Vincent Jarry, *La démocratie des murmures* (Paris: Éditions Excès, 2019).
19. Judith Butler, *Notes Toward A Performative Theory of Assembly* (Cambridge, MA: Harvard University Press, 2015), 156–157.
20. Gaétan Supertino, "'Gilets Jaunes': Les 'portes-paroles' se suivent et ne se ressemblent pas," *Europe1*, December 3, 2018, https://www.europe1.fr/politique/gilets-jaunes-les-porte-parole-se-suivent-et-ne-se-ressemblent-pas-3812957.
21. Naturally, this raises myriad questions about meaning, interpretation, and representation, especially about the giving of meaning or the very possibility of giving meaning, and about linguistic structuralism, who determines meaning, and how meaning emerges—important questions that would require lengthier treatment. There is much more to say, of course, but that should not stop us in the urgency of this political moment in France. I earlier addressed many of these questions through a *lecture croisée* of Sartre, Lévi-Strauss, Bourdieu, and Butler in Bernard E. Harcourt, *Language of the Gun: Youth, Crime, and Public Policy* (Chicago: University of Chicago Press, 2006), some of which I took up again in an essay titled "An Answer to the Question: 'What Is Post-Structuralism?,'" *Public Law and Legal Theory Working Paper Series* no. 156 (2007), https://ssrn.com/abstract=970348.
22. According to two surveys conducted by YouGov in 2016, "12 percent of people who voted in the primary and reported voting for Sanders also voted in November and reported voting for Trump." The RAND Presidential Election Panel Survey, on the other hand, concluded, "Among voters who reported supporting Sanders as of March 2016, 6 percent then reported voting for Trump in November." Voters switching parties in the general election after their candidate loses in the primaries is not a uniquely Sanders/Trump phenomenon, though. To put these Sanders/Trump voter percentages in perspective, "Sanders supporters were about as likely to vote for Trump as Rubio's supporters were to vote for Clinton, and far less likely than Kasich supporters were to vote for Clinton." John Sides, "Did Enough Bernie Sanders Supporters Vote for Trump to Cost Clinton the Election?" *Washington Post*, August 24, 2017, https://www.washingtonpost.com/news/monkey-cage/wp/2017/08/24/did-enough-bernie-sanders-supporters-vote-for-trump-to-cost-clinton-the-election/.
23. Chantal Mouffe, *For a Left Populism* (New York: Verso, 2018), 22.
24. What are the odds of getting the exact same head count two weeks in a row? And why is it 84,000 both times, not rounded up to 85,000? The Yellow Vest movement began to contest those numbers, but the media was surprisingly silent and, oddly, did not offer any independent count.
25. "Les gilets jaunes restent mobilisés après le lancement du débat national," *Le Monde*, January 19, 2019, https://www.lemonde.fr/societe/article/2019/01/19/a-paris-les-gilets-jaunes-s-elancent-des-invalides-en-denoncant-les-violences-policieres_5411608_3224.html.
26. Donna J. Haraway, "Tentacular Thinking," Chapter 2, in Donna J. Haraway, *Staying with the Trouble: Making Kin in the Chthulucene* (Durham, NC: Duke University Press, 2016), 47.

18. What More Am I To Do?

1. Bruno Latour, "Why Has Critique Run Out of Steam? From Matters of Fact to Matters of Concern," *Critical Inquiry* 30, no. 2 (2004): 225–248.
2. Bryan Stevenson and Ruth Friedman, "Deliberate Indifference: Judicial Tolerance of Racial Bias in Criminal Justice," *Washington and Lee Law Review* 51, no. 2 (Spring 1994): 509–527 ("Albert Jefferson faced three all-white juries when the state used a total of twenty-four strikes to eliminate every black person summoned for service on each occasion"). See also Transcript of Postconviction Rec. at 39–56, *Jefferson v. State*, CC-8-87 (Chambers County Cir. Ct. Jan. 25, 1989).

3. Carol S. Steiker and Jordan M. Steiker, "Sober Second Thoughts: Reflections on Two Decades of Constitutional Regulation of Capital Punishment," *Harvard Law Review* 109, no. 2 (December 1995): 437; 429–430.
4. In their more recent work, *Courting Death*, Steiker and Steiker have a different take on the history and legitimacy of the death penalty as it has been carried out since 1995. Carol S. Steiker and Jordan M. Steiker, *Courting Death* (Cambridge, MA: Harvard University Press, 2016). They diagnose the same overregulation and underregulation, and argue, as they did in 1995, that "the death penalty is, perversely, both over- and underregulated." Again, they show that the jurisprudence that has been created is "at once so messy and so meaningless," Steiker and Steiker, *Courting Death*, 155. However, they take a different position on legitimation since the mid-1990s. In the first few decades, they argue, "the Court's interventions strengthened the status of the death penalty as a form of punishment in the eyes of the actors within the capital system and of the public at large." Steiker and Steiker, *Courting Death*, 156; see also 188. But all of this changed in the mid-1990s. "The legitimating effects of the death penalty, while powerful, eventually were undermined by a confluence of factors, not least of which was the discovery of numerous wrongly convicted inmates on American death rows," they write (Steiker and Steiker, *Courting Death*, 192). It is in this sense that the Supreme Court ultimately "regulated the death penalty to death" (Steiker and Steiker, *Courting Death*, 4). Instead of legitimating, it began to undermine: "constitutional regulation began to reveal some of its destabilizing potential" (Steiker and Steiker, *Courting Death*, 192). That may be a premature assessment, given the election of Donald Trump and his appointments to the Supreme Court. But in all fairness, the book was written with the expectation that Hillary Clinton would be elected president.
5. Slavoj Žižek, "How to Begin from the Beginning," in *The Idea of Communism*, vol. 1, ed. Costas Douzinas and Slavoj Žižek (New York: Verso, 2010), 217.
6. Walter Benjamin, "Critique of Violence," in *Reflections: Essays, Aphorisms, Autobiographical Writings*, ed. Peter Demetz, trans. Edmund Jephcott (New York: Schocken Books, 1978), 299.
7. Stefano Harney and Fred Moten, *The Undercommons: Fugitive Planning and Black Study* (Wivenhoe, UK: Minor Compositions, 2013), 42.
8. See Bernard E. Harcourt, *Language of the Gun: Youth, Crime, and Public Policy* (Chicago: University of Chicago Press, 2006), 124. I read *Les Mains sales* in the late 1970s, in my teens, and was so taken by it that more than twenty-five years later, I framed one of my monographs—a qualitative social scientific investigation of the meaning of gun carrying to incarcerated youths at a juvenile facility in Tucson, Arizona—through Sartre's play.
9. Jean-Paul Sartre, "L'écrivain et sa langue" (interview with Pierre Verstraeten), *Revue d'Esthétique*, vol. 18, fasc. 3–4 (July–December 1965): 306–334, 311; I also discuss this in *Language of the Gun*, 114–116.
10. Gayatri Chakravorty Spivak, "Can the Subaltern Speak?" in *Can the Subaltern Speak? Reflections on the History of an Idea*, ed. Rosalind C. Morris (New York: Columbia University Press, 2010), 62–63.
11. Audre Lorde, "The Master's Tools Will Never Dismantle the Master's House," in *Sister Outsider: Essays and Speeches by Audre Lorde* (Berkeley, CA: Crossing Press, 2007), 110–113.
12. Sara Ahmed, *Living a Feminist Life* (Durham, NC: Duke University Press, 2017), 160.
13. Jacques Derrida, *Séminaire. 1999–2000*, vol. 1 of *La peine de mort*, ed. Geoffrey Bennington, Marc Crépon, and Thomas Dutoit (Paris: Galilée, 2012), 51–52.
14. Derrida, *Séminaire*, 199; 121.
15. "The Auschwitz Album: Last Moments Before the Gas Chambers," Yad Vashem, accessed August 20, 2019, http://www.yadvashem.org/yv/en/exhibitions/album_auschwitz/last-moments.asp.
16. "The Gas Chambers," Yad Vashem, accessed August 20, 2019, www.yadvashem.org/odot_pdf/Microsoft%20Word%20-%206234.pdf.
17. Mike Cason, "Alabama AG's Office Silent on New Execution Method," Al.com, August 14, 2019, https://www.al.com/news/2019/08/alabama-ags-office-silent-on-new-execution-method.html.

18. The social science evidence is overwhelming. See *Death Penalty Sentencing: Research Indicates Pattern of Racial Disparities*, Report to Senate and House Committees on the Judiciary, prepared by the U.S. General Accounting Office, February 1990.
19. Derrida, *Séminaire*, 243–244.
20. See generally Bryan Stevenson, *Just Mercy: A Story of Justice and Redemption* (New York: Spiegel & Grau, 2014).
21. David Garland, "Penality and the Penal State," *Criminology* 51, no. 3 (2013): 483–484.
22. David Garland, *Peculiar Institution: America's Death Penalty in an Age of Abolition* (Cambridge, MA: Harvard University Press, 2012), 311; 312.
23. The Invisible Committee, *Now* (Cambridge, MA: MIT Press (Semiotext(e)), 2017), 81.
24. For Stathis Gourgouris's statement, see Bernard E. Harcourt, Judith Revel, Emmanuelle Saada, Jesús Velasco, Jackie Wang, and McKenzie Wark, "Praxis 2/13: The Invisible Committee," public seminar, Columbia University, October 03, 2018, New York, video at 1:51:50 mark, http://blogs.law.columbia.edu/praxis1313/2-13/; for his article, see Stathis Gourgouris, "Preliminary Thoughts on Left Governmentality," *Critical Times* 1, no. 1 (2018): 99–107, https://ctjournal.org/index.php/criticaltimes/article/view/14.
25. Michel Foucault, *Qu'est-ce que la critique?* ed. Henri-Paul Fruchaud and Daniele Lorenzini (Paris: Vrin, 2015), 37; 37, 38.
26. On Foucault and neoliberalism, see, e.g., Daniel Zamora, "Can We Criticize Foucault?" *Jacobin*, December 10, 2014, https://www.jacobinmag.com/2014/12/foucault-interview/.
27. Foucault, *Qu'est-ce que la critique?* 37. ("*Comment ne pas être gouverné* comme cela, *par ceux-là, au nom de ces principes-ci, en vue de tels objectifs et par le moyen de tels procédés, pas comme ça, pas pour ça, pas par eux?*")
28. The Invisible Committee, *Now*, 86; 87.
29. The Invisible Committee, *Now*, 88.
30. *The Urban Dictionary*, s.v. "biglaw," last modified October 26, 2009, https://www.urbandictionary.com/define.php?term=biglaw.
31. Michael Hardt and Antonio Negri, *Commonwealth* (Cambridge, MA: The Belknap Press of Harvard University Press, 2011), 8.
32. Étienne Balibar, "Law, Property, Politics: A Rejoinder to Mikhaïl Xifaras' 'The Role of Critical Theory,'" *Praxis 13/13* (blog), December 3, 2018, http://blogs.law.columbia.edu/praxis1313/etienne-balibar-law-property-politics/, 6.
33. Mikhaïl Xifaras, "The Role of the Law in Critical Theory," *Praxis 13/13* (blog), December 2, 2018, http://blogs.law.columbia.edu/praxis1313/mikhail-xifaras-the-role-of-the-law-in-critical-theory-the-role-of-property-in-the-commons/, draft at 31 (on file with author), 37 ("*Hâtons-nous de rendre la critique (interne) du droit populaire.*").
34. Michael Hardt and Antonio Negri, *Assembly* (New York: Oxford University Press, 2017), 133, xx, 39, 69, 70.
35. François Mitterrand, quoted in Robert Badinter, *L'Abolition* (Paris: Fayard, 2000), 230.
36. Foucault, *The Punitive Society*, 272–273.
37. Hardt and Negri, *Assembly*, 71.
38. Victor Hugo, *Écrits sur la peine de mort* (Arles, France: Actes Sud, 2002), 186–187, quoted in Derrida, *Séminaire. La peine de mort*, 153.
39. Jeffrey M. Jones, "U.S. Death Penalty Support Lowest Since 1972," *Gallup*, October 26, 2017, https://news.gallup.com/poll/221030/death-penalty-support-lowest-1972.aspx; "2018 Pew Poll Finds Uptick in Death Penalty Support, Though Still Near Historic Lows," Death Penalty Information Center, https://deathpenaltyinfo.org/facts-and-research/public-opinion-polls/national-polls-and-studies.
40. Lawrence Sherman, "Trust and Confidence in Criminal Justice," *National Institute of Justice Journal* 248 (2002): 22–31.

41. Judith Butler, *Notes Toward a Performative Theory of Assembly* (Cambridge, MA: Harvard University Press, 2015), 153.
42. Butler, *Notes Toward a Performative Theory of Assembly*, 156; 156.
43. Butler, *Notes Toward a Performative Theory of Assembly*, 173.
44. Chantal Mouffe and Ernesto Laclau, *Hegemony and Socialist Strategy* (New York: Verso, 1986).
45. Butler, *Notes Toward a Performative Theory of Assembly*, 7; 16; 18.
46. Butler, *Notes Toward a Performative Theory of Assembly*, 165.
47. Allegra McLeod, "Law, Critique, and the Undercommons," in *A Time for Critique*, ed. Didier Fassin and Bernard E. Harcourt (New York: Columbia University Press, 2019), 252–270.
48. Shaila Dewan, "Inside America's Black Box: A Rare Look at the Violence of Incarceration," *New York Times*, March 30, 2019, https://www.nytimes.com/2019/03/30/us/inside-americas-black-box.html.

19. Crisis, Critique, Praxis

1. So, for several years, overlapping the open-access publication of the first edition of this manuscript, I invited other critical thinkers to concretely say what they believed was to be done in these times of acute crisis. Bernard E. Harcourt, *Critique & Praxis: A First Draft* (New York: Columbia Center for Contemporary Critical Thought, 2018), http://harcourt.praxis.law.columbia.edu/.
2. Bruno Latour, *Down to Earth: Politics in the New Climatic Regime* (Cambridge: Polity, 2018); Donna J. Haraway, *Staying with the Trouble: Making Kin in the Chthulucene* (Durham, NC: Duke University Press, 2016), 31, 47, and 184n50; Jason Moore, ed., *Anthropocene or Capitalocene?* (Oakland, CA: PM Press, 2016); Nancy Fraser, "Legitimation Crisis? On the Political Contradictions of Financialized Capitalism," *Critical Historical Studies* 2, no. 2 (2015): 157–189; Wendy Brown, "Neoliberalism's Frankenstein: Authoritarian Freedom in Twenty-First Century 'Democracies,'" *Critical Times* 1 (2018): 60–79.
3. Voltaire, *Candide ou l'Optimisme* (Paris: Gallimard, 2007), 154.
4. Peter W. Singer, "National Security Pros, It's Time to Talk About Right-Wing Extremism," *Defense One*, February 28, 2018, https://www.defenseone.com/threats/2018/02/national-security-pros-its-time-talk-about-right-wing-extremism/146319/; Christian Picciolini, "Op-Ed: White Men Can Be Terrorists Too," *Los Angeles Times*, October 7, 2018, https://www.latimes.com/opinion/op-ed/la-oe-picciolini-white-supremacists-20181007-story.html.
5. The Editorial Board, "The New Radicalization of the Internet," *New York Times*, November 24, 2018, https://www.nytimes.com/2018/11/24/opinion/sunday/facebook-twitter-terrorism-extremism.html.
6. Paul Street, "Signs of Creeping Fascism Are All Around Us," *truthdig*, November 14, 2018, https://www.truthdig.com/articles/the-signs-of-creeping-fascism-are-all-around-us/.
7. Alison Kaplan Sommer, "How Did the Term 'Globalist' Become an Anti-Semitic Slur? Blame Bannon," *Haaretz*, March 13, 2018, https://www.haaretz.com/us-news/.premium-how-did-the-term-globalist-became-an-anti-semitic-slur-blame-bannon-1.5895925; Ian Schwartz, "Trump: Nationalism Means I Love the Country; I'm Not a Globalist, I Want to Take Care of U.S. First," *RealClearPolitics*, October 29, 2018, https://www.realclearpolitics.com/video/2018/10/29/trump_nationalism_means_i_love_the_country_im_not_a_globalist_i_want_to_take_care_of_us_first.html.
8. Ben Zimmer, "The Origins of the 'Globalist' Slur," *Atlantic*, March 14, 2018, https://www.theatlantic.com/politics/archive/2018/03/the-origins-of-the-globalist-slur/555479/; Yvette J. Dean, "Trump Attacks Koch Brothers with Anti-Semitic Dog Whistle," *Jerusalem Post*, July 31, 2018, https://www.jpost.com/American-Politics/Trump-attacks-Koch-brothers-with-antisemitic-dog-whistle-563841.
9. Anti-Defamation League (ADL), "Quantifying Hate, a Year of Anti-Semitism on Twitter," accessed August 22, 2019, from https://www.adl.org/resources/reports/quantifying-hate-a-year-of-anti-semitism-on-twitter.

10. "Trump Declares Himself a Nationalist," CNN, accessed August 22, 2019, from https://www.cnn.com/videos/politics/2018/10/23/president-trump-nationalist-globalist-rally-sot-vpx.cnn.
11. Richard Wolf, "Travel Ban Lexicon: From Candidate Donald Trump's Campaign Promises to President Trump's Tweets," *USA TODAY*, April 24, 2018, https://www.usatoday.com/story/news/politics/2018/04/24/travel-ban-donald-trump-campaign-promises-president-tweets/542504002/.
12. Peter Baker and Maggie Haberman, "Trump Widens War on Black Critics While Embracing 'Inner-City Pastors,'" *New York Times*, July 29, 2019, https://www.nytimes.com/2019/07/29/us/politics/trump-al-sharpton.html.
13. Talia Kaplan, "Trump Ramps up War of Words with Elijah Cummings, Calls Congressman 'Racist,'" Fox News, July 28, 2019, https://www.foxnews.com/politics/trump-elijah-cummings-president-calls-congressman-racist.
14. Colby Itkowitz, "Trump Attacks Rep. Cummings's District, Calling It a 'Disgusting, Rat and Rodent Infested Mess,'" *Washington Post*, July 27, 2019, https://www.washingtonpost.com/politics/trump-attacks-rep-cummingss-district-calling-it-a-disgusting-rat-and-rodent-infested-mess/2019/07/27/b93c89b2-b073-11e9-bc5c-e73b603e7f38_story.html.
15. Matthew Yglesias, "Trump's Racist Tirades Against 'The Squad,' Explained," *Vox*, July 18, 2019, https://www.vox.com/2019/7/15/20694616/donald-trump-racist-tweets-omar-aoc-tlaib-pressley.
16. Peter Baker, "Trump Declares a National Emergency, and Provokes a Constitutional Clash," *New York Times*, February 15, 2019, https://www.nytimes.com/2019/02/15/us/politics/national-emergency-trump.html.
17. Christine Wang, "Trump Website Takes Down Muslim Ban Statement After Reporter Grills Spicer in Briefing," *CNBC*, May 8, 2017, http://www.cnbc.com/2017/05/08/trump-website-takes-down-muslim-ban-statement-after-reporter-grills-spicer-in-briefing.html.
18. Chris Cillizza, "Donald Trump's Incredibly Unpresidential Statement on Charlottesville," CNN, August 13, 2017, https://www.cnn.com/2017/08/12/politics/trump-charlottesville-statement/index.html.
19. George T. Shaw, "Introduction: An Alternative to Failure," in *A Fair Hearing: The Alt-Right in the Words of Its Members and Leaders*, ed. George T. Shaw (Budapest, Hungary: Arktos Media Ltd, 2018), ix.
20. Shaw, "Introduction: An Alternative to Failure," x; x.
21. Richard Spencer, "Stop Watching Football," in *A Fair Hearing: The Alt-Right in the Words of Its Members and Leaders*, 101.
22. Shaw, "Introduction: An Alternative to Failure," xi.
23. Shaw, "Introduction: An Alternative to Failure," xii.
24. TOI Staff, "Trump Closing Campaign Ad Revives Remarks Seen as Striking Anti-Semitic Tones," *Times of Israel*, November 6, 2016, https://www.timesofisrael.com/trump-closing-campaign-ad-seen-as-striking-anti-semitic-tones/.
25. Donald Trump (@realDonaldTrump), "I have asked Secretary of State @SecPompeo to closely study the South Africa land and farm seizures and expropriations and the large scale killing of farmers. 'South African Government is now seizing land from white farmers.' @TuckerCarlson @FoxNews," Twitter, August 22, 2018, 10:28 p.m., https://twitter.com/realDonaldTrump/status/1032454567152246785?.
26. Natalie Nougayrède, "Steve Bannon Is on a Far-Right Mission to Radicalise Europe," *The Guardian*, June 6, 2018, https://www.theguardian.com/commentisfree/2018/jun/06/steve-bannon-far-right-radicalise-europe-trump.
27. Guillaume Faye, *Why We Fight: Manifesto of the European Resistance* (London: Arktos Media, 2011), 263–271.
28. Daniel Friberg, *The Real Right Returns: A Handbook for the True Opposition* (London: Arktos Media, 2015), 3; 3; 3; 19; 8; 10; 9; 10; Scott Horsley, "President Trump Says Europe Is 'Losing Its Culture,'" NPR, July 12, 2018, https://www.npr.org/2018/07/12/628639813/president-trump-says-europe-is-losing-its-culture.

29. Faye, *Why We Fight*, 77; 78; 260; Friberg, *The Real Right Returns*, 10.
30. Samuel Moyn, "The Alt-Right's Favorite Meme Is 100 Years Old," *New York Times*, November 13, 2018, https://www.nytimes.com/2018/11/13/opinion/cultural-marxism-anti-semitism.html.
31. Shaw, "Introduction: An Alternative to Failure," xi; Spencer, "Stop Watching Football," 97; Jared Taylor, "Race Realism," 115-125, in *A Fair Hearing: The Alt-Right in the Words of Its Members and Leaders*, 124.
32. "POTUS and Political Warfare," prepared by Richard Higgins of the National Security Council (Washington DC, 2017), 2, https://www.documentcloud.org/documents/3922874-Political-Warfare.html#document/p1.
33. Leonard Greene, "Trump Called for Death Penalty After Central Park Jogger Attack, and Still Has No Sympathy for Accused Despite Convictions Overturned," *New York Daily News*, July 19, 2018, https://www.nydailynews.com/new-york/ny-news-trump-death-penalty-central-park-five-20180713-story.html.
34. Sarah Burns, "Why Trump Doubled Down on the Central Park Five," *New York Times*, October 17, 2016, https://www.nytimes.com/2016/10/18/opinion/why-trump-doubled-down-on-the-central-park-five.html.
35. Paul Street, "Signs of Creeping Fascism Are All Around Us," *truthdig*, November 14, 2018, https://www.truthdig.com/articles/the-signs-of-creeping-fascism-are-all-around-us/.
36. "WATCH: 'That's Such a Racist Question,' Trump Tells NewsHour's Yamiche Alcindor," November 7, 2018, https://www.youtube.com/watch?v=7bSMiSTdthE&feature=youtu.be (emphasis added).
37. Dara Lind, "Trump's 'Animals' Remark and the Ensuing Controversy, Explained," *Vox*, May 21, 2018, https://www.vox.com/2018/5/18/17368716/trump-animals-immigrants-illegal-ms-13.
38. Z. Byron Wolf, "Trump Basically Called Mexicans Rapists Again," CNN, April 6, 2018, https://www.cnn.com/2018/04/06/politics/trump-mexico-rapists/index.html.
39. Ali Vitali, Kasie Hunt, and Frank Thorp V, "Trump Referred to Haiti and African Nations as 'Shithole' Countries," NBC News, January 11, 2018, https://www.nbcnews.com/politics/white-house/trump-referred-haiti-african-countries-shithole-nations-n836946.
40. Faye, *Why We Fight*, 72-262; Friberg, *The Real Right Returns*.
41. Friberg, *The Real Right Returns*, 24; Collin Liddell, "A Normie's Guide to the Alt-Right," in *A Fair Hearing: The Alt-Right in the Words of Its Members and Leaders*, 15; 16.
42. Shaw, "Introduction: An Alternative to Failure," xi; xi; Friberg, *The Real Right Returns*, 60; 61; 6; Faye, *Why We Fight*, 37.
43. Augustus Invictus, "Physical Removal: More Than a Meme," in George T. Shaw, ed., *A Fair Hearing: The Alt-Right in the Words of Its Members and Leaders*, 210.
44. Matt Novak, "Why Are Trump Supporters Offering People 'Free Helicopter Rides' Online?" *Gizmodo*, accessed August 22, 2019, https://gizmodo.com/why-are-trump-supporters-offering-people-free-helicopte-1829705238.
45. *The Urban Dictionary*, s.v. "Right Wing Death Squad," last modified Febraury 21, 2019, https://www.urbandictionary.com/define.php?term=Right%20Wing%20Death%20Squad.
46. Invictus, "Physical Removal," 214; Faye, *Why We Fight*, 29; Higgins, "POTUS and Political Warfare," 3.
47. Higgins, "POTUS and Political Warfare," 1.
48. Herbert Marcuse, *Counterrevolution and Revolt* (Boston: Beacon Press, 1972), 25 (quoting William Shirer).
49. David Neiwert, "Right-Wing Extremists Are Already Threatening Violence over a Democratic House," November 16, 2018, https://www.washingtonpost.com/outlook/2018/11/16/right-wing-extremists-are-already-threatening-violence-over-democratic-house/.
50. Facundo Alvaredo, Lucas Chancel, Thomas Piketty, Emmanuel Saez, and Gabriel Zucman, "Global Inequality Dynamics: New Findings from WID.WORLD," NBER Working Paper 23119 (February 2017), http://www.nber.org/papers/w23119.

51. Noah Kirsch, "The 3 Richest Americans Hold More Wealth than Bottom 50 Percent of the Country, Study Finds," *Forbes*, November 9, 2017, https://www.forbes.com/ . . ./the-3-richest-americans-hold-more-wealth-than-bottom-50; "Bill Gates, Jeff Bezos and Warren Buffett Have More Wealth than Half the Population of the US Combined," CNBC, November 9, 2017, https://www.cnbc.com/2017/11/09/gates-bezos-buffett-have-more-wealth-than-half-the-us-combined.html.
52. Josh Harkinson, "America's 100 Richest People Control More Wealth than the Entire Black Population," *Mother Jones*, December 2, 2015, http://www.motherjones.com/politics/2015/12/report-100-people-more-wealth-african-american-population/.
53. For details, see "Outrageous Wealth Disparity in America. 400 Richest More Wealth than Bottom 64 Percent," GlobalResearch, November 9, 2017, https://www.globalresearch.ca/outrageous-wealth-disparity-in-america-400-richest-more-wealth-than-bottom-64/5617370.
54. Venkat Venkatasubramanian, *How Much Inequality Is Fair?* (New York: Columbia University Press, 2017), 8–9; see also Bernie Sanders, *Guide to Political Revolution* (New York: Henry Holt, 2017), 60.
55. Jackie Wang, *Carceral Capitalism. Essays on the Contemporary Continuum of Incarceration: The Biopolitics of Juvenile Delinquency, Predatory Policing, the Political Economy of Fees and Fines, and Algorithmic Policing.* (Cambridge, MA: Semiotext(e), 2018).
56. Samuel Moyn, *Not Enough: Human Rights in an Unequal World* (Cambridge, MA: Harvard University Press, 2018), 2.
57. See, e.g., Thomas Piketty, "Vers une économie politique et historique: Réflexions sur le capital au XXIe siècle," *Annales. Histoire, Sciences Sociales* 1, no. 70 (2015): 125–138; Alvaredo et al. "Global Inequality Dynamics: New Findings from WID.WORLD." This new research has begun to extend the analysis of *Capital in the Twentieth Century* to China, Brazil, India, the Middle East, and other areas of the world. Thomas Piketty, *Capital in the Twenty-First Century* (Cambridge, MA: Harvard University Press, 2014).
58. Bruno Latour, *Down to Earth: Politics in the New Climatic Regime* (Cambridge: Polity, 2018), 2.
59. Latour, *Down to Earth*, 21–22; 19.
60. Latour, *Down to Earth*, 18; 1.
61. Latour, *Down to Earth*, 20.
62. Thomas Piketty, *Le Capital au XXIème siècle* (Paris: Le Seuil, 2013).
63. Piketty, "Vers une économie politique et historique"; Piketty, *Capital in the Twenty-First Century.*
64. Sanders, *Guide to Political Revolution*, back cover.
65. Sanders, *Guide to Political Revolution*, 46–47, 60–61, 4–5, 154–155, 81, 103, 119, 153, xii.
66. Certain passages in Horkheimer's work resonate with my argument about neoliberal penality. See, e.g., Max Horkheimer, "Traditional and Critical Theory," in *Critical Theory: Selected Essays*, trans. Matthew J. O'Connell et al. (New York: Continuum, 1992), 215. ("If we take seriously the ideas by which the bourgeoisie explains its own order—free exchange, free competition, harmony of interests, and so on—and if we follow them to their logical conclusion, they manifest their inner contradiction, and therewith their real opposition to the bourgeois order.")
67. Max Horkheimer and Theodor Adorno, *Dialectic of Enlightenment*, trans. John Cumming (New York: Continuum, 1996), 221 (in "Notes and Drafts," just before "Isolation by Communication").
68. See, especially, the work of and surrounding Esteban Pérez Caldentey. Esteban Pérez Caldentey and Matías Vernengo, eds., *Ideas, Policies, and Economic Development in the Americas* (New York: Routledge, 2007); Esteban Pérez Caldentey and Matías Vernengo, eds., *Why Latin American Nations Fail: Development Strategies in the Twenty-First Century* (Oakland: University of California Press, 2017).
69. This may entail limited state monopolies in certain areas, mixed with highly regulated private markets in other sectors, regulated for just distribution. There is no abstract litmus test or label to apply—just a constant vigilance of the economic outcomes to ensure equality and social justice.

70. Clifford Geertz, *After the Fact: Two Countries, Four Decades, One Anthropologist* (Cambridge, MA: Harvard University Press, 1995), 19.
71. Friedrich Nietzsche, *Daybreak: Thoughts on the Prejudices of Morality*, ed. Maudemarie Clark and Brian Leiter, trans. R. J. Hollingdale (Cambridge: Cambridge University Press, 1997), Aphorism 432 (emphasis added); see also Foucault's Nietzsche manuscripts, folio 407 (in preparation for the McGill 1971 conference on Nietzsche) in Fonds Michel Foucault, NAF 28730, Boîte 65, Bibliothèque nationale de France.
72. Georges Duby, "Avant-propos," in *Le dimanche de Bouvines* (Paris: Gallimard, 1973).
73. Michel Foucault, *The Punitive Society: Lectures at the Collège de France 1972–1973*, ed. Bernard E. Harcourt, trans. Graham Burchell (New York: Picador, 2015), 164–165.
74. John Christopher Barry brought this to my attention in June 2019, after a seminar at the EHESS where I juxtaposed Axel Honneth and Sara Ahmed in what Barry correctly called an effort at a "*grand écart théorique.*"
75. Walter Benjamin, "Brecht's *Threepenny Novel*," in Walter Benjamin, *Understanding Brecht*, trans. Anna Bostock (New York: Verso, 1998), 81.

Conclusion

1. Donna J. Haraway, *Staying with the Trouble: Making Kin in the Chthulucene* (Durham, NC: Duke University Press, 2016), 31.
2. Haraway, *Staying with the Trouble*, 31.
3. Haraway, *Staying with the Trouble*, 57.
4. Haraway, *Staying with the Trouble*, 57.
5. Bernard E. Harcourt, Amy Allen, Carolin Emcke, and Heather Ann Thompson, "Praxis 13/13: The Space of Praxis," public seminar, Columbia University, May 8, 2019, New York, http://blogs.law.columbia.edu/praxis1313/13-13/.
6. Karl Marx, "Manifesto of the Communist Party," in *The Marx-Engels Reader*, ed. Robert C. Tucker, trans. Ronald Rogowski, 2nd ed. (New York: Norton, 1978), 473.
7. Nancy Fraser and Axel Honneth, *Redistribution or Recognition. A Political-Philosophical Exchange* (New York: Verso, 2003); Kimberlé Crenshaw, "Mapping the Margins: Intersectionality, Identity Politics, and Violence Against Women of Color," *Stanford Law Review* 43, no. 6 (1991): 1241–1299.
8. Immanuel Kant, "An Answer to the Question: 'What Is Enlightenment?' " *Political Writings*, 2nd ed., ed. Hans Reiss, 54–63 (Cambridge: Cambridge University Press, 1991), 59.
9. Seyla Benhabib, *Critique, Norm, and Utopia: A Study of the Foundations of Critical Theory* (New York: Columbia University Press, 1986), 20; Reinhart Koselleck, *Critique and Crisis: Enlightenment and the Pathogenesis of Modern Society* (Cambridge, MA: MIT Press, 1988), 103-109.
10. Bruno Latour, *Down to Earth: Politics in the New Climatic Regime* (Cambridge: Polity, 2018), 106.

Postscript

1. United Nations, Intergovernmental Panel on Climate Change (V. Masson-Delmotte, P. Zhai, H. O. Pörtner, D. Roberts, J. Skea, P. R. Shukla, A. Pirani, W. Moufouma-Okia, C. Péan, R. Pidcock, S. Connors, J. B. R. Matthews, Y. Chen, X. Zhou, M. I. Gomis, E. Lonnoy, T. Maycock, M. Tignor, T. Waterfield, eds.), *Special Report on Global Warming of 1.5°C*, 2018, https://www.ipcc.ch/sr15/chapter/spm/.

Bibliography

Ackerman, Bruce. *Revolutionary Constitutions: Charismatic Leadership and the Rule of Law.* Cambridge, MA: Harvard University Press, 2019.

Adorno, Theodor W. "The Actuality of Philosophy." *Telos* 1997, no. 31 (1997): 120–133.

Adorno, Theodor W. "Marginalia on Theory and Praxis." In *Critical Models: Interventions and Catchwords*, trans. Henry W. Pickford, 259–278. New York: Columbia University Press, 1998.

Adorno, Theodor W. *Negative Dialectics.* New York: Continuum, 1973.

Adorno, Theodor W., Else Frenkel-Brunswik, Daniel J. Levinson, and R. Nevitt Sanford. *The Authoritarian Personality.* New York: Verso, 2019.

Agamben, Giorgio. *Creation and Anarchy: The Work of Art and the Religion of Capitalism.* Stanford, CA: Stanford University Press, 2019.

Agamben, Giorgio. *The Highest Poverty: Monastic Rules and Form-of-Life.* Stanford, CA: Stanford University Press, 2013.

Agamben, Giorgio. *Homo Sacer: Sovereign Power and Bare Life.* Trans. Daniel Heller-Roazen. Stanford, CA: Stanford University Press, 1998.

Ahmed, Sara. *Living a Feminist Life.* Durham, NC: Duke University Press, 2017.

Ahmed, Sara. *The Promise of Happiness.* Durham, NC: Duke University Press, 2010.

Ahmed, Sara. *Willful Subjects.* Durham, NC: Duke University Press, 2014.

Akbar, Amna. "Gross Collective Action." *Praxis 13/13* (blog). October 21, 2018. http://blogs.law.columbia.edu/praxis1313/amna-a-akbar-gross-collective-action/.

Alcoff, Linda Martín. *Real Knowing: New Versions of the Coherence Theory.* Ithaca, NY: Cornell University Press, 1996.

Ali, Tariq. *The Dilemmas of Lenin: Terrorism, War, Empire, Love, Revolution.* New York: Verso, 2017.

Allen, Amy. "Beyond Kant Versus Hegel: An Alternative Strategy for Grounding the Normativity of Critique." In *Feminism, Capitalism, and Critique: Essays in Honor of Nancy Fraser*, ed. Banu Bargu and Chiara Bottici, 243–261. New York: Palgrave Macmillan, 2017.

Allen, Amy. "Discourse, Power, and Subjectivation: The Foucault/Habermas Debate Reconsidered." *Philosophical Forum* 40, no. 1 (2009): 1–28.

Allen, Amy. *The End of Progress: Decolonizing the Normative Foundations of Critical Theory.* New York: Columbia University Press, 2016.

Althusser, Louis. "Ideology and Ideological State Apparatus (Notes Towards an Investigation)." In *Lenin and Philosophy and Other Essays*, trans. Ben Brewster, 85–126. New York: Monthly Review Press, 2001.

Althusser, Louis, Étienne Balibar, Roger Establet, Pierre Macherey, and Jacques Rancière. *Reading Capital: The Complete Edition.* Trans. Ben Brewster and David Fernbach. New York: Verso, 2016.

Alvaredo, Facundo, Lucas Chancel, Thomas Piketty, Emmanuel Saez, and Gabriel Zucman. "Global Inequality Dynamics: New Findings from WID.WORLD." NBER Working Paper 23119 (February 2017). http://www.nber.org/papers/w23119.

Anderson, Perry. *Considerations on Western Marxism.* London: NLB, 1976.

Anderson, Perry. "On the Concatenation in the Arab World," *New Left Review* 68 (March–April 2011): 5–15. https://newleftreview.org/issues/II68/articles/perry-anderson-on-the-concatenation-in-the-arab-world.

Anderson, Perry. "Two Revolutions." *New Left Review* 61 (2010): 59–96. https://newleftreview.org/issues/II61/articles/perry-anderson-two-revolutions.

Antonio, Robert J. "Immanent Critique as the Core of Critical Theory: Its Origins and Developments in Hegel, Marx, and Contemporary Thought." *British Journal of Sociology* 32, no. 3 (1981): 330–345.

Arendt, Hannah. *Crises of the Republic.* New York: Harcourt, 1972.

Arendt, Hannah. *Eichmann in Jerusalem: A Report on the Banality of Evil* (New York: Penguin, 1977).

Arendt, Hannah. *The Human Condition,* 2nd ed. Chicago: University of Chicago Press, 1998.

Arendt, Hannah. *The Life of the Mind.* Orlando, FL: Harcourt, 1978.

Arendt, Hannah. *On Revolution.* New York: Penguin, 2006 [1963].

Arendt, Hannah. "Truth and Politics." *New Yorker,* February 5, 1967, 49–88.

Armey, Dick, and Matt Kibbe. *Give Us Liberty: A Tea Party Manifesto.* New York: HarperCollins, 2010.

Artières, Philippe, Laurent Quéro, and Michelle Zancarini-Fournel, eds. *Le Groupe d'information sur les prisons: Archives d'une lutte 1970–1972.* Paris: Éditions de l'IMEC, 2003.

Asad, Talal. "The Limits of Religious Criticism in the Middle East." In Talal Asad. *Genealogies of Religion: Discipline and Reasons of Power in Christianity and Islam,* 200–236. Baltimore: John Hopkins University, 1993.

Asad, Talal. "Thinking About Tradition, Religion, and Politics in Egypt Today." *Critical Inquiry* 42, no. 1 (Autumn 2015): 166–214.

Astor, Dorian, and Alain Jugnon, eds. *Pourquoi nous sommes nietzschéens.* Brussels, Belgium: Les Impressions Nouvelles, 2016.

Austin, J. L. *How to Do Things with Words.* Ed. J.O. Urmson and Marina Sbisà. New York: Oxford University Press, 2011.

Badinter, Robert. *L'Abolition.* Paris: Fayard, 2000.

Badiou, Alain. "The Affirmative Dialectics." In *The Seoul Conference,* vol. 3 of *The Idea of Communism,* ed. Costas Douzinas and Slavoj Žižek, 127–136. New York: Verso, 2016.

Badiou, Alain. *The Communist Hypothesis.* Trans. David Macey and Steve Corcoran. New York: Verso, 2010.

Badiou, Alain. *The Meaning of Sarkozy.* Trans. David Fernbach. London: Verso, 2008.

Baehr, Peter. *The Unmasking Style in Social Theory.* London: Routledge, 2019.

Balibar, Étienne. "Communism as Commitment, Imagination, and Politics." In *The New York Conference,* vol. 2 of *The Idea of Communism,* ed. Slavoj Žižek, 13–35. New York: Verso, 2013.

Balibar, Étienne. "Critique in the 21st Century." *Radical Philosophy* 200 (2016). https://www.radicalphilosophy.com/article/critique-in-the-21st-century.

Balibar, Étienne. "Dire, contredire: Sur les formes de la *parrêsia* selon Foucault." In Étienne Balibar, *Libre parole,* 81–120. Paris: Galilée, 2018.

Balibar, Étienne. *Equaliberty: Political Essays.* Trans. James Ingram. Durham, NC: Duke University Press, 2013.

Balibar, Étienne. "'Gilets jaunes': The Meaning of the Confrontation." *openDemocracy.* December 20, 2018. https://www.opendemocracy.net/can-europe-make-it/etienne-balibar/gilets-jaunes-meaning-of-confrontation.

Balibar, Étienne. "Gilets jaunes: Le sens du face à face." *Praxis 13/13* (blog). January 12, 2019. http://blogs.law.columbia.edu/praxis1313/etienne-balibar-gilets-jaunes-le-sens-du-face-a-face/.

Balibar, Étienne. "The Idea of Revolution: Yesterday, Today, and Tomorrow." *Uprising 13/13* (blog). August 27, 2017. http://blogs.law.columbia.edu/uprising1313/etienne-balibar-the-idea-of-revolution-yesterday-today-and-tomorrow/.

Balibar, Étienne. "Law, Property, Politics: A Rejoinder to Mikhaïl Xifaras' 'The Role of Critical Theory.'" *Praxis 13/13* (blog). December 3, 2018. http://blogs.law.columbia.edu/praxis1313/etienne-balibar-law-property-politics/.

Balibar, Étienne. *Libre Parole.* Paris: Éditions Galilée, 2018.

Bantigny, Ludivine. "Un Événement." *Praxis 13/13* (blog). January 12, 2019. http://blogs.law.columbia.edu/praxis1313/ludivine-bantigny-un-evenement/.

Bardawil, Fadi. "Critical Blind Spots: Rethinking Left Criticism in the Wake of the Syrian Revolution." In *A Time for Critique*, ed. Didier Fassin and Bernard E. Harcourt, 174–192. New York: Columbia University Press, 2019.

Bargu, Banu. *Starve and Immolate: The Politics of Human Weapons.* New York: Columbia University Press, 2014.

Barthe, Yannick, and Cyril Lemieux. "Quelle critiques après Bourdieu?" *Mouvements* 5, no. 24 (2002): 33–38.

Bataille, Georges. *Erotism: Death and Sensuality.* Trans. Mary Dalwood. San Francisco: City Lights Publishers, 1986.

Bataille, Georges. Foreword to Marquis de Sade, *120 Days of Sodom.* Sun Vision Press, 2012.

Bataille, Georges. "*Sur Nietzsche.*" In *La Somme athéologique*, vol. 6 of *Oeuvres complètes.* Paris: Gallimard, 1973.

Bataille, Georges et al., eds. "Nietzsche et les Fascistes: Une Réparation." *Acéphale: Religion, sociologie, philosophie* 2 (1937): 17–21.

Baudrillard, Jean. *Le miroir de la production ou l'illusion critique du matérialisme historique.* Paris: Casterman, 1973.

Baudrillard, Jean. *The Mirror of Production.* Trans. Mark Poster. St. Louis: Telos, 1975.

Bauer, A. J., Christine Baumgarthuber, Jed Bickman, Jeremy Breecher, and the Writers for the 99 Percent. *Occupying Wall Street: The Inside Story of an Action That Changed America.* Chicago: Haymarket, 2011.

Bayat, Asef. *Revolution Without Revolutionaries: Making Sense of the Arab Spring.* Palo Alto, CA: Stanford University Press, 2017.

Bayoumi, Soha. "Revolution, Hope, and Actors' Categories. Or What's an Engaged Scholar to Do?" October 22, 2017 (on file with author).

de Beauvoir, Simone. *All Said and Done.* New York: Putnam, 1974.

de Beauvoir, Simone. *Faut-il brûler Sade?* Paris: Gallimard, 1955 (originally published under the title *Privilèges*).

de Beauvoir, Simone. *The Second Sex.* Trans. Constance Borde and Sheila Malovany-Chevallier. New York: Vintage, 2011.

Beck, Glenn. *Glenn Beck's Common Sense: The Case Against an Out-of-Control Government, Inspired by Thomas Paine.* New York: Threshold, 2009.

Becker, Gary S., François Ewald, and Bernard E. Harcourt. "Becker and Foucault on Crime and Punishment." In *Neoliberalism (cont'd)*, vol. 9 of *Carceral Notebooks*, ed. Bernard E. Harcourt, 5–45. New York: U.S. Lithograph, 2013.

Becker, Gary S., François Ewald, and Bernard E. Harcourt. "Becker on Ewald on Foucault on Becker: American Neoliberalism and Michel Foucault's 1979 *Birth of Biopolitics* Lectures." In *Neoliberalism and Risk*, vol. 7 of *Carceral Notebooks*, ed. Bernard E. Harcourt, 1–35. New York: U.S. Lithograph, 2011.

Benhabib, Seyla. "Carl Schmitt's Critique of Kant: Sovereignty and International Law." *Political Theory* 40, no. 6 (2012): 688–713.

Benhabib, Seyla. "Claiming Rights Across Borders: International Human Rights and Democratic Sovereignty." *American Political Science Review* 103, no. 4 (2009): 691–704.

Benhabib, Seyla. "Critique and Emancipation: Comments Prepared for the *Emanzipation Conference*." Lecture, Humboldt-Universität zu Berlin, May 25, 2018 (draft on file with author).

Benhabib, Seyla. *Critique, Norm, and Utopia: A Study of the Foundations of Critical Theory*. New York: Columbia University Press, 1986.

Benhabib, Seyla. *Dignity in Adversity: Human Rights in Turbulent Times*. New York: Polity, 2011.

Benhabib, Seyla. "Epistemologies of Post-Modernism." *New German Critique* Fall 1984, no. 33 (1984): 103–127.

Benhabib, Seyla. *Exile, Statelessness, and Migration: Playing Chess with History from Hannah Arendt to Isaiah Berlin*. Princeton, NJ: Princeton University Press, 2018.

Benhabib, Seyla. "Feminism and Postmodernism: An Uneasy Alliance." In *Feminist Contentions: A Philosophical Exchange*, ed. Seyla Benhabib, Judith Butler, Drucilla Cornell, Nancy Fraser, and Linda Nicholson, 17–34. New York: Routledge, 1995.

Benhabib, Seyla. *Situating the Self: Gender, Community and Post-modernism*. London: Polity, 1992.

Benhabib, Seyla. "Subjectivity, Historiography, and Politics: Reflections on the 'Feminism/Postmodernism Exchange.'" In *Feminist Contentions: A Philosophical Exchange*, ed. Seyla Benhabib, Judith Butler, Drucilla Cornell, Nancy Fraser, and Linda Nicholson, 107–125. New York: Routledge, 1995.

Benhabib, Seyla, Judith Butler, Drucilla Cornell, Nancy Fraser, and Linda Nicholson, eds. *Feminist Contentions: A Philosophical Exchange*. New York: Routledge, 1995.

Benjamin, Walter. *The Correspondence of Walter Benjamin, 1910–1940*. Ed. Gershom Scholem and Theodor W. Adorno. Trans. Manfred R. Jacobson and Evelyn M. Jacobson. Chicago: University of Chicago Press, 1994.

Benjamin, Walter. *Illuminations*, ed. Hannah Arendt. New York: Schocken, 1968.

Benjamin, Walter. *Reflections: Essays, Aphorisms, Autobiographical Writings*. Ed. Peter Demetz. Trans. Edmund Jephcott. New York: Schocken, 1978.

Benjamin, Walter. *Understanding Brecht*. Trans. Anna Bostock. New York: Verso, 1998.

Bernstein, Eduard. *The Preconditions of Socialism*. Ed. and trans. Henry Tudor. Cambridge: Cambridge University Press, 1993.

Bernstein, Jay. *Torture and Dignity: An Essay on Moral Injury*. Chicago: University of Chicago Press, 2015.

Bernstein, Richard J. *Praxis and Action: Contemporary Philosophies of Human Action*. Philadelphia: University of Pennsylvania Press, 1971.

Best, Stephen, and Sharon Marcus. "Surface Reading: An Introduction." *Representations* 108, no. 1 (2009): 1–21.

Bey, Hakim. *The Temporary Autonomous Zone*. New York: Autonomedia, 1985.

Bhabha, Homi K. "Foreword." In Frantz Fanon, *The Wretched of the Earth*, vii–xli. New York: Grove, 2004.

Bhabha, Homi K. *The Location of Culture*. New York: Routledge, 1994.

Bhabha, Homi, and Steven Pinker. "Does the Enlightenment Need Defending?" Institute of Art and Ideas, September 10, 2018. https://iai.tv/articles/does-the-enlightenment-need-defending-auid-1149.

Bilgrami, Akeel. "Gandhi, the Philosopher." In Akeel Bilgrami, *Secularism, Identity, and Enchantment*. Cambridge, MA: Harvard University Press, 2014.

Biondi, Charleyne. "La dissidence civique dans l'impasse démocratique: Le cas Edward Snowden." Masters thesis, Institut d'études politiques, Paris, 2015.

"#BlackLivesMatter." *Uprising 13/13* (blog). November 9, 2017. http://blogs.law.columbia.edu/uprising1313/4-13/.

Black Lives Matter Global Network. "Herstory." Black Lives Matter. Accessed August 8, 2019, from https://blacklivesmatter.com/about/herstory/.

Blanchot, Maurice. *Lautréamont et Sade*. Paris: Minuit, 1949.

Blumenkranz, Carla, Keith Gessen, Mark Greif, Sarah Leonard, Sarah Resnick, Nikil Saval, Eli Schmitt, and Asta Taylor, eds. *Occupy!* New York: Verso, 2011.

Bobbio, Norberto. *Left and Right: The Significance of a Political Distinction*. Chicago: University of Chicago Press, 1996.

Boltanski, Luc. *De la critique. Précis de sociologie de l'émancipation*. Paris: Gallimard, 2009.

Boltanski, Luc. "Sociologie critique et sociologie de la critique." *Politix* 3, no. 10 (1990): 124–134.

Boltanski, Luc, and Eve Chiapello. *Le Nouvel esprit de capitalisme*. Paris: Gallimard, 1999.

Boltanski, Luc, and Laurent Thévenot. *On Justification: Economies of Worth*. Princeton, NJ: Princeton University Press, 2006.

Bonsu, Janae, and Terrance Laney. "Agenda to Keep Us Safe." *BYP100*. 2016. http://agendatobuildblackfutures.org/wp-content/uploads/2016/01/BYP100-Agenda-to-Keep-Us-Safe-AKTUS.pdf.

Bookchin, Murray. *Social Anarchism or Lifestyle Anarchism: An Unbridgeable Chasm*. Chico, CA: AKPress, 1995.

Bourdieu, Pierre. *Language and Symbolic Power*. Cambridge, MA: Harvard University Press, 1991.

Brown, Wendy. "Neoliberalism's Frankenstein: Authoritarian Freedom in Twenty-First-Century 'Democracies.'" *Critical Times* no. 1 (2018): 60–79.

Brown, Wendy. *Undoing the Demos*. New York: Zone, 2015.

Buck-Morss, Susan. *Dialectics of Seeing: Walter Benjamin and the Arcades Project*. Cambridge, MA: MIT Press, 1989.

Buck-Morss, Susan. *The Origin of Negative Dialectics: Theodor W. Adorno, Walter Benjamin, and the Frankfurt School*. New York: Free Press, 1979.

Butler, Judith. "Beauvoir on Sade: Making Sexuality into an Ethic." In *The Cambridge Companion to Simone de Beauvoir*, ed. Claudia Card, 168–188. Cambridge: Cambridge University Press, 2003.

Butler, Judith. "For a Careful Reading," In *Feminist Contentions: A Philosophical Exchange*, ed. Seyla Benhabib, Judith Butler, Drucilla Cornell, Nancy Fraser, and Linda Nicholson, 127–143. New York: Routledge, 1995.

Butler, Judith. "Contingent Foundations: Feminism and the Question of 'Postmodernism.'" In *Feminist Contentions: A Philosophical Exchange*, ed. Seyla Benhabib, Judith Butler, Drucilla Cornell, Nancy Fraser, and Linda Nicholson, 35–57. New York: Routledge, 1995.

Butler, Judith. *Gender Trouble: Feminism and the Subversion of Identity*. New York: Routledge, 1990.

Butler, Judith. *Giving an Account of Oneself*. New York: Fordham University Press, 2003.

Butler, Judith. *Notes Toward a Performative Theory of Assembly*. Cambridge, MA: Harvard University Press, 2015.

Butler, Judith. "Protest, Violent and Nonviolent." *The Big Picture, Public Books*, October 13, 2017. http://www.publicbooks.org/the-big-picture-protest-violent-and-nonviolent/.

Butler, Judith. "Sex and Gender in Simone de Beauvoir's Second Sex." *Yale French Studies* no. 72 (1986): 35–49.

Butler, Judith. "What Is Critique? An Essay on Foucault's Virtue." *European Institute for Progressive Cultural Policies*, May 2001. http://eipcp.net/transversal/0806/butler/en.

Butler, Paul. "Gideon's Muted Trumpet." *New York Times*, March 17, 2013.

Call, Lewis. *Postmodern Anarchism*. Lanham, MD: Lexington, 2000.

Camp, Jordan, and Christina Heatherton, eds. *Policing the Planet: Why the Policing Crisis Led to Black Lives Matter*. New York: Verso, 2016.

Camus, Albert. "L'Homme révolté." In *Essais d'Albert Camus*, ed. R. Quilliot and L. Faucon. Paris: Gallimard, 1965.

Castoriadis, Cornelius. *L'Institution imaginaire de la société*. Paris: Seuil, 1975.

Castoriadis, Cornelius. *The Imaginary Institution of Society*. Trans. Kathleen Blamey. Cambridge: Polity Press, 1987.

Cavarero, Adriana. *Horrorism: Naming Contemporary Violence*. New York: Columbia University Press, 2008.

Cavin, Susan. "OSS & the Frankfurt School: Recycling the 'Damaged Lives of Cultural Outsiders.'" Paper presented at the 2004 meeting of the American Sociological Association, San Francisco, August 15, 2004. http://citation.allacademic.com/meta/p_mla_apa_research_citation/1/1/0/1/8/pages110188/p110188-1.php.

Celikates, Robin. "Civil Disobedience as a Practice of Civic Freedom." In *On Global Citizenship: James Tully in Dialogue*, ed. David Owen, 207–228. New York: Bloomsbury, 2014.

Celikates, Robin. "Democratizing Civil Disobedience." *Philosophy and Social Criticism* 42, no. 10 (2016): 982–994.

Césaire, Aimé. *And the Dogs Were Silent*. In *Lyric and Dramatic Poetry*. Trans. Clayton Eshleman and Annette Smith. Charlottesville: University of Virginia Press, 1990.

Chakrabarty, Dipesh. "The Climate of History: Four Theses." *Critical Inquiry* 35, no. 20 (2009): 17–40.

Chakrabarty, Dipesh. *Provincializing Europe: Postcolonial Thought and Historical Difference*. Princeton, NJ: Princeton University Press, 2000.

Chatterjee, Partha. *The Nation and Its Fragments: Colonial and Postcolonial Histories*. Princeton, NJ: Princeton University Press, 1993.

Clover, Joshua. *Riot. Strike. Riot*. New York: Verso, 2016.

Cobb, Jelani. "The Matter of Black Lives." *New Yorker*, March 14, 2016.

Cohen, Cathy J. "Deviance as Resistance: A New Research Agenda for the Study of Black Politics." *Du Bois Review* 1, no. 1 (2004): 27–45.

Cohen, Cathy J. "The Radical Potential of Queer? Twenty Years Later." *GLQ: A Journal of Lesbian and Gay Studies* 25, no. 1 (2019): 140–144. https://muse.jhu.edu/.

Cohen, Cathy J., and Sarah J. Jackson. "Ask a Feminist: A Conversation with Cathy J. Cohen on Black Lives Matter, Feminism, and Contemporary Activism." *Signs: Journal of Women in Culture and Society* 41, no. 4 (Summer 2016): 1–18.

Cohen, Jean. "What's Wrong with (Theories of) Left Populism?" Paper presented at the *Constellations Conference* at Columbia University, New York, November 30, 2018 (on file with author).

Coleman, Gabriella. *Hacker, Hoaxer, Whistleblower, Spy: The Many Faces of Anonymous*. London: Verso, 2015.

Coleman, Gabriella. "From Internet Farming to Weapons of the Geek." *Current Anthropology* 58, no. 15 (February 2017): S92.

Connolly, William E. "The Desire to Punish," In William E. Connolly, *The Ethos of Pluralization*, 41–74. Minneapolis: University of Minnesota Press, 1995.

Conrad, Joseph. *The Secret Agent*. Ed. John Lyon. Oxford: Oxford University Press, 2008.

Courtois, Kalinka. "The '*Groupe d'information sur les prisons*': French Intellectuals and Activism Post May '68." PhD diss., Columbia University, 2019.

Couture, Tony. "Feminist Criticisms of Habermas's Ethics and Politics." *Dialogue: Canadian Philosophical Review/Revue canadienne de philosophie* 34, no. 2 (1995): 259–280.

Crenshaw, Kimberlé. "Mapping the Margins: Intersectionality, Identity Politics, and Violence Against Women of Color." *Stanford Law Review* 43, no. 6 (1991): 1241–1299.

Crutzen, Paul J., John R McNeill, and Will Steffen. "The Anthropocene: Are Humans Now Overwhelming the Great Forces of Nature?" *Ambio* 36, no. 8 (2007): 614–621.

Cumming, Robert Denoon, ed. *The Philosophy of Jean-Paul Sartre.* New York: Vintage, 1965.

Davidson, Arnold. "In Praise of Counter-conduct." *History of the Human Sciences* 24, no. 4 (2011): 25–41.

Davis, Angela Y. *Are Prisons Obsolete?* New York: Seven Stories Press, 2003.

Davis, Angela Y. *Freedom is a Constant Struggle: Ferguson, Palestine, and the Foundations of a Movement.* Chicago: Haymarket, 2016.

Dean, Jodi. "Claiming Division, Naming a Wrong." *Theory & Event* 14, no. 4. (2011). https://muse.jhu.edu/.

Dean, Jodi. *The Communist Horizon.* New York: Verso, 2012.

Descombes, Vincent. *Le Même et l'autre.* Paris: Minuit, 1979.

Defert, Daniel. "Chronologie." In *1954–1969*, vol. 1 of *Dits et Écrits*, ed. Daniel Defert, François Ewald, and Jacques Lagrange, 13–64. Paris: Gallimard, 1994.

Defert, Daniel. *Une Vie politique. Entretiens avec Philippe Artières et Eric Favereau, avec la collaboration de Joséphine Gross.* Paris: Seuil, 2014.

Deleuze, Gilles, ed. *Cahiers de Royaumont. Nietzsche.* Paris: Minuit, 1967.

Deleuze, Gilles. "Conclusions sur la volonté de puissance et l'éternel retour." In *Cahiers de Royaumont. Nietzsche*, 275–287. Paris: Minuit, 1967.

Deleuze, Gilles. *Différence et répétition.* Paris: Presses Universitaires de France, 1968.

Deleuze, Gilles. "Écrivain non: Un nouveau cartographe." *Critique* 343 (December 1975): 1207–1227.

Deleuze, Gilles. *Foucault.* Trans. Séan Hand. Minneapolis: University of Minnesota Press, 1988.

Deleuze, Gilles. "Mystère d'Ariane Selon Nietzsche." In Gilles Deleuze, *Critique et Clinique*, 126–134. Paris: Minuit, 1993.

Deleuze, Gilles. *Nietzsche, sa vie, son œuvre: avec un exposé de sa philosophie.* Paris: Presses universitaires de France, 1965.

Deleuze, Gilles. "Nietzsche." In *Gilles Deleuze: Pure Immanence: Essays on a Life*, ed. John Rajchman, trans. Anne Boyman, 53–102. New York: Zone, 2001.

Deleuze, Gilles. *Nietzsche et la philosophie.* Paris: Presses Universitaires de France, 1962.

Deleuze, Gilles. *Nietzsche and Philosophy.* Trans. Hugh Tomlinson. New York: Columbia University Press, 2006.

Deleuze, Gilles. *Présentation de Sacher-Masoch: Le froid et le cruel.* Paris: Minuit, 1967.

Deleuze, Gilles, and Félix Guattari. *Anti-Oedipus: Capitalism and Schizophrenia.* Trans. Robert Hurley, Mark Seem, and Helen R. Lane. Minneapolis: University of Minnesota Press, 1983.

Deleuze, Gilles, and Félix Guattari. *A Thousand Plateaus: Capitalism and Schizophrenia.* Trans. Brian Massumi. Minneapolis: University of Minnesota Press, 1987.

Delmas, Candice. *A Duty to Resist: When Disobedience Should Be Uncivil.* New York: Oxford University Press, 2018.

Delmas, Candice. "The Ethics of Government Whistleblowing." *Social Theory and Practice* 41, no. 1 (January 2015): 77–105.

Derrida, Jacques. *Séminaire La peine de mort. Volume I (1999-2000)*, ed. Geoffrey Bennington, Marc Crépon, and Thomas Dutoit. Paris: Galilée, 2012.

Derrida, Jacques. *Éperons. Les styles de Nietzsche.* Paris: Flammarion, 1978.

Derrida, Jacques. *De la grammatologie.* Paris: Minuit, 1967.

Derrida, Jacques. *Limited Inc.* Evanston, IL: Northwestern University Press, 1988.

Derrida, Jacques. "Apparition of the Inapparent: The phenomenological 'conjuring trick.'" In Jacques Derrida, *Specters of Marx*, trans. Peggy Kamuf, 156–221. New York: Routledge Classics, 1994.

Desautels-Stein, Justin. *The Jurisprudence of Style: A Structuralist History of American Pragmatism and Liberal Legal Thought.* Cambridge: Cambridge University Press, 2018.

Dilts, Andrew. "To Kill a Thief: Punishment, Proportionality, and Criminal Subjectivity in Locke's 'Second Treatise.' " *Political Theory* 40, no. 1 (2012): 58–83.

Donzelot, Jacques. *L'invention du social: Essai sur le déclin des passions politiques.* Paris: Fayard, 1984.

Donzelot, Jacques. *La Police des familles.* Paris: Minuit, 1977.

Dosse, François. *Histoire du structuralisme.* 2 vols. Paris: Éditions La Découverte, 1992.

Drolc, Nicolas, dir. *Sur les toits.* 2014; Nancy, France: Les Films Furax.

DuBois, Page. *Torture and Truth.* New York: Routledge, 1991.

Du Bois, W. E. B. *The Souls of Black Folks.* Mineola, NY: Dover, 1994.

Duby, Georges. *Le dimanche de Bouvines.* Paris: Gallimard, 1973.

Dumézil, Georges. *Servius et la fortune: Essai sur la fonction sociale de louange et de blâme et sur les éléments indo-européens du cens romain.* Paris: Gallimard, 1943.

Elden, Stuart. *Foucault: The Birth of Power.* Cambridge: Polity, 2017.

Ellenberger, Henri F. *The Discovery of the Unconscious: The History and Evolution of Dynamic Psychiatry.* New York: Basic Books, 1970.

Éribon, Didier. "Habermas, le 'moderne.'" *Libération,* March 9, 1983, 33.

Evans, Caroline. *Fashion at the Edge: Spectacle, Modernity, and Deathliness.* New Haven, CT: Yale University Press, 2007.

Ewald, François. *The Birth of Solidarity: The History of the French Welfare State.* Ed. Melinda Cooper. Trans. Timothy Scott Johnson. Durham, NC: Duke University Press, forthcoming.

Ewald, François, and Bernard E. Harcourt. "Situation du cours." In Michel Foucault, *Théories et institutions pénales. Cours au Collège de France,* 243–282. Paris: Gallimard, 2015.

Fanon, Frantz. *The Wretched of the Earth.* Trans. Richard Philcox. New York: Grove, 2004.

Farge, Arlette, and Michel Foucault, eds. *Le Désordre des familles: Lettres de cachet des Archives de la Bastille au XVIIIe siècle.* Paris: Gallimard, 1982.

Fassin, Didier. "The Endurance of Critique." *Anthropological Theory* 17, no. 1 (2017): 4–29.

Fassin, Didier. "How Is Critique?" In *A Time for Critique,* ed. Didier Fassin and Bernard E. Harcourt, 13–35. New York: Columbia University Press, 2019.

Fassin, Didier. *Punir, une passion contemporaine.* Paris: Seuil, 2016.

Fassin, Didier. *The Will to Punish.* Oxford: Oxford University Press, 2017.

Fassin, Didier, and Bernard E. Harcourt, eds. *A Time for Critique.* New York: Columbia University Press, 2019.

Faye, Guillaume. *Why We Fight: Manifesto of the European Resistance.* London: Arktos Media, 2011.

Federici, Silvia. *Wages Against Housework.* Montpelier, UK: Falling Wall Press, 1975.

Feenberg, Andrew. *The Philosophy of Praxis: Marx, Lukács and the Frankfurt School.* New York: Verso, 2014.

Ferry, Luc, and Alain Renaut, eds. *Why We Are Not Nietzscheans.* Trans. Robert de Laoiza. Chicago: University of Chicago Press, 1997.

Feyerabend, Paul. *Against Method.* New York: Verso, 2010.

Finchelstein, Federico. *From Fascism to Populism in History.* Berkeley: University of California Press, 2017.

Finlayson, James Gordon. *The Habermas-Rawls Debate.* New York: Columbia University Press, 2019.

Finlayson, James Gordon, Fabian Freyenhagen, and James Gledhill, eds. *Habermas and Rawls: Disputing the Political.* New York: Routledge, 2011.

Fischel, Joseph J. *Sex and Harm in the Age of Consent.* Minneapolis: University of Minnesota Press, 2016.

Fontaine, Claire. "1977: The Year That Is Never Commemorated." Draft dated 2017 (on file with author).

Fontaine, Claire. "Insurrection Mao." *Uprising 13/13* (blog). September 27, 2017. http://blogs.law.columbia.edu/uprising1313/claire-fontaine-insurrection-mao/.

Ford, Richard T. "Beyond 'Difference': A Reluctant Critique of Left Identity Politics." In *Left Legalism/Left Critique,* ed. Wendy Brown and Janet Halley, 38–79. Durham, NC: Duke University Press, 2002.

Forst, Rainer. *Justification and Critique*. Trans. Ciaran Cronin. Cambridge: Polity, 2014.

Forst, Rainer. "Noumenal Power." *Journal of Political Philosophy* 23, no. 2 (2015): 111–127.

Forst, Rainer. "Noumenal Power Revisited: Reply to Critics." *Journal of Political Power* 11, no. 3 (2018): 294–321.

Forstenzer, Joshua. "Something Has Cracked: Post-Truth Politics and Richard Rorty's Postmodernist Bourgeois Liberalism." Ash Center Occasional Papers Series, Ash Center for Democratic Governance and Innovation, Harvard Kennedy School, Cambridge, MA, July 2018.

Forti, Simona. "The Modern Concept of Revolution." September 11, 2017 (draft on file with author).

Foucault, Michel. "Adorno, Horkheimer, and Marcuse: Who Is a 'Negator of History'?" In *Remarks on Marx: Conversations with Duccio Trombadori*, trans. R. James Goldstein and James Casciato, 115–130. New York: Semiotexte, 1991.

Foucault, Michel. *The Archaeology of Knowledge and the Discourse on Language*. London: Tavistock Publications, 1972.

Foucault, Michel. *Les Aveux de la chair. Histoire de la sexualité, Volume 4*. Ed. Frédéric Gros. Paris: Gallimard, 2018.

Foucault, Michel. *The Birth of Biopolitics: Lectures at the Collège de France, 1978–1979*. Ed. Michel Senellart. Trans. Graham Burchell. Basingstoke, UK: Palgrave Macmillan, 2008.

Foucault, Michel. *The Birth of the Clinic: An Archaeology of Medical Perception*. Trans. A. M. Sheridan Smith. New York: Vintage, 1994.

Foucault, Michel. "Confinement, Psychiatry, Prison." Interview by David Cooper et al. In *Politics, Philosophy, Culture: Interviews and Other Writings 1977–1984*, ed. Lawrence D. Kritzman, trans. Alan Sheridan, 178–210. New York: Routledge, 1988.

Foucault, Michel. *Le Courage de la vérité*. Ed. Frédéric Gros. Paris: Gallimard/Seuil, 2009.

Foucault, Michel. *The Courage of Truth: The Government of Self and Others II: Lectures at the Collège de France, 1983–1984*. Ed. Frederic Gros. Trans. Graham Burchell. Basingstoke, UK: Palgrave Macmillan, 2011.

Foucault, Michel. *Discipline and Punish: The Birth of the Prison*. Trans. Alan Sheridan. New York: Vintage, 1979.

Foucault, Michel. *Discourse and Truth, and Parrēsia*. Ed. Henri-Paul Fruchaud, Daniele Lorenzini, and Nancy Luxon. Chicago: University of Chicago Press, 2019.

Foucault, Michel. *Dits et Écrits*. Ed. Daniel Defert, François Ewald, and Jacques Lagrange. 4 vols. Paris: Gallimard, 1994.

Foucault, Michel. *Dits et Écrits*. Ed. Daniel Defert, François Ewald, and Jacques Lagrange. 2 vols. Paris: Gallimard, 2001.

Foucault, Michel. *The Essential Works of Foucault* (1954–1984). Vol. 1, *Ethics: Subjectivity and Truth*. Ed. Paul Rabinow. Trans. Robert Hurley. New York: New Press, 1997.

Foucault, Michel. *The Essential Works of Foucault* (1954–1984). Vol. 2, *Aesthetics, Methods and Epistemology*. Ed. James D. Faubion. Trans. Robert Hurley. New York: New Press, 1998.

Foucault, Michel. *The Essential Works of Foucault* (1954–1984). Vol. 3, *Power*. Ed. James D. Faubion. Trans. Robert Hurley. New York: New Press, 2000.

Foucault, Michel. *On the Government of the Living: Lectures at the Collège de France, 1979–1980*. Ed. Michel Senellart. Trans. Graham Burchell. Basingstoke, UK: Palgrave Macmillan, 2014.

Foucault, Michel. *The Hermeneutics of the Subject: Lectures at the Collège de France, 1981–1982*. Ed. Frédéric Gros. Trans. Graham Burchell. New York: Picador, 2005.

Foucault, Michel. *History of Madness*. Ed. Jean Khalfa. Trans. Jonathan Murphy and Jean Khalfa. New York: Routledge, 2009.

Foucault, Michel. *The History of Sexuality*. Vol. 1, *An Introduction*. Trans. Robert Hurley. New York: Vintage, 1990.

Foucault, Michel. *The History of Sexuality*. Vol. 2, *The Use of Pleasure*. Trans. Robert Hurley. New York: Vintage, 1990.

Foucault, Michel. *The History of Sexuality*. Vol. 3, *The Care of the Self*. Trans. Robert Hurley. New York: Vintage, 1988.

Foucault, Michel. *"Il faut défendre la société." Cours au Collège de France, 1976*. Ed. Mauro Bertani and Alessandro Fontana. Paris: Gallimard/Seuil, 1997.

Foucault, Michel. "Les intellectuels et le pouvoir." Interview by Gilles Deleuze. Special issue, *L'Arc: Gilles Deleuze* no. 49 (2eme trimestre 1972): 3–10.

Foucault, Michel. *Introduction à l'*Anthropologie. In Immanuel Kant, *Anthropologie du point de vue pragmatique*, 11–79. Paris: Vrin, 2008.

Foucault, Michel. *Leçons sur la volonté de savoir. Cours au Collège de France (1970–1971)*. Ed. Daniel Defert. Paris: Gallimard/Seuil, 2011.

Foucault, Michel. *Lectures on the Will to Know: Lectures at the Collège de France, 1970–1971 and Oedipal Knowledge*. Ed. Arnold Davidson. Trans. Graham Burchell. Basingstoke, UK: Palgrave Macmillan, 2013.

Foucault, Michel. *Maladie mentale et personalité*. Paris: Presses universitaires de France, 1954.

Foucault, Michel. *Mal faire, dire vrai. Fonction de l'aveu en justice*. Ed. Fabienne Brion and Bernard E. Harcourt. Louvain, Belgium: Presses universitaires de Louvain, 2012.

Foucault, Michel. *Les Mots et les choses: Une archéologie des sciences humaines*. Paris: Gallimard, 1966.

Foucault, Michel. *Naissance de la biopolitique. Cours au Collège de France (1978–1979)*. Ed. Michel Senellart. Paris: Gallimard, 2004.

Foucault, Michel. *Naissance de la clinique. Une Archéologie du regard médical*. Paris: Presses Universitaires de France, 1963.

Foucault, Michel. "Nietzsche, Genealogy, History." In *The Foucault Reader*, ed. Paul Rabinow, 76–100. New York: Pantheon, 1984.

Foucault, Michel. *Oeuvres*. Ed. Frédéric Gros. 2 vols. Paris: Gallimard/Pléiade, 2015.

Foucault, Michel. *The Order of Things: An Archaeology of the Human Sciences*. Trans. Alan Sheridan. New York: Vintage, 1994.

Foucault, Michel. *Penal Theories and Institutions*. Ed. Bernard E. Harcourt. Trans. Graham Burchell. New York: Palgrave Macmillan, 2019.

Foucault, Michel. *The Politics of Truth*. Ed. Sylvère Lotringer. Los Angeles: Semiotext(e), 2007.

Foucault, Michel. *Power/Knowledge: Selected Interviews and Other Writings, 1972–1977*. Ed. Colin Gordon. Trans. John Mepham. New York: Pantheon, 1980.

Foucault, Michel. *Psychiatric Power: Lectures at the Collège de France, 1973–1974*. Ed. Jacques Lagrange. Trans. Graham Burchell. Basingstoke, UK: Palgrave Macmillan, 2006.

Foucault, Michel. *The Punitive Society: Lectures at the Collège de France 1972–1973*. Ed. Bernard E. Harcourt. Trans. Graham Burchell. New York: Picador, 2015.

Foucault, Michel. *Qu'est-ce que la critique?* Ed. Henri-Paul Fruchaud and Daniele Lorenzini. Paris: Vrin, 2015.

Foucault, Michel. "Qu'est-ce que la critique? [Critique et *Aufklärung*]." *Bulletin de la société française de philosophie* 84, no. 2 (1990): 35–63.

Foucault, Michel. *Sécurité, Territoire, Population. Cours au Collège de France, 1977–1978*. Ed. Michel Senellart. Paris: Gallimard, 2004.

Foucault, Michel. *Security, Territory, Population: Lectures at the Collège de France, 1977–1978*. Ed. Michel Senellart. Trans. Graham Burchell. Basingstoke, UK: Palgrave Macmillan, 2007.

Foucault, Michel. *La Sexualité, Cours donné à l'université de Clermont-Ferrand. 1964, suivi de Le Discours de la sexualité, Cours donné à l'université de Vincennes. 1969*. Ed. Claude-Olivier Doron. Paris: Gallimard/Seuil, 2018.

Foucault, Michel. *La Société punitive. Cours au Collège de France (1972–1973)*. Ed. Bernard E. Harcourt. Paris: Gallimard/Seuil, 2013.

Foucault, Michel. *"Society Must Be Defended": Lectures at the Collège de France, 1975–1976*. Ed. Mauro Bertani and Alessandro Fontana. Trans. Arnold I. Davidson. New York: Picador, 2003.

Foucault, Michel. *Subjectivité et vérité. Cours au Collège de France (1980–1981)*. Ed. Frédéric Gros. Paris: EHESS/Gallimard/Seuil, 2014.

Foucault, Michel. *Subjectivity and Truth: Lectures at the Collège de France, 1980–1981*. Ed. Frédéric Gros. Trans. Graham Burchell. London: Palgrave Macmillan, 2017.

Foucault, Michel. *Surveiller et punir. Naissance de la prison*. In *Michel Foucault: Oeuvres*. Vol. 2, ed. Bernard E. Harcourt, 261–613. Paris: Gallimard/La Pléiade, 2015.

Foucault, Michel. *Théories et institutions pénales. Cours au Collège de France. 1971–1972*. Ed. Bernard E. Harcourt. Paris: Gallimard/Seuil, 2015.

Foucault, Michel. *La Volonté de savoir*. Paris: Gallimard, 1976.

Foucault, Michel. "What Is Enlightenment?" In *The Foucault Reader*, ed. Paul Rabinow, 32–50. New York: Pantheon, 1984.

Foucault, Michel. *Wrong-Doing, Truth-Telling: The Function of Avowal in Justice*. Ed. Fabienne Brion and Bernard E. Harcourt. Trans. Stephen W. Sawyer. Chicago: University of Chicago Press, 2014.

Foucault, Michel, and Gilles Deleuze. "Intellectuals and Power: A Conversation Between Michel Foucault and Gilles Deleuze." In *Language, Counter-memory, Practice: Selected Essays and Interviews*, ed. Donald F. Bouchard, trans. Donald F. Bouchard and Sherry Simon, 214–215. Ithaca, NY: Cornell University Press, 1977.

Fraser, Nancy. "Legitimation Crisis? On the Political Contradictions of Financialized Capitalism." *Critical Historical Studies* 2, no. 2 (2015): 157–189.

Fraser, Nancy. "Legitimation Crisis? On the Political Contradictions of Financialized Capitalism." Paper presented at the Legal Theory Workshop at Columbia University in New York on April 20, 2015 (on file with author).

Fraser, Nancy, and Axel Honneth. *Redistribution or Recognition? A Political-Philosophical Exchange*. New York: Verso, 2003.

Fraser, Nancy, and Rahel Jaeggi. *Capitalism: A Conversation in Critical Theory*. New York: Polity, 2018.

Freire, Paulo. *Pedagogy of the Oppressed*. New York: Continuum, 1968.

Freud, Sigmund. *The Future of an Illusion*. Ed. and trans. James Strachey. New York: Norton, 1961.

Freud, Sigmund. *Die Zukunft einer Illusion*. Leipzig, Germany: Internationaler Psychoanalytischer Verlag, 1928.

Friberg, Daniel. *The Real Right Returns: A Handbook for the True Opposition*. London: Arktos Media, 2015.

Gallop, Jane. *Reading Lacan*. Ithaca, NY: Cornell University Press, 1985.

Gandhi, M. K. *Non-Violent Resistance (Satyagraha)*. New York: Dover Publications, 2001.

Garcia, Vivien. *L'anarchisme aujourd'hui*. Paris: L'Harmattan, 2009.

Garland, David. *Peculiar Institution: America's Death Penalty in an Age of Abolition*. Cambridge, MA: Harvard University Press, 2012.

Garland, David. "Penality and the Penal State." *Criminology* 51, no. 3 (2013): 475–517.

Geertz, Clifford. *After the Fact: Two Countries, Four Decades, One Anthropologist*. Cambridge, MA: Harvard University Press, 1995.

General Accounting Office, United States. *Death Penalty Sentencing: Research Indicates Pattern of Racial Disparities*. Report to Senate and House Committees on the Judiciary. February 1990.

Geuss, Raymond. *The Idea of a Critical Theory: Habermas and the Frankfurt School.* Cambridge: Cambridge University Press, 1981.

Geuss, Raymond, and Lawrence Hamilton. "Human Rights: A Very Bad Idea: Interview with Raymond Geuss." By Lawrence Hamilton. *Theoria: A Journal of Social and Political Theory* 60, no. 135 (June 2013): 83–103.

Gilmore, Ruth Wilson. *Golden Gulag: Prisons, Surplus, Crisis, and Opposition in Globalizing California.* Berkeley: University of California Press, 2007.

GIP. "Manifeste du GIP," February 8, 1971. In Michel Foucault, *Dits et Écrits*, vol. 1: *1954–1975*, ed. Daniel Defert, François Ewald, and Jacques Lagrange. Paris: Gallimard/Quarto, 2001.

Goldstein, Emmanuel. "Hacktivism and the Hacker Promise." *Uprising 13/13* (blog). March 16, 2018. http://blogs.law.columbia.edu/uprising1313/emmanuel-goldstein-hacktivism-and-the-hacker-promise/.

Gooding-Williams, Robert. *In the Shadow of Du Bois: Afro-Modern Political Thought in America.* Cambridge, MA: Harvard University Press, 2015.

Gooding-Williams, Robert. *Zarathustra's Dionysian Modernism.* Palo Alto, CA: Stanford University Press, 2002.

Gourgouris, Stathis. "Preliminary Thoughts on Left Governmentality." *Critical Times* 1, no. 1 (2018): 99–107. https://ctjournal.org/index.php/criticaltimes/article/view/14.

Gourgouris, Stathis, Jacques Lezra, and Ann Stoler, eds. *Political Concepts—A Lexicon in Formation: Thinking with Balibar.* New York: Fordham University Press, 2020.

Gosse, Van. "A Movement of Movements: The Definition and Periodization of the New Left." In *A Companion to Post-1945 America*, ed. Jean-Christophe Agnew and Roy Rosenzweig, 277–302. Hoboken, NJ: Blackwell Publishing, 2006.

Greenberg, Jack. *Litigation for Social Change: Methods, Limits, and Role in Democracy.* New York: Association of the Bar of the City of New York, 1974.

Greenwald, Glenn. *No Place to Hide: Edward Snowden, the NSA, and the U.S. Surveillance State.* New York: Metropolitan, 2014.

Gros, Frédéric. *Désobéir.* Paris: Albin Michel, 2017.

Grossman, Cathy Lynn. "Religion Colors Money Views; Survey Reveals Many See God Steering Economy, Government as Meddlers." *USA Today*, September 20, 2011.

Guercio, Francesco, trans. "*A/Traverso*, Notebook #1 (October 1975), Part ¼," *Uprising 13/13* (blog). September 27, 2017. http://blogs.law.columbia.edu/uprising1313/francesco-guercio-annotated-translation-of-atraverso-notebook-1-october-1975-part-14/.

Habermas, Jürgen. *Between Facts and Norms: Contributions to a Discourse Theory of Law and Democracy.* Cambridge, MA: MIT Press, 1996.

Habermas, Jürgen. "Concluding Remarks." In *Habermas and the Public Sphere*, ed. Craig Calhoun, 462–479. Cambridge, MA: MIT Press, 1992.

Habermas, Jürgen. *Legitimation Crisis.* Trans. Thomas McCarthy. Boston: Beacon, 1975.

Habermas, Jürgen. *The New Conservatism: Cultural Criticism and the Historians' Debate.* Trans. Shierry Weber Nicholsen. Cambridge, MA: MIT Press, 1991.

Habermas, Jürgen. *The Philosophical Discourse of Modernity.* Trans. Frederick Lawrence. Cambridge: Polity, 1987.

Habermas, Jürgen. "Reconciliation Through the Public Use of Reason: Remarks on John Rawls's Political Liberalism." *Journal of Philosophy* 92, no. 3 (1995): 109–131.

Habermas, Jürgen. *The Structural Transformation of the Public Sphere: An Inquiry into a Category of Bourgeois Society.* Trans. Thomas Burger. Cambridge, MA: MIT Press, 1991.

Hacking, Ian. "Making Up People." In *Historical Ontology*, ed. Ian Hacking, 99–114. Cambridge, MA: Harvard University Press, 2002.

Hacking, Ian. *The Taming of Chance*. New York: Cambridge University Press, 1990.

Halberstam, Jack. "Strategy of Wildness." *Praxis 13/13* (blog). February 25, 2019. http://blogs.law.columbia.edu/praxis1313/jack-halberstam-strategy-of-wildness/.

Halberstam, Jack. "The Wild Beyond: With and for the Undercommons." Introduction to Stefano Harney and Fred Moten, *The Undercommons: Fugitive Planning & Black Study*, 5–12. Wivenhoe, UK: Minor Compositions, 2013.

Hall, Stuart, Chas Critcher, Tony Jefferson, John Clarke, and Brian Roberts. *Policing the Crisis: Mugging, the State, and Law and Order*. London: MacMillan, 1978.

Halley, Janet. "Sexuality Harassment." In *Directions in Sexual Harassment Law*, ed. Catherine MacKinnon and Reva Siegel, 80–104. New Haven, CT: Yale University Press, 2002.

Hallward, Peter. "Communism of the Intellect, Communism of the Will." In *The Idea of Communism*. vol. 1, ed. Costas Douzinas and Slavoj Žižek, 111–130. New York: Verso, 2010.

Haraway, Donna J. *Staying with the Trouble: Making Kin in the Chthulucene*. Durham, NC: Duke University Press, 2016.

Harcourt, Bernard E. *Against Prediction: Profiling, Policing, and Punishing in an Actuarial Age*. Chicago: University of Chicago Press, 2007.

Harcourt, Bernard E. "The Collapse of the Harm Principle." *Journal of Criminal Law and Criminology* 90, no. 1 (1999): 109–194.

Harcourt, Bernard E. "Counter-Critical Theory: An Intervention in Contemporary Critical Thought and Practice." *Critical Times: Interventions in Global Critical Theory* 1, no. 1 (2018): 5–22.

Harcourt, Bernard E. *The Counterrevolution: How Our Government Went to War Against Its Own Citizens*. New York: Basic Books, 2018.

Harcourt, Bernard E. *Exposed: Desire and Disobedience in the Digital Age*. Cambridge, MA: Harvard University Press, 2015.

Harcourt, Bernard E. "Foreword to the Supreme Court Review: 'You Are Entering a Gay and Lesbian-Free Zone': On the Radical Dissents of Justice Scalia and Other (Post-) Queers [Raising Questions about *Lawrence*, Sex Wars, and the Criminal Law]." *Journal of Criminal Law and Criminology* 94, no. 3 (2004): 503–549.

Harcourt, Bernard E. *The Illusion of Free Markets: Punishment and the Myth of Natural Order*. Cambridge, MA: Harvard University Press, 2011.

Harcourt, Bernard E. *Language of the Gun: Youth, Crime, and Public Policy*. Chicago: University of Chicago Press, 2006.

Harcourt, Bernard E. "Political Disobedience." In *Occupy: Three Inquiries in Disobedience*, ed. W. J. T. Mitchell, Bernard E. Harcourt, and Michael Taussig, 45–91. Chicago: University of Chicago Press, 2013.

Harcourt, Bernard E. "Radical Thought from Marx, Nietzsche, and Freud, Through Foucault, to the Present: Comments on Steven Lukes's 'In Defense of False Consciousness.'" *University of Chicago Legal Forum* 2011, no. 1 (2011): 29–51.

Harding, Luke. *The Snowden Files: The Inside Story of the World's Most Wanted Man*. New York: Vintage, 2014.

Hardt, Michael, and Antonio Negri. *Assembly*. New York: Oxford University Press, 2017.

Hardt, Michael and Antonio Negri. *Commonwealth*. Cambridge, MA: The Belknap Press of Harvard University Press, 2011.

Harney, Stefano, and Fred Moten. *The Undercommons: Fugitive Planning & Black Study*. Wivenhoe, UK: Minor Compositions, 2013.

Harris, Cheryl. "Whiteness as Property." In *Critical Race Theory*, ed. Kimberlé Crenshaw, Neil T. Gotanda, Gary Peller, and Kendall Thomas, 276–291. New York: New Press, 1996.

Hartman, Saidiya. "Venus in Two Acts." *Small Axe*, no. 26, 12 (2), June 2008: 1–14.

Harvey, David. *A Brief History of Neoliberalism.* Oxford: Oxford University Press, 2005.

Harvey, David L. "Introduction." *Sociological Perspectives* 33, no. 1 (1990): 1–10.

Hayek, F. A. *The Road to Serfdom.* Ed. Bruce Caldwell. Chicago: University of Chicago Press, 2007.

Hayes, Chris. *A Colony in a Nation.* New York: Norton, 2017.

Hegel, G. W. F. *Elements of the Philosophy of Right.* Ed. Allen W. Wood. Trans. H. B. Nisbet. Cambridge: Cambridge University Press, 1991.

Hegel, G. W. F. *Phenomenology of Spirit.* Trans. A. V. Miller. Oxford: Oxford University Press, 1981.

Hessel, Stéphane. *Indignez-vous.* Montpellier, France: Indigène editions, 2010.

Hill-Collins, Patricia. *Black Feminist Thought: Knowledge, Consciousness, and the Politics of Empowerment.* New York: Routledge, 2009.

Hobbes, Thomas. *Leviathan.* Ed. Richard Tuck. Cambridge: Cambridge University Press, 1996.

Holliday, Darryl. "The New Black Power: They're Young. They're Radical. They're Organized. And They're a Thorn in Rahm's Side." *Chicago Magazine*, February 22, 2016. http://www.chicagomag.com/Chicago-Magazine/March-2016/black-leaders/.

Homza, Lu Ann. *The Spanish Inquisition, 1478–1614: An Anthology of Sources.* Indianapolis: Hackett Publishing, 2006.

Honig, Bonnie. *Political Theory and the Displacement of Politics.* Ithaca, NY: Cornell University Press, 1993.

Honneth, Axel. *Critique of Power: Reflective Stages in a Critical Social Theory.* Trans. Kenneth Baynes. Cambridge, MA: MIT Press, 1991.

Honneth, Axel. *The Idea of Socialism: Towards a Renewal.* Cambridge: Polity, 2017.

Horkheimer, Max. *Critical Theory: Selected Essays.* Trans. Matthew J. O'Connell et al. New York: Continuum, 1992.

Horkheimer, Max. *Eclipse of Reason.* London: Bloomsbury, 1974.

Horkheimer, Max. "The Latest Attack on Metaphysics." In *Critical Theory: Selected Essays*, trans. Matthew J. O'Connell et al., 132–187. New York: Continuum, 1992.

Horkheimer, Max. "Traditional and Critical Theory." In *Critical Theory: Selected Essays*, trans. Matthew J. O'Connell et al., 188–252. New York: Continuum, 1992.

Horkheimer, Max, and Theodor W. Adorno. *Dialectic of Enlightenment.* Trans. John Cumming. New York: Continuum, 1996.

Howard, Dick. "An Interview with C. Castoriadis." *Telos* 23 (1975): 134.

Hoy, David, ed. *Foucault: A Critical Reader.* Oxford: Basil Blackwell, 1986.

Hoy, David. "Power, Repression, Progress: Foucault, Lukes, and the Frankfurt School." In *Foucault: A Critical Reader*, 123–148. London: Basil Blackwell, 1986.

Hugo, Victor. *Écrits sur la peine de mort.* Arles, France: Actes Sud, 2002.

Husserl, Edmund. *The Crisis of European Science and Transcendental Phenomenology.* Trans. David Carr. Evanston: Northwestern University Press, 1970.

Indivisible: A Practical Guide for Resisting the Trump Agenda. Last updated 12/14/2016. http://election.princeton.edu/wp-content/uploads/2016/12/Indivisible_-A-Practical-Guide-For-Resisting-the-Trump-Agenda-Google-Docs.pdf.

Invisible Committee, The. *The Coming Insurrection.* Cambridge, MA: MIT Press (Semiotext(e)), 2009.

Invisible Committee, The. *Now.* Cambridge, MA: MIT Press (Semiotext(e)), 2017.

Invisible Committee, The. *To Our Friends.* Cambridge, MA: MIT Press (Semiotext(e)), 2015.

Irigaray, Luce. *Ce Sexe qui n'en est pas un.* Paris: Minuit, 1977.

Irigaray, Luce. *This Sex Which Is Not One.* Trans. Catherine Porter with Carolyn Burke. Ithaca, NY: Cornell University Press, 1985.

Iyengar, Shanto, and Douglas S. Massey. "Scientific communication in a post-truth society." *PNAS* 116, no. 16 (2019): 7656–7661.

Jaeggi, Rahel. *Critique of Forms of Life*. Trans. Ciaran Cronin. Cambridge, MA: The Belknap Press of Harvard University Press, 2018.

Jaeggi, Rahel. "Ideology as Social Practice." Paper presented at Columbia University Political Theory Workshop, February 6, 2019 (on file with author).

Jaeggi, Rahel. "Rethinking Ideology." In *New Waves in Political Philosophy*, ed. Boudewijn de Bruin and Christopher F. Zurn, 63–86. New York: Palgrave Macmillan, 2009.

Jameson, Frederic. *Marxism and Form: Twentieth Century Dialectical Theories of Literature*. Princeton: Princeton University Press, 1971.

Jarry, Vincent. *La démocratie des murmures*. Paris: Éditions Excès, 2019.

Jay, Martin. *The Dialectical Imagination: A History of the Frankfurt School and the Institute for Social Research, 1923–1950*. Berkeley: University of California Press, 1973.

Jennings, Michael W. *Dialectical Images: Walter Benjamin's Theory of Literary Criticism*. Ithaca, NY: Cornell University Press, 1987.

Jonsson, Stefan. "Aesthetic Dimensions of Contemporary Protest: Methodological Considerations on Monstrous Events." Paper presented May 11, 2018, at Yale University, New Haven, CT (on file with author).

Kakutani, Michiko. *The Death of Truth: Notes on Falsehood in the Age of Trump*. New York: Tim Duggan, 2018.

Kanō, Jigorō, and T. Lindsay. "Jujutsu and the Origins of Judo." In *Transactions of the Asiatic Society of Japan*, Vol. 15. Yokohama, Japan: R. Meiklejohn and Co., 1887.

Kant, Immanuel. "An Answer to the Question: 'What Is Enlightenment?'" In *Political Writings*, ed. Hans Reiss, 54–63, 2nd ed. Cambridge: Cambridge University Press, 1991.

Kant, Immanuel. "On the Common Saying: That May Be Correct in Theory, But It Is of No Use in Practice." In *Practical Philosophy*, ed. Mary Gregor, 273–310. Cambridge: Cambridge University Press, 1996.

Kant, Immanuel. *Critique of Practical Reason*. Ed. Mary Gregor. Trans. Mary Gregor. Cambridge: Cambridge University Press, 1997.

Kant, Immanuel. *Critique of Pure Reason*. Trans. Norman Kemp Smith. New York: St. Martin's, 1965.

Katznelson, Ira. *Fear Itself: The New Deal and the Origins of Our Time*. New York: Norton, 2013.

Kavanagh, Jennifer, and Michael D. Rich. *Truth Decay: An Initial Exploration of the Diminishing Role of Facts and Analysis in American Public Life*. Santa Monica, CA: RAND Corporation, 2018. https://www.rand.org/pubs/research_reports/RR2314.html.

Kazanjian, David. *The Colonizing Trick: National Culture and Imperial Citizenship in Early America*. Minneapolis: University of Minnesota Press, 2003.

Kelley, Robin D. G. "Coates and West in Jackson." *Boston Review*, December 22, 2017. http://bostonreview.net/race/robin-d-g-kelley-coates-and-west-jackson.

Kelly, Michael, ed. *Critique and Power: Recasting the Foucault/Habermas Debate*. Cambridge, MA: MIT Press, 1994.

Kennedy, David. "The International Human Rights Movement: Part of the Problem?" *European Human Rights Law Review* 15, no. 3 (2001): 101–125.

Kennedy, Duncan. *A Critique of Adjudication: Fin de Siècle*. Cambridge, MA: Harvard University Press, 1997.

Kennedy, Duncan. "Critique of Rights in Critical Legal Studies," in *Left Legalism/Left Critique*. Ed. Wendy Brown and Janet Halley, 178–228. Durham, NC: Duke University Press, 2002.

Kennedy, Duncan. "The Stakes of Law, or Hale and Foucault!" *Legal Studies Forum* XV, no. 4 (1991): 327–366.

Kiéfer, Audrey. *Michel Foucault: Le GIP, l'histoire et l'action.* Philosophy thesis, Université de Picardie Jules Verne d'Amiens, France, 2006.

King, Martin Luther, Jr. *A Testament of Hope: The Essential Writings of Martin Luther King, Jr.* San Francisco: Harper & Row, 1986.

Klossowski, Pierre. *Nietzsche et le cercle vicieux.* Paris: Mercure de France, 1969.

Kofman, Sarah. *Nietzsche et la métaphore.* Paris: Éditions Galilée, 1972.

Kofman, Sarah. *Nietzsche et la scène philosophique.* Paris: Éditions Galilée, 1979.

Kojève, Alexandre. *Introduction to the Reading of Hegel: Lectures on the* Phenomenology of Spirit. Ed. Allan Bloom. Trans. James H. Nichols, Jr. Ithaca, NY: Cornell University Press, 1980.

Koopman, Colin. "Conduct and Power: Foucault's Methodological Expansions in 1971." In *Active Intolerance: Michel Foucault, the Prisons Information Group, and the Future of Abolition*, ed. Perry Zurn and Andrew Dilts, 59–74. New York: Palgrave Macmillan, 2016.

Koopman, Colin. "Critical Problematization in Foucault and Deleuze: The Force of Critique Without Judgment." In *Between Deleuze and Foucault*, ed. Nicolae Morar, Thomas Nail, and Daniel Smith, 87–119. Edinburgh: Edinburgh University Press, 2016.

Koopman, Colin. *Genealogy as Critique: Foucault and the Problems of Modernity.* Bloomington: Indiana University Press, 2013.

Koopman, Colin. *How We Became Our Data: A Genealogy of the Informational Person.* Chicago: University of Chicago Press, 2019.

Koopman, Colin. "Problematization in Foucault's Genealogy and Deleuze's Symptomatology." *Angelaki: Journal of the Theoretical Humanities* 12, no. 2 (April 2018): 187–203.

Koselleck, Reinhart. *Critique and Crisis: Enlightenment and the Pathogenesis of Modern Society.* Cambridge, MA: MIT Press, 1988.

Koselleck, Reinhart. "Historical Criteria of the Modern Concept of Revolution." In Reinhart Koselleck, *Futures Past: On the Semantics of Historical Time*, trans. Keith Tribe. New York: Columbia University Press, 2004.

Koselleck, Reinhart. "Vergangene Zukunft. Zur Semantik geschichtlicher Zeiten." *Zeitschrift für Philosophische Forschung* 34, no. 3 (1980): 461–464.

Lacan, Jacques. *Écrits.* Paris: Éditions du Seuil, 1966.

Lacan, Jacques. *Le Séminaire de Jacques Lacan, Livre XI, "Les quatre concepts fondamentaux de la psychanalyse."* Paris: Seuil, 1973.

Lacoue-Labarthe, Philippe, and Jean-Luc Nancy. *Retreating the Political.* New York: Routledge, 1997.

Latour, Bruno. "Anthropology at the Time of the Anthropocene. A Personal View of What Is to Be Studied." Lecture to the American Association of Anthropologists, Washington, DC, 2014.

Latour, Bruno. *Down to Earth: Politics in the New Climatic Regime.* Cambridge: Polity, 2018.

Latour, Bruno. "Why Has Critique Run Out of Steam? From Matters of Fact to Matters of Concern." *Critical Inquiry* 30, no. 2 (2004): 225–248.

Laugier, Sandra, and Albert Ogien. *Pourquoi désobéir en démocratie?* Paris: La Découverte, 2011.

Lecourt, Dominique. "The Sadism of Foucault." Paper presented at the Foucault Colloquium, Créteil, Paris, 2014.

Lenin, Vladimir Ilyich. "The Tasks of the Proletariat in the Present Revolution" [a.k.a. "The April Theses"]. *Pravda* no. 26, April 7, 1917.

Lenin, Vladimir Ilyich. *What Is To Be Done? Burning Questions of Our Movement.* New York: International Publishers, 1929.

Leshem, Dotan. *The Origins of Neoliberalism: Modeling the Economy from Jesus to Foucault.* New York: Columbia University Press, 2016.

Levi, Simona. "Working Notes for a R-evolution." *Uprising 13/13* (blog). March 12, 2018. http://blogs.law.columbia.edu/uprising1313/simona-levi-working-notes-for-a-r-evolution/.

Levitin, Daniel J. *Weaponized Lies: How to Think Critically in the Post-Truth Era.* New York: Penguin Random House, 2016.

Lewandowsky, Stephan, Ullrich K. H. Ecker, and John Cook. "Beyond Misinformation: Understanding and Coping with the 'Post-Truth' Era." *Journal of Applied Research in Memory and Cognition* 6, no. 4 (2017): 353–369.

Lezra, Jacques. "Solidarity." In *Political Concepts—a Lexicon in Formation: Thinking with Balibar*, ed. Stathis Gourgouris, Jacques Lezra, and Ann Stoler. New York: Fordham University Press, 2020.

Livingston, Alexander. *Freedom Now: Inventing Civil Disobedience in Twentieth-Century America* (book project).

Lobkowicz, Nicholas. *Theory and Practice: History of a Concept from Aristotle to Marx.* Notre Dame, IN: University of Notre Dame Press, 1967.

Locke, John. "Second Treatise on Government." In *Two Treatises of Government*, ed. Peter Laslett, 265–428. Cambridge: Cambridge University Press, 1988.

Lorde, Audre. "The Master's Tools Will Never Dismantle the Master's House." In Audre Lorde, *Sister Outsider: Essays and Speeches*, 110–113. Berkeley, CA: Crossing Press, 2007.

Lorenzini, Daniele. *La Force du vrai. De Foucault à Austin.* Lormont, France: Le Bord de l'eau, 2017.

Lorenzini, Daniele. "On Possibilising Genealogy." Draft presented at the Columbia Center for Contemporary Critical Thought's "Critical Work" workshop on April 19, 2019 (draft on file with author).

Lorenzini, Daniele, and Martina Tazzioli. "Critique's Others, Desubjugation, History. The Re-appropriation of Problems Beyond the Quest for Evidence." Working paper, August 1, 2019 (draft on file with author).

Lukes, Steven. "In Defense of 'False Consciousness.'" *University of Chicago Legal Forum* 2011 (2011): 29–52. http://chicagounbound.uchicago.edu/uclf/vol2011/iss1/3/.

Lukes, Steven. "The Grand Dichotomy of the Twentieth Century." In *The Cambridge History of the Twentieth Century Political Thought*, ed. Terence Ball and Richard Bellamy. Cambridge: Cambridge University Press, 2003.

Lukes, Steven. *Power: A Radical View.* New York: Palgrave Macmillan, 2005.

Lukes, Steven. "Power, Truth and Epistemic Closure." *Praxis 13/13* (blog). September 9, 2018. http://blogs.law.columbia.edu/praxis1313/steven-lukes-power-truth-and-epistemic-closure/.

Luxemburg, Rosa. *The Crisis in the German Social Democracy: The Junius Pamphlet (1919).* Whitefish, MO: Kessinger, 2010.

Luxemburg, Rosa. *Organizational Questions of Russian Social Democracy.* Creative Commons: 2017. Originally published in 1904. https://archive.org/details/Leninism_Or_Marxism_New.

Luxemburg, Rosa. *Reform or Revolution and Other Writings.* Mineola, NY: Dover, 2006.

Lyons, David. *Confronting Injustice: Moral History and Political Theory.* Oxford: Oxford University Press, 2013.

Macpherson, C. B. *The Political Theory of Possessive Individualism: From Hobbes to Locke.* Oxford: Oxford University Press, 1962.

Madar, Chase. *The Passion of Bradley Manning: The Story Behind the Wikileaks Whistleblower.* New York: Verso, 2013.

Maharawal, Manissa. "Standing Up." In *Occupy!* ed. Carla Blumenkranz et al. New York: Verso, 2011.

Mahmood, Saba. *Politics of Piety: The Islamic Revival and the Feminist Subject.* Princeton, NJ: Princeton University Press, 2005.

Mannheim, Karl. *Ideology and Utopia: An Introduction to the Sociology of Knowledge.* New York: Harcourt, Brace and Company, 1940.

Mantena, Karuna. "The Power of Nonviolence." *Aeon*, March 11, 2016. https://aeon.co/essays/nonviolence-has-returned-from-obscurity-to-become-a-new-force.

Mantena, Karuna. "Showdown for Nonviolence: The Theory and Practice of Nonviolent Politics." In *To Shape a New World: Essays on the Political Philosophy of Martin Luther King, Jr.*, ed. Tommie Shelby and Brandon M. Terry, 78–101. Cambridge, MA: Belknap Harvard University Press, 2018.

Manza, Jeff, and Christopher Uggen. *Locked Out: Felon Disenfranchisement and American Democracy.* New York: Oxford University Press, 2006.

Marchart, Oliver. *Post-Foundational Political Thought: Political Difference in Nancy, Lefort, Badiou and Laclau.* Edinburgh: Edinburgh University Press, 2007.

Marcuse, Herbert. *Counterrevolution and Revolt.* Boston: Beacon, 1972.

Marcuse, Herbert. *One-Dimensional Man.* Boston: Beacon, 1964.

Marx, Karl. "Afterword (Second German Ed.)." In *Capital: A Critique of Political Economy*, ed. Frederick Engels, trans. Samuel Moore and Edward Aveling. Moscow: Progress Publishers, 1965.

Marx, Karl. *Capital: A Critique of Political Economy.* Vol. 1. Trans. Ben Fowkes. New York: Vintage, 1976.

Marx, Karl. "Economic and Philosophical Manuscripts of 1844." In *The Marx-Engels Reader*, 2nd ed., ed. Robert C. Tucker, trans. Ronald Rogowski, 66–125. New York: Norton, 1978.

Marx, Karl. "Eleventh Thesis." In *The German Ideology.* London: Lawrence and Wishart, 1938.

Marx, Karl. "On the Jewish Question." In *The Marx-Engels Reader*, 2nd ed., ed. Robert C. Tucker, trans. Ronald Rogowski, 26–52. New York: Norton, 1978.

Marx, Karl. "For a Ruthless Criticism of Everything Existing," originally in the *Deutsch-Franzosische Jahrbucher* (1844), reproduced in *The Marx-Engels Reader*, 2nd ed., ed. Robert C. Tucker, trans. Ronald Rogowski, 12–15. New York: Norton, 1978.

Marx, Karl, and Frederick Engels. *Manifesto of the Communist Party.* Ed. Frederick Engels. New York: International Publishers, 1948.

Massey, Douglas S. *Categorically Unequal: The American Stratification System.* New York: Russel Sage Foundation, 2008.

Mauvaise Troupe Collective. *The Zad and NoTAV: Territorial Struggles and the Making of a New Political Intelligence.* Trans. Kristin Ross. New York: Verso, 2018.

Maxwell, Lida. *Insurgent Truth: Chelsea Manning and the Politics of Outsider Truth-Telling.* New York: Oxford University Press, 2019.

May, Todd. *Nonviolent Resistance: A Philosophical Introduction.* Cambridge: Polity, 2015.

May, Todd. *The Political Philosophy of Poststructuralist Anarchism.* University Park: The Pennsylvania State University Press, 1994.

Mbembe, Achille. *Critique of Black Reason.* Durham, NC: Duke University Press, 2017.

Mbembe, Achille. "Necropolitics." *Public Culture* 15, no. 1 (2003): 11–40.

McBride, Keally. *Tea Party Rules: Rousseau's American Tour 2011* (2017), unpublished manuscript (draft on file with author).

McCarthy, Thomas. "The Critique of Impure Reason: Foucault and the Frankfurt School." *Political Theory* 18, no. 3 (1990): 437–469.

McCarthy, Thomas. *Race, Empire, and the Idea of Human Development.* Cambridge: Cambridge University Press, 2009.

McIntyre, Lee. *Post-Truth.* Cambridge, MA: MIT Press, 2018.

McLeod, Allegra. "Law, Critique, and the Undercommons." In *A Time for Critique*, ed. Didier Fassin and Bernard E. Harcourt, 252–270. New York: Columbia University Press, 2019.

Mehta, Uday Singh. "Gandhi on Democracy, Politics and the Ethics of Everyday Life," *Modern Intellectual History* 7, no. 2 (2010): 355–371.

Merleau-Ponty, Maurice. *Phénoménologie de la perception*. Paris: Gallimard, 1945.

Mertes, Tom, ed. *A Movement of Movements: Is Another World Really Possible?* New York: Verso, 2004.

Michelman, Frank. "Law's Republic." *Yale Law Journal* 97, no. 8 (1988): 1493–1537.

Mitchell, W. J. T., Michael Taussig, and Bernard E. Harcourt. *Occupy: Three Inquiries in Disobedience*. Chicago: University of Chicago Press, 2013.

Moore, Jason, ed. *Anthropocene or Capitalocene?* Oakland, CA: PM Press, 2016.

Morris, Rosalind, ed. *Can the Subaltern Speak? Reflections on the History of an Idea*. New York: Columbia University Press, 2010.

Morris, Rosalind. "Unpopular Politics: The Collective, the Communist and the Popular in Recent Thai History." In *The Seoul Conference*, vol. 3 of *The Idea of Communism*, ed. Slavoj Žižek and Alex Taek-Gwang Lee, 212–239. New York: Verso, 2016.

Mouffe, Chantal. *For a Left Populism*. New York: Verso, 2018.

Mouffe, Chantal, and Ernesto Laclau. *Hegemony and Socialist Strategy*. New York: Verso, 1986.

Moyn, Samuel. *Not Enough: Human Rights in an Unequal World*. Cambridge, MA: Harvard University Press, 2018.

Müller, Jan-Werner. *What Is Populism?* Philadelphia: University of Pennsylvania Press, 2016.

Muñoz, José Esteban. *Disidentifications: Queers of Color and the Performance of Politics*. Minneapolis: University of Minnesota Press, 1999.

Myers, Ella. *Worldly Ethics: Democratic Politics and Care for the World*. Durham, NC: Duke University Press, 2013.

Negri, Antonio. "French Insurrection." *Verso* (blog). December 8, 2018. https://www.versobooks.com/blogs/4158-french-insurrection.

Negri, Antonio. "Gilets jaunes: Un contropotere." *Praxis, 13/13* (blog). January 11, 2019. http://blogs.law.columbia.edu/praxis1313/antonio-negri-gilets-jaunes-un-contropotere/.

Negri, Antonio. "Reflections on the Seventh Round of the *Gilets Jaunes*." EuroNomade. January 5, 2019. http://www.euronomade.info/?p=11480.

Nehamas, Alexander. "The Genealogy of Genealogy: Interpretation in Nietzsche's Second 'Untimely Meditation' and in 'On the Genealogy of Morals.' " In *Nietzsche, Genealogy, History: Essays on Nietzsche's Genealogy of Morals*, ed. Richard Schacht, 269–283. Berkeley: University of California Press, 1994.

Neumann, Franz. *Behemoth: The Structure and Practice of National Socialism*. Oxford: Oxford University Press, 1942.

Neumann, Franz, Herbert Marcuse, and Otto Kirchheimer. *Secret Reports on Nazi Germany: The Frankfurt School Contribution to the War Effort*, ed. Raffaele Laudani. Princeton, NJ: Princeton University Press, 2013.

Newman, Saul. *Power and Politics in Poststructuralist Thought: New Theories of the Political*. New York: Routledge, 2005.

Nietzsche, Friedrich. *Daybreak: Thoughts on the Prejudices of Morality*. Ed. Maudemarie Clark and Brian Leiter. Trans. R. J. Hollingdale. Cambridge: Cambridge University Press, 1997.

Nietzsche, Friedrich. *The Gay Science*. Ed. Bernard Williams. Trans. Josefine Nauckhoff. Cambridge: Cambridge University Press, 2001.

Nietzsche, Friedrich. *On the Genealogy of Morals*. Trans. Walter Kaufmann and R. J. Hollingdale. New York: Vintage, 1989.

Nietzsche, Friedrich. *Thus Spoke Zarathustra*. Ed. Adrian del Caro and Robert B. Pippin. Cambridge: Cambridge University Press, 2006.

Nietzsche, Friedrich. "On Truth and Lie in a Nonmoral Sense (1873)." In *On Truth and Untruth: Selected Writings*, ed. and trans. Taylor Carman, 17–49. New York: HarperCollins, 2010.

Nietzsche, Friedrich. *Twilight of the Idols and the Anti-Christ.* Trans. R. J. Hollingdale. New York: Penguin, 1990.

Nietzsche, Friedrich. *Will to Power.* Ed. Walter Kaufman. Trans. Walter Kaufman and R. J. Hollingdale. New York: Vintage, 1968.

Obarrio, Juan. *The Spirit of the Laws in Mozambique.* Chicago: University of Chicago Press, 2014.

Ockham, William of. *Breviloquium de principatu tyrannico.* In *Opera Politica*, Vol. 4. Ed. Hilary Seton Offler, 97–260. Oxford: Oxford University Press, 1997.

O'Connor, Cailin, and James Owen Weatherall. *The Misinformation Age: How False Beliefs Spread.* New Haven, CT: Yale University Press, 2018.

Pagès, Ghislaine. "Revolutionary in Rhetoric Only." *Praxis 3/13* (blog). October 24, 2018. http://blogs.law.columbia.edu/praxis1313/ghislaine-pages-revolutionary-in-rhetoric-only/.

Palin, Sarah. *Going Rogue: An American Life.* New York: HarperCollins Publishers, 2009.

Parla, Ayse. "Critique Without a Politics of Hope?" In *A Time for Critique*, ed. Didier Fassin and Bernard E. Harcourt, 52–70. New York: Columbia University Press, 2019.

Patton, Paul. *Deleuze and the Political.* London: Routledge, 2000.

Patton, Paul. *Deleuzian Concepts: Philosophy, Colonization, Politics.* Stanford, CA: Stanford University Press, 2010.

Peeters, Rik, and Marc Schuilenburg. "Gift Politics: Exposure and Surveillance in the Anthropocene." *Crime, Law, and Social Change* 68, no. 5 (2017): 563–578.

Peillon, Antoine. *Coeur de boxeur. Le vrai combat de Christophe Dettinger.* Paris: Les liens qui libèrent, 2019.

Pérez Caldentey, Esteban, and Matías Vernengo, eds. *Ideas, Policies, and Economic Development in the Americas.* New York: Routledge, 2007.

Pérez Caldentey, Esteban, and Matías Vernengo, eds. *Why Latin American Nations Fail: Development Strategies in the Twenty-First Century.* Oakland: University of California Press, 2017.

Perroux, François. *La Co-existence pacifique*, Vol. 3. Paris: Presses Universitaires de France, 1958.

Pierce, Lee. "Review of *Notes Toward a Performative Theory of Assembly*, by Judith Butler." *Philosophy & Rhetoric* (2017): 356–362.

Piketty, Thomas. *Le Capital au XXIème siècle.* Paris: Seuil, 2013.

Piketty, Thomas. *Capital in the Twenty-First Century.* Cambridge, MA: Harvard University Press, 2014.

Piketty, Thomas. "*Vers une économie politique et historique: Réflexions sur le capital au XXIe siècle.*" *Annales. Histoire, Sciences Sociales* 1, no. 70 (2015): 125–138.

Pinker, Steven. *Enlightenment Now: The Case for Reason, Science, Humanism, and Progress.* New York: Penguin, 2018.

Plato. *The Collected Dialogues of Plato.* Ed. Edith Hamilton and Huntington Cairns (Princeton: Princeton University Press, 1989.

Popper, Karl. *The Logic of Scientific Discovery.* New York: Routledge, 2002.

Poulantzas, Nicos. *L'État, le Pouvoir, le Socialisme.* Paris: Presses universitaires de France, 1978.

Poulantzas, Nicos. *State, Power, Socialism.* Trans. Patrick Camiller. New York: Verso, 2014.

Protevi, John. *Edges of the State.* Minneapolis: University of Minnesota Press, 2019.

Rajchman, John. *The Deleuze Connections.* Cambridge, MA: MIT Press, 2000.

Rajchman, John. "Introduction." In Gilles Deleuze, *Gilles Deleuze: Pure Immanence: Essays on a Life*, ed. John Rajchman, trans. Anne Boyman, 7–23. New York: Zone, 2001.

Rancière, Jacques. *Disagreement. Politics and Philosophy.* Trans. Julie Rose. Minneapolis: University of Minnesota Press, 1999.

Rancière, Jacques. *The Ignorant Schoolmaster: Five Lessons in Intellectual Emancipation.* Stanford: Stanford University Press, 1991.

Ransby, Barbara. "Black Lives Matter Is Democracy in Action." *New York Times*, October 21, 2017.

Ransom, John S. *Foucault's Discipline: The Politics of Subjectivity*. Durham, NC: Duke University Press, 1997.

Rao, Anupama. *The Caste Question: Dalits and the Politics of Modern India*. Berkeley: University of California Press, 2009.

Rawls, John. "Justice as Fairness: Political Not Metaphysical." *Philosophy and Public Affairs* 14, no. 3 (Summer 1985): 223–251.

Rawls, John. "Political Liberalism: Reply to Habermas." *Journal of Philosophy* 92, no. 3 (1995): 132–180.

La Révolte de la prison de Nancy. 15 January 1972. Documents et propos de Michel Foucault, Jean-Paul Sartre et de militants du Groupe d'information sur les prisons. Paris: Le Point du jour, 2013.

Robcis, Camille. "Radical Psychiatry, Institutional Analysis, and the Commons." *Praxis 13/13* (blog). December 4, 2018. http://blogs.law.columbia.edu/praxis1313/camille-robcis-radical-psychiatry-institutional-analysis-and-the-commons/.

Rorty, Richard. *Achieving Our Country: Leftist Thought in Twentieth-Century America*. Cambridge, MA: Harvard University Press, 1998.

Rorty, Richard. *Philosophy and the Mirror of Nature*. Princeton, NJ: Princeton University Press, 1979.

Rorty, Richard, and Pascal Engel. *What's the Use of Truth?* Trans. William McCuaig. New York: Columbia University Press, 2016.

Rosenberg, Alan, and Joseph Westfall. *Foucault and Nietzsche: A Critical Encounter*. New York: Bloomsbury, 2018.

Rosenberg, Gerald N. *The Hollow Hope: Can Courts Bring About Social Change?* Chicago: University of Chicago Press, 1991.

Roudinesco, Elisabeth. *Jacques Lacan and Co.: A History of Psychoanalysis in France, 1925–1985*. Trans. Jeffrey Mehlman. Chicago: University of Chicago Press, 1990.

Rousseau, Jean-Jacques. *On the Social Contract*. Ed. Roger D. Masters. Trans. Judith R. Masters. New York: St. Martin's Press, 1978.

Rusche, Georg, and Otto Kirchheimer. *Punishment and Social Structure*. New York: Routledge, 2017.

Ruyter-Harcourt, Isadora. "Insanity and Social Status in Classical Rome." Ancient Studies thesis (with distinction), Barnard College, Columbia University, May 2015 (draft on file with author).

Saar, Martin. *Genealogie als Kritik: Geschichte und Theorie des Subjekts nach Nietzsche und Foucault*. Frankfurt: Campus, 2007.

Saar, Martin. "Genealogy and Subjectivity." *European Journal of Philosophy* 10, no. 2 (2002): 231–245.

Saar, Martin. "X—What Is Social Philosophy? Or: Order, Practice, Subject." *Proceedings of the Aristotelian Society* 118, no. 2 (2018): 207–223.

Sade, Marquis de. *120 Days of Sodom* [orig. 1785]. New York: Sun Vision Press, 2012.

Said, Edward. *Culture and Imperialism*. New York: Vintage, 1993.

Said, Edward. *Orientalism*. New York: Vintage, 2003.

Salecl, Renata. *Choice*. London: Profile, 2010.

Sandel, Michael J. *Liberalism and the Limits of Justice*. New York: Cambridge University Press, 1982.

Sanders, Bernie. *Guide to Political Revolution*. New York: Henry Holt, 2017.

Sartre, Jean-Paul. *Critique of Dialectical Reason*. Vol. 1, *Theory of Practical Ensembles*. Ed. Jonathan Reé. Trans. Alan Sheridan-Smith. New York: Verso, 2004.

Sartre, Jean-Paul. "L'écrivain et sa langue." Interview with Pierre Verstraeten. *Revue d'Esthétique*, 18, fasc. 3–4 (July–December 1965): 306–334.

Sartre, Jean-Paul. *Les Mains sales*. Paris: Gallimard, 1948.

Sartre, Jean-Paul. Préface to Frantz Fanon, *Les Damnés de la terre*. Paris: Maspéro, 1961.

Sartre, Jean-Paul. Preface to Frantz Fanon, *The Wretched of the Earth*, xliii–lxii. New York: Grove, 2004.

Sartre, Jean-Paul. *Les séquestrés d'Altona*. Paris: Gallimard, 1960.

Scahill, Jeremy. "The Counterinsurgency Paradigm: How U.S. Politics Have Become Paramilitarized." *Intercept*, November 25, 2018. https://theintercept.com/2018/11/25/counterinsurgency-us-drone-strikes/.

Scheuerman, William E. *Civil Disobedience*. Cambridge: Polity, 2018.

Scheuerman, William E. "The Frankfurt School at War." Review of *Secret Reports on Nazi Germany*, by Franz Neumann, Herbert Marcuse, and Otto Kirchheimer. *Foreign Affairs*, July/August 2013.

Scheuerman, William E. "Whistleblowing as Civil Disobedience: The Case of Edward Snowden." *Philosophy and Social Criticism* 40, no. 7 (2014): 609–628.

Scott, James C. "The Infrapolitics of Subordinate Groups." In *Domination and the Arts of Resistance*, 183–201. New Haven, CT, and London: Yale University Press, 1990.

Sedgwick, Eve Kosofsky. *Epistemology of the Closet*. Berkeley: University of California Press, 1990.

Shaw, George T., ed. *A Fair Hearing: The Alt-Right in the Words of Its Members and Leaders*. London: Arktos Media, 2018.

Shelby, Tommie. *Dark Ghettos: Injustice, Dissent, and Reform*. Cambridge, MA: Harvard University Press, 2016.

Shelby, Tommie, and Brandon M. Terry, eds. *To Shape a New World: Essays on the Political Philosophy of Martin Luther King, Jr.* Cambridge, MA: Harvard University Press, 2018.

Sherman, Lawrence W. "Trust and Confidence in Criminal Justice." *National Institute of Justice Journal* 248 (2002): 22–31.

Simon, John K. "Michel Foucault on Attica: An Interview" (translated and edited from a taped conversation), *Social Justice* 18, no. 3 (1991) (reprinted from *Telos*, no. 19, Spring 1974).

Smeltzer, Joshua. "Review of *Assembly*, by Michael Hardt and Toni Negri." *LSE Review of Books*, January 31, 2018. https://blogs.lse.ac.uk/lsereviewofbooks/2018/01/31/book-review-assembly-by-michael-hardt-and-antonio-negri/.

Snowden, Edward. *Permanent Record*. New York: Metropolitan, 2019.

Sophocles. *Oedipus the King*. In *The Three Theban Plays: Antigone, Oedipus the King, Oedipus at Colonus*. Trans. Robert Fagles. New York: Penguin, 1982.

Sorel, Georges. *Réflexions sur la violence*. Paris: Rivière, 1910.

Spivak, Gayatri Chakravorty. "Can the Subaltern Speak?" In *Marxism and the Interpretation of Culture*, ed. Cary Nelson and Lawrence Grossberg. Urbana: University of Illinois Press, 1988.

Spivak, Gayatri Chakravorty. "Can the Subaltern Speak?" In *Can the Subaltern Speak? Reflections on the History of an Idea*, ed. Rosalind C. Morris, 21–78. New York: Columbia University Press, 2010.

Spivak, Gayatri Chakravorty. *A Critique of Postcolonial Reason: Toward a History of the Vanishing Present*. Cambridge, MA: Harvard University Press, 1999.

Stanley, Jason. *How Fascism Works: The Politics of Us and Them*. New York: Random House, 2018.

Steiker, Carol S., and Jordan M. Steiker. *Courting Death*. Cambridge, MA: Harvard University Press, 2016.

Steiker, Carol S., and Jordan M. Steiker. "Sober Second Thoughts: Reflections on Two Decades of Constitutional Regulation of Capital Punishment." *Harvard Law Review* 109, no. 2 (December 1995): 357–438.

Steiner, Uwe. *Walter Benjamin: An Introduction to His Work and Thought*. Trans. Michael Winkler. Chicago: University of Chicago Press, 2010.

Stevenson, Bryan. *Just Mercy: A Story of Justice and Redemption*. New York: Spiegel & Grau, 2014.

Stevenson, Bryan, and Ruth Friedman. "Deliberate Indifference: Judicial Tolerance of Racial Bias in Criminal Justice." *Washington and Lee Law Review* 51, no. 2 (Spring 1994): 509–527.

Stiglitz, Joseph. "Democracy in the Twenty-first Century." *Social Europe*, September 01, 2014. https://www.socialeurope.eu/democracy.

Stoler, Ann Laura. "Ann Stoler on Reading Foucault Today." *Foucault 13/13* (blog). November 19, 2015. http://blogs.law.columbia.edu/foucault1313/2015/11/19/ann-stoler-on-society-must-be-defended-reading-foucault-today/.

Stoler, Ann Laura. *Duress: Imperial Durabilities in Our Times.* Durham, NC: Duke University Press, 2016.

Stoler, Ann Laura. "Internal Frontiers." In *Political Concepts—a Lexicon in Formation: Thinking with Balibar,* ed. Stathis Gourgouris, Jacques Lezra, and Ann Stoler. New York: Fordham University Press, 2020.

Stoler, Ann Laura. *Race and the Education of Desire: Foucault's History of Sexuality and the Colonial Order of Things.* Durham, NC: Duke University Press, 1995.

Taussig, Michael. "I'm So Angry I Made A Sign." In *Occupy: Three Theories in Disobedience,* ed. W. J. T. Mitchell, Bernard E. Harcourt, and Michael Taussig, 3–44. Chicago: University of Chicago Press, 2013.

Taylor, Keeanga-Yamahtta. *From #BlackLivesMatter to Black Liberation.* Chicago: Haymarket, 2016.

Terry, Brandon. "MLK Now." *Boston Review,* January 9, 2018, 9–30.

Terry, Brandon. "Requiem for a Dream: The Problem-Space of Black Power." In *To Shape a New World,* ed. Tommie Shelby and Brandon M. Terry, 290–324. Cambridge, MA: Harvard University Press, 2018.

Thiele, Leslie Paul. "The Agony of Politics: The Nietzschean Roots of Foucault's Thought." *American Political Science Review* 84, no. 3 (1990): 907–925.

Thoreau, Henry David. *On the Duty of Disobedience.* Chicago: Charles H. Kerr, 1989.

Tiisala, Tuomo. "Review of *Foucault and Nietzsche: A Critical Encounter,* edited by Alan Rosenberg and Joseph Westfall." *Notre Dame Philosophical Reviews* (2018). https://ndpr.nd.edu/news/foucault-and-nietzsche-a-critical-encounter/.

Tiqqun. "L'Hypothèse cybernétique." *Tiqqun* 2 (2001): 40–83.

Tomba, Massimiliano. *Insurgent Universality: An Alternative Legacy of Modernity.* New York: Oxford University Press, 2019.

Tomba, Massimiliano. "Justice and Divine Violence: Walter Benjamin and the Time of Anticipation." *Theory & Event* 20, no. 3 (2017): 579–598.

Tronti, Mario. *Sull'autonomia del politico.* Milan, Italy: Feltrinelli, 1977.

Tuck, Richard. "The Left Case for Brexit." *Dissent Magazine,* June 6, 2016.

Tufekci, Zeynep. *Twitter and Tear Gas: The Power and Fragility of Networked Protest.* New Haven, CT: Yale University Press, 2017.

United Nations, Intergovernmental Panel on Climate Change (V. Masson-Delmotte, P. Zhai, H. O. Pörtner, D. Roberts, J. Skea, P.R. Shukla, A. Pirani, W. Moufouma-Okia, C. Péan, R. Pidcock, S. Connors, J. B. R. Matthews, Y. Chen, X. Zhou, M. I. Gomis, E. Lonnoy, T. Maycock, M. Tignor, T. Waterfield, eds.). *Special Report on Global Warming of 1.5°C,* 2018, https://www.ipcc.ch/sr15/chapter/spm/.

Uprising 13/13. "13 Forms of Uprising/13 Seminars at Columbia." Accessed July 16, 2019. http://blogs.law.columbia.edu/praxis1313/.

Urbinati, Nadia. "Political Theory of Populism." *Annual Review of Political Science* 22, no. 1 (2019): 111–127.

Velasco, Jesús. "The Revolution Has Been Printed." *Uprising 13/13* (blog). September 22, 2017. http://blogs.law.columbia.edu/uprising1313/jesus-r-velasco-the-revolution-has-been-printed/.

Venkatasubramanian, Venkat. *How Much Inequality Is Fair?* New York: Columbia University Press, 2017.

Voltaire. *Candide ou l'Optimisme.* Paris: Gallimard, 2007.

Wacquant, Loïc. *Punishing the Poor.* Durham, NC: Duke University Press, 2009.

Wallerstein, Immanuel. "How to Fight a Class Struggle, Commentary No. 491." February 15, 2019. https://www.iwallerstein.com/how-to-fight-a-class-struggle/.

Walsh, Mary. "Review of *Notes Toward a Performative Theory of Assembly,* by Judith Butler." *The Review of Politics* 79, no. 1 (Winter 2017): 180–183.

Walzer, Michael. "Liberalism and the Arts of Separation." *Political Theory* 12, no. 3 (August 1984): 315–330.

Wang, Jackie. *Carceral Capitalism. Essays on the Contemporary Continuum of Incarceration: The Biopolitics of Juvenile Delinquency, Predatory Policing, the Political Economy of Fees and Fines, and Algorithmic Policing.* Cambridge, MA: Semiotext(e), 2018.

Weheliye, Alexander G. *Habeas Viscus: Racializing Assemblages, Biopolitics, and Black Feminist Theories of the Human.* Durham, NC: Duke University Press, 2014.

Wheatland, Thomas. *The Frankfurt School in Exile.* Minneapolis: University of Minnesota Press, 2009.

White, Hayden. *Metahistory: The Historical Imagination in 19th-Century Europe.* Baltimore: Johns Hopkins University Press, 2014.

Wilder, Gary. *Freedom Time: Negritude, Decolonization, and the Future of the World.* Durham, NC: Duke University Press, 2014.

Williams, Michael. *Unnatural Doubts: Epistemological Realism and the Basis of Skepticism.* Cambridge: Basil Blackwell, 1991.

Williams, Patricia J. *The Alchemy of Race and Rights.* Cambridge, MA: Harvard University Press, 1991.

Wizisla, Erdmut. *Walter Benjamin and Bertolt Brecht—The Story of a Friendship.* New Haven, CT: Yale University Press, 2009.

Wolin, Richard. *The Wind from the East: French Intellectuals, the Cultural Revolution, and the Legacy of the 1960s.* Princeton, NJ: Princeton University Press, 2010.

Woodly, Deva. "#BlackLivesMatter and the Democratic Necessity of Social Movements." *Uprising 13/13* (blog). November 1, 2017. http://blogs.law.columbia.edu/uprising1313/deva-woodly-blacklivesmatter-and-the-democratic-necessity-of-social-movements/.

Worthen, Hana. "Review of *Notes Toward a Performative Theory of Assembly*, by Judith Butler." *Critical Inquiry.* February 8, 2016.

Xifaras, Mikhaïl. "The Role of the Law in Critical Theory." *Praxis 13/13* (blog). December 2, 2018 (draft on file with author).

Young, Iris Marion. *Justice and the Politics of Difference.* Princeton, NJ: Princeton University Press, 1990.

Zamora, Daniel. "Can We Criticize Foucault?" *Jacobin*, December 10, 2014. https://www.jacobinmag.com/2014/12/foucault-interview/.

Zaretsky, Eli. "Nancy Fraser and the Left: A Searching Idea of Equality." In *Feminism, Capitalism, and Critique: Essays in Honor of Nancy Fraser*, ed. Banu Bargu and Chiara Bottici, 263–279. New York: Palgrave Macmillan, 2017.

Zaretsky, Eli. *Why America Needs a Left: A Historical Argument.* Cambridge: Polity, 2012.

Zedong, Mao. *Selected Works of Mao Tse-tung.* 5 vols. Peking: Foreign Languages Press, 1967.

Zerilli, Linda M.G. *A Democratic Theory of Judgment.* Chicago: University of Chicago Press, 2016.

Zernike, Kate. *Boiling Mad: Inside Tea Party America.* New York: St. Martin's, 2010.

Žižek, Slavoj. "From *Che vuoi?* to Fantasy: Lacan with Eyes Wide Shut." In *How to Read Lacan*, ed. Slavoj Žižek, 40–60. New York: Norton, 2007.

Žižek, Slavoj, "How to Begin from the Beginning." In *The Idea of Communism.* Vol. 1, ed. Slavoj Žižek and Costas Douzinas, 209–226. New York: Verso, 2010.

Žižek, Slavoj, ed. *The New York Conference.* Vol. 2 of *The Idea of Communism.* New York: Verso, 2013.

Žižek, Slovoj. "No Way Out? Communism in the Next Century." In *The Idea of Communism.* Vol. 3, ed. Slavoj Žižek and Alex Taek-Gwang Lee, 240–257. New York: Verso, 2016.

Žižek, Slavoj. *The Plague of Fantasies.* New York: Verso, 1997.

Žižek, Slavoj. "Shoplifters of the World Unite." *London Review of Books*, August 19, 2011.

Žižek, Slavoj. *Violence: Six Sideways Reflections.* New York: Picador, 2008.

Žižek, Slavoj, and Costas Douzinas, eds. *The Idea of Communism.* Vol. 1, New York: Verso, 2010.

Žižek, Slavoj, and Alex Taek-Gwang Lee, eds. *The Seoul Conference.* Vol. 3 of *The Idea of Communism.* New York: Verso, 2016.

Zola, Émile. *The Dreyfus Affair: J'accuse and Other Writings.* Trans. Eleanor Levieux. New Haven, CT: Yale University Press, 1996.

Zurn, Perry and Andrew Dilts, eds. *Active Intolerance: Michel Foucault, the Prisons Information Group, and the Future of Abolition.* New York: Palgrave Macmillan, 2016.

Zurn, Perry and Andrew Dilts, special eds. *Challenging the Punitive Society,* Volume 12 (2016) of *Carceral Notebooks.* New York: U.S. Lithograph, 2016.

Acknowledgments

As I mention in closing in chapter 18, this book was born of decades of clashes and conflicts between my political activism and my critical theorizing. In those political interventions, I have been accompanied and supported by close colleagues, without whom I would not have managed, and to whom I owe a great deal of thanks, especially Bryan Stevenson, Steve Bright, Tom Durkin, Ruth Friedman, George Kendall, Randy Susskind, Max Stern, Jeff Fagan, W. J. T. Mitchell, Mick Taussig, Alexis Hoag, and Noah Smith-Drelich. I have also had the great privilege and blessing to learn from and think closely with brilliant critical thinkers, to whom I am deeply indebted, including Sheldon Wolin, Rüdiger Bittner, Seyla Benhabib, Richard Tuck, Duncan Kennedy, Étienne Balibar, Homi Bhabha, Daniel Defert, Carolin Emcke, François Ewald, Frédéric Gros, Didier Fassin, Fabienne Brion, Raymond Geuss, Axel Honneth, Bonnie Honig, Janet Halley, David Kennedy, Daniele Lorenzini, Steven Lukes, Martha Minow, Frank Michelman, Toni Negri, Judith Revel, Martin Saar, Carol Steiker, Ann Stoler, Brandon Terry, Massimiliano Tomba, Jesús Velasco, Bernie Yack, and Linda Zerilli. All the errors in this book are mine, but many more have been avoided due to generous and productive conversations with them and support from them.

I want to extend a special thanks to Mia Ruyter, my best interlocutor, critic, and political companion for decades of confronting theory and praxis with me; and to my editor, Eric Schwartz at Columbia University Press, for all his support, encouragement, and ideas about publishing in the digital age. Leonard Benardo was a crucial interlocutor at several pivotal moments, and I thank him dearly for that.

This book would not have appeared without the brilliant editorial assistance of Fonda Shen, who was indispensable in editing, referencing, and preparing the manuscript for publication, and the extraordinary shepherding of Lowell Frye at Columbia University Press. Ghislaine Pagès provided outstanding assistance at every stage of the manuscript, and to her, I am always deeply indebted.

My thinking about critical praxis grew over seminars, workshops, and discussions with a number of extraordinary thinkers, and I want especially to thank Amna Akbar, Amy Allen, Charleyne Biondi, Judith Butler, Jean Cohen, Andrew Dilts, Joseph Fischel, Michael Hardt, Jeremy Kessler, Clécio Lemos, Karuna Mantena, Allegra McLeod, Uday Mehta, Sam Moyn, David Pozen, John Rajchman, Kendall Thomas, Mikhaïl Xifaras, and Camila Vergara for their generosity in thinking with me. I am also especially indebted to a brilliant group of young scholars and former students who provoked and inspired so much of my thinking on critical theory and praxis, including Ibai Atuxta, Tommaso Bardelli, Christopher Berk, Yuna Blajer, Marcus Board, Kyla Bourne, Sabina Bremner, Kalinka Courtois, Corentin Durand, Shawn Fagan, Maxime Gaborit, Samuel Galloway, Shai Gortler, Gilles Gressani, Dawn Helphand, Daniel Henry, Diana Kim, Tyson Leuchter, Kate Levine, Dimitri M'Bama, Ray Noll, Alexander de la Paz, Josh Sellers, Michi Soyer, Tuomo Tiisala, Sherod Thaxton, and Daniel Wyche. Anna Krauthamer, Beth Manchester, Claire Merrill, and Ghislaine Pagès have been extraordinary in helping to organize those seminars, and I am deeply grateful to them.

Parts of this book were presented, critiqued, and discussed in different workshops, and I want to extend a special thanks and my gratitude for those often sharp, but always productive exchanges: with Martin Saar, Rainer Forst, and the participants at the Colloquium at the Goethe University, Frankfurt am Main, on December 20, 2018; to Michael Hardt, Michael Gillespie, Geneviève Rousselière, Fadi Bardawil, Alexander Kirshner, Patrick Giamario, Elliot Mamet, and the other participants in the Duke Political Theory Workshop on February 1, 2019; to Christian Emden, Uwe Steiner, Robert Werth, James Faubion, Kathleen Canning, Aysha Pollnitz, and other members of the Rice University Humanities Center and Program at the Politics, Law, and Social Thought workshop on February 22, 2019; to Veena Das, Heba Islam, Sabrina Axster, Erin Aeran Chung, P. J. Brendese, Stuart Schrader, and Mariam Banahi, and others at the Johns Hopkins University conference on surveillance through the Program in Racism, Immigration, and

Citizenship (RIC) on April 5, 2019, as well as to all the student protesters at Johns Hopkins University, who inspired us with their militancy; to Patchen Markell, Aziz Rana, Jordan Jochim, and the participants at the Cornell Political Theory Workshop on November 15, 2018; and to Massimiliano Tomba, Banu Bargu, and colleagues at the conference at the Humanities Center at the University of California, Santa Cruz, History of Consciousness, on April 15, 2019. I am deeply indebted for these conversations.

I dedicate this book to Isadora Ruyter-Harcourt and Léonard Ruyter-Harcourt with all my admiration, love, confidence, and hope for the future.

Name Index

Thinkers with extensive page locators are given fuller treatment in the concept index

Concept Index